SOUTH-WESTERN
MATHEMATICS
OF MONEY

CHERYL CLAYTON
Richardson High School
Richardson, Texas

MP01AA
PUBLISHED BY
SOUTH-WESTERN PUBLISHING CO.
CINCINNATI, OH   DALLAS, TX   LIVERMORE, CA

Senior Acquisitions Editor: Eve Lewis
Production Editor: Mark Cheatham
Editorial Production Manager: Carol Sturzenberger
Designer: Barbara Libby
Marketing Manager: Gregory Getter

Cover photographs © Comstock, Inc.

ISBN: 0–538–61450–1

Library of Congress Catalog Card Number: 90–63343

1 2 3 4 5 6 7 8 9 Ki 8 7 6 5 4 3 2 1

Printed in the United States of America

PREFACE

As young people who are finishing the last years of high school, you are becoming independent adults in a highly complex world. As you accomplish this transition, you prepare yourselves by accepting responsibility for the many choices you face. You realize that you must learn to function as adults in a society that is changing more rapidly than ever before. One facet of teenage life does not change, however. Teenagers have always wanted the freedom to choose their own friends, to make decisions independently of their parents, and to make and spend their own money. And you still do.

Young people in your generation are entering the job market in large numbers even before completing high school. Many are finding the realities of acquiring, handling, and spending money to be a challenging and sometimes overwhelming task. *Mathematics of Money* offers assistance in two important ways. It helps you to:

- Sharpen the mathematical skills you need to manage your own finances
- Become aware of some of the inducements and temptations you will face as you choose how to spend your money.

Many tools are now available to assist you to become informed consumers and capable money managers. The availability of home computers, with their accompanying software, and sophisticated calculators, which are truly miniature computers, is mushrooming so quickly that you will have access to a wide variety of technological capabilities about which we can only speculate today.

The readings in *Mathematics of Money* give you sketches of life that might seem familiar. We observe one student who has probably overdrawn his bank account wondering if he can stuff twenty-dollar bills back into the Automatic Teller Machine. Another student, whose father carries too many credit cards, is embarrassed in a restaurant when the father accidentally scatters his cards on the floor. One student considers moving into an apartment with her friend, since she has a job as a clerk in a toy store. One of her disgruntled customers threw a toy and knocked over a building block display when she told him that his credit card had been rejected.

You are encouraged to bring into the classroom materials and observations from your own life. You will make connections with your own experiences—connections that will be of interest to your fellow students. You will have opportunities to explore the real world of work, banking, apartment hunting, and paying bills.

The book begins by telling how money can be earned. The characters in the first two chapters show us the differences between earning wages, earning a salary, working on commission, and operating a small business. They wonder why amounts of money are deducted from their paychecks; not enough is left over to buy a new tire for his car as one character had planned.

In Chapters 2 and 3, the characters share with us some of their experiences with using checking and savings accounts. You will have the opportunity to write thousands of dollars in checks to the top winners in a major U.S. golf tournament. One of the characters is intrigued by the idea that because of compound interest, money that is left sitting, under proper conditions, seems to put down roots and grow new money!

In Chapters 5, 6, and 7 our characters reveal to us the very pervasive and persuasive world of credit. Their eyes are opened to the large sums of money banks and lenders are acquiring from willing consumers who are paying high rates of interest on their credit purchases. In our world of immediate gratification, we consumers have listened to the siren's call: "Have your credit card ready." We have learned to carry a wallet full of credit cards. We have mastered the art of paper shuffling so well that we can have the money chasing its tail around in circles for years without ever making any progress in reducing our debt.

Chapter 8, which reviews various forms of advertising and some of the messages in them, has a definite bearing on the decision-making process. Many of the the topics presented in *Mathematics of Money* involve enticing customers to relinquish dollar bills from their wallets. Examining the process and form by which these enticements are delivered to us allows us to make more intelligent purchasing decisions.

Chapters 9 and 10 show our characters handling investments, shopping for life insurance, and planning for retirement. You will have an opportunity to handle vast amounts of (fictitious!) money as you make your own stock purchase decisions.

Chapter 11 shows our characters facing their responsibilities as taxpayers and making their way through the 1040 forms. They will see a connection between how much was taken out of their paychecks in Chapter 1 and how much of that money will be kept by the IRS. One character discovers "Tax Freedom Day."

Chapters 12 and 13 give our characters the chance to calculate the costs of owning and operating their cars. One of our young drivers describes a vivid and frightening lesson on the necessity of good auto insurance. Several other characters give us tips on making travel plans that illustrate how family members who take trips together can return home still speaking to one another.

The housing chapters, 14 and 15, follow our graduating high school students as they move out of their own homes and into apartments. They discover the many financial and life-style decisions they must make when choosing and sharing an apartment. Parents of our characters share with them some of the many responsibilities of home ownership. One character encourages his family to move into a new house so that he will no longer have to share a bedroom with his brother. The brother frequently complains about our character's posters, music, closet space, and clothes on the floor.

The last chapter is a culmination of the preceding ones. You will create family budgets for several fictitious families. You will analyze the fixed and variable expenses each family faces, compare these with their monthly income, then make adjustments in whatever expenses you can. Just as many families discover each month—if there are more bills than money to pay them—someone may get left out. If that someone is not to be the grocer, another source of spending may have to be reduced. Most of us want more than we have rather than less; our characters will share some ideas about staying within the budget.

As you, like the characters in the book, approach adulthood and work your way through the transition, you will face many financial decisions. *Mathematics of Money* offers assistance in financial planning so that the choices you make to establish an independent life style in your own apartment or house will be informed choices.

ABOUT THE AUTHOR

Cheryl Clayton, M.Ed.

The author has taught at Richardson High School, in Richardson, Texas for the past twelve years, where she originated the popular mathematics of consumer economics course on which this book is based. She was awarded a summer workshop grant from the National Endowment for the Humanities in 1988. Her career has included teaching fundamentals of mathematics, algebra, geometry, trigonometry, analytic geometry and consumer mathematics at the junior high and high school levels. At Oak Ridge High School in Orlando, Florida she was honored as teacher of the year in 1971. She attended Texas Christian University where she received a Bachelor's degree in 1966; in 1979 she took a Master's degree in Education from North Texas State University. She is married, has two sons, and lives in Dallas.

Consultants

Barbara O. Eatherly
North Lamar High School
Paris, Texas

Linda George
J.J. Pearce High School
Richardson, Texas

Paula Ordeneaux
Dulles High School
Sugarland, Texas

CONTENTS

CHAPTER **1** PERSONAL EARNING POWER

This chapter opens the book with a look at earning power. When you come to the end of Chapter 16, you will again be looking at income, this time as a part of a total family budget. In between, you will study banking accounts—both checking and savings, starting your own business, using consumer credit, responding to advertising, making investments, buying life insurance and annuities, paying income tax, making car payments, and the budget-making process itself.

You will handle real-life materials—such as newspaper job ads; abstract concepts—such as standard of living and demographics; and complex systems—such as compound interest and the Consumer Price Index. You will polish your mathematical skills in every context and explore the consumer world outside the classroom.

In this chapter you will be introduced to Alex and his friends. They are fictitious, but the decisions they face are very real. Every year many young people make choices like the ones you will see them making as they approach the end of their high school experience.

We will see how Alex carefully considers the balance between the time and effort required in taking a part-time job and the financial rewards of working. He sees how the information he reads in newspaper job ads translates into a paycheck for regular and overtime hours. Alex's friend Betty will help us compare the consistent income of a salaried job with the variable income of a job paid by commission. When a salesperson is on a commission, he or she may make recommendations to the customer that differ from those a salaried salesperson would make. Betty tells us why.

Another friend, Luis, will see how and why deductions are made from his paycheck. His first paycheck from the grocery store where he works comes as a surprise to Luis. He had expected to receive his full hourly rate, but he received noticeably less.

Daphne, a year younger than Alex and his classmates, watches her older brother Darrin make career decisions and begins to think about making her own. She learns about sources of help in exploring the world of work. She also learns how a person's income is enhanced by benefits received in addition to pay.

Alex, Betty, Luis, and Daphne have looked forward to this time when they will no longer have all their decisions made for them. They are glad to begin taking charge of their own lives. At the same time, the importance of some of those decisions is becoming clear to them, and accepting the responsibility for their choices is not as easy as it was when the choices were fewer.

Perhaps you are facing some of the same choices that confront Alex and his friends. This chapter is intended to increase your personal income earning power by providing some tools you may find helpful in making informed decisions.

Alex and his classmates are entering their last year of high school. Many of his friends have already had summer jobs. Some have more spending money than he has, and they do not always have to tell their parents how they spend it. Some have started saving money for college or for other schooling.

Alex's parents have been asking him what he plans to do after graduation. His girlfriend, Alice, is planning to go to State University next fall. He hates the thought of being away from Alice for long—they plan to get married when she finishes her law degree, but that could be a while. If Alex goes to State to be with Alice, he may decide to study accounting, but he is not really skilled in mathematics. What Alex really enjoys is tinkering around with the van that his parents bought him when he learned to drive.

Alex could use some extra cash: the van needs a few parts, and he would like to take Alice to the spring prom. Alex's older sister Karen rode to the prom last year in a chauffeured limousine—Alex can just imagine what that cost! Then there is always the question of more school: tuition, books, fees, money, money, money!

The $483 that Alex saved from mowing lawns this summer is almost gone. Alex has been thinking about getting a job after school, partly as a way of earning extra cash but also as a way of getting a taste of what it will be like in the work world. If he can find a way to choose a career he would really like, he may decide he needs more training, and getting a job might bring in the extra money to pay for it.

OBJECTIVES: In this section, we will help Alex to:

- *compute the earnings of a part-time job*
- *compare an hourly wage with a weekly or monthly salary*
- *plan a part-time work schedule that leaves time for studies and social life*

EARNING INCOME

Alex already knows a few facts about money. He knows that his family's **standard of living** is determined by the amount of income his parents earn. **Income** is the money received from investments or from a person's activities at work or in business. His family, like most Americans, depends on their labor for their primary income. Approximately 9 out of 10 American workers earn income in the form of wages or salary. A **wage** is an hourly or daily rate of pay, while a **salary** is a weekly, monthly, or yearly rate. Most clerical workers and people who do physical labor are wage earners, and professional and technical workers are salary earners. About 10% of all workers are in business for themselves and earn **self-employment income** instead of wages or salaries. These include such people as physicians, shopkeepers, writers, photographers, and farmers.

You may have wondered why a few baseball players have actually been paid over one million dollars for a season while the President of the United States earns $200,000 a year, or why an actor who becomes a star earns far more than a professional accountant or teacher. Income from labor reflects social values, the monetary worth of the labor, and the demand for the labor in relation to the number of people able to do the job.

Alex began examining the classified ads in the employment section of the Sunday newspaper. He did not see any ads offering million-dollar salaries to baseball players. He did find, however, that part-time jobs available to students pay a specific amount for each hour worked. The amount is an **hourly rate**. The hours the employee is required to work each week are the employee's **regular hours**.

Some weeks an employee will be asked or allowed to work more than the required amount of hours: these extra hours are called **overtime hours**. The hourly rate for these overtime hours is generally greater than the regular hourly rate.

The ads stating weekly, monthly, and yearly salaries did not specify how many hours the employee must work. Salaried employees receive the same salary each pay period whether they work the minimum number of hours required or put in extra time during weekends and evenings.

Ask Yourself

1. If an employee is paid by the hour and works more than the required number of hours in a week, the employee is generally paid more for the extra hours. What are the extra hours called?

2. If an employee is paid a monthly salary, will he or she be paid more for working extra hours on the weekend?

3. Workers in which kinds of jobs earn hourly or daily wages?

4. If you were earning a salary of $2000 a month and took a new job at $3000 a month, what would be the effect on your standard of living?

SHARPEN YOUR SKILLS

___ Skill 1 ___

Alex's friend Ed delivers pizzas. The hourly rate he earns is $3.40. He also receives tips from his customers if the pizza is still hot and if the order is properly filled.

During the first week of February, Ed worked 16 1/2 hours and received $28.50 in tips.

Question   How much money did Ed make that week?

Solution   Use paper and pencil or a calculator. Express the number of hours as a decimal.

$3.40 hourly rate	$56.10 regular wages
x 16.5 number of hours	+28.50 tips
$56.10 regular wages	$84.60 total wages

Ed earned $84.60 that week.

___ Skill 2 ___

If he works more than 20 hours in one week, Ed receives 1 1/2 times his regular hourly rate of $3.40 for the extra hours.

During the second week of February there was an ice storm. Many people ordered pizza to be delivered. That week Ed worked 26 hours and received $43.75 in tips.

Question   How much money did Ed make that week?

Solution   Use paper and pencil or a calculator. Express the overtime rate as a decimal. Find the number of hours of overtime (26 – 20).

$3.40 regular hourly rate
x   1.5 overtime rate
$5.10 hourly overtime rate

$5.10 hourly overtime rate
x   6 overtime hours
$30.60 overtime wages

$ 3.40 regular hourly rate
x   20 regular hours
$68.00 regular wages

$30.60 overtime wages
  68.00 regular wages
+43.75 tips
$142.35 total wages

Ed earned $142.35 that week.

—————— Skill 3 ——————

Alex wondered how salaries stated by the week, month, and year compared with hourly wages. He devised a plan to find out, assuming 40 work hours = 1 week, 52 weeks = 1 year, and 12 months = 1 year. (A 52-week year generally means 50 weeks of work plus two weeks of paid vacation.)

Questions   How much is the monthly salary for each of the jobs shown in the advertisements? Who makes the most?

1.   **2.**   **3.**

RECEPTIONIST must have good phone skills. $6.50 hr. to start. Hours: 8:30am-5pm. Equal Oppty Employment. Call Monday–Thursday only.

COMMUNITY WORK Start a new career with the state's oldest consumer group. Great future! No experience nec. Paid training, holidays, vacations. Up to $350 per wk.

ADMINISTRATIVE ASSISTANT Social service agency seeks Admin. Asst. for data entry. Must have exp. with dBase III systems. Typing 40 wpm. Sal. $15K + benefits.

Solutions   **1.** $6.50   hourly rate
                        x   40   hours per week
                        $260.00   weekly salary

                        $260.00   weekly salary
                        x   52   weeks per year
                        $13,520.00   yearly salary

$$\frac{\$13,520}{12} = \$1126.67 \quad \text{monthly salary}$$

The receptionist makes $1126.67 per month.

2. $350.00   weekly rate
          x   52   weeks per year
          $18,200.00   yearly salary

$$\frac{\$18,200.00}{12} = \$1516.67 \quad \text{monthly salary}$$

The community worker makes $1516.67 per month.

3. $15,000   yearly salary

$$\frac{\$15,000}{12} = \$1250.00 \quad \text{monthly salary}$$

The administrative assistant makes $1250.00 per month.

The community worker makes the most in a month.

_____ Skill 4

Alex wonders if he will have time to spend with Alice and keep up with his school work if he tries to work 20 to 25 hours per week. Alex made this schedule to see how many hours he could work each week.

Sunday	Monday–Thursday	Friday	Saturday
Off until: 3 P.M.	School until: 4 P.M.	School until: 4 P.M.	Up at: 9 A.M.
Work: 3 – 7	Work: 4:30 – 7:30	Work: 4:30 – 6:30	Work: 11 – 5
Schoolwork 8 – 10		See Alice 7 – 11	

Alex realized he could work the following number of hours each week:

Day	Sun.	Mon.	Tues.	Wed.	Thurs.	Fri.	Sat.	Total
Hours	4	3	3	3	3	2	6	24

However, Alex does not want to work on both Saturday and Sunday.

Questions 1. If Alex works Sunday but not Saturday, how many hours could he work each week?

2. If he works Saturday but not Sunday, how many hours could he work in the week?

Solutions Use mental math or paper and pencil.

1. Sunday through Friday = 18 hours   (4+3+3+3+3+2 = 18)

2. Monday through Saturday = 20 hours (3+3+3+3+2+6 = 20)

EXERCISE YOUR SKILLS

1. What is the major difference between the way the pay is computed for salaried employees and for hourly employees?

2. Why would an employer be willing to pay extra money for overtime hours?

3. Why would a salaried employee be willing to work extra hours if his or her salary will remain the same?

4. Why do many professional baseball players earn more money each year than the President of the United States?

5. If a student takes a part-time job, what do you think is the maximum number of hours he or she should be allowed to work per week? Be sure to take into consideration the time needed to keep up with school work.

———   **Activity 1**   ———

Find the salary earned by each of the following "employees" for one week.

NOTE: Save your results to use in Activity 2, which follows.

1. I am the tape recorder in the French language lab. I make $11.50 per hour, and I worked 29 1/2 hours this week. I received a bonus of $3.50 when I taught the students how to say "I love you" in French.

2. I am the light that turns on when you open the refrigerator door. My door was open 22 1/2 hours this week. My salary is $10.00 per hour. I did not receive a bonus because I was on when my owner knocked over a bottle of juice on his toe.

3. I am the pay telephone outside the principal's office. I work all the time, but only got paid $12.00 per hour for 29 hours this week. I got a $25.00 bonus from a guy whose girlfriend told him through me that she had decided not to break up with him after all.

4. I am the gate that goes up and down to let cars into the airport. I made $9.50 per hour for 29 1/2 hours of work this week.

5. I dispense tokens for video games. I eat five-dollar bills and spit out 20 tokens at a time. I worked 27 hours last week. I earned $13.00 per hour and received an extra $1.00 when the tokens got stuck and a little girl kicked me.

6. I am the golf cart that Carla pulls around the golf course. I carry all of her clubs and the lucky red charm that her brother gave her. I worked 31 hours this week and made $14.00 per hour. I received a $20 bonus when Carla made her first eagle.

7. I am the gremlin who rings the tardy bell 20 seconds early before selected classes. I only work when I can make someone late for math class. This week I worked 28 hours and got paid $14.50 per hour. I get no bonuses because no one likes me.

8. I am the book cover that keeps slipping off your school book. I worked 26 hours last week and got $12.00 per hour. My bonus was taken back when the guy who had written a phone number on me accidentally threw me away.

_____ Activity 2 _____

1–8. Assume that the employees named in Activity 1 received 1 1/2 times their regular hourly rate for all hours they worked over 20. Find each new weekly salary including bonuses and overtime.

_____ Activity 3 _____

Assuming a 40-hour work week, 52 weeks per year, and 12 months per year, find the monthly salary of each job described in the classified ads shown below. (Use the highest pay rate mentioned.)

1.

HEALTH CARE. Better Life Health Care Personnel is looking for respiratory therapist. Earn as much as $17.85/hr.

2.

Health Care
NURSES
RNs UP TO $35/HR.

3.

Maintenance: *MECHANIC* Center Manuf. is in need of a person with 3-5 yrs exp. in machine repair/punch press. $10.70/hr

4.

Mold Maker
Jr. MOLD MAKER We pay as high as $8.50 after 1 yr.

5.

General Retail Clerk
Are you getting nowhere with that same old job? Earn $450 to $600 per week. No exp. nec.

6.

Hair Dresser
English and Spanish speaking. Guaranteed pay $300 / wk to start. Apply in person only.

7.

Sales!
Interesting inside sales position. Start at $5.75/hr.

8.

DRIVERS
Drivers for local messenger. Earn $450 per week. Must have own car and good drive record.

9.

Data Processing
COBOL/DOS
Lead Programmer
Analyst
$40,000/yr

_____ Activity 4 _____

Answer the following questions about arranging a work schedule.

You are only allowed to work on Saturday or Sunday, never both on the same weekend. You may work past 8 P.M. only two nights each week. Your work week starts on Monday. The hours of available work are as follows:

Mon.–Thurs.	2 P.M. to 11 P.M.
Friday	4 P.M. to midnight
Saturday	9 A.M. to midnight
Sunday	2 P.M.. to 11 P.M.

1. What is the maximum number of hours you could work in one week?

2. You devise the following schedule:

Monday	4 P.M. to 11 P.M.	Thursday	4 P.M. to 8 P.M.
Tuesday	4 P.M. to 8 P.M.	Saturday	1 P.M. to 6 P.M.
Wednesday	4 P.M. to 11 P.M.	Friday and Sunday	off

How many hours will you work each week?

3. Your boss changes your schedule to the following:

Monday	4 P.M. to 8 P.M.	Friday	4 P.M. to 8 P.M.
Wednesday	4 P.M. to 11 P.M.	Sunday	4 P.M. to 11 P.M.
Thursday	4 P.M. to 8 P.M.	Tuesday and Saturday	off

How many hours will you work each week?

4. Devise a schedule that would allow you to work the following hours.

    a. 20 hours   **b.** 25 hours   **c.** 30 hours

5. You make $6.40 per hour. How much will you make if you follow the schedule from problem **4. a.**?   **4. b.**?   **4. c.**?

6. If you make 1 1/2 times your regular hourly rate for any hours over 20, how much will you make in problem **4. a.**?   **4. b.**?   **4. c.**?

Betty goes to high school with Alex. She knows Alex is trying to decide if getting a part-time job is worth the effort and time involved. She and Alex were dating before Alex met Alice. In fact, she was with Alex when he went looking for the van.

Alex and his parents seemed to know a lot about car salespeople when they were picking out the van. At one of the lots they visited, a saleswoman kept trying to push Alex's father and mother into choosing a certain van. It was a gorgeous, current-year model. Betty noticed, as the saleswoman kept saying, it was "loaded." It had all the extras: "power this" and "power that," a really plush interior, all kinds of built-in storage spaces and gimmicks—and a very powerful engine. Of course it had a powerful price tag, too. Betty guessed it cost more than Alex's parents wanted to spend. After all, Alex just needed transportation to and from school.

As they left that car lot and drove toward the one where Alex would eventually buy the van, Betty asked why the saleswoman seemed so eager to sell the most expensive van they had. "Oh, she works on a commission, Betty—you see, the more money we spend, the more she makes! Perhaps she has not stopped to realize that if she does not sell us what we want, she will not make anything!"

Betty was not sure she understood how a person's earnings could be affected by the price of a van. She decided to find out.

OBJECTIVES: In this section, we will help Betty to:

- *determine how much a salesperson earns when the salesperson's pay is based on a commission*
- *discover why the earnings of a person who works on commission can vary from month to month*

EARNING COMMISSIONS

People whose salaries depend upon how much they sell in a given period of time are said to be paid on **commission**. These salespeople receive a percent of each amount they bring in. For example, Jason, who works at a used-car lot, earns a 15% commission on every car he sells. Today Jason sold a car for $6000. His earnings are 15% of $6000.

$$6000 \times 0.15 = \$900$$

The more cars Jason sells, the more money he makes. If he sells no cars in a particular day, he earns no money that day.

Some salespeople earn a regular salary plus a commission. The ad pictured here is offering a weekly salary plus a commission. If the headline is to be believed, the salesperson could earn $50,000 in a year. But he or she would probably have to make a lot of sales to earn that much.

Auto

$50,000+ POTENTIAL

We are seeking 2 aggressive self-motivated people to add to our highly successful team. Previous auto experience helpful. For those people with HEAVY RETAIL SALES EXP. We have an intensive in-house training program to launch a successful sales career. We offer:

- Weekly salary & comm.
- New demo.
- Top medical ins. program.
- Heavy advertising.
- Excellent service dept. to keep your customers happy.

Suppose the weekly salary is $300; for 52 weeks the salary would be $15,600 (300 x 52 weeks). If the salesperson earns 10% commission on all sales and sells $344,000 worth of cars during the year, he or she would earn:

$15,600 $300 x 52 = regular salary
+ 34,400 $344,000 x 0.10 = commission
$ 50,000   total for the year

If these are new cars, this could mean somewhere between 25 and 40 cars per year. If the commission rate is less than 10%, the salesperson would have to sell more cars to make the same amount.

Sales companies will also encourage their salespeople to sell more by offering them a **graduated commission**. If they sell up to a specified amount, their commission rate will be a certain percent; if they sell more than that amount, their percent increases.

For example, a real estate salesperson may receive 4% of the selling price of homes selling for up to $100,000. If the salesperson sells a home for $250,000, he or she may receive 6% of the amount of the sale price that is over $100,000.

$100,000 x 0.04 = $4000	4% of the minimum
$250,000 – 100,000 = $150,000	amount over $100,000
$150,000 x 0.06 = $9000	6% of the excess
$4000 + $9000 = $13,000	total commission

PUSH MONEY

Consumers are easily influenced when they lack adequate product information. Unfortunately, in a great number of stores salespeople are not informed enough about a product to give adequate information. They are just trained to take your orders. Others may be well informed, but the consumer has no way of knowing if the salesperson is being paid **push money**. Push money is a cash incentive given to the salesperson by the manufacturer for selling that manufacturer's products. Push money is different from a commission, which is money paid by the store. Store commissions are given to salespeople for selling all products in the store. Push money is paid by the manufacturer for the sale of a particular product. If you see salespeople pushing Product A this week, it may be that the commission plus push money on that product is better than on other products. The next week, the same salesperson may tell you that Product B is superior. Let the Buyer Beware!

As Betty was seeking out information about salespeople whose earnings depend upon a commission, she discovered the following classified ads in the employment section of her Sunday newspaper. They seemed very attractive to her, and she wondered why jobs with such high pay even needed to be advertised. Betty assumed many people would be eager to earn such income. Perhaps there was more to it than she could tell from the ads.

Marketing
ENTRY LEVEL
MANAGEMENT

- Seeking bright, aggressive, college degreed individuals for continued development and expansion of a major national transportation company opening 32nd office on way to 50 locations in the next 2 yrs.

- Our entry-level management training program is designed for motivated individuals wanting to pursue a successful career in general management, learning all aspects of how to run a business with regards to management, marketing, and administration.

- First yr income between $18,000 & $20,000. All promotions to management from within based on performance and merit.

- 4 yr college degree required.

- Benefits include profit sharing, medical & life insurance as well as a training program.
- Management incomes yearly from $27,000 – $50,000.

ALL YOU NEED IS THE DESIRE TO EARN MORE MONEY than you have ever earned before!! Energy and commitment a necessity. College a plus. Take this oppty. to do yourself a favor. Call today for details. $1500/mo start.

$$$
AUTO SALES

Midland County's largest used car dealer needs two strong, exper. salespeople. We stock 150 cars under $6,000 retail and we can get your deals done! Salary to $200/week for the right person. Bilingual a big plus but not necessary. 5 day week, insurance, strong advertising and stronger traffic make this one of the top sales jobs in town. If you have the references and past earnings to prove you're one of the best we want to talk to you!

Betty remembered talking with a friend who sells cars. Betty found out that if there is a rebate or discount given on a car, that affects how much commission is earned. Suppose a car is priced at $6000 and a $420 discount is offered to make the customer want to buy the car. The salesperson receives commission only on $5580 ($6000 – $420 = $5580). Betty realizes that finding a job requires a lot of research. She cannot just read the ads.

Ask Yourself

1. How can people earn such high pay?

2. How does a graduated commission work?

3. What is push money?

4. How is push money different from a commission?

5. How could a computer spreadsheet program be used to find commissions, wages, and salaries?

SHARPEN YOUR SKILLS

———— Skill 1 ————

Betty's friend Rosalie is a salesperson at a department store. She sells small appliances and housewares. Among the many items she sells is a fancy ceramic mug.

COMPUTER MUG of glazed earthenware with terminal and keyboard as handle. Dishwasher-safe. For hot liquids, cold beverages, pencils, more. Holds 14 oz.
#45678 mug   **$12.95**

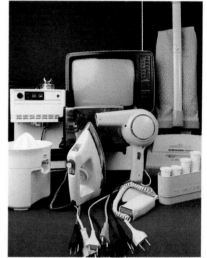

This week Rosalie sold 25 mugs at $12.95 each and earned 7% commission.

Question   To the nearest penny, how much did Rosalie earn from the sales of these mugs?

Solution $ 12.95   price of mug
            x   25   number of mugs
            $323.75   total sales

            $ 323.75   total sales
            x   0.07   commission rate
            $22.6625   earnings $22.66 to the nearest cent

Rosalie earned $22.66 as her commission on the mugs.

_____ Skill 2 _____

The car salesperson described in this ad will earn $300 per week plus a commission. William has accepted the job. His first 4 weeks on the job, he sold 3 cars for a total of $19,500. His commission rate is 8%.

Auto Sales
EARN $100,000 OR MORE $300 Sal./Wk + Commission We are fast growing firm. We are looking for a strong sales background. Must be good in paperwork & honest.

Question   How much did William earn during those 4 weeks?

Solution

$ 300	per week	$19,500	total sales
x 4	number of weeks	x 0.08	commission rate
$1200	regular salary	$1560.00	commission

$1200 + $1560 = $2760   total earnings

William earned $2760 as his salary plus commission during the 4 weeks.

_____ Skill 3 _____

Yvette is a real-estate salesperson. Her earnings are based on a graduated commission. She receives 4% of any sale up to $100,000. For any amount over $100,000, she receives 6% commission.

Questions How much will she make selling each home described here?

1. MINT CONDITION!! $109,000
You'll appreciate love and care that went into this stunning 3 bdrm, 2 bath home. Vaulted ceilings, custom drapes, mst. bath w/whirlpool/double vanity.

2. 1005 Maple $189,900
Stunning custom in Maple Estates! Porte cochere, antique brick, soaring clgs, skylit kitchen, microwave, plant ledges, gorgeous cabinets, split bdrms, custom drapes & MORE!!!

Solutions

1. $100,000		**2.** $100,000
x 0.04	rate up to $100,000	x 0.04
$4000	first commission	$4000
$109,000		$189,900
−100,000		−100,000
$ 9,000	amount over $100,000	$ 89,900
$ 9,000	amount over $100,000	$ 89,900
x 0.06	rate over $100,000	x 0.06
$540	second commission	$5394
$4000	first commission	$4000
540	second commission	5394
$4540	total commission	$9394

EXERCISE YOUR SKILLS

1. If a salesperson is earning a commission, why is it to his or her advantage for you to buy the more expensive items?

2. If a person works on a commission basis, he or she cannot predict exactly what next month's income is going to be. How can he or she then handle money so there is enough to pay bills?

3. Imagine that you work on commission in a large department store. During the month before Christmas and Hanukkah your division has a high volume of sales and your salary is three times what it was the previous month. Would you be tempted to spend most of your earnings, assuming next month's salary will be as high? Why or why not?

4. Reread each ad that Betty read in this section. Decide what is positive and what is negative about each position. Make a list of questions you would ask if you went for an interview for each job. Which jobs appeal most to you? Which jobs appeal least to you?

_____ **Activity 1** _____

Find the total sales amount and the commission that would be paid to a salesperson for each of the following items. Costs and commission rates are shown. You may use a spreadsheet program or draw a table like the following to complete the exercises.

Number Sold	Price	Comm. Rate	Total Sales	Comm.

	Number Sold	Price	Commission Rate		Number Sold	Price	Commission Rate
1.	21	$16.75	9%	**2.**	16	$21.90	8.5%
3.	40	$105.60	9.25%	**4.**	36	$2.80	8%
5.	5	$1034.60	9.75%	**6.**	14	$21.95	7.5%
7.	3	$408.10	11.2%	**8.**	32	$3.75	10%
9.	12	$22.80	8.2%	**10.**	19	$7.99	9.5%

_____ Activity 2 _____

Carole and several of her friends have jobs working for base salaries plus commissions. Find the month's earnings for each person. Base salary, commission rate, and the amount of sales are shown. Again, draw a table or use a spreadsheet program.

	Name	Base Salary	Comm. Rate	Total Sales		Name	Base Salary	Comm. Rate	Total Sales
1.	Carole	$350	12%	$6125	**2.**	Isabel	$475	11 1/2%	$6250
3.	Jose	$1000	8 1/2%	$7100	**4.**	Joanna	$2150	7 1/2%	$7350
5.	Paul	$900	9%	$6975	**6.**	Gabe	$2500	7%	$7475
7.	Archie	$650	10 1/2%	$6500	**8.**	Ellen	$1225	8%	$7225
9.	Ivy	$3000	6 1/2%	$7600	**10.**	Peter	$725	10%	$6675
11.	Fumiko	$850	9 1/2%	$6800	**12.**	Angel	$500	11%	$6375

_____ Activity 3 _____

Samantha sells cars. Her earnings are based on a graduated commission. She receives 3% of her total sales up to $20,000. In addition, she receives 4 1/4% of all sales over $20,000. Find Samantha's total earnings for each week.

1. The first week, Samantha sold these five cars:

$10,171 BRAND NEW!	5 YEARS YOUNG! $5,450
Already Discounted $2,108 2.4 liter, Fuel Injected Engine. AM/FM stereo with cassette. Power steering. Power brakes. Remote fuel door release. Power trunk release. Carpeted floor mats.	4x4, 2 dr., 5 spd w/4 wheel drive, A/C.
	6 YEAR OLD VAN $3,995
	Auto, sunroofs, ice maker, too many extras to list!
11 YEAR-OLD BEAUTY $1,750	LATEST MODEL!!
2 dr., Auto, A/C, AM/FM cass., Pwr. windows & seats.	Selling Price $7,188 Rebate – 800 SALE PRICE $6,388

2. The second week, Samantha sold cars that cost $6399, $2495, $6350, $7450, and $10,188.

3. The third week, Samantha sold these five cars:

> a sport coup for $9988, less a $200 rebate
> a used car for $3995
> a convertible for $7995, less a $1000 discount
> a used car for $3450
> a new car for $14,495, less a $1500 discount

4. The fourth week the dealer decided to offer $500 off the base price of all cars sold. Samantha sold cars with base prices of $7371, $3495, $4495, $8950, and $9388.

Eduardo is a real-estate salesperson. He specializes in selling houses. His earnings are based on a graduated commission. He receives 2% on each sale up to $100,000 and 3% of the amount above $100,000. How much would Eduardo earn for selling each of these houses?

5. BEAUTY & SPACE $199,900

5 bedrooms, 3 1/2 baths, formal living and dining. Study. Master bedroom. Lots of storage. Jacuzzi.

6. LOCATION PLUS $149,900

4 bedrooms, 2 1/2 baths, formal living and dining. Family room. Game room.

7. LOW MAINTENANCE YARD $139,950

4 bedrooms, 2 1/2 baths. Large living room, formal dining and breakfast area.

8. PRICED TO SELL $108,500

Imagine yourself in this 2000 plus square foot home. 4 bedrooms, 2 baths.

9. Assume Eduardo sold house 5 in January, house 6 in February, house 7 in March and house 8 in April. Graph his income for the first four months of the year.

10. If Eduardo were paid a monthly salary of $3,000 instead of commissions, how would the graph of his income change?

DEDUCTIONS: WHO GETS WHAT?

Luis has known Alex and Betty since they were in the 7th grade together. He and Alex have been comparing notes lately about the increasing costs of dating, keeping a car running, and getting any kind of schooling after high school. Luis realized three years ago that the only way to come up with the money he needed was to find a job. He started out stocking the shelves at the supermarket, then he bagged groceries for awhile. Now he runs the cash register and sometimes gets to work behind the deli counter.

What a shock it had been to Luis the first time he received a weekly paycheck. He knew he had worked 18 hours; he was supposed to get $3.75 an hour, and he figured the $67.50 was just enough to buy one new tire for his car. When he saw the check was only for $55.34, he immediately wanted to know what had happened to the rest of his money.

Luis knew that all the deductions from his check were somehow related to the mass of papers that got spread around the dining room table every April. His mother would scribble calculations on sheets of paper—she had been glad when calculators became solar powered because she used to deplete at least one battery every April. These calculators were accompanied by materials about taxes—but it was all very mysterious, so Luis didn't ask questions. After April 15th, all the papers seemed to vanish for another year.

When Luis began to investigate, he learned that the taxes collected by the federal government every year are used for a multitude of purposes. Highways, libraries, nutrition, national parks, airports, and agriculture would not be the same without the input of federal tax dollars. The nation's defense and the feeding of hungry children are supported by taxes as well.

Luis has heard his parents mention Medicare frequently in the last year. His grandfather has been hospitalized for a chronic illness and had numerous medical tests and treatments. Some of these costs are covered by Medicare—another service courtesy of taxes.

OBJECTIVES: In this section, we will help Luis to:

- *understand why income taxes are deducted from a paycheck and what they are used for*
- *learn what social security taxes are for*
- *realize why a new employee fills out a W-4 form*
- *calculate take-home pay by subtracting deductions from gross pay*

TAXES— A TOOL OF GOVERNMENT

Luis's taxes, and yours, too, of course, are used to support federal, state, and local governments in their several roles. In our society, government performs several broad economic functions. It provides public goods and services such as national parks and public highways; promotes economic growth and full employment; redistributes income to those in need; corrects cases of market failure created by monopolies; and establishes the legal framework for protecting the rights of citizens.

Luis knows that parks, highways, schools, and the police department are supported by taxes. He does not know how the government promotes a more equitable distribution of income. The government can, in effect, transfer money among people in society so that some are paying for government benefits given to others. Taxes, of course, are the government's major means of making these **transfer payments**. Social security programs, welfare, disabled veterans' programs, and disaster relief are a few examples of the redistribution of income accomplished through government taxation and spending in our society.

Luis knows that, as a citizen, he is also entitled to suggest changes in the way his taxes are spent. The legislators representing him are the people who can make changes. An important consideration in every tax decision made by legislators is the effect the change in tax policy will have on workers, consumers, business and industry, and the economy in general. Changes in tax policy sound easy to make, but in practice they are not. No one likes tax increases. Legislators realize this fact and avoid raising taxes whenever it is possible for them to do so.

WHY SOCIAL SECURITY?

So the government is funded by income taxes. Is social security just another form of the same thing?

From the time we are born until the time we die, we are all affected by the need for **income security**. Children are certainly affected if their parents lose the ability to earn an income. Young adults are concerned about how they would survive if they were injured or disabled. Middle-aged people are concerned about how their children would be supported and educated if they were to die or become disabled. Older retired people often worry about living expenses because their incomes are considerably lower than those they earned before retirement.

In 1935, the United States government started a **social security system** to help protect its citizens from economic insecurity. Simply put, the social security system is insurance that is compulsory for most workers. The social security system provides a base on which individuals may build protection for themselves and for their dependents. The cost is paid by both the worker and the employer.

Most employed people have social security taxes, called FICA (Federal Insurance Contributions Act) taxes, deducted from their paychecks. Employers also contribute to the program by matching the amounts paid by the employees. A percent of the employee's salary is paid into the social security trust fund, which entitles the employee to social security benefits.

A few of the benefits paid for by social security include the following:

Disability Insurance. Income to individuals who become disabled and cannot work. Disability income benefits are paid, after a five-month waiting period, when it is determined that the physical or mental disability is severe enough to prevent the person from working for at least a year.

Survivor's Insurance. Money for monthly living expenses to survivors of deceased workers who were eligible for social security. These benefits go to children and in some cases to a widow or widower.

Health Insurance. A two-part health insurance program called Medicare for persons over age 65. Medicare consists of hospital insurance and medical insurance.

Retirement Insurance. Monthly social security payments may be made to a retired worker and to the worker's spouse.

FORMS

When Luis first began his job at the supermarket, he was asked to fill out a **Form W-4—Employee's Withholding Allowance Certificate.** The information he put on this form determines the amount of money that his employer will deduct from his paycheck for income taxes. The amount will depend on his income level, his marital status, and the number of withholding allowances that he claims on this form.

- Cut along this line and give this form to your employer. Keep the rest for your records. - - - - - - - - - - - - -

Form **W-4** Department of the Treasury Internal Revenue Service	**Employee's Withholding Allowance Certificate** ▶ **For Privacy Act and Paperwork Reduction Act Notice, see instructions.**	OMB No. 1545-0010 19 _ _

1 Type or print your full name   Luis Estevez

2 Your social security number   123-45-6789

Home address (number and street or rural route)   456 Cedar Street

City or town, state, and ZIP code   Inland, In. 12345

3 Marital Status   ☒ Single   ☐ Married
☐ Married, but withhold at higher Single rate
Note: *If married, but legally separated, or spouse is a nonresident alien, check the Single box.*

4 Total number of allowances you are claiming (from the Worksheet on page 3)   1

5 Additional amount, if any, you want deducted from each pay (see Step 4 on page 2) . . . . $

6 I claim exemption from withholding because (see Step 2 above and check boxes below that apply):
  a ☐ Last year I did not owe any Federal income tax and had a right to a full refund of **ALL** income tax withheld, **AND**
  b ☐ This year I do not expect to owe any Federal income tax and expect to have a right to a full refund of **ALL** income tax withheld. If both a and b apply, enter the year effective and "EXEMPT" here . . . . ▶ Year 19
  c If you entered "EXEMPT" on line 6b, are you a full-time student? . . . . ☐ Yes ☐ No

Under penalties of perjury, I certify that I am entitled to the number of withholding allowances claimed on this certificate or, if claiming exemption from withholding, that I am entitled to claim the exempt status

Employee's signature ▶   Date ▶ , 19

7 Employer's name and address (**Employer: Complete 7, 8, and 9 only if sending to IRS**)

8 Office code

9 Employer identification number

It is not necessary for his employer to withhold any tax from Luis's income if he did not have any income tax liability (that is, did not owe any taxes) last year and if he does not expect to have any tax liability this year.

This procedure is especially useful for students who have part-time or summer jobs and do not earn enough money to pay any income tax.

READING YOUR PAYCHECK

Luis was really looking forward to his first paycheck. He knew that his income from this job would be the first step toward financial independence. His first check is shown below. He also received a pay statement summarizing his deductions.

Pay Statement

Evans Foods
1000 Center Street
Inland, IN 12345

Pay Statement

Check No.	Name			Social Security Number		
3705	Luis Estevez			123-45-6789		

Pay Date	Pay Period			Type		
07/10/–	07/03/– – 07/09/–			Salary		

	Gross Pay	Federal Inc. Tax	FICA	State Inc. Tax	Other	Net Pay
	$90.00	$5.00	$6.89			$78.11

Pay Check

Evans Foods
1000 Center Street
Inland, IN 00000

July 10 19 _____

PAY TO THE ORDER OF _Luis Estevez_ $ | 55.34 |

fifty-five and 34/100 _____ DOLLARS

Commercial Bank
Inland, Indiana

FOR _____   _Amelia Evans, manager_

Young workers are often surprised by the difference between **gross pay** (or total pay) and their **take-home pay** (or net pay). Take-home pay is the amount left over after federal and state taxes and other deductions have been taken out of the check. A **deduction** is an amount of money subtracted from a person's gross pay for such items as FICA tax, insurance, federal and state income taxes, and union dues. After deductions, your take-home pay is likely to be about 20% to 30% less than your gross pay.

Ask Yourself

1. What are five broad economic functions of our government?

2. What are four examples of the redistribution of income the government accomplishes through taxation and spending?

3. Who pays for social security?

4. How is the amount your employer withholds for income tax determined?

5. When you first get a job, which federal tax form will you be asked to complete and submit to your employer?

6. How is take-home pay computed?

SHARPEN YOUR SKILLS

———— Skill 1 ————

Luis is still working at the supermarket; since he has been there over a year, he is now making $4.50 per hour. This week he worked 20 hours.

Question   How much is his gross pay for this week?

Solution $4.50 x 20 = $90.00   gross pay

———— Skill 2 ————

Luis entered one withholding allowance on his W-4 form. This information will be used to locate the amount to withhold on a table like the following:

The wages are —		And the number of withholding allowances claimed is —							
At least	But less than	0	1	2	3	4	5	6	7
		The amount of income tax to be withheld shall be —							
80	85	9	3	0	0	0	0	0	0
85	90	10	4	0	0	0	0	0	0
90	95	10	5	0	0	0	0	0	0
95	100	11	5	0	0	0	0	0	0
100	105	12	6	0	0	0	0	0	0
105	110	13	7	1	0	0	0	0	0
110	115	13	8	2	0	0	0	0	0

Questions   1. How much will be withheld for income tax?

2. How much will be deducted for social security?

Solutions   1. Notice his wages, $90.00, belong on the line "at least 90, but less than 95." Read across to the withholding allowance column headed 1. The number in that column is the dollar amount to be withheld. The amount withheld for income tax from Luis's check will be $5.

2. The deduction for social security is read from the Social Security Employee Tax Table:

7.65% Social Security Employee Tax Table

Wages at least	But less than	Tax to be withheld	Wages at least	But less than	Tax to be withheld	Wages at least	But less than	Tax to be withheld	Wages at least	But less than	Tax to be withheld
51.18	51.31	3.92	63.86	63.99	4.89	76.54	76.67	5.86	89.22	89.35	6.83
51.31	51.44	3.93	63.99	64.12	4.90	76.67	76.80	5.87	89.35	89.48	6.84
51.44	51.57	3.94	64.12	64.25	4.91	76.80	76.93	5.88	89.48	89.61	6.85
51.57	51.70	3.95	64.25	64.38	4.92	76.93	77.06	5.89	89.61	89.74	6.86
51.70	51.84	3.96	64.38	64.51	4.93	77.06	77.19	5.90	89.74	89.87	6.87
51.84	51.97	3.97	64.51	64.65	4.94	77.19	77.33	5.91	89.87	90.00	6.88
51.97	52.10	3.98	64.65	64.78	4.95	77.33	77.46	5.92	90.00	90.14	6.89
52.10	52.23	3.99	64.78	64.91	4.96	77.46	77.59	5.93	90.14	90.27	6.90
52.23	52.36	4.00	64.91	65.04	4.97	77.59	77.72	5.94	90.27	90.40	6.91
52.36	52.49	4.01	65.04	65.17	4.98	77.72	77.85	5.95	90.40	90.53	6.92
52.49	52.62	4.02	65.17	65.30	4.99	77.85	77.98	5.96	90.53	90.66	6.93
52.62	52.75	4.03	65.30	65.43	5.00	77.98	78.11	5.97	90.66	90.79	6.94
52.75	52.88	4.04	65.43	65.56	5.01	78.11	78.24	5.98	90.79	90.92	6.95
52.88	53.01	4.05	65.56	65.69	5.02	78.24	78.37	5.99	90.92	91.05	6.96

Notice that the table is in four columns across. Again find Luis's wages, "at least 90, but less than 90.14." Read the dollar amount in the column labeled "Tax to be withheld." Luis's deduction for social security is $6.89. You can also use your calculator to find 7.65% of wages. $90.05 x 0.0765 = $6.89

_____ Skill 3 _____

Question   How much is Luis's take-home pay?

Solution   Take-home pay = gross pay – income tax withholding – social security deduction

For Luis, take-home pay = $90.00 – 5.00 – 6.89 = $78.11

EXERCISE YOUR SKILLS

1. Why is it difficult to make changes in the tax policies?
2. Why did the government start the social security system?
3. If the social security taxes you are paying now are being transferred to current beneficiaries, who will pay for the benefits you will receive in the future?
4. Why do you suppose that social security, unlike private insurance, is not voluntary for the majority of workers?
5. How do the provisions for retirement benefits under social security eliminate certain economic risks?

_____ Activity 1 _____

Find the gross pay for each person.

1. A person works 120 hours in a month and earns $5.00 per hour.

2. A person earns a salary of $350 per month plus a commission of 10% on sales. Sales for the month were $30,500.

_____ Activity 2 _____

Find the monthly deductions for each person whose gross pay is listed below. For income tax withholding, use the table in the Reference Section at the back of the book labeled "Married Persons—Monthly Payroll Period." Use your calculator or the "Social Security Employee Tax Table" also in the Reference Section, to find the social security deduction. The number of withholding allowances is given. Record your answers in a table like the one shown below.

Note: Keep this table to record your answers for Activity 3.

Monthly Salary	Withholding Allowances	Income Tax Withholding	Social Security (FICA)	Take-home Pay

	Monthly Salary	Withholding Allowances		Monthly Salary	Withholding Allowances
1.	$2400	0	2.	$3400	5
3.	$1280	5	4.	$2000	3
5.	$2550	4	6.	$2640	1
7.	$4720	2	8.	$4000	5
9.	$3000	3	10.	$5000	1
11.	$700	3	12.	$5250	4
13.	$4600	1	14.	$2208.33	5
15.	$1666.67	0	16.	$2500	1
17.	$1500	5	18.	$1500	4
19.	$4166.67	2	20.	$3500	3

_____ Activity 3 _____

Find the take-home pay for each situation in Activity 2.

EMPLOYMENT OPPORTUNITIES: SO MANY CHOICES

Daphne is one year younger than Alex and his classmates, but she has been in some classes with them. Her older brother Darrin graduated from the high school four years ago and has had trouble finding a direction for himself since then. Daphne and Darrin have had long talks about "life after high school," and Daphne hopes to learn from Darrin's experience.

Darrin left for State University the year after graduating from high school. He was full of ambition and hoped to major in aeronautical engineering. He knew he could not be an astronaut, which is what he had really wanted to do ever since the family visited Cape Canaveral when he was 11. Darrin's eyesight was not good enough to qualify him for astronaut training, so he had decided to try to participate in the space program in some other way.

Darrin's first year at State was tough. About mid-October he began to wish he had not skimmed through some of those higher-level science and mathematics courses he had taken in high school. But he had only taken them because his friends had.

He stayed at State only one year then came home and enrolled in a community college for a year. After that he dropped out and took a job. He moved out of the family house into an apartment. He planned to save his money and go back to State the following year. But he discovered living in an apartment was too expensive, and he moved back home again.

Daphne is glad to have Darrin at home, but all the changes have really been hard on the family. She would like a clearer picture of what is waiting for her out there before she wastes a lot of time and money. She would prefer training for a career for which she has the interest and the skills. She would also like some idea that she will be able to find a job at the end of the training.

OBJECTIVES: In this section, we will help Daphne discover how to:

- *identify career fields suited to talents and interests*
- *investigate jobs and their educational requirements*
- *predict what the job market will be like in several years*
- *understand what financial benefits in addition to pay are included as a part of employment*

**CHOOSING
A CAREER**

Daphne wonders why Darrin is having such a hard time choosing a career. She knows it is probably one of the most important decisions people have to make in their lives. But studies have shown that fewer than 50% of the people surveyed enjoy their work. More people could have jobs they enjoy if they took more time to assess their interests and abilities. A career choice is important, not only because of the tremendous amount of time spent on the job, but also because of the influence the career choice has on the quality of your life—your income, self-esteem, and satisfaction. Daphne knows that some people have fewer choices than others. But because she is fortunate enough to have choices, she wants to make them carefully.

The number of occupations in the United States can be counted in the thousands. Some occupations require long periods of education or training. A few jobs do not. But most require some post-high-school education or training. Perhaps some workers, like Darrin, had missed an opportunity to benefit from the education they were being offered. Of the 40 occupations with the largest projected job growth in the next decade, only one in four will require a college degree or specialized technical training, according to employment projections published by the U.S. Bureau of Labor Statistics. This agency groups occupations in 13 clusters of related jobs, as follows:

Industrial production	Office
Service	Education
Sales	Construction
Transportation	Scientific and technical
Mechanics and repairers	Health
Social science	Social service
Art, design, and communication	

With the large number of occupational choices in front of her, Daphne wonders: "Where do I begin?"

If you are asking that same question, start with what you know about your own interests and abilities. Do you like frequent contact with other people, or do you prefer to spend a lot of time alone? Are you a good follower or someone whose greatest rewards come from directing others in a work effort? Identify your personal strengths in skills such as communication, social work, computation, investigation, manual work, creative efforts, interpersonal relations, and management.

The next step is to match your individual talents, interests, and goals with those required by various fields of work. A good place to begin is with the *Occupational Outlook Handbook* published by the Bureau of Labor Statistics. Numerous other sources are available in school and public libraries. Interviewing people in a field that interests you is also helpful in answering many questions. Remember, too, that as the demand for goods and services changes, workers often have to change jobs. It is estimated that college-educated workers change jobs an average of four to eight times in their lifetimes. Workers with high school educations change jobs more frequently.

Education makes a difference in occupational choice, weekly earnings, and lifetime income. According to the most recent available data, people who have postsecondary education can expect to earn more than $1,400,000 in their lifetimes. This is nearly two and a half times the $600,000 likely to be earned by workers who had fewer than eight years of schooling and more than one and a half times as much as high school graduates. In order to maximize income, it pays to acquire additional education and training.

Job opportunities and occupational trends are being changed by **technology**. Technology enables machines or labor-saving methods to be used to produce goods and services rather than labor. As a percent of the total work force, the number of blue-collar workers (carpenters, plumbers, and factory workers, for example) is decreasing and the demand for white-collar workers (office workers, salespeople, and technicians, for example) is increasing. The changing nature of business due to technology requires workers to have better training in order to fill new types of jobs.

FRINGE BENEFITS

Wages and salary are only one kind of financial reward for work. Paid vacations, life and health insurance, free uniforms, retirement plans, stock options, and discounts on company products are also part of total earnings. These other benefits are called **fringe benefits**. These fringe benefits are often called "perks." Fringe benefits are like a hidden paycheck within a paycheck. Between 10% and 25% of total employee compensation consists of fringe benefits. According to one source, company benefits can add as much as 37 cents to every dollar earned. In other words, employees earning $18,000 actually cost their employers between $20,000 and $25,000 when the cost of fringe benefits is added.

Ask Yourself

1. According to the U.S. Bureau of Labor Statistics, 40 occupations have the largest projected job growth in the next decade. How many will require a college degree or specialized technical training?

2. The material you have just read suggests that you begin considering the choice of a career by identifying your own interests and abilities. Name eight skills in which you might have strength.

3. Another step is to match your interests and talents with those required by various fields of work. What publication offered by the Bureau of Labor Statistics can you consult for this information?

4. How has technology affected the percent of blue-collar workers in the total work force?

SHARPEN YOUR SKILLS

_____ Skill 1 _____

Nathan earns $8.10 per hour. He works 40 hours per week for 50 weeks a year, and also gets 2 weeks of paid vacation. His other benefits cost his employer $3000 per year.

Question   Find the yearly company cost of his salary and benefits?

Solution   Use a calculator or pencil and paper. Remember, 50 weeks of work plus 2 weeks vacation = 52 weeks.

$8.10 x 40 = $324 weekly pay

$324 x 52 = $16,848 yearly pay

$16,848 + $3000 = $19,848

The yearly company cost for Nathan's salary plus benefits is $19,848.

Yolanda earns $54,000 a year. The company fringe benefits cost 18% of each employee's salary.

Question   Find the yearly company cost for Yolanda's fringe benefits.

Solution   Use a calculator or pencil and paper.

Write 18% as a decimal (0.18). Find 18% of $54,000. The yearly company cost for her benefits is $9,720.

EXERCISE YOUR SKILLS

1. From your experience, what are some examples of jobs that are open and available at the same time people are looking for employment and cannot find a job?

2. Why would workers with a high school education change jobs more frequently than college-educated workers?

3. An interview with someone who is already working in a field you are considering is helpful in answering some of your questions. What are six questions you might ask in such an interview?

_____ Activity 1 _____

Find the yearly company cost for each job.

1. Salary of $20,000 a year plus benefits of $4000.

2. Wages of $6.55 per hour. Work week of 40 hours. Work 50 weeks a year, plus 2 weeks paid vacation. Other benefits of $2200.

3. Salary of $3,400 a month plus benefits equal to 12% of the salary.

4. Wages of $11.15 per hour. Work 40 hours a week, 40 weeks per year, plus 1 week paid vacation. Other benefits are 25% of the salary.

EXTEND YOUR UNDERSTANDING
PROJECT 1–1: COLLEGE INFORMATION

Obtain information from colleges you might wish to attend.

Assignments

1. Call or write three colleges for a copy of their college catalog.

2. Make a chart comparing costs of tuition; room and board; transportation to school; personal expenses; and so on. **Note:** Transportation to school may or may not be important depending upon how many times during each year you return home.

3. List the field(s) of study you are considering.

4. List the degrees or majors offered by each school.

5. Bring in three college catalogs. Turn in your cost comparison chart. Turn in a list of majors and degrees offered.

6. Write about which college you think you would like to attend and explain why.

Extension

Interview people who have attended college. Write a one-page report on their experiences.

PROJECT 1–2: CAREER INTERVIEW

Assignment

1. Make arrangements for an interview with someone who has a job in a career field or occupational area that interests you.

2. Prepare for the interview by making a list of questions that you would like answered. The following list of job topics should help you prepare questions for the interview.

Place of work and daily tasks	Hours worked
Working environment	Education required
Appearance needed for job	Experience needed
Special talents needed	Strength needed
Hazards at work	Time pressures on job
Entry-level earnings	Top-level earnings
Type of work—easy/hard	Future of job potential
Fringe benefits of job	Security of job
Work as part of a team	Work individually

3. Complete the interview. Write a report that summarizes what you have learned. Include specific questions and answers from your interview.

CHAPTER 1 KEY TERMS

Section 1–1

hourly rate
income
overtime hours
regular hours
salary
self-employment income
standard of living
wage

Section 1–2

commission
graduated commission
push money

Section 1–3

deduction
disability insurance
form W-4
gross pay
health insurance
income security
retirement insurance
social security system
survivor's insurance
take-home pay
transfer payments

Section 1–4

fringe benefits
technology

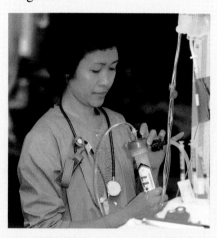

CHAPTER 1 REVIEW

1. If your company requires a lot of overtime, would you prefer to work for an hourly rate or for a monthly salary? Why?

2. Why would you not trust the advice of a salesperson whom you knew was getting push money?

3. Why is your take-home pay less than your gross earnings?

4. Why would you expect people with little education and/or job training to have more difficulty getting a job than a person with a college degree and work experience?

Find the total weekly pay based on an overtime rate of 1 1/2 times the regular hourly rate for all hours over 20.

	Number of Hours	Wages/Hour	Bonuses
5.	42	$ 6.50	$10.00
6.	35.5	$18.75	$20.00
7.	40	$21.50	$41.00

Find the total number of hours you would work during the week if you worked the following hours:

8. Saturday 3 – 8 P.M.   Sunday 3 – 8 P.M.   Monday 4 – 11 P.M.
    Tuesday off   Wednesday 4 – 8 P.M.   Thursday 6 – 10 P.M.

9. Assume you work the schedule in Problem 8. Find your total weekly salary if you make $4.50 per hour and an overtime rate of 1 1/2 times your regular hourly rate for any time over 20 hours.

Find the amount of total sales and the total commissions made, based on the given information.

	Number of Items	Price of Each	Commission Rate	Total Sales	Commission
10.	25	$ 108.92	15%		
11.	3	$3405.00	8.2%		
12.	42	$ 23.50	6.3%		
13.	150	$ 19.95	7%		

Solve each problem.

14. Your salary is $300 per week plus 15% commission. What is your week's pay if your total sales for the week is $4175?

15. Your graduated commission pays you 3% on all sales up to $7000, and 5% on all sales over $7000. What is your pay if your total sales are $10,800?

Use the tables in the Reference Section to find the income tax and social security withholding for each single person making the monthly salaries given below. What will the take-home pay be for each person?

	Monthly Salary	Withholding Allowances	Withholding	Social Security	Take-home Pay
16.	$ 1500	0			
17.	$ 2728	5			
18.	$1731.20	5			

CHAPTER 1 TEST

1. If you work 60 hours each week, would you earn more money working for $6 an hour or for $1200 a month?

2. Would you buy a car from a salesperson if you knew he or she was getting push money? Why?

3. How does your take-home pay differ from your gross earnings?

4. Why might there be unemployed people in a city that has 100 openings for employment?

5. If your pay is $500 per week plus 12% commission, what is your week's pay if your total sales are $2723?

6. Your graduated commission pays 3% for sales up to $8500 and 5% on sales over $8500. Find your pay for total sales of $12,600?

Find the total weekly pay based on an overtime rate of 1 1/2 times the regular hourly rate for all hours over 20.

7. You work 43 1/2 hours at $2.75 per hour and receive $17.50 in tips.

8. You work 37 hours at $2.85 per hour and receive $25.00 in tips.

Assume 40 hours = 1 work week, 52 weeks = 1 year, 12 months = 1 year. Find the hourly, weekly, and yearly salaries for the following pay rates.

9. $6392 per month   10. $1276.80 per week   11. $31.70 per hour

Find the amount of total sales and total commission made based on the information shown.

12. You sell 17 items at $35 each. Your commission rate is 12.8%.

13. You sell 78 items at $383.60 each. Your commission rate is 3%.

14. You sell 5 items at $2050.00 each. Your commission rate is 10%.

Use the tax tables in the Reference Section to complete the following chart.

	Monthly Salary	Withholding Allowances	Withholding	Social Security	Take-home Pay
15.	$3456	3			
16.	$5000	4			
18.	$4000	1			

In this skills preview, you will review skills that you will need to complete the exercises in the next two chapters. If you do not know how to complete any exercises. be sure to ask for help.

Round to the nearest whole number.

1. 2.7   **2.** 17.3   **3.** 208.9   **4.** 5,627.85

Round to the nearest cent.

5. $2.176   **6.** $10.5823   **7.** $0.765   **8.** $373.1649

Find each product.

9. $6.23   **10.** $245   **11.** $3,000   **12.** $60,000
        x 16   x 0.6   x 0.17   x 0.065

13. $70.50   **14.** $25.82   **15.** $109.85   **16.** $753.50
        x 0.4   x .0.14   x 1.75   x 0.0175

Write each of the following in words.

17. $57.00   **18.** $15.25   **19.** $378.49   **20.** $14,250

Use the table to answer each question.

21. How many more units did Ann sell than Beth?

22. What were the total sales?

23. Make a bar graph to show the information given in the table.

	SALES	
	Units	**Dollars**
Tom	450	$900
Beth	300	$575
Angel	650	$1200

24. The principal of a loan is $600, the interest rate is 18%, and the time is 3 years. Use the formula **i = prt** (**interest = principal x rate x time**) to find the interest.

Plot graphs of the following three functions by selecting values of x and calculating the corresponding values of y.

25. $y = 2x + 3$ **26.** $y = x + 7$ **27.** $y = -2x - 1$

28. Graph the inequality $y \leq x - 5$

29. On a separate graph, show the graph of $y > x + 1$

Use a calculator to compute the following numbers and write them in standard form.

30. 4^2 **31.** 7^3 **32.** 6^4 **33.** 2^7

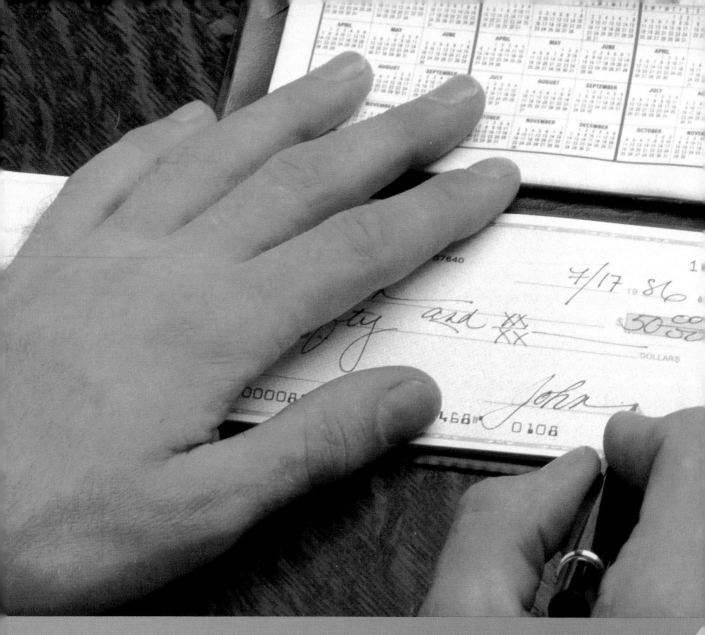

CHAPTER 2 CHECK OUT THE ACCOUNT

In this chapter, the young people in our class will be introduced to the use of a checking account in a bank. Jeff will examine the differences among services offered with a checking account at different banks and will compare the charges involved at each bank. He will use the cost of checks, service charges, extra fees, and interest earned to calculate a new checking account balance at the end of a month.

Latoya will show us how to write a check, endorse it correctly, and keep a proper check register. She imagines herself the treasurer of the Eldorado Open Golf Tournament, writing checks for thousands of dollars to the winners. Someday she may in fact have responsibility for large amounts of money, if she pursues her interest in business and finance.

Larry will discover the necessity of keeping a close watch on how much money he has in his checking account and will go through the process of reconciling his check register with a bank statement. He is fascinated by automated teller machines, or ATMs, which will give him money at convenient locations all over town just for entering the correct codes. But he is still a little uncertain about exactly what happens at the other end—in his checking account at the bank. He needs to learn more.

Many young people open their own checking accounts when they begin working at regular jobs and handling money that is truly their own. A checking account can be a very helpful way of using money safely and efficiently. But it needs to be managed carefully, so that you always know how much money you have!

CHOOSING A BANK: IS THERE A DIFFERENCE?

Jeff has been keeping track of his own money ever since he started receiving a dollar a week in allowance when he was seven. Jeff's older brother, Jeremy, never seems to know where all his money goes, but Jeff keeps very careful records of what he has earned, spent, and saved. Jeff earned $305 last summer tutoring some of his classmates as they took algebra in summer school. He only spent $15 of his summer earnings and saved the rest.

Jeremy has asked to borrow money from Jeff several times. The last time he borrowed $25 for a gift he wanted to buy for his girlfriend, Ellen. Jeremy did not pay the money back when he said he would. Jeff has decided to open a checking account so his money will be a little safer. He will be doing some more tutoring now that semester exams are coming up, and he knows a bank account will help him keep track of his income in preparation for filing a tax return next spring.

Jeff also has bills to pay now, too, since he applied for a gasoline credit card in his own name. Jeff does quite a lot of driving when he does the tutoring. He also pays the automobile insurance premium.

Jeff knows that different banks offer many of the same services, but that service charges, interest rates, and minimum balance requirements can vary from bank to bank. Before he chooses which bank to go to, he will investigate the differences.

OBJECTIVES: *In this section, we will help Jeff to:*

- *learn what different types of checking accounts are available*
- *compare the costs of banking services offered by various banks*

CHECKING ACCOUNTS

The check is the most widely used means of transferring money. Nearly 90 percent of all monetary transactions, such as buying goods and paying rent, are made with checks. **Checks** are orders written by a depositor directing a bank to pay out money. Checks are safe and convenient. They provide proof of payment and records for tax and budget purposes.

Most young people open their first checking account shortly after they go to work or to college. When a person opens a checking account, the bank and the customer establish a contractual agreement that allows the customer to deposit money in the bank and to write checks on the account. The bank agrees to maintain the account, provide records, and honor checks when they

are presented for collection. When a customer writes a check, it is a demand on the customer's deposits. It is for this reason that checks are called **demand deposits.**

Following is an explanation of the different types of checking accounts available.

Cost-Per-Check Accounts. Cost-per-check accounts are considered thrift accounts or minimum use accounts. Generally, one has to maintain a minimum balance and pay a fee for each check. The fee may range from $0.02 to $0.25 per check. Some banks also charge a maintenance fee that ranges from $0.50 to $2.50 per month even if there is no activity in the account.

Minimum-Balance Accounts. Minimum-balance accounts require the customer to maintain a certain balance, often $300, but sometimes as much as $500 or more. The minimum balance may be a low balance or an average balance. With a **low-balance account,** the customer is charged a service fee even if the account falls below the minimum only one day in a month. An **average-balance account** can drop to zero as long as the customer deposits enough money during the month to bring the account average for the month up to the minimum required. Some banks advertise minimum-balance accounts as "free checking accounts." They may be low-cost accounts, but they are not free.

Free Checking Accounts. Some banks provide totally free checking; that is, there are no minimum balance requirements or service charges. Such accounts are the best type for checking account customers. Free checking is provided by some banks in the belief that checking account customers will also use the bank's other services such as savings accounts, consumer loans, and safe-deposit boxes.

NOW (Negotiable Order of Withdrawal) Accounts. One type of checking service that appears to be gaining acceptance is an interest-bearing account known as a **NOW account.** NOW accounts earn interest at the rate of 5 1/4% a year. The drawback to NOW accounts is the minimum balance requirement. If the account balance falls below the required balance, the bank charges a monthly service fee or a check handling fee.

Ask Yourself

1. Why is a check referred to as a demand deposit?

2. Are minimum-balance accounts free?

3. Does a NOW account require a minimum balance?

SHARPEN YOUR SKILLS

___ Skill 1 ___

In a Presto+ Account at Preston State Bank, the cost of using Presto+ checks is $0.0225 per check. If the number of checks written in a month is over 20, an additional $0.15 is charged for each check over 20. A minimum balance of $500 is required in order to avoid a service charge. For balances of $200 to

$499.99, the service charge is $5.00. Interest is paid on the beginning balance at 0.45% per month.

To find Jeff's new balance, the bank will subtract the cost of checks, the charge for more than 20 checks, and the service charge from his beginning balance and add the amount of interest.

Note: For these and the following calculations, assume that the amount deposited in the month exactly equals the amount withdrawn in the form of checks written. While this is not likely to be the case in reality, it allows you to see in these examples what the effect of the fees and service charges is.

Question   If Jeff writes 25 checks this month, how much will the checks cost him?

Solution   Use pencil and paper or a calculator.

$0.0225   cost per check
x   25   number of checks
$0.5625   charge for checks

This is $0.56 to the nearest cent.

$0.15   cost per check
x   5   number of checks over 20
$0.75   charge for checks over 20

Jeff's total charge for checks will be $0.56 + $0.75 = $1.31.

Question   If Jeff's beginning balance is $450, how much interest will he earn this month?

Solution $450.00   beginning balance
x0.0045   rate of interest
$ 2.025   interest earned

The total interest earned will be $2.03, to the nearest cent.

Question   What is Jeff's new balance?

Solution
Beginning balance			$450.00
Charges			
	Cost of checks	$0.56	
	Charge for checks over 20	0.75	
	Service charge	5.00	
	Total charges	$6.31	–6.31
Balance after charges			$443.69
	Interest		+2.03
	Ending balance		$445.72

Jeff's new balance is $445.72.

EXERCISE YOUR SKILLS

1. What three things does a bank agree to do as its part of the contractual agreement entered into when a person opens a checking account?

2. Why would a cost-per-check account be considered a thrift account?

3. What is the difference between a low-balance account and an average-balance acount?

_____ **Activity 1** _____

Find the interest, charges, and new balance for each bank account described.

1. In a Presto+ Account:

   Interest is paid at the rate of 0.45% per month on the beginning balance.

   There is no service charge if the balance is $500 or more. For balances of $200–$499.99, the service charge is $5.00. For balances under $200, the service charge is $6.00.

   The cost of Presto+ checks is $0.0225 per check. If the number of checks written in a month is over 20, Presto+ also charges an additional $0.15 for each check over 20.

	Beginning Balance	Number of Checks	Interest Earned	Service Charges	Cost of Checks	Extra Charges	New Balance
a.	$650	18					
b.	$625	26					
c.	$480	20					
d.	$190	31					

2. At First Bank:

   No interest is paid on the balance.

   There are no service charges.

The cost per check is $0.0225. If the beginning balance is below $1000, First Bank charges an additional $0.23 for each check written.

	Beginning Balance	Number of Checks	Interest Earned	Service Charges	Cost of Checks	Extra Charges	New Balance
a.	$650	18					
b.	$625	26					
c.	$480	20					
d.	$190	31					

3. At Second Bank:

Interest is paid on the beginning balance at the rate of 0.5% per month.

The service charge is $3.00 per month.

The cost per check is $0.0225. There are no additional charges whether or not a minimum balance is maintained.

	Beginning Balance	Number of Checks	Interest Earned	Service Charges	Cost of Checks	Extra Charges	New Balance
a.	$650	18					
b.	$625	26					
c.	$480	20					
d.	$190	31					

4. At Third Bank:

Interest is paid at the rate of 0.52% per month on the beginning balance.

There are no service charges.

The cost per check is $.0025. If the beginning balance is below $500, Third Bank charges $0.25 for every check written.

	Beginning Balance	Number of Checks	Interest Earned	Service Charges	Cost of Checks	Extra Charges	New Balance
a.	$650	18					
b.	$625	26					
c.	$480	20					
d.	$190	31					

Latoya receives a weekly check from the restaurant, the Hometown Diner, where she works after school. The weekly paychecks are printed on a computer, but they are all signed by the manager. Latoya imagines how good it would feel to sign thousands of dollars' worth of checks every month. Latoya's parents write checks to pay the bills that come to their house every month. They do not seem to enjoy the task all that much, but maybe that is because there are usually more bills than there is money to pay them with.

Some of Latoya's earnings are used to help pay those bills. Latoya would like to help write the checks, too, and keep track of how much money they have in their checking account. What Latoya really wants to do is to write checks for a large corporation for thousands of dollars of someone else's money! But for the moment, she will settle for learning how to write a proper check and maintain an accurate check register. She plans to open her own checking account when she feels comfortable with these procedures.

OBJECTIVES: In this section, we will help Latoya to:

- *write checks and maintain a check register*
- *endorse checks properly*
- *make a bank deposit*

WRITING AND ENDORSING CHECKS

Most people make money transactions through the use of checks. When checks are properly written, as shown below, they provide proof of payment and are an excellent record of transactions. However, it is important to prevent someone from altering your checks. You must carefully fill in the **payee** (the person to whom the check is written), sign it as the **drawer** (the person from whose account the funds are to be withdrawn), and keep a careful record in your check register. A **check register** is a separate form on which a checking account holder keeps a record of deposits and checks written.

Endorsements. It is also important to sign and endorse checks properly. Banks and other businesses that cash or accept checks for payment are careful that the signature on the front of the check, or the endorsement on the back, is that of the person presenting the check for payment. That is why businesses often ask for identification that includes a picture and a signature before accepting a check from a person they do not know.

```
LATOYA S. MARSHALL                                           0 0 1
2501 Maple Avenue
Inland, IN 24680                                    _____ , 19 _____
Telephone 555-1234

                                                          ┌──────────────┐
                                                       $  │              │
Pay to the order of _____  └──────────────┘

_____ Dollars
┌──┐
│L │  Inland Bank
│ B│  15 Commercial Street
└──┘  Inland, IN 12345
For: _____     _____
                                        Signature
```

An **endorsement** is a signature and a message to the bank telling it to cash a check, deposit it, or transfer your right to the check to someone else. It is written on the back of the check, at the left-hand end. Endorsements are made on the back of the check exactly as your name appears on the face of the check. Even if your name is misspelled, you should sign it as it is written on the face, and then add the correct spelling. There are three common types of endorsements: blank, restrictive, and full.

A **blank endorsement** is your signature only. A check with a blank endorsement is like cash. Anyone who has possession of the check can present it for payment at a bank. For this reason, you should not blank endorse a check unless you are at the bank.

A **restrictive endorsement** is your signature and a message that limits the use of the check. A restrictive endorsement usually reads "For deposit only." This type of endorsement allows you to send the check by mail for deposit without fear of loss. If a check endorsed "for deposit only" is lost or stolen, it cannot be cashed.

A **full endorsement** is your signature and a message that directs the transfer of the check to someone else whom you designate. A full endorsement is written: "Pay to the order of…" followed by the name of the recipient and your signature. This endorsement transfers the right of payment to the new payee.

Blank Endorsement

Restrictive Endorsement

Full Endorsement

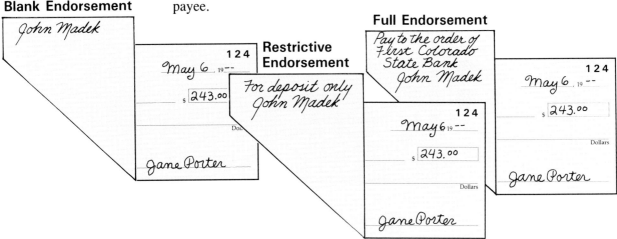

Ask Yourself

1. Why do many people use checks for money transactions?
2. Why is it important to write checks properly?
3. Why is it important to endorse checks properly?

SHARPEN YOUR SKILLS

———— Skill 1 ————

Latoya has been given the following procedures for writing a check and keeping a record of it in her check register. The numbers of the steps correspond to the circled numbers in the illustration. **Note:** You should always use permanent ink for writing a check, never pencil or erasable ink.

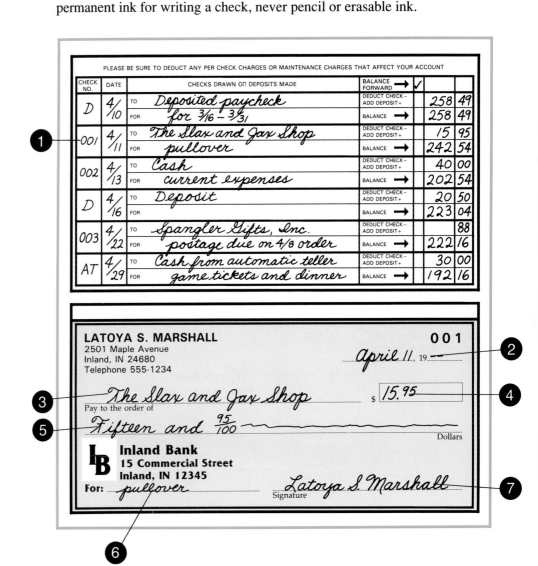

1. In the check register, before actually writing the check, record the payee, the purpose of the check, and the amount of the check. Record the check number.

2. On the check itself, write the date. The date can be important if the check is ever needed as proof of payment.

3. Designate the payee.

4. Write the amount of the check, in numbers, next to the dollar sign.

5. Spell out the amount of the check on the middle line and draw a line to fill in the space to the word "Dollars."

6. Write the purpose for which each check is written on the line (which may be labeled "For") at the bottom of the check.

7. Sign your name as the drawer on the signature line.

Latoya read about the Eldorado Open Golf Tournament played in her city on March 4 of this year. She imagined what it would be like to write the checks to the winners for such large amounts. She also imagined seeing her own name—Latoya Marshall—on the winners list! Following is the list as it appeared in her local paper:

Cynthia Alvarez	$352,000
Mark Louis	104,533
Janet Altshul	104,533
Sol Prim	53,200
Peggy Race	28,350
Bruce Dunn	28,350
Kate Schultz	21,700
Calvin Price	16,892
Pablo Chosa	8,442
Tina Marin	5,700

Question   How would Latoya make out the largest check?

Solution   Following is a check correctly made out to the largest winner, Cynthia Alvarez for $352,000.

The total prize amount was $723,700. The checks would be written from a special account that should have a balance of $0.00 when the checks are all written.

Question   What would the check register look like when all the prize checks have been written?

Solution   Beginning with the initial balance, the amount of a check is subtracted to create a new balance as shown below. Notice that the initial deposit is entered at the top. All checks are recorded with a date and description; then the amount is subtracted from the previous balance.

CHECK NUMBER	DATE	CHECKS/DEPOSITS	AMOUNT	BALANCE
	3/1	Initial deposit – prize money	$723,700	$723,700
001	3/4	To: Cynthia Alvarez For: 1st place	352,000	371,700
002	3/4	To: Mark Louis For: 2nd place	104,533	267,167
003	3/4	To: Janet Altshul For: 2nd place	104,533	162,634
004	3/4	To: Sol Pilgrim For: 3rd place	53,200	109,434
005	3/4	To: Peggy Race For: 4th place	28,350	81,084
006	3/4	To: Bruce Dunn For: 4th place	28,350	52,734
007	3/4	To: Kate Schultz For: 5th place	21,700	31,034
008	3/4	To: Calvin Price For: 6th place	16,892	14,142
009	3/4	To: Pablo Chosa For: 7th place	8,442	5,700
010	3/4	To: Tina Marin For: 8th place	5,700	0

———   **Skill 2**   ————————————————————————

Latoya has learned that she should endorse a check on the back of the check exactly as her name appears on the face of the check. Even if her name is misspelled, she should sign it as it is written on the face, and then add the correct spelling. She must be sure to include restrictions (such as "For deposit only") when they are needed.

Latoya has received the following paycheck from the restaurant.

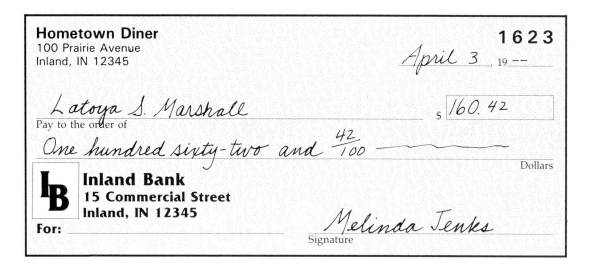

She wants to deposit it in her new checking account. She is at the bank.

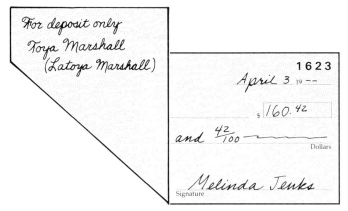

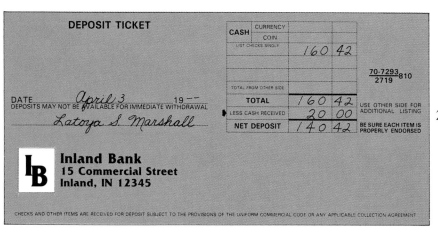

Questions

1. How should she endorse the check?
2. How should she complete the deposit slip if she wants $20 back in cash?

Solutions

1. Her signature should appear on the back of the check exactly as it appears on the front. Since the manager at the restaurant used Latoya's full name, including her middle initial, she should do the same. Because she is at the bank, she does not need to write any more.
2. Notice how the deposit slip is completed. Generally, if you withdraw cash, you must sign the deposit slip as shown.

Now Latoya has received a check from her grandfather. He has used his pet name for her on the face of the check: Toya. She plans to mail the check to the bank.

Question How should she endorse the check?

Solution Latoya should write her name on the back of the check exactly as it appears on the face, and then write her full name. She should add restrictions to her endorsement to protect the check in case it is lost, since she is not at the bank to make the deposit. Of course, she also needs to complete a deposit slip and include it with the check.

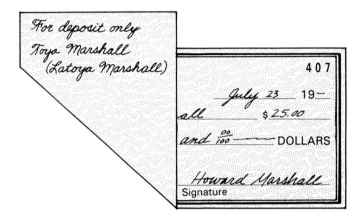

EXERCISE YOUR SKILLS

1. Why should you write checks in ink?

2. Why should you not sign a blank endorsement unless you are at the bank?

3. What does an endorsement do?

_____ **Activity 1** _____

Imagine that you have been shopping all around town. Your check register now looks like the following:

CHECK NUMBER	DATE	CHECKS/DEPOSITS		AMOUNT
301	1/15	To: Panasonic Bike Shop	For: Bicycle	$ 181.50
302	1/18	To: Brian's Sports	For: Helmet	25.00
303	1/20	To: Friendly Feet	For: Shoes	25.00
304	1/21	To: 50K Ride-A-Thon	For: Entry Fee	5.00
305	1/23	To: Gargantua's Dept. Store	For: Socks	14.26
306	1/23	To: Pandora's Hi Fashion	For: Shorts	15.04
307	1/25	To: Amalgam Dept. Store	For: Bike Rack	115.00

	1/25		Deposit – Paycheck			311.19
308	1/25	To:	Sweatshirts Outrageous	For:	Jacket	71.81
309	1/25	To:	Bike World	For:	Tires	111.26
310	1/25	To:	Bruce's Sports	For:	Racing Pedals	40.17
	1/25		Deposit – Savings			200.00
311	1/25	To:	Camper's Delight	For:	Back Pack	98.50
312	1/25	To:	Light The Night	For:	Lantern	24.00
313	1/25	To:	Army Surplus	For:	Mess Kit	25.00
314	1/25	To:	Cash			50.00
315	1/25	To:	Sounds Galore	For:	Tapes	63.00
	1/25		Deposit – Loan			120.00
316	1/25	To:	Rent–A–Tent	For:	Tent	125.00
317	1/26	To:	Cash			25.00
318	1/28	To:	The Grocer	For:	Groceries	55.30
319	1/30	To:	Energy Source	For:	Batteries	9.50
	2/1		Deposit – Tutoring			100.00
320	2/1	To:	County Vehicles	For:	Registration	5.00
321	2/1	To:	Biking News	For:	Magazine	18.28
322	2/3	To:	Ozurka	For:	Water	4.50
323	2/4	To:	Familiar Pharmacy	For:	First Aid	7.55
324	2/5	To:	Emergency	For:	Clinic	15.00
325	2/5	To:	Familiar Pharmacy	For:	Medicine	9.11
326	2/6	To:	Sticks and Stones	For:	Crutches	95.00
327	2/6	To:	Forever Photo	For:	Album	11.71

> **Note:** Your teacher should furnish you with a check register and blank checks for this exercise. If not, sketch your own—**DO NOT WRITE IN THE TEXTBOOK.**

1. Write checks for the first eight purchases in the register.

2. Add the deposits and subtract the payments as they appear in the check register to reach a final balance. Note that the beginning balance is $660.00. The final balance should be $145.70.

_____ Activity 2 _____

1. You have received a check from your part-time job. Your boss used your full name, including your middle initial. You are at the bank. Show how you would endorse the check.

2. You have received a check from your part-time job. Your boss used your full name, including your middle initial. This time you are going to mail the check to the bank. Show how you would endorse the check.

3. Your aunt mailed you a check. She used your nickname, "Rusty," instead of your real name. You are at the bank. Show how you would endorse the check.

4. Your father gave you a check. He used your first initial and last name only. You want to give the check to your friend, Judy Bruns, to repay a loan she made you. Show how you would endorse the check.

Larry still watches in fascination as the $10 and $20 bills come tumbling down out of the automated teller machine at the convenience store down the street. The first time Larry used the machine he wasn't sure he would know what buttons to push, but the instructions on the computer screen were very simple; after one visit Larry was confident he could operate them all. In fact, one weekend Larry spent Saturday afternoon driving around town locating other machines that would accept his card, and he came home with $240 in his pocket in tens and twenties. Driving around so much had made Larry a little hungry; he spent some money for pizza, some for a beef sandwich, some more for popcorn, and finally some for frozen yogurt.

Next to the yogurt store was one of Larry's favorite haunts—the music store. Larry spotted a new tape he wanted, and bought two copies—the extra one for his girlfriend, Lorrie Anne. Larry considered making some notes on the amounts of money he had spent, but he forgot about it while he was thinking how much Lorrie Anne would like the present.

As Larry was gathering up his keys and change and getting ready to drive to Lorrie Anne's house, one of the slips of paper from the ATM, which Larry had wadded up and stuck in his pocket, fell to the floor and caught Larry's attention. Printed near the end of the receipt was "Available Balance: $14.78." "Wait a minute, now," Larry thought. "I wrote two checks yesterday that haven't reached the bank yet. They totaled more than $150. How can I only have $14.78 left? Why, I deposited $300 two days ago! What became of the $300?"

Larry had a sinking feeling he knew what had become of the money. What would happen at the bank tomorrow if those checks he wrote went through his account? Larry began to wonder if there were any way of stuffing some of that cash back into the machine.

OBJECTIVES: In this section, we will help Larry to:

- *assess the advantages and disadvantages of using electronic fund transfers*
- *reconcile a bank statement and a check register balance*

AUTOMATED TELLER MACHINES (ATMs)

No longer do customers have to rush to the bank before it closes. **Automated teller machines** allow customers easy access to their accounts during banking or nonbanking hours. By using a special ATM card and punching in a personal identification number, a customer can deposit or withdraw money and even obtain a loan at the site of an automated teller. Automated tellers are placed in convenient locations such as airports, shopping malls, and street corners. The machines may be located on the premises of the financial institution.

Many transactions can be performed with the use of these machines. In addition to withdrawing funds from either your savings or checking account, or making a loan, you can use the machines to make payments on loans and credit card accounts, make deposits, transfer funds from one account to another, or determine the current balance in your savings or checking account.

But what if your ATM card is lost, stolen, or used without permission? If you lose or misplace your ATM card, you must notify the bank immediately. Usually, the most you will have to pay if you notify the bank within two business days is $50.

Follow these rules of bookkeeping when using electronic fund services:

1. Always keep the record of your transaction. Check the date, amount, location, and type of transaction. You will later use this information to verify your monthly statement.

2. If a mistake is made at the time of the transaction, call your bank for direct customer service. If you cannot get service at the time, contact the bank as soon as possible.

3. Enter your debit transactions (that is, money taken out) in your check register just as you would a check transaction. This practice allows you to maintain an accurate running total of how much money you have.

The Checkless Society. A few years ago, people thought the checkless society, in which all transactions were made electronically, would be upon us in full force by the late 1980s. This was not to be, however. Many bank customers are still reluctant to use money stations and computers. They fear breakdowns of the electronic equipment or computer errors that could tie up their funds for days or weeks. Nonetheless, electronic banking is widely used and will continue to grow.

KEEPING A RECORD OF YOUR MONEY

Customers receive monthly **statements** from their banks that reflect all checking account transactions: deposits, checks cleared, service charges, and the ending balance of the account at the close of the statement period. Several days elapse from the time the statement is prepared to the time the statement is received by the customer. During this time, additional checks may be written and deposits made and recorded in the register. Also, if the owner of the checking account has written a check but the recipient has not yet cashed it, the bank will not have subtracted the amount of that check from the account. Such checks are called **outstanding checks**. Each of these reasons will cause the customer's check register and statement to differ. The process of finding the correct balance is called **reconciliation**. (The procedure to follow for reconciling your bank statement and check register is described in detail in Sharpen Your Skills.)

After the reconciliation procedure is completed, the adjusted balances should agree. They represent the correct amount of money that remains in the checking account.

When you have your own checking account, each month, after you reconcile the account, make a notation or underscore the balance. This will tell you that your account was in balance.

If the check register and statement do not agree, you should first check your own arithmetic, and then—even though the statement was probably created on a computer and is therefore likely to be accurate—check the bank's arithmetic as well. You will have received your checks back from the bank with your statement. These are called **canceled checks**. Compare these checks with your register to see whether you missed any outstanding checks.

INLAND BANK
BANK STATEMENT

TO:
LARRY LENDER
4115 N. LINCOLN
INLAND, IN 12345

ACCOUNT NUMBER:
75-197-66

DATE	YOUR BALANCE WAS	WE SUBTRACTED NO.	CHECKS	SERVICE CHARGE	WE ADDED NO.	DEPOSITS	MAKING YOUR PRESENT BALANCE
8/31/--	186.43	14	586.65	1.90	2	706.09	303.97

DATE	CHECKS			DEPOSITS	BALANCE
8/2				286.75	473.18
8/6	125.00				348.18
8/9	23.46	40.00			284.72
8/10	9.45	15.00			260.27
8/12	15.74	139.00			105.33
8/15	34.10				71.43
8/16				419.34	490.77
8/17	21.19				469.58
8/19	8.00				461.58
8/22	14.86	10.00	45.00		391.72
8/27	85.85				305.87
8/31	1.90SC				303.97

Please notify bank immediately of any change of address. The account will be considered correct if errors are not reported immediately.

Symbol code:
SC   Service Charge
OD   Overdrawn Account
SP   Stop Payment
EC   Error Correction

Compare the amount you recorded for each check with the register amount and the statement amount for that check. When you find an error, recalculate the balance affected and compare it with the other balance.

If there is still no agreement, report the matter to the bank. You should do this within ten working days of receiving the statement. Bank bookkeeping departments work with customers to determine if there has been an error by the bank and will help customers find the reason for the differences. Some banks charge a fee for assistance with reconciliation.

YOU CAN EASILY
BALANCE YOUR CHECKBOOK
BY FOLLOWING THIS PROCEDURE

FILL IN BELOW AMOUNTS FROM YOUR CHECKBOOK AND BANK STATEMENT

BALANCE SHOWN ON
  BANK STATEMENT $_____

ADD DEPOSITS
  NOT ON STATEMENT $_____

                                _____
                                _____
                    TOTAL $_____

SUBTRACT CHECKS ISSUED
  BUT NOT ON STATEMENT

#_____ $_____
_____   _____
_____   _____
_____   _____
_____   _____
_____   _____
_____   _____
_____   _____
_____   _____
_____   _____

          TOTAL $_____
          BALANCE $_____

BALANCE SHOWN IN
  YOUR CHECKBOOK $_____

ADD ANY DEPOSITS AND
  OTHER CREDITS NOT
  ALREADY ENTERED IN $_____
  CHECKBOOK
                               _____
                               _____
                    TOTAL   _____

SUBTRACT SERVICE
  CHARGES AND OTHER
  BANK CHARGES NOT IN
  CHECKBOOK
              $_____
              _____

          TOTAL $_____
          BALANCE $_____

THESE TOTALS REPRESENT THE CORRECT AMOUNT OF MONEY YOU HAVE IN THE
BANK AND SHOULD AGREE. DIFFERENCES, IF ANY, SHOULD BE REPORTED TO THE BANK
WITHIN TEN DAYS AFTER THE RECEIPT OF YOUR STATEMENT

Ask Yourself

1. What should you do if you lose your ATM card?

2. If you lose your ATM card, for how much will you probably be liable if you notify the bank within two days?

3. What is a monthly statement?

4. What are outstanding checks?

SHARPEN YOUR SKILLS

Larry has received the following monthly statement from his bank.

INLAND BANK

BANK STATEMENT

TO:
LARRY LENDER
4115 N. LINCOLN
INLAND, IN 12345

ACCOUNT NUMBER:
75-197-66

DATE	YOUR BALANCE WAS	WE SUBTRACTED NO.	CHECKS	SERVICE CHARGE	WE ADDED NO.	DEPOSITS	MAKING YOUR PRESENT BALANCE
9/30/--	303.97	12		2.30	2		140.22

DATE	CHECKS			DEPOSITS	BALANCE
					303.97
9/1	100.25				203.72
9/3	7.50				128.72
9/9				200.00	328.72
9/11	14.00				114.72
9/16	12.95	15.45			86.32
9/19				200.00	286.32
9/21	11.15	20.00	34.50		220.67
9/24	5.40	7.75			207.52
9/28	65.00				142.52
9/30	2.30SC				140.22

Please notify bank immediately of any change of address. The account will be considered correct if er-

Symbol code:
SC   Service Charge

Question   How can you use the reconciliation worksheet to compare your check register and statement?

Solution   We will use Larry's statement and the reconciliation form shown below.

1. Enter the balance shown on the bank statement and the balance shown in your check register. Larry's balances are shown.

2. Add to the bank statement balance any deposits and other credits not shown on the bank statement. (If the bank statement shows a deposit that you had failed to enter in your check register, that deposit should be added to your check register balance.) Larry has made one deposit of $50.00 since this statement was issued.

3. List any outstanding checks. Larry has written two checks that had not yet cleared when the statement was issued. They total $63.05.

YOU CAN EASILY BALANCE YOUR CHECKBOOK BY FOLLOWING THIS PROCEDURE

FILL IN BELOW AMOUNTS FROM YOUR CHECKBOOK AND BANK STATEMENT

BALANCE SHOWN ON BANK STATEMENT $ 140.22	BALANCE SHOWN IN YOUR CHECKBOOK $ 255.57
ADD DEPOSITS NOT ON STATEMENT $ 50.00	
TOTAL $ 190.22	ADD ANY DEPOSITS AND OTHER CREDITS NOT ALREADY ENTERED IN CHECKBOOK $ _____
	TOTAL _____
SUBTRACT CHECKS ISSUED BUT NOT ON STATEMENT	
#218 $ 25.00	
221 38.05	
	SUBTRACT SERVICE CHARGES AND OTHER BANK CHARGES NOT IN CHECKBOOK $ 2.30
TOTAL $ 63.05	TOTAL $ 2.30
BALANCE $ 127.17	BALANCE $ 127.17

THESE TOTALS REPRESENT THE CORRECT AMOUNT OF MONEY YOU HAVE IN THE BANK AND SHOULD AGREE. DIFFERENCES, IF ANY, SHOULD BE REPORTED TO THE BANK WITHIN TEN DAYS AFTER THE RECEIPT OF YOUR STATEMENT

4. Subtract from your check register balance the amount of any bank charges shown on your statement. Be sure to deduct these charges in your check register also. Larry's statement shows an unrecorded charge of $2.30.

5. Add to your check register any interest paid on your checking account that month. Larry's account does not pay any interest.

6. The two balances should now be in agreement. If they are not, double check your check register additions and subtractions. Larry's balances agree.

Check Register

CHECK NUMBER	DATE		CHECKS/DEPOSITS	AMOUNT	BALANCE $1840 63
201	3/7	TO:	FOREVER PHOTOS	183 70	
		FOR:	CAMERA		1656 93
202	3/8	TO:	LIGHTNING DEVELOPING	63 50	
		FOR:	PICTURES		1593 43
203	3/8	TO:	WE-HAVE-IT DEPT. STORE	23 80	
		FOR:	ALBUMS		1569 63
204	3/9	TO:	FLASH BACK	12 95	
		FOR:	CAMERA CASE		1556 68
	3/10	TO:	DEPOSIT	363 90	
		FOR:	PAYCHECK		1920 58
205	3/12	TO:	M-MART	12 50	
		FOR:	FILM		1908 08
	3/15	TO:	ATM	50 00	
		FOR:	CASH		1858 08
206	3/17	TO:	CAMERA CASE	85 60	
		FOR:	LENSES		1772 48
	3/17	TO:	DEPOSIT	250 00	
		FOR:			2022 48
201	3/17	TO:	ATM	50 00	
		FOR:	CASH		1972 48
207	3/19	TO:	LIGHTNING DEVELOPING	26 85	
		FOR:	CHEMICALS		1945 63
208	3/21	TO:	ELECTRIC COMPANY	95 75	
		FOR:	ELECTRIC BILL		1849 88

EXERCISE YOUR SKILLS

1. What are three advantages of using ATMs?

2. What is one disadvantage of an ATM?

3. Why have we not become a checkless society?

4. Why is the current balance in your check register you receive often different from the balance on the bank statement?

5. What steps can you take to reconcile your check register and your bank statement if the initial reconciliation process does not yield a balance?

_____ Activity 1 _____

Shown below and on the left are a portion of Rachel's check register and a statement from her bank. Reconcile her bank statement with her check register. Ask your teacher for a blank reconciliation worksheet or make your own like the one on the next page.

Checking Account Statement

ACCT. 190-12566
DATE 3/31/--
PAGE 1

National City Bank

RACHEL ROSEN
717 NORTH WILSON PLACE
INLAND, IN 12345

BALANCE FORWARD	NO. OF CHECKS	TOTAL CHECK AMOUNT	NO. OF DEP.	TOTAL DEPOSIT AMOUNT	SERVICE CHARGE	BALANCE THIS STATEMENT
1840.63	7	577.80	2	613.90	6.50	1870.23

CHECKS AND OTHER DEBITS		DEPOSITS AND OTHER CREDITS	DATE	BALANCE
201	183.70		3/10	1656.93
202	63.50		3/10	1593.43
203	23.80		3/11	1569.63
204	12.95	363.90	3/11	1920.58
205	12.50		3/15	1908.08
206	85.60		3/20	1822.48
208	95.75	250.00	3/22	1976.73
	50.00ATM		3/23	1926.73
	50.00ATM		3/24	1876.73
	6.50SC		3/25	1870.23

PLEASE EXAMINE AT ONCE.

IF NO ERRORS ARE REPORTED
WITHIN 10 DAYS, THE ACCOUNT WILL
BE CONSIDERED CORRECT.

PLEASE ADVISE US
IN WRITING OF ANY CHANGE
IN YOUR ADDRESS

KEY TO SYMBOLS

AD	AUTOMATIC DEPOSIT	DM	DEBIT MEMO
AP	AUTOMATIC PAYMENT	EC	ERROR CORRECTED
AR	AUTOMATIC REVERSAL	IE	INTEREST EARNED
CB	CHARGE BACK	OD	OVERDRAWN
CC	CERTIFIED CHECK	RC	RETURN CHECK CHG
CM	CREDIT MEMO	RT	RETURN ITEM
CO	CHARGE OFF	SC	SERVICE CHARGE

YOU CAN EASILY
BALANCE YOUR CHECKBOOK
BY FOLLOWING THIS PROCEDURE

FILL IN BELOW AMOUNTS FROM YOUR CHECKBOOK AND BANK STATEMENT

BALANCE SHOWN ON
BANK STATEMENT $ _____

ADD DEPOSITS
NOT ON STATEMENT $ _____

                        _____
                        _____
              TOTAL $ _____

SUBTRACT CHECKS ISSUED
BUT NOT ON STATEMENT

#_____ $ _____
_____   _____
_____   _____
_____   _____
_____   _____
_____   _____
_____   _____
_____   _____
_____   _____
_____   _____

              TOTAL $ _____
              BALANCE $ _____

BALANCE SHOWN IN
YOUR CHECKBOOK $ _____

ADD ANY DEPOSITS AND
OTHER CREDITS NOT
ALREADY ENTERED IN $ _____
CHECKBOOK
                        _____
                        _____
                        _____
              TOTAL   _____

SUBTRACT SERVICE
CHARGES AND OTHER
BANK CHARGES NOT IN
CHECKBOOK

              $ _____
              _____
              _____

              TOTAL $ _____
              BALANCE $ _____

THESE TOTALS REPRESENT THE CORRECT AMOUNT OF MONEY YOU HAVE IN THE
BANK AND SHOULD AGREE. DIFFERENCES, IF ANY, SHOULD BE REPORTED TO THE BANK
WITHIN TEN DAYS AFTER THE RECEIPT OF YOUR STATEMENT

EXTEND YOUR UNDERSTANDING
PROJECT 2–1: BANKING INSTITUTIONS

Knowledge of financial institutions and the ability to compare their services are prime factors in good management of personal or business income. As you learned in the chapter, different institutions offer different services, charge different service fees, and pay different interest rates.

Assignment Gather information about a commercial bank and a savings and loan association in your community. Compare your information with that of your classmates. Below are some possible questions. Your teacher has a form available for you to use in completing this project.

1. Are checking accounts available?
2. What are the service charges?
3. Are savings accounts available?
4. What method is used to determine interest paid?
5. Are credit card services available?
6. Are special checks provided?
7. Are ATM cards available?
8. Does the institution have deposit insurance?
9. For what amount are the accounts insured?
10. Can electronic fund transfers be made?
11. Can customers obtain loans?
12. What types of loan are available?
13. Are safe-deposit boxes available?
14. Is estate planning guidance available?
15. Is tax assistance or counseling provided?
16. Is a travel service available?
17. List any other financial advisory services that are provided.

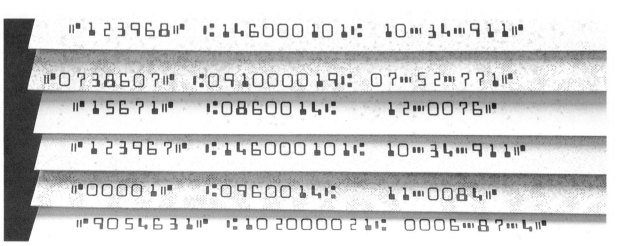

PROJECT 2–2: AUTOMATED TELLER MACHINES

Automated teller machines allow customers 24-hour access to banking services. Because anyone can walk or drive up to a machine and use it, various security precautions are taken by banking institutions to protect against theft. To use your card, you must insert it into the machine and also punch your personal identification number (PIN) into the machine's keyboard. When you receive a card from the bank, they sometimes allow you to choose your own 4- or 5-digit PIN. If anyone else should find out what your PIN is, he or she could take money from your account.

Assignment 1. Visit local banks and find how you obtain a PIN. Some people use their birthdate as their PIN. Is this a good idea? Why or why not?

2. Visit local banks and find what security precautions they take with regard to ATM cards.

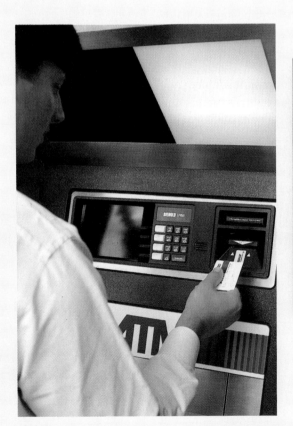

CHAPTER 2 KEY TERMS

Section 2–1

average-balance account
checks
cost-per-check account
demand deposit
low-balance accounts
minimum-balance account
NOW account

Section 2–2

blank endorsement
check register
drawer
endorsement
full endorsement
payee
restrictive endorsement

Section 2–3

automated teller machine (ATM)
canceled checks
outstanding checks
reconciliation
statement

CHAPTER 2 REVIEW

1. The cost of Presto+ checks is \$0.0225 per check, unless the number of checks written is over 20; then there is an additional charge of \$0.15 for each check over 20. No service charge is charged for beginning balances of \$500 and above, \$5.00 is charged for beginning balances of \$200.00–\$499.99, and \$6.00 is charged for beginning balances below \$200. Presto+ accounts pay interest of 0.45% per month on the beginning balance. Assume that deposits and the total amount of checks written are equal. Copy the chart below and complete it using the information given.

	Beginning Balance	Number of Checks	Cost of Checks	Extra Charges	Service Charge	Interest Earned	New Balance
a.	\$ 500	20					
b.	1000	10					
c.	600	16					
d.	400	24					
e.	300	30					
f.	100	32					

2. Find the new balance at the end of each transaction. The beginning balance is $0.00.

Date	Check No.	Check/Deposit	Amount	Balance
2-17		Deposit	$455.78	_____
2-18	405	Ravine Variety	85.95	_____
2-18	406	Power & Light	38.58	_____
2-18	407	Douglas Water	7.45	_____
2-19	408	Folly Gasoline	14.76	_____
2-20	409	Folly Service Station	53.90	_____
2-20		Deposit	104.88	_____
2-21	410	Bay Oil Company	16.28	_____
2-22	411	Shamrock Gifts	17.00	_____
2-23	412	VISA	18.81	_____

3. Reconcile the bank statement and check register summarized below.

BANK STATEMENT

Date	Transaction	Amount	New Balance
6-11	Balance forward	$400.00	$400.00
6-12	ATM cash withdrawal	50.00	350.00
6-12	Check #435	19.37	330.63
6-14	Check #437	35.00	295.63
6-17	Check #436	40.55	255.08
6-19	Deposit	50.00	305.08
6-19	ATM cash withdrawal	25.00	280.08
6-21	Check #439	11.16	268.92
6-22	Check #438	1.00	267.92
6-25	Service charge	5.00	262.92

CHECK REGISTER

Date	Transaction	Amount	New Balance
6-05	Balance forward	$400.00	$400.00
6-11	Check #435	19.37	380.63
6-12	ATM cash	50.00	330.63
6-12	Check #436	40.55	290.08
6-13	Check #437	35.00	255.08
6-14	Check #438	1.00	254.08
6-15	Check #439	11.16	242.92
6-19	ATM cash	25.00	217.92
6-19	Deposit	50.00	267.92
6-25	Deposit	40.00	307.92
6-26	Check #440	65.00	242.92

1. The cost of Presto+ checks is $0.0225 per check, unless the number of checks written is over 20; then there is an additional charge of $0.15 for each check over 20. No service charge is charged for beginning balances of $500 and above, $5.00 is charged for beginning balances of $200.00–$499.99, and $6.00 is charged for beginning balances below $200. Presto+ accounts pay interest of 0.45% per month on the beginning balance. Assume the deposits and amounts of checks are equal. Copy the chart below and complete it using the information given.

	Beginning Balance	Number of Checks	Cost of Checks	Extra Charges	Service Charge	Interest Earned	New Balance
a.	$ 400	20					
b.	300	10					
c.	150	20					
d.	500	24					
e.	1000	32					

2. Find the new balance at the end of each transaction. The beginning balance is $0.00.

Date	Check No.	Check/Deposit	Amount	Balance
4-15		Deposit	$1214.85	_____
4-15	415	VISA	101.97	_____
4-18	416	Craft Supply Co.	34.85	_____
4-19	417	Village Variety	83.66	_____
4-20		Deposit	320.00	_____
5-27	418	Republic Bank	120.00	_____
5-29	419	Telephone Co.	53.14	_____

3. Reconcile the bank statement and check register shown below.

BANK STATEMENT

Date	Transaction	Amount	New Balance
4-2	Balance forward	$200.00	$200.00
4-4	Check #426	35.00	165.00
4-5	ATM cash withdrawal	40.00	125.00
4-6	Check #425	13.19	111.81
4-18	ATM cash withdrawal	25.00	86.81
4-20	Service charges	8.30	78.51

CHECK REGISTER

Date	Transaction	Amount	New Balance
4-1	Balance forward	$200.00	$200.00
4-1	Check #425	13.19	186.81
4-2	Check #426	35.00	151.81
4-5	ATM cash	40.00	111.81
4-18	ATM cash	25.00	86.81
4-22	Deposit	500.00	586.81
4-22	Check #427	413.00	173.81

CUMULATIVE REVIEW

1. You worked 10 hours at $5.25 per hour. You received $11.50 in tips. Find your total wages.

2. You worked 24 hours at $4.90 per hour. You received 1 1/2 times your hourly rate for any hours over 20. Find your total wages.

3. You worked the schedule shown below. You earned the same as in Problem 2. Find your total wages for the week.

Monday	Tuesday	Wednesday	Thursday	Friday	Saturday
4–7	4–7	5–10	4–7	4–7	9–2

4. You earn a base salary of $400 per month plus commission of 8% of sales. If your sales for one month are $4000, how much will you earn that month?

5. As a realtor, you sold a house for $210,000. You earn 4% commission on the first $100,000 and 5% commission on any amount over $100,000. How much commission did you earn on the house?

6. You earned $95.75. Your income tax withholding is $5 and your social security withholding is $7.32. Find your take-home pay.

7. You earned $113.25. Your income tax withholding is $13 and your social security withholding is 7.65% of your earnings. Find your take-home pay.

8. You earn $7.10 per hour. You work 40 hours a week for 50 weeks. You get 2 weeks of paid vacation, plus $2500 fringe benefits. Find your yearly earnings, including benefits.

9. You wrote 25 checks one month. The bank charges $0.025 per check for the first 20 checks and $0.10 for each check over 20. How much are the charges for that month?

10. You earn $46,000 per year, plus 16% of your salary in fringe benefits. Find your yearly earnings, including benefits.

11. Your uncle wrote you a check and used your full legal name. Write your name as you would to endorse the check.

12. What is a blank endorsement? When is the only time you should use it?

13. You wrote a check for $24.65. You had $95.16 in your checking account. Show how you would enter this check in your check register.

14. Your checkbook balance shows $140.23. You have outstanding checks totaling $23.34. The bank shows your balance as $116.89. Does your account balance?

15. Why is it important to reconcile your checkbook every month?

In the same high school class as Alex and his pals and Jeff and his buddies, we find Maria and her friends facing some of the same tough choices. Most of these classmates have earned some money of their own and are enjoying the sense of independence it has brought them. They are eager to be out of school and completely on their own; at the same time, most of them also realize the importance of choosing a career they will find satisfying. For many, this choice means attending college for further training, delaying total independence for a while. Many of these students' parents have already been saving money toward this extra education, and they have been encouraging their sons and daughters to prepare for the future by saving as well.

In this chapter, Maria and her friend Nelson will help us examine how people go about saving money for expenditures that require more cash than can be found easily in a regular salary. Maria dreams of buying her own car. She saves money toward the car each month. In the process, she learns about different savings institutions and the way they pay interest on her money—as if she were making them a loan. Nelson looks into interest in greater detail, discovering it matters how often interest is paid on a savings account as well as what the annual interest rate is.

Their friend Olivia will help to explain the impact of the Federal Reserve System upon the majority of consumers. She discovers that transferring money great distances, even across the country, takes only minutes. And that the Federal Reserve System plays a key role in managing the country's money supply.

SECTION 3–1
SAVINGS:
SAVE NOW—BUY LATER

Maria does not think of herself as extravagant, but since she got her job and has had more money of her own, she has noticed several items she would like to buy. She finally did get a car just three months ago, when she could prove to her father that she would be able to make the payments on it, pay for the insurance, and buy the gasoline. Her father helped her pick out the little car; it only had 14,000 miles on it and had been owned and maintained by a large national car rental chain. So far she has not had to buy so much as a new tire for it.

Convincing Dad that she could keep up the payments had not been easy. Just being able to drive herself to school and to work made it worth going through what he had required before Maria could get the car.

For six months, Maria contributed half of her paycheck each week from the fast food restaurant to a savings account at the bank. Dad told her to keep the money to spend while she is at college next year; he wanted to see whether Maria would be able to save money for the car. After six long months, Dad was convinced.

Maria will share with us some of what she has learned about saving money. She has decided it isn't so hard after all, and maybe she will save more to buy some of the things she did without during the six months. Perhaps she can even take her friend Melody out to lunch to celebrate Melody's birthday.

OBJECTIVES: In this section, we will help Maria to:

- *recognize why people save money*
- *identify the places where people commonly deposit savings: commercial banks, savings banks, savings and loan associations, and credit unions*
- *explain the factors that will influence the amount of money earned at financial institutions: interest rate, compounding, liquidity*
- *explain the differences between regular savings accounts and certificates of deposit*

WHY PEOPLE SAVE

To Maria's father, it was obvious that the family needed another car when Maria began working. Maria is a safe driver and was using Dad's car for many of the family errands. Still, there were times when arranging transportation for everyone took skillful coordination. Maria's parents have been saving for several years for her education in addition to maintaining a regular savings account for emergencies. As most people do, Maria's family knows that unknown events cause problems for many families and individuals. Loss of income due to an accident, illness, or unemployment is quite common. Financial advisors recommend a savings of three to six months' salary to cover sickness or unemployment.

The self-discipline and consistency it takes to maintain a habit of saving each month are admirable qualities to develop. Maria's father wanted to help Maria follow through with her plan to pay for the car and at the same time develop the self-discipline of saving.

People have many reasons for saving—for a vacation, for stereo or sports equipment, or for a major appliance. Many young people save to help pay for college. Some people save to earn income. When money is set aside and used by someone else, it earns interest; in other words, money that is invested makes more money.

WHERE PEOPLE SAVE

Once Maria had made a firm decision to build a savings account, she had to decide where she would keep it. She knew there were several options available.

People usually save through commercial banks, savings and loan associations, and credit unions. Savings in these institutions are usually safe and secure and offer a relatively fixed rate of return on money.

Commercial banks offer a wide variety of services that make the bank the center of an individual's or a family's financial affairs. Some of the services offered by commercial banks are checking accounts, savings accounts, credit cards, loans, financial counseling, safe-deposit boxes, traveler's checks, money orders and transfers, and trust and investment services.

Savings banks operate in much the same way as commercial banks in that they offer such services as savings accounts, check cashing, safe-deposit boxes, and savings-bank life insurance. They also specialize in real estate loans. Savings banks are commonly found in the northeastern part of the United States.

Savings and loan associations generally lend money for home purchases and home construction. They are sometimes called **thrift institutions**.

Credit unions are not-for-profit savings and lending financial institutions. Membership in a credit union is made up of individuals who are all members of the same professional organization, church, company, or other group. Maria's father, along with 7500 other federal employees, is a member of the Federal Employees Credit Union in their county. Loans are made to credit union members from the savings of other members.

HOW TO SELECT A SAVINGS ACCOUNT

After Maria discovered the many different types of savings institutions eager to use her money, she began to wonder why she should choose one place over another.

When Maria's money is put to work, she should expect it to work as hard as possible. **Interest** is the return savers get from letting someone else use their money, and it is the most important factor in determining the amount of money a savings account will earn. Calling around to various institutions, Maria realized that interest rates vary from place to place.

The liquidity of a savings account will also influence how much the account earns. **Liquidity** means the ease and speed with which savings can be converted to cash. The longer the savers are willing to tie up their money, the higher the interest rate they will receive.

Regular savings accounts are the most flexible, or liquid; that is, deposits and withdrawals can be made at any time. Regular savings accounts allow you to deposit small amounts of money and to withdraw your savings whenever you want to. The family's emergency fund savings are in a regular savings account.

A **certificate of deposit (CD)** is less liquid than a regular savings account. The certificate of deposit is a special form which records the amount of savings a person has placed in a special account. The family has placed Maria's school tuition money in certificates of deposit because they know when they will want to withdraw it.

The CD specifies a fixed amount of money that must be deposited and a period of time during which the saver promises not to withdraw money from the account. The interest rates for six-month certificates are tied to the weekly U.S. Treasury bill interest rate.

Since the bank has the use of the family's money for a guaranteed period of time, they can afford to pay a higher rate of interest than on a regular savings account. The federal government has imposed stringent penalty regulations for early withdrawal from a certificate of deposit. The family can be penalized three months' interest on certificates of less than one year if they withdraw the money before the time upon which they agreed.

Ask Yourself

1. What emergencies do people usually save for?

2. How much do financial advisors recommend that people save to cover sickness or unemployment?

3. Name 3 types of institutions where people usually keep their savings.

4. Name 4 of the services offered by commercial banks.

5. Which individuals would belong to the same credit union?

6. What is interest?

SHARPEN YOUR SKILLS

_____ Skill 1 _____

Question   Maria can save $85 per week from her paycheck. How much will she save after 6 weeks?

Solution   Use mental calculation or paper and pencil.

The amount Maria can save is

```
$ 85   weekly savings
x   6   number of weeks
$510   total saved
```

Maria can save $510 in 6 weeks.

_____ Skill 2 _____

Maria's savings of $85 per week are earning interest at the rate of 5% per year.

Questions

1. How much will she save in 52 weeks?

2. If interest is paid at the end of the year on the balance as of that time, how much interest will her savings account earn in a year?

3. How much will be in her account after the interest is added?

Solutions   Use pencil and paper or a calculator.

1.
```
    $85   weekly savings
x   52   number of weeks
    170
    425
$4420   total saved
```

In 52 weeks, Maria will save $4420.

$$I = P \times R \times T$$

2. To answer this question, Maria will use the following formula:

$$I = P \times R \times T$$

I = Interest
P = Principal
R = Annual interest rate
T = Time in years

To figure out her interest, Maria puts her figures into the equation:

I = P x R x T

I = $4420 x .05 x 1

I = $221.00

Maria's savings of $4420 will earn $221 in interest in a year.

3. $4420   money saved
   + 221   interest earned
   $4641

Maria will have $4641 in her account at the end of the year.

Note: The kind of interest Maria is calculating is called simple interest. Banks usually offer compound interest, which will be described in the next section.

_____ Skill 3 _____

Maria's friend Dwight wants to buy a golf bag. He finds one on sale for $59.84. The sale price is in effect for 1 month.

Golf Bag ....SALE $59.84
Less than half original price!
Genuine Leather, sturdy con-
struction. Just like the pros use!

Question   If he can save $22 per week, will he have enough money to buy the golf bag before the sale is over?

Solution   Use mental arithmetic or pencil and paper.

```
                     2.72      weeks needed
amount saved   $22)$ 59.84     cost of golf bag
each week         44
                 ───
                 158
                 154
                 ───
                  44
                  44
                 ───
                   0
```

Round answer to 3 weeks.

Yes, Dwight will have enough money before the sale is over.

Skill 4

Maria's sister Sarita would like to buy these items. She can save $25 each week from her salary.

1. Audio Box
3-bank EQ.Local-distance switch
Time/frequency display switch.
Reg. $75.00   Sale $59.87

2. TEMPLAR Quartz Switch
Yellow case with black band. Measures elapsed time and lap time.
$89.99   Reg. $135.00

3. Sale $109.00   Reg. $119.95
Huffy 26" 10-Speed Bicycle
Men's or Women's mountain bike style. Front and rear brakes.

4. Zental   35mm Camera
$139.92   Completely automatic
Sale   No focusing—Auto flash
Uses 2 AA batteries

Question   How many weeks will Sarita have to save to buy each item?

Solution   Sarita will make a graph to find out how many weeks she has to save. Each level of $25 on the graph equals 1 week of savings for Sarita. The more weeks she saves, the more items she can buy.

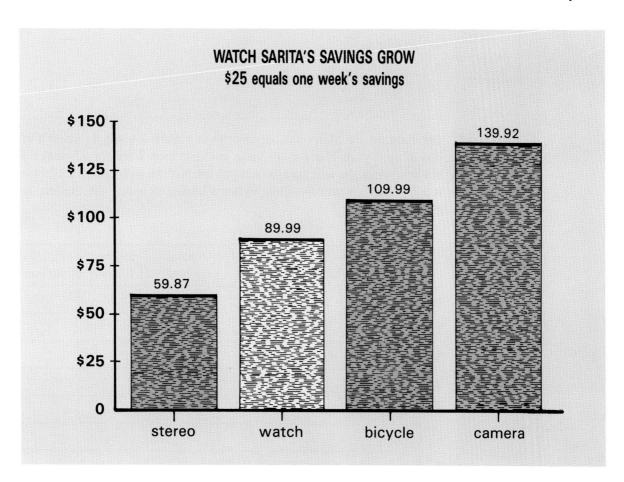

EXERCISE YOUR SKILLS

1. Why would less-liquid savings accounts earn higher interest than more-liquid ones?

2. Why do you think the government imposes stiff penalties for withdrawing money from a certificate of deposit?

3. Why should savers deposit emergency savings in a regular savings account rather than in a certificate of deposit?

_____ **Activity 1** _____

Maria and her father determined that if she could save $60 each week, she could afford to buy a car. At that rate, how much could she save by the end of each time period given below?

1. 4 weeks

2. 8 weeks

3. 12 weeks

4. 26 weeks

5. 1 year (52 weeks)

_____ **Activity 2** _____

The bank where Maria has her savings is paying 5% simple interest at the end of each year. Maria saves these amounts each week for 52 weeks. Find out how much she will save, how much interest she will earn (Recall: $I = P \times R \times T$), and how much will be in her account, including the interest, at the end of the year.

	Amount Saved per Week	Number of Weeks	Total Saved	Interest Earned	Total in Account
1.	$ 10	52	$520	$26	$546
2.	15	52			
3.	20	52			
4.	25	52			
5.	30	52			
6.	50	52			
7.	100	52			

_____ **Activity 3** _____

Dwight is considering buying a few other items besides the golf clubs. Find how much he can save and how long he will have to save in order to be able to afford each item below if he can save the stated amounts.

1. Sale $139.99 ....Reg. $159.95
Murray's "Pro-Master" 3–9 irons, pitching wedge, 1–3–5 woods. Lightweight steel shafts. Stainless steel woods.

Amount Saved per Week	Number of Weeks Needed	Total Saved
$15	10	$150
20	7	140
25		
50		

2. Diamond/Sapphire Ring
14K gold. Elegant setting
Regular $275.00
Special Price $199.99

Amount Saved per Week	Number of Weeks Needed	Total Saved
$15		
20		
25		
50		

3. Sale $149.99 ....Reg. $199.95
Teak Portable CD Player 3-beam laser pick-up. Music shuffle for random playback. Uses 4 AA batteries (not included).

Amount Saved per Week	Number of Weeks Needed	Total Saved
$15	10	$150
20		
25		
50		

4. Calculator Plus
Business graphics and time management functions. 6.5 K bytes user memory. Lightweight. Alphanumeric display.
Reg. $209.00
Sale price $179.99

Amount Saved per Week	Number of Weeks Needed	Total Saved
$15		
20		
25		
50		

5. Save $50

Sale $369.99   Reg. 419.99
25" Remote Stereo Color TV 1-
78-channel cable compatible.
Random access touch tuning, programmable. On-screen display.

Amount Saved per Week	Number of Weeks Needed	Total Saved
$15		
20		
25		
50		

_____ **Activity 4** _____

Use the following list of items for Problems 1–3.

   a.   Car stereo system $139.99
   b.   Portable AM/FM Stereo $219.99
   c.   Computer $499.00
   d.   Auto-Focus Camera $189.99
   e.   VCR $199.99
   f.   Keyboard $129.99
   g.   Camcorder $999.99
   h.   Watch $149.99

1. List these items and their prices in sequence from least expensive to most expensive. Use letters **a** through **h** to identify the order.

2. Draw a graph or use a computer spreadsheet/graphing program to show how many weeks it will take to save enough money to buy each item on the list if you save $25 each week.

3. Draw another graph showing the number of weeks needed if you save $40 each week.

COMPOUND INTEREST: MONEY THAT GROWS

While Maria was saving money so her father would believe she could buy the car, her friend Nelson was paying close attention. He knew there were times Maria was tempted to spend some of her savings, but he saw that those savings were growing even faster than she was putting the money in. Maria explained that her savings were earning interest; Nelson saw this as the bank's way of rewarding her for keeping her money in the bank. The idea of earning money without having to work for it appealed to Nelson, who is reluctant to find an after-school job.

Nelson prefers to spend his extra time in the computer lab, writing programs. One of his favorite programs received recognition at a science competition; it is a simulation that projects the changing growth patterns of the great forests in this hemisphere and the impact those changes could have on human lives. Nelson became interested in the topic when a lumber company wanted to cut some of the trees from a national forest where he and his family have gone camping.

As a result of his study, Nelson learned how long it takes to grow new trees; he began to wonder if growing new money from old money was anything like that.

OBJECTIVES: In this section, we will help Nelson to:

- *compute the total interest for a savings account when the interest is compounded annually, semiannually, quarterly, or monthly*
- *compute interest in a savings account using a compound interest table*
- *compute interest in a savings account using a compound interest formula*

COMPOUND INTEREST

Just as Maria discovered that interest rates vary in different institutions, Nelson found that the way interest is calculated can vary, too.

Interest is always expressed as an annual percent. This means that if Maria kept $1000 in a savings account for one year with interest of 5%, she would earn $50 **simple interest.**

I = Interest; P = Principal; R = Rate of Interest; T = Time
I = P x R x T or $1000 x .05 x 1 (year) = $50

However, in practice, interest is not calculated that way. All savings institutions **compound** interest at least semiannually. This means that twice a year the interest earned is added to the previous balance, so that the principal balance on which interest is paid becomes greater and greater. Every six months, half the yearly interest will be added to the balance.

To find half of the yearly interest, the yearly rate is divided by 2. If the yearly rate is 5%, the semiannual rate is 5% divided by 2, or $2\frac{1}{2}$%.

When interest is added to an account four times a year, it is referred to as being compounded quarterly. The process for finding interest that is compounded quarterly is similar to the one for finding interest that is compounded semiannually, but interest will be calculated and paid four times a year, and the interest rate used every three months is the yearly rate divided by 4.

Compound interest is always figured on whole dollar amounts. The interest on $354.85, for instance, is figured on $354.00.

RULE OF 72

The Rule of 72 offers an easy and fast way to determine how long it will take for a sum of money to double. To apply the rule, simply divide the growth rate into 72. For example, if your $5,000 savings account is growing at an average rate of 10%, in roughly 7 years your money will have doubled to $10,000 (72/10 = 7.2).

Another use for the rule is to determine how long it will take for the dollar to lose half its purchasing power. If inflation stays at 6%, it will take 12 years for the dollar's purchasing power to drop by 50% (72/6 = 12).

The Rule of 72 is handy when calculating how long it will take you to save for special uses, such as college expenses, retirement, and so on.

Ask Yourself

1. What is simple interest?

2. What is compound interest?

3. Do you think you will earn more interest on a savings account if the compounding is done quarterly rather than semiannually?

4. What do you give up in order to earn interest in a savings account?

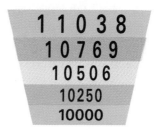

SHARPEN YOUR SKILLS

_____ Skill 1 _____

Nelson's parents have a certificate of deposit in the amount of $10,000; it is held by a bank that pays 5% interest, compounded semiannually.

Question   How much will they have in this account after 2 years?

Solution   Remember, the semiannual rate for 5% annual interest is $2\frac{1}{2}\%$.

$$
\begin{array}{ll}
\$\ \ 10,000 & \text{principal balance} \\
\underline{\text{x}\ \ \ \ 0.025} & \text{semiannual rate} \\
\$\ 250.000 & \text{semiannual interest}
\end{array}
$$

This interest will be added to the principal balance of $10,000, so the next time interest is paid, it will be computed on a balance of $10,250. Each time, the interest is added to the balance before the next interest is calculated.

At the end of 2 years, the family's balance sheet would look like this:

Time Period	Interest Earned	Principal Balance
Beginning	$ 0.00	$ 10,000.00
First half-year	250.00	10,250.00
End of 1st year	256.25	10,506.25
Third half-year	262.65	10,768.90
End of 2nd year	269.20	11,038.10

At the end of 2 years, Nelson's parents will have earned $1038.10 in compound interest on their certificate of deposit.

$$
\begin{array}{ll}
\$\ 11,038.10 & \text{ending balance} \\
\underline{-\ 10,000.00} & \text{beginning balance} \\
\$\ \ 1,038.10 & \text{interest earned}
\end{array}
$$

Recall that compound interest is paid on whole dollar amounts, so the interest on $10,506.25, for example, is found by multiplying the rate times $10,506.

Suppose the family had their $10,000 in a bank paying 5% interest that is compounded quarterly.

Question   How much interest will the money earn in 2 years? Remember, the quarterly interest rate is found by dividing the annual rate by 4: $5\% \div 4 = 1\frac{1}{4}\%$

INTEREST COMPOUNDED

JANUARY	JULY
FEBRUARY	AUGUST
MARCH	SEPTEMBER
APRIL	OCTOBER
MAY	NOVEMBER
JUNE	DECEMBER

Quarterly

JANUARY	JULY
FEBRUARY	AUGUST
MARCH	SEPTEMBER
APRIL	OCTOBER
MAY	NOVEMBER
JUNE	DECEMBER

Semiannually

JANUARY	JULY
FEBRUARY	AUGUST
MARCH	SEPTEMBER
APRIL	OCTOBER
MAY	NOVEMBER
JUNE	DECEMBER

Annually

Solution

$$\begin{array}{ll}
\$ \quad 10{,}000 & \text{principal balance} \\
\underline{\times \quad 0.0125} & \text{quarterly rate} \\
50000 & \\
20000 & \\
\underline{10000} & \\
\$125.0000 & \text{quarterly interest}
\end{array}$$

Their balance sheet would look like the following:

Time Period	Interest Earned	Principal Balance
First quarter	$125.00	$10,125.00
Second quarter	126.56	10,251.56
Third quarter	128.14	10,379.70
Fourth quarter (1 year)	129.74	10,509.44
Fifth quarter	131.36	10,640.80
Sixth quarter	133.00	10,773.80
Seventh quarter	134.66	10,908.46
Eighth quarter (2 years)	136.35	11,044.81

At the end of two years, Nelson's family will have earned $1,044.81 in compound interest on their money.

$$\begin{array}{ll}
\$11{,}044.81 & \text{ending balance} \\
\underline{-\ 10{,}000.00} & \text{original balance} \\
\$ \ 1{,}044.81 & \text{interest earned}
\end{array}$$

———— **Skill 2** ————————————————————

The bank may use compound interest tables to find the interest for their savings accounts. The tables give the amount that $1.00 is worth after each year at various rates of interest.

Questions   How much would the family's $10,000 be worth after 2 years, if the interest is figured using a table and is compounded as follows:

1. Annually   **2.** Semiannually   **3.** Quarterly

Solutions   Use a calculator.

An annual interest-compounding table appears in the Reference Section at the end of this book. A small portion of that table is shown here.

1. Find the amount $1.00 is worth after 2 years under the 5% column.

ANNUAL INTEREST COMPOUNDING	
Years	**5%** **Nominal** **Annual Rate**
1	1.0500 000 000
2	1.1025 000 000
3	1.1576 250 000
4	1.2155 062 500
5	1.2762 815 625

One dollar is worth $1.102500 after 2 years.

Ten digits after the decimal are shown on the table. Table values can be rounded to any number of digits depending upon the accuracy required. In these examples, table values will be rounded to 6 digits after the decimal.

Multiply the value of $1.00, as found in the table, by $10,000.

$10,000 x 1.102500 = $11,025.00

The family's $10,000 would be worth $11,025.00 after 2 years.

2. Use a semiannual interest compounding table (shown in full in the Reference Section) to find the worth of $1.00 after 2 years.

SEMIANNUAL INTEREST COMPOUNDING	
	5% **Nominal** **Annual Rate**
Half Years 1	1.0250 000 000
Years	
1	1.0506 250 000
2	1.1038 128 906
3	1.1596 934 182
4	1.2184 028 975
5	1.2800 845 442

The worth of $1.00 after 2 years is $1.103813, with accuracy to 6 digits.

Multiply the value of $1.00 by $10,000.

$10,000 x 1.103813 = $11,038.13

The family's $10,000 would be worth $11,038.13 after 2 years.

3. Use a quarterly interest compounding table.

QUARTERLY INTEREST COMPOUNDING	
Quarters	5% Nominal Annual Rate
1	1.0125 000 000
2	1.0251 562 500
3	1.0379 707 031
Years	
1	1.0509 453 369
2	1.1044 861 012
3	1.1607 545 177
4	1.2198 895 477
5	1.2820 372 317

The worth of $1.00 after 2 years is $1.104486.

Multiply the value of $1.00 by $10,000.

$10,000 x 1.104486 = $11,044.86

The family's $10,000 would be worth $11,044.86 after 2 years.

_____ Skill 3 _____

Another way to find compound interest is to use the following formula:

$$A = P(1 + i/n)^{nt}$$

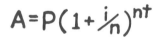

A = Amount of final balance
P = Initial deposit or principal balance
i = Interest rate per year
n = Number of times interest is paid each year
t = Number of years money is deposited

Notice in the formula that the interest rate per year is expressed as a decimal (5 percent as .05); *nt* means *n* times *t*; the superscript or raised *nt* means that the value will be raised to the power of *nt*. Recall, for instance, that y^2 is *y* times *y*, y^3 is *y* times *y* times *y*, and so on. You will see how this works as you go through the examples.

Question　How much will $5000 be worth at 8% interest at the end of 3 years if interest is compounded as follows:

1. Annually
2. Semiannually
3. Quarterly
4. Monthly

Solution   Substitute these values into the formula: $P = \$5000$
$i = 8\%$ or 0.08

The final balance at the end of 3 years is $6298.56

1. Compounding annually
For 3 years, $n = 1$; $t = 3$
$A = \$5000 \, (1 + 0.08)^{1 \times 3}$
$A = \$5000 \, (1.08)^3$
$A = \$5000 \, (1.259712)$
$A = \$6298.56$

The final balance at the end of 3 years is $6326.60.

2. Compounding semiannually
For 3 years, $n = 2$; $t = 3$
$A = \$5000 \, (1 + 0.04)^{2 \times 3}$
$A = \$5000 \, (1.04)^6$
$A = \$5000 \, (1.265319)$
$A = \$6326.60$

The final balance at the end of 3 years is $6341.21.

3. Compounding quarterly
For 3 years, $n = 4$; $t = 3$
$A = \$5000 \, (1 + 0.02)^{4 \times 3}$
$A = \$5000 \, (1.02)^{12}$
$A = \$5000 \, (1.268242)$
$A = \$6341.21$

The final balance at the end of 3 years is $6341.21.

4. Compounding monthly
For 3 years, $n = 12$; $t = 3$
$A = \$5000 \, (1 + 0.00667)^{12 \times 3}$
$A = \$5000 \, (1.00667)^{36}$
$A = \$5000 \, (1.270388)$
$A = \$6351.94$

The final balance at the end of 3 years is $6351.94.

As you would expect, the more often interest is compounded, the higher the total interest earned in a year. The following graph shows the different results when 5% interest on $5000 is compounded at different intervals, as just calculated.

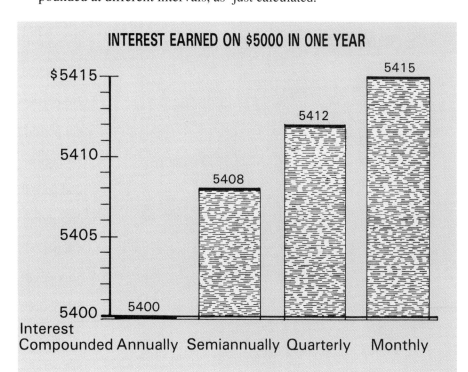

INTEREST EARNED ON $5000 IN ONE YEAR

EXERCISE YOUR SKILLS

1. Interest that is compounded annually is paid every _____ months.

2. Interest that is compounded semiannually is paid every _____ months.

3. Interest that is compounded quarterly is paid every _____ months.

4. 5% interest compounded annually means _____ % paid every _____ months.

5. 6% interest compounded quarterly means _____ % paid every _____ months.

_____ **Activity 1** _____

Use a calculator to find the amount of interest and the new balance that will accumulate over 2 years on the following principal amounts at the given interest rate with interest compounded as shown. The first few are done for you as examples.

Principal	Interest Rate	Compounded	Interest Earned		New Balance
1. $1000	6%	Annually	1st period:	$60	$1060.00
			2nd period:	$63.60	$1123.60
2. $1000	6%	Semiannually	1st period:	$30	$1030.00
			2nd period: _____		_____
			3rd period: _____		_____
			4th period: _____		_____
3. $1000	6%	Quarterly	1st period:	$15	
			2nd period: _____		_____
			3rd period: _____		_____
			4th period: _____		_____
			5th period: _____		_____
			6th period: _____		_____
			7th period: _____		_____
			8th period: _____		_____

(continued)

Principal	Interest Rate	Compounded	Interest Earned		New Balance
4. $5000	8%	Annually	1st period:	$400	
			2nd period: _____		_____
5. $5000	8%	Semiannually	1st period:	$200	
			2nd period: _____		_____
			3rd period: _____		_____
			4th period: _____		_____
6. $5000	8%	Quarterly	1st period:	$100	_____
			2nd period: _____		_____
			3rd period: _____		_____
			4th period: _____		_____
			5th period: _____		_____
			6th period: _____		_____
			7th period: _____		_____
			8th period: _____		_____
7. $10,000	12%	Annually	1st period:	$1200	_____
			2nd period: _____		_____
8. $10,000	12%	Semiannually	1st period: _____		_____
			2nd period: _____		_____
			3rd period: _____		_____
			4th period: _____		_____
9. $10,000	12%	Quarterly	1st period: _____		_____
			2nd period: _____		_____
			3rd period: _____		_____
			4th period: _____		_____
			5th period: _____		_____
			6th period: _____		_____
			7th period: _____		_____
			8th period: _____		_____

_____ **Activity 2** _____

1. Use the compound interest tables in the Reference Section to find the final balances at the end of each year for the principal amounts listed in Activity 1.

2. Use the formula—$A = P(1 + i/n)^{nt}$—to calculate the final balances at the end of 2 years for the principal amounts listed in Activity 1.

3. How do your answers compare when you use these three different means of calculation? Do they agree to the nearest penny? To the nearest $0.10?

_____ **Activity 3** _____

Calculate the interest that will accumulate over 3 years on a principal amount of $3000 when 8% interest is compounded annually, semiannually, quarterly, and monthly. Then graph your results to show the comparison, using graph paper and pencil or a spreadsheet and a graphing computer program.

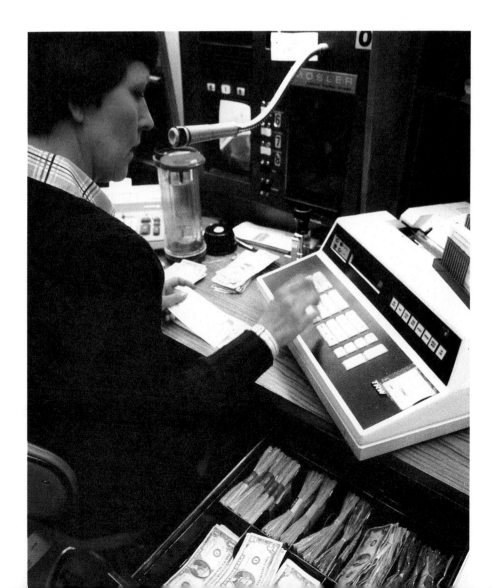

As long as she can remember, Olivia has been receiving money from her Aunt Millicent on her birthday. Aunt Millicent lives way out in California—Olivia lives in Indiana—but every November a $20 check arrives with a card. Olivia is not that fond of her younger brother, Orson, so she doesn't quite understand why Mom seems so fond of her sister Millicent. But Mom even flew to California last year and stayed three weeks when Aunt Millicent had surgery.

Olivia knew that Mom needed more money in California than she had taken with her, and she had been able to cash a check out there at Aunt Millicent's bank. Olivia thought it was quite amazing that the California bank could somehow take the cash that Mom had in the bank in Indiana and give it to Mom in California in a matter of minutes. Dad said it had something to do with Federal Reserves and "computers taking over the world." Dad has a tendency to exaggerate; many times he has reminded Olivia of how much more you could buy with $20 when he was a kid.

Olivia herself has noticed that Aunt Millicent's birthday check doesn't buy as much as it used to. Olivia assumed that meant she was growing up and the new clothes she now wanted to buy cost more than the clothes she used to buy. The way her father talks about inflation and taxes and government spending and cost-of-living increases reminds her of something she heard about the Federal Reserve System in economics class. Olivia decided to find out more about how the Federal Reserve System works.

OBJECTIVES: In this section, we will help Olivia to:

- *describe the organization of the Federal Reserve System*
- *list four important functions of the Federal Reserve System*
- *describe how the Federal Reserve System controls monetary policy*
- *observe and calculate the multiplier effect*

FUNCTIONS OF THE FEDERAL RESERVE SYSTEM

The Federal Reserve System consists of 12 Federal Reserve banks, 25 branches, a board of governors, and a Federal Open Market Committee. The following map of the Federal Reserve System shows the locations of the district banks and branches. Olivia has seen this map in her economics class and has noticed that she lives in district 7, while Aunt Millicent lives in district 12.

ORGANIZATION OF THE FEDERAL RESERVE SYSTEM

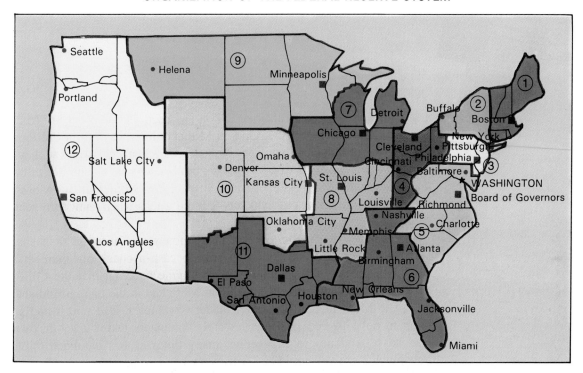

LEGEND

▬ BOUNDARIES OF FEDERAL
RESERVE DISTRICTS

★ BOARD OF GOVERNORS OF
THE FEDERAL RESERVE
SYSTEM

• CITY WHERE A BRANCH OF
FEDERAL RESERVE BANK
IS LOCATED

BOUNDARIES OF FEDERAL
RESERVE BRANCH
TERRITORIES

■ CITY WHERE FEDERAL
RESERVE BANK IS LOCATED

③ FEDERAL RESERVE DISTRICT
NUMBER. THIS NUMBER APPEARS
ON THE CURRENCY ISSUED BY
THE FEDERAL RESERVE BANK
IN THE DISTRICT.

Source: Board of Governors of the Federal Reserve System, *Federal
Reserve Bulletin* 73, no. 2 (February 1987): A86.

The important functions of the Federal Reserve System are the following:

1. To act as a central bank.
2. To serve as a bank for the United States government.
3. To supervise financial institutions.
4. To regulate and manage the nation's money supply.

A Central Bank. The Federal Reserve System issues one type of currency, the **Federal Reserve note.** This paper money is our main currency and is accepted as legal tender. **Legal tender** is any kind of money that by law must be acceptable in paying debts and taxes.

This currency is printed by the Bureau of Printing and Engraving. In addition to issuing currency, the Federal Reserve banks act as a major clearinghouse for the collection and return of checks so that depositors' accounts are credited quickly. When Olivia deposits Aunt Millicent's check in her bank, the bank transmits this information electronically to the Federal Reserve bank in its district. This Federal Reserve bank sends the information to the Federal Reserve bank in Aunt Millicent's district, which in turn contacts Aunt Millicent's bank. The use of computers has made this process very fast, so the banks complete these transfers in a day or two.

In its role as a central bank, the Federal Reserve supplies cash to meet the special needs of financial institutions—for instance, during holidays when consumer demand for cash is high.

The Government's Bank. The Federal Reserve System handles the flow of income and expenditures for the federal government. The issuance of Medicare payments, for instance, may come from a Federal Reserve bank.

Supervision of Financial Institutions. All member banks are supervised and regulated by the Federal Reserve System. Periodically, the Federal Reserve System examines the books of member banks to determine if they are conforming to Federal Reserve standards.

Regulation and Management of the Nation's Money Supply. Olivia's father comments about inflation relate to the Federal Reserve's most important function: the regulation and management of the nation's **money supply**—the total amount of coins and currency and demand deposits in circulation in the economy. The Federal Reserve System tries to maintain the right amount of money in circulation. If there is too much money, inflation results. If the money supply is too low, recession and unemployment result.

If business activity is slowing down and unemployment begins to rise, the Federal Reserve banks will try to expand the money and credit supply. To do this, financial institutions will be encouraged to borrow money from the Federal Reserve banks at low interest rates. With low interest rates, businesses are encouraged to borrow money to expand their operations, and wage earners are encouraged to borrow money to build more homes and buy more goods. On the other hand, if business activity expands too rapidly (characterized by rising prices, too much borrowing and spending by businesses and consumers, full employment, and job vacancies), the Federal Reserve banks will try to reduce the money and credit supply. If the money supply is limited, the interest rates rise, and businesses and individuals are discouraged from borrowing.

By maintaining a balance in the amount of money in circulation, the Federal Reserve is able to ensure that credit is plentiful enough to allow expansion of the economy but not so plentiful that rapid inflation occurs.

The consumer price index (CPI) compiled monthly by the Bureau of Labor Statistics, measures the change in price over time of a specific group of goods and services used by the average household. (You will learn more about the CPI in Chapter 9.)

This group, or "market basket," consists of about 400 goods and services in the areas of food, housing, transportation, clothing, entertainment, and medical and personal care. The CPI can be used to compare inflation from month to month or year to year.

Following the law of supply and demand, when interest rates are low and the money supply increases, people spend more freely. Suppliers can raise their prices because demand is greater than the supply of goods or services. Thus, inflation occurs. When interest rates are high and money is tight, people buy less goods and services. Therefore, merchants have an over supply of inventory and must lower their prices to attract buyers. By controlling the money supply, the Federal Reserve also affects the prices consumers pay for goods and services.

CREATION OF DEPOSITS

Depository institutions (banks) must deposit a percentage of their customers' deposits with the Federal Reserve System. This deposit is known as a **required reserve**. This reserve is a safeguard against a financial institution's investing (making loans and buying government securities) too much or all of its customers' deposits.

The major and minor controls on deposits in financial institutions have been shown to be quite powerful tools wielded by the Federal Reserve System. The real strength lies, however, in the **multiplier effect** that initial deposits create.

For any given demand deposit, a financial institution has the right to invest or extend loans from the **excess reserves**. As an example, assume that the reserve requirement is 20%; that leaves 80% in excess reserves. This is illustrated, in the following example, by the simple balance sheet for a $1,000 demand deposit. The financial institution actually created an extra $800 of money or credit. This was done by lending the $800 rather than holding it in the reserve or in the vault.

Initial Deposit			
Assets		**Liabilities**	
Required Reserves (20%)	$200	Demand Deposit	$1,000
Loans and Investments (80%)	800		
Total	$1,000	Total	$1,000

If the $800 that was used in making loans is deposited by the borrower in the same or another institution, still more money or credit can be created. The next illustration shows the balance sheet for this new deposit. The second deposit created an extra $640 of money or credit.

Second Deposit			
Assets		**Liabilities**	
Required Reserves (20%)	$160	Demand Deposit	$800
Loans and Investments (80%)	640		
Total	$800	Total	$800

We can also expect this $640 to be deposited by the new borrower. The multiplier effect continues as follows: $128 is held in reserve (20% of $640), and $512 is put out in loans or other investments. The cycle continues until there is not a penny left to deposit. By this time, the original $1,000 deposit will have enabled close to $4,000 in extra money or credit to be created.

The Federal Reserve System uses the reserve requirements to manage the money supply. If the reserve requirement is increased, then the multiplier effect for creating new money or credit is reduced. This is known as a **tight money policy**. If the reserve requirement is reduced, then the multiplier effect is increased. This is known as an **easy money policy.**

Economic conditions and personal behavior can prevent the multiplier effect from reaching its full force. For example, if the economy is in a period of inflation, and interest rates are quite high, businesses and consumers may not wish to borrow money. Thus, the lack of demand for money means that not all the excess reserves available will be loaned out, and the multiplier effect will be reduced. If the economy is in a period of recession, businesses and consumers may be afraid to borrow even though interest rates are low. This, too, tends to keep the multiplier effect from reaching its full potential, since financial institutions are not able to make loans. The multiplier effect can reach its full potential in creating new money and credit only when the demand for money (loans) equals the supply.

Another condition that can keep the multiplier effect from reaching its full potential is personal behavior regarding money and financial institutions. Some people do not trust depository institutions but keep their money instead at home or in safe-deposit boxes. If this money does not get into circulation (through spending or depositing), then the multiplier effect is diminished.

Olivia and her brother Orson will certainly do their part to keep their money in circulation. They aren't very big savers, and they do spend whatever comes their way. Perhaps the owner of the music store, where a lot of their money goes, will allow the bank to use its deposits.

Ask Yourself

1. What states make up district 12 of the Federal Reserve System?

2. What are 4 important functions of the Federal Reserve System?

3. What is legal tender?

4. How does the Federal Reserve System try to expand the money supply?

5. What is a reserve requirement?

6. What is the difference between a tight money policy and an easy money policy?

SHARPEN YOUR SKILLS

Skill 1

Observe the results of the multiplier effect on an initial deposit of $1,000. The following spreadsheet shows the first ten levels. Use the tables that appeared in the story for this section to help you follow the spreadsheet on the facing page.

Questions   What is the total amount of extra money or credit created through 5 levels of the multiplier effect? Through 10 levels?

RESULTS OF MULTIPLIER EFFECT ON $1000 DEPOSIT

Level	Assets		Liabilities		Totals
					$1000.00
1	Reserves Loans Total	$ 200.00 800.00 1000.00	Demand Deposit Total	$1000.00 $1000.00	800.00
2	Reserves Loans Total	160.00 640.00 800.00	Demand Deposit Total	800.00 800.00	640.00
3	Reserves Loans Total	128.00 512.00 640.00	Demand Deposit Total	640.00 640.00	512.00
4	Reserves Loans Total	102.40 409.60 512.00	Demand Deposit Total	512.00 512.00	409.60
5	Reserves Loans Total	81.92 327.68 409.60	Demand Deposit Total	409.60 409.60	327.68
6	Reserves Loans Total	65.54 262.14 327.68	Demand Deposit Total	327.68 327.68	262.14
7	Reserves Loans Total	52.43 209.71 262.14	Demand Deposit Total	262.14 262.14	209.71
8	Reserves Loans Total	41.94 167.77 209.71	Demand Deposit Total	209.71 209.71	167.77
9	Reserves Loans Total	33.55 134.22 167.77	Demand Deposit Total	167.77 167.77	134.22
10	Reserves Loans Total	26.84 107.38 143.22	Demand Deposit Total	134.22 134.22	107.38
				Total	$4570.51

Solutions	For 5 levels,	For 10 levels,
	$1000.00	$3689.28
	800.00	262.14
	640.00	209.72
	512.00	167.77
	409.60	134.22
	327.68	107.38
	$3689.28	$4570.51

The total amount of extra money or credit created through 5 levels of the multiplier effect is:

$3689.28
– 1000.00
$2689.28

The total amount of extra money or credit created through 10 levels of the multiplier effect is:

$4570.51
– 1000.00
$3570.51

EXERCISE YOUR SKILLS

1. Does one bank actually send cash to another bank across the country to cash a check drawn on an account there? Why or why not?

2. What happens if there is too much money in circulation?

3. How does the multiplier effect work?

4. In what ways is the multiplier sometimes stopped?

_____ Activity 1 _____

Use a spreadsheet computer program, or make a spreadsheet yourself on paper, to show the multiplier effect on the amounts below if the Federal Reserve requirement is 20%. Show the first 10 levels, and find the total extra money or credit that is generated.

1. $500

2. $2,500

3. $12,500

EXTEND YOUR UNDERSTANDING
PROJECT 3–1 SAVINGS ACCOUNTS

As you know, there are many different kinds of savings accounts. These accounts may vary greatly.

Assignment   Visit local banks and savings and loan associations to find information on various types of savings accounts.

1. Name of institution
2. Types of accounts available
3. Rate of interest for each type of account
4. Minimum balance requirements
5. How interest is compounded
6. When interest is paid

PROJECT 3–2 FEDERAL RESERVE SYSTEM

As you learned in this chapter, the Federal Reserve System is a very important agency. It acts as a fiscal agent for the U. S. government. The Federal Reserve banks regulate our economy by regulating the money supply.

Assignment   Gather information about a Federal Reserve System by doing research at your local library, by interviewing bankers, and/or by reading news magazines and newspapers. Answer the following questions.

1. What Federal Reserve District do you live in?
2. How does the Federal Reserve System actually process your checks?
3. What is the current condition of the money supply?
4. Is the Federal Reserve currently trying to expand or reduce the money and credit supply?
5. What are the current implications of the above activity?
6. What is the current required reserves for banks?

KEY TERMS

CHAPTER 3 REVIEW

How much can be saved over the following time periods if $45 can be saved each week?

1. 4 weeks
2. 12 weeks
3. 26 weeks
4. 1 year (52 weeks)

How long will it take to save $165 if you can save the following amounts each week? What is the total amount saved in that time period?

	Amount Per Week	Number of Weeks	Total Amount Saved
5.	$15		
6.	$25		
7.	$50		

Assume the bank is paying 6% simple interest and you have deposited the amounts listed below each week. Find the total you can save in a year (52 weeks), the amount of interest you will receive, and the total amount that will be in your account after the interest is paid.

	Amount Saved Per Week	Total Amount Saved	Interest Earned	Total in Account
8.	$25.00			
9.	$32.50			
10.	$68.00			
11.	$110.00			

You have a savings account with $6000 in it. Your bank pays 7% interest. Find the value of this account at the end of each year for the next 5 years if the interest is compounded:

12. annually
13. semiannually
14. quarterly
15. monthly

Use either the table in the Reference Section or the compound interest formula ($A = P (I + i/t)^{nt}$) to perform these calculations.

Solve.

16. Find the extra money or credit that is generated because of the multiplier effect if the Federal Reserve requirement is 20%. Begin with $2000 and show the first 6 levels.

How much can be saved over the following time periods if $75 can be saved each week?

1. 4 weeks **2.** 12 weeks

3. 26 weeks **4.** 1 year (52 weeks)

How long would it take to save $355 if you can save the following amounts each week? What is the total amount saved in that time period?

	Amount Per Week	Number of	Total Amount Saved
5.	$15		
6.	25		
7.	50		

Assume the bank is paying 8.5 percent simple interest and you have deposited the amounts listed below each week. Find the total you can save in a year (52 weeks), the amount of interest you will receive, and the total amount that will be in your account after the interest is paid.

	Amount Saved Per Week	Total Amount Saved	Interest Earned	Total in Account
8.	$35.00			
9.	$42.50			
10.	$96.80			
11.	$125.00			

You have a savings account with $8500 in it. Your bank pays 7% interest. Find the value of this account at the end of each year for the next 4 years if the interest is compounded as shown below. Use either the table in the Reference Section or the compound interest formula ($A = P (I + i/n)^{nt}$) to perform these calculations.

12. annually **13.** semiannually

14. quarterly **15.** monthly

Solve.

16. Find the extra money or credit that is generated because of the multiplier effect if the Federal Reserve requirement is 20%. Begin with $300 and show the first 6 levels.

In this skills preview, you will review skills that you will need to complete the exercises in the coming chapters. If you do not know how to complete any exercises, be sure to ask for help.

Complete each table.

	Committee	Money Raised	Money Spent	Balance Left
1.	Travel	$400.00	$350.00	
2.	Entertainment	$834.25		$260.83
3.	Correspondence		$250.00	$694.00

	Number Sold	Price Each	Total Sales
4.	12	$2.00	
5.	23		$76.59
6.		$12.65	$771.65

Make a line graph to show the following information.

Number of units sold	5	10	15	20	25	30
Profit	$2	$4	$6	$8	$10	$12

Use your graph to answer questions 7 and 8.

7. What will the profit be if 40 units are sold?

8. Which equation would describe your line graph?
   a. $p = n/5$ b. $p = n/5 - 3$ c. $p = 2(n/5)$

Find each of the following percents.

9. 20% of $1000

10. 30 is what percent of 100?

11. 10% of $444

12. 50 is 10% of what number?

13. 15% of $230.45

14. 200 is what percent of 5000?

Solve.

15. You borrowed $500 from a bank. You paid it back by making 5 payments of $105 each. How much interest did you pay on the loan?

4 A VENTURE INTO BUSINESS

Evelyn and three of her friends have decided to find out if they can operate a small business to make extra money for college. They have consulted several books on the subject. They have read suggestions about everything from house- and pet-sitting to selling popcorn and soft drinks at ball games to singing telegrams and printing mailing labels.

They realize that a lot of factors must be considered when selecting a business. Whether or not they can provide their labor at a reasonable cost is one consideration. Determining the other costs of producing and marketing their service or product is another. They will also want to know what effects competition will have on their sales. They must be able to measure their profits against the costs.

This chapter will demonstrate how labor and production costs, competition, and profit all play a part in determining which particular businesses are worth pursuing.

Evelyn is a natural business manager and entrepreneur. She first focuses on the possibility of starting a word-processing business. She has identified a market among fellow students who do not have access to computers. She has already done some typing for people including her new business partner Greg.

Greg will help Evelyn do the typing. He is a design student who has another talent that could be turned into a business idea, painting. He has already made some sweatshirts with painted designs on them.

Their friend Freda is brought into the business because of her marketing abilities. Her talent for selling people things that they do not need is outstanding. Her record-keeping and savings are not as impressive.

They all need the services of the fourth partner, Hari. He is comfortable with figures, so he will keep the company records. He has a computer spreadsheet program that allows him to find the break-even point for small businesses. The group can decide how many items they will produce and exactly how much to charge for them.

In the process of starting their business, the students learn about weekly payroll records and deductions for federal income tax and social security. They discover that the company must match employees' social security contributions, so the cost to the company for each employee is actually higher than the stated wages.

EMPLOYEES ARE PART OF THE COMPANY

Evelyn is a junior in high school. She is aware of the serious thoughts her friend Daphne has been having about preparing herself for a career. She is also in need of some extra money but is not quite ready to enter the part-time work force the way Luis has.

Evelyn has done some baby-sitting from time to time for friends of her parents. She has also watered plants and fed pets for neighbors on vacation. She wonders if there are other services she might also be able to offer for which adults or students would be willing to pay. After all, walking a dog twice a day does not really bring in much revenue.

She and her friends have been studying business principles in their economics class, and they are investigating several ideas they have for services or products they could sell without having to invest large sums of money.

One of these services is word processing. Evelyn's family bought a computer several years ago, and Evelyn has used it as a word processor to prepare reports and essays for school. She has also learned how to prepare a spreadsheet and has experimented with some functions the spreadsheet program enables her to do. She realizes that the computer could help her in several ways as she considers this business decision. It could be used to provide a service, and it could also be used to organize the records of her company.

Some of her classmates do not have access to a word processor. Or if they do have one, they do not know how to type. Perhaps they would be willing to pay to have research papers professionally typed and printed on a word processor. What is more, there is a college nearby which Evelyn now sees as being full of potential customers. There is no end to the term papers and research papers college students must write. Word processing is clearly a business worth considering.

If Evelyn and her friends decide to offer this service, they will have to charge a fair and reasonable price so it will be worth the time and effort they will have to spend. Managing any business requires making many decisions. Evelyn will investigate some of these decisions.

OBJECTIVES: In this section, we will help Evelyn to:

- *examine some of the functions of management in a business*
- *prepare a payroll showing wages, salaries, deductions, and take-home pay for employees in a small company*
- *use a spreadsheet to display payroll information*

LABOR

If Evelyn and her friends are going to invest their physical effort, mental effort, and skills in a new venture, they want to see a return on their investment. The efforts and skills they invest are their **labor.** The word labor is also used for those workers who do not share in the ownership or the executive decision making of the company they work for. In a small company like Evelyn's, all the employees perform the functions of labor, management, and ownership. Even in very large firms, labor is sometimes represented on management boards. This is because workers have unique experience and insight into the production process.

MANAGEMENT

Management is one key to a successful business operation. Suppose Evelyn decides on the best idea there is and acquires the most intelligent and industrious labor force. She cannot have a successful business without good organization and management. In all businesses, plans must be made, workers hired, raw materials obtained, and equipment purchased or built. Putting all these factors together for the first time is called **entrepreneurship**. This is the role Evelyn is fulfilling now, as she envisions a business and seeks to make it real.

MARKET ECONOMY

As manager, Evelyn must be aware that it is her responsibility to sell the best product at the lowest price and still make the highest profit possible. In a **market economy**, profit is the incentive, or reason, for the **producers** to satisfy the wants of **consumers**, or users of the service or product. The owners of property are free to determine how they can most efficiently use available resources. Evelyn's competition—that is, other businesses that offer the same product or service—may have more efficient operations. She must find out what competition she has.

In a market economy, consumers influence what will be produced by the way they spend their income. Of course, businesses try to influence consumer demand through advertising and other selling activities, but the final decision is made by the consumers. Consumers decide whether or not to buy, in what quantities, and at what price. Because of the competitive nature of business, if consumers cannot obtain what they want from one producer, there is usually another producer happy to satisfy them.

If a product or service is of high quality, it will usually sell for a higher price than one of low quality. In other words, in a competitive market, we pay for our resources—whether labor or materials—according to how they satisfy wants.

Evelyn and her friends are looking closely at the possibility of starting a word-processing business. Evelyn and her friend Greg would do the typing. Both are good typists, and Greg has learned how to use Evelyn's computer. Their friend Freda would be responsible for advertising. She would deliver flyers to neighborhood homes and students at school. She would also contact people at the community college and ask to put up posters in the student recreation center and some of the classroom buildings. Another friend, Hari, would be in charge of the finances. He has a special skill with figures and can show Evelyn how to set up their records.

They hope to provide a high quality service at a competitive price and still be able to pay reasonable wages and manage their other resources as well.

Ask Yourself

1. What incentive do businesses have to satisfy the wants of consumers?

2. How do consumers influence what will be produced?

3. How do businesses attempt to influence consumers in their choices?

SHARPEN YOUR SKILLS

_____ Skill 1 _____

Evelyn would like to keep good records of the wages each person earns in the business. She and Hari have worked out the following spreadsheet on her computer as a sample of the records they will keep. The first record is a weekly report of each person's gross pay (earnings) and take-home pay.

Below is a spreadsheet they set up on the computer. It covers all the company's employees, summarizing the information relevant to their paychecks. The number of exemptions and marital status are used in calculating the amounts that will be deducted when the paychecks are written.

If they did not have a computer they would have made the spreadsheet with pencil and paper and used a calculator to compute the figures.

PAYROLL REGISTER for WEEK 3/1–3/7 EARNINGS					
Employee	Number of Exemptions	Marital Status	Hourly Rate	Hours Worked	Gross Pay
Evelyn	0	S	$5.50	14	$ 77.00
Greg	1	S	$5.50	12	$ 66.00
Freda	0	S	$4.50	16	$ 72.00
Hari	1	S	$4.50	4	$ 18.00
Total Payroll					$233.00

Notice that Evelyn and Hari have assigned hourly wages to each worker and estimated the hours each would work in one week. Evelyn would work 14 hours. At her pay rate of $5.50 per hour, that would be $77 in the sample week. That amount is her total, or gross, pay. Freda, earning $4.50 per hour and working 16 hours, would earn $72. The total cost of gross pay for the four employees is $233 for this week.

_____ Skill 2 _____

The number of exemptions and the marital status included in the table are used to calculate social security (FICA) and income tax deductions. The income tax deductions are shown in this table.

Income Tax Withholding— Percentage Method

SINGLE Persons–WEEKLY Payroll Period

(For Wages Paid After December 19   )

And the wages are–		And the number of withholding allowances claimed is–								
At least	But less than	0	1	2	3	4	5	6	7	8
		The amount of income tax to be withheld shall be–								
$0	$25	$0	$0	$0	$0	$0	$0	$0	$0	$0
25	30	1	0	0	0	0	0	0	0	0
30	35	1	0	0	0	0	0	0	0	0
35	40	2	0	0	0	0	0	0	0	0
40	45	3	0	0	0	0	0	0	0	0
45	50	4	0	0	0	0	0	0	0	0
50	55	4	0	0	0	0	0	0	0	0
55	60	5	0	0	0	0	0	0	0	0
60	65	6	0	0	0	0	0	0	0	0
65	70	7	1	0	0	0	0	0	0	0
70	75	7	2	0	0	0	0	0	0	0
75	80	8	2	0	0	0	0	0	0	0
80	85	9	3	0	0	0	0	0	0	0
85	90	10	4	0	0	0	0	0	0	0
90	95	10	5	0	0	0	0	0	0	0
95	100	11	5	0	0	0	0	0	0	0
100	105	12	6	0	0	0	0	0	0	0
105	110	13	7	1	0	0	0	0	0	0
110	115	13	8	2	0	0	0	0	0	0
115	120	14	8	2	0	0	0	0	0	0
120	125	15	9	3	0	0	0	0	0	0
125	130	16	10	4	0	0	0	0	0	0
130	135	16	11	5	0	0	0	0	0	0
135	140	17	11	5	0	0	0	0	0	0
140	145	18	12	6	0	0	0	0	0	0
145	150	19	13	7	1	0	0	0	0	0
150	155	19	14	8	2	0	0	0	0	0
155	160	20	14	8	2	0	0	0	0	0
160	165	21	15	9	3	0	0	0	0	0
165	170	22	16	10	4	0	0	0	0	0
170	175	22	17	11	5	0	0	0	0	0
175	180	23	17	11	5	0	0	0	0	0
180	185	24	18	12	6	0	0	0	0	0
185	190	25	19	13	7	1	0	0	0	0
190	195	25	20	14	8	2	0	0	0	0

Hari and Evelyn used tax calculation tables like the one shown and those found in the Reference Section at the back of the book to calculate the deductions.

PAYROLL REGISTER for WEEK 3/1–3/7 DEDUCTIONS					
Employee	Gross Pay	Federal Income Tax	FICA (Social Security)	Total Deductions	Take-Home Pay
Evelyn	$ 77.00	$ 8.00	$ 5.89	$13.89	$ 63.11
Greg	66.00	1.00	5.05	6.05	59.95
Freda	72.00	7.00	5.51	12.51	59.49
Hari	18.00	0.00	1.38	1.38	16.62
Totals	$233.00	$16.00	$17.83	$33.83	$199.17

From Evelyn's gross pay of $77, $8 will be withheld for income tax. Using the FICA tables found in the Reference Section, you can see that $5.89 will be withheld for social security. Evelyn's total deductions are $13.89. Taking $13.89 from her gross pay leaves $63.11. That amount is referred to as her take-home pay.

In an actual payroll, a deduction for state income tax would usually be made as well. State income tax is figured in the same way as federal income tax, using tables, but the percent varies from one state to another.

Figures for the other workers are calculated in the same way. Notice that Greg makes $66, which is less than Freda's income of $72, yet he takes home slightly more than she does—$59.95 compared to $59.49. This is because Greg claims one exemption while Freda claims none. You can see in the tax deduction calculation tables how this difference affects take-home pay.

_____ Skill 3 _____

Because the company acts as the employer, with Evelyn and her friends as employees, the company must match the contributions made to FICA from each employee's earnings. As you saw in Chapter 1, social security payments are used to fund retirement benefits. People who are currently retired receive funds paid in by current workers and their employers.

The next table shows a monthly record for one employee (Evelyn) and the amount of matching FICA funds to be sent to the government for that employee for that month. Notice that the first line shows the same information that appeared in the first two tables for Evelyn for the week of 3/1–3/7. The next three lines summarize the next three week's earnings and deductions for her.

MONTHLY PAYROLL SUMMARY Employee: Evelyn				
Week	Gross Pay	Deductions		Take-Home Pay
		Fed. Inc. Tax	FICA	
3/1–3/7	$ 77.00	$ 8.00	$ 5.89	$ 63.11
3/8–3/14	55.00	5.00	4.21	45.79
3/15–3/21	88.00	10.00	6.73	71.27
3/22–3/28	66.00	7.00	5.05	53.95
Totals	$286.00	$30.00	$21.88	$234.12

Special forms are available from the Internal Revenue Service for depositing these tax amounts with the government. If Evelyn and her friends start their business, they will be responsible for keeping records like these and making these deposits.

EXERCISE YOUR SKILLS

1. What are four of the factors involved in entrepreneurship?
2. What are four responsibilities of good management?
3. What is the investment that workers make in a business?

___ Activity 1 ___

Prepare a handwritten table or computer spreadsheet to illustrate four weekly payrolls for each of the following employees. Copy and complete this form for each week.

PAYROLL REGISTER for WEEK _____ EARNINGS					
Employee	Number of Exemptions	Marital Status	Hourly Rate	Hours Worked	Gross Pay
Total Payroll					$

PAYROLL REGISTER for WEEK 3/1–3/7 EARNINGS							
Employee	Number of Exemptions	Marital Status	Hourly Rate	Hours Worked (Week)			
				1	2	3	4
Catlyn	0	S	$3.75	16	14	21	32
Sara	1	S	$4.50	20	28	25	18
Joleen	0	S	$8.00	26	16	16	24
Hernando	1	S	$6.24	14	10	30	20

_____ Activity 2 _____

Prepare a handwritten table or computer spreadsheet to illustrate 4 weekly payroll registers for each of the employees in Activity 1. Copy and complete this form for each week. Refer to the tables for Federal Income Tax Withholding and Social Security Employee Tax (FICA) in the Reference Section of this book to find the deductions in each of the following problems.

PAYROLL REGISTER for WEEK 3/1–3/7 DEDUCTIONS					
Employee	Gross Pay	Federal Income Tax	FICA (Social Security)	Total Deductions	Take-Home Pay
	$	$	$	$	$
Totals	$	$	$	$	$

_____ Activity 3 _____

Prepare a monthly summary for each employee from Activities 1 and 2. Show the weekly totals for payroll information. Use a spreadsheet program or make your own tables by hand.

MONTHLY PAYROLL SUMMARY Employee: _____				
Week	Gross Pay	Deductions		Take-Home Pay
		Fed. Inc. Tax	FICA	
	$	$	$	$
Totals	$	$	$	$

SECTION 4–2
FLUCTUATING FACTORS OF PRODUCTION

Greg wants to go into business with Evelyn to earn some extra money. His parents have limited the amount of money they are spending for Greg's clothes and entertainment because they are trying to save money for his college tuition and expenses. Greg is a good student with a talent in art, and he may receive a scholarship to college. He wants to study fashion design or fashion merchandising.

Greg and Evelyn have discussed their mutual interests in starting a small business that can be managed in their own homes. Greg likes the word-processing idea. He is a good typist, but he does not have a computer. Evelyn typed his 15-page English paper last year. In return, Greg painted a beautiful eagle on a sweatshirt for Evelyn. Many of their friends admired the sweatshirt. That suggested another possible business idea! Greg is wondering what costs would be involved in painting designs on sweatshirts or T-shirts to sell to his friends. He also would need to know what prices they would have to sell sweatshirts for in order to be competitive and still make a profit.

OBJECTIVE: In this section, we will help Greg to:

- *examine the many costs of producing items for sale in a small business*

ADD-ON COSTS

Greg has contacted a wholesale supplier who is willing to provide plain T-shirts and sweatshirts for a reasonable price. Transforming a plain T-shirt into a painted one is a matter of having the proper paints, a place to work, design ideas, and enough time to do the painting.

Greg is aware that it takes a long chain of events to turn a **commodity** into a consumer good. In this chain are costs—referred to as **add-on costs**—that contribute to the price of the end product. Add-on costs are those that add to the price of a raw commodity as it goes through the processing and marketing steps in the channel of distribution. Add-on costs cover such things as labor, advertising, energy, and transportation.

Labor. At every stage of the production process, labor costs are incurred. The business partners set wages for themselves that are then figured as costs of the business. These contribute to the add-on cost of any final product. Labor costs include not only wages but also employee benefits such as pension

115

plans and medical, dental, and life insurance. Evelyn and Hari have already designed a spreadsheet to keep track of the basic labor costs they would incur. Greg will also have to take this into consideration when marketing T-shirts and sweatshirts.

Packaging. Packaging costs reflect both the material and the design of the package. Packaging plays an important role in the marketing of a product. Frequently, a product's package is responsible for a buyer's initial reaction; therefore, packaging is often designed to project a particular image or attract a specific audience. Greg thinks the artistic design he will paint on his shirts, while not actually a package, will project an image he can sell.

Advertising. This category includes all kinds of materials and activities used to promote sales of a particular product. In addition to media promotion (television, magazine, and radio), promotional materials might include educational pamphlets, booklets, posters, and other publications. Advertising costs vary greatly from one product to another. Evelyn and Greg have discussed wearing some of the shirts as a kind of "walking advertisement" for their products. When Evelyn wears the shirt Greg made for her last year, a lot of their friends ask where they can get one like it.

Energy. Energy expenditures cover electricity, fuel oil, natural gas, or any other energy source used in the manufacturing, distribution, and sales of a product. Energy is necessary to complete each step in the marketing and distribution chain. For example, storage may require energy for special heat and humidity controls. Evelyn and Greg have discussed with their parents the idea of paying a portion of the **utility** (energy) bills for the home they decide to work in.

Transportation. The cost of transportation is added to the cost of a product at practically every step in the marketing and distribution channel. Transportation costs include fuel, maintenance and upkeep, depreciation, and even labor costs. Transportation for this group mainly involves Freda's driving to deliver flyers and posters and talking with people, plus transporting their finished products to their customers.

Ask Yourself

1. What do labor costs include, besides wages?
2. What are several ways of advertising a product?
3. What do energy expenditures cover?

SHARPEN YOUR SKILLS

Skill 1

Evelyn, Greg, Freda, and Hari sat down to figure out the costs involved in producing and selling hand-painted T-shirts and sweatshirts. They came up with the following lists:

Materials	12 T-shirts	$66.00, or $5.50 per shirt
	12 sweatshirts	$90.00, or $7.50 per shirt
	Paints	$30.00, or $1.25 per shirt

Labor	$5.00 per hour (for one week)	
	Evelyn and Greg, 15 hours each	$150.00
	Freda and Hari, 10 hours each	$100.00

| Packaging | Small plastic bags—$2.00 per 100 ($0.02 per shirt) |

| Advertising | Flyers, distribute 100 per week, $5.00 per 100 |

| Energy | Part of utility bill at Evelyn's house—$2.50 per week |

| Transportation | Freda's car—$25 per week |

They decided to find the total weekly cost of producing 12 T-shirts and 12 sweatshirts. They compiled their list this way:

Materials:	T-shirts	12 x $5.50	$ 66.00
	Sweatshirts	12 x $7.50	90.00
	Paints	24 x $1.25	30.00
Labor for week		50 x $5.00	250.00
Packaging		24 x $0.02	0.48
Advertising			5.00
Energy			2.50
Transportation			25.00
TOTAL COST FOR 24 SHIRTS, MADE IN 1 WEEK			$468.98

EXERCISE YOUR SKILLS

1. What add-on costs increase the price of a commodity?

2. How does packaging play a role in marketing a product or service?

3. In what way does transportation add to the cost of a product?

4. When you purchase a nationally advertised item, are you paying for any advertising costs?

—————   **Activity 1**   ————————————————————

Find the cost of producing the stated amounts of each of the following items. You may assume that the advertising, energy, and transportation costs are the same for every item, as follows:

Advertising	$ 5.00
Energy	2.50
Transportation	25.00
Total	$32.50

> **Note:** After you have completed these problems, keep your work. You will need the information again in the activities for Sections 4–3 and 4–4.

1. Three students have decided to sell bumper stickers advertising school spirit slogans. How much will it cost to produce 200 stickers each week if the costs include:

Labor	45 hours at $4.50 per hour
Materials	$1.04 per sticker

    Plus advertising, energy, and transportation costs

2. Four students have decided to appliqué letters on towels to personalize them. They think they can prepare 100 towels per week. How much will these 100 towels cost to make, if the costs include:

Labor	60 hours at $4.00 per hour
Materials	towels at $2.00 each letters at $0.20 per towel
Packaging	cardboard boxes at $0.10 each

    Plus advertising, energy, and transportation costs

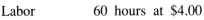

3. Two students will sell personalized note paper with 50 sheets per package. How much will it cost to produce 100 packages in a week, if the costs include:

   Labor   30 hours at $5.00 per hour
   Materials   paper at $5.00 for 500 sheets
               printing at $0.02 per sheet
   Packaging   wrappers at $0.02 per package
   Plus advertising, energy, and transportation costs

4. Two students plan to sell pennants with the school logo on them. How much will it cost to produce 200 pennants in a week, if the costs include:

   Labor   40 hours at $4.50 per hour
   Materials   pennants at $1.00 each
               paints at $0.20 per pennant
   Plus advertising, energy, and transportation costs

5. Three students will use a home computer to print personalized greeting cards. How much will it cost to produce 50 boxes of 20 cards each, if the costs include:

   Labor   60 hours at $4.00 per hour
   Materials   paper at $25.00 for 5000 sheets
               printer ribbons at $6.00 to print 500 pages
   Packaging   boxes at $0.20 each
   Plus advertising, energy, and transportation costs

6. Four students want to make hand-painted coffee mugs for use in the car. How much will it cost to produce 50 mugs, if the costs include:

   Labor   50 hours at $5.00 per hour
   Materials   mugs at $3.00 each
               paints at $0.40 per mug
   Packaging   boxes at $0.15 each
   Plus advertising, energy, and transportation costs

7. Two students plan to sell tennis balls at the tennis courts. They will purchase the tennis balls through a discount store and resell them. How much will it cost to sell 100 cans of tennis balls, if the costs include:

   Labor   20 hours at $4.00 per hour
   Materials   balls at $2.75 per can
   Plus advertising, energy, and transportation costs

8. Two students plan to order school book bags from a manufacturer and sell them in their school. They will paint the school's insignia on the bags. How much will it cost to prepare and sell 50 book bags, if the costs include:

   Labor   35 hours at $4.50 per hour
   Materials   bags at $4.00 each
   Plus advertising, energy, and transportation costs

9. Three students plan to personalize and sell lunch boxes. How much will it cost to produce 50 boxes, if the costs include:

Labor   60 hours at $4.00 per hour
Materials   boxes at $4.00 each
             paints at $0.80 per box
Plus advertising, energy, and transportation costs

10. Three students want to buy and resell tennis racket covers with the state university emblem on them. How much will it cost to produce 50 tennis racket covers, if the costs include:

Labor   40 hours at $5.00 per hour
Materials   covers at $4.00 each
Packaging   plastic bags at $0.03 each
Plus advertising, energy, and transportation costs

11. Three students will personalize bookmarks for sale. How much will it cost to prepare 200 bookmarks, if the costs include:

Labor   50 hours at $4.50 per hour
Materials   bookmarks at $0.80 each
             adding names at $0.12 each
Plus advertising, energy, and transportation costs

12. Four students will try selling carrot cookies. How much will it cost to produce 100 dozen cookies, if the costs include:

Labor   72 hours at $4.50 per hour
Materials   supplies for 20 dozen at $25.00
Packaging   boxes at $0.20 each
Plus advertising, energy, and transportation costs

13. Two students will order stadium blankets for use at football games. How much will it cost to prepare 25 blankets, if the costs include:

Labor   35 hours at $5.00 per hour
Materials   blankets at $8.00 each
Packaging   plastic bags at $0.15 each
Plus advertising, energy, and transportation costs

14. Three students will personalize acrylic desk organizers. How much will it cost to produce 50, if the costs include:

Labor   48 hours at $4.00 per hour
Materials   organizers at $6.00 each
             paints at $0.30 each
Packaging   boxes at $0.10 each
Plus advertising, energy, and transportation costs

> **Note:** After you have completed these problems, keep your work. You will need the information again in the activities for Sections 4–3 and 4–4.

Freda has sold everything from automobile sunglasses to video tapes, from book bags to personalized towels. She even sold some of her brother's Boy Scout note cards when he ordered too many boxes and her parents said they could never use them all in a year.

Freda has always been a good salesperson. She has a knack for understanding people and exactly what motivates them to buy something they might not know they want or need. Freda can point out to them exactly how their lives would be enhanced by whatever she is selling at the moment. She also knows how good she is at selling. Her keen perception of people's partly subconscious motivations makes it easy.

Acquiring money has encouraged Freda to keep on selling even though she never seems able to hold onto her profits. Keeping track of her cash flow is not easy for Freda. She does not even always know if she has made a profit or not. Her savings account has not grown much, but a lot of cash has passed through her hands every month.

When Freda learned that Evelyn and Greg were planning to start a business together, she offered to go in with them. Maybe Evelyn and Greg can help her evaluate where all her money goes. In return, Freda can help them understand the effects of competition on sales, and they can all make a profit.

After all, Freda did sell the most fruit in the school last year. She even received a plaque from the fruit company! She has never been bothered by the competition. She either has more desire to sell than others do, or a keener understanding of her customers, or both.

In the course of evaluating businesses, the partners will learn about the fixed costs and variable costs involved. Labor, transportation, advertising, and fuel are considered fixed expenses. The materials that go into their product and packaging are variable expenses. They will also learn how nonprice competition can be just as important as price setting in drawing customers.

OBJECTIVES: In this section, we will help Freda to:

- *explain how competition works*
- *find the profit or loss from the sales of their company's products or services*

COMPETITION

Competition is a rivalry among sellers for consumers' dollars or a rivalry among producers for the factors of production. Competition keeps producers from charging unreasonably high prices and making excessive profits. Certain conditions have to exist for competition to work the way it is supposed to:

- There should be a large number of buyers and sellers.
- Buyers should have sufficient information regarding the nature of the product, particularly price and quality.
- Buyers should also have alternatives, that is, substitutes and similar products to choose from.
- There should be easy entry into the market for new producers who are attracted to profits.

Profit is the difference between receipts and costs. That is, the amount that remains after the amount it costs to produce an item is subtracted from the amount received from selling it. If the cost to produce the items is greater than the amount received from selling them, the business suffers a **loss**.

Competition works in this way: If profits for a business get too high, other businesses will move in and take away customers by offering a lower price or a better product. **Price competition** involves taking business away from a competitor by lowering prices. Evelyn, Greg, and Freda are hoping to offer a service or product that is not being offered by competitors in their area or is not being offered at a price as low as theirs. In order to arrive at prices at which they can afford to sell, they must analyze their total costs, which consist of **fixed costs**—like their wages—plus **variable costs**—like material costs.

There are other ways to compete for consumers' dollars. Winning business away from a competitor by product differentiation, advertising, high-quality customer service, or product design or improvement is called **nonprice competition**. If Greg's painted shirts are of better quality or have more appealing designs than those currently available, people will buy them. Improvement, such as the improvement of automobile gas consumption, can be beneficial to consumers. But some forms of nonprice competition may not be beneficial to consumers. For example, product differentiation can involve excessive advertising to emphasize a minute product difference or to create an imaginary difference. This actually may raise the cost of the product with no resulting advantage to consumers.

Sellers go to a great deal of expense and effort to convince consumers that their products taste better, work harder, make us more attractive, or keep us healthier than competing products. Consumers must be careful to scrutinize these claims and do their own comparisons to discover what differences do in fact exist.

The right to compete is important in our market economy. Everyone is free to enter a trade or business and to compete with others. Several federal laws have been passed to assure competition. These laws prevent businesses from agreeing upon prices and thereby eliminating the effects of competition. Public utilities—such as water, electricity, telephone, and public transportation—

are an exception to the rules of competition. A public utility usually has exclusive rights to provide services to a community, since one large utility company can often operate more efficiently than several smaller firms would.

Ask Yourself

1. What conditions must be present for competition to work?
2. What is nonprice competition?
3. Why are most public utilities exempt from the laws that govern competition?

SHARPEN YOUR SKILLS

Evelyn and her friends have decided to analyze their costs by dividing them into two groups, as follows:

Fixed costs   Costs that remain the same each week, assuming the employees work the same number of hours: labor, transportation, advertising, and energy.

Variable costs   Costs that vary according to how many items the employees produce: materials and packaging.

This is a simplified scheme, but it is practical for Evelyn, Greg, and Freda to use. In reality, variations would occur. Labor and energy costs, for instance, would probably increase when the quantity of product increases.

Question What profit would the T-shirt and sweatshirt company make in one week, if they produced and sold 24 shirts?

Solution Use the following information about the fixed and variable costs to calculate the total costs.

Fixed Costs

Labor for week	50 hours x $5.00	$250.00
Advertising		5.00
Energy		2.50
Transportation		25.00
TOTAL FIXED COSTS		$282.50

Variable Costs

Materials:		
T-shirts	12 x $5.50	$ 66.00
Sweatshirts	12 x $7.50	90.00
Paints	24 x $1.25	30.00
Packaging	24 x $0.02	0.48
TOTAL VARIABLE COSTS		$186.48

Total costs can be calculated as follows:

Total Costs = Fixed Costs + Variable Costs

$282.50 + $186.48 = $468.98

Freda has advised them to sell the 12 T-shirts for $15.00 each and the 12 sweatshirts for $25.00 each. If they do this, they will receive:

12 x $15.00	$180.00
12 x $25.00	300.00
TOTAL RECEIPTS	$480.00

Profit would then be figured as follows:

Profit = Total Receipts – Total Costs

$480.00 – $468.98 = $11.02

Their profit would be $11.02.

A profit of $11.02 does not seem very high. But they have already included, as part of the costs, their wages for the week. So the company does not have to make a very large profit in order for its employees to be paid. It only needs to break even.

Since the profit for 24 shirts was not outstanding, Freda suggests they consider selling 30 shirts (15 of each kind) in a week. She thinks they could make more shirts in the same amount of time (using the same amount of energy and requiring the same advertising and transportation), but their material costs would go up. So would their receipts, of course.

Question   What would the company's profit be if they made and sold 30 shirts in one week?

Solution   Their costs would look like this:

Fixed Costs = $282.50 (They stay the same.)

To find the variable costs, they must first compute the cost per shirt for each kind.

	Sweatshirts			*T-shirts*	
Materials			Materials		
Sweatshirts	$7.50		T-shirts	$5.50	
Paint	1.25		Paint	1.25	
Package	0.02		Package	0.02	
TOTAL	$8.77		TOTAL	$6.77	

Then they can calculate the variable costs:

15 x $8.77	$131.55	total cost for sweatshirts
15 x $6.77	$101.55	total cost for T-shirts
TOTAL	$233.10	

Variable Costs = $233.10

Total Costs = $282.50 + $233.10 = $515.60

Selling the shirts at the same prices as before, their receipts would be:

15 x $15.00	$225.00
15 x $25.00	375.00
TOTAL RECEIPTS	$600.00

Their profit would then be figured as follows:

Profit = $600.00 – $515.60 = $84.40

Next, Evelyn, Greg, and Freda decide to figure the profits they would make in the word-processing business.

Question   What profit would the word-processing business make in one week?

Solution

Fixed Costs

Labor for week	50 hours x $5.00	$250.00
Advertising (print and distribute 100 flyers)		5.00
Energy (part of utility bill)		5.00
Transportation (driving to solicit business, deliver finished product)		25.00
TOTAL FIXED COSTS		$285.00

Variable Costs

Materials (per page):

Computer paper	$0.005
Printer ribbon	$0.012
TOTAL COST PER PAGE	$0.017

If they could type 100 pages per week, the variable costs per week would be:

100 x $0.017 = $1.70

Total costs could then be calculated as follows:

Total Costs = Fixed Costs + Variable Costs

$285.00 + $1.70 = $286.70

If they sold their services for $2.00 per page, their receipts would be:

100 x $2.00 = $200.00

Their receipts would be *less than* their costs, so they would have a loss.

Total Costs – Total Receipts = Loss

$286.70 – $200.00 = $86.70

Even though they would still receive a salary, they do not want to operate at a loss. They decided to try another approach. Perhaps they could type 200 pages per week, at the same fixed costs.

Question   What would the word processing profit be if they typed 200 pages per week?

Solution   Their costs would look like this:

Fixed Costs = $285.00

To find their variable costs, they must multiply the cost per page by the new number of pages:

200 x $0.017 = $3.40

Their variable costs would be $3.40.

Total costs can be calculated as follows:

Total Costs = Fixed Costs + Variable Costs

$285.00 + $3.40 = $288.40

Their total costs would be $288.40.

To find their receipts from typing, they must multiply the price per page by the new number of pages:

200 x $2.00 = $400.00

Their profit would then be figured as follows:

Profit = Total Receipts – Total Costs

$400.00 – $288.40 = $111.60

They would make a profit of $111.60 if they could produce 200 pages per week.

EXERCISE YOUR SKILLS

1. Since a primary motive of business is to make as large a profit as possible, what prevents a business from demanding excessively high prices for its products and services?

2. When would product differentiation be of benefit to a consumer?

3. Why is there a law preventing businesses from agreeing on prices to be charged for products or services?

_____ Activity 1 _____

For these problems, use the production costs you determined in Activity 1 in Section 4–2. You can assume that fixed costs include labor, advertising, energy, and transportation and that variable costs include materials and packaging.

Find the profit or loss for selling each product at the given price and in the quantities listed. You may wish to use a spreadsheet, either computer-generated or hand-drawn, like this one.

Quantity			
Fixed Costs ($32.50 + labor)			
Variable Costs			
Total Costs			
Receipts			
Profit or Loss			

> **Note:** After you have completed these problems, keep your work. You will use it in future activities.

1. Bumper stickers selling for $2.00 each, produced and sold in the following quantities:
    a. 200   **b.** 300   **c.** 400

2. Personalized towels selling for $5.00 each, produced and sold in the following quantities:
    a. 100   **b.** 200   **c.** 300

3. Personalized note cards selling for $3.00 a pack, produced and sold in the following quantities:
    a. 100   **b.** 200   **c.** 300

4. Pennants with the school logo selling for $2.00 each, produced and sold in the following quantities:
    a. 200   **b.** 300   **c.** 400

5. Personalized greeting cards selling for $10.00 per pack, produced and sold in the following quantities:

    a. 25 packs   **b.** 50 packs   **c.** 75 packs

6. Hand-painted coffee mugs selling for $10.00 each, produced and sold in the following quantities:
    a. 25   **b.** 50   **c.** 75

7. Tennis balls selling for $4.00 per can, acquired and sold in the following quantities:
    a. 100   **b.** 200   **c.** 300

8. School book bags selling for $7.50 each, produced and sold in the following quantities:
    a. 25   **b.** 50   **c.** 75

9. Personalized lunch boxes selling for $8.00 each, produced and sold in the following quantities:
    a. 25   **b.** 50   **c.** 75

10. Tennis racket covers selling for $10.00 each, acquired and sold in the following quantities:
    a. 25   **b.** 50   **c.** 75

11. Personalized bookmarks selling for $1.50 each, produced and sold in the following quantities:
    a. 200   **b.** 300   **c.** 400

12. Carrot cookies selling for $5.00 per dozen, produced and sold in the following quantities:
    a. 75 dozen   **b.** 100 dozen   **c.** 125 dozen

13. Stadium blankets selling for $20.00 each, acquired and sold in the following quantities:
    a. 25   **b.** 50   **c.** 75

14. Desk organizers selling for $10.00 each, prepared and sold in the following quantities:
    a. 25   **b.** 50   **c.** 75

Note: Keep your work. You will need it for activities in Section 4–4.

Hari is not very well-known among his classmates. He is soft-spoken and shy. He usually sits around reading, studying, working mathematics problems, and drawing graphs of changes in the stock market.

Hari has money invested in several large companies. He has been subscribing to a business newspaper since he was nine years old. He always seems to have the newest, most sophisticated calculator of anyone in the class. He still remembers the day Mr. Newton, the mathematics teacher, first showed him a calculator with a tiny screen that could show the graphs of mathematical functions. He would love to have a calculator like that.

As Evelyn, Greg, and Freda became more serious about forming their own company, they realized that Hari would be the perfect choice for a partner who could keep track of their profits and let them know if they need to make changes. Hari was surprised and pleased when they asked him to become their partner. He has had a lot of experience now in tracking other people's businesses in the stock market. He has also been an owner himself, in a small way, by purchasing stock. But he has never had the experience of helping to run a company himself.

OBJECTIVES:　　*In this section, Hari will show how to:*

- *use algebra to complete a spreadsheet to determine profit or loss*
- *graph the cost = sales break-even point for the company*

PROFIT

Evelyn and her friends, like other producers, are not guaranteed an income when they start a business. All producers hope for a profit, and it is the idea of making a profit that frequently is their strongest motivation. Freda understands this motive very well. She has sometimes done work for the sheer satisfaction of it. And she has also been motivated by a desire to help people, to furnish them with things they may need or enjoy. But in the final analysis she works to earn an income. And in this she is like most people.

Profit is the incentive or reward for organizing the factors of production and for supplying products and services. The concept of profit also caused Evelyn, Greg, and Freda to shift their efforts from one quantity of their product to another quantity because they found they could make a better profit by making more. One figure a business will want to know is the "cost = sales" **break-even point**. If they make too few items for their fixed costs, they will lose money. If they make too many items, they may be left with unsold **inventory,** or stock on hand.

129

Usually, the more **efficient** a business is, the greater its profits will be. A business also increases its chances for greater profits by offering consumers better products, lower prices, and better services than competing firms. Thus, consumers benefit from the efforts of businesses to make a greater profit by making their operations more efficient.

People would be considered unwise if they were to invest their savings in a business in which there was no chance to make a profit. Furthermore, businesses could not continue to operate long if their income was only great enough to meet costs. Large corporations are no different in this respect from business enterprises owned and operated by a single individual. They too must make a profit to remain in operation.

A portion of the profits of corporations is kept for use in the business—to pay expenses in years when business is not good, to build new buildings, and to buy and replace machines, equipment, and materials. Profits are also used to expand business activities which, in turn, create more jobs for more people.

Ask Yourself

1. What are several motivations people have for working?

2. How can a business increase its chances for higher profits?

3. How do businesses use their profits?

SHARPEN YOUR SKILLS

Hari has learned how to create a spreadsheet and a graph that will illustrate the cost=sales break-even point for a company. He and his friends know that if the amount of their total sales is less than their costs, their company will suffer a loss. The only way to make a profit is to have total sales exceed costs.

_____   Skill 1   _____

Question   How can a business decide how much of a product to make and sell?

Solution   Recall the figuring that Hari and his friends did when they were thinking of producing 30 shirts, 15 of each kind. They arrived at these figures:

Fixed Costs = $288.50 per week
Variable Costs = $8.77 per sweatshirt and $6.77 per T-shirt

If they produce an equal number of sweatshirts and T-shirts, they can consider the variable cost per shirt to be the average of the variable costs for the two kinds, or $7.77. Likewise, they can consider an average sale price to be $20.00, assuming that they will sell an equal number of shirts at $15.00 and $25.00.

Hari's spreadsheet computer program has used these figures to compute additional information as shown in the following spreadsheet.

1	2	3	4	5	6	7
Fixed Costs	Variable Costs (per unit)	Number Produced	Total Costs	Average Sale (per unit)	Total Sales	Profit (Loss)
$282.50	$7.77	10	$360.20	$20.00	$200.00	($160.20)
$282.50	$7.77	14	$391.28	$20.00	$280.00	($111.28)
$282.50	$7.77	18	$422.36	$20.00	$360.00	($62.36)
$282.50	$7.77	22	$453.44	$20.00	$440.00	($13.44)
$282.50	$7.77	26	$484.52	$20.00	$520.00	$35.48
$282.50	$7.77	30	$515.60	$20.00	$600.00	$84.40

Notice that the information in columns 1, 2, and 5 is the same in all rows. It was furnished by Hari when he set up the spreadsheet. For column 3, Hari specified the quantity of shirts to be produced and sold. To get the information in the other columns, Hari had to provide the needed formulas or questions. He provided these formulas:

Column 4:   **Total Costs =**
Fixed Costs + (Variable Costs) (Number Produced)

Column 6:   **Total Sales = (Number Produced) (Average Sales)**

Column 7:   **Profit (Loss) = Total Sales – Total Costs**

Notice that if the difference between total sales and total costs is negative, a loss is produced. The loss is shown in parentheses ($160.20).

_____ **Skill 2** _____

Question   How can the information from a spreadsheet, such as the one just developed, be shown as a graph?

Solution   Hari's program will automatically produce a graph that looks like the one below:

Notice that one line shows total costs and the other shows total sales. You can see the change from a loss to a profit as more shirts are produced. The point at which the two lines cross is called the cost = sales break-even point. Using the graph, can you tell that approximately 23 shirts is the break-even point?

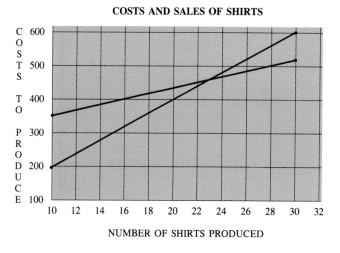

COSTS AND SALES OF SHIRTS

NUMBER OF SHIRTS PRODUCED

Another way of looking at it is shown in the next graph. Any combination of shirts and costs in the striped area will yield a loss. Any combination in the solid area will yield a profit.

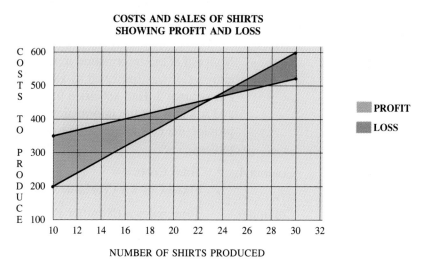

**COSTS AND SALES OF SHIRTS
SHOWING PROFIT AND LOSS**

NUMBER OF SHIRTS PRODUCED

_____ Skill 3 _____

You can see from the spreadsheet and graph that the break-even point is about 23 shirts.

Question   Can the break-even point be found by using an equation?

Solution   The break-even point can be found by using the following mathematical equation:

$$\textbf{Break-even Point} = \frac{\textbf{Fixed Costs}}{\textbf{Sales Price – Variable Costs per Unit}}$$

Hari knows that his fixed costs are \$282.50. His average sale price is \$20 and his variable costs per unit are \$7.77. He can put them in the formula as follows:

$$\frac{\$282.50}{\$20 - \$7.77} = 23.09894$$

Rounded to the nearest whole number, the answer is 23 shirts.

EXERCISE YOUR SKILLS

1. How do consumers benefit from the efforts of businesses to make a greater profit?

2. How can a small business decide how much of which items to produce?

3. Why can businesses not operate on a nonprofit basis?

4. How is each line in Hari's graph generated?

_____ Activity 1 _____

Use your results from Activity 1 in Section 4–3 to make a new spreadsheet, that shows the same information as in Hari's spreadsheet, for each of the exercises in that activity. You can use a computer program, a programmable calculator, or pencil and paper.

> **Note:** Save your results for the next activity.

_____ Activity 2 _____

Use your information from Activity 1 to make a graph for each of the exercises. Give the approximate cost = sales break-even point for each item.

_____ Activity 3 _____

Use the formula from Skill 3 to compute the break-even points for each of the exercises in Activity 2.

EXTEND YOUR UNDERSTANDING
PROJECT 4–1: RETAIL SALES PROJECT

Work in small groups to set up imaginary companies. Select items or services that your company would like to sell or provide for potential customers. You may use information given within the chapter as cost basis, or do your own research to find the costs of producing various services or products. You must document (tell how you arrived at these costs) for each product or service your company decides to produce.

Assignment

1. Decide what product or service your company is going to provide. Write a description of that product or service. Be sure to include all elements including advertising, energy use, transportation, and packaging. If possible, furnish drawings, photographs, or other examples of your product or service.

2. Decide on the number of hours per week each employee (member of the group) will work. Use a different number of hours for each person. Decide how much each person will earn per hour. Decide the marital status and number of exemptions for each employee.

3. Complete a Payroll Register for 4 consecutive weeks (one month) to show each employee's earnings. This register must show name, number of exemptions, marital status, hourly rate, hours worked, gross pay, federal income tax deduction, FICA deduction, total deductions, and take-home pay.

4. Furnish a monthly payroll summary for each employee.

5. List your fixed costs and variable costs. Make a computer or handwritten spreadsheet to show fixed costs, variable costs, number produced, total costs, average sale (or sale per unit), total sales, and profit or loss. **Note:** Your spreadsheet should have some entries that result in a loss and others that result in a profit.

6. Make a line graph that shows the break-even point for your company's chosen business venture.

Extensions

1. After you have completed a plan for your company, get together with other groups in your class and try to sell them your product. Plan an ad campaign and a product presentation designed to convince them to buy your product.

2. On the basis of feedback obtained from other groups, redesign your product or service to be more useful or attractive to potential customers.

3. Listen in turn to other groups' presentations and give them feedback about their product or service. Try to make your comments useful to them in redesigning their product or rethinking their service.

PROJECT 4–2: SECOND RETAIL SALES PROJECT

Work in small groups. If you chose a product for Project 4–1, repeat the procedure but choose a service for Project 4–2. If you chose a service for Project 4–1, repeat the procedure but choose a product for Project 4–2. Change the number of hours and hourly wage for each employee. Change each of the fixed and variable costs.

PROJECT 4–3: RECOGNIZING DIFFERENCES

Interview several people that run a small business. Try to find some people who offer a product and others who offer a service. Write a paper that explains the differences in expenses and profit between a business that furnishes a service versus one that furnishes a product and vice versa.

CHAPTER 4 KEY TERMS

CHAPTER 4 REVIEW

Find the following earnings:

	Number of Hours	Hourly Rate	Weekly Earnings		Number of Hours	Hourly Rate	Weekly Earnings
1.	38	$3.35		**2.**	26	$7.50	
3.	41	$22.70		**4.**	22	$14.80	

Find the weekly take-home pay for each of these single people if each claims one withholding allowance (exemption). Use the tables for Federal Income Tax Withholding and Social Security Tax (FICA) in the Reference Section of this text.

	Gross Pay	Federal Income Withholding Tax	Soc. Sec. (FICA)	Take-Home Pay
5.	$127.30			
6.	$195.00			
7.	$930.70			
8.	$325.60			

Duanita and Alisha want to make and sell stuffed kittens. Use the information given in the box to help you find the total production costs involved in manufacturing the amounts of toys indicated in Problems 9, 10, and 11.

Production Costs			
Fixed Costs		**Variable Costs**	
Labor	$3.50 per hour for 30 hours	Materials	$2.25 each
		Packaging	$0.02 each
Advertising	$3.00		
Energy	$3.58		
Transportation	$5.92		

9. 20 kittens   **10.** 40 kittens   **11.** 60 kittens

Duanita and Alisha will sell the stuffed kittens for $7.00 each. Use the production costs found in Problems 9–11 to find the amount of profit or loss from the sale of each group of toys.

12. 20 kittens   **13.** 40 kittens   **14.** 60 kittens

Use your results from Problems 9–14 to make a spreadsheet that shows the following information for producing and selling 20, 40, and 60 kittens.

	Fixed Costs	Variable Costs (per unit)	Number Produced	Total Costs	Average Sale (per unit)	Total Sales	Profit (Loss)
15.			20				
16.			40				
17.			60				

18. Make a graph that shows total costs.

19. On the same graph as Problem 18, show total sales.

20. Find the break-even point for these sales.

Use the information you learned in this chapter to answer each of the following questions:

21. What factors are important to know before deciding to start a business? Explain your answer.

22. Why is it important to know how much profit (or loss) a business makes?

23. If a company does not make enough money to break even, what kinds of changes should they consider making?

24. After 1 year, the employees in Oscar's company expected to receive a raise in salary. What should Oscar consider before deciding whether to give them raises and how much the raises should be?

Find the weekly earnings for each of the following:

1. 42 hours at $4.80 per hour
2. 33 hours at $17.25 per hour
3. 27 hours at $7.50 per hour
4. 36 hours at $23.45 per hour

Find the weekly take-home pay for each weekly gross pay of these single people. Each claims one withholding allowance (exemption). Use the tables for Federal Income Tax Withholding and Social Security Tax (FICA) in the Reference Section of the book.

5. $201.60
6. $569.25
7. $202.50
8. $844.20

Bruce and Akira want to sell stadium cushions. Use the information given in the box to help you find the total production cost involved in manufacturing the numbers of cushions indicated in Problems 9, 10 and 11.

Production Costs			
Fixed Costs		**_Variable Costs_**	
Labor	$3.25/hour for 30 hours	Materials	$1.40 each
Advertising	$2.00	Packaging	$0.50 each
Energy	$2.58		
Transportation	$4.42		

9. 30 cushions
10. 60 cushions
11. 90 cushions

Use the costs found above to find the amount of profit or loss for selling the following numbers of cushions at $5.00 each.

12. 30 cushions
13. 60 cushions
14. 90 cushions

Use your results from above to make a spreadsheet that shows the following for producing and selling 30, 60, and 90 cushions.

	Fixed Costs	Variable Costs (per unit)	Number Produced	Total Costs	Average Sale (per unit)	Total Sales	Profit (Loss)
15.			30				
16.			60				
17.			90				

18. Make a graph that shows total costs, total sales, and the break-even point for the cushion sales.

CUMULATIVE REVIEW

1. You work 26 hours at $6.22 per hour. You receive $12.50 in tips. You receive 1 1/2 times your hourly rate for any hours over 20. Find your total wages.

2. You work the schedule shown below. You earn $5 per hour. You receive $22 in tips. Find your total wages for the week.

Monday	Tuesday	Wednesday	Thursday	Friday	Saturday
3–6	3–7	3–6	3–6	4–9	8–12

3. You sold a house for $110,000. You earn 4% commission on the first $100,000 and 6% commission on anything over $100,000. How much commission did you earn?

4. You earned $94.00. Your income tax withholding is $13 and your social security withholding is 7.65% of your earnings. Find your take-home pay.

5. You earn $9.30 per hour. You work 35 hours a week for 50 weeks. You get 2 weeks of paid vacation, plus 18% of your base salary in fringe benefits. Find your yearly earnings, including benefits.

6. You wrote 33 checks one month. The bank charges $0.0225 for the first 20 checks and $0.08 for each check over 20. How much are the charges for that month?

7. Your employer made out your paycheck with your first and middle initials and full last name. Write your name as you would to endorse the check.

8. You write a check for $243.50. You had $982.61 in your checking account. Show how you would enter this check in your check register.

9. You save $28 per week. You want to buy a stereo that costs $189. How many weeks must you save before you can get the stereo?

10. What would the simple interest be on $500 at 8.5% for one year if interest is paid semi-annually?

11. Use the formula $A = P(1 + i/n)nt$ to find the interest for one-half year if the principal is $1000, the rate is 8%, and the interest is compounded quarterly.

12. The fixed costs of producing hand-painted sweatshirts are $285 per week. The variable costs are $8 per shirt plus $1 per shirt for paints. What is the cost of producing 25 shirts in one week?

13. Using the information from Problem 12, what would the profit or loss be if each sweatshirt is sold for $20?

14. Make a line graph that shows the break-even point for the information in Problems 13 and 14.

Using someone else's money while we wait to acquire our own gives us an inflated sense of wealth. As Americans, we can now buy practically anything that is for sale without using money we currently possess. By presenting a credit card, we can eat in a fine restaurant and we can have our teeth fixed. We can fly across the country and we can attend a baseball game; we can have the lawn mower repaired and the poodle groomed.

Homes and cars have been sold on the installment plan for many years because consumers wanted to have these items before they could save enough cash to purchase them. Bankers were willing to finance these purchases provided they could enter an agreement that would guarantee repayment of the borrowed money. Bankers also recognized an opportunity to make more money in the process. Homeowners have been willing to repay two or three times as much as they borrowed since that was the only way they could afford to buy a home.

Once bankers realized what money could be made by extending credit, they had to find a way to convince Americans, who thought of themselves as honest and hard-working, that owing money and being in debt is really fine, as long as they can keep up the payments. We consumers have not been hard to convince. Skillful advertisers understand our basic desires for more than we have; once we allow the genie out of the bottle to grant us just a small wish, we have found it difficult to restrain ourselves from asking for more. Banks have capitalized on this false sense of wealth we enjoy, too, by offering more and more credit to those of us who are able to keep up with the monthly payments.

Owning something now that we can't afford to pay for now, except in small monthly installments, is a very attractive and luxurious way to live, but we can overextend ourselves easily without even realizing it. We may choose to continue to enjoy the genie's power, but as intelligent consumers, we can at least be aware of the hazards. We can pay attention to the high price of spending what we do not have, and we can notice who is receiving all that extra money.

In this chapter, three of our high-school students will examine some of the facets of installment buying. They will highlight some of the risks and suggest some ways of reducing the cost.

Patrick knows Maria quite well and is impressed by her ability to save so much money from her weekly paycheck. Patrick has a job at Paradise Department Store; he is a cashier in the camera/luggage department. Patrick will graduate from high school this year and plans to attend a community college for at least a year or two. He and his father have been trying to save money for the tuition to the state university, but there hasn't been a lot left over each month since his mother died three years ago. They lost her income, and her illness used up a lot of their savings, so if Patrick wants to go to college he will have to help pay the expenses.

Patrick knows that Maria's father will help her borrow the money for a car. Maria will be making monthly payments to the bank to pay back the loan. Patrick wonders if he can also borrow money from the bank for school tuition. Maria told him something about paying back more than he borrowed. Patrick isn't sure that is particularly fair, but he may be willing to pay the bank a fair profit if he can borrow the money.

OBJECTIVES: In this section, we will help Patrick to:

- *identify the major functions of credit*
- *recognize the features of installment credit*
- *determine the cost of using credit*
- *compute the amount repaid for a loan*

NATURE OF CREDIT

"Buy now, pay later," is a phrase Patrick has heard many times, especially in commercial advertising. The use of credit has become a way of life for many consumers; Patrick thinks he can handle it, too. His economics teacher mentioned that the word credit actually means debit. People don't like to be in debt, so they use the word credit instead.

Credit is a form of debt that occurs whenever cash, goods, or services are provided in exchange for a promise to pay at a future date. If the car dealership where Maria will buy her car could not give credit to its customers, it would sell very few cars. Many people cannot afford to pay cash for a large purchase such as an automobile. Instead, they borrow the amount they need to pay for the car, then pay back that amount plus interest. The total amount they pay to the bank is known as the **deferred payment price**. The deferred payment price is considerably more than the original loan amount.

This difference can be called **interest** or **finance charge**. Minus the loan amount, it is the amount of profit made by the bank or lending institutions. For the person who borrowed the money, this interest is the price he or she pays for the privilege of using someone else's money.

If a bank or credit union has faith in Patrick's ability to pay them back at some time in the future, he will be allowed to borrow his tuition money.

FUNCTIONS OF CREDIT

Patrick has discovered several positive effects of people's using credit. They are:

1. Credit stabilizes the economy. Credit steadies economic activity as it allows individuals and businesses to buy goods and services even when their income is temporarily limited. Business managers and bankers assume that enough income will eventually be available.

2. Credit promotes business growth. When Evelyn went into business, she and her friends were able to borrow some of the money they needed to establish their company. Many people start new businesses, and thousands of others continue in business, through the use of credit.

3. Credit expands production. By borrowing, Patrick may increase his earning power and his eventual productivity because he will be getting more education. Similarly, a business that must sell what it produces will have no income until its products are sold. The initial costs of production must be financed by funds already in the company or by borrowed funds.

4. Credit raises the standard of living. If Alex and Alice do get married in a few years, they will not need to wait for their savings to build up before buying things that make life comfortable—such as a home, a car, furniture, appliances, a stereo, a television, nice clothing, vacations, and so on.

USING INSTALLMENT CREDIT

Using installment credit means buying something and then making regular payments over a period of months. Maria will be using installment credit when she buys her car. Purchases made on an installment plan usually carry the following restrictions:

1. A down payment is required.

2. A substantial finance or carrying charge is added to the price.

3. Payments of equal amounts are spread over a specified period of time.

4. If payments are not made as scheduled, protection is provided to the seller in the form of a security agreement.

RULE OF 78s

Most creditors will allow a borrower to prepay the balance of an installment loan. This right of prepayment (paying off the contract before it comes due) saves the borrower interest charges. However, the amount saved by prepaying the loan will vary according to each loan agreement. Many stores apply the Rule of 78 to buyers who prepay a loan. The reasoning behind this procedure is that lenders are entitled to more interest in the early months of the contract when their risks are greater and less interest near the maturity date when their risks are less.

Here is how the rule works. Write the numbers 1 through 12 in a column. Add the numbers. The total is 78. The first month's interest charge (on a 12-month contract) is 12/78 of the total finance charge. The last month's interest is 1/78 of the total finance charge.

Suppose you bought a microwave oven for $360, putting $60 down. Then you signed a contract stating that the balance of $300 was to be paid in 12 equal installments with interest at 21 percent a year ($63 total interest or $5.25 interest each month). At the time of your 9th installment, you decide to prepay the contract. Applying the Rule of 78s, the store would charge you a total of $58.15 interest (72/78 of $63), representing a savings of $4.85 in interest ($63 − $58.15). The 72 is computed by adding the numbers in the column from 12 through 4 (12 + 11 + 10 + 9…4). The last three numbers in the column, which are not counted, represent the three months still remaining in the contract.

Ask Yourself

1. What are 4 major functions of credit?

2. What are 3 restrictions of installment credit?

3. What must a bank have faith in when it approves a loan to a person?

SHARPEN YOUR SKILLS

_____ Skill 1 _____

Suppose that Maria finds a car that costs $6500. She buys the car on the installment plan at $12\frac{1}{2}$% interest for 3 years.

Questions **1.** How much will Maria's monthly payments be?

2. How much will Maria have paid for the car at the end of 3 years?

Solutions **1.** To find the monthly payment for a loan amount, use an amortization table. There is an amortization table at $12\frac{1}{2}$% in the Reference Section at the back of this book. A portion of that table is reproduced below. Since 6500 is not listed under "Amount," you can find the payments for $6000 and $500 and add them together. Find $6000 and $500 under the column marked "Amount". Find the monthly payment for each under the column marked 3 years.

12½% Amortization Table
MONTHLY PAYMENT
Necessary to amortize a loan

TERM AMOUNT	1 YEAR	2 YEARS	3 YEARS	4 YEARS
$ 25	2.23	1.19	.84	.67
50	4.46	2.37	1.68	1.33
75	6.69	3.55	2.51	2.00
100	8.91	4.74	3.35	2.66
200	17.82	9.47	6.70	5.32
300	26.73	14.20	10.04	7.98
400	35.64	18.93	13.39	10.64
500	44.55	23.66	16.73	13.29
600	53.45	28.39	20.08	15.95
700	62.36	33.12	23.42	18.61
800	71.27	37.85	26.77	21.27
900	80.18	42.58	30.11	23.93
1000	89.09	47.31	33.46	26.58
2000	178.17	94.62	66.91	53.16
3000	267.25	141.93	100.37	79.74
4000	356.34	189.23	133.82	106.32
5000	445.42	236.54	167.27	132.90
6000	534.50	283.85	200.73	159.48
7000	623.59	331.16	234.18	186.06
8000	712.67	378.46	267.63	212.64
9000	801.75	425.77	301.09	239.22
10000	890.83	473.08	334.54	265.80

	Loan Amount	Monthly Payment
	$ 6000	$ 200.73
	+ 500	+ 16.73
Totals	$ 6500	$ 217.46

Maria's monthly payment will be $217.46.

2. The total payments are found by multiplying the monthly payment by the number of months in 3 years.

$ 217.46   monthly payment
x 36   months in 3 years
$ 7828.56   total payments, or
deferred payment price

If Maria buys a new car, it will cost $12,825. She can get a loan for that amount for 4 years at $12\frac{1}{2}\%$ interest.

Questions 1. How much would Maria's monthly payment be?

2. How much would Maria have paid for the car at the end of 4 years?

Solutions 1. Look again at the amortization table. Since $12,825 is not listed under "Amount," break it down into parts that are listed in the column as shown below, and find the monthly payment for each part under the column marked 4 years.

	Loan Amount	4 Years Payment
	$ 10,000	$ 265.80
	2,000	53.16
	800	21.27
	+ 25	+ 0.67
Totals	$ 12,825	$ 340.90

2. The total payments are found by multiplying the monthly payment by the number of months in 4 years.

$ 340.90   monthly payment
x 48   months in 4 years
$16,363.20   total payments, or
deferred payment price

EXERCISE YOUR SKILLS

1. Why is the term credit used instead of debt?

2. How does the use of credit raise the standard of living?

3. Why do you think consumers are willing to pay substantial finance charges as part of repaying an installment loan?

4. Who receives the revenue from finance charges paid by consumers?

5. What do you think the bank or other lending institutions would do if a borrower did not make the payments on an installment loan?

_____ **Activity 1** _____

Patrick is an excellent student and will probably receive a scholarship for college, but his father has explained that part of the money for attending college will have to be borrowed. Patrick is considering applying to several different colleges and would like to know how much he will have to pay back if he borrows the amounts of money needed for these schools.

1. Use the amortization table for $12\frac{1}{2}\%$ interest in the Reference Section of this book to find the monthly payment for the loan amounts listed below over the periods of 3 years, 4 years, and 5 years.

2. Find the total payments for each time period.

3. Record your results in a table like the following.

Note: Save your table to use in the activity in Section 5–2.

	Loan Amount	Number of Years	Monthly Payment	Total Payments
a.	$6500	3	217.46	217.46 x 36 = $7828.56
		4	172.77	172.77 x 48 =
		5		
b.	9500	3		
		4		
		5		
c.	6000	3		
		4		
		5		
d.	12000	3		
		4		
		5		
e.	17500	3		
		4		
		5		
f.	11650	3		
		4		
		5		
g.	8775	3		
		4		
		5		
h.	5525	3		
		4		
		5		

PROBLEMS WITH CREDIT: THE GENIE GRANTS TOO MANY WISHES

Joan could tell Patrick a few things about credit. The first installment loan her family took out seemed reasonable; it was a mortgage for the home they are buying. With Mom and Dad both working they were making the payments easily enough. Then they decided to buy another car; it was the first car they ever bought new, and Joan is learning to drive in it. Joan is not sure how much it cost, but she has heard her parents arguing about it.

Then last year, after a series of violent thunderstorms, the roof in the den started to leak, so the family took out a second mortgage on the house to pay for a new roof. They will be paying on this mortgage for another six years. They also borrowed money to replace the air conditioning and heating system, and then to put in new carpets—the old ones were damaged by rain from the leaking roof.

All these payments were manageable until Mom lost her job four months ago. The electronics company where she has been working was forced to eliminate some jobs in her department because the company lost money last year.

Joan's parents have really been on edge lately, especially as more bills arrive everyday. They even borrowed more money from the credit union to pay some of the bills, and now they are having trouble making those payments. Joan will be glad when her mother finds another job; maybe she and Dad won't yell at each other so much, and they can get back to normal. All the family members are a little stunned by recent events and are wondering how they managed to get into such a mess so quickly.

OBJECTIVES: In this section, we will help Joan to:

- *cite several problems with using credit*
- *recognize indications that a family has used credit too much*
- *compute the percent of the original loan that is paid in interest*
- *find the cost of buying an automobile on the installment plan*

CREDIT: TOOL OR TRAP?

Other Americans, like Joan's family, borrow money from a bank or other financial institution in order to obtain the use of merchandise before paying for it. Americans are heavy credit users; almost everyone arranges to use some sort of credit in a lifetime, especially for expensive purchases such as a new roof and air-conditioning system. So what went wrong for Joan's parents and what can be a problem for millions of other credit users like them?

1. Credit is rented money. We must pay heavily for the privilege of using it. Banks and lending institutions encourage us to indulge in this privilege because they receive the profits.

2. Credit ties up future income. When credit purchases are made, we are actually spending future income or earnings. Too much future income tied up in making credit payments can be a burden. If that income happens to disappear suddenly, making the payments may become impossible.

3. Credit makes it easy to overspend. Businesses with products or services to sell are cashing in on consumers' willingness to use credit to pay for something they might never have bought if they had to pay cash. If a furniture store owner can make bedroom suites more accessible to potential customers by offering "Convenient credit terms—No payments until June," the owner will sell more bedroom suites.

Credit demands careful management. Unwise use of credit can cause people, businesses, and even governments to go bankrupt. Excessive debt can undermine the debtor's job, marriage, and even health. Many consumers suffer from the stress and strain of debt problems.

One convenient yardstick for measuring your ability to handle debt is as follows: No matter what your income, 10% of take-home pay, excluding a home mortgage, is a comfortable amount to spend making payments on credit accounts or **installment loans**; 15% is a manageable amount; and 20% or more is a dangerous credit overload. It may not be obvious when you are passing these limits in credit usage. But there are other signs to look for. Some other indications of credit overload are when an individual or family

- is forced to miss some installment payments in order to pay the monthly mortgage payment
- has to seek a new loan before an old one is repaid
- can pay only the minimum amount due on credit card accounts but continues to use the cards
- has taken out loans to combine debts or has asked for extensions on existing loans
- has begun to receive repeated overdue notices from creditors
- has little or no savings or has drawn on savings to pay regular bills that once were paid out of monthly income
- has telephone calls or letters from creditors demanding payment of overdue bills

Wisely used, installment buying can be a benefit to consumers, business, and the economy in general. But it can be harmful if abused.

1. What are three problems with using credit?

2. What are four of the seven indicators that an individual or a family has abused credit and is suffering from a credit overload?

3. Why is it easy to borrow too much?

SHARPEN YOUR SKILLS

_____ Skill 1 _____

The interest or finance charge that is added to a loan amount is a substantial amount of money. If the loan amount is $6500, and the loan is repaid in 3 years at $12\frac{1}{2}\%$, the total payments are $7828.56. (See Sharpen Your Skills in Section 5–1 for this calculation.)

Question   What is the percent of interest on the original loan?

Solution   To find the amount of interest, subtract the loan amount from the total payments.

$$\begin{array}{rl} \$7828.56 & \text{total payments} \\ -\,6500.00 & \text{original loan amount} \\ \hline \$1328.56 & \text{amount of interest} \end{array}$$

Then find the percent by dividing the amount of interest by the loan amount. Round your answer to the nearest whole percent.

$$\$1328.56 \div 6500 = 0.2044$$

$$0.2044 = 20\% \text{ to the nearest whole percent}$$

The interest is 20%.

EXERCISE YOUR SKILLS

1. Why should a family not take out a new loan to help make payments on a previous loan, if they are having difficulty?

2. What part of a family's income can go to make payments on installment loans before the family has a dangerous credit overload?

3. How can excessive debt damage a consumer's health?

_____ Activity 1 _____

Before going off to college, Patrick is considering taking a short vacation in Colorado to backpack with friends. If he did this every summer he would not be able to earn as much money working at summer jobs as he had planned. He realizes this would mean it would take longer to repay his tuition loan. Joan, who is an excellent mathematics student, has explained to Patrick that if he extends the time during which he must repay the tuition loan to 5 years, the interest he pays will be a greater percentage of the loan amount.

1. Use the results from Activity 1 in Section 5–1 to find the amount of interest paid on each loan amount.

2. Find the percent of the loan amount paid in interest to the nearest whole percent.

3. Record your results in a table like the following.

> **Note:** Save your table to use in Activity 1 in Section 5–3.

	Loan Amount	Years	Total Payments	Amount of Interest	Percent of Interest
a.	$6500	3	$7828.56	$1328.56	20%
		4	8292.96	1792.96	
		5			
b.	9500	3			
		4			
		5			
c.	6000	3			
		4			
		5			
d.	12000	3			
		4			
		5			
e.	17500	3			
		4			
		5			
f.	11650	3			
		4			
		5			
g.	8775	3			
		4			
		5			
h.	5525	3			
		4			
		5			

4. Did the percent of interest increase as the loan amounts increased? Did the percent of interest increase as the time periods increased?

CREDIT MANAGEMENT: THE GENIE CAN BE CONTROLLED

Raul wants to take Joan to the prom this spring, but she has not been willing to discuss it. Raul and Joan have dated regularly for a year and a half and they know each other quite well. Raul knew when Joan's mother lost her job, and he has guessed that the financial outlook at their house has not been comfortable. Raul thinks that Joan does not have the money for a new dress for the prom. He is trying to think of some way to help out with this problem.

Raul would like to avoid making the same mistakes Joan's family has made. Before he considers using installment credit, he will explore ways to reduce the cost and to figure out whether he can afford it.

OBJECTIVES: In this section, we will help Raul to:

- *follow some suggestions from financial advisors about how to use installment credit wisely*
- *determine how much can be saved by varying payment plans on an installment loan*

GUIDELINES FOR USING CREDIT WISELY

Credit can be an important tool in money management if it is used wisely. Raul has found the following suggestions from the financial advisors and credit counselors about the proper use of credit.

Limit Installment Debt to 15% to 20% of Take-Home Pay. Monthly installment payments (excluding a home mortgage) of 15% to 20% of take-home pay is usually considered to be a manageable amount. Any amount above 20% will reduce an individual's ability to pay for food, shelter, transportation, clothing, and other essentials. Sylvia Porter, a columnist and authority on money matters, recommends: Do not owe more than one-third of your **discretionary income** for the year. Discretionary income is the income you have left after you pay for the basic needs of food, clothing, and shelter.

Purchase Durable Products That Will Outlast the Payment Period. If credit is going to be used for items that do not appreciate (increase in value), it is wise to restrict its use to the purchase of durable products such as household appliances or cars. And it is important to choose those products carefully. Certainly it will be difficult to make payments on a car for two years if the car only lasted six months.

If you are thinking of borrowing money or opening a charge account, always remember that your first step should be to figure out how much it will cost you and whether you can afford it. Then you can shop around for the best terms.

WAYS TO REDUCE THE COST OF INSTALLMENT LOANS

Raul has also discovered the following means of keeping credit costs down.

Have a Short Payment Period. Some consumers have the idea that paying for a product or service over a longer period of time does not cost more. Actually, the longer the payment period and the smaller the payments, the greater the cost of financing the item.

Make a Large Down Payment. Usually the consumer is required to pay for a portion of a purchase in cash. This portion is called the **down payment**. The larger the down payment, the less the borrower has to borrow. Money is saved by paying a larger portion in cash and financing—that is, borrowing— a smaller portion.

Compare Interest Rates. The interest rate on a loan can vary dramatically from lender to lender, so it is wise to shop for interest just as you would shop for the product itself, looking for the best value.

Ask Yourself

1. What are two guidelines for using credit wisely?

2. If you are thinking about borrowing money, what should be your first step?

3. What are three ways of reducing the cost of installment loans?

SHARPEN YOUR SKILLS

_____ Skill 1 _____

Maria is trying to decide if it is better to finance her car for 3 years or to extend the loan to 5 years. She may buy a car that costs $14,950 at $12\frac{1}{2}\%$ interest.

Question How much money can Maria save on the car if she finances it over a period of 3 years rather than 5 years?

Solution Find the down payment:

$14,950	cost of car
x 0.10	percent of down payment
$1,495.00	down payment

Find the loan amount:

$14,950	cost of car
– 1,495	down payment
$13,455	loan amount

Find monthly payments, total payments, and total cost for 3 years and 5 years. Use the amortization table for $12\frac{1}{2}\%$ interest in the Reference Section of this book. **Note:** Use $13,450 as the basis for calculations, ignoring the final $5.

3 Years	5 Years	
$449.98	$302.61	monthly payment
x 36	x 60	number of months
$16,199.28	$18,156.60	total payments
+ 1,495.00	+ 1,495.00	down payment
$17,694.28	$19,651.60	total cost

Find the amount that would be saved if the loan were financed over 3 years rather than 5 years.

$19,651.60	total cost in 5 years
–17,694.28	total cost in 3 years
$ 1,957.32	savings

Maria can save $1957.32 by choosing the 3-year repayment plan.

Note: The cost of the car remained the same in this problem; the only change was the time period during which the loan was financed. A savings of almost $2000 on a car that costs almost $15,000 could be considered a substantial savings. Of course, the consumer must also recognize that the monthly payments are higher in the shorter time period. The consumer must decide which plan is best under the circumstances, but the consumer should be aware that the difference between the two plans is significant.

_____ **Skill 2** _____

1. Maria realizes that it might make a difference if she changed the down payment amount. She will compare her previous findings (with a down payment of 10%) with amounts she would pay if she made a down payment of 20% or 30%.

Question   How do the total payments for a loan compare when down payments of 10%, 20%, and 30% are made?

Solution   Maria already has the following information:

Loan	Total Cost	
Amount	**3 Years**	**5 Years**
$13,455	$17,694.28	$19,651.60

She then follows the steps shown in Skill 1.

Find the down payment:

$14,950	cost of car (from Skill 1)
x .20	percent of down payment
$ 2,990	down payment

Find the loan amount:

$14,950	cost of car
− 2,990	down payment
$11,960	loan amount

Find the monthly payments, total payments, and cost for 3 and 5 years. (Ignore any remainder of the loan amount that is below the minimum shown on the table.)

3 Years	**5 Years**	
$ 399.79	$ 268.86	monthly payments
x 36	x 60	number of months
$14,392.44	$16,131.60	
+ 2,990.00	+ 2,990.00	down payment
$17,382.44	$19,121.60	total cost

Total payments with a 20% down payment:

	Down				
Full	**Payment**	**Loan**	**Total Cost**		
Cost	**20%**	**Amount**	**3 Years**	**5 Years**	
$14,950	$2,990.00	$11,960.00	$17,382.44	$19,121.60	

Total payments with a 30% down payment are figured the same way, with the following results:

Full Cost	Down Payment 30%	Loan Amount	Total Cost	
			3 Years	5 Years
$14,950	$4,485.00	$10,465.00	$17,040.72	$18,591.60

The corresponding amounts can be compared as shown below:

	10% Down	20% Down	30% Down
3 Years	$17,694.28	$17,382.44	$17,040.72
5 Years	19,651.60	19,121.60	18,591.60

Therefore, with a down payment of 20%, she would save $311.84 over 3 years, or $530 over 5. With a down payment of 30%, she would save $653.56 over 3 years, or $1060 over 5.

2. Laurie has been thinking of buying a portable keyboard. She has looked at different shops and found that she can purchase one with a loan at 10% interest at one shop and $12\frac{1}{2}$% at another. She is curious about what difference the percent of interest would make in the total cost of a loan to purchase the keyboard.

Question   What would be the difference in total payments between a loan with 10% interest and a loan with $12\frac{1}{2}$% interest when the loans are for the same amount and both are repaid over 2 years?

Solution   The 10% and $12\frac{1}{2}$% amortization tables in the Reference Section are used to find the total repayment amounts.

Years	Total Loan Amount	Total Cost	
		10% Interest	$12\frac{1}{2}$% Interest
2	$650.00	$720.00	$738.24

The total repayment amounts are compared:

	$738.24	repayment amount at 12 1/2%
	−720.00	repayment amount at 10%
Savings	$ 18.24	difference in total amounts

3. Bernard has collected prices and loan amounts on a harp he wants to buy. The loans have different down payments, time periods, and rates of interest.

Question   How could he construct a spreadsheet to help him compare the loans?

Solution   Using amortization tables for 10% and $12\frac{1}{2}$% (as they appear in the Reference Section of this book), he found the costs of a $1200 loan over 1, 2, and 3 years.

He put them into a spreadsheet like the following:

Years	Down Payment	Total Cost	
		10% Interest	**$12\frac{1}{2}$% Interest**
1	10%	1134.24	$1149.36
	20%	1002.36	1015.68
2	10%	1190.88	1220.64
	20%	1052.40	1198.32
3	10%	1249.20	1294.92
	20%	1104.12	1265.04

EXERCISE YOUR SKILLS

1. What is discretionary income?

2. Why does increasing the size of your down payment for a purchase save you money in the long run?

3. Why would a bank or lending institution encourage you to make a smaller down payment and increase the time period for your installment loan?

_____   **Activity 1** _____

Raul's parents decided to allow him to take one of their two cars to college; Raul's brother, Julio, is now old enough to drive the second one. Their father received an increase in salary this year and is now ready to buy another car for the family; he wants to find the most economical way to do it.

SKILLS PREVIEW

Round to the nearest cent.

1. $2.30562   **2.** $450.271   **3.** $583.24

Write each percent as a decimal.

4. 18%   **5.** 1.5%   **6.** 235%

Find each sum or difference.

7. $7856.92
   +6134.75

8. $875.36
   −624.95

9. $10,951.82
   −9,994.44

Find each product or quotient. Round your answers to the nearest cent.

10. $625
   x36

11. $725.35
   x0.25

12. $1436.25
   x0.0175

13. 18)$256.85   **14.** 2.5)$800   **15.** 0.015)$1600

Find each of the following. Round your answers to the nearest cent.

16. 10% of $500   **17.** 8% of $6500

18. 15% of $450   **19.** 18% of $520.50

You borrowed $800 and made 12 payments of $71.27 each to pay off a loan.

20. What is the total amount you paid?

21. How much interest did you pay?

The graph shows percents of cars available at a car lot. There are 200 cars in all.

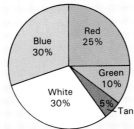

22. How many red cars are there?

23. How many of the available cars are green?

24. How many of the cars are white or tan?

25. What percent of the cars are red or blue?

CHAPTER **6** **CREDIT CARDS: PLASTIC MONEY**

The focus of the American economy has gradually shifted away from an independent, agrarian existence. In that setting, people offered services or goods that they could produce in exchange for goods and services they needed. One local merchant ordered and had delivered by wagon all the manufactured items that the local farmers could not create for themselves. If an item was not available through this merchant, and the farmer or one of his neighbors couldn't make it or grow it, the farmer could either travel many miles by wagon or train to a larger city in search of it, or do without the item.

The acquisition of wealth and what wealth can provide is an attractive incentive. In America today, the production and distribution of goods and services is big business. We have become very specialized in what we, as individuals, can offer to others in exchange for the many creations we receive from them.

Our economy is so specialized that companies exist not only to create products and services but also to convince us that we all should acquire more of these products. Large companies spend millions of dollars every year advertising their products and supporting advertising agencies. Another segment of big business was developed to process all the money exchanged among the other businesses. Banks offer many services that keep our economy flowing.

One major service offered to consumers by banks, retailers, and other companies is the credit or charge card. Bankers and merchants have realized that if they make credit convenient and painless to consumers, merchants will sell more, and the banks can charge both the merchants and the customers for the service. For the consumer, handing over the plastic card is much easier than handing over the dollar bills, so we have a tendency to spend more.

In this chapter, three of our high school students will take a closer look at the costs and the conveniences of using credit cards. At the end of the chapter, they will pose the question: Is the convenience worth the costs? You will consider the evidence with them and come to your own conclusions.

HOW MANY CARDS = ONE WALLET FULL?

Sylvia Shawn enjoys spending money. She has a bumper sticker on her car that reads "When the Going Gets Tough, the Tough Go Shopping." Sylvia's mother rarely takes her shopping; Sylvia's parents are divorced, and she lives with her mother, so Sylvia really looks forward to the two weekends every month she spends with her father. He always takes her to really great places to shop. Paying for everything seems simple for him, but he rarely carries any cash.

On a typical Saturday visit, their first stop will be at a gas station to fill up his yellow sports car. Sylvia usually picks up a snack and a drink as well; Dad grabs several packs of baseball cards, too, and pays for all this with his handy oil company credit card. Then they are off to Sylvia's favorite shopping mall, where Dad waits patiently while Sylvia tries on eight or ten outfits before selecting two or three to buy.

Once again, Mr. Shawn pulls out a trusty credit card to pay for the new clothes; he has had a credit card for each department store they go to, and every card is well used. One Saturday, Sylvia selected a new set of earrings, a purse, and a pair of shoes to go with one of her new outfits, plus a whole line of makeup products she had been wanting to try. All these purchases were added to Mr. Shawn's **charge account** when he flashed a magic card.

Since Sylvia will be going away to college next year, her father has been helping her pick out an elaborate nine-piece set of luggage in marine blue. For this purchase, Dad has another plastic card, a VISA card. Dad has several VISA cards he carries from different banks around the country. He calls them his "plastic money" cards. His VISA card is shown below:

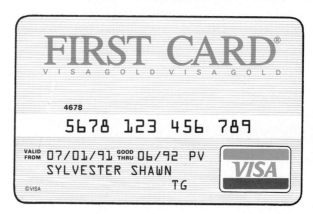

VISA, The Three Bands Design, and the Dove Design are registered trademarks of Visa International and are reproduced with permission.

When they finish shopping, Sylvia's father often takes her to a fancy restaurant for dinner. For this he has still another kind of card, American Express; he uses it for restaurant meals, airline tickets, car rentals, and other travel expenses. He calls it his "entertainment expense account" card.

Sylvia still doesn't understand how he got so many cards, and why he doesn't just carry real money instead. Sylvia's mother has several credit cards but she rarely uses them. She manages her money carefully.

Sylvia knows there is a lot of disagreement between her parents about the use of credit cards. Sylvia would like to have a few cards of her own, but she wonders if that is a good idea. She wants to know more.

OBJECTIVES: In this section, we will help Sylvia to:

- ⬤ *describe how credit cards are used*
- ⬤ *identify three categories of credit cards and several companies that offer the cards in each category*
- ⬤ *describe the ways of receiving or applying for a card*
- ⬤ *identify advantages and disadvantages of credit cards*

USING CREDIT

Every time Sylvia's father finds a charge slip like the one below, he is increasing his debt.

▶ answering machines · baseball cards · Civil War chess sets · dentures · earrings · funerals · garage door openers · greeting cards · ice cream · perfume · knife sharpeners · lawyer's fees · measles shots · electronic games · oil paintings · postage stamps · quilts · chocolate candy · subway rides · theater tickets · underwear · manicures · visits to the vet · waterbeds · photocopies · yardwork · admissions to the zoo, and · · · ·

At left are some of the thousands of things he could pay for with a credit card.

We are bombarded by voices from the media telling us to buy more and more and charge it all on our "VISA or MasterCard." Drowned out in the noise are the quiet voices from our past that told us that "saving is honorable" and "borrowing is irresponsible" and that living beyond one's means is not something to be proud of.

Sylvia has noticed the many items advertised on television that she could order by phone through a special 800 number or by mail if she had a credit card. She is particularly interested in the many compact disc recordings she could order if her mother would allow her to use a credit card.

Of course, Sylvia doesn't yet own a compact disc player, but she will as soon as she saves enough money. Her mother still believes the credit cards should only be used for convenience, not as a way of borrowing money for things she could not otherwise afford.

As Sylvia has watched her father with his cards, she has learned what they are, what kinds there are, and how the credit card companies know what has been purchased with the cards.

CREDIT CARD: WHAT IS IT AND HOW DOES IT WORK?

A **credit card** is a small plastic card—about 2" by 3½"—that identifies the holder and extends the cardholder an unsecured line of credit. Most cards entitle the holder to charge purchases up to a maximum **credit limit**. The cardholder agrees, when he or she signs the application for the card, to pay for purchases according to the credit card terms: time limits and grace periods, interest rates, and so on. Examples of companies issuing these cards are local department stores, national retail chains, car rental companies, travel and entertainment companies, airlines, telephone companies, oil companies, hotel/motel chains, and commercial banks. The card issuer receives reports of what the holder has charged from all the businesses to which the holder has presented the card. The issuer then bills the holder once a month for the total of the charges. The holder writes one check to the issuing company; it then disburses payments—that is, sends the appropriate amount of money—to the various businesses. Most cards entitle the holder to charge purchases up to a maximum credit limit.

In the case of bank cards, a merchant turns in the charge to his or her bank. The bank notifies the cardholder's bank that a purchase has been made. The cardholder's bank then bills the cardholder for all purchases that month. The cardholder writes one check to the bank. Through the bank card system, the card issuer then pays the merchant's bank. The merchant's bank has already paid the merchant.

TYPES OF CARDS

Credit cards can be divided into four categories: (1) single-purpose cards; (2) multipurpose travel, food, and entertainment cards; (3) all-purpose bank credit cards; and (4) debit cards.

Single-purpose cards include those from oil companies such as Exxon, Mobil, Shell, and Standard Oil; and those from department stores such as Sears and Montgomery Ward. Sylvia's father uses an oil company card and cards from the stores in the mall, all single-purpose cards. There is no fee for the card, and the card allows the owner to make purchases or obtain services at the store, station, or company that issued it. The purpose of this kind of card is to encourage you to shop exclusively with this particular company. If you have a credit card from one specific oil company and not another, perhaps you will buy more of your gasoline from that company.

Multipurpose travel and entertainment cards include American Express, Diners Club, and Carte Blanche. There is an annual membership fee for these cards. For this membership fee, these cards provide a variety of services which some credit cards do not provide, such as guaranteed check cashing at hotels and airline counters, free travel insurance, and emergency card replacement. Usually no credit limit is imposed on the cardholder. However, these are charge cards, not credit cards, so the cardholder is expected to pay the entire unpaid balance upon being billed.

All-purpose bank cards include VISA, MasterCard, and Discover cards. These cards are widely accepted by retailers as well as by restaurants, hotels, airlines, and other companies that wish to cash in on the boost in sales that accompanies the acceptance of credit cards. Some banks offer cardholders special purchase insurance and world-wide travel assistance.

Another advantage is that cardholders also are covered by Regulation Z which is the regulation that inforces the Truth in Lending Act passed by Congress. These regulations protect consumers in cases of error, if merchandise is not received, and/or if services are not rendered. Card users may receive more protection than if they had paid by check or cash since it may be easier to get a credit on their credit card than to get a cash refund.

These cards can also be used to get instant loans up to a limited amount at the bank, credit union, or 24-hour teller facility. Sylvia has explained to her mother that the card can be used to obtain cash right out of an Automatic Teller Machine (ATM). Some banks provide special checks you can use to pay for something or to make a deposit into your regular checking or savings account. A credit limit is imposed on the cardholder.

Debit cards are essentially electronic checks. They enable cardholders to use their ATM cards to pay for purchases at local stores. The cardholder's financial institution deducts the purchase amount from the consumer's checking account instead of posting it to a credit account. The bank cards enable the merchant to use the credit card company's existing authorization, draft transmission, and settlement systems. This kind of card is widely used outside the United States, and may become popular in America in the near future.

WHAT DOES IT COST?

If you use a single-purpose card or an all-purpose card, a **finance charge** is levied on unpaid balance. Rates vary from state to state but are typically 18% yearly (1½% per month). To the right is a sample credit card billing statement. It is the VISA statement Mr. Shawn received for his purchase of luggage for Sylvia during their day of shopping.

The finance charge will be added each month unless the

entire balance due is paid by a certain date. The monthly statement will tell you how much time you have to pay the bill before a finance charge is added to the cost of the purchases. Many institutions also charge a membership fee—$15, $25, or $30 or more a year—for the use of their cards.

Sylvia's mother knows that the interest rates for cash advances are even higher than the rates on purchases. She has discouraged Sylvia from considering the credit card as a source of instant, borrowed cash from a machine.

HOW DO YOU GET A CREDIT CARD?

Sylvia would like to be able to walk into a music store, pick up several cassette tapes and CDs and maybe a new set of headphones, not even notice the prices, then hand the clerk a shiny plastic card with her name stamped in bold letters on it. Her father told Sylvia that if she wants a card she should apply for one. Applications for VISA and MasterCard are available at almost any bank. Merchants who honor the single- and multipurpose cards have applications for them.

Referred By: _____

(_____) _____   _____
Phone Number   VISA/MasterCard Account Number (excluding the first four digits)

APPLY FOR VISA OR MASTERCARD WITH NO ANNUAL FEE

PLEASE TELL US ABOUT YOURSELF

Print full name	Last	First	Middle	
Your Home Address Number and Street				☐ Own ☐ Rent
City, Town or Post Office		State	Zip Code	
Home Phone and Area Code ( )			Years at Current Address	
Previous Home Address			Years at Previous Address	
City, Town or Post Office		State	Zip Code	
Social Security Number		Date of Birth		
Drivers License No. and State				

PLEASE TELL US ABOUT YOUR JOB

Business Name or Employer		Position	
Check Here if ☐ Retired ☐ Self Employed		If Retired, Indicate Former Employer	
Business Address, Number and Street			
City, Town or Post Office		State	Zip Code
Business Phone and Area Code ( )		Ext.	Years at Job

FOLD   FOLD

PLEASE GIVE US SOME FINANCIAL INFORMATION

Yearly Income $	Monthly Rent or Mortgage $

You need not include spouse's income, alimony, child support, or maintenance payments paid to you if you are not relying on them to establish credit worthiness.

Additional Income $	Source(s) of Other Income

YOUR CARD CHOICE   FOR FREE ADDITIONAL CARD

I am applying for (check one) ☐ VISA ☐ MasterCard If not specified, this will be considered a VISA request.	Would you like an additional card for ☐ Yes a member of your family or household? ☐ No	If yes, name and relationship:

PLEASE SIGN THIS AUTHORIZATION

I give the above information for the purpose of obtaining credit and authorize the obtaining of information concerning any statements made herein—including the procurement of consumer credit reports and answering of questions about your credit experience with me. I authorize Gary-Wheaton Bank, National Association, a subsidiary of First Chicago Corporation, and its affiliates, any of which may issue the card applied for in this application, to share this application and information obtained concerning this application.

I agree to be bound by the terms and conditions set forth in the cardholder agreement that will be mailed to me with my card.

X_____
Applicant's Signature   Date

Annual % Rate	Annualized Membership Fee	Minimum Finance Charge	Variable Rate Index and Spread	Grace Period	Balance Calculation Method	Cash Advance, Transaction, Overlimit, and Late Fees
None	None	Not Applicable	For Purchases: 25 Days For Cash Advance: None	Average Daily Balance (including new transactions)	Cash Advance Fee: None; Transaction Fee: None; Overlimit Fee: None; Late Fee: $5.00

Residents of Illinois may contact the Illinois Commissioner of Banks and Trust Companies for comparative information on interest rate charges, fees, grace periods, at: State of Illinois—C.I.P., P.O. Box 10181, Springfield, Illinois 62791, 1-800-634-5452.

All disclosure information provided is accurate and subject to change from the revision date indicated on this document.

Sylvia began gathering a collection of these applications. They asked a lot of questions, some of which Sylvia could answer easily. However, the questions about occupation, monthly income, checking account, other credit references, whether she was renting or buying her home, and how long she had held her current job, were more difficult for Sylvia. She realized that having no employment and no income except her weekly $10 allowance from Mom would probably make it difficult to have her application accepted. Sylvia sent in several of them anyway just to see what would happen. About two months later, the rejection letters started arriving. However, she did receive a nice letter from one of the oil companies asking her to re-apply when she graduates from high school and begins working. One of the banks suggested that if one of her parents would apply with her and guarantee the payments, they would reconsider her application.

At one time issuers of bank cards, in an attempt to get established and to build their volume, sent out cards to people who had not applied for them and whom they had not screened carefully. As a result, many people who were poor **credit risks** received cards; other people, who had no desire for cards, also received them. Congress has since made it illegal for a bank to provide a credit card to a person that has not applied for it.

Sylvia and her father are well aware of the advantages of credit cards; they put together the following list.

Advantages of Credit Cards

1. Credit cards are a very convenient and simple way to buy.

2. Payment for purchases can be delayed until a predetermined date. (Dad likes this one particularly well.)

3. A record of purchases is made automatically.

4. The danger of losing money while shopping is minimized, since cash is not needed at the time of purchase.

5. It is easy to order merchandise by mail or telephone using credit cards.

6. Salespeople and business owners may come to recognize frequent charge customers; this can result in better service for the customers.

7. You can pay for several purchases at one time.

8. Credit cards enable customers to take advantage of sales.

9. When you need extra cash, you don't have to ask; you just use your own previously established line of credit. Many banks even provide this cash through ATMs.

FIRST CARD
VISA GOLD VISA GOLD
4678
5678 123 456 789
VALID FROM 07/01/91 GOOD THRU 06/92 PV
SYLVESTER SHAWN
TG
VISA

Sylvia's mother, on the other hand, has compiled the following list of cautions.

Disadvantages of Credit Cards

1. A credit card is a disadvantage for people who have a tendency to spend beyond their income or their ability to pay. It is imperative that credit card users are responsible.

2. Using the charge card does not have the same impact on the shopper as paying cash. At least when you hand cash to the clerk, you cannot spend the same cash again — it is gone. But you will get your credit card back, to use again in the next store. Therefore, you may forget how much you have charged until the bill comes at the end of the month.

3. Since so many charges can be made on the telephone and through the mail, anyone who knows your credit card number, your name, and some other information that is easily obtainable, can make unauthorized charges to your account without even having your card.

4. Credit cards can be stolen by the same thief who would steal your cash, so you should protect them as you would cash. If they are stolen, notify the company immediately or you could be held liable for unauthorized purchases. Cardholders are not liable for charges once they have notified their issuing company, and in no case are they liable for more than $50 once the company has been notified.

Ask Yourself

1. What are 2 companies that offer credit or charge cards in each of the following categories?

   a. Single-purpose cards

   b. Multipurpose travel and entertainment cards

   c. All-purpose bank cards

2. How can you get a credit or charge card?

3. What are 4 advantages of these cards?

4. What are 2 disadvantages of these cards?

SHARPEN YOUR SKILLS

_____ Skill 1 _____

Suppose you owe a balance of $1500 on your VISA account. Your bank only requires that you pay 10% of what you owe each month as a minimum payment. However, the bank also charges 1.5% of the amount you owe as a finance charge.

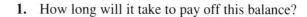

Questions 1. How long will it take to pay off this balance?

2. How much interest will you pay over the period of time it takes to pay off the balance?

Solutions 1. Set up a chart like the one below and compute each part. You may wish to use a computer spreadsheet program to create your chart and calculate the contents.

Beginning balance shown is $1500.00

Interest = Balance x 1.5%, rounded to the nearest penny.

$1500.00 x 0.015 = $22.50

Amount Owed = Balance + Interest

$1500.00 + 22.50 = $1522.50

Payment = 10% x Amount Owed, rounded to the nearest dollar.

$1522.50 x 0.10 = $152

Next Balance = Amount Owed – Payment

Continue finding each new balance until the amount owed is less than $200; after that make payments of $20 each until the amount owed is less than $20; then make the last payment equal to the final amount owed.

	Balance	Interest	Amount Owed	Payment
1.	$ 1500.00	$ 22.50	$1522.50	$ 152
2.	1370.50	20.56	1391.06	139
3.	1252.06	18.78	1270.84	127
4.	1143.84	17.16	1161.00	116
5.	1045.00	15.68	1060.68	106
6.	954.68	14.32	969.00	97
7.	872.00	13.08	885.08	89
8.	796.08	11.94	808.02	81
9.	727.02	10.91	737.93	74
10.	663.93	9.96	673.89	67
11.	606.89	9.10	615.99	62
12.	553.99	8.31	562.30	56
13.	506.30	7.59	513.89	51
14.	462.89	6.94	469.83	47
15.	422.83	6.34	429.17	43

	Balance	Interest	Amount Owed	Payment
16.	386.17	5.79	391.96	39
17.	352.96	5.29	358.25	36
18.	322.25	4.83	327.08	33
19.	294.08	4.41	298.49	30
20.	268.49	4.03	272.52	27
21.	245.52	3.68	249.20	25
22.	224.20	3.36	227.56	23
23.	204.56	3.07	207.63	21
24.	186.63	2.80	189.43	20
25.	169.43	2.54	171.97	20
26.	151.97	2.28	154.25	20
27.	134.25	2.01	136.26	20
28.	116.26	1.74	118.00	20
29.	98.00	1.47	99.47	20
30.	79.47	1.19	80.60	20
31.	60.66	.91	61.57	20
32.	41.57	.62	42.19	20
33.	22.19	.33	22.52	20
34.	2.52	.04	2.56	2.56

To pay off this VISA balance, you must make 34 payments.

2. Total the Interest column.

The total interest paid is $243.56

EXERCISE YOUR SKILLS

1. What is the major difference between what you must pay each month to American Express and to VISA?

2. Why do you think a bank would refuse to issue a credit card to someone who has no regular monthly income?

3. How might consumers keep track of how much they have charged on their credit cards before the monthly bills come?

4. Why do you think some credit card holders insist on tearing up the carbon papers that are a part of the credit card slip they have just signed?

_____ **Activity 1** _____

Karl and Aubrey's parents have three MasterCard and VISA accounts from different banks and are making the minimum payments required each month. Aubrey is trying to convince them that making larger payments each month would eventually reduce the amount of interest they pay each year.

Since interest on credit card accounts is no longer allowed as an itemized deduction on their income tax return, Aubrey's mother is considering his argument. This activity will help show Aubrey's mother how much interest she is paying during the first year under each payment plan.

1. Determine the amount of interest paid over one year on a VISA account with a monthly interest rate of 1.5% and monthly payments of 10% of the amount owed. Set up a chart like the following and compute the figures to fill it. A few of the figures are already entered for you.

	Balance	Interest	Amount Owed	Payment
a.	$2000.00	$30.00	$2030.00	$203
b.	1827.00			
c.				
d.				
e.				
f.				
g.				
h.				
i.				
j.				
k.				
l.	739.71			

What is the total interest?

2. Set up a chart like the one in Problem 1, using a beginning balance of $4690, a monthly interest rate of 1.5%, and a monthly payment of 10% of the amount owed. The 12th balance is $1732.66. Total the interest through 12 payments.

3. In the same way, find the total interest for 12 payments with a beginning balance of $1358. The 12th balance is $501.40.

Note: Save your results to use for Activity 1 in Section 6–2.

Trevor lives next door to Sylvia and her mother. He and Sylvia used to play together as kids; Trevor and his younger sister, Tracey, spent a lot of time in Sylvia's playroom. Sylvia always wanted to pretend they were a family so she could take Tracey shopping for new clothes and toys. Then she would pull out her credit cards to pay for everything. Since she had always seen her father with his cards, Sylvia assumed that it was the way things were done. Sylvia also liked Trevor and wanted to include him in their game.

Trevor's mother had given them some outdated cards to play with. She had cut off a part of each card so it couldn't be used for a real purchase.

Trevor realized even then how much Sylvia enjoyed shopping on credit. Trevor's parents have their share of credit cards, also, but they don't use them as much as Sylvia's father does. Last year Trevor's parents decided to open a special charge account at a national department store to buy a big-screen television set. Trevor watched as his father and mother signed the contract. He noticed several items in bold print on the contract; among them were finance charge, annual percentage rate, and total finance price. Trevor's mother told him that the Truth in Lending Act requires this information as part of every installment contract. His parents were especially interested in the annual percentage rate and the total financed price, since these were what determined how much the television set actually would cost them.

Trevor is learning that not only can the same television set cost different amounts at different stores, but the financing terms can also differ. He has decided to investigate the Truth in Lending Act more fully.

OBJECTIVES: In this section, we will help Trevor to:

- *describe the requirements made by the Truth In Lending Act*
- *define annual percentage rate and finance charge*
- *determine the amount of interest paid on revolving charge accounts over a period of time*

THE COST OF CREDIT

The Consumer Credit Protection Act, commonly known as the **Truth in Lending Act,** requires that creditors tell consumers the exact cost of buying on credit. The purpose of the law is to assure full disclosure of all credit costs so that consumers can compare costs. Disclosure of costs must be made in writing before credit is extended. In the contract that Trevor's parents signed to buy the television set, the following items were disclosed.

Annual Percentage Rate (APR). This is the percent cost of credit on a yearly basis. The borrower does not have to know how to compute the APR but should know that the APR is the key to comparing costs. Assume that you wish to borrow $1000 with a dollar finance charge of $80. It might appear that the $80 represents 8 percent of $1000. Actually, if you could keep the full $1000 for the whole year and pay it all back at one time, the APR would be 8%. But with installment contracts, you do not have the full $1000 for the entire year. If the $1000 is repaid in 12 equal payments of $90 each, the money you borrowed and get to keep, and the balance of the debt, decreases each month. At the end of six months, you have only $500 of the amount you originally borrowed. In fact, you have less and less of the $1000 each month, and you owe less and less. By the last month, all but $90 of the original loan has been repaid. In this example, the $80 finance charge on $1000 amounts to 14.5% for the year.

Finance charge. This is the total dollar amount it costs to use credit. The finance charges include interest (the cost of using someone else's money) and sometimes other costs.

Late payment penalties. If you are late making your scheduled payment, your lender may charge a penalty.

Total financed price. This is the total dollar amount you will actually pay by the end of the contract.

Prepayment penalty. If you wish to pay off the balance before the due date, your lender may also charge a penalty, but if so, this penalty must be stated in the contract.

Number of Payments. In addition, the total number of payments to be made must be stated. If the customer can avoid additional interest charges, he or she must be told how this can be done. The difference in interest rates for different kinds of loans must also be disclosed. If the company charges a higher rate of interest for cash advances than for regular purchases, the customer must be given this information in the credit agreement.

Notification. Any changes in the terms of the loan must be communicated to the borrower at least 15 days before they take effect.

Cooling Off Period. You have three days in which to change your mind about the purchase you have financed. This applies to almost all purchases, but does not apply to a first mortgage.

Limited Liability. This law sets the limit of $50 on your liability for unauthorized purchases when your credit card is stolen or lost. As you have read, this is the highest amount for which you will be responsible if you report the loss promptly.

Ask Yourself

1. What are 6 items that must be disclosed in writing in a credit contract.

2. What is a finance charge?

3. What is a prepayment penalty

SHARPEN YOUR SKILLS

Skill 1

Another important consideration is the minimum monthly payment. This amount is usually set by the lending institution, but you can set your own monthly payment so long as it is above the required amount. The amount of the payment of course affects the length of time it will take you to pay off the total loan. It also affects the amount of interest you will pay. To see how this is so, consider the following example.

You are making minimum monthly payments on your MasterCard account and your current balance is $785.00. Suppose your bank requires a minimum payment per month of 10% of the unpaid balance (rounded to the nearest whole dollar), and the interest rate is 1.5% per month. If the amount owed drops below $20, the minimum payment is the total amount owed.

Questions   **1.** How much interest will you have paid in the first year?

2. If the minimum payment were 5% of the amount owed, how much interest would you pay in the first year?

Solutions   **1.** Set up a chart like the one below and compute each part.

First Balance = $785.00

Interest = Balance x 1.5%, rounded to the nearest penny.

$785.00 x 0.015 = $11.78

Amount Owed = Balance + Interest

$785.00 + 11.78 = $796.78

Payment = 10% of Amount Owed, rounded to the nearest whole dollar.

$796.78 x 0.10 = $80

Next Balance = Amount Owed – Payment

$796.78 – 80 = $716.78

Work through the first 12 payments, and then total the interest column.

	Balance	Interest	Amount Owed	Payment
a.	$785.00	$11.78	$796.78	$80
b.	716.78	10.75	727.53	73
c.	654.53	9.82	664.35	66
d.	598.35	8.98	607.33	61
e.	546.33	8.19	554.52	55
f.	499.52	7.49	507.01	51
g.	456.01	6.84	462.85	46
h.	416.85	6.25	423.10	42
i.	381.10	5.72	386.82	39
j.	347.82	5.22	353.04	35
k.	318.04	4.77	322.81	32
l.	290.81	4.36	295.17	30

Total Interest $90.17

The interest paid in the first year is $90.17.

2. Work through the problem again, through the first year, this time using 5% of the amount owed as the payment; then total the interest column.

	Balance	Interest	Amount Owed	Payment
a.	$785.00	$11.78	$796.78	$40
b.	756.78	11.35	768.13	38
c.	730.13	10.95	741.08	37
d.	704.08	10.56	714.64	36
e.	678.64	10.18	688.82	34
f.	654.82	9.82	644.64	33
g.	631.64	9.47	641.11	32
h.	609.11	9.14	618.25	31
i.	587.25	8.81	596.06	30
j.	566.06	8.49	574.55	29

	Balance	Interest	Amount Owed	Payment
k.	545.55	8.18	553.73	28
l.	525.73	7.89	533.62	27

Total Interest $116.62

The interest paid in the first year would be $116.62. The lower minimum payment increased the amount paid in interest. Over the life of the loan, paying back at 5%, you would pay $119.61 in interest.

_____ Skill 2 _____

To show how the amount of interest varies when you change the amount of the monthly payment on a loan, you can construct a bar graph.

Question   How would you make a bar graph for the loans considered in Skill 1?

Solution   You would label the x-axis with the range of dollar amounts appropriate to the interest amounts. In this case, $80 through $130 by $10 amounts. You would label the y-axis with the loan terms, in this case monthly payments of 10% and 5%. The graph looks like the one below.

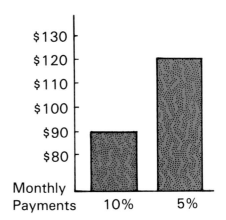

EXERCISE YOUR SKILLS

1. What is the difference between the finance charge and the total financed price?

2. Why was the Truth in Lending Act passed?

3. Assuming the annual percentage rate (APR) is the same in both instances, which do you think would cost more when paying off a debt—making larger payments for a short period of time or making smaller payments for a longer period?

_____ **Activity 1** _____

Determine the increase in the interest paid on a MasterCard account over a period of one year if the payment is changed from 10% to 5% per month, by computing the interest on each of the amounts used in Activity 1 in Section 6–1. Change the payment to 5% of the amount owed.

Set up a chart similar to the one below for each of the following amounts:

1. $2000; the 12th balance is $1338.75.
2. $4680; the 12th balance is $3142.37.
3. $1358; the 12th balance is $910.09.

	Balance	Interest	Amount Owed	Payment (5% of Amount Owed)
a.	$2000.00	$30.00	$2030.00	$102
b.				
c.				
d.				
e.				
f.				
g.				
h.				
i.				
j.				
k.				
l.	1338.75			

What is the total interest?

How much more interest is paid during the year for each of the amounts under the second payment plan? (Compare your answers with those from Activity 6–1.)

4. Since Christmas and Hanukkah shopping entices many consumers to buy more than they do at other times of the year, many banks open new MasterCard and VISA accounts for potential shoppers in preparation for the holiday season. Different banks offer different interest rates for these accounts. Compare the amounts of interest paid over a period of 1 year on different accounts if the interest rates are different.

First, show the first 12 payments on a balance of $2500 at an interest rate of 21% per year. (21% divided by 12 = 1.75% per month.) Assume the payment is 10% of the amount owed, rounded to the nearest dollar. Total the interest through the first 12 payments.

	Balance	Interest	Amount Owed	Payment
a.	$2500.00	$43.75	$2543.75	$254
b.	2289.75			
c.				
d.				
e.				
f.				
g.				
h.				
i.				
j.				
k.				
l.				

What is the total interest?

Work the problem again, using an interest rate of 14% per year. (14% divided by 12 = 1.17% per month.) The other conditions are the same.

	Balance	Interest	Amount Owed	Payment
a.	$2500.00	$29.25	$2529.25	$253
b.	2276.25			
c.				
d.				
e.				
f.				
g.				
h.				
i.				
j.				
k.				
l.				

What is the total interest?

How much more interest is paid during the first year if the bank's interest rate is 21% rather than 14%?

Note: Save your results from Activity 1 for use in the next activity.

_____ **Activity 2** _____

Make a bar graph to illustrate the differences in the amounts of interest paid on the loans considered in Activity 1.

Ursula likes her clerking job at Joyful Toys. She started working there eight months ago when she turned 16 and got her driver's license. In dealing with the customers, however, there is one thing she does not enjoy doing. Each time a customer presents a credit card for a purchase, Ursula must run the card through a computer scanner to verify that this customer's bank will approve the charge. Sometimes the credit is denied. Ursula does not like having to inform the customer of this fact.

Once when this happened, a customer became angry and acted as though Ursula were at fault. He yelled at her and demanded to see the store manager. As he left he hurled a handful of action figures and a model rocket he was holding toward the display case, knocking over a tower of blocks and almost breaking the glass. The store manager did not blame Ursula for the mess, nor for the fact that several customers left while all this was happening, but it made her very uncomfortable.

Ursula knows that if a customer's credit is not verified by the computer, sometimes the bank that issued the card will not repay the local merchant. In that case, Joyful Toys simply loses the entire cost of the purchased items. The store already must pay a service fee to the bank each time a credit purchase is made.

When Ursula handles a customer's credit card she must be careful to process the information correctly. After verifying the charge with the customer's bank, she makes an imprint of the card on the sales slip. On the imprint she circles the expiration date — that is the date, printed on the card, on which the customer must renew the card. After that date, the card is no longer valid.

Ursula then asks the customer to sign the sales slip and to write down his or her telephone number. The phone number is not required by the credit card company but it is an additional precaution the store manager takes to make certain that the customers are legitimate. Finally, before handing the customer his or her copy of the sales slip, Ursula compares the customer's signature on the sales slip with the signature on the card itself. She can then be satisfied that she has done everything possible to verify the customer's right to use the card. After all this she usually smiles and wishes the customer a good day!

OBJECTIVES: *In this section, we will help Ursula to:*

- *identify costs paid by retailers for selling on credit*
- *find the average daily balance and determine what effect it has on making payments on a credit card account*

COST OF CHARGE ACCOUNTS

Retailers selling on credit who issue their own cards incur extra costs on every sale. The extra costs result principally from the following:

- The clerical work necessary for recording sales and collecting accounts

- Losses because of customers who fail to make payments

- An increased tendency of charge customers to return goods for exchange

Retailers who fail to investigate a customer's ability to pay before charging sales to his or her account are apt to have high losses from failure to collect debts. One may well expect to find high prices in stores that recklessly advertise generous credit terms to everyone. Stores that have sound credit policies have practically no losses from customers who fail to make payments. Retailers who accept VISA, MasterCard, and American Express, instead of issuing their own cards, pay a fee to the banks; therefore it is the banks in these cases who deal with the additional costs.

Banks issuing all-purpose credit cards like American Express, VISA, and MasterCard, collect from participating retailers a percentage of every sale made on their card. This charge covers the card-issuing companies who stand to lose money if the cardholders fail to pay for the purchases they charged. Even though the salesperson takes every precaution, a few illegitimate uses of credit cards are bound to slip through. It is these losses the credit card company must make good.

Banks, in turn, pass these costs along to their credit card customers by charging interest on unpaid balances. The maximum amount of interest the bank can charge the customer is determined by state laws. Differences in state interest rate limitations has caused at least one large bank to move its national credit card operation from New York to South Dakota. In South Dakota, the amount of interest the bank can charge is higher than it could charge in New York.

Most banks will allow the cardholder to pay off a new balance with no interest due if payment is made within 25 days of the billing date. If the cardholder does not wish to pay the entire balance due, he or she can make a minimum payment (on some types of credit card accounts) and be charged interest on the remainder. Interest of 1.5% a month on the **average daily balance** is a standard charge, but different states have different rates.

The average daily balance is found by figuring the unpaid balance for each day of the billing cycle, adding these balances together, and dividing the total by the number of days in the billing cycle.

Banks encourage regular users of credit cards to continue to use their cards as long as they also continue to make monthly payments of these debts. As long as the customers go on borrowing, the interest keeps on growing, and so does the profit to the bank. Credit card users should pay close attention to what the convenience of credit is costing them in dollars per year, and ask themselves whether the convenience is really worth the price.

Ask Yourself

1. Why do banks who issue VISA, Discover, and MasterCard charge the retailers who accept these cards?

2. How is the average daily balance found?

3. How is the maximum amount of interest charged by a bank determined?

SHARPEN YOUR SKILLS

A Discover account had daily balances and payments as follows:

From 5/1 through 5/16, the daily balance was $385.00.

On 5/17, a payment was made of $80.00.

From 5/18 through 5/30, the daily balance remained at $305.00

Question   What was the average daily balance?

Solution   First, find the sum of daily balances.

Dates	Payment	End of Day Balance	Number of Days	Sum of Daily Balances
5/1–5/16		$385.00	16	$ 6,160.00
5/17	$80.00	305.00	1	305.00
5/18–5/30		305.00	13	3,965.00
			Total:	$10,430.00

Find the total number of days in the billing cycle.

16 + 1 + 13 = 30 days

Divide the sum of daily balances by the number of days to get the average daily balance.

$\dfrac{\$10,430.00}{30} = \$347.67$ rounded to the nearest penny

Question   What is the finance charge and the new balance of the Discover account if the monthly interest rate is 1.5%?

Solution   Find the unpaid balance.

Previous Balance – Payments = Unpaid Balance

$385.00 – 80.00 = $305.00

Find the finance charge.

Monthly Rate x Average Daily Balance = Finance Charge

0.015 x $347.67 = $5.22

Find the new balance

Unpaid Balance + Finance Charge = New Balance

$305.00 + $5.22 = $310.22

EXERCISE YOUR SKILLS

1. Why does a clerk use a computer scanner to check a customer's credit card that is presented for a purchase?

2. Why should credit card users pay close attention to the cost of credit?

3. If a credit card holder promptly reports the loss of a card, who is responsible for unauthorized charges over $50 made on the card?

———— **Activity 1** ————

Find the average daily balance, the finance charge, and the new balance in each of the following situations. Assume the finance charge is 1.5% of the average daily balance. Complete the table and calculate the amounts for each problem. Use the procedure shown for Problem 1.

1.

Billing Periods	Payment	End of Day Balance	Number of Days	Sum of Balances
1/1-1/7		$1948.50	7	13,639.50
1/8		1850.50		
1/9-1/31		1850.50		

Average Daily Balance = _____ x 0.015 = Finance Charge

Previous Balance – Payment = Unpaid Balance

$1948.50 – $98.00 = $1850.50

Unpaid Balance + Finance Charge = New Balance

$1850.50 + _____ = _____

2.

Billing Periods	Payment	End of Day Balances	Number of Days	Sum of Balances
2/1–2/10		$1878.59	10	
2/11	$93.00	1785.59		
2/12–2/28		1785.59		

3.

Billing Periods	Payment	End of Day Balance	Number of Days	Sum of Balances
3/1–3/15		$1812.87		
3/16	$88.00	1724.87		
3/17–3/31		1724.87		

4.

Billing Periods	Payment	End of Day Balance	Number of Days	Sum of Balances
4/1–4/12		$1751.38		
4/13	$83.00	1668.38		
4/14–4/30		1668.38		

5.

Billing Periods	Payment	End of Day Balance	Number of Days	Sum of Balances
5/1–5/20		$1693.90		
5/21	$79.00	1614.90		
5/22–5/31		1614.90		

6.

Billing Periods	Payment	End of Day Balance	Number of Days	Sum of Balances
6/1–6/13		$1639.89		
6/14	$75.00	1564.89		
6/15–6/30		1564.89		

7.

Billing Periods	Payment	End of Day Balance	Number of Days	Sum of Balances
7/1–7/18		$1588.85		
7/19	$71.00	1517.85		
7/20–7/31		1517.85		

8.

Billing Periods	Payment	End of Day Balance	Number of Days	Sum of Balances
8/1–8/9		$1541.24		
8/10	$68.00	1473.24		
8/11–8/31		1473.24		

9.

Billing Periods	Payment	End of Day Balance	Number of Days	Sum of Balances
9/1–9/13		$1495.60		
9/14	$64.00	1431.60		
9/15–9/30		1431.60		

10.

Billing Periods	Payment	End of Day Balance	Number of Days	Sum of Balances
10/1–10/21		$1453.49		
10/22	$61.00	1392.49		
10/23–10/31		1392.49		

EXTEND YOUR UNDERSTANDING
PROJECT 6–1: SHOPPING ON CREDIT

1. Call or visit 25 different merchants in your area, including at least 3 department stores.

2. Find out which credit cards are accepted by these stores. Try to find at least 5 places that accept credit cards other than MasterCard or Visa.

3. Make a poster presenting the information you gathered, including the name and address of each store and the hours they are open.

4. Write a 1-page report on what you learned through this project. Include comments about the following:

   - Why do so many merchants accept MasterCard, VISA, and Discover cards?
   - What, if any, are the differences among MasterCard, VISA and Discover?
   - What advantage do merchants gain from accepting credit cards?
   - What are the disadvantages of credit cards for merchants and consumers?
   - What department stores issue their own credit cards? What are the advantages and disadvantages of these cards to the merchants and the consumers?

PROJECT 6–2: AUDIO-VISUAL PRESENTATIONS

Use the kinds of techniques you see in advertising to point out some of the disadvantages or advantages to the use of credit cards. First, discuss with a small group of your classmates how you feel about using credit cards. Then choose one of the following activities to complete independently or with a group of classmates.

1. Create a poster presenting one or more of the following:

   - advantages of using credit cards;
   - disadvantages of using credit cards;
   - a collage of available credit cards—include a wide variety, such as diner's cards, oil company cards, department store cards, and bankcards.

   Illustrate the poster and make it eye-catching or humorous.

2. Draw a cartoon illustrating some negative aspect or disadvantage of credit buying. Exaggeration is permissible in cartoons to emphasize your point.

3. Write a humorous skit to illustrate the negative aspects of using credit cards and perform your skit for your class.

CHAPTER 6 KEY TERMS

CHAPTER 6 REVIEW

1. Find the total interest through the first 6 payments on this MasterCard account. Use monthly interest rate of 1.5% (18% per year), and make payments of 10% of the amount owed, rounded to the nearest dollar. Copy and complete this chart.

	Balance	Interest	Amount Owed	Payment
a.	1200.00			
b.				
c.				
d.				
e.				
f.				

What is the total interest?

2. Find the total interest through the first 6 payments on this MasterCard account. Use monthly interest rate of 1.75% (21% per year), and make payments of 5% of the amount owed, rounded to the nearest dollar. Copy and complete this chart.

	Balance	Interest	Amount Owed	Payment
a.	1200.00			
b.				
c.				
d.				
e.				
f.				

What is the total interest?

3. Find the average daily balance using the information shown below.

Dates	Payment	End of Day Balance	Number of Days	Sum of Balances
6/1–6/16		$1250.75		
6/17	$125.00	1125.75		
6/18–6/30		1125.75		

4. Find the average daily balance, the finance charge, and the new balance in the following situation. Assume the finance charge is 1.5% of the average daily balance. Copy and complete the computation given below the data.

Dates	Payment	End of Day Balance	Number of Days	Sum of Balances
7/1–7/18		$9871.60		
7/19	$493.00	9378.60		
7/20–7/31		9378.60		

Average Daily Balance = _____ x 0.015 = _____ Finance Charge

Previous Balance – Payment = Unpaid Balance

_____ – _____ = _____

Unpaid Balance + Finance Charge = New Balance

_____ + _____ = _____

1. Find the total interest through the first 6 payments on this VISA account. Use monthly interest rate of 1.5% (18% per year), and make payments of 10% of the amount owed, rounded to the nearest dollar. Copy and complete the chart.

	Balance	Interest	Amount Owed	Payment
a.	2350.65			
b.				
c.				
d.				
e.				
f.				

What is the total interest?

2. Find the total interest through the first 6 payments on this VISA account. Use monthly interest rate of 1.75% (21% per year), and make payments of 5% of the amount owed, rounded to the nearest dollar. Copy and complete the chart.

	Balance	Interest	Amount Owed	Payment
a.	2350.65			
b.				
c.				
d.				
e.				
f.				

What is the total interest?

3. Find the average daily balance using the information shown below.

Dates	Payment	End of Day Balance	Number of Days	Sum of Balances
7/1–7/18		$987.60		
7/19	$49.00	938.60		
7/20–7/31		938.60		

CUMULATIVE REVIEW

1. You earn $7.25 per hour. You worked 46 hours last week. You receive 1½ times your hourly rate for any hours over 40. Find your total wages for last week.

2. You sold a house for $210,000. You earn 5% commission on the first $100,000 and 6% commission on any amount over $100,000. How much commission did you earn?

3. You worked 35 hours a week for 50 weeks. You get 2 weeks of paid vacation, plus 25% of your base salary in fringe benefits. You earn $4500 per month. Find your yearly earnings, including benefits.

4. The bank charges $0.02 for the first 20 checks and $0.09 for each check over 20. How much are the charges if you write 25 checks in a month?

5. You received a check made out to your first name, middle initial and full last name. Write your name as you would to endorse the check.

6. You write a check for $110.23. How would you write that amount in words on the check?

7. What would the simple interest be on $600 at 10.5% for one year, if interest is paid semiannually?

8. Your fixed costs for your business are $200 per week. The variable costs are $5.10 per item. What is the cost if you produce 80 items in one week?

9. Using the information from Problem 8, what would the profit or loss be if each item sold for $9.50?

10. You borrowed $3400 for 3 years. You pay $111 per month. What is the deferred payment price?

11. In Problem 10, how much interest did you pay?

12. You have a choice of paying $450 a month for 3 years or $300 a month for 5 years for a $13,500 loan. How much will you save if you pay the loan off in 3 years?

13. You borrowed $7500 and paid $1500 in interest in one year. Find the percent of the loan paid in interest for that year.

14. Your credit card charges 1.5% interest per month. You pay 10% of the balance each month. Complete a table using the following columns, for 3 months. Your beginning balance is $540.

    Balance   Interest   Amount Owed   Payment

15. You balance from the first of the month through the 15th was $450. Then you make a payment of $100 on the 16th. You made no more charges or payments through the 31st of the month. Find your average daily balance.

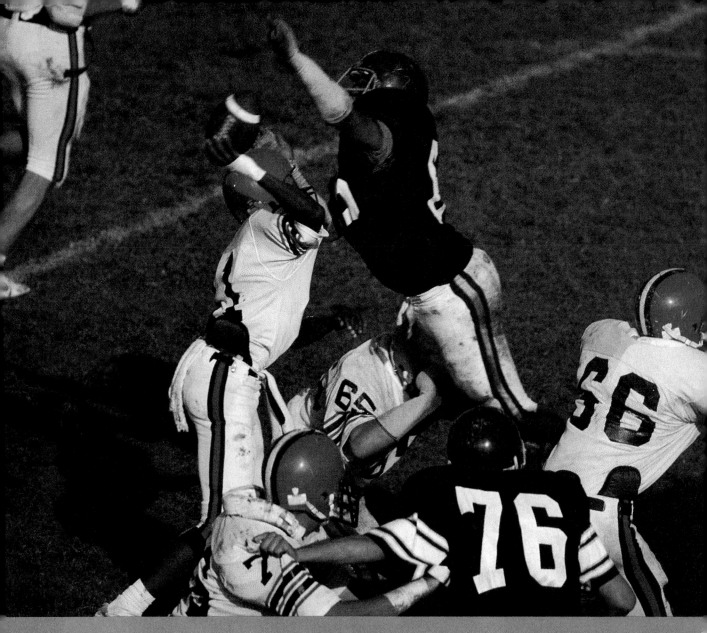

200

Using a little bit of credit grants us a small wish from the genie. Since the price is barely noticeable, we find it easy to ask for just a little bigger wish next time. If we keep paying the very minor charge every month, the genie will grant us a little more and a little more. Before we even realize that the small payments have gradually increased to large payments, the genie has lured us into the quicksand of too many debts and we are sucked under. We can no longer afford to buy things we really need because all of our extra money goes toward keeping up the minimum payments for the things we bought last year. Our wants have become needs because we are accustomed to a certain style of living, and the harder we try to pay them off and get out of debt, the farther behind we get. As with other addictions, when we most need "just a little bit more"—because we suddenly realize we are in over our heads—our sources disappear. As the saying goes, we have been given "just enough rope to hang ourselves."

Fortunately for most "credit card junkies," we do not have to go completely under in a mire of unpaid bills and declare bankruptcy before someone will help us out. Though stuffing the genie back into the bottle is a little like stuffing an inflatable air mattress back into its original bag, if we keep punching at it hard enough and long enough, our credit load can be deflated. Congress has passed a few laws to help protect us from ourselves. But part of the price we pay for living in a free society is the opportunity to make bad choices at times and the responsibility for coping with the consequences of those choices.

In this chapter, our teenagers will observe more of the ways we use credit. They will see how we can get credit, even more credit than we need. They will also spell out some of the warning signs of trouble with credit, as well as some of the hazards we face once we are in over our heads. Finally, they will point out for us some steps we can take to get ourselves back out safely.

LIMITING CREDIT

Vernon lives in a suburban area near a major city; his parents are both college graduates with well-paying jobs. Vernon has played football for the high school team for several years; he can run the 100-meter dash in close to 10 seconds on a good day, so he usually plays a running back position for the team. He caught two touchdown passes and one 43-yard pass last year in the regional championship game.

Vernon's visibility on the football field has focused attention on the rest of his life style. When he and his girlfriend, Veronica, go out to dinner, Vernon often picks up the tab for several other friends who happen to stop over to their table to talk football. Vernon carries his father's American Express card for such expenditures.

Of course, Vernon has to dress well for these occasions. Vernon has stopped asking his mother to select his clothes for him, since she does not always understand the importance of maintaining his image. She has, however, allowed Vernon to use her VISA card to buy his clothes, as long as he does not charge too much in any one month. Last month, when Vernon bought new snakeskin boots with silver trim, she did insist that he not use the card again until the boots were completely paid for.

Vernon has wondered if his friends get to use their parents' credit cards very often. Vernon carries his own gasoline credit card, and he has been allowed to order a few "Have Your Credit Card Ready" items he has seen advertised on television, but his parents have been very firm about how much he can charge each month. Vernon would like to get his own VISA card so he wouldn't have to be so limited, but he is already making car payments for his brand new car out of his weekly paychecks. Paying for the car and the insurance premiums for it (which are almost as much) leaves Vernon barely enough to take Veronica out every weekend.

Why do Vernon's parents set limits on their spending? He will try to find out.

OBJECTIVES: In this section, we will help Vernon to:

- *recognize the different ways of using credit cards*
- *observe which people are likely to use credit each way*
- *determine whether and in what ways a consumer should use credit*
- *calculate what credit purchases a family can afford*

WHO GETS CREDIT AND HOW THEY USE IT

Our level of income determines how much credit we can get. Vernon's family—with its high income—has been offered quite a lot of credit. People with a higher-than-average education are more likely to be offered credit cards than those with less education. Young families with children are more likely to use cards but are also more likely to incur debt with their cards.

Likewise, those who live in the suburbs tend to use their credit cards more than families living in central cities or rural areas.

Vernon's family falls into the category of people who use the cards as a convenience, instead of carrying large amounts of cash or writing many checks. They pay their credit card charges promptly, within the 20-to-25-day period required, and pay little or no interest.

The other group of card users, of which they do not wish to be a part, use the credit card's revolving installment loan features, almost never completely paying off their debts, making the minimum required payments, and paying interest to the bank with every payment.

Should you use a credit card? According to the experts, the answer to this question is *no* if the following are true:

- You use the card as an excuse to overspend.
- You frequently buy things you do not need on impulse.
- You are often late making scheduled payments.
- You have no steady income.

The answer is *yes* if the following are true:

- You have handled credit responsibly in the past.
- You use the card as a budgeting convenience.
- You recognize the dangers as well as the attraction.

To use credit cards to your best advantage, do the following:

1. Keep only cards that you will actually use fairly often. For most people in the middle-income bracket, a couple of oil company cards for gasoline and one bank card are enough. The business person may wish to use a travel-entertainment card also.

2. Consider every charged purchase as though you were paying cash. Ask yourself: Can I repay the charge promptly and easily?

3. Do not spend more than 20% of take-home pay on credit payments. As described in earlier chapters, if a family uses more than this amount on credit payments (not including the mortgage payment), it is suffering a credit overload.

4. At the beginning of each month, set a limit on the total amount of charges you will be able to repay easily. Stay within that limit and repay the charges promptly to avoid additional interest charges.

5. Keep your receipts until you receive your statement to verify your spending with the statement.

Ask Yourself

1. What are 2 ways in which consumers can use credit cards?

2. Why do you think charging only what you can pay for each month is a good idea?

3. What are 3 reasons for not using a credit card?

SHARPEN YOUR SKILLS

------ Skill 1 ------

Vernon's family income is $4550 in take-home pay each month. They limit their installment debt to 20% of their take-home pay.

Questions
1. How much can they pay toward installment debts?

2. Can they afford to make a car payment of $225 a month?

3. How much would be left over for other credit purchases?

4. If they take on no other installment debts this month, which of the items shown below is the most expensive one they can afford to charge this month?

SUPER BUY   **$899⁹⁹**

VHS CAMCORDER WITH CASE!
8:1 POWER ZOOM LENS WITH MACRO.

SALE $229⁹⁹   COUNTRY STYLE CAMEL BACK HARDWOOD DAYBED WITH GOLDEN OAK FINISH. Multiple spindles and turnings.
Trundle . . . Super buy

SALE $599⁹⁹
26" Stereo Remote Color TV
Sleep timer. 147 channels, cable compatible.

Solutions
1. $4550 x 20% =
   4550 x 0.2 = $910.00

2. Since the car payment of $225 is less than $910, they can afford it.

3. Left over for other credit purchases will be:

   $910 – 225 = $685

4. The most expensive gift they can afford to charge is the color television.

EXERCISE YOUR SKILLS

1. How can you use credit cards to your best advantage?

2. Why is it easier to overspend when you are using a credit card?

3. What might the outcome be if a family suffers from a credit overload?

___ **Activity 1** ___

The take-home pay for seven families is shown below, along with a description of the car or truck each family is buying. The monthly payment for the vehicle is shown in the ad. Each family wishes to keep its credit purchases to a maximum of 20% of their take-home pay. They are also considering buying the items shown on the following catalog pages. Answer the following questions for each of the families.

1. If the family could only buy 1 item, which one is the most expensive they could afford?

2. If each family can buy 2 items, which are the 2 most expensive they could buy?

3. Which families can afford the sofa?

4. Family B wants to buy the camcorder, the dishwasher, the dining set, and the silver bowl. How many months will it take them to pay for these items if they only spend 20% of their take-home pay on credit purchases and they are already making the car payment of $238?

Family A	
Take-Home Pay	$3150
20% of Take-Home	$ 630
Car Payment	

Description of Car:

4-DOOR AUTOMATIC
• Air Conditioning
• Power Group
• Tilt Steering Wheel
• Polycast Wheels

$151 mo.*/$9188

Description of Car:

Family B	
Take-Home Pay	$2270
20% of Take-Home	
Car Payment	

GL 4-DOOR SEDAN
• Manual Air Conditioning
• Stereo Radio W/Cassette Player
• Power Door Locks
• Six-Way Power Driver's Seat
• Power Side Windows
• 3.0L EFI V6 Engine
• Automatic Overdrive Transmission

$238 mo.*/$12,895

Family C	
Take-Home Pay	$1495
20% of Take-Home	
Car Payment	

Description of Car:

- Bucket Seats
- Preferred Equipment Package
- Electronic AM/FM Stereo w/ Cass.
- 6-Way Power Driver's Seat
- Rear Window Defroster
- V6 Engine

$235 mo.*/$12,895

Family D	
Take-Home Pay	$4280
20% of Take-Home	
Car Payment	

Description of Car:

WAGON 2WD
- Air Conditioning
- Clearcoat Paint

$222 mo.*/$12,294

Family E	
Take-Home Pay	$2190
20% of Take-Home	
Car Payment	

Description of Car:

SUPER CAB PICKUP
- Air Conditioning

$199 mo.*/$12,795

Family F	
Take-Home Pay	$1640
20% of Take-Home	
Car Payment	

Description of Car:

SUPER CAB AUTOMATIC
- AM-FM Stereo
- Cassette – Chrome
- Tachometer
- Automatic
- V-6

$179 mo.*/$10,395

Family G	
Take-Home Pay	$3000
20% of Take-Home	
Car Payment	

Description of Car:

AUTOMATIC
- Power Steering
- Elec AM/FM Stereo Radio w/cass/clk
- Sliding Rear Window
- Tachometer
- Air Conditioning

$159 mo.*/$9489

SALE 369⁹⁹

REG. 799.99

5 PIECE DINING SET with oak finished hardwood table and four cane back chairs with castors.

CLOSEOUT 899⁹⁹

WAS 1799.99

DOUBLE PILLOWBACK STYLE 2 PIECE SECTIONAL SOFA. Includes incliner unit on each end. Polyester/cotton upholstery.

SPECIAL BUY 499⁹⁹

26" STEREO REMOTE COLOR TV.
MTS broadcast stereo sound system. Sleep timer.

SALE 249⁹⁹

6 DISC CD CHANGER WITH REMOTE.
32 track programmable. 8 X oversampling.

SUPER BUY 899⁹⁹

VHS CAMCORDER WITH CASE!
8:1 power zoom lens. 2 lux. A/V dubbing. 10 watt color light.

SUPER BUY 399⁹⁹

BUILT-IN DISHWASHER.
3 level wash. Filtered wash/rinse.

SALE 1099⁹⁹

20.2 CU. FT. SIDE BY SIDE FROSTLESS REFRIGERATOR.

SALE 139⁹⁹

AM/FM AUTO REVERSE CASSETTE CAR STEREO.

SALE 199⁹⁹

REMOVABLE AM/FM CASSETTE CAR STEREO. Speakers.

A. 9" candlesticks, pair _____ $50.00
B. Set of 4 napkin rings _____ 20.00
C. Salt and pepper set _____ 45.00
D. 4 1/2" console candlesticks, pair _____ 40.00
E. Silverplated tray. Gift boxed. _____ $50.00
F. Traditional 8" bowl crafted in solid
   brass and silverplate. Gift boxed _____ $40.00

Daryl has watched in fascination as his father unfolds his packet of credit cards. He has five oil company cards, six charge accounts at department stores, an American Express card; an ATM cash card, four MasterCards, and six VISA cards. Just carrying that many cards around must be a chore, Daryl thinks. How in the world could anyone manage to acquire so many cards, much less need them all? And what about when the bills come—there must be a lot of checks to write each month. Daryl carries only four cards: his driver's license, his school library card, a credit card for gasoline, and his ID card for the video rental store.

When Daryl asked his father about all the credit cards, he explained that his credit rating is excellent. He has lived in the same house for eight years, he has been a high salaried employee at the same business for 12 years, he has bought three different cars with installment loans, making prompt payments every month, and he is 41 years old. Creditors are more than willing to give him credit because he has shown he is capable and consistent when paying his debts. Over a four-year period, 12 different banks from around the country offered him credit cards; he took most of them up on their offers, realizing how easy it was to use the cards to buy much more than he could afford to pay for with cash. Now he makes the minimum payment each month to each bank and continues to use almost all the credit available to him on each card so he can continue spending the way he has been.

Watching his father writing all the checks each month, Daryl is not sure that carrying 23 credit cards is truly necessary. But he would like to know how to get at least one general purpose card for himself. Since he has never had one and probably doesn't even have a credit rating, he is wondering where to begin.

OBJECTIVES: In this section, we will help Daryl to:

- *determine a credit rating in two ways—the judgment of the creditor and the score on a credit-scoring table*
- *find out how to get credit for the first time*

HOW CREDIT IS GRANTED

A person's **credit rating** is an indication of his or her ability to secure goods, services, and money in return for the promise to pay. Daryl knows that a favorable credit rating does not come automatically. His father's good rating has developed as a result of slow growth. It has been nurtured, fostered, strengthened, and improved. It is an asset of tremendous value to those who develop it over a long period of years. But it can be easily destroyed. It is sensitive to abuse, and it usually continues only as long as it is justified. Daryl's father has so much credit now that, were he to apply for more, he would probably be told he already has sufficient credit.

Judgment of Creditor. Sometimes the decision of whether to grant credit lies with the **creditor**. In that case, the creditor will consider the "three C's" of credit—capacity, character, and collateral.

1. Capacity. Do you have the capacity to repay the loan? How long have you worked, how much do you earn? The creditor will also ask about your expenses such as rent, mortgage, car payments, and the like.

2. Character. Have you been responsible about meeting financial obligations in the past? Daryl's father's prompt payment of his automobile installment loans in the past shows he has met his obligations responsibly.

3. Collateral. Is the creditor protected from loss if you fail to pay? Creditors want to know if you have a savings account or other assets (car, home, or other valuable assets) to offer as **security** for a loan.

Credit-Scoring Systems. Because of laws that prohibit discrimination, large credit-lending institutions have developed credit-scoring systems that could be considered more objective than personal judgment. Credit-scoring systems work on the principal that the factors that make up credit worthiness can be given points. Such a scoring system is shown on the next page.

The ideas behind the scoring table are as follows:

In general, you are a better credit risk if you are older. However, people in their mid-30s often face the unforeseen expenses of divorce, or other causes of financial stress, so their credit rating points are lower.

You are considered more stable the longer you have lived in the same place, and your score will go up if you own your home rather than rent it. People with cars get more points than those without, and newer car owners generally earn more points than older car owners.

Another factor to be considered is how long you have held the same job. What kind of job you have, your income, and amount of current debt also make a difference.

Having either a savings account or a checking account is good, and you score more points if you have both.

People who already have one or more credit cards in good standing score higher than those who have none. Department store charge cards, travel and entertainment cards, and oil company cards usually rate somewhat lower than all-purpose bank cards.

If you have borrowed recently at high interest from a finance company, you will probably lose several points. If you have applied and been turned down for credit more than once in the last six months, you may have difficulty getting new credit at all.

Hypothetical Credit-Scoring Table

Fill out your credit profile by answering the nine questions below in Table 1. Circle the one response that applies to you, and then find your total score by adding up the points you got for each response. The points are found in the lower right-hand corner of each box. (For example: if you are 25 years old, you get 12 points.) Once you've totaled your score, look at Table 2 to find out how good a credit "bet" you may be.

1.

1. age?	under 25 — 12	25–29 — 5	30–34 — 0	35–39 — 1	40–44 — 18	45–49 — 22	50 or over — 31	
2. time at address?	less than 1 yr. — 9	1–2 yrs. — 0	2–3 yrs. — 5	3–5 yrs. — 0	5–9 yrs. — 5	10 yrs. or more — 21		
3. age of auto?	none — 0	0–1 yrs. — 12	2 yrs. — 16	3–4 yrs. — 13	5–7 yrs. — 3	8 yrs. or more — 0		
4. monthly auto payment?	none — 18	less than $125 — 6	$126-$150 — 1	$151-$199 — 4	$200 or more — 0			
5. housing cost?	less than $274 — 0	$275-$399 — 10	$400 or more — 12	owns clear — 12	lives with relatives — 24			
6. checking and savings accounts	both — 15	checking only — 2	savings only — 2	neither — 0				
7. finance company reference	yes — 0	no — 15						
8. major credit cards?	none — 0	1 — 5	2 or more — 15					
9. ratio of debt to income?	no debts — 41	1%–5% — 16	6%–15% — 20	16% or over — 0				

2.

A lender using this scoring table selects a cutoff point from a table like this, which gauges how likely applicants are to repay loans.

Total Score	Probability of Repayment
90	89 in 100
95	91 in 100
100	92 in 100
105	93 in 100
110	94 in 100
115	95 in 100
120	95.5 in 100
125	96 in 100
130	96.25 in 100

Source: Federal Reserve Board. Developed by Fair, Isaac, and Co., Inc. Modified to update.

First-Time Credit. Daryl is most interested in how to get credit for the first time. Credit is one of those things that is easy to get if you have had it before. But what about getting credit for the first time? Below are some suggestions for Daryl to help him establish a good credit reputation. He could:

- Open a charge account at a retail store where his parents have an account.
- Establish checking and savings accounts at the local bank.
- Get one of his parents to **cosign** a small loan. By cosigning, Daryl's father promises to pay if Daryl does not. When Daryl repays on time, he establishes a good credit record.
- Join a credit union.
- Be a responsible employee. Creditors generally ask for length of employment at a job and for personal references.

As Daryl begins to establish his own credit rating, he will be careful not to abuse it. He will treat it as the valuable asset that it is and continue to strengthen it as time goes on.

Ask Yourself

1. What are the "3 Cs" that creditors use to judge a person's acceptability for credit?

2. How does a lending institution determine the credit worthiness of an applicant?

3. How might you establish a good credit reputation?

SHARPEN YOUR SKILLS

_____ Skill 1 _____

Following are the facts about Daryl's father relevant to his credit rating:

1. He is 41 years old.
2. He has lived at his current address for 8 years.
3. His current car is 2 years old.
4. His monthly car payment is $0.00.
5. His housing cost is $482 per month.
6. He has a checking account and a savings account.
7. He has not been referred to a finance company.
8. He has 23 major credit cards.
9. His ratio of debt to income is 20%.

Question   How would a potential creditor rate his credit worthiness?

Solution   Use the credit-scoring table shown earlier in this section to find the credit score for Daryl's father. His points will be as follows:

	Points
1.	18
2.	5
3.	16
4.	18
5.	12
6.	15
7.	15
8.	15
9.	+ 0
Total Score	114

According to the credit-scoring system the probability that he will repay a loan is 94 in 100.

EXERCISE YOUR SKILLS

1. Why is it important to establish a favorable credit rating?

2. If you were a lender, what is the minimum score on the credit-scoring table you would accept for a loan applicant? Why?

3. It has been said that a person's credit rating is one of his or her most valuable assets. Do you agree or disagree with this statement? Why?

_____ Activity 1 _____

Use the credit-scoring table shown earlier in this section to find the credit score for each family described below.

1. **Family 1**
    - Age of the head of the household—35
    - Lived at the current address—4 years
    - Age of their current car—3 years
    - Monthly car payment—$165
    - Housing cost—$650
    - They have a checking account and a savings account.
    - They have not been referred to a finance company.
    - They have 7 major credit cards.
    - Their ratio of debt to income is 12%.

2. **Family 2**
    - Age of the head of the household—48
    - Lived at the current address—12 years
    - Age of their current automobile—5 years

- Monthly car payment—$0.00
- Housing cost—$385
- They have a checking account and a savings account.
- They have not been referred to a finance company.
- They have 6 major credit cards.
- Their ratio of debt to income is 19%.

3. **Family 3**
   - Age of the head of the household—26
   - Lived at the current address—2 years
   - Age of their current car—1 year
   - Monthly car payment—$364
   - Housing cost—$741
   - They have a checking account but not a savings account.
   - They have not been referred to a finance company.
   - They have 12 major credit cards.
   - Their ratio of debt to income is 24%.

4. **Family 4**
   - Age of the head of the household—43
   - Lived at the current address—16 years
   - Age of their current car—1 year
   - Monthly car payment—$0.00
   - Housing cost—$640
   - They have a checking account and a savings account.
   - They have not been referred to a finance company.
   - They have 3 major credit cards.
   - Their ratio of debt to income is 8%.

5. **Family 5**
   - Age of the head of the household—32
   - Lived at the current address—3 years
   - Age of their current car—1 year
   - Monthly car payment—$237
   - Housing cost—$853
   - They have a checking account but not a savings account.
   - They have been referred to a finance company.
   - They have 12 major credit cards.
   - Their ratio of debt to income is 32%.

6. **Family 6**
   - Age of the head of the household—52
   - Lived at the current address—22 years
   - Age of their current car—3 years
   - Monthly car payment—$0.00
   - Housing cost—$332
   - They have a checking account and a savings account.
   - They have not been referred to a finance company.
   - They have 8 major credit cards.
   - Their ratio of debt to income is 4%.

7. **Family 7**
   - Age of the head of the household—34
   - Lived at the current address—6 months
   - Age of their current car—8 years
   - Monthly car payment—$0.00
   - Housing cost—$213
   - They have a checking account but not a savings account.
   - They have not been referred to a finance company.
   - They have 2 major credit cards.
   - Their ratio of debt to income is 8%.

8. **Family 8**
   - Age of the head of the household—23
   - Lived at the current address—17 years
   - Age of their current car—1 year
   - Monthly car payment—$233
   - Housing cost—$150
   - They have a checking account and a savings account.
   - They have not been referred to a finance company.
   - They have 1 major credit card.
   - Their ratio of debt to income is 3%.

Using credit to buy things that he could not otherwise afford has great appeal for Daryl. His father has now acquired thousands of dollars of debt by being such a good credit customer. The interest alone that he pays each year on his various credit accounts runs into the thousands of dollars.

Many consumers like him are willing to pay large amounts of money in interest to banks and to merchants. Larger businesses that can afford to absorb the occasional losses from customers who get behind in their payments have discovered how lucrative it is to extend credit.

Daryl is learning of the many ways merchants have found to cash in on the extra profits to be had if they can entice their customers to buy on credit terms. Daryl will share some of these discoveries with us.

OBJECTIVES: In this section, we will help Daryl to:

- *discover how merchants manipulate credit income and entice customers with*
  - *cash discounts*
  - *rent-to-own plans*
  - *credit offered at lower than market rates*
  - *cash-back plans*

SPECIAL CREDIT PLANS

Cash Discounts. Since stores must pay credit card companies 4 to 7 percent for the privilege of accepting their card and may base their prices on their own costs, many customers who pay cash feel they are entitled to discounts on their purchases. Stores now have the right to offer **cash discounts** as long as the offer is made to all potential customers. The law does prohibit retailers from adding extra charges to credit card purchases specifically to cover the credit card company fees.

Rent-To-Own Plans. Another credit plan that does not sound like a credit plan because the payments are almost painless is the **rent-to-own plan**. Why wait until you have several hundred dollars available before you can buy that new television or stereo system or dining room suite? Rent it now, with low, easy, weekly payments of only $25; then if you decide to buy, all your rental goes toward the purchase price.

Of course, if you decide you cannot afford it or do not want it, you just take it back and the rental agency keeps all the money you paid in, since, after all, you were only renting. But you were spared the embarrassment and blemish to your credit rating of having broken an installment loan contract and having your furniture repossessed. You just changed your mind and took it back; and what do you have in return for all that money you paid in rental fees? Probably nothing.

Now if you decide to keep the furniture or the TV or the stereo, all your weekly rental fees will go toward the purchase price of the item. But, notice how many weeks it takes to complete the payments. You will still most likely pay considerably more than you would have paid to buy the item outright.

This plan is especially attractive to young people who have not established a credit rating yet and would not be able to qualify for an installment loan. People who already have over-extended their credit and are not eligible for any more may decide to extend themselves even further by using this plan.

Credit at Lower Than Market Rates. One particularly attractive incentive used to promote sales is the extension of credit terms at an interest rate that is lower than the **market rate**—that is, the rate currently available on the open market. Automobile companies use this device extensively. Since the dealers can offer to finance the loan through the company's own finance corporation, it can offer a lower interest rate than one that might be available through your bank.

As an example, General Motors may finance your car loan at 6.5% when the best rate your bank or credit union can offer is 13.5%. The loan costs you less, but GMAC (the finance company owned by General Motors) gets the interest you would otherwise have paid to the bank. General Motors also makes a profit on the sale of the car.

Cash-Back Plans. Offered by some automobile dealers as an alternative to a low interest rate on the loan is a **rebate** plan called the cash-back. In effect, a lower purchase price is offered. The customer must carefully consider the details of the financing deal. Just looking at the lowest purchase price—or the lowest interest rate—or the highest rebate is not enough.

Ask Yourself

1. Why might merchants be willing to offer a discount for a cash purchase?

2. What is a rent-to-own plan?

3. What companies often offer credit at interest rates lower than those offered by banks?

SHARPEN YOUR SKILLS

Look carefully at this ad:

NEW LUXURY MODEL

$1000 CASH BACK

– OR –

$750 CASH BACK **Plus**

6.9% APR

– OR –

2.9% APR
Available

FACTORY AIR

- Wide Vinyl Bodyside Mold
- AM/FM 4 Speaker Stereo
- Tinted Glass
- Power Steering
- Interval Wipers
- Rear Window Defroster

- Instrumentation Group
- Digital Clock w/over Console Light/Security Group
- Dual Elect. Mirrors
- Luxury Wheel Covers
- 1.9L EFI Engine

MSRP	$10,154
FACTORY DISC.	–744
FACTORY REBATE	1000
OUR DISC	1035

YOUR PRICE $7375

The ad does not state what interest rate you pay if you choose the $1000 cash back. You can assume that if you choose this method of payment, you will have to seek financing from a bank or other source. Typical bank financing would be 13 3/4% over 48 months.

_____ Skill 1 _____

Question   Which plan would yield the lowest price to the consumer?

Solution   **Plan 1**   Purchase price $7375 (rebate $1000)
Financed at 13 3/4% over 48 months (from a bank)
Monthly payment $200.63
Total Financed Price $9630.24 (monthly payment x 48)

Plan 2   Purchase price $7625 (rebate $750)
Financed at 6.90% over 48 months
Monthly payment $181.64
Total Financed Price $8718.72 (monthly payment x 48)

Plan 3 Purchase price $8375 (no rebate)
Financed at 2.9% over 48 months
Monthly payment $189.00
Total Financed Price $9072.00 (monthly payment x 48)

In this example it appears that the lowest cost to the customer is Plan 2—the $750 rebate and financing at 6.9%.

___ **Skill 2** _____

Questions **1.** Which plan would provide the highest profit to the car dealer?

2. Why would the dealer encourage the customer to choose one method of payment over another?

Solutions **1.** Looking at Plan 2—which is the most attractive to the customer—the dealer receives interest on the loan which can be figured as follows:

$$\$8718.72 - 7625.00 = \$1093.72 \text{ interest}$$

The dealer will probably also receive the extra $250 in rebate from the company:

$$\$1000 - 750 = \$250$$

In all, the dealer receives:

Interest	$1093.72
Rebate	+ 250.00
Profit	$1343.72

In Plan 3, the figures would be:

Interest	$ 697
Rebate	+1000
Profit	$1697

In Plan 1, the dealer would receive no interest and no rebate, so the dealer's profit in that case would be zero.
(Profit here refers to additional income over any profit built into the car's price in the first place. In Chapter 12 you will see in detail what the dealer's profit is on the car itself.)

Therefore, the most advantageous plan for the dealer would be Plan 3.

2. When the car company is offering a rebate, the dealer would have the greatest incentive to encourage you to take the lowest financing through the dealer itself and forgo the rebate.

EXERCISE YOUR SKILLS

1. If you were offered a discount for paying cash, would you still use a credit card for a purchase? Why?

2. How would you rate the using of rent-to-own plans?

3. Why is it wise to shop around for a loan when you are buying a car?

___ Activity 1 ___

For each of the cars described below, find the total loan amount; then use amortization tables at 5%, 8 3/4%, and 13% in the Reference Section of this book to find the monthly payment. Finally, find the total financed price for each car sales plan. Which of the financing plans offers the lowest total financed price? Copy and complete the table for each problem.

> **Note:** Save your results to use in the next activity.

1. Car Price $10,100

	Plan A	**Plan B**
Rebate	$900	none
Loan Amount		
Rate/Time	13%/48 months	5%/48 months
Monthly Payment		
Total Financed Price		

2. Car Price $12,000

	Plan A	Plan B	Plan C
Rebate	$1500	$800	none
Loan Amount			
Rate/Time	13%/48 months	8 3/4%/48 months	5%/48 months
Monthly Payment			
Total Financed Price			

3. Car Price $9400

	Plan A	Plan B	Plan C
Rebate	$1500	$1200	none
Loan Amount			
Rate/Time	13%/48 months	8 3/4%/48 months	5%/48 months
Monthly Payment			
Total Financed Price			

4. Car Price $6500

	Plan A	Plan B	Plan C
Rebate	$1500	$1000	none
Loan Amount			
Rate/Time	13%/48 months	8 3/4%/48 months	5%/48 months
Monthly Payment			
Total Financed Price			

5. Car Price $13,800

	Plan A	Plan B	Plan C
Rebate	$2000	$1000	none
Loan Amount			
Rate/Time	13%/48 months	8 3/4%/48 months	5%/48 months
Monthly Payment			
Total Financed Price			

Remember: Save your results for Activity 2.

_____   **Activity 2**   _____

Find which plan will provide the dealer with the most profit for each car sales deal in Activity 1. To find the profit for the dealer under each plan, find the amount of interest the dealer will receive under each plan; then add the rebate the dealer will receive if it does not go to the customer. Copy and complete the table for each problem.

1.

Plan A		Plan B	
Interest		Interest	
Rebate		Rebate	
Profit		Profit	

2.

Plan A		Plan B		Plan C	
Interest		Interest		Interest	
Rebate		Rebate		Rebate	
Profit		Profit		Profit	

3.

Plan A		Plan B		Plan C	
Interest		Interest		Interest	
Rebate		Rebate		Rebate	
Profit		Profit		Profit	

4.

Plan A		Plan B		Plan C	
Interest		Interest		Interest	
Rebate		Rebate		Rebate	
Profit		Profit		Profit	

5.

Plan A		Plan B		Plan C	
Interest		Interest		Interest	
Rebate		Rebate		Rebate	
Profit		Profit		Profit	

CREDIT CARD PROTECTION

Sylvia Shawn's mother has several credit cards of her own, even though she and Mr. Shawn are divorced. Mrs. Shawn was able to get credit in her own name after the divorce even though all of the accounts were in Mr. Shawn's name while they were still married. When Mrs. Shawn applied for the cards, she was helped by something called equal credit opportunity.

Sylvia remembers what a hassle it was for Mr. Shawn after his credit cards were stolen once. He had left them in the glove compartment of his car one day at the golf course. Sylvia was with him. As they left the golf course and stopped to buy gasoline, he realized the whole packet of credit cards had been taken. He spent the next three hours making phone calls to all the banks and charge account offices; but before the information could even be entered into the various computer networks, the thief had spent over $10,000.

For the next three months, Mr. Shawn dealt with the credit card companies, as bills for $2650 worth of ski equipment, $3240 worth of video cameras, video cassette recorders, televisions, and a $4500 computer system were all billed to his now-closed accounts.

Mr. Shawn discovered that under the Fair Credit Reporting Act and the Fair Credit Billing Act his credit rating would be preserved, and he would only have to pay the first $50 of the unauthorized charges on each card. (This was still a substantial amount because he had so many cards.) But he also learned what a nuisance it is to have all your credit accounts changed and to have to wait for new cards to arrive from every creditor.

Sylvia has learned from his experience that credit cards are just as valuable as cash, and she will share some of the other information about consumer credit laws that she has learned.

OBJECTIVES: In this section, we will help Sylvia to:

- *appreciate how consumers are protected by:*
  - *the Fair Credit Reporting Act*
  - *the Fair Credit Billing Act*
- *understand the effect of the*
  - *Equal Credit Opportunity Act for consumers*
- *recognize ways to protect credit cards*
- *calculate credit account interest, payments, and balances*

CONSUMER RIGHTS

The **Fair Credit Reporting Act** prevents credit agencies from giving out wrong credit information about consumers. An individual who has been denied credit, employment, or insurance because of an inaccurate credit agency report may ask to know the source of the report. The individual may then have incorrect information and any information that cannot be proven removed from the file. The act also allows consumers the right to examine information in their credit files, and when they feel they have been misrepresented they can add a short statement to the files giving their side of the story.

Under the **Fair Credit Billing Act**, consumers can preserve their credit ratings while settling disputes with stores and credit card companies. During this time the creditor cannot report you as delinquent to any credit agency for your failure to pay the portion of your bill that is under dispute.

The **Equal Credit Opportunity Act** is directed toward credit discrimination on the basis of sex, marital status, race, color, religion, age, or national origin. This means, for instance, that women applying for credit must be judged by the same standards as men. If they have a steady income and can qualify in other respects as good credit risks, they are equally entitled to credit.

The law specifically says that creditors cannot:

► deny credit on the basis of sex, marital status, race, color, religion, national origin, or age (if old enough to enter into a binding contract),

► deny credit because an applicant receives any income from a public program,

► ask questions concerning birth control practices and plans for children, or assume that a female applicant is likely to become pregnant and have an interruption of income,

> ▶ ask about an applicant's marital status (unless a spouse will be contractually liable for the loan, a spouse's income is counted on to repay a loan, or a spouse plans to use the loan),

> ▶ refuse to consider part-time income of a working spouse, alimony, child support, or social security payments,

> ▶ cancel a divorced or widowed person's credit when a marriage ends unless the income has dropped so much that the person may not be able to pay.

The act does not entitle you to credit whenever you want it. You must still pass the creditor's tests that indicate your financial ability and willingness to repay the debt.

HOW TO PROTECT YOUR CREDIT CARDS

If your credit cards are stolen, the most you will have to pay in charges you did not authorize is $50 per card. But, if you carry 23 cards as Daryl's father does, that is still a possible $1100 if a thief works quickly before you notice your cards are gone.

So it pays you to take what steps you can to protect yourself.

> ▶ Destroy any cards that you do not really use. Cut unwanted cards in half and throw them away.

> ▶ Make a list of all the credit cards you are keeping (with the account numbers and the name and address of each issuer); keep the list at home; do not carry it with you.

> ▶ Be sure you get your card back every time you use it. Dishonest employees of legitimate establishments may retain your card to give to fraudulent users.

> ▶ Do not leave your credit card in the glove compartment of your car. This is one of the first places a credit card thief looks.

> ▶ Do not underestimate the value of your card. It is the equivalent of cash. Remember, the thief does not underestimate its value.

Ask Yourself

1. How does the Fair Credit Reporting Act protect consumers?
2. How does the Fair Credit Billing Act protect consumers?
3. What does the Equal Credit Opportunity Act prevent?
4. What are 3 ways in which you can protect your credit cards?

SHARPEN YOUR SKILLS

_____ Skill 1 _____

Many consumers continue to add new purchases to their all-purpose credit card accounts before they have paid for earlier ones. Grace is trying to convince her mother not to charge any more purchases of baseball cards until she has paid for the four gifts she bought during the fall. They have decided to follow the account carefully for one year. Grace's mother will make minimal purchases and see if she can bring the balance down.

Question After 12 months, will Grace's mother owe more or less than she did at the beginning of the year?

Solution Look at the following record of the account.

New purchases are added before the next balance on each of the lines indicated. We will enter an interest rate of 1.5% per month (18% per year) and make monthly payments of 10% of the amount owed, rounded to the nearest dollar. We will find the total amount of interest paid over one year.

	Purchases	Balance	Interest	Amount Owed	Payment
a.	$ 0.00	$1265.80	$18.99	$1284.79	$128
b.	0.00	1156.79	17.35	1174.14	117
c.	250.75	1307.89	19.62	1327.51	133
d.	0.00	1194.51	17.92	1212.43	121
e.	75.00	1166.43	17.50	1183.93	118
f.	0.00	1065.93	15.99	1081.92	108
g.	0.00	973.92	14.61	988.53	99
h.	380.50	1270.03	19.05	1289.08	129
i.	0.00	1160.08	17.40	1177.48	118
j.	0.00	1059.48	15.89	1075.37	108
k.	45.90	1013.27	15.20	1028.47	103
l.	0.00	925.47	13.88	939.35	94

Total Interest $203.40.

After 12 months, Grace's mother owes less than she did at the beginning.

EXERCISE YOUR SKILLS

1. Why is it important for people to be able to examine information in their credit files?

2. What might happen if consumers were not protected by the Fair Credit Billing Act?

3. How does the Equal Credit Opportunity Act help a woman who becomes divorced or widowed?

———— Activity 1 ————

Show the first 12 payments and find the total interest paid over a year on the following MasterCard accounts. Remember that new purchases are added before the next balance on each of the lines indicated; an interest rate of 1.5% per month (18% per year) is charged; and monthly payments are 10% of the amount owed, rounded to the nearest dollar.

For every account, tell whether the person owes more or less than at the beginning of the year.

1.

	Purchases	Balance	Interest	Amount Owed	Payment
a.	$ 0.00	$554.75			
b.	$76.35				
c.	0.00				
d.	75.99				
e.	22.80				
f.	0.00				
g.	97.88				
h.	75.00				
i.	31.00				
j.	66.00				
k.	67.00				
l.	0.00				

Total Interest = ?

2.

	Purchases	Balance	Interest	Amount Owed	Payment
a.	$ 0.00	$875.66			
b.	0.00				
c.	0.00				
d.	0.00				
e.	0.00				
f.	158.00				
g.	0.00				
h.	85.00				
i.	92.00				
j.	0.00				
k.	0.00				
l.	123.00				

Total Interest = ?

3.

	Purchases	Balance	Interest	Amount Owed	Payment
a.	$ 0.00	$1450.63			
b.	0.00				
c.	0.00				
d.	234.00				
e.	0.00				
f.	0.00				
g.	0.00				
h.	0.00				
i.	314.00				
j.	45.00				
k.	68.00				
l.	0.00				

Total Interest = ?

Sylvia and Daryl were engaged in a conversation and stumbled onto the topic of credit card use. They began to compare facts about their fathers and their use of credit cards. One credit story led to another, and by the end of the conversation, Sylvia and Daryl were both relieved to know they weren't alone in having serious doubts about some of the choices made by their respective fathers. Daryl was especially relieved to know he did not have the only father in town whose stack of credit cards was so thick he appeared to be shuffling a deck of playing cards every time he used one. Once when his father dropped them all on the floor in a restaurant, Daryl was so embarrassed as his father crawled around under the table retrieving them, he rushed out to the parking lot to wait, wishing he could pretend he did not know the man on the floor with the cards.

Daryl's father was embarrassed, too, but not as much as when he was so far behind in paying all the credit bills that he actually considered trying to pawn some of the new video equipment he had just purchased. At times he has even considered filing for bankruptcy, but he knows that is a drastic step. If a person ever declares bankruptcy, he or she cannot even consider asking for any credit for at least seven years and may be turned down even then.

Sylvia and Daryl are discussing some less radical methods of helping their fathers with their finances.

OBJECTIVES: In this section, we will help Sylvia and Daryl to:

- *discover what happens if debtors cannot pay their debts*
- *recognize the signs of carrying too much debt*
- *find out how to get out of credit difficulty safely*
- *calculate percent of take-home pay that credit payments require*

DEBT COLLECTION PRACTICES

Creditors often employ professional **collection agencies** to collect overdue accounts and **repossess** articles on which money is due. The collection process has been known to include everything from collection letters, late-night telephone calls, and abusive language to threats of having consumers fired from their jobs because of nonpayment of debt. In order to stop these practices, Congress passed the **Fair Debt Collection Practices Act**, which declares that the following collection actions are illegal.

▶ Threatening violence, using obscene language, publishing shame lists of debtors, and making harassing phone calls at night

▶ Calling a debtor at work or contacting a debtor's employer

▶ Claiming that the collector is from a state or federal agency or is a government official

▶ Revealing the existence of a bad debt to third parties such as neighbors or employers

▶ Using false or deceptive means to obtain information about a debtor

The act also provides that debtors also have the right to notify a collection agency in writing that they do not wish to hear from the agency again, except for legal notices and notices of possible further action.

It is important to note that the law applies only to debt collection agencies—not to banks and other financial institutions or stores.

Garnishment. Creditors can use a legal procedure, known as **garnishment**, to withhold a part of a debtor's earnings for the payment of a debt. The law also prohibits an employer from firing an employee because of garnishment of wages for indebtedness.

DEBT PROBLEMS

What kinds of families face these problems? Following is a profile of a family that has problems with debt. It shows characteristics that can be considered typical.

▶ The family is young, with more than the average number of children but only an average income.

▶ The parent or parents are impulsive shoppers, are carefree, and do not postpone buying things when they want them; they cave in easily to high-pressure salesmen.

▶ The family does not read much, not even the daily newspaper. Television is the major form of entertainment and the way the family gets their news and information. And television disproportionately influences the family's buying decisions.

▶ The parent or parents tend to blame their situation on "unavoidable circumstances" (such as pregnancy, temporary unemployment, the purchase of a new car) and do not take responsibility for their problems.

▶ The family moves more often than the average family.

▶ No one assumes clear responsibility for managing the family finances.

▶ The family has a single adult at its head (either by choice or as a result of divorce, separation, or the death of a partner).

Clear Danger Signals. Following are questions to ask yourself if you think you may be crossing into the danger zone of too much debt:

▶ Do you continually lengthen the repayment periods on your installment loans and make smaller and smaller down payments?

▶ Do the balances on your revolving charge accounts continue to go up?

▶ Do the bills for this month begin piling up before you have finished paying last month's bills?

▶ Are you slowly, but steadily, using a larger part of your income to pay your debts each month?

▶ Are you taking cash advances on your credit card to pay such regular monthly bills as utilities, rent, and food?

SOLUTIONS TO DEBT PROBLEMS

Is there a safe way out? Sylvia and Daryl are convinced there are some ways to end the ever increasing debt spiral. They have found the following information to share with us.

Wage Earner Plan—Chapter XIII. Chapter XIII of the Federal Bankruptcy Act is an alternative to declaring bankruptcy. Chapter XIII allows the debtor, creditors, and a judge, acting together, to set a monthly amount for the debtor to pay over an extended repayment period. This is called a **wage earner plan.** The debts are not wiped out, but the court takes a portion of each paycheck and distributes it to the creditors. Chapter XIII does not require the debtor to give up assets such as personal property and real estate.

Usually, as part of this arrangement, the debtor cannot make additional credit purchases from a creditor until the original debt has been paid.

Bankruptcy. Straight bankruptcy, also called **liquidation bankruptcy,** requires debtors to sell most of their assets at public sale through a trustee in return for a discharge from most, if not all, of their outstanding debts. The concept behind bankruptcy is to wipe out all debts and give the debtor a new start.

The wage earner plan and bankruptcy are drastic moves, but not as drastic as the next two that Sylvia and Daryl found.

Pawn Shops and Loan Sharks. When individuals or families are not able to get loans from financial institutions such as banks or small finance companies, they sometimes turn to pawn shops and loan sharks. This form of money borrowing can be very expensive and should be avoided.

For a cash loan, **pawnbrokers** accept **collateral** such as jewelry, art objects, watches, and clothing. The pawnbroker actually lends only about 40% resale value of the article at a high interest rate of 36 to 50%. The pawnbroker keeps the collateral for the period of the loan and returns it when the loan has been repaid. Problems occur when people do not save the money to repay the loan and they lose their collateral, which was worth more than the loan.

Desperate or unknowing borrowers may turn to **loan sharks.** These are illegal credit lenders who charge very high rates for money; for example, they will give you $50 now in exchange for your giving them $75 when you get paid. Usually such loans are for one week or one month.

Most states have laws governing small loan practices, but some do not. Some unscrupulous lenders operate without a license in states that do have regulatory laws.

Rates are not quoted by illegal or unethical lenders because they are extremely high—ranging from 100 to 500%. Collection practices often involve threats of harm and violence. Sylvia and Daryl hope their fathers will not turn to pawnbrokers or loan sharks.

Credit Counseling. Sylvia and Daryl prefer the final method they have found, credit counseling, as the first step toward regaining financial stability. They have recommended it to their fathers. To begin with, they have been told, a person seeking counseling should contact his or her local bank. Many banks are now offering credit counseling to customers who find themselves in difficulty.

Another resource available is the National Foundation for Consumer Credit; it is located at 1819 H Street N.W., Washington, DC 20006. It will provide you with the address of one of the consumer credit counseling services near you. These are nonprofit organizations, backed by local banks, merchants, and educators, and they are set up to provide financial counseling to anyone, but will offer special help to overburdened families in an effort to find ways to get them out of trouble.

Another agency offering help is the Family Service Agency. Hundreds of Family Service Agencies either offer financial counseling or can refer you to some agency which does. If you do not know which agency offers such help in your area, write to the Family Service Association of America, at 44 East Twenty-third Street, New York, NY 10010.

Ask Yourself

1. What action might a creditor use if debtors do not pay their debts?

2. What are 3 signs of carrying too much debt?

3. What is a safe way to get out of debt?

SHARPEN YOUR SKILLS

_____ Skill 1 _____

As our teenage experts have noticed several times in these chapters, a family that spends more than 20% of their take-home pay on installment payments and credit accounts is in danger of a credit overload. Daryl and Sylvia have decided to look at specific family budgets to determine how well the families are handling credit.

Questions 1. What percent of the family's take-home pay goes toward paying credit bills?

2. Is this family spending too much of their salary paying these bills?

Solutions   The family's budget this month looks like this:

Income

Take-Home Pay	$4550.00

Expenses

Mortgage Payment	462.00
Utilities	185.00
Telephone	45.00

Cable Television	53.00
Gasoline and Car Repairs	220.00
Food	650.00
Savings	450.00
*Car Payment	225.00
*Credit Union Loan	75.00
*MasterCard	120.00
*VISA	95.00
Charge Accounts:	
*Sears	135.00
*Foley's Garage	25.00
*American Express	140.00
Everything Else	1670.00

The entries that count as credit payments are marked with an asterisk. (A mortgage is not counted as part of the credit expenses.) The total of these payments is $815.00.

As a percent of their take-home pay, the family is spending:

$815/4550 = .179 or 18%

The family spends 18% on credit payments.

They are not spending too much, but they are approaching the 20% limit.

EXERCISE YOUR SKILLS

1. Why do you think the law prohibits an employer from firing an employee because of garnishment of wages for indebtedness?

2. Why is an impulsive shopper in greater risk for financial problems?

3. Why would Sylvia and Daryl recommend credit counseling as the first step toward regaining financial stability?

Activity 1

Following are the monthly budgets for four families. Their incomes range from $1850.00 (Family D) to $5400.00 (Family B). You will notice that they all have some expenses that they pay by choice (for example, cable television) and some they pay by necessity (food and mortgage). Their credit payments are marked with asterisks. For each family, determine if they are in danger of credit overload. To do this you will find what percent of their take-home pay goes toward the payment of credit bills.

Is the family spending too much of their income on these bills? Can you suggest any adjustments they could make to reduce their expenses, if necessary?

1. **Family A**

   ### Income

Take-Home Pay	$3290.00

   ### Expenses

Mortgage Payment	$650.00
Utilities	148.00
Telephone	43.00
Cable Television	53.00
Gasoline and Car Repairs	183.50
Food	580.00
Savings	330.00
*Car Payment	165.00
*MasterCard	56.00
*American Express	140.00
*VISA	45.00
Charge Accounts:	
*Sears	77.00
Everything Else	819.50

2. **Family B**

   ### Income

Take–Home Pay	$5400.00

   ### Expenses

Rent	$852.00
Utilities	118.70
Telephone	43.60
Sports Club Fee	53.00
Gasoline and Car Repairs	126.00
Food	580.00
Savings	540.00
*Car Payment	237.00
*MasterCard	89.00
*American Express	140.00
*VISA	102.00
Charge Accounts:	
*Hardware Store	34.00
*Penneys	15.00
Everything Else	2469.70

3. Family C

Income

Take-Home Pay	$3210.00

Expenses

Mortgage Payment	$640.00
Utilities	235.00
Telephone	74.00
Sports Club Fee	53.00
Gasoline and Car Repairs	54.00
Food	620.00
Savings	321.00
*Car Payment	0.00
*MasterCard	79.00
*American Express	140.00
*VISA	42.00
Charge Accounts:	
*Pharmacy	34.00
*Montgomery Ward	65.00
Everything Else	853.00

4. Family D

Income

Take-Home Pay	$1850.00

Expenses

Mortgage Payment	$150.00
Utilities	83.00
Telephone	26.00
Cable Television	33.00
Gasoline and Car Repairs	68.50
Food	225.00
Savings	185.00
*Car Payment	233.00
*MasterCard	26.00
*VISA	35.00
Charge Accounts:	
*Sears	45.00
Everything Else	740.50

EXTEND YOUR UNDERSTANDING
PROJECT 7–1: CREDIT COUNSELOR

You have learned that people who are in financial difficulties sometimes talk to a credit counselor. This project is designed to help you learn more about what a credit counselor does to help people. You will also determine what a credit counselor might recommend to people who need to get their finances back on track.

Assignment

1. Work with a group of classmates to complete this project.

2. Interview several credit counselors at local banks or other financial institutions in your neighborhood.

3. Write to the following organizations for information about organizations in your area that you can contact:

   National Foundation for Consumer Credit
   1819 H Street N.W.
   Washington, DC 20006

   Family Service Association of America
   44 East Twenty-third Street
   New York, NY 10010

4. Contact the consumer credit counseling services in your neighborhood to find out what services they offer.

5. Investigate the education and training that is required for a person to become a credit counselor.

6. Try to interview people who have used credit counseling services to find out what advice they were given and how they were helped.

7. Discuss the information that you obtain with the students in your group and organize the information for a written report.

8. Write a report about the education and training a credit counselor is required to receive, the work of a credit counselor, the availability of positions for credit counselors in your area, other areas where credit counselors might find employment, and any other information that you obtain.

PROJECT 7–2: COMPARING SPENDING HABITS

When you are trying to make comparisons of spending habits, the more information you are able to obtain, the more accurate your comparison will be. Therefore, this project might best be completed as a class project.

Assignment

1. Divide the class into 2 groups. One group will interview adults and the other will interview people who are under age 18.

2. Each half of the class may then be subdivided into smaller groups with each small group assigned to a specific group—such as freshmen, sophomores, juniors, and seniors. The adults might be divided in groups such as singles under 25, singles over 25, married people under 30, married people over 30, or other such groups the class decides upon.

3. Each group is to interview a specified number of people in the appropriate group (10–20 by each student in a group).

4. Gather information about the spending habits of these groups of people such as:

   > What is their income?
   > How much of their income do they save?
   > How much do they pay in taxes?
   > How much do they spend on items such as food, clothing, transportation, housing, utilities, insurance, recreation, and any other items that the groups decide on?

5. After all the information is gathered, organize the data in a chart that is set up by your group.

6. Compare your information to the findings of other groups.

7. Work as a whole to combine the information gathered by each group into a single set of graphs, such as circle graphs, to show the percent of income each of the various age groups spends on different categories.

CHAPTER 7 KEY TERMS

CHAPTER 7 REVIEW

1. Use the credit-scoring table in the Reference Section of your book to determine the credit scores for the following families.

	Family A	Family B
Age of head of household	40	30
Years at current address	12	5
Age of current car	5	1
Monthly auto payments	none	$265
Housing cost	$385	$540
Checking and saving accounts	both	both
Referred to a finance company?	no	no
Major credit cards	5	3
Ratio of debt to income	10%	15%

2. Why do you think financial advisors recommend a 20% limit for credit payments other than a home mortgage?

3. Why might it be wise for young people to establish credit while they are still living with their parent or parents?

4. Why should people be careful about cosigning loans for friends?

5. Do you think the Equal Credit Opportunity Act is a good law? Why?

6. If a family's take-home pay is $3500 a month, how much can they afford to spend for credit payments each month?

7. Find the total financed price, the total interest, and the dealer's profit for each car sale plan below if the car price is $12,500.

	Plan A	Plan B	Plan C
Rebate	$1200	$750	none
Loan Amount			
Time of Loan	48 months	48 months	36 months
Monthly Payment	$276.02	$283.21	$370.58
Total Financed Price			
Total Interest			
Dealer's Profit			

8. For an all-purpose credit account, set up a chart to show the first 6 monthly payments and find the total interest paid over 6 months at 1.5% interest per month. The beginning balance is $500 and you make monthly payments of 10% of the amount owed. During the second month, you make an additional purchase of $125.

9. If a family has an income of $3600 a month and makes the following payments during the month, what percent of their income are they spending to pay credit bills? Do they owe too much money in installment payments? Explain.

Mortgage—$645, car payment—$225, utilities—$160, cable television—$51, gas and car repairs—$230, savings—$360, Sears—$102, VISA—$68, MasterCard—$85, food—$640, American Express—$175, everything else $821.

1. Would a family be more likely to be approved for a loan if they had a score on the credit-scoring table (in the Reference Section of this book) of 62 or a score of 95?

2. Which one or more of these credit collection methods is legal?

   a. Publishing a list of debtors

   b. Collectors posing as government officials

   c. Garnishment of wages

   d. Sending a notice of an overdue payment

3. What is the difference between a wage earner plan under Chapter XIII and a declaration of bankruptcy?

4. Find the total financed price, the total interest, and the dealer's profit for each car sale plan if the car price is $13,800.

	Plan A	Plan B
Rebate	$1500	none
Loan Amount		
Time of Loan	48 months	48 months
Monthly Payment	$293.28	$306.88
Total Financed Price		
Total Interest		
Dealer's Profit		

5. For an all-purpose credit account, set up a chart to show the first 6 monthly payments and find the total interest paid over 6 months at 1.5% interest per month. The beginning balance is $650 and you make monthly payments of 10% of the amount owed. During the third month, you make a new purchase of $89.78.

6. If a family has an income of $3100 a month and makes the following payments during the month, what percent of their income are they spending to pay credit bills? Do they owe too much money in installment payments? Explain.

   Mortgage—$478, car payment—$237.50, utilities—$120, Sears—$120, VISA—$45, car repairs—$140, MasterCard—$88, food—$620, and American Express—$320

SKILLS PREVIEW

In this skills preview, you will review skills that you will need to complete the exercises in Chapters 8 and 9. If you do not know how to complete any exercises, be sure to ask for help.

Find each of the following numbers. Round your answer to the nearest tenth.

1. 23.2% of $92.5 million   **3.** 18.2% of $91.2 million

2. 61.5% of $80.1 million   **4.** 5.8% of $6.5 million

Find each of the following. Round your answer to the nearest tenth of a percent.

5. $16.5 million is what percent of $80 million?

6. $26.8 million is what percent of $85.5 million?

7. $39,530,600 is what percent of $78,200,000?

8. $2655 is what percent of $50,000?

Complete the table.

	Old Amount	New Amount	Amount of Increase or Decrease
9.	$ 3,650	$ 3,400	
10.	$ 27,674	$ 21,325	
11.	$1,753,109	$2,156,232	
12.	$ 378.76	$ 753.90	

Multiply.

13. 5 x 6 3/4   **14.** 9 x 11 5/8

15. 27 x 15 3/8   **16.** 105 x 48 1/4

Divide. Round to the nearest whole number.

17. $60,000 ÷ 72 1/2   **18.** $75,000 ÷ 61 7/8

19. $9800 ÷ 28 1/4   **20.** $50,000 ÷ 40 1/8

21. Develop a bar graph using the following numbers. Use the horizontal axis for days and the vertical axis for the numbers.

Day	1	2	3	4	5	6
Number	6 1/2	5 3/4	8 1/2	9	5	4 1/2

Find each of the following. Round to two decimal places.

22. $\left(\dfrac{360}{111.9}\right)$ x $100   **23.** $\left(\dfrac{960}{145}\right)$ x $100   **24.** $\left(\dfrac{261}{81.5}\right)$ x $100

CHAPTER 8

ADVERTISING: THE BRIDGE FROM SELL TO SALE

Advertising is all around us. We sometimes complain about it as we do about the weather. At times we might wish to tell advertisers how to do their jobs, or at least how not to do them, but few of us would actually want them to disappear entirely. Though we may tolerate advertising as a necessary evil—like dentistry and taxes—at some level we must admit we need it.

We as consumers are becoming more clever at avoiding advertising, but when we really *want* to find an appliance on sale or the new convenience foods that are available we do use it. As we become more adept at dodging commercials (for instance, by using our VCRs to record television programs for later viewing, at which time we can skip over the commercials), advertisers counter with more clever ways of getting their messages across.

Today we have a greater portion of our income to spend on discretionary items than our parents and grandparents. Consequently, we expect to maintain a better standard of living than they did. Manufacturers are more than willing to make products to enhance our lifestyles. When they do, they must inform us of their new creations; and they must keep us buying the old ones, too, so that they can continue to afford to come up with more new ones.

Much of our economy depends upon our selling things to one another. The teenagers we will meet in this chapter will help us discover what part advertising plays in this process. Felix is especially vulnerable to certain ads—those that suggest if he buys the advertised product he will feel a part of a wonderful group of people, all more glamourous than himself. This Join-the-Crowd formula is a successful advertising tool.

Yvonne and her twin sister Yvette are aware of the advertising coming our way on television and radio, in magazines, on billboards, and in the mail. They recognize messages in ads based on the appeal of science and nutrition. They are also aware of the federal regulations prohibiting unfair advertising practices—such as the omission of significant facts or the tendency to deceive. Other practices they identify are tricky but not strictly illegal.

Finally, Yvette learns how advertisers carefully target specific groups of buyers. Advertisers use sophisticated techniques to reach their audience. Our teens are learning to be sophisticated members of the audience.

SECTION 8–1
IS ADVERTISING WORTH THE PRICE?

Felix thinks of himself as a part of the fringe. He has never been in the inner circle at school, in fact he feels happy when some of his classmates do speak to him from time to time. Some of the guys make fun of his uncommon name, and he has never had the nerve to ask a girl for a date. He did go to one of the school parties last year but he didn't know any of the new dances and he felt he made a fool of himself. Felix decided not to go to any more school parties until he learned the new dances and felt he was a part of the group.

Lately Felix has been listening to advertisements for products that are supposed to make him feel more like one of the crowd. He persuaded his mother to buy him new boots, but so far he has not noticed any new friends flocking around him.

Felix is beginning to wonder how much of the advertising he can believe. Is he reading more into the message than he is supposed to? Has advertising always been this way? Felix will take a closer look at exactly what advertising is and at some of the messages he finds particularly persuasive.

OBJECTIVES: In this section, we will help Felix to:

- *determine what advertising is and how it developed*
- *categorize advertising as informative or persuasive*
- *classify some of the common messages seen in advertising*
- *examine where the advertising money goes*

WHAT IS ADVERTISING?

One of the most explicit definitions of an advertisement is, "any paid-for communication intended to inform and/or influence one or more people." Advertisements, and advertisers, have been paying to inform and influence the rest of us for quite a while, at least since the days of ancient Greece.

The development of mass production, followed by mass consumption, which brought about mass retailing, encouraged manufacturers to **brand** their products. That is, they gave them identifying names and characteristics to make them stand out in the market. Another factor crucial to the development of advertising was the growth of education and literacy in the second half of the nineteenth century. In those days, advertisements were seen in the press and on posters, but advertisers quickly recognized the opportunity offered by the developments in transportation. Streetcars, buses, and hot-air balloons soon were seen as mobile billboards. One of the first forms of advertising was the sign announcing a business or professional office.

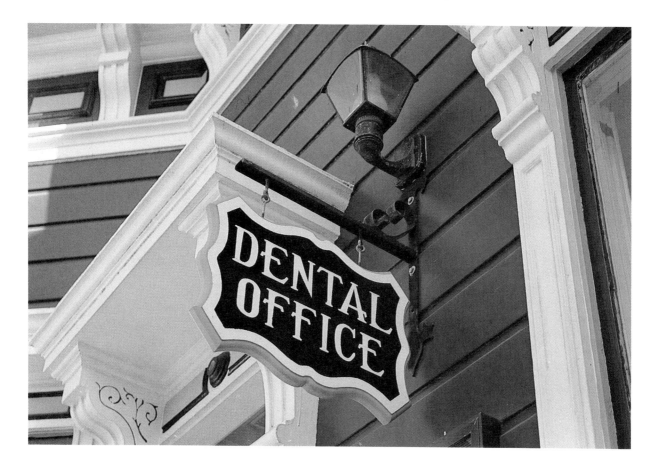

The introduction of commercial television in the 1950s allowed advertisers the unique opportunity to broadcast sounds and pictures into millions of homes. Advertising became a multi-billion dollar industry. In the U.S. alone, $87.8 billion dollars were spent on advertising in 1984.

Advertising has traditionally been seen as a sometimes clever, often wasteful, and always manipulative business. It has been accused of creating desires for things people do not really need. However, new evidence is suggesting that advertising actually keeps prices down by stimulating competition. In this new view, advertising is being seen as the consumer's friend.

INFORMATION OR PERSUASION?

Advertisements and commercial messages about products and services are everywhere. Advertising plays an important communication function in our marketplace. For Felix and other consumers, it is another source of information about products, services, or ideas that are available. But advertising is more than information: it is also persuasion. For the merchant, advertising is designed to sell products. It is not unbiased or objective with regard to a product or service being advertised. **Advertising,** then, both promotes and presents information about goods and services.

Advertising in our society has critics as well as defenders. Critics claim that it:

- promotes materialism and causes people to buy what they do not need and cannot afford,
- creates artificial wants that result in wasted productive resources,
- reduces price competition and creates competition that is based on false, insignificant, or nonexistent differences in products,
- promotes unnecessary competition between brands, which results in higher prices,
- lowers the general level of taste,
- plays upon consumers emotions and motivations,
- provides little or no useful information for consumers.

On the other side are the defenders of advertising. For the defenders, advertising is merely a helpful aid in purchasing goods or services. The proponents of advertising claim that it:

- provides information about new or unknown products and about changes in technology,
- communicates details of performance or other characteristics of existing products,
- promotes changes in aspirations and living standards by exposing people to goods, services, and new ideas,
- contributes to more leisure time by promoting timesaving products and services,
- communicates new ideas and facts,
- reduces the cost of newspapers, magazines, television, and radio programs through commercial sponsorship,
- supplies daily price information, including money-saving specials and sales,
- tells consumers the location of specific sellers, thereby saving consumers time and money in finding products and services,
- entertains people, amuses them, and gives them aesthetically pleasing images.

In today's marketplace, advertising is an essential tool of business. Advertising can be useful to consumers if they know what product or service they want, and if they can overlook emotional appeals to buy a particular product or service. The consumer must respond to advertising intelligently, deciding for himself or herself what part of the message is useful information and what part is not.

THE LANGUAGE OF ADVERTISING

Some consumers laugh at ads. Others claim disbelief and ignore them. Some think ads are harmless nonsense. Some enjoy them. Regardless of their attitudes, consumers need to know something about the language of advertising. Many consumer decisions are based unknowingly on the appeals of ads. In this chapter we will look at some of the typical messages. While many messages do not fit neatly into one category or another, and some may seem to belong to several categories, many have fairly strong messages that can be identified. Following are some typical messages.

Join the Crowd. The appeal in this message is to go along with others, be a member of the "in" group—a discriminating crowd that has good taste, good looks, good minds, money, and success. This message is aimed especially at teenagers, because being a member of the right group is particularly important to them.

Remember Me? A famous person, usually an actor or sports personality, appears to use the product and lends credibility to it.

"Listen. I love today's western look, right down to the boots," says the famous country singer. Announcer: "What does this fabulous model have to say about our skin cream? Her skin says it all."

Young and Beautiful. The implied message in these ads is that if you use this product, you, too, will be as young and beautiful as the people in them. An underlying theme to these messages is that youth and beauty are particularly desirable states. If you aren't young, you certainly want to look as young as you can for as long as possible. And if you are attractive, members of the opposite sex will be drawn to you, just as they are in these ads.

Bigger than Life. The claims in these ads make the products appear exaggerated, either in size or in what they are able to do.

"Use this film, and every photograph you take will look professional."

WHERE THE MONEY GOES

Close to $100 billion is spent for advertising every year in the United States alone. This amount is several percent of the total value of all goods and services produced in the U.S. In 1984, about 56% of the total expenditure was for national advertising and about 44% for local advertising. Newspapers accounted for the greatest portion, followed by television, direct mail, radio, magazines, business and farm publications, and outdoor media, in that order.

The following graph shows the percent of the total advertising expenditures for each medium.

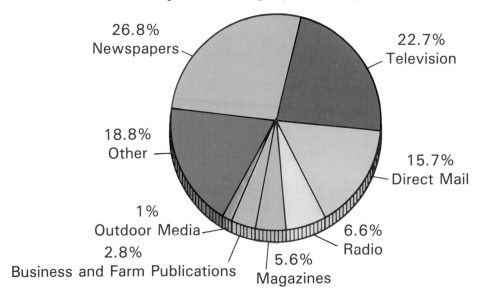

Percentage of Advertising Expenditures by Medium, 1984

26.8% Newspapers

22.7% Television

18.8% Other

15.7% Direct Mail

1% Outdoor Media

2.8% Business and Farm Publications

5.6% Magazines

6.6% Radio

Ask Yourself

1. What is advertising?

2. What developments encouraged manufacturers to identify their products by brand?

3. What are the claims of some of the critics of advertising?

SHARPEN YOUR SKILLS

_____ Skill 1 _____

Question   According to the graph "Percent of Money Spent for Advertising by Medium," what percent of advertising expenditures went to television?

Solution   22.7% was spent on television.

Question   If $87.8 billion were spent in 1984, how much money was spent on television advertising?

Solution   22.7% of $87.8 billion = 0.227 x $87,800,000,000
                        = $19,930,600,000 or $19.9 billion

_____ Skill 2 _____

Suppose that $100 billion were spent on advertising in 1989.

Question   What percent increase would there be in the amount of money spent for television advertising from 1984 to 1989?

Solution   To find the percent of increase, find the difference between the two totals. Then divide the difference by the first (earlier) amount.

1984 $19,930,600,000
1989 0.227 x $100,000,000,000 = $22,700,000,000

$$\begin{array}{r} \$22,700,000,000 \\ -19,930,600,000 \\ \hline \$ \ 2,769,400,000 \end{array}$$ $\dfrac{\$2,769,400,000}{19,930,600,000} = 0.139$

There would be a 13.9% increase in television advertising spending from 1984 to 1989.

EXERCISE YOUR SKILLS

1. How do informative ads differ from persuasive ads?

2. How are some messages in advertising particularly aimed at teenagers?

3. Why do you think the greatest portion of money spent for advertising goes for newspaper advertisements?

_____ Activity 1 _____

1. In 1982, the amount spent on advertising was $67.9 billion. Assume the percents were the same as those in the graph "Percent of Money Spent for Advertising by Medium." How much was spent on advertising through each of the following media?

   a. Newspapers   **e.** Magazines

   b. Television   **f.** Business and farm publications

   c. Direct mail   **g.** Outdoor media

   d. Radio

2. In 1984, the amount spent on advertising was $87.8 billion. The percents spent for each medium are shown on the graph "Percent of Money Spent for Advertising by Medium." How much was spent on advertising through each of the media listed in Problem 1?

3. If the amount spent on advertising in 1990 was $105.3 billion, and the percents the same as those in the graph, how much was spent on advertising through each of the media listed in Problem 1?

_____ Activity 2 _____

What percent increase in the amount of money spent on advertising through the following media was there between 1982 and 1990? (Use the amounts of money given in Problems **1** and **3** of Activity 1.)

1. Newspapers   5. Magazines

2. Television   6. Business and farm publications

3. Direct mail   7. Outdoor media

4. Radio

WHOSE TARGET ARE YOU TODAY?

Yvonne and her twin sister, Yvette, watch quite a lot of television, and they each subscribe to one magazine. Cable television also comes into their home on two of their television sets, and their family subscribes to one movie channel. Yvonne usually prefers watching movies that are broadcast on the movie channel because they are not interrupted with commercials. She views commercials as totally unrelated to the movie, coming close to destroying the continuity of some scenes.

Yvonne also has a rental card from a video store, which she uses quite often. Recently, however, she has noticed that even rented movies use some of the space at the beginning or end to advertise other movies or other products. And recognizable products appear in some of the scenes.

Yvonne is quite annoyed with so much advertising bombarding her from all directions. Every 30-minute television show has 7 minutes of commercials and 23 minutes of program. Ads show up all through her favorite magazine; along every highway they drive on; even in the mail and over the telephone. Yvonne is wondering what life would be like if there were no advertising.

Yvonne has even been called on the telephone to answer survey questions about the number and ages of the people in her family, how much education they have, what income group they fall into, and many other questions. Yvonne has read about being part of a target audience. With so much advertising around, she has really felt like a target at times, and whoever is shooting at her has incredible aim!

Yvonne also wonders why she sees so much advertising of products that have been around for as long as she can remember and must be familiar to everyone. Yvonne will investigate her questions more thoroughly.

OBJECTIVES: In this section, we will help Yvonne to:

- *examine some of the consequences that might result if advertising disappeared*
- *examine advertising from the advertiser's point of view, including the idea of a target market*
- *consider four reasons for advertising products that have already been established*
- *discuss the characteristics of advertising in newspapers and magazines*
- *classify advertising according to four typical messages*

ADVERTISING: DO WE NEED IT?

Advertising is an integral part of our lives. Without it we would notice a significant change. Posters and billboards would vanish, as would most television stations—with all the news, sports, entertainment, and drama programs people have come to depend on. The only magazines and newspapers that could continue to function would be much smaller and more expensive. But the really brutal impact would be on the process of mass production and mass consumption, on the price and availability of products in the stores, on the economy, and on employment.

HOW DO ADVERTISERS VIEW ADVERTISING?

Advertising is not simply created, paid for, and then shown to the public. Extensive research is done by advertising agencies, both before and after the ads are created and distributed. Advertisers are particularly interested in the **target market** for their products. They do exhaustive surveys and analyze thousands of bits of information about their potential customers.

Such studies characterize consumers on the basis of their **demographics**: age, sex, income level, family size, level of education, employment, and so on. These studies also reveal the reading and buying habits of various groups. One way companies get specific information is from the consumers themselves. Every time you purchase an item and are asked to send in a product registration card, you are probably adding your name to another list which classifies you according to your spending and hobby habits and which may be used later as a mailing list.

Advertisers analyze which combination of media will reach their target market in the most efficient way. After a new product is on the market and has been advertised, they do more surveys to find out how customers were influenced by the advertising. Advertisers are also aware that customers are generally reluctant to admit that advertising has any influence on what they purchase.

Advertising must not merely inform people about a product, it must also persuade them to buy it. The products advertised do not have to be new ones. In fact, far more money is spent advertising existing products than new ones.

WHY ADVERTISE ESTABLISHED PRODUCTS?

Established products are still advertised because, first, though the products may not be new, the customers are. For instance, very few people are truly interested in baby products until they have a baby in the family. Suddenly they notice ads for baby food, diapers, and strollers. Children become interested in foods, toys, and video games. Teenagers notice music, makeup, fashion, and movies; young adults buy cold drinks, cars, exercise equipment, home furnishings, and appliances. And, if we are to believe what advertisers show us, old people are interested in products that help relieve their physical ailments—reclining chairs, antacids, and pain relievers—and money for retirement—life insurance and mutual funds.

Second, products are constantly being changed and improved to keep up with technological advances and new demands. Consumers now are asking for more convenience and more nutrition in their foods, while at the same time demanding less damage to the environment by their waste products and automobiles. Although the words "new" and "improved" may be the most overworked in advertising language, manufacturers are often changing their products to stay ahead of the competition.

Third, consumers do forget about products unless they are frequently reminded of them.

Fourth, manufacturers advertise to build up their brand image and to add to their perceived value.

THE MEDIA

Newspapers. More advertising money is spent in newspapers than in any other medium: today it is up to 41% of the advertising revenue, as compared to 33% for television. This may seem surprising, since television costs so much more, but there are a great many more newspapers than television stations. One of the big advantages of a newspaper, from an advertiser's point of view, is that a newspaper can provide a wide variety of audiences in terms of numbers and demographics.

Unlike television, a newspaper can provide information that a reader can keep for future reference. A newspaper can also include a coupon offering money off the price of a product or offering the reader a chance to send for further information.

The charge for newspaper space is determined by the number of single-column centimeters. An ad can be created to fit almost any size and shape. Newspapers have fewer restrictions than television on the types of advertising they can accept; they can still advertise products that can no longer be advertised on television.

Two primary disadvantages are: (1) advertising nationally means advertising in a number of different newspapers, which can also require the creation of many different ads; (2) newspapers are not as effective at creating images as television, with its color, movement, and sound. Newsprint is not particularly high quality paper, and photographs do not reproduce as well.

Magazines. The greatest advantage of a magazine, to an advertiser, is that specific groups of people choose to buy specific magazines. Many magazines are so specialized that the ads can be designed for the particular needs of their audience.

Magazines also use higher quality paper than newspapers, and more color pages, but their production deadlines are longer, so the advertiser's copy cannot be as timely. Obviously, like newspapers, they cannot provide movement and sound. Unlike newspapers, magazines make a national campaign easier to plan because many of them circulate nationally.

MORE MESSAGES FOUND IN ADVERTISING

In the last section, you saw several typical advertising messages. Following are some more messages you can find in advertisements you see every day.

Act Now. In this type of ad, the message urges the consumer to "hurry on down" to buy the product "while supplies last." These products are only available for a limited time. If a low sale price is also mentioned in the ad, the ad also contains a Save Money message.

Save Money. These ads indicate that the product is economical to use, or that the price for buying the product is especially low. You will save money because this car gets more miles to a gallon of gasoline; or these products are offered at a special sale price.

Scientific or Statistical. This claim uses a scientific proof, data, or a "mystery" ingredient to establish superiority. The scientific claim is especially effective in today's climate of reliance on experts. We tend to take the word of a doctor or researcher about things we cannot find out for ourselves. These claims are often stated in such a way that they do not really amount to an endorsement. For instance, they might say "Doctors have found that our product is superior," without telling how many doctors and how qualified they were. Or, they use language such as, "Our product can be an effective addition to a balanced diet," which does not actually promise that it will be.

"Our breath mints contain a sparkling drop of freshness." "Our cleanser is 45% more powerful than the next leading brand."

Healthy or Nutritious. If you buy these products, you are choosing products that will be good for your health—that is the message. With so many people interested in good nutrition and in staying healthy, a lot of advertisers are emphasizing these aspects of their products. Many manufacturers are developing food products that are low in cholesterol, low in fat and sodium, low in sugar and calories, and high in fiber.

Ask Yourself

1. What significant changes might you notice if there were no advertising?

2. Why is it necessary to continue to advertise established products?

3. What are two disadvantages of newspaper advertising?

SHARPEN YOUR SKILLS

Question   How can you tell what appeal an advertisement is making?

Solution   Keep in mind the list of message types examined to this point:

Remember Me	**Bigger than Life**
Act Now	**Join the Crowd**
Young and Beautiful	**Healthy or Nutritious**
Save Money	**Scientific or Statistical**

Ask yourself the following questions about an ad:

- What part of me is this appealing to?
- What ideals is it setting up?
- What does it suggest is wrong?
- How does it suggest things can be improved?
- What will go wrong if I don't buy the product?

Most ads appeal to you in more than one way. But they can often be analyzed, as in the following examples.

	Advertisements	Interpretation
1.	"Move to Exotic Highland Acres ...just a few miles from your present home. Scenic beauty, healthy air, friendly neighbors, exciting activities, and stimulating community events every single night."	As you read this ad or hear it over the radio, you begin to feel it sounds too good to be true. It is appealing to the longing for something Bigger than Life.
2.	"Safe and sane exercise. Our European-trained aerobic fitness experts and latest pro-balanced equipment available to you daily for your own computer-personalized routine."	With its technical sounding terms and reliance on professional qualifications, this ad appeals to the desire for a Scientific foundation to a process.
3.	"Your mother wouldn't tell you about us...because our social and personal development tips make you irresistible! Hire a personal secretary to handle your calendar if you subscribe to TEEN MAKEOVERS, the magazine for winning teens."	At first it may seem this appeals to Beauty and Youth, but as you continue to listen or read on you see the appeal is pitched most strongly to the desire to Join the Crowd.

	Advertisements	Interpretation
4.	"Tired? Nervous? Sick of Worry? Just swallow one small pill daily, use our breathing techniques, and eat a sensible diet. In no time, your worries will be memories."	This is a straightforward appeal to the desire for things Healthy and Nutritious.
5.	"What do Paul Bunyan and Moby Dick have in common? They both never existed. But if they had, no doubt they would have used Snow White Wash...a giant in the laundry department."	These famous characters do not have anything really to do with the product, but they catch your attention through the appeal of celebrity endorsements, called Remember Me?
6.	"Fabulous Mountain Tours... Everything included in one low price. Meals, guides, tents, tent poles, tent stakes...even firewood. Leave your cash at home, the rest is on us."	The low price is an appeal to Save Money. In addition the ad appeals to the fantasy of having things simple and carefree.
7.	"Only a few select home sites remain in beautiful Lorraine Acres. Off the Interstate at Stateline Road, this lovely, all-new development is filling up fast. Your neighbors are already moving in...what's keeping you?"	Whenever you begin to feel anxious that there will not be enough of a product left for you, you are subject to the Act Now appeal. This one adds the Join the Crowd appeal to it, suggesting that it is *the* place to be.
8.	"Hair too straight? Too curly? Too dark? Too pale? Look at these photos of actual HairWonder customers. Then hurry in to get your own dream haircut. Don't feel less than gorgeous any more.	Youth and Beauty are the strongest appeal in this direct beauty service ad. Some ads use beautiful people, some suggest a beautiful you, this one does both.

EXERCISE YOUR SKILLS

1. How are you affected by advertising?

2. How do advertisers determine the target market for their products?

3. What is the greatest advantage of magazine advertising over other media?

_____ **Activity 1** _____

Classify each of the advertising messages that follow according to the categories listed below. (**Note:** Some messages will fit into more than one category.)

Remember Me	**Act Now**
Bigger than Life	**Young and Beautiful**
Save Money	**Join the Crowd**
Scientific or Statistical	**Healthy or Nutritious**

Messages

1. Kangaroo Express: Speediest Service at Lowest Prices

2. Extended Warranty Service Plan provides carefree years of driving

3. Zipp International Mail Service now offers one flat rate to over 200 countries worldwide—Just $12.50 for a 2 oz. letter.

4. Accept Nothing Less—With Ultissimo, any possibility in the cosmos is available.

5. Look at the ultraplush interior and you won't believe the price!

6. AstroCar provides the luxury-car lease with the compact-car price.

7. New 4WD Cardinal: Four-wheel drive, rear anti-lock brakes, and safety are standard equipment.

8. How can you cut costs and maintain quality? Employ Pristine Temporary Services.

9. The New Panther Convertible—Sunbathe While You Soar Like the Wind.

10. This famous movie star knows how to throw the perfect beach party. First, find a secluded spot. And, like this star, always serve Surfer's Sizzlers.

11. Fresh Pick: The Most Selective Packers in the Field. We could have just given you the finest vegetables around—But we went a step beyond and added super-seasoned sauce to make our veggies the most mouthwatering delights to accompany any main course.

12. My Lady's Chocolates: Under the guidance of royal chocolateers, every morsel of My Lady's chocolate became a queenly delight. A gift of regal taste.

13. Add a secret touch to your recipes—honey, peanut butter, and chocolate—Now there's a treat too delectable to refuse!

14. Save up to 45% with our famous jewelry discounts—Anything less would be grand larceny.

15. Buy from the source—Cut out 3 markups. No better buy available. G.I.A. Certified diamonds: our only quality.

16. Dane Imports—By acclaimed Scandinavian craftsmen at 20% to 30% lower than retail prices. Less money buys a lot more.

17. With elegance at this price, how can you afford not to splurge? Sweep that special someone away for a romantic weekend...but don't reveal the special weekend rates.

18. Sure you've heard a few hundred miracle skin care claims and you're skeptical—But now listen to a few hundred dermatologists who say: Only MagiAge contains the active ingredient we recommend to remove age spots.

19. "Until I tried Softfeet Soles, I thought aching feet were part of being me."

20. The Creaminess You Love Without Cholesterol! Try the only whipped topping flavored like real whipping cream, but without the calories and cholesterol.

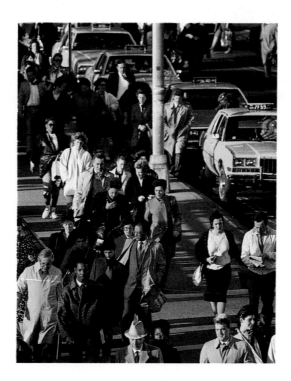

y at El Torito with the

ADVERTISING OUTDOORS AND BY MAIL

Yvonne's twin sister, Yvette, has also noticed an abundance of advertising in all forms. She is particularly annoyed when she sees the words "Suggested Manufacturer's Retail Price" because she realizes that stores generally sell below that price and still make a profit.

Yvette remembers the day her parents purchased a new washing machine, because the one that had been around for 15 years finally gave up. They needed one quickly and inexpensively so they looked in the Sunday paper to see what was being advertised on sale. They found a simple washer without a lot of fancy settings advertised at what they considered a good price. When they got to the store, the salesperson showed them the advertised model, but then immediately tried to convince them that what they really needed, with their large family, was a much fancier model—with a fancier price tag!

They left the store and went to another outlet of the same chain and dealt with a different salesperson. That salesperson sold them the washer they had come to buy in the first place. Yvette's father commented he had never seen a better example of the old "bait and switch" routine.

Yvette wonders whether some advertising practices are illegal. She finds the language in some ads really confusing. In fact, it seems to be intended to confuse. Yvette has particularly noticed the ads that use comparative words— better, stronger, lower, faster—without the comparison. They never say what the product is better, stronger, lower, or faster than!

OBJECTIVES: In this section, we will help Yvette to:

- *identify some of the federal regulations against deceptive practices found in ads*
- *discuss characteristics of advertising on billboards, business to business, by direct response, and direct mail*
- *classify advertising according to five claims*

FEDERAL REGULATIONS

Government regulations attempt to keep advertising fair, honest, and moral. In 1914, Congress created the Federal Trade Commission (FTC) and gave it the power to deal with abuses in interstate advertising. The criteria used by the Federal Trade Commission to determine if an ad is misleading or deceptive are:

259

- Tendency to deceive. Proof of actual deception is not essential. If an advertisement has a tendency to mislead or deceive, the FTC can stop the ad.
- Actual truthfulness. The purpose of the law against deceptive advertising is the protection of the consumer. Nothing less than literal truthfulness is tolerated. According to the FTC, the important criterion is the impression that the advertisement is likely to make upon the general public.
- Omission of important facts. The FTC has concluded that even though every sentence considered separately is true, the advertisement as a whole may be misleading because factors are omitted that should be mentioned or because the message is composed in such a way as to mislead.
- Double meaning. Because the purpose of the law is to prohibit advertising that has the tendency and capacity to deceive, an advertisement that can be interpreted to have two meanings is illegal if one of the meanings is false or misleading.

DECEPTIVE PRACTICES

The following are some advertising practices that have been found deceptive.

Bait and Switch. A product is advertised at an exceptionally low price, but consumers go to the store only to find that the merchandise is not available or is less desirable than another product. The salesperson then directs their attention to another model that costs more.

Advertised Specials. Stores often advertise items on special sale. When consumers arrive, they may be told, "We sold out earlier than we expected." The FTC has ruled that stores ought to have advertised specials readily available at the advertised price during the advertised sale period.

"Buy One—Get One Free" or **"Free gift."** Some ads offer a free gift, but the usual price of the product may have been increased to cover the cost of the gift. The FTC has ruled that a merchant must not directly and immediately recover the cost of the free merchandise.

False Price Comparisons. "Retail Value, $25.95; Our Price $14.95." When price comparisons are made between one store and others in an area, the comparisons must be based on an actual price, not an artificial price.

Manufacturer's Retail List Price. "Suggested Retail List Price $24.95; Our Price $20.95." Many consumers believe that a manufacturer's list price is the price at which an article is generally sold. Manufacturers do provide retailers with suggested prices. Because of competition and widespread disregard for these suggested prices, however, such terms are not dependable indicators of actual regular prices.

MORE MEDIA

Billboards. The billboard is still the purest form of advertising, so-called because the message must be quickly read and easily understood. People can usually give only a few seconds' notice to billboards. However, billboards are on display day and night. People driving the same route to work or to shop will see the same signs numerous times.

Advertisers have difficulty measuring the audience impact of a billboard—a fact seen as a distinct disadvantage by advertisers.

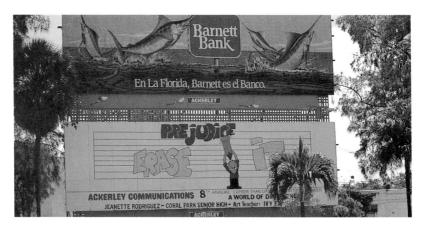

Business-to-Business. Many companies exist to offer services to other companies and are never in contact with the general public. Advertising agencies are a good example; they design the advertising package to sell a particular product that is manufactured by a separate business which hires them and which actually creates and sells the products. Advertisers promote the use of **business-to-business advertising**.

Direct Response. When advertisers use the **direct response** method, they have included a coupon, order blank, or some other means of soliciting a response from the customer.

Customers place orders from catalogs and receive their products by mail. Advantages include the elimination of wholesalers' and retailers' costs, and the company does not have to arrange for the distribution of its products. The disadvantages to the customer are that he or she cannot see the product before buying it and must usually pay the transportation costs.

Direct Mail. Direct mail advertising differs from direct response advertising in that it does not try to persuade the recipient to return a coupon or order form. The cost of **direct mail** is high compared with other media because of the cost of postage. However, advertisers can use selective mailing lists and send their message only to people in their target market. Thus, only the people who might be interested in the product will receive the advertisement.

Advertisers also like the fact that the results of the ad can be measured more accurately than for some other media. They can determine rather easily if the ad was effective by surveying a sample of the target audience.

Creating the mailing list is the key, of course. Research has become so sophisticated that a system now exists which can describe a person's lifestyle and purchasing habits based on his or her address and neighborhood.

Research has also shown that 18% of this direct mail is still thrown away, unread, as "junk mail." That leaves 82% that at least gets read first.

MORE MESSAGES

Several more of the typical messages found in advertising are described below.

New and Improved. The word "new" has a magical appeal to it. On a national basis, a product can be called new for only six months. The "improved" claim does not mean changed for the better. It means changed or different from before. In place of new and improved, watch for words that suggest new, but don't mean new—"introductory, now, today's, announcing, revolutionary, presenting, a fresh way to...."

> "Our new improved dog food with high quality protein. Now it's actually better at helping your dog stay healthy." "Now double-protection toothpaste. Fights cavities and freshens breath." "New improved furniture polish—Now polish as often as you want without the worry of build-up."

"Ours Is Better than Theirs." Two or more products are described in the ad, but the one being advertised is always better in some way than the others. Advertisements may also make a general claim, saying the product is better than all the others in the category, or some such vague comparison. If the comparison is only implied, such as "Lower in Fat," but the ad does not tell you what it is lower than, the message is an **unfinished claim**.

Unfinished Claim. The unfinished claim does not finish a comparison. The ad claims that the product is better or has more of something but does not tell you what it is better than.

> "Our TV gives you more." "Twice as much of the pain reliever doctors recommend most." "Our creamer gives coffee more body, more flavor." "Quieter, smoother ride." "More active ingredients...and more effective, too."

Weasel Claim. A weasel word is a modifier that makes the statement meaningless. Some commonly used **weasel words** are: helps, like, virtual, acts, works, can be, up to, as much as, refreshes, comforts, fights, the feel of, the look of.

> "Helps control dandruff symptoms with regular use." "Leaves dishes virtually spotless." "Fights bad breath." "Looks, smells, tastes like real eggs."

Unique Claim. This claim states that no other product is like the product advertised; it's unique; it has something no other product has.

> "There's no other mascara like it." "Either way, liquid or spray, there's nothing else like it." "Our ambassador service—it's the only one of its kind."

Ask Yourself

1. What are three deceptive practices used in ads that are against federal regulations?

2. Why are billboards the "purest" form of advertising?

3. What is business-to-business advertising?

4. How are direct response and direct mail advertising alike?

SHARPEN YOUR SKILLS

Question   How can you tell what claim an advertisement is making?

Solution   Keep in mind the list of claim types examined in this section:

New and Improved	**Unique Claim**
Unfinished Claim	**Weasel Claim**
"Ours is Better than Theirs"	

Ask yourself the following questions about an ad:

- What am I supposed to conclude from this ad?
- What comparison is it making?
- Does it actually make a claim, or does it leave the comparison vague?
- Is it suggesting a change has been made?
- Is it suggesting there is no other product like it?

Many ads make more than one claim. For example, a common format is to compare two products, find one superior, and then reveal that the other was the old version of the new! In other words, a New and Improved ad in the form of an "Ours is Better than Theirs" ad.

	Advertisements	**Interpretation**
1.	Nothing like this glue has ever existed before. You must try it to appreciate it. Send for your free sample today. Amaze yourself. Amaze your friends. Accept no substitutes.	This is clearly a Unique Claim. Unique claims suggest that there is something inherently good in being unmatched. It is possible that something that is one-of-a-kind will be superior, but there is no guarantee.

	Advertisements	Interpretation
2.	S o f t e r . . . S m o o t h e r . . . Warmer...More comfortable. What more could your baby want in a diaper?	This ad is all comparative adjectives without the other half of the comparison, making it an Unfinished Claim. Notice how comparative words are often used as stronger-seeming forms of their own roots (soft, smooth, warm, comfortable).
3.	You told us you loved our headbands...but we didn't make them in enough colors. Well, now we do.	This ad suggests the company actually listens to its customers, which is flattering. And now they have improved their product, just for you. New and Improved.
4.	We challenged the leading brand to a wear test, and we won hands down. Now, what excuse do you have for not buying CALICO Socks?	Clearly an "Ours is Better than Theirs" ad. Often these involve a side-by-side comparison or survey of consumers in which one brand comes out on top.
5.	Could this be wood? It's not, but you'll never tell. Our product looks, feels, fools, like the real thing. And has many comparable uses.	Does this product seem worthwhile? Do you have a good picture of what it looks like and can be used for? What does comparable mean? Is that the same as actual? The ad suggests a lot with Weasel Claims.

EXERCISE YOUR SKILLS

1. What are some deceptive practices in advertising that are not covered by federal regulations?

2. Why is it difficult for advertisers to measure the audience impact of billboards?

3. Do you think that unfinished claims and weasel claims are deceptive advertising? Why?

_____ **Activity 1** _____

Classify each of the advertising messages listed below into one of the following categories of claims. (Note: Some may fit more than one category.)

> **Unique Claim**   **New and Improved**
> **Unfinished Claim**   **Weasel Claim**
>   **"Ours Is Better Than Theirs"**

1. Daily use prevents nearly all plaque buildup.

2. Larry Lend's Import Car of the Year has the unique performance and styling it takes to satisfy even the most demanding driver.

3. Nothing fights foot odor better.

4. Try some and you'll taste that pure eating pleasure—Heavenly Dark Chocolate.

5. The car for the Human Race—it's a Steller.

6. Take your CALL card every where you go. All around the world, businesses are counting on CALL. Unlike other cards, with the CALL card there are no hidden charges, whether you dial direct or use an operator.

7. In Touch with the Future—Sleep Master Sleep System.

8. Not all brands are as choosy about their beef as Tenderline Special Dinner.

9. You're not going to find luxury like this in any import—None of them have anything like our convertible, the world's biggest seller.

10. Imitation cheese is made mostly from oil and water—hardly any milk. But a 3/4 oz. slice of Dairy Singles is made from six ounces of milk. That's why it tastes better. So give your family Dairy Singles and get a great big grin.

11. Beauty Builds a Better Bed.

12. Taste tests prove it! Solo is the best tasting among all national brands.

13. No other fruit drink has the great taste of all natural Super Fruit. It's the only one.

14. Created for the pleasure of sun-lovers and performance-lovers alike, the 500 convertible is, first and foremost, a luxury car. Second, it is a truly integrated convertible—unlike some other models.

15. It's indeed a rare sensation to drive the Jazzy MT-5. It rides like the wind. You feel a part of the car, as you feel the amazing custom engineering. Jazzy: It's a special treat.

SECTION 8–4
ADVERTISING WITH SIGHTS AND SOUNDS

Zelda is known to advertisers as a "grazer." She uses the remote control device with her cable television set to graze her way through a dozen other channels while the commercial break is showing on the channel she was watching. If she sees anything particularly interesting she may stop and watch a new program.

Zelda also uses her VCR to record a lot of the programs she really wants to watch because when she plays the tape, she can speed through the commercials without having to watch them at normal speed. If she does watch a program when it is aired, the commercial break may be the time she chooses to fix a snack for herself or carry out the garbage.

Advertisers have to be especially clever and creative to make a commercial that Zelda will actually watch. They are aware that many consumers now are capable of doing what Zelda does, so they spend a great deal of money studying the potential market for a product; then they create the advertising based on an appeal to that specific market.

When they finally do create the kind of commercial they think will appeal to the grazers, advertisers spend a lot more money to buy the particular air time they think their target market is most likely to be watching.

Zelda might be easier to reach on the radio, since she does drive to and from school every day with the radio on. She also listens to the radio as she dresses in the morning, and when she is helping her parents clean house or make dinner.

OBJECTIVES: In this section, we will help Zelda to:

- *examine the characteristics of advertising on radio and television*
- *compute the costs of airing commercials on television*
- *analyze demographic data about television audiences*

ADVERTISING ON RADIO

Listeners to radio are allowed to use their imagination to envision the products being advertised. Like television, radio is a fleeting medium which can provide the listener with a few details and no permanent record of what has been said. Unlike television, however, radio is very portable, and can be a welcome friend while the listener is engaged in a variety of other activities. You can listen to the radio while driving, jogging, mowing the lawn, shaving, attending sporting events, or walking the dog.

266

Radio is a **timely medium**, which means it can react quickly to changes in the news, and it can give current price information. Advertisers who wish to remind their potential customers about a product as close as possible to the time they make a purchase will be interested in the following results of a study by the Radio Advertising Bureau.

The percents show the portion of the audience reached by each medium within one hour of their day's largest purchase:

Radio	51%
Television	16%
Newspapers	9%
Magazines	6%

As a part of the same study, figures were given to show the time elapsed between exposure to each medium and the day's largest purchase. Again, radio led with one hour and 57 minutes, followed by television with 3 hours and 24 minutes, then newspapers, 3 hours and 42 minutes, and magazines, 4 hours. Omitted from the study were posters—a medium considered very effective in reaching customers close to the time of purchase.

ADVERTISING ON TELEVISION

Television is an intrusive medium. Advertising on television intrudes its way into our homes practically uninvited, and it is a popular medium to advertisers for that very reason. Television advertising is very expensive, however, since producing a television commercial is like producing a very short movie—the actors, script, theme, set, music, direction, and filming all can cost large sums of money.

The advertiser must also purchase the air time, the price for which is determined by the number of people watching a particular program. An advertiser might well spend as much as $1 million to show a 30-second spot four or five times during the Super Bowl, or as little as a few thousand dollars for the same number of showings during Sunday morning news broadcasts. The more people who are watching a program, the higher the rates for advertising during that program. Only companies with fairly large advertising budgets can afford nationwide commercial television advertising.

BUYING COMMERCIAL TIME

As an advertising medium, television is unique. It is the only medium to deliver sights and sounds, instantaneously. It reaches high numbers of people at one time. It can be used to reach local, regional, and national audiences. And, because of its broad reach, it is very expensive. A company has to plan its use of television time very carefully in order to make the best use of its advertising money.

Television commercials come in several lengths—all the way from 10-second IDs (so-named because they accompany the station identification breaks) to 120-seconds or a full two minutes. The 60-second commercial used to be the standard. High costs caused advertisers to start buying 30-second **spots**—as commercial message slots are called—and an interesting thing happened. They found that, in fact, the 30-second spot was more effective than the 60-second one. The audience apparently learns as much in the shorter time and does not get more information than it can absorb. Advertisers of extremely popular brands are increasingly choosing 15-second commercials, again because of the high cost of television time. Their brands are so recognizable that it takes only 15-seconds to get their message across to the people.

The actual cost of a spot depends on many factors. As you might guess, the advertising time on a very popular television show is more expensive than on a less popular one. In general, **primetime** (Monday–Saturday 8:00–11:00 P.M. Sunday 7:00–11:00 P.M.) is more expensive than daytime or late-night. Certain times of the year more people are viewing television, and bargains can be found in the off seasons. January and February are heavy viewing months, July and August light months. Finally, if you are willing to accept any slot that has not been purchased by another advertiser, you will often pay less for it. If you can condense your message into 10 seconds—only about $7\frac{1}{2}$ of them with sound—you will pay less than for longer commercials.

The television stations and advertisers engage in heavy bargaining before agreeing on the final price for commercial time. During the negotiations, the station may promise to deliver a certain size audience or an audience with certain demographics. If the audience turns out not to be as promised, the station compensates the advertiser with free commercial time or with a credit. An advertiser usually buys a number of spots at one time, so as to strike a deal on the whole package. The package is usually made up of some less popular times along with some prestigious ones.

ANALYZING THE AUDIENCE

Television stations typically carry 6 minutes of commercials per hour during primetime, 12 minutes per hour during the day. With the typical commercial now 30 seconds long, this means a greater number of commercials in any one break. Advertisers worry that their message will not stand out among all the other ads, announcements, and station and network promotions. This effect is called **clutter**. One thing advertisers do to counteract clutter is to aim their messages at audiences that are most likely to respond. A desirable audience may already be disposed to like their products, may have a greater need for their products, or may have a large amount of disposable income.

Television shows are compared by means of ratings. A **rating point** is 1% of all television households or persons tuned to a station or network at a given time. If a particular show has a 10% rating, that means 10% of those watching television at that time were watching that show. Typical ratings during primetime are around 18%, high ratings are around 30%, and the very highest historically are about 50%—for the SuperBowl.

How do the stations know how many people are watching? They learn not only how many people but who they are—in demographic terms—from rating services. These services use several methods to collect their data. The first is an electronic recorder that indicates whether a set is turned on and where it is tuned. To get more information about the people watching, rating companies typically rely on diaries. These are records kept by family members. They are asked to record when they come into the room and when they leave. This gives the rating companies very specific information about the people their programs and advertisers are reaching.

The more detailed their information, the better for those potential advertisers who have specific target markets in mind. The families selected to participate in the rating system are chosen very carefully. They are selected on the basis of their demographic characteristics so that they reflect the tastes of the population as a whole.

To the costs of air time, advertisers must add the cost of making the commercials they will air. The most expensive may cost over $200,000. The least expensive, perhaps $5,000. Primetime commercials typically are more elaborate and cost more to make than those run during the daytime or late at night.

How do companies determine how much they can afford to spend? One measure they use is their cost per 1000 audience members. They look at the numbers predicted to be in the audience. They determine they can afford to pay a certain amount for each 1000 reached, say $7.50. If the expected audience for a program is 2,500,000, that means the company could spend $7.50 x (2,500,000 ÷ 1000) or $18,750 for a commercial to air on that program. If they cannot make and air a commercial for that amount, they could consider placing the commercial on a show that draws more viewers or increasing the amount they are willing to spend to reach each 1000 viewers. Of course, many companies in this position opt for radio or newspaper advertising instead.

JUDGING THE RESULTS

Television advertising would not be so expensive if it were not effective. But advertisers are always seeking feedback about how effective their commercials are. Historically such data has been hard to obtain. How do you know when a person's mind has been changed? Traditionally researchers have used audience surveys to get this information. They interviewed people who had seen the commercials during their usual television viewing, or they set up special screenings of commercials and invited an audience in. They asked about likeability, communication, recall, and the effect on attitudes.

Now there is a promising means of obtaining direct feedback from the point of sale. Scanners that are connected to terminals at the checkout counters of retail and grocery stores collect sales data automatically. Then researchers study the data to see whether the currently running ads have had the desirable effect. Their statistics tell them to what extent the audience has been influenced to buy the advertised product.

Ask Yourself

1. What makes television unique as an advertising medium?

2. What are two of the reasons for the popularity of the 30-second spot?

3. What is meant by primetime?

SHARPEN YOUR SKILLS

_____ Skill 1 _____

Following are figures for a television advertising campaign for fruit juice.

Commercial		Times Aired			Audience Size
Juice Pack	M	12:30p	8:30p	11:30p	100,000
	T	7:15a	9:15p	11:45p	129,000
	W	12:30p	8:30p	11:30p	140,000
	Th	7:15a	9:15p	11:45p	195,000
	F	12:30p	8:30p	11:30p	165,000
	S	7:15a	9:15p	11:45p	76,000
	Su	10:00a	3:30p	9:30p	53,000

Cost to make commercial: $35,000
Cost for 1 week air time: $15,000
Planned length of campaign: 10 weeks

Question   How much did the advertiser pay per 1000 people in the audience?

Solution   Find the total number of people in the audience that week by adding the audience size column. It comes to 858,000.

Divide the cost of producing the commercial by the number of weeks it will run.

$35,000 ÷ 10 = $3,500

Add together the costs of making and airing the commercial for one week.

$ 3,500
  15,000
$18,500

Divide the total audience by 1000.

698,000 ÷ 1000 = 698

Divide the cost of making and running the commercial for the week by the number of 1000s reached.

$$\frac{\$18,500}{698} = \$26.50$$

The advertiser paid $26.50 for every 1000 people reached.

_____ Skill 2 _____

Following are the local demographics for the several shows on which the Juice Pack advertisers are considering advertising.

Program	Program A	Program B	Program C
Women			
Total 18+	108,000	54,000	330,000
18–24	11,000	25,000	88,000
25–34	26,000	17,000	98,000
35–49	32,000	9,000	78,000
50–75	39,000	3,000	64,000
Men			
Total 18+	88,000	86,000	225,000
18–24	7,900	29,000	69,000
25–34	21,000	24,000	78,000
35–49	25,000	16,000	47,000
50–75	35,000	17,000	31,000
Teens			
12–17	8,000	6,000	24,000
Children			
2–5	200	120	3,000
6–11	1,200	2,000	8,000

Questions

1. How many women watch Program B?

2. How many children under 11 watch Program C?

3. Which program seems to appeal more to men than to women?

4. Which program is more popular with older adults than with younger?

5. If the Juice Pack company wanted to reach teenagers, which program would give them the largest audience of teens?

6. If they wanted to reach parents of young children, which show or shows would most likely work?

7. What do you think would be a good mix of spots to buy to sell the Juice Pack?

Solutions

1. 5400

2. 11,000

3. Program B

4. Program A

5. Program C

6. Programs B and C would be strongest

7. One possibility would be to try to reach children who then might convince their parents to buy the juice. Or you might aim directly for the adults either as consumers or as buyers.

EXERCISE YOUR SKILLS

1. How do advertisers and television stations typically arrive at a cost for spots?

2. Why is clutter a problem?

3. How are rating points calculated?

_____ Activity 1 _____

Following are the costs to make and air a nail polish commercial.

Cost to make commercial: $12,000
Cost for 1 week air time: $989.00
Planned length of campaign: 15 weeks

The commercial was aired on the following schedule.

	Audience Size		
Day	**Men**	**Women**	**Children**
M	60,000	29,000	17,000
T	25,000	59,000	20,000
W	39,000	16,000	12,000
Th	48,000	10,000	8,000
F	70,000	8,000	4,000
S	12,000	28,000	11,000
Su	32,000	24,000	30,000
Totals:			
Cost per 1000 viewers:			

1. How many people did the advertiser reach each day?

2. How much did the advertiser pay to reach each 1000 women?

3. How much did the advertiser pay to reach each 1000 men?

4. How much did the advertiser pay to reach each 1000 in the entire week?

5. Would you consider the money spent on reaching the men a waste? Why or why not?

_____ **Activity 2** _____

Program	Program X	Program Y	Program Z
Women			
Total 18+	310,000	248,000	85,000
18–24	111,000	45,000	4,000
25–34	67,000	57,000	12,000
35–49	43,000	62,000	15,000
50–75	89,000	84,000	54,000
Men			
Total 18+	346,000	218,000	87,000
18–24	123,900	35,000	9,000
25–34	89,000	45,000	8,000
35–49	36,000	65,000	13,000
50–75	98,000	73,000	56,000
Teens			
12–17	12,000	9,000	4,000
Children			
2–5	300	180	500
6–11	600	120	900

1. Which show is watched by more children between the ages of 2 and 5 than between 6 and 11?

2. Which show is watched by more women than men?

3. Which show attracts mostly viewers over 50?

4. With regard to these 3 shows, do teenagers show the same viewing behavior as their parents or do they differ?

5. On which show or shows would you advertise baby food?

6. On which show would you advertise property in a retirement community?

7. If you believed that adults between the ages of 35 and 49 were earning the highest incomes, which program would you use to reach them?

EXTEND YOUR UNDERSTANDING
PROJECT 8–1: CLASSIFYING ADVERTISING TECHNIQUES

This project is designed to help you identify advertising techniques that you find in ads and commercials from various sources. Work with a group of your classmates to complete the project in order to study a large number of different kinds of ads.

Assignment

1. Collect 25 to 30 ads from magazines, newspapers, direct mail, or other printed materials.

2. Tape record the commercials on your favorite radio station for several hours. (If several people do this, you can cover a whole day.)

3. Videotape the commercials on your favorite TV channel for several hours.

4. Work with your group to classify each commercial into one of the 12 advertising techniques discussed in the chapter.

5. Make a summary sheet to organize your findings as to which techniques were used on radio, on television, and in printed material.

6. Draw some conclusions from your findings such as how different techniques are used for programs that attract different audiences, what times of the day different techniques are used, what reasons you can think of for this, and so on.

Share your ads and your conclusions with the other groups in your class. Did their findings agree with yours? Why do you think this might be so?

PROJECT 8–2: COST OF ADVERTISING ON TELEVISION

This project is designed to help you find out how costs of television advertising are determined. Work with a group of your classmates to complete the activity.

The prices of television advertising depend on the ratings of the shows on which the commercials appear. Use reference books or contact a television station in your area to find out how the costs are calculated.

Assignment

1. Calculate the cost of a 30-second and a 60-second spot on some of the top shows.

2. Watch some of the shows to determine which advertisers have commercials on these shows.

What conclusions about these advertisers can you draw from their willingness to spend this amount of money on advertising?

Extension

1. Write a television commercial for either a real product or a made-up product.

2. Present the commercial to your class.

3. If possible, videotape the commercial and watch it on television.

4. Which of the advertising techniques discussed in the chapter did you use in your commercial? Who was your target group?

CHAPTER 8 KEY TERMS

Section 8–1

advertising
brand

Section 8–2

target market
demographics

Section 8–3

bait and switch
business-to-business advertising
direct mail
direct response
unfinished claim
weasel words

Section 8–4

clutter
primetime
rating point
timely medium

CHAPTER 8 REVIEW

1. Do you consider advertising to be an asset or a detriment to your life?

2. What kinds of advertisements and commercials do you enjoy, if any? Are you ever persuaded to buy things you do not really need by these ads?

3. What products might you expect to be advertised using Join the Crowd messages?

4. To what groups of people might Scientific or Statistical, or Healthy or Nutritious, messages be targeted?

5. What do you think should be done about deceptive advertising practices that are not against federal regulations?

6. If you were an advertiser, from which television networks would you prefer to buy advertising spots? Why?

7. **a.** If the amount spent on advertising for one year was $75.8 billion, and 23.5% was spent on television ads, how much money was spent on television ads?

   b. If 27.6% was spent on newspaper ads, how much money was spent on newspaper ads?

c. If the following year $500,000 more was spent on television ads, what was the percent of increase?

Following are the local demographics for two shows on which Arctic Toothpaste is going to advertise.

	Program A	Program B
Women		
Total 18+	159,000	105,000
18–24	14,000	14,000
25–34	26,000	52,000
35–49	39,000	22,000
50–75	80,000	17,000
Men		
Total 18+	141,000	195,000
18–24	9,000	32,000
25–34	21,000	88,000
35–49	35,000	39,000
50–75	76,000	36,000

8. Which program has more appeal for women?

9. Which program has more appeal for men?

10. What percent of total women watching Program A is between 18 and 24?

11. What percent of total men watching Program B is between 35 and 49?

12. What is the total number of adult viewers of Program A?

13. What is the total number of viewers between 35 and 49 watching Program A?

14. If Arctic Toothpaste decided to launch a new denture toothpaste, which program would give more viewers between 50 and 75?

15. Which program would you expect to be watched by more boys under 18 — Program A or B?

16. In general, are the viewing patterns of men and women more similar on Program A or B?

1. How do its proponents defend advertising?

2. Why do manufacturers continue to advertise established products?

3. What is deceptive about Unfinished Claims?

4. Why are advertisers better able to target their audience on cable television than on other television networks?

5. What message is carried by ads that say Remember Me?

6. How would you classify the following advertising message? "One of a Kind! No other diamond ring has this design!"

7. **a.** If the amount spent on advertising for one year was $68.9 billion, and 21.4% was spent for cable television ads, how much money was spent on cable television advertising?

   b. If during the following year $760,000 more was spent on cable television advertising, what was the percent of increase?

Following are figures for a television advertising campaign for Aloft Airlines. They are reviewing their costs and have to decide how to change their schedule of commercials to get better results.

Commercial	Times Aired	Total Audience
Aloft Airlines	M 6:00a, 7:00p	216,000
	T 12:30p, 11:30p	149,000
	W 6:00a, 7:00p	176,000
	Th 12:30p, 11:30p	134,000
	F 6:00a, 7:00p	164,000
	S 9:00a, 9:30p	274,000
	Su 11:00a, 6:00p	315,000

8. What is their largest weekday audience?

9. How much did the advertisers pay per 1000 viewers on Sunday if their cost to produce the commercial was $200,000, it will run for 10 days, and it cost them $7000 for airtime that day?

10. How much did the advertisers pay per 1000 viewers on Friday if their production costs were the same as in Problem 2 and their airtime cost $2500?

11. If all costs are the same Monday and Wednesday, which is the better day for Aloft Airlines to advertise?

12. Do you think that if they changed their commercial times on Tuesdays and Thursdays to the hours they have Monday, Wednesday, and Friday they would reach more viewers or fewer? Why?

CUMULATIVE REVIEW

1. You earned $165.00. Your income tax withholding is $21 and your social security withholding is 7.65%. Find your take-home pay.

2. You sold a house for $185,000. You earn 5% commission on the first $100,000 and 6% commission on any amount over $100,000. How much commission did you earn?

3. The bank charges $0.025 for the first 20 checks and $0.0825 for each check over 20. What are the charges for 35 checks in a month?

4. Your fixed costs for your business are $325.50 per week. The variable costs are $7.10 per item. What is the cost if you produce 120 items in one week? What would the profit or loss be if each item sold for $9.95?

5. You borrowed $13,500 for 5 years. You pay $359 per month. What is the deferred payment price? How much interest did you pay?

6. You have a choice of paying $487.50 a month for 4 years or $375 a month for 6 years for a $19,500 loan. How much will you save if you pay the loan off in 4 years?

7. For an all-purpose credit account, set up a chart to show the first 6 monthly payments and find the total interest paid over 6 months at 1.5% interest per month. The balance is $825 and you make monthly payments (rounded to the nearest dollar) of 10% of the amount owed. During the second month, you make an additional purchase of $145.

8. Find the total financed price, the total interest, and the dealer's profit for each car sale plan if the car price is $10,500.

	Plan A	Plan B
Rebate	$500	none
Loan Amount		
Time of Loan	48 months	48 months
Monthly Payment	$276.25	$292.50
Total Financed Price		
Total Interest		
Dealer's Profit		

9. **a.** If the amount spent on advertising for one year was $72.6 billion, and 26.2% was spent on newspaper ads, how much money was spent on newspaper ads?

   b. If during the following year $650,000 more was spent on newspaper ads, what was the percent of increase?

CHAPTER **9**

INVESTMENTS IN STOCKS AND BONDS

Wall Street is more than a place; for many of us Wall Street embodies wealth. It is an arena in which millions of dollars circulate daily. Portions of companies, even whole companies, are bought and sold to other companies and to wealthy investors, and the money flashes by as numbers on computer screens.

Many companies, however, are owned by thousands of stockholders, so the opportunity for stock ownership is available to the smaller, wage-earning investor. Companies which listed over 100,000 stockholders in 1990 include Westinghouse, Atlantic Richfield, Eastman Kodak, Texaco, Chrysler, Occidental Petroleum, Mobil, Ford, Sears, and Southwestern Bell, to name a few.

So much money circulating will be tempting to unscrupulous deal makers. They will try to take advantage of others who view participation in the action on Wall Street as a chance to get rich. That much money also tempts the amateur investor to try to anticipate what will happen to prices of certain stocks in the future. If the investor guesses well, the stocks he or she buys will increase in value and can be sold for a profit.

Four of our high-school students, Jeff, Maria, Nelson, and Olivia whom we have already met in earlier chapters, will investigate various aspects of stock investments.

Included in their study will be the differences among stocks, bonds, and mutual funds, and some of the consequences of speculating. They will examine some of the ways to avoid risky investment schemes and some of the factors that affect stock prices.

SECTION 9–1
STOCKING UP

Jeff owns some stock that his grandfather bought for him when he was three years old. Granddad retired seven years ago from a large aerospace engineering firm that offered stock ownership as part of the employee benefit plan. Granddad had also been able to buy some of the shares for Jeff, as a way of saving towards Jeff's college costs.

Jeff didn't know much about stock when Granddad gave him the stock certificates when he was 16, but now that the time is approaching for him to go to college, he has been more interested in what the certificates mean and in what they are worth. Jeff has received regular checks from the company four times a year ever since he has owned the stock. Now that he has his own checking account, he keeps these funds there. Dad says the payments are dividend checks, and though the amounts have varied over the years, the accumulation is quite impressive to Jeff.

Jeff's parents have bought a $50 U.S. savings bond for Jeff every month since he was five years old, but Jeff is still unsure that these investments will be worth enough, considering the high price of college. Will he need to continue working this summer doing tutoring in algebra? Should he find a job that pays more? Or, should he cash in the bonds and invest the money in mutual funds? His father owns some shares in a mutual fund that he buys through an employee benefit plan. Every Sunday he carefully reads the business section of the newspaper and the five issues of *The Wall Street Journal* that have come during the week. Dad says he is more than willing to let the mutual fund manage his investments. The daily and weekly changes in the business world are so varied and complex that only a computer system and constant attention could keep track of them all. Dad says no thanks, he will take his roller coaster rides at the amusement park instead. Jeff will try to discover why investing in the stock and bond market might be compared to a ride on a roller coaster.

OBJECTIVES: In this section, we will help Jeff to:

- *examine several types of investments, including stocks, bonds, and mutual funds*
- *calculate the number of shares an investor can buy at a specified price*
- *read newspaper stock trading listings*

STOCKS

Jeff's shares of stock represent ownership in the company. Such a company, a business made up of a number of owners, is called a **corporation**. When Granddad bought stock in the corporation, he was buying a share in the ownership. If the corporation is successful, he will take part in its success through **dividends** (the part of the profits of a corporation that each stockholder receives). The dividends from Granddad's company have been issued four times a year.

Granddad and Jeff could also make money on their stock through a **capital gain**, or an increase in the market value of the shares of stock. However, to make money that way, they would have to sell the stock for more than Granddad paid for it. Jeff is glad the company continues to be profitable.

On the other hand, if the corporation is not successful, it may pay no dividends, the value of the stock may decrease, and Granddad and Jeff may even lose their investment.

A corporation may have both common stock (like Jeff's) and preferred stock.

Common Stock. Owners of common stock of a corporation are entitled to participate in the earnings and in the election of a board of directors. A corporation makes no promise or guarantee that a dividend will be paid. If a corporation does not make a sufficient profit, it will not pay a dividend, since a dividend is a share of profits.

Preferred Stock. The owners of preferred stock also have a share in the ownership of a corporation. Usually they do not have a right to vote in the election of corporate directors. They do, however, receive their fixed share of profits before the common stockholders are paid any dividends.

Newspaper Stock Listings. The current prices of stocks and other information are printed in newspapers after the close of trading every day. In simplified form, the information is printed as follows:

52-Week		Stock	Div	High	Low	Last	Change
High	Low						
$35\frac{3}{4}$	$19\frac{3}{4}$	GROW	1.10	$22\frac{1}{8}$	$21\frac{5}{8}$	22	$+\frac{1}{4}$

The abbreviated name of the company is GROW. The highest and lowest prices in the previous 52 weeks (one year) are shown first. The dividend is $1.10 per share per year. Today's high and low are shown next. Then the closing cost for today and finally the change from yesterday. In this case, stock in the GROW company varied from $22\frac{1}{8}$ to $21\frac{5}{8}$, ending at 22, which was up $\frac{1}{4}$ from the day before.

BONDS

When you buy a **bond**, you lend money to either a corporation or a government. You get three things when you buy a bond: (1) the bond issuer's promise to pay back the entire amount to you; (2) a maturity date, which is

the date it may be redeemed; and (3) a promise to pay interest at a specified interest rate. For example, if you buy a "$1000 Joy 8⅛ 95" bond from Joy Motor Company, you will be paid an annual interest rate of 8⅛ percent, or $81.25 per $1000, until 1995. At the date of maturity (1995), Joy will pay back the $1000, or face value, of the bond. If you were to sell the bond before the maturity date, the chances are it would be worth less than the full face value.

Municipal bonds. These bonds are issued by states, cities, counties, school districts, and other governmental bodies to raise money for schools, hospitals, streets, and so forth. **Corporate bonds** are issued by private companies to raise money for plant expansion or other company operations.

U.S. Savings Bonds. Jeff's parents have purchased over $6000 in U.S. savings bonds for Jeff. Like many other Americans, they appreciate the payroll savings plan in which individuals buy a bond each month through a payroll deduction.

U.S. savings bonds are backed by the power of the government to tax, and the country's faith in the government to pay its debts. Although sometimes criticized for being too low, the interest rate on U.S. savings bonds is guaranteed. They are considered a secure form of savings because if they are lost, stolen, or destroyed, they will be replaced upon receipt of a valid claim.

MUTUAL FUNDS

Jeff's father's company assists its employees in buying mutual funds, as well. A **mutual fund** is a means of pooling funds with thousands of other people in order to acquire a wide variety of stocks, bonds, and other types of investments. This is particularly helpful to small investors, such as Jeff's father, who do not have enough money to **diversify** (buy a well-balanced assortment of investments) or enough knowledge to make sound stock and bond investment decisions.

When investors buy a share in a mutual fund, they are buying shares in a mutual fund company that will then purchase the different stocks, bonds, and other investments. A person who invests in mutual funds is a part owner of a company that owns many different types of **securities**. Instead of investing $1000 in one particular corporation, Jeff's father can buy $1000 worth of shares in a mutual fund, and have an interest in perhaps 100 or more different corporations.

Ask Yourself

1. What are you buying when you buy stocks?

2. What do you actually do when you buy a bond?

3. What is a mutual fund?

SHARPEN YOUR SKILLS

Skill 1

Jeff would like to know how many shares of the mutual fund he could buy if he cashed in his U.S. savings bonds. He has $2200 in bonds that are matured, and the mutual fund is selling for 33⅜ dollars per share today.

Questions   **1.** How many shares could he buy?

2. How much will the shares cost him?

Solutions   **1.** Stock prices are quoted in fractional parts of $1.00.

That means $0.25 = ¼; $0.50 = ½; and $0.75 = ¾.

To determine what ⅛, ⅜, ⅝, and ⅞ are equivalent to in cents, divide the numerator by the denominator.

⅛ = 0.125   ⅜ = 0.375   ⅝ = 0.625   ⅞ = 0.875

The price of one share of a mutual fund is 33⅜ or $33.375.

To find how many shares he can buy, divide the amount he has ($2220) by the price per share (33.375):

2200 ÷ 33.375 = 65.92

Jeff knows he cannot buy a part of a share, so he drops the decimal portion of the number.

Jeff can buy 65 shares.

2. To find how much the shares will cost, multiply the number of shares by the price per share:

65 x 33.375 = $2169.38 (rounded to the nearest penny)

Notice that the fractional portion of a cent is used in the intermediate calculations, but the result is rounded to the nearest penny.

_____ Skill 2 _____

Jeff has been reading the newspaper stock–trading listings in order to learn about how the prices of stocks are reported. Following is a partial listing for one day.

| 52-Week | | | | | | | |
High	Low	Stock	Div	High	Low	Last	Change
53¼	39½	BLK	1.25	41½	40¾	41	−¼
163	135¼	BXCO	2.00	137¼	136¾	137¼	+¾
4¾	2¼	MAL		2⅝	2½	2⅝	+⅛
12¾	7⅝	TEM	0.75	11⅛	11	11⅛	+¼

Questions

1. What was the closing price for TEM today?

2. What was the highest price at which BLK traded today?

3. How does BXCO's closing price today compare with its closing price yesterday?

4. How much did the BXCO stock fluctuate during trading today?

5. What was the closing price of BXCO yesterday?

6. What is the annual dividend per share paid by BLK?

7. Which company does not pay a dividend?

8. Which companies closed at their high prices for the day? Which did not?

9. What is the highest price for which MAL has traded in the previous 52 weeks? What is the lowest?

Solutions

1. 11⅛ (or $11.125)

2. 41½ (or $41.50)

3. Up ¾

4. 137¼ − 136¾ = ½

5. 137¼ − ¾ = 136 ½

6. $1.25

7. MAL

8. TEM, BXCO, and MAL closed at their high for the day; BLK did not.

9. 4¾ is the highest price for which MAL has traded in the previous 52 weeks; 2¼ is the lowest.

EXERCISE YOUR SKILLS

1. What is the risk involved in buying stocks?

2. Who is more likely to realize a financial gain, the owner of common stock or the owner of preferred stock? Why?

3. For what purposes might your city or town raise money by issuing municipal bonds for sale?

———— Activity 1 ————

Use the prices per share shown below to find the number of shares of stock you can afford to purchase if you have $50,000 to invest in each of the following companies. Also, find the total cost of the shares in each company. Round all money amounts to the nearest penny. Remember that you cannot purchase part of a share of stock.

Company	Price per Share	Number of Shares	Total Cost
1. Adore	6½	7692	$49,998.00
2. ATR	24⅞	_____	_____
3. ACDn	9⅛	_____	_____
4. ACDln	10¾	_____	_____
5. ACD Mn	8⅞	_____	_____
6. ACD Sc	10⅝	_____	_____
7. ACD Sp n	9	_____	_____
8. AMRE	3¼	_____	_____
9. AR Intl	4⅞	_____	_____
10. ARR	53⅝	_____	_____
11. ARO	6¼	_____	_____
12. ATA	38⅝	_____	_____
13. AVP	18⅜	_____	_____
14. ACO Lab	47¼	_____	_____
15. Apme C	9⅞	_____	_____

Activity 2

Use the following segment from a newspaper stock trading listing for one day to answer the following questions.

52-Week High	52-Week Low	Stock	Div	High	Low	Last	Change
57¾	40¾	LOL	1.42	41⅜	41	41¼	−⅛
49⅞	29⅜	LUKO	0.97	30	29⅝	29⅝	——
91⅛	67	MIMT	2.24	81¾	80¼	81¼	−¼
24	15⅝	NAJ	0.46	17¾	17⅜	17⅝	−⅛
36⅜	22	NOLT	0.64	24¼	23⅞	24¼	+¼

1. Which stock finished up for the day?
2. Which stock closed at the same price it closed at yesterday?
3. How much did NAJ fluctuate during the day today?
4. Which stock fluctuated by exactly ½ during the day?
5. What is the difference between yesterday's closing price and today's closing price for NAJ?
6. Which stock pays the highest dividend?
7. If you had 100 shares of NOLT, how much would you receive in dividends over the year?
8. By how much does LOL's closing price today differ from its high for the last 52 weeks?
9. Which stock closed today exactly 2 above its low for the last 52 weeks?

JK

7¾	5⅝	JHM LP	1.19e	19.4	5	170	6¼	6⅛	6⅛	...
30	14¼	JWP s		...	11	4243	16⅞	15⅝	16¾	+ 1
11⅛	6¾	Jackpot	.32b	4.5	13	35	7¼	7	7⅛	...
27¼	12¼	Jacobs s		...	18	120	23⅝	22⅞	23⅝	+ ⅝
14½	6½	Jakart n		...	...	59	7½	7¼	7½	...
29¼	18½	JRiver	.60	2.6	33	2113	23⅜	22¾	23⅜	+ ⅜
45⅞	32½	JRvr pf	3.37	9.3	...	223	36¼	36¼	36¼	...
46⅜	34⅛	JRvr pf	3.50	9.4	...	209	37¼	37	37⅛	− ⅛
7¾	1¾	Jamswy	.08	3.8	7	223	2¼	2⅛	2⅛	− ⅛
16¾	7⅜	JpOTC n		...	...	80	9⅛	8⅞	8⅞	− ½
45½	32½	JeffPl	1.52	4.4	8	182	35¾	34¾	34¾	− ¾
24¾	22⅛	JerC pf	2.18	9.3	...	4	23⅝	23⅝	23⅝	+ ¼
74⅛	51⅛	JohnJn	1.36	2.1	20	7949	66½	65⅜	65¾	− ½
32¼	17⅛	JohnCn	1.20	5.2	11	363	24	23⅛	23⅛	− 1⅛
30⅜	22½	Josten	.80	2.7	20	1761	30	29¾	30	+ ⅛
26	11	KLM	1.02e	8.5	8	151	12⅛	12	12	− ⅛
37¼	23⅜	K mart	1.72	6.3	16	3416	27¾	27⅛	27⅜	− ½
26½	21	KN Eng	1.12	4.5	13	108	25½	25⅛	25⅛	...
22⅛	13¾	KanPip	2.20	14.2	...	138	15⅝	15⅜	15½	+ ⅛
6¼	3⅛	Kaneb		...	...	894	4¾	4½	4½	− ⅛
36⅛	29⅛	KCtyPL	2.68	8.5	9	335	31⅜	31⅛	31⅜	+ ⅜
25¼	22¾	KCPL pf	2.20	9.2	...	6	24	24	24	+ ⅜
50¾	35½	KCSou	1.08	2.8	7	136	38¾	38	38	− 1
27	19⅝	KanGE	1.72	6.4	15	585	26⅞	26¾	26¾	− ⅛
25⅛	19¾	KansPL	1.80	8.4	10	223	21½	21¼	21½	− ⅛
27¾	14¾	Katyln		...	5	62	15¾	15½	15½	+ ½
15⅝	5⅜	KaufBH	.30	4.4	3	1448	7	6⅜	6¾	+ ¼
74	58¾	Kellogg	1.92	2.7	19	2345	72⅛	69⅞	70½	− 1⅞
25⅜	5¼	Kellwd	.80	9.1	12	385	8⅞	8⅜	8¾	+ ½
51	17⅛	Kemper	.92	4.6	58	876	20	18⅞	19⅞	+ ⅝
9⅜	6⅛	KmpHi	1.20	17.5	...	794	6⅞	6⅝	6⅞	+ ¼
9⅞	7⅝	KmplGv	.88	10.1	...	2287	8¾	8½	8¾	...
10¾	7	KmpMl	1.40	18.4	...	380	7¾	7⅝	7⅝	− ⅛
12	10⅜	KmpMu	.87	7.8	...	633	11⅛	10⅞	11⅛	+ ¼
12	10⅛	KmpStr	.90	8.4	...	276	10¾	10⅝	10¾	+ ⅛
37	24¼	Kenmt	1.16	4.3	9	585	27	26⅝	27	− ¼
14⅞	7¼	KentEl		...	12	37	10⅛	9¾	10⅛	+ ⅜
21⅜	17¼	KyUtil	1.46	6.9	10	1339	21⅛	21	21⅛	− ⅛
13⅝	4½	KerrGl	.33i	...	...	48	5¼	4⅞	4⅞	− ⅛
21	12¾	KerG pf	1.70	12.7	...	2	13⅜	13⅜	13⅜	− ⅛
53⅝	43⅜	KerrMc	.33i	...	16	1191	44⅞	44¼	44½	− ⅜
29¼	16⅞	Keycp	1.36	6.3	6	218	21⅞	21¼	21⅝	− ¼
25¾	11¼	KeyCo s		...	6	17	12¾	12⅝	12¾	− ¼
29¾	16½	KeyInt	.60	2.2	21	209	27½	26⅝	27¼	+ ½
83¼	61½	KimbCl	2.72	3.4	15	1738	80¼	79¾	80⅛	+ ⅛
9½	2⅝	KimEn s		...	19	80	3¾	3⅝	3¾	− ⅛
30	18⅛	KngWd s		...	11	591	23⅛	22¾	22⅞	...
9⅞	8¼	KBAust	1.06e	11.9	...	60	9	8⅞	8⅞	...
58⅜	37	KnghtR	1.32	3.3	12	402	40⅝	40	40	− ⅞
13½	6¼	Knogo	.30	4.3	41	213	7¼	7	7	− ⅛
25½	6½	Koger	1.00	15.1	110	955	6¾	6½	6⅝	...
14⅛	6⅛	Kolmor	.32	5.1	5	36	6⅜	6¼	6¼	− ⅛
37⅞	11⅜	Korea	1.94e	14.1	...	346	14	13¾	13¾	− ¼
17	10⅝	Kroger		...	...	915	13	12½	12⅝	+ ⅛
13⅛	8½	Kuhlm	.60	5.8	12	23	10⅝	10⅜	10⅜	− ⅛
126	72	Kyocer	.61r	.7	40	3	93¾	93¼	93¼	− 1½
14½	6¾	Kysor	.60	8.1	...	40	7½	7⅜	7⅜	− ⅛

Maria's savings account keeps growing as she continues to add to it, proving to her father that she can afford to make payments on a car. He cosigned the loan papers with Maria and they purchased a recent model small car from the rental car retail sales lot.

Maria's father told her to keep the money she had saved over the past six months, and to use it for college in the next few years. Maria has been having doubts about going to college, but she has not mentioned them to Dad yet. She is wondering if she could invest her savings in the stock market and make more money. Maria has a good friend, Clarence Jr. (called Cal), whose father has been able to study the stock market very thoroughly for a number of years and has owned thousands of shares of stock in various companies.

Clarence Sr. hasn't always done really well on the market, however. Cal still talks about October 19, 1987, known as Black Monday in business circles. The Dow Jones average dropped 508 points that day, losing 22.6% of its value, along with the value of a lot of his father's investments. Money discussions at Cal's house were so tense for the next few months that Cal used to come over to talk with Maria and her family in order to get away from the tension and to have someone sympathetic to talk with.

Finally Cal's family had sold their large home in the exclusive area of town and bought a much smaller house in another suburb farther away from the city. Clarence Sr. also sold his luxury car and bought a used one inexpensively from the car dealership. Cal gave up his vision of having his own car at 17, though some of his friends are finding a way to get their own cars.

Maria wonders how investing in stocks can cause such an upheaval in a family. She has watched some of the changes in the stock prices and thinks she could make some good choices that might make her wealthy if she had the money to invest. Maria will find out how stocks are bought and sold, and other things she will need to know if she is considering investing some of her real money in real stocks.

OBJECTIVES: In this section, we will help Maria to:

- *discover what factors must be considered before deciding to buy stock*
- *understand the process that takes place when stocks are traded*
- *calculate profit or loss from buying and selling shares of stock*

Clarence Sr. is not unlike many other businesspeople in this country who have watched their acquaintances acquire large sums of money by learning how to "play the market." Unfortunately for him, somewhere along the line his perspective changed. He crossed over the line between **investing** in stocks and **speculating**, or gambling with money his family needed to secure its financial independence.

Investing, (rather than speculating) in stable, long-term, growth stocks as an intelligent means of building up the family's savings is one way of participating in our growing economy. These investments can be a good hedge against inflation, and stocks, unlike some other forms of investment, are easy to liquidate if you need cash.

Cal's family always knew that there was some risk involved with stock ownership. Perhaps Clarence Sr. was very careful at first with his choice of stocks. Then, as those choices paid well and he was able to make bigger profits, he was swept along by the tide of his increasing fortune and he began to take bigger risks. When the market dropped so suddenly in October of 1987, some of the riskier companies lost so much of their value that he was forced to sell many of his holdings at a loss.

The line between investing safely and gambling with the mortgage money (that is, with money needed for essentials) is hard to define, and it differs in every family. As has happened to those who gamble on other events with unpredictable outcomes (horse racing, sporting events, card games, and so on) Clarence Sr. became intoxicated by the rewards. The thrill of winning became more important than the actual cash, and risking the family's financial security became easier each time.

Clarence Sr. was lucky that he could still afford to buy any house and car. He and his family have decided that he does not have the emotional temperament to handle stock investments. He would say you should consider all of the following points before you invest in stocks.

1. Be sure you can afford to lose what you risk.

2. Determine a specific investment goal.

3. Ask yourself if you have the emotional temperament suited to handling the ups and downs of investing.

4. Plan to spend time as well as money.

5. Choose an experienced, reputable broker to give you guidance and advice.

6. Do not expect too much, too soon.

7. After you have set your goals and objectives, stick to them.

8. Be aware that you buy individual stocks, not the stock market averages.

9. Have an overall family investment plan to protect you from falling into hit-or-miss investing.

THE PROCESS OF BUYING AND SELLING

If Maria decides she can fulfill all of these requirements, then she will open an account with a **broker**, that is, a salesperson who specializes in buying and selling stocks and bonds. Only brokers can trade stock, but Maria can instruct the broker when to buy or sell. Maria must pay the broker a **commission**, which in this case is a fee for services the broker performs when he or she buys or sells the stocks or bonds. Commission rates vary according to the brokerage house and the size of the trade.

Many investors purchase a hundred shares of a particular stock, which is called a **round lot**. A trade of fewer than 100 shares is called an **odd lot**. Maria will pay a higher broker commission if she buys or sells odd lots because they are less convenient.

Stocks are traded in national and regional stock exchanges. The biggest of these is the New York Stock Exchange, where over 84 percent of all listed securities are bought and sold. The American Stock Exchange is the other national exchange. The over-the-counter market is also a national network of dealers and brokers who trade among themselves by telephone, telegraph, or teletype.

Buying and selling stocks on a security exchange is carried on by means of the auction method. A stock may be offered for sale at a certain price, or someone may bid for the same stock at a different price. A sale is made when someone buys the stock at the price offered.

Maria can instruct her broker to purchase or sell shares of stock for her within a certain price range and the broker will follow her instructions. But she has been cautioned to:

- be aware of what she is risking when she buys stocks;

- follow the good advice of her broker. The broker will not be right every time, but he or she has more experience than Maria does, and can be more objective in evaluating the market in general.

Ask Yourself

1. How does investing in stocks differ from speculating?

2. What are three points you should consider before you invest in stocks?

3. Why should investors follow the good advice of their stock brokers?

SHARPEN YOUR SKILLS

_____ **Skill 1** _____

Question How much would it cost for Maria to buy 250 shares of stock at 17¾?

Solution The purchase price of one share is 17¾, or $17.75.

The total cost of the shares is the number of shares times the purchase price of each share:

$$250 \times \$17.75 = \$4437.50$$

_____ **Skill 2** _____

Question How much profit would Maria make if she bought 300 shares of stock at 23¼ and sold them at 25⅝?

Solution The total purchase price of the shares is the number of shares times the price per share:

$$300 \times \$23.25 = \$6975.00$$

The total selling price of the shares is the number of shares times the selling price per share:

$$300 \times \$25.625 = \$7687.50$$

The profit is the difference between total purchase price and total selling price:

$$\$7687.50 - 6975.00 = \$712.50$$

_____ **Skill 3** _____

Questions

1. If the purchase price of a share of stock drops from $45 to $40, what is the percent of decrease?

2. If the new price of a share of stock is $40, down 11% from the original price, what was the original price of the share?

3. If the purchase price of a share of stock increases from $45 to $60, what was the percent of increase?

4. If the new price of a share of stock is $60, which is 33⅓% higher than the original price, what was the original price of the stock?

Solutions

1. The percent of decrease is the difference between the old price and the new price, divided by the new price:

    $$\$45 - \$40 = \$5$$

    $$\frac{\$5}{\$45} = \$11\%$$

2. To find the original price of an item when it has decreased, use the following equation:

    $$\frac{\text{Decreased Value}}{100\% - \text{Percent of Change}}$$

    In this problem,

    $$100\% - 11\% = 89\%$$

    $$\frac{\$40}{89\%} = \$44.94$$

    or $45, rounded to the nearest dollar.

    The old price, therefore, was $45.

3. To find the percent of increase, subtract the new price from the old price and divide the difference of these numbers by the original price.

    $$\$60 - \$45 = \$15$$

    $$\frac{\$15}{\$45} = 33.333\%$$

4. To find the original price of an item after a percent increase, use the following formula:

    $$\frac{\text{Increased Value}}{100\% + \text{Percent of Change}}$$

    In this problem, the new or increased value is $60. The percent increase is 33⅓. Therefore,

    $$\frac{\$60}{133⅓} \ (100\% + 33⅓\%) = \$45$$

EXERCISE YOUR SKILLS

1. Why is a person's emotional temperament important when handling investments?

2. How should an investor determine how much money to invest in stocks?

3. Why might it be wiser for some people to invest in U. S. savings bonds than in stocks?

——— Activity 1 ———

Find the cost of these shares of stock at the price listed. Round your answers to the nearest penny. The first one is done for you.

1. 300 shares at 21⅛ = 300 x 21.125 = $6337.50

2. 225 shares at 63¼

3. 500 shares at 416⅜

4. 45 shares at 32½

5. 150 shares at 150

6. 40 shares at 16⅝

7. 340 shares at 42¾

8. 700 shares at 51⅞

9. 1000 shares at 73

10. 600 shares at 82⅛

11. 750 shares at 91¼

12. 820 shares at 102⅜

13. 635 shares at 121½

14. 999 shares at 34⅝

15. 345 shares at 100

——— Activity 2 ———

Fill in this chart to find the profit or loss from buying these shares at the first price and selling them at the second price.

	Company	Number of Shares	First Price	First Total	Second Price	Second Total	Difference (Pr/Loss)
1.	AP & P	306	41⅞	$12,813.75	43⅜	$13,272.75	$459 Pr
2.	Zola	215	10¼		12½		
3.	ABM	400	42½		40⅞		
4.	Lands	6000	20		23		
5.	Dr. Pop	150	29⅜		26⅜		
6.	Doledo	310	9⅞		11¼		
7.	GTC	450	117½		126		

	Company	Number of Shares	First Price	First Total	Second Price	Second Total	Difference (Pr/Loss)
8.	Binbury	55	65⅝		63¼		
9.	Elm Ind.	785	11¾		9		
10.	5-N	56	71½		75⅛		
11.	Shagly	587	10¼		12⅛		
12.	ChicaM	540	112		115½		
13.	Gensi	103	27⅜		26		
14.	ETS	1500	73		75⅝		
15.	Gengt	800	46⅝		43⅝		
16.	UPF&G	385	15¼		13		
17.	Otten	750	27		29⅞		
18.	Sprou	1000	48½		52¾		
19.	CallasW	420	62¾		61		
20.	FepDel	110	112⅛		100¾		

Note: Save your chart for the next activity.

___ **Activity 3** _____

For each of the stocks in Activity 2, calculate the percent of increase or decrease in stock price.

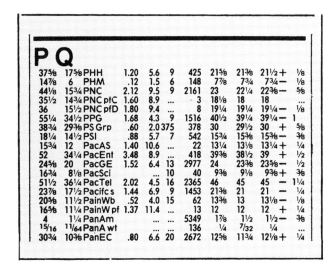

Nelson watched Maria's savings account grow while she was saving for the car. Nelson explained to Maria the effects of compound interest, and they were both intrigued by the idea that an amount of money seems to take on a life of its own and begins to grow without their having to do anything.

Nelson knows Maria is watching the stock market and thinking about the risks involved in investing real money. Nelson and Maria have spent time discussing the problem Clarence Sr. has been having since the value of his investments took such a beating on Black Monday.

Nelson and Maria worked together in economics class on a project that allowed them to simulate gambling with stock investments. They did not use real money, and they did not have to know a great deal about the companies they chose. Nelson and Maria did quite well, earning a profit of $12,650 over a six-week period, having started with $100,000 of fictitious money to invest.

Nelson and Maria understand, though, having watched what happened to Cal and his family, that investing real money is much more serious. A wise investor must not view investments as a gamble and must not be so greedy that he or she is willing to jump into any investment scheme that promises large, fast profits. If a plan seems too good to be true, it probably is.

OBJECTIVES: In this section, we will help Nelson to:

- *examine ways to avoid risky investment schemes*
- *graph changes in various company stock prices over short periods of time*
- *calculate the changes in an investor's stock holdings over a period of time*

INVESTMENT SCHEMES

Nelson has seen some of these ads in the newspapers:

"Worried about inflation? Diamonds will protect you." "Need extra money? Earn $350 weekly part-time—$750 weekly full time . . . $45,000 potential . . . operate out of your home . . . all you have to do is stuff envelopes." (In this one, they just don't tell you where the envelopes come from; in many cases, you have to entice other people to send them to you, and all it costs you to find this out is a mere $50–$75!) "Make quick money—join a pyramid club. For only $1000 you can earn $16,000."

These investment scams and many more like them are common. Unfortunately, they are hard to stamp out. Most operate on the principle that greed will overcome common sense.

After the stock market crash of 1929, Congress established the **U.S. Securities and Exchange Commission (SEC)**, a federal agency whose purpose is to correct the unsound stock selling practices and schemes that were prevalent prior to the crash. The commission has two basic responsibilities, which are:

> - To see that companies that offer securities for sale in interstate commerce (that is, in more than one state) file with the commission and make available to investors complete and accurate information;
> - To protect investors against misrepresentation and fraud in the issuance and sale of securities.

The SEC requires disclosure of facts that are essential for informed analysis, but it cannot keep us from becoming greedy and wishing to obtain fortunes with no effort. The SEC can tell us the truth about legitimate companies, but it cannot keep us from buying securities or making other investments that have little or no value.

If Nelson or Maria, or any of us, does buy into a scam and lose large sums of money, we have practically no recourse. Defrauded investors generally must use the courts to recover money. The investor's best protection is the following SEC advice.

> - Do not deal with strange security firms or salespersons. Consult your banker or other experienced people you know and trust.
> - Be sure you understand the risk of loss.
> - Tell the salesperson to put all the information in writing or to mail you a written statement.
> - Give at least as much consideration to investing as you would to buying other valuable products or property.
> - Do not speculate or play the market.
> - Do not listen to high-pressure sales talk.
> - Beware of tips, rumors, and promises of spectacular profits.

HAS THE BROKER GOT A DEAL FOR YOU?

While the great majority of brokers are very honest, you may occasionally run into a con artist who is only interested in taking your money. Be very wary of anyone who does the following:

> - Plugs one certain stock and refuses to sell you anything else.
> - Promises a quick, sure profit.
> - Claims to have inside information.
> - Urges you to hurry "before the price goes up".
> - Does not have a reputation that you can check on.

If you wind up falling for some slick operator's con game at some time during your life, take comfort from this fact: Almost everyone will get stung at least once, some of us will even get greedy twice. When you do decide to invest, try not to risk more than you can afford to lose, because you may possibly end up losing money even when you make investments thoughtfully.

Ask Yourself

1. What is the U.S. Securities and Exchange Commission?

2. What are the basic responsibilities of the U. S. Securities and Exchange Commission?

3. How might defrauded investors recover money?

SHARPEN YOUR SKILLS

——— Skill 1 ————————————————————————

Nelson has made notes on the closing price of stock in NR300, a company listed on a regional stock exchange in his area. His list of closing prices is as follows:

APR 11	39.25
APR 18	40.75
APR 25	45.125
MAY 2	41.5
MAY 9	50
MAY 16	39.75
MAY 23	48.75
MAY 30	43
JUN 6	42.375

Notice that the prices are stated in up to three decimal places. If there are no fractions of a dollar, only the whole dollar amount is shown.

Question   How can Nelson graph this price information?

Solution   Nelson put the price information on the vertical axis and the dates on the horizontal axis. He plotted the price for each date, then connected the points to make the following graph, which shows the changes in the stock's price over 8 weeks.

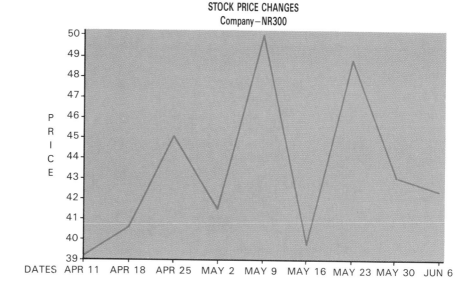

STOCK PRICE CHANGES
Company – NR300

Skill 2

Nelson plans to buy and sell shares of this and other stocks. He will need to keep track of the number of shares he owns after each trade.

Question   How many shares will Nelson own each week in the NR300 company if he makes the following trades:

1st week	Buy 250 shares
2nd week	Sell 100 shares
3rd week	Buy 125 shares
4th week	Buy 300 shares
	Sell 400 shares
5th week	Buy 175 shares
	Sell 50 shares
6th week	Buy 200 shares

Solution   The following chart will help Nelson to keep track of his holdings. Each time he buys shares he adds them to what he owns. Each time he sells shares, he subtracts them from his holdings.

Week 1			Week 2			Week 3		
Buy	Sell	Own	Buy	Sell	Own	Buy	Sell	Own
250	0	250	0	100	150	125	0	275

Week 4			Week 5			Week 6		
Buy	Sell	Own	Buy	Sell	Own	Buy	Sell	Own
300	400	175	175	50	300	200	0	500

EXERCISE YOUR SKILLS

1. Why should you beware of ads that promise unreasonable earnings or deals?

2. Why do some people lose money on investments despite the protection offered by the U.S. Securities and Exchange Commission?

3. When should you suspect that a broker may be trying to involve you in a swindle?

Activity 1

Graph the changes in stock prices shown below and on the next page. Show three stocks on each graph, using a different kind of line or color for each one.

Stock 1	Day	Graph 1	Graph 2	Graph 3	Graph 4	Graph 5
	1	6	16¼	22	3	9¼
	2	6⅜	17½	24¾	3⅜	10½
	3	7⅛	18⅛	23¼	4⅛	11⅛
	4	6¼	16½	21¼	3¼	9½
	5	7½	16	26¼	4½	9
	6	6¾	18¼	28¼	3¾	11¼
	7	6⅝	19¾	24¼	3⅝	12¾
	8	7	20	22½	4	10½
	9	7⅞	19¼	27⅝	4⅞	12¼
	10	8	17⅛	24	5	10⅛

Stock 2	Day	Graph 1	Graph 2	Graph 3	Graph 4	Graph 5
	1	6⅛	16⅝	26½	3⅛	9⅝
	2	6⅛	18½	24½	3⅝	11½
	3	7¼	17¾	22¼	4¼	10¾
	4	6½	16⅞	23½	3½	9⅞
	5	6¾	19½	26¼	3¾	12½
	6	7¾	18⅜	21½	4¾	11⅜
	7	6	19½	23¾	3	13
	8	7½	16	21	4½	9
	9	6½	17⅞	28¾	3½	10⅞
	10	6¼	19⅛	22¾	3¼	11⅛

Stock 3	1	$7\frac{1}{8}$	$17\frac{5}{8}$	$27\frac{3}{4}$	$4\frac{1}{8}$	$10\frac{5}{8}$
	2	$7\frac{3}{8}$	$19\frac{1}{2}$	$26\frac{3}{4}$	$4\frac{3}{8}$	$12\frac{1}{2}$
	3	$7\frac{3}{4}$	$16\frac{3}{4}$	23	$4\frac{3}{4}$	$9\frac{3}{4}$
	4	$7\frac{5}{8}$	$18\frac{1}{2}$	29	$4\frac{5}{8}$	$11\frac{1}{2}$
	5	8	$17\frac{3}{8}$	$21\frac{3}{4}$	5	$10\frac{3}{8}$
	6	6	$16\frac{1}{8}$	25	3	$9\frac{1}{8}$
	7	$6\frac{7}{8}$	$18\frac{3}{4}$	$28\frac{1}{4}$	$3\frac{3}{8}$	$11\frac{3}{4}$
	8	$6\frac{1}{8}$	$17\frac{1}{4}$	$27\frac{1}{4}$	$3\frac{1}{8}$	$10\frac{1}{4}$
	9	$6\frac{1}{4}$	$18\frac{7}{8}$	$25\frac{1}{2}$	$3\frac{1}{4}$	$11\frac{1}{8}$
	10	$7\frac{3}{4}$	$16\frac{3}{8}$	$27\frac{1}{2}$	$4\frac{3}{4}$	$9\frac{3}{8}$

——— Activity 2 ———

Use the information below to fill out a weekly chart showing the number of shares bought and sold in each company and how many shares are owned at the end of each week. Companies may be traded more than once in a week.

Week 1:   Feb 1 – 5
Week 2:   Feb 8 – 12
Week 3:   Feb 15 – 19
Week 4:   Feb 22 – 26
Week 5:   Mar 1 – Mar 5
Week 6:   Mar 7 – Mar 11

		Date	**Buy or Sell**	**Company**	**Number of Shares**	**Own**
Week 1	**a.**	2/1	B	AP & P	350	350
	b.	2/1	B	Zoca Zl	200	200
	c.	2/1	B	Graft	160	160
	d.	2/1	B	Gepsi	300	300
	e.	2/2	B	Cara Lou	500	500
	f.	2/2	B	Zola	1,000	1,000
	g.	2/2	B	Elmland	30,000	30,000
	h.	2/3	B	Disnel	450	450
	i.	2/3	B	ADK	50	50
	j.	2/4	B	Parity	196	196

	Date	Buy or Sell	Company	Number of Shares	Own
Week 2 a.	2/8	B	AP & P	275	_____
b.	2/8	B	Zoca Zl	400	_____
c.	2/9	B	Graft	300	_____
d.	2/9	B	Gepsi	160	_____
e.	2/10	B	Cara Lou	450	_____
f.	2/10	B	Zola	50	_____
g.	2/11	B	Elmland	2,000	_____
h.	2/11	B	Disnel	196	_____
i.	2/12	B	ADK	250	_____
j.	2/12	B	Parity	112	_____
Week 3 a.	2/16	S	AP & P	300	_____
b.	2/16	S	Zoca Zl	295	_____
c.	2/16	S	Graft	240	_____
d.	2/17	S	Gepsi	160	_____
e.	2/17	S	Cara Lou	250	_____
f.	2/18	S	Zola	480	_____
g.	2/18	S	Elmland	10,000	_____
h.	2/19	S	Disnel	280	_____
i.	2/19	S	ADK	100	_____
j.	2/19	S	Parity	120	_____
Week 4 a.	2/22	B	AP & P	250	_____
b.	2/22	S	Zoca Zl	200	_____
c.	2/23	B	Graft	250	_____
d.	2/23	S	Gepsi	150	_____
e.	2/24	B	Cara Lou	120	_____
f.	2/24	S	Zola	300	_____
g.	2/25	B	Elmland	180	_____
h.	2/25	S	Disnel	120	_____
i.	2/26	B	ADK	200	_____
j.	2/26	S	Parity	50	_____

		Date	Buy or Sell	Company	Number of Shares	Own
Week 5	a.	3/1	B	AP & P	700	_____
	b.	3/1	B	Zoca Zl	120	_____
	c.	3/1	B	Graft	200	_____
	d.	3/2	B	Gepsi	650	_____
	e.	3/2	S	Cara Lou	620	_____
	f.	3/2	S	Zola	150	_____
	g.	3/2	S	Elmland	14,500	_____
	h.	3/3	S	Disnel	50	_____
	i.	3/3	B	ADK	120	_____
	j.	3/3	B	Parity	400	_____
Week 6	a.	3/7	B	AP & P	295	_____
	b.	3/7	B	Zoca Zl	400	_____
	c.	3/7	S	Graft	120	_____
	d.	3/8	S	Gepsi	250	_____
	e.	3/8	B	Cara Lou	180	_____
	f.	3/8	B	Zola	450	_____
	g.	3/8	S	Elmland	7,000	_____
	h.	3/9	S	Disnel	190	_____
	i.	3/9	B	ADK	190	_____
	j.	3/9	B	Parity	370	_____
	k.	3/10	S	AP & P	385	_____
	l.	3/10	S	Zoca Zl	95	_____
	m.	3/10	B	Graft	275	_____
	n.	3/11	B	Gepsi	125	_____
	o.	3/11	S	Cara Lou	100	_____
	p.	3/11	S	Zola	280	_____
	q.	3/11	B	Elmland	5,000	_____
	r.	3/11	S	Disnel	25	_____

STOCK PRICES AND INFLATION

Olivia and Patricia were partners in the economics class stock market competition. The stocks they chose did not do as well as Nelson and Maria's, possibly because Olivia and Patricia were not quite as willing to gamble large sums of money. Olivia and Patricia did take the time to keep track of the prices of some of the stocks for a while before they chose which ones they would buy.

One of the newspapers they read discussed the "bear market" conditions that were continuing, and Olivia was not sure what bears had to do with stock prices going down. Nelson and Maria had discovered that not all the stocks go down at the same time.

Olivia also remembers from her study of the Federal Reserve System that the economy in the United States is affected by inflation. Though the rates of inflation have varied from year to year, Olivia knows from her study of history that fairly steady inflation has affected salaries and prices for a number of years. One means of measuring the effects of this inflation is the Consumer Price Index.

Olivia has often heard her parents speak of nickel postage stamps and the 10-cent newspapers as though their childhood was not that long ago. To Olivia, 35 years might as well be a hundred, but she does know that most adults talk that way. She decides that when she is an adult, she will remember what she thought when she was a teenager, and not tell her children about how low prices were when she was a kid.

OBJECTIVES: In this section, we will help Olivia to:

- *examine what causes stock prices to change*
- *understand the effects of inflation as charted by the Consumer Price Index*
- *use the CPI to calculate changes in prices of products*

BULL AND BEAR MARKETS

Since Olivia has been reading the business section of the newspaper, she has noticed the writers refer to bull and bear markets as though bulls and bears had something to do with stock prices. After extensive research, she has finally discovered the connection, probably created by some clever broker 100 years ago and passed along by other clever brokers through the years. In

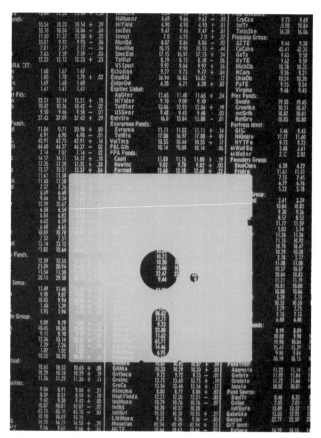

a **bear market** stock prices are going down; in a **bull market** prices are going up.

The reason the term bull is linked with an uplift in prices is probably the tendency of a bull to lift and throw up an object with its horns. The bear is generally more cautious, trying to knock its opponent down.

WHAT CAUSES STOCK PRICES TO CHANGE?

Olivia's discovery of fighting bulls and bears was intriguing, but she realized the bull and the bear are only reflections of trends. What Olivia would really like to know is how to predict today which stock prices will be higher tomorrow. Why do the prices change at all? Recall that stocks are sold by the auction method: If no one really wants a stock, the selling price will be low; if lots of people want it, they can out bid each other and drive the price up. The value of a share of stock at any given moment is exactly equal to what someone else is willing to pay for it.

Olivia knows that to become wealthy with stock investments, she must sell her stocks at higher prices than she paid for them. She also knows that the investors who have become wealthy have been especially well informed about which companies will continue to grow, expand, and become profitable. Other investors will want to buy stocks in companies they believe will make money.

Some investors are even able to predict what factors will affect the volatile prices of stocks in general; those who knew what to trade before Black Monday (October 19, 1987) might even have made money while others were losing it. However, Olivia and Patricia, and many of the rest of us, are not that good at predicting the future. In fact, in recent years, some stock brokers who have helped create the future of stock prices have been convicted of illegal **insider trading**, that is, they made their trading decisions with the benefit of information that should only have been known within the companies themselves.

There are probably as many ways of studying the stock market and trying to predict the future as there are people investing in it. People look at patterns and trends in the market, the political situation and state of the economy, and most importantly, the companies themselves. Serious investors believe in the company, know as much as possible about its future plans, and can give the investment a chance to grow along with the company.

THE CONSUMER PRICE INDEX

Inflation affects the cost of every product and service we purchase because, in effect, it cheapens the value of a dollar bill. While it is also true that in many jobs, salaries have also increased, we may be making more money now than we were 10 years ago and still not be able to buy as much.

Olivia's understanding of inflation from her study of the Federal Reserve System helped her to realize why her aunt's $20 birthday check does not buy as much as it used to. She had thought that her new clothes just cost more than the children's clothes she used to buy. This may be true, but because of inflation, children's clothes would probably cost more now as well.

The **Consumer Price Index (CPI)** is an economic yardstick that can help Olivia to judge the changes in the buying power of the dollar. Economists use the CPI to measure **inflation** (a general increase in prices) or **deflation** (a general decrease in prices).

The Bureau of Labor Statistics (BLS) compiles and publishes two CPIs. The CPI-W (wage-earners and clerical workers) represents the experience of urban wage-earners and clerical workers and includes approximately 40% of the population. The CPI-U is a broader index that covers about 80% of the population. The CPI-U (for all urban consumers) includes such diverse groups as salaried workers, the unemployed, the retired, and the self-employed. The BLS checks prices of a **market basket** of goods and services throughout the country. The market basket of some 400 items includes everyday purchases such as housing, clothing, and professional services (health care, entertainment, and recreation).

The CPI measures the changes in the cost of the same market basket of goods and services over time.

The following chart shows the breakdown of the CPI for all urban consumers in various categories.

CONSUMER PRICE INDEX FOR ALL URBAN CONSUMERS 1984 = 100		
Group	**March 1989**	**March 1988**
All items	122.3	116.5
Food	123.5	115.9
Apparel and upkeep	119.3	114.3
Men's and boys' apparel	115.9	111.6
Women's and girls' apparel	119.4	115.3
Footwear	114.1	107.3
Housing, total	121.5	117.0
Rent	138.6	132.9
Gas and electricity	104.8	101.7
Fuel oil, coal, bottled gas	81.5	80.5
House operation	110.5	108.3
House furnishings	105.1	104.7
Transportation	111.9	106.5
Medical care	146.1	136.3
Personal care	123.6	118.1
Entertainment	124.7	119.0
Personal and educational expenses	154.6	145.0

Source: The 1990 Information Please Almanac

Notice the "1984 = 100" at the top of the chart. This is a revision of the earlier CPI which used 1967 as its base year. The chart illustrates that the market basket of items that cost $100 in 1984 cost the higher amounts shown in 1988 and 1989. Looking at all the items together, they cost $122.30 in March of 1989 and $116.50 in March of 1988.

Olivia has made this graph of the changes in the CPI from 1984 through 1989.

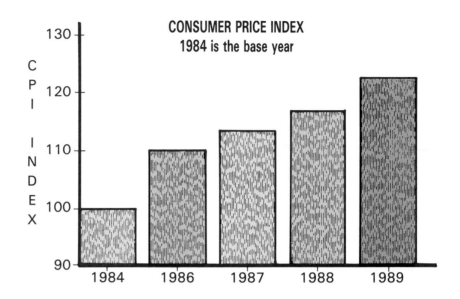

1. What is a bear market?

2. What is a bull market?

3. What determines the price of stocks?

4. What is the Consumer Price Index?

SHARPEN YOUR SKILLS

_____ Skill 1 _____

Olivia's mother has flown to Sacramento several times in the past 10 years to visit her sister. Each time she has paid more for her airline ticket. To determine if her airline ticket prices increased at the same rate as the CPI, Olivia will do some calculations for us.

Question   If the ticket in 1989 cost $450, how much should it have cost in 1984?

Solution   Refer to the Consumer Price Index for all urban consumers in Section 4. This question can be answered in two different ways (by using the all-items line of the CPI chart or the transportation line) which yield different results.

1. Using the all-items line—

   The all-items line was $122.30 in 1989.

   First, divide $450.00 by the CPI amount:

   $450 \div 122.30 = 3.6795$ rounded to 4 decimal places

   Next, multiply the result by $100:

   $3.6795 \times \$100 = \$367.95$

   In March 1989, this ticket should have cost $367.95.

2. Using the transportation line—

   The transportation line was $111.90 in 1989.

   First, divide $450.00 by the CPI:

   $450 \div 111.90 = 4.0214$ rounded to 4 decimal places

   Next, multiply the result by $100:

   $4.0214 \times \$100 = \$402.14$

   In March 1984, this ticket should have cost $402.14. Clearly it makes a difference which figure you use from the CPI. In general, the closer you can get to the specific item, the more accurate the results will be.

Question   If an airplane ticket cost $300 in 1984, how much should it have cost in 1989, using the transportation part of the CPI?

Solution   Divide 300 by 100:

$300 \div 100 = 3$

Multiply the result by the transportation CPI:

$3 \times \$111.90 = \$335.70$

The ticket that cost $300 in 1984 should have cost $335.70 in 1989.

EXERCISE YOUR SKILLS

1. How do economists use the Consumer Price Index?

2. How does inflation affect you?

3. Why is the cost of a market basket of 400 items a better indication of the Consumer Price Index than the cost of a few selected items would be?

_____ **Activity 1** _____

1. Use the Consumer Price Index chart (in Section 4) for all urban consumers to find the expected cost of each of these items in 1989. Assume that the cost of the item increased at the same rate as the Consumer Price Index. The price of each item in 1984 and the category to which it belongs are shown.

	Category	Item	Price in 1984	Price in 1989
a.	All items	Car	$ 9,650.00	$11,801.95
b.	Food	Apple	0.30	_____
c.	Apparel and upkeep	Clothing	22.50	_____
d.	Men's and boys' apparel	Jacket	43.80	_____
e.	Footwear	Shoes	97.50	_____
f.	Housing, total	House	65,000.00	_____
g.	Rent	Rent	335.00	_____
h.	Gas and electricity	Electricity	107.60	_____
i.	Fuel oil, coal, gas	Oil	98.50	_____
j.	Transportation	Ticket	374.20	_____

2. Below are the costs of selected items in 1989. Use the Consumer Price Index chart for all urban consumers to find the amount each of these items should have cost in 1984. Assume that the cost of each item increased at the same rate as the Consumer Price Index.

	Category	Item	Price in 1984	Price in 1989
a.	All items	Lawn mower	_____	$ 235.80
b.	Apparel and upkeep	Cleaning	_____	17.65
c.	Women's and girls' apparel	Skirt	_____	93.40
d.	Housing, total	House	_____	98,000.00
e.	House operation	Maintenance	_____	375.00
f.	House furnishings	Couch	_____	425.00
g.	Medical care	Doctor	_____	45.00
h.	Personal care	Make-up	_____	23.00
i.	Entertainment	Sports event	_____	42.00
j.	Personal and educational expenses	Tuition	_____	1,850.00

EXTEND YOUR UNDERSTANDING
PROJECT 9-1: COMPANIES LISTED ON THE
NEW YORK STOCK EXCHANGE

Assignments

- Select four of the companies listed on the NYSE.

- Follow the stock prices for your companies over the period of the project.

- Graph the changes in prices for your companies.

- Find out where the company has a regional or national headquarters by contacting a local branch office, or by reading a label from one of their products.

- Write a letter to the regional or national headquarters and request a copy of the company's annual report.

- Turn in copies of the letters you wrote, the annual reports you received from the companies, and any other information they sent you.

Extensions

- Find products produced by your companies.

- Make a poster showing photographs of local offices of your companies, their products, and any other available pictures.

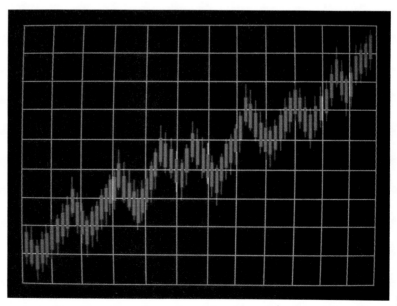

PROJECT 9–2: CAREER—INVESTMENT BROKER

Assignments

- Work with a group of your classmates to complete this activity.
- Find out what the educational requirements are for an investment broker.
- Find out where investment brokers work—independently or for investment groups.
- Determine the availability of job opportunities for investment brokers in your area and in other areas of the country.
- Find out what the salary ranges and possibilities are for investment brokers.
- Make a poster to summarize your findings.

Extensions

- Discuss your findings with other groups in your class.
- Prepare a leaflet describing a career as an investment broker. Try to encourage young people to enter the field of investment brokers.

V

34¼	11⅝	VF Cp	1.00	6.8	7	1091	15	14½	14¾	−¼
7	5/16	VMG n	.30j	...	...	371	⅝	½	9/16	+1/16
18¼	6	Valhi	.20	3.4	9	73	6	d5¾	5⅞	−¼
20	13½	Valero	.28	1.4	12	2004	20	19¾	19⅞	−⅛
28⅞	26½	Valer pf	3.44	12.4	...	1	27¾	27¾	27¾	...
18⅜	12⅝	ValNG	2.50	15.4	9	116	16¼	16	16¼	+⅛
1½	⅝	Valeyln		...	...	10	¾	¾	¾	+1/16
18⅝	7¼	VanDrn	.60	6.2	8	91	9¾	9¼	9¾	+⅝
9¾	8⅝	VKmpM	.72	7.8	...	261	9¼	9⅛	9¼	+⅛
8⅜	4	VKMT	.97	22.8	...	251	4⅜	4¼	4¼	−⅛
12½	10⅜	VKMI n	.87	8.3	...	103	10½	d10¼	10½	−⅛
10⅜	4¾	VKML	1.13	20.5	21	78	5½	5⅜	5½	...
25¾	23¼	VKmL pf	2.37	9.8	...	59	24½	24⅛	24⅛	−⅛
13¾	4⅜	Varco		...	35	1166	8⅝	8⅜	8⅜	−⅜
34¾	20	Varian	.26	.8	49	964	31¼	31	31⅛	−⅛
3½	1¾	Varity		...	6	2596	2⅛	1⅞	2⅛	...
23½	14½	Varity pf	1.30	8.3	...	48	15¾	15½	15⅝	...
10	4	VenSt n		...	...	9065	9½	8½	9	+¼
14	12⅝	VestSe	1.20a	9.1	11	24	13⅜	13⅛	13⅛	−⅛
1⅝	1/32	viVestr		...	...	175	⅛	1/16	⅛	+1/32
10¾	7⅞	VinPt n		...	...	460	8	7⅞	7⅞	−⅛
58	52	VaEP pf	5.00	9.1	...	z50	55	55	55	−½
90¼	81	VaEP pf	7.72	9.0	...	z10	85½	85½	85½	+1½
102⅜	96	VaEP pf	8.60	8.8	...	z20	98	98	98	−½
84⅜	75½	VaEP pf	7.20	9.0	...	z150	80⅛	80⅛	80⅛	+⅛
87	78⅜	VaEP pf	7.45	9.1	...	z30	82¼	82¼	82¼	+¼
23⅛	10	Vishay	1.03t	8.4	7	94	12¼	12	12¼	...
43⅛	16⅞	VistaCh	1.80	7.6	4	513	24⅞	23½	23¾	−1¼
18⅜	8¾	VistaRs		...	13	16	9⅜	9	9⅛	−⅜
24¼	15¼	Vivra s		...	...	15	23¼	23¼	23¼	−¼
23⅞	14¼	Vons		...	21	176	19½	19	19⅛	−¼
46¾	29⅜	VulcM	1.20	3.7	11	50	32¾	31¾	32¾	+1

CHAPTER 9 KEY TERMS

CHAPTER 9 REVIEW

1. How can you make money from stocks?

2. Why is buying bonds the same as lending money to a municipality or a corporation?

3. How is a mutual fund helpful to small investors?

4. What should the most important factor be in deciding whether or not to buy stock?

5. What method is used to buy and sell stocks on a security exchange?

6. How does the U.S. Securities and Exchange Commission help to protect investors?

7. Why do people try to predict the future of the stock market?

Find the profit from buying 2500 shares at the low price and selling them at the high price. Round all money amounts to the nearest penny.

	Company	Low	Total Value	High	Total Value	Profit
8.	Disnel	63¼		68½		
9.	AP & P	18½		20¼		
10.	Banter	24⅜		26⅞		
11.	Donnzl	49⅛		53		
12.	W Kodik	47		50½		
13.	Soeing	16⅞		21⅜		
14.	Zola	43½		45		

Begin with a balance of $200,000 worth of stock; find the new balance at the end of each transaction.

	Company	Price Share	Number of Shares	Buy/Sell	Total Value	Balance
15.	Vo Comp	31⅝	1500	B		
16.	Trysler	48⅝	500	B		
17.	Abon	46⅜	250	B		
18.	ETRA	37½	1000	S		
19.	XXMc	96¼	300	S		
20.	Cortez	70¾	50	B		
21.	Imoco	51⅛	700	S		
22.	Zelta	75¼	500	B		
23.	DeBont	26¾	925	S		
24.	Tobit	54½	3000	S		
25.	Diticorp	40	400	B		

Find the whole number of shares that can be bought in the companies listed below if you can spend $80,000 in each company. Find the total value of these shares.

	Company	Price/Share	Number of Whole Shares	Total Value
26.	Z Mart	73⅜		
27.	Croler	64⅝		
28.	Zaxta	85⅛		
29.	Zwag	61⅞		
30.	Int Br	21¼		
31.	Hex Inst	31¾		
32.	Disnel	40⅛		
33.	SwBall	3		
34.	Algin	28¼		
35.	Ballad	38½		

Use graph paper to graph the following points in the sequence shown. (Let 1 square = ¼ dollar.)

36. 6¾, 4, 7¼, 3¾, 5¼, 2½, 4¾, 3¼, 5½

37. 15¼, 11⅛, 13⅜, 12⅞, 14⅝, 11½, 13¾, 12½, 15

CHAPTER 9 TEST

1. Should you buy stocks for short-term or for long-term investments? Why?

2. Which is generally a more secure investment—stocks or bonds? Why?

3. Why should people with a small amount of savings probably not invest in the stock market?

4. What do you think is the greatest cause of people losing large amounts of money from stock investments?

5. a. If you bought 1000 shares of stock at a price of 62½, what would be the total cost of your stock?
   b. If after two years, you sold the 1000 shares at a price of 69¾, what would be the total amount you received?
   c. How much would you lose or gain on the 1000 shares of stock?

6. Find the number of whole shares that can be bought in the companies listed below if you can spend $100,000 in each company.
   a. Z Mart at 65¼ per share
   b. Zaxta at 87½ per share
   c. Int Br at 26⅜ per share
   d. Disnel at 38¾ per share
   e. Algin at 25⅞ per share
   f. Ballad at 37¼ per share

7. Find the total value of the shares of stock for **a–f** in Problem 6.

8. Graph the following changes in stock prices:

   4½   3¼   4¾   6   6⅝   5½   8¾   3¼   6⅛

9. Use the Consumer Price Index in Section 4 of this chapter to find the expected cost of each of the following items in 1989. The price for each item in 1984 is given.
   a. Women's jacket $50.75
   b. House $77,000
   c. Rent $435
   d. Gas (home heating) $223
   e. Fuel oil $128
   f. Airline ticket $395

Begin with stock worth $225,000; find the new balances.

	Company	Price Share	Number of Shares	Buy/Sell	Total Value	Balance
10.	Vo Comp	29⅝	500	B		
11.	Trysler	48½	450	S		
12.	Abon	44	50	B		
13.	ETRA	37⅞	2000	S		
14.	XXMc	94¼	300	S		
15.	Cortez	68¾	750	B		

In this skills preview, you will review skills that you will need to complete the exercises in Chapters 10 and 11. If you do not know how to complete any exercises, be sure to ask for help.

Find each sum or difference.

1. $1374 $\underline{-1120}$	**2.** $1366 $\underline{-\ 363}$	**3.** $2689 $\underline{-\ 1811}$
4. $35,600 $\underline{+53,200}$	**5.** $42,100 $\underline{+26,950}$	**6.** $53,960 $\underline{.+45,920}$
7. $10,160.50 $\underline{+\ 1,735.60}$	**8.** $11,200.30 $\underline{+\ 1,650.90}$	**9.** $10,596.20 $\underline{+\ 1,956.56}$
10. $ 895 1215 6526 $\underline{+\ 325}$	**11.** $ 965 1395 5905 $\underline{+\ 465}$	**12.** $ 860 1426 6449 $\underline{+\ 523}$

13. $42,000 - [$5200 + 2($2000)]

14. $56,500 - ($3100 + $2000)

Find each product.

15. 6.5 x $23,500

16. 8.5 x $30,000

17. 7.5 x $65,000

18. $\dfrac{$200,000}{$100,000}$ x 1374

19. $\dfrac{$50,000}{$100,000}$ x $918

20. $\dfrac{$300,000}{$100,000}$ x $2689

21. $5000
$\underline{\text{x } 126.870568}$

22. $2000
$\underline{\text{x } 104.819598}$

23. $4000
$\underline{\text{x } 95.025516}$

24. $3500
$\underline{\text{x } 152.667084}$

25. $1555 x 12

26. $2450 x 12

27. 0.075 x $3550

28. 0.075 x $4455

29. Find 33% of the difference between $65,000 and $44,900.

To teenagers, retirement is a lifetime away. They see examining types of life insurance—and comparing them with other savings instruments—as more appropriate for their parents than for them. Since teenagers generally do not provide the major portion of the income for a family, they may be right. They rarely need any life insurance at all. Yet they may play a helpful role in their families, and prepare for their own futures, by being well informed.

Many families have been convinced by salespeople that, because life insurance is inexpensive for teens, they should certainly have some! Other families have been convinced that cash-value life insurance is a good investment because they can borrow from the policy when their teenagers are ready to go to college. Some experts would argue that other forms of investment may offer a larger return.

Older people often live for many years past retirement. Many find that the fixed-income pension plans on which they depend are not adequate to meet the rising costs of living. Their grown children may help them out financially, just at the time when they are raising their own families. They must help support two generations in addition to their own. For parents, investment in retirement plans can help ease the financial burden on their children.

If the teenagers in this chapter take a closer look at the financial decisions their parents are making, they may be more understanding when their parents turn down some of their requests. Maybe they will even be able to help their parents plan wisely for their retirement. What is more, our teenagers will be working for their own money very soon; if they are not well informed, they might be easily enticed into buying insurance they do not really need.

In 1988, there were 8.020159 trillion dollars worth of life insurance in force in the United States. The insurance industry is one of the most powerful in our nation. As a group, insurance companies own a great deal of the business property in our country. As all of this suggests, they are succeeding in selling a great deal of life insurance.

Until last year, Lily had rarely thought about life insurance. Her mother tried once to discuss it with her, but Lily never did really understand. At the time she ranked their conversation right up there among the most boring they had ever had. Discussing Grandmother's cataract surgery or viewing her cousin's 243 slides of his recent vacation was more exciting.

Last year, though, the father of Lily's very close friend, Annika, was killed in an automobile accident. Annika and her mother found dealing with this traumatic shock extremely difficult. Annika explained to Lily that the adjustment was complicated by the fact that her father did not have much life insurance. Her mother struggled to pay the bills with the income from her job. She hoped to find a better-paying job, without having to move. She knew how much it would mean to Annika to stay with her friends and finish her senior year at the same high school.

After eight months, however, Annika's mother finally found a better job in another city, and they had to move away. Lily knew that she would miss her friend very much; she was also confused about how life insurance could have such a dramatic effect on her life.

Perhaps she will start another conversation with her mother about the life insurance situation in their family. After all, both her parents provide income, and they share the housework, cooking, cleaning, and caring for the children. If either of her parents suddenly died, what financial changes would Lily have to face?

OBJECTIVES: In this section, we will help Lily to:

- *understand what life insurance is*
- *evaluate who needs life insurance*
- *determine how much life insurance a family should buy*

LIFE INSURANCE

Life insurance is a nice way of saying death insurance. If Annika's father had purchased adequate life insurance, his wife would have received enough money to replace the income lost when he died. **Life insurance** is a contract to pay a specified amount of money to a designated person upon the death of the policy holder. If Annika's father had not been supporting a family, however, he probably would not have needed life insurance at all.

How Does Insurance Work? All types of insurance are based on two ideas—risk sharing and statistical probability. Every person faces financial risks that can result from such unpredictable events as accidents, fires, floods, illness, or the death of someone who is contributing to one's support. These risks of loss can be lessened by being shared. A large group of people pay money into a central pool. Those who have contributed have the right to call on that reserve when they suffer a loss. Insurance organizations have formed for the purpose of managing and disbursing this money to people as the need arises. The amount of money that must be collected is based on the likelihood, or statistical probability, of each disaster's occurring.

Who Needs Life Insurance? When one member of the family is the only provider, that person's death would cause the greatest financial trouble. Although Annika's father did not provide all the income for their family, he contributed enough that his family depended upon having it. His insurance should have been enough to replace the long-term income that his **dependents** (his wife and children, in this case) lost when he died.

Today, with the growing number of women who provide substantial income to the family, women must consider their own needs for life insurance. If a wife and mother dies, her husband and her children have to replace her income. In many families, the husband and wife contribute equally, and in others a woman is the main or sole provider. Even if one of the parents does not work outside the home, or for pay, that parent might need to have life insurance. This is because the family would have to hire someone else to do the childcare, housework, and so on, which that parent had been doing.

Many parents buy insurance for their children, but the money is most likely misspent. Insurance salespeople use several arguments to encourage the purchase of a family policy that may include coverage for the children or an individual policy for a child or teenager. One such argument is that the cost for a young person's insurance is small, but so is the likelihood of that young person's death.

Life insurance is best purchased for the protection of dependents. If you are a high school student, or soon to be a college student, and have no dependents, you probably do not need life insurance.

How Much Insurance is Needed? Annika knew her father did have some life insurance. The problems arose because he evidently did not have enough. Although the insurance company will gladly sell as much insurance to an individual as the person wants to buy, there are some general guidelines that may be helpful in determining how much a family should have. An ideal goal would be to have the insurance provide enough income for the family to continue its current standard of living. According to one major financial services company, accomplishing this goal does not require 100% of current take-home pay. The goal is to replace the net income, that is the amount that remains after income tax and social security have been deducted. Seventy-five percent income replacement will do, but at least 60% would be needed to avoid a serious lowering of the family's standard of living.

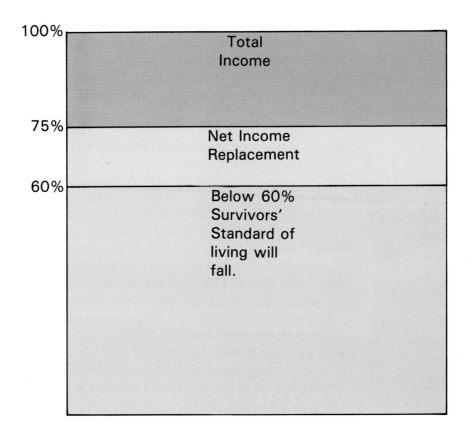

Ask Yourself

1. What is life insurance?

2. Who needs life insurance?

3. How much life insurance does a person need?

SHARPEN YOUR SKILLS

_____ Skill 1 _____

Annika's father was earning $30,000 per year when he was 35 years old.

Question   How much insurance should he have bought to provide 75% income replacement?

Solution   Look at the Multiples-of-Salary Chart for Net Income Replacement on the facing page.

Multiples-of-Salary Chart for Net Income Replacement

Present Age

Present Gross Earnings	25 Years		35 Years		45 Years		55 Years	
	75%	60%	75%	60%	75%	60%	75%	60%
$ 7,500	4.0	3.0	5.5	4.0	7.5	5.5	6.5	4.5
9,000	4.0	3.0	5.5	4.0	7.5	5.5	6.5	4.5
15,000	4.5	3.0	6.5	4.5	8.0	6.0	7.0	5.5
23,500	6.5	4.5	8.0	5.5	8.5	6.5	7.5	5.5
30,000	7.5	5.0	8.0	6.0	8.5	6.5	7.0	5.5
40,000	7.5	5.0	8.0	6.0	8.0	6.0	7.0	5.5
65,000	7.5	5.5	7.5	6.0	7.5	6.0	6.5	5.0

Find the income level of $30,000 in the left-hand column. Then read across to the column for 35 years and 75%. The number 8.0 appears in that space. To find the amount of insurance needed, multiply the annual salary by this factor.

$$8.0 \times \$30,000 = \$240,000$$

Annika's father should have purchased $240,000 worth of life insurance at age 35 to replace 75% of his income.

EXERCISE YOUR SKILLS

1. Why do people need life insurance?

2. Which member or members of a family should be covered by life insurance?

3. About how much life insurance does a person need if that person's annual salary is $40,000?

_____ Activity 1 _____

Use the Multiples-of-Salary Chart in Skill 1, to find the amount of life insurance each of these income earners should buy under the conditions described.

Present Earnings	Age	Income Replacement	Amount of Insurance
$65,000	35	75%	$357,500
65,000	45	60%	
40,000	55	75%	
40,000	25	60%	
30,000	35	75%	
30,000	45	60%	
23,500	55	75%	
23,500	25	60%	
15,000	35	75%	
15,000	45	60%	

Manuel knows Lily is upset because their friend Annika had to move away. He knew Joan's family had been in financial difficulty when her mother lost her job, but Annika's mother's situation is even worse. Manuel shares Lily's new interest in life insurance because of the sudden death of their friend's father.

Manuel will help Lily research the subject and investigate the different types of life insurance that exist and what they cost. Manuel is still doubtful that the types and costs of life insurance will be a hot topic any time soon, but he has become intrigued. He will take a closer look.

OBJECTIVES: In this section, we will help Manuel to:

● *examine the kinds of life insurance available*
● *calculate the cost of various amounts of life insurance*

LIFE INSURANCE— TWO TYPES

Manuel's older brother, Martin, is married and has a young child. Manuel's research will be of use to Martin and his wife as they decide what kind of insurance they need. Manuel explained that they can choose from two basic types. Essentially, all life insurance can be classified as either pure protection—called **term insurance**—or protection plus savings—called **cash-value insurance**.

Term Insurance. If Martin and his wife choose term insurance, they will be protected for a certain period of time, usually five or ten years. If the insured person, often simply called the **insured**, dies during the term, the **beneficiary** receives the **face value** of the policy. That means, for instance, that if Annika's father had had $100,000 worth of term insurance, she and her mother would have received the full $100,000 on his death. If the insured does not die during the term, the policy expires or must be renewed another term. Term insurance is generally the cheapest insurance available until a person reaches approximately age 50. Because it can be increased or decreased at the end of each term, term insurance provides considerable flexibility.

Manuel discovered three common types of term insurance. **Group life insurance**, which people can buy through their place of employment, provides insurance for a large number under a single policy without the need for medical examinations.

A policy of the second type—**renewable-convertible term**—covers a person for the period of time identified (one year, five years, ten years) and can be renewed without a medical examination.

The third alternative is **decreasing term**. The amount of the benefit the insurance company will award the survivors decreases over time. This is appropriate for a family in which the children will grow up and move out of the home. When they are no longer dependents, the parents no longer need as much insurance. The appeal of decreasing term is that the premiums are lower than for renewable term insurance.

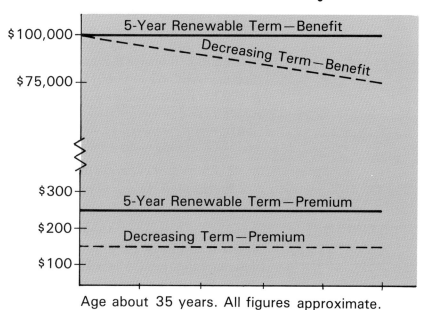

5-Year Renewable Term vs. Decreasing Term

Age about 35 years. All figures approximate.

Cash-Value Insurance. If Martin and his wife choose cash-value insurance they will be buying protection plus savings. As they pay the premiums, the policy will build up cash value much like a savings account.

Manuel learned about three traditional types of cash-value insurance. The first is **ordinary life**, also called straight life or whole life. With this insurance policy, you pay premiums that are more than enough to buy the insurance coverage you need. The excess is invested for you, adding to the cash value of the policy. You have the alternative of cashing in the policy, that is, taking out the money and the interest it has earned. The rate of interest tends to be low in comparison with other forms of investment.

Limited payment insurance has a smaller number of higher premium payments. The purchaser pays higher premiums, but the policy is paid up to its cash value in fewer years.

If the couple wants a policy in which the cash value buildup is accomplished quickly, they would choose an **endowment policy**. An endowment policy is protection plus savings, but the emphasis is on the savings. Because of this rapid accumulation over a short period of time, the premiums on endowment policies are very high.

The types of life insurance and their characteristics are summarized in the chart that follows.

LIFE INSURANCE	
Term Insurance	
Group Life Insurance	Purchased through work, the policy takes advantage of group rates
Renewable-Convertible Term	For 1, 5, or 10 year terms; can be renewed
Decreasing Term	Pays higher death benefit at first, lower later; costs less than renewable
Cash-Value Insurance	
Ordinary Life	Combines savings with insurance; can also be cashed in for accumulated value; also called whole life or straight life
Limited Payment	Higher premiums paid more quickly build up the cash value of the policy earlier
Endowment	Very high premiums build up cash value even faster

WHAT DOES IT COST?

The cost of life insurance varies widely from company to company. The range between the most expensive and the least expensive can be as much as 100%. **Comparison shopping** is the best way to find the best price for both term insurance and cash-value whole life insurance.

Ask Yourself

1. What are the two basic types of life insurance?

2. What is a beneficiary?

3. What are the advantages of decreasing term insurance?

SHARPEN YOUR SKILLS

_____ Skill 1 _____

The following table shows the comparative premium rates from one company for two of the major types of insurance, for men only. (The rates for women are somewhat lower because they have longer life expectancies.)

Comparison Table for Term and Whole Life Premiums Policy face value is $100,000.			
Age	5-Year Renewable Term	Whole Life	First Year Difference
20	$205	$ 775	$ 570
25	207	918	711
30	218	1,112	894
35	254	1,374	1,120
40	363	1,729	1,366
45	562	2,127	1,565
50	878	2,689	1,811

Ramón is a 30-year-old father who is comparing the premiums for different types of life insurance.

Questions

1. How much would 5-year-term insurance for $100,000 cost Ramón per year?

2. How much would the same amount of whole life insurance cost him?

3. In one year, how much would he save by buying term insurance instead of whole life?

Solutions   Use the table shown above.

1. Reading across the line for age 30, the number under 5-year-renewable term is 218. Ramon's annual premium would be $218.

2. The figure in the whole life column is 1,112, meaning $1,112.

3. To find the difference, subtract as follows:

$1,112   premium for whole life
− 218   premium for term
$ 894   difference

Ramón would save $894 by buying term insurance.

EXERCISE YOUR SKILLS

1. Why is group life insurance usually less costly than individual policies?

2. What is the advantage of limited payment insurance?

3. Why might insurance salespeople not necessarily recommend the best type of life insurance for your family?

_____ **Activity 1** _____

1. Use the Comparison Table for Term and Whole Life Insurance in Skill 1 to find the yearly premium for the amounts of insurance listed below for men at the ages shown.

Note: To find the cost of $50,000 worth of life insurance, divide the $100,000 premium by 2. To find the cost of $200,000 worth, multiply by 2.

	Amount of Insurance	Age	Type	Premium
a.	100,000	25	Term	
b.	100,000	25	Whole Life	
c.	200,000	35	Term	
d.	200,000	35	Whole Life	
e.	300,000	45	Term	
f.	300,000	45	Whole Life	
g.	50,000	30	Term	
h.	50,000	30	Whole Life	
i.	150,000	40	Term	
j.	150,000	40	Whole Life	
k.	250,000	50	Term	
l.	250,000	50	Whole Life	

2. For each set of costs in Problem 1, which is the less expensive? By how much?

While Lily and Manuel are taking a new look at life insurance, Eleanor has concerns of her own. Her grandmother retired this year from college teaching; her grandfather retired three years ago from a job with the civil service. Their financial security has been on Eleanor's mind.

Eleanor has always enjoyed visiting with her grandparents—they are more tolerant than her parents. Grandmother understands her newly acquired adulthood. Eleanor has had her driver's license for over a year now, and her grandmother lets Eleanor drive her car.

Before Grandmother retired, she could always take Eleanor and her parents out to eat at nice places. She sometimes took Eleanor shopping, and if she sent Eleanor to the grocery store, she let her keep the change. Since Grandmother retired this year, though, she is not as free with her cash. Grandfather has had a series of health problems, and the medical bills have been coming more regularly. Medicare and social security have only covered part of their expenses. Eleanor is not certain of the details, but she knows the retirement plans that they receive do not provide them with as much as they earned when they were both working.

Furthermore, they must make additional insurance payments to cover their medical costs. In an effort to keep down its enormous costs, Medicare has set caps on the amounts it considers reasonable for a given operation or medical procedure. The difference between the amount Medicare reimburses the patient (which is often 80% of the cap amount) and the amount the doctor or hospital actually charges, which may be much more, must be paid by the patient. For this reason, patients like Eleanor's grandparents often carry supplemental medical insurance to help them pay the difference.

Eleanor's mother is talking about helping her parents financially, as well as re-evaluating her own retirement plans. As Eleanor thinks about helping her parents in their old age, she is becoming interested in talk of tax shelters and IRAs. She may help her parents make wise choices as they plan for their retirement.

OBJECTIVES: In this section, we will help Eleanor to:

- *examine reasons for investing in retirement plans such as tax-deferred annuities and Individual Retirement Accounts (IRAs)*
- *calculate the future value of regular compound interest investments*
- *compare the future value of cash-value life insurance with the future value of the same amount invested at compound interest*

SOCIAL SECURITY IS NOT ENOUGH

Living too long is a risk that everyone faces—that is, living too long to support oneself. Eleanor prefers that her grandparents have a long and comfortable retirement.

Grandmother and Grandfather tried to plan ahead for their retirement. They knew that social security was never intended to provide sole support in retirement. It was designed only to provide a supplement to income from savings and other assets. Even though social security benefits will automatically increase if the cost of living rises more than three percent, the recipients will receive far less income than they enjoyed in their working years. Among those tools which people can use to supplement their social security benefits are annuities and Individual Retirement Accounts.

ANNUITIES

Eleanor's grandmother did place some of her income from college teaching in a tax-deferred annuity. An **annuity** is an investment plan that provides income upon retirement. Annuities are usually purchased through insurance companies and offer two advantages—forced savings and tax deferral. Grandmother chose to make payments into her annuity through a **payroll deduction**, the amount she requested was automatically deducted from her paycheck each month.

Since she has retired, Grandmother can draw the money back out of the company that kept it for her. She has also received interest on the money. She must now pay taxes on her income from the annuity, but her tax rate will be less now that she is earning less income. That is the benefit of such an annuity.

INDIVIDUAL RETIREMENT ACCOUNTS (IRAs)

An **Individual Retirement Account (IRA)** is a tax-sheltered retirement plan that allows workers to deduct up to $2000 a year each from their adjusted gross income when they prepare their tax returns. An IRA is not available to workers whose adjusted gross income (before the IRA deduction) is $50,000 or more for couples or $35,000 for singles, and who are covered by employers' pension plans.

Money can be withdrawn from an IRA, but the owner will pay a tax penalty and possibly an interest penalty. Unless the owner of an IRA becomes disabled, the earliest age at which he or she can withdraw from the IRA without penalty is 59½. The money itself in an IRA plan is placed in certificates of deposit, mutual funds, stocks, or bonds—almost any investment instrument so long as the account is handled separately from other investments as an IRA account. And each person must have his or her own IRA account.

INSURANCE vs. INVESTMENTS

Eleanor is especially curious about cash-value life insurance as an investment plan when she compares it to investing in a mutual fund or a certificate of deposit that pays compound interest.

The CVLI/BTID Controversy. A controversy has arisen in the last few years because of the large amounts of cash-value life insurance that have been sold, while consumers, perhaps mistakenly, assumed this was a good plan for savings. Some in the insurance industry have begun to realize that consumers can save a great deal more money by buying term insurance and investing the money they save. They invest the difference in instruments such as mutual funds or CDs that pay compound interest.

Strong opinions have been expressed on both sides of the CVLI/BTID controversy. The name stands for Cash-Value Life Insurance/Buy Term, Invest the Difference. Consumers must make their own decisions about buying life insurance, and these decisions should be based on careful research. The availability and cost of different types of life insurance vary from company to company. So it is a complex task to compare the policies available and select the most appropriate.

To make such comparisons yourself, you must have available the life insurance premiums and pay out policies as well as the compound interest figures such as those shown in the Reference Section of the book. The interest rate of course fluctuates, so you must learn the current rate and make some projection about rates in the future. Remember, though, that if you invest through an insurance company, they will be making a profit on your money. If you can find comparable rates yourself, you may come out ahead.

Careful decision making can lead to higher yields. Even our teenagers, who look at retirement as many years in the future, know there is a difference between having $20,000 at retirement—and having $200,000!

Ask Yourself

1. What are tax-deferred annuities?

2. What are Individual Retirement Accounts?

3. What is the earliest age at which you can withdraw money from an IRA without penalty?

SHARPEN YOUR SKILLS

────── Skill 1 ──────────────────────────

Eleanor's father and mother are both 43, and they have just opened IRA accounts that they hope will supply them with extra money when they retire at age 65, which will be 22 years from now. They will deposit $2000 dollars into each account every year, and the accounts will pay 8% interest, compounded annually.

Question   By the time they are 65, how much money will each parent have in his or her account?

Solution   To determine the future value of money that is deposited into an interest-bearing account on a regular basis, you would use a table like the one on the page following.

FUTURE WORTH OF ONE DOLLAR PER PERIOD WITH INTEREST PAYABLE AT END OF EACH PERIOD (COMPOUNDED ANNUALLY)

Years	8% Annual Rate
1	1.0000000
21	50.4229214
22	55.4567552
23	60.8932956
24	66.7647592
25	73.1059400
26	79.9544151
27	87.3507684
28	95.3388298
29	103.9659362
30	113.2832111

This table shows what would happen if every year (annually) $1.00 were put into an account paying 8% compound interest. Notice that after 22 years, there would be approximately $55.46.

However, Eleanor's parents don't put just $1.00 in their accounts, they put in 2000 times that much—$2000.00 every year. To find out how much money Eleanor's parents would each have, multiply the amount they save every year by the number indicated in the table. (To ensure accuracy, the number from the table should be correct to 6 decimal places.)

$$\$2000 \times 55.456755 = \$110,913.51$$

When they retire, Eleanor's parents will each have $110,913.51 in their accounts.

_____ Skill 2 _____

Suppose Eleanor's grandfather had purchased $50,000 worth of whole life insurance when he was 20.

1. How much would his annual premium be?

2. How much would he pay for the insurance over 40 years?

Solutions

1. See Comparison Table for Term and Whole Life Premiums in the Reference Section. The premium for $50,000 of insurance is ½ times the premium for $100,000.

   The premium would be:

   $$\$775.00 \div 2 = \$387.50$$

The total paid in 40 years would be:

$$\begin{array}{r} \$\quad 387.50 \\ \text{x}\qquad 40 \\ \hline \$15,500.00 \end{array}$$

He would have paid $15,500 in premiums over 40 years.

Question If he had invested the $387.50 premium money every year in a savings account or mutual fund that paid 8½% interest, compounded semiannually, how much would his savings be worth at the end of 40 years?

Solution Use the Future Worth Table (for semiannual compounding, payable at the end of each period) in the Reference Section of this book. Under the column headed 8½%, read down to 40 years. The amount in the table is:

633.668480   correct to six decimal places

To find how much his savings would be worth, multiply the table amount by the amount saved every year.

$$\begin{array}{r} \$\quad 387.50 \\ \text{x}\,633.668480 \\ \hline \$\ 122,773.27 \quad \text{rounded to the nearest penny} \end{array}$$

His savings would be $122,773.27.

_____   Skill 3   _____

Suppose Eleanor's grandfather paid his premiums semiannually (every 6 months) instead of annually.

Question How much would his monthly premium be?

Solution $387.50 ÷ 2 = $193.75 per month

Question If, instead of paying the insurance premiums, he had invested the $193.75 every 6 months in a savings account or mutual fund that paid 8½% interest, compounded semiannually, how much would his savings be worth at the end of 40 years?

Solution Since he would be adding money to the account every 6 months (semiannually), we need to use a Compound Interest Table that shows semiannual compounding instead of annual compounding. Use the table called Future Worth of One Dollar Per Period with Interest Payable at End of Each Period—Compounded Semiannually in the Reference Section of this book. Under the column headed 8½%, read down to 40 years. The amount in the table is:

633.668480 (correct to 6 decimal places)

To find how much his savings would be worth, multiply the amount saved every 6 months by the number from the table.

193.75 x 633.668480 = $122,773.27

_____ Skill 4 _____

Following is a table showing the cash value (or accumulation of savings) of a whole life insurance policy of $100,000 over the first 20 years.

Accumulated Cash Value of $100,000 Whole Life Policy					
Year	Person's Age	Cash Value	Year	Person's Age	Cash Value
1	25	$ 0	11	35	$ 6454
2	26	700	12	36	7293
3	27	1500	13	37	8241
4	28	2300	14	38	9313
5	29	3100	15	39	10523
6	30	3503	16	40	11891
7	31	3958	17	41	13437
8	32	4473	18	42	15184
9	33	5054	19	43	17158
10	34	5712	20	44	19388

Question If Eleanor's grandfather had bought $100,000 worth of whole life cash-value insurance at age 25, what would the cash value have been when he was 44?

Solution Looking at the table, you see the value at age 44 would have been $19,388.

EXERCISE YOUR SKILLS

1. Why should people invest in retirement plans such as tax-deferred annuities and Individual Retirement Accounts?

2. What are two advantages of purchasing tax-deferred annuities through payroll deductions?

3. Who is _not_ eligible for an IRA?

_____ Activity 1 _____

Use the table below to answer the questions that follow.

Future Worth of One Dollar Per Period With Interest Payable at the End of Each Period	
Years	8% Annual Rate
	1.0000000
20	45.7619643
25	73.1059400
30	113.2832111

1. If you contribute $2000 a year to an IRA account beginning at age 45, how much will you have in your account at age 65?

2. If you begin contributing the same amount at age 40, how much will you have at age 65?

3. If you begin contributing the same amount at age 35, how much more will you have at age 65 than if you began at age 45? At age 40?

_____ Activity 2 _____

1. Suppose you purchase $100,000 worth of whole life insurance when you become 25. Use the Comparison Table for Term and Whole Life Insurance on the facing page to find the premium per year. Then calculate how much you will pay in premiums in 40 years.

2. If you invested the amount of the insurance premium in Problem 1 in a savings account at 8½% interest, how much would your account be worth at the end of 40 years? Use the Future Worth Table for annual compounding payable at the end of each period in the Reference Section to help calculate the amount.

3a. Using the table showing the cash value of a whole life policy in the Reference Section, what would be the cash value in 40 years.

3b. Which of the investments, cash value of the insurance policy or the annual compounding in Problem 2, will give you the greatest earnings on your money? How much more?

_____ Activity 3 _____

1. If you pay the premium on the insurance in Activity 2 semiannually, how much will your premiums be?

2. Use the Future Worth Table (for semiannual compounding) in the Reference Section of the book to find how much money you would have at the end of 40 years if you invested the premiums from Problem 1 in a savings account every 6 months and earned 8½% interest.

3. Which will be worth more—the cash value of the insurance policy in Problem 1 or the semiannual compounding investing in Problem 2? How much more?

_____ Activity 4 _____

1. Use the Accumulated Cash Value table in Skill 4 to answer this question.

   If a person buys $100,000 worth of whole life insurance at age 25, how much will the cash value of the policy be when he or she is each of the following ages?

   a. 30   **b.** 35   **c.** 40   **d.** 42

2. Use the Future Worth Table (for monthly compounding payable at the end of each period) in the Reference Section of the book as well as the table in Skill 4 to answer this question.

   Assume a person's premium for $100,000 worth of whole life insurance purchased at age 25 was $840 per year. If he or she invested this money at 8½% interest compounded monthly, what would it be worth after the following periods?

   Sample

After 40 years, at age 65
$840 ÷ 12 = $70
4038.652333
x   70
$ 282,705.66

   a. After 5 years, at age 30   **c.** After 15 years, at age 40

   b. After 10 years, at age 35   **d.** After 17 years, at age 42

3. What is the difference between the cash value of the $100,000 policy at each age and the invested savings at 8½% interest for items **a**, **b**, **c**, and **d** of Problem 2?

EXTEND YOUR UNDERSTANDING
PROJECT 10–1: COMPARING TYPES OF AVAILABLE INSURANCE

Work with a group of your classmates to complete this activity.

1. Each member of the group should chose two insurance companies that sell policies in your area.

2. Find out what types of life insurance policies each company sells.

3. Obtain a list of the premiums for each type of policy.

4. Create a bulletin board to display your findings.

1. Discuss your findings with the other members of your group.

2. Evaluate the various policies and premiums. Decide which company and which policy provide the best investment at the lowest cost.

3. Prepare a brochure stating which policy is the best and why. Make the brochure colorful and eye-catching so it might be used as an advertisement for the policy.

PROJECT 10–2: HOW ARE INSURANCE PREMIUMS DETERMINED?

1. Contact various insurance companies to find out what statistics they use to determine the premiums for different types of life insurance.

2. Contact people (actuaries) who compile the statistics used by insurance companies to determine premiums. Find out how they compile the statistics.

3. Write a report summarizing your findings.

1. Use reference books such as a world almanac to study the changes in the life expectancy of men and women over the last century.

2. Compare the changes in life expectancies with the changes in life insurance premiums over the years for which you can find figures. How do they compare?

CHAPTER 10 KEY TERMS

Section 10–1

dependents
life insurance

Section 10–2

beneficiary
cash-value insurance
comparison shopping
decreasing term
endowment policy
face value
group life insurance
insured
limited payment insurance
ordinary life
renewable-convertible term
term insurance

Section 10–3

annuity
Individual Retirement
    Account (IRA)
payroll deduction

CHAPTER 10 REVIEW

1. Why is it important for people to have adequate life insurance?

2. How does a person decide whether to purchase term insurance or cash-value insurance?

3. Why might young families be wise to purchase decreasing term insurance?

4. Why do people need retirement plans other than social security?

Use the Multiples of Salary Chart in the Reference Section to find the amount of life insurance each of these income earners should buy.

5. Juanita is 35 years of age and has gross earnings of $40,000. She n e e d s 60% income replacement.

6. Joshua is 45 years of age and has gross earnings of $30,000. He needs 75% income replacement.

Use the Comparison Table for Term and Whole Life Premiums in the Reference Section to find the yearly premium for the amounts of insurance listed below.

7. $50,000 whole life insurance at 25 years of age

8. $150,000 term insurance at 45 years of age

9. $200,000 term insurance at 40 years of age

10. $250,000 whole life insurance at 35 years of age

Use the Future Worth Table for 8% Annual Compounding (End of Period) in the Reference Section to answer the following questions:

11. If André contributes $2000 a year to an IRA account beginning at age 35, how much will he have in his account at age 65?

12. If André and his wife each begin contributing $2000 a year at age 40, how much will they each have in their accounts at age 65?

13. If you begin contributing $2000 a year to an IRA account at age 30, how much more will you have in the account at age 60 than if you begin to contribute the same amount at age 40?

Use the Comparison Table for Term and Whole Life Premiums. Accumulated Cash Value of $100,000 Whole Life Policy, and the Future Worth Tables in the Reference Section of the book to answer the following questions.

14. If Miguel purchases $150,000 worth of whole life insurance when he is 35 years old, how much will he pay in premiums in 30 years?

15. If Miguel invested the amount of the insurance premiums in Problem 14 in an annual compounding interest account at 8½% interest, how much would his account be worth at the end of 30 years?

16. Will the cash value of the insurance policy (Problem 14) or the investment (Problem 15) give Miguel the greatest earnings on his money? How much more?

17. If Miguel paid the premium on the insurance in Problem 14 monthly, how much would his monthly premiums be?

18. If he invested the monthly premiums in an account which compounded interest monthly at a rate of 8%, how much money would he have in his account at the end of 30 years?

19. How much more than the cash value of the insurance policy in Problem 14 will the investment account in Problem 18 be worth?

20. Which will be worth more—the savings account in Problem 15 or the savings account in Problem 18? How much more?

CHAPTER 10 TEST

1. Why do life insurance needs vary from family to family?

2. How does term insurance differ from cash-value insurance?

3. How does decreasing term insurance help families to meet their financial needs at an affordable cost?

4. Use the Multiples of Salary Chart in the Reference Section to find the amount of life insurance a 40-year-old who has gross earnings of $45,000 would need in order to provide 60% income replacement.

5. Use the Comparison Table for Term and Whole Life Premiums in the Reference Section to find the yearly premium for $125,000 of whole life insurance purchased at the age of 30.

6. Use the following table to find how much will be in an IRA account at age 65 if contributions of $2000 a year were begun at age 35.

FUTURE WORTH OF ONE DOLLAR PER PERIOD WITH INTEREST PAYABLE AT END OF EACH PERIOD (COMPOUNDED ANNUALLY)	
Years	**8% Annual Rate**
1	1.0000000
20	45.7619643
21	50.4229214
22	55.4567552
23	60.8932956
24	66.7647592
25	73.1059400
26	79.9544151
27	87.3507684
28	95.3388298
29	103.9659362
30	113.2832111

7. Use the Comparison Table for Term and Whole Life Premiums in the Reference Section to find how much will be paid in premiums in 35 years for a whole life insurance policy of $100,000 purchased at age 30.

8. Use the Future Worth Table (for semiannual compounding payable at the end of each period) in the Reference Section to find how much would be in the saving account at the end of 35 years if the premiums paid in Problem 7 were invested at 8½%.

9. Which would be worth more at the end of 35 years—the cash value of the insurance policy or the savings account? How much more?

1. What would the simple interest be on $950 at 9.5% for one year if interest is paid semi-annually?

2. You have a choice of paying $395 for 3 years or $260 a month for 5 years for a $12,500 loan. How much will you save if you pay the loan off in 3 years?

3. Your credit card charges 1.5% interest per month. You pay 10% of the balance each month. Complete a table using the following columns for 3 months. Your beginning balance is $690.

Balance	Interest	Amount Owed	Payment

4. Your family's take home pay is $4300 a month; how much can you afford to spend for credit card payments each month?

5. For an all-purpose credit account, set up a chart to show the first 6 monthly payments and find the total interest paid over 6 months at 1.5% interest per month. The beginning balance is $720 and you make monthly payments of 10% of the amount owed. During the second month, you make an additional purchase of $125.

6. Find the total financed price, the total interest, and the dealer's profit for each car sale plan if the car price is $12,900.

	Plan A	Plan B
Rebate	$1500	none
Loan Amount		
Time of Loan	48 months	48 months
Monthly Payment	$295.60	$305.10
Total Financed Price		
Total Interest		
Dealer's Profit		

7. a. If you bought 1500 shares of stock at a price of 58¼, what would be the total cost of your stock?

   b. If after two years, you sold the 1500 shares at a price of 65½, what would be the total amount you received?

   c. How much did you lose or gain on the 1500 shares of stock?

8. Begin with a balance of $150,000 worth of stock; find the new balance at the end of each transaction.

Company	Price/Share	Number of Shares	Buy/Sell	Total Value	Balance
Von Comp	33⅜	2000	B		
Abon	42½	500	B		
Etra	39¾	1500	S		
XXMC	98¼	450	B		
Imoco	48⅜	600	S		
Zelta	82½	400	B		
Diti Corp	50	200	B		

9. Find the number of whole shares that can be bought in the companies listed below if you can spend $150,000 in each company.

a.   B Mart at 83½ per share
b.   Zionel at 53¾ per share
c.   Haxta at 65⅛ per share
d.   Dallard at 35⅜ per share

10. Use the Multiples of Salary Chart in the Reference Section to find the amount of life insurance a 35-year-old who has gross earnings of $40,000 would need in order to provide 75% income replacement.

11. Use the Comparison Table for Term and Whole Life Premiums in the Reference Section to find the yearly premium for $200,000 of whole life insurance purchased at the age of 35.

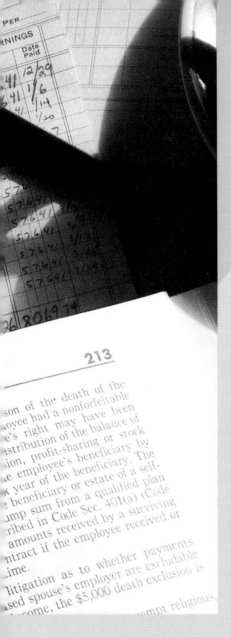

Whether or not we agree with the exact way our tax dollars are spent, most of us would not be willing to do without the many services our governments provide.

Taxes, for most of us, are the biggest single item in our family budgets. The average worker/taxpayer works every year from January 1 to May 1 to earn enough to fulfill his or her tax obligations to the different levels of government. Perhaps we are fortunate that this segment of our salary never reaches our hands; it is withheld by our employers and paid to the Internal Revenue Service (IRS) before we even see it. Otherwise, many of us might find handing it over in a lump sum to be very difficult indeed.

Even so, once a year by the April 15 deadline, each of us who has had an income must calculate for the IRS exactly how much we owe for the previous year. Some of us are entitled to get back some or all of the money that has been withheld; others will owe more. We compute our income taxes by filling out IRS forms. Because we earn and use our incomes in so many different ways, the forms devised by the IRS must accommodate many possibilities. They take some getting used to.

Attempts have been made to keep the forms simple enough for ordinary taxpayers. In this chapter, three of our high school students will examine the three tax return forms that are used by individuals. They will demonstrate the ease with which many individuals can complete these forms themselves. They will also indicate sources of assistance if we still need it; that is, assistance with the forms. When it comes to paying the bill, we are on our own!

Luis had big plans for his first paycheck. His car needed some tires, and the amount he would receive for his first week's work should be just enough. He was quite surprised when he received the check—$12.16 was missing! He examined the stub more closely and noticed that several deductions had been made from his salary.

The largest one got his attention; it said "Federal Income Tax Withheld." He remembers the mass of papers his father and mother shuffle and sort during the first week of April every year, accompanied by mumblings about government spending, depreciation, deductions, and Schedule A. It is now his turn to deal with income taxes.

Luis is determined to figure out what it all means. He received his W-2 form from his employer, and he knows he must file a federal income tax return. He expects to receive a refund. He wonders if the amount withdrawn from his paycheck will be enough to cover his taxes. Luis plans to compare the amounts that are withdrawn from his weekly check with the amounts of taxes shown on the tax table. If he gets back as much as he thinks he will, he can buy a whole new set of tires for his car.

OBJECTIVES: In this section, we will help Luis to:

- *realize how much of the year an employee works to pay income taxes*
- *discover some of the characteristics of the federal income tax system*
- *find how much income tax will be owed in specific cases*
- *compare the tax owed with the amount withheld by the employer*

**THE PRICE TAG
ON GOVERNMENT**

Taxes are what we pay for civilized society.

Oliver Wendell Holmes, Jr.

In this world nothing is certain but death and taxes.

Benjamin Franklin

The income tax has made more liars out of the American people than golf has.

Will Rogers

A newspaper article entitled "Tax Freedom Day" caught Luis's attention. Since he first realized all his earnings were being taxed by the federal government, he has noticed such articles. As he read, he discovered that the Tax Foundation Incorporated, a private organization, calculates an annual Tax Freedom Day. This is the day each year when the average American will stop working to pay for government services. To Luis, this meant that if he was working full time and receiving a full salary, the amount of money that he would pay the government in taxes would be equivalent to what he would earn from the beginning of January to May 1st.

The cost of government as measured by the number of working days has increased considerably between 1930 and 1980. See the following table. The Tax Foundation estimates that typical workers pay approximately a third of their earnings into local, state, and federal taxes. Luis certainly hopes these governments are using his money wisely.

Tax Freedom Days

1930	February 13
1940	March 8
1950	April 3
1960	April 17
1970	April 28
1975	April 28
1980	May 1
1981	May 4
1982	May 3
1983	April 30
1984	April 28
1985	May 1
1986	May 1

Source: Tax Foundation Incorporated

HOW DID THIS HAPPEN?

Luis wondered if governments in our country have always needed so much money. As he investigated, he discovered that for its first 100 years, the United States relied upon taxes on certain goods manufactured here and on products that were brought in from other countries. Then our country changed from a rural-agricultural society to an industrial society, and the role of the federal government grew. The income of the federal government had to be increased. The 16th Amendment, adopted in 1913, gave Congress the power to pass income tax laws. We now have taxes on income, sales, and property.

United States Individual Income Tax. Luis also discovered some features of the elaborate process we go through to supply funds to our government. The **income tax** is a tax on an individual's earnings from wages, salary, tips, interest, rents, dividends, and capital gains and is the largest revenue producing tax for the federal government. Each year, on or before April 15, American citizens like Luis and his parents determine their tax liability and voluntarily pay the amount due or request a refund if they have one coming.

Following are some of the characteristics of our income tax system.

Ability to Pay. The federal income tax is based on one's ability to pay. Basically, this means that the individual income tax rate takes a proportionately higher share from Luis's parents' income than it will from his. The more you earn, the more you pay.

Voluntary Compliance. Another characteristic of the federal personal income tax is voluntary compliance. The Internal Revenue Service relies on Luis, and on all the rest of us, to know our tax responsibilities and to meet them faithfully. If some of our citizens, like Al Capone for instance, evade their responsibility and do not pay their taxes voluntarily, they can be imprisoned, since tax evasion is illegal.

Pay-As-You-Earn. A feature particularly helpful to Luis, especially when he realizes that almost one quarter of his income goes to the government, is the pay-as-you-earn feature. As we receive income subject to a tax, we pay the tax. This system helps prevent Luis, and other taxpayers from owing large amounts of taxes at the end of the year. Luis's employer is responsible for withholding tax from his paycheck and depositing it with the IRS. Luis learned how much had been withheld from his paycheck during the year when he received his Form W-2 from his employer.

1 Control number		For Paperwork Reduction Act Notice, see back of Copy D. OMB No. 1545-0008	For Official Use Only ▶	
2 Employer's name, address, and ZIP code		3 Employer's identification number		4 Employer's State number
		5 Statutory employee ☐ De-ceased ☐ Pension plan ☐ Legal rep. ☐ 942 emp. ☐ Sub-total ☐ Deferred compensation ☐ Void ☐		
		6 Allocated tips		7 Advance EIC payment
8 Employee's social security number	9 Federal income tax withheld	10 Wages, tips, other compensation		11 Social security tax withheld
12 Employee's name (first, middle, last)		13 Social security wages		14 Social security tips
		16*		16a Fringe benefits incl. in Box 10
15 Employee's address and ZIP code		17 State income tax	18 State wages, tips, etc.	19 Name of State
		20 Local income tax	21 Local wages, tips, etc.	22 Name of locality

Form **W-2 Wage and Tax Statement**   Copy A For Social Security Administration   Department of the Treasury
                                            *See Instructions for Forms W-2 and W-2P   Internal Revenue Service

FORM W-2   Form W-2 is a wage and a tax statement. Every employer Luis works for during the year must send him a W-2 form for the period that he worked.

This form provides him with a record of wages earned as well as federal, state, and other taxes withheld during the year. Luis must submit a copy of each Form W-2 with his tax return.

TAX TABLES

Your **tax liability**, or the amount you owe, can be found on the tax tables. Before you use the tables, however, you need to find your **taxable income**. Taxable income is the amount of money you actually make during the year *minus* certain deductions that are allowed by the government. For example, if you make $7000 a year, the government might allow you to subtract $3100 dollars from that amount before you figure your taxes. In that case, your taxable income would be $7000 – $3100 or $3900.

After you know your taxable income, you use the appropriate table for your filing status. A portion of one is shown in Skill 1 below. There are columns for single people, married people filing jointly, married people filing separately, and the head of a household. Read down the income column until you find your taxable income. Then read across to the column in which you belong. The amount shown is your tax. (For married couples, if one income is lower than the other, filing a **joint return** often results in lower taxes.)

Ask Yourself

1. How long does the average person have to work in order to earn the amount of money paid to the government in taxes?

2. What is an income tax?

3. What are two characteristics of our income tax system?

SHARPEN YOUR SKILLS

_____ Skill 1 _____

Elizabeth's taxable income for the past year was $2,975.

Question   How much tax does she owe?

Solution   Use the portion of the tax table shown on the next page. Read down the income column (headed "If 1040A line 19, or 1040EZ line 5 is—") to find 2,975.

Notice 2,975 is listed twice, once under the column marked "At least" and once under "But less than." Use the line where 2,975 is shown under the "At least" column.

Read across to the column headed "Single."

The amount in that column is 448. Elizabeth owes $448.00 in income tax for the year.

Tax Table

For persons with taxable incomes of less than $50,000

If 1040A, line 19, OR 1040EZ, line 5 is—		And you are—			
At least	But less than	Single (and 1040EZ filers)	Married filing jointly *	Married filing sepa-rately	Head of a house-hold
		Your tax is—			
2,700	2,725	407	407	407	407
2,725	2,750	411	411	411	411
2,750	2,775	414	414	414	414
2,775	2,800	418	418	418	418
2,800	2,825	422	422	422	422
2,825	2,850	426	426	426	426
2,850	2,875	429	429	429	429
2,875	2,900	433	433	433	433
2,900	2,925	437	437	437	437
2,925	2,950	441	441	441	441
2,950	2,975	444	444	444	444
2,975	3,000	448	448	448	448

_____ Skill 2 _____

Taxpayers whose taxable income is over $50,000 do not use the same tax tables. Instead they use the Tax Rate Schedules—X, Z, Y-1, or Y-2.

Schedule X, for filers who are single, is shown below.

Caution: Use ONLY if your taxable income (Form 1040, line 37) is $50,000 or more. If less, use the **Tax Table.**

19 _ _ Tax Rate Schedules

Schedule X—Use if your filing status is **Single**

If the amount on Form 1040, line 37 is: Over—	But not over—	Enter on Form 1040, line 38	of the amount over—
$0	$18,550	. . . . . . .15%	$0
18,550	44,900	$2,782.50 + 28%	18,550
44,900	93,130	10,160.50 + 33%	44,900
93,130	. . . .	Use **Worksheet** to figure your tax.	

Question   If Marilyn, who is single, has taxable income of $50,000, how much is her tax?

Solution   Use Schedule X, for singles.

$50,000 is between $44,900 and $93,130 so you should follow these instructions:

Marilyn's tax is $10,160.50 + 33% of the amount over $44,900.

Step 1   Subtract $44,900 from $50,000:

$50,000 – 44,900 = $5,100

Step 2   Find 33% of $5,100:

$5,100 x .33 = $1,683.00

Step 3   Add $1,683.00 to $10,160.50:

$1,683.00 + 10,160.50 = $11,843.50

Marilyn's total tax owed is $11,843.50.

_____   **Skill 3**   _____

Luis's monthly income for this year was $675.

Questions

1. What was his total income?

2. What was his taxable income?

3. How much income tax does he owe?

4. How much was withheld from his checks?

5. Will he get a refund or owe additional taxes? How much?

Solutions

1. His yearly income would be:

$675 x 12 = $8,100

2. To find his taxable income you must make some adjustments that will be more fully explained in the next section. For now you should:

Subtract his standard deduction:

$8,100 – 3,100 = $5,000

Subtract the amount for one withholding allowance of $2,000:

$5,000 – 2,000 = $3,000

His taxable income is $3,000.

3. Use the Tax Table in the Reference Section to find the tax on $3,000 for a single person.

The amount is $454.

SINGLE Persons–MONTHLY Payroll Period

(For Wages Paid After December 1989)

And the wages are–		And the number of withholding allowances claimed is–				
At least	But less than	0	1	2	3	4
		The amount of income tax to be withheld shall be–				
$0	$105	$0	$0	$0	$0	
105	110	1	0	0	0	
110	115	2	0	0	0	
115	120	3	0	0	0	
120	125	3	0	0	0	
125	130	4	0	0	0	
130	135	5	0	0	0	
135	140	6	0	0	0	
140	145	6	0	0	0	
145	150	7	0	0	0	
150	160	8	0	0	0	
160	170	10	0	0	0	
170	180	11	0	0	0	
180	190	13	0	0	0	
190	200	14	0	0	0	
200	210	16	0	0	0	
210	220	17	0	0	0	
220	230	19	0	0	0	
230	240	20	0	0	0	
240	250	22	0	0	0	
250	260	23	0	0	0	
260	270	25	0	0	0	
270	280	26	1	0	0	
280	290	28	2	0	0	
290	300	29	4	0	0	
300	320	32	6	0	0	
320	340	35	9	0	0	
340	360	38	12	0	0	
360	380	41	15	0	0	
380	400	44	18	0	0	
400	420	47	21	0	0	
420	440	50	24	0	0	
440	460	53	27	1	0	
460	480	56	30	4	0	
480	500	59	33	7	0	
500	520	62	36	10	0	
520	540	65	39	13	0	
540	560	68	42	16	0	
560	580	71	45	19	0	
580	600	74	48	22	0	
600	640	78	52	27	1	
640	680	84	58	33	7	
680	720	90	64	39	13	
720	760	96	70	45	19	
760	800	102	76	51	25	
800	840	108	82	57	31	
840	880	114	88	63	37	
880	920	120	94	69	43	
920	960	126	100	75	49	
960	1,000	132	106	81	55	
1,000	1,040	138	112	87	61	
1,040	1,080	144	118	93	67	
1,080	1,120	150	124	99	73	
1,120	1,160	156	130	105	79	
1,160	1,200	162	136	111	85	
1,200	1,240	168	142	117	91	
1,240	1,280	174	148	123	97	
1,280	1,320	180	154	129	103	
1,320	1,360	186	160	135	109	
1,360	1,400	192	166	141	115	
1,400	1,440	198	172	147	121	
1,440	1,480	204	178	153	127	
1,480	1,520	210	184	159	133	
1,520	1,560	216	190	165	139	
1,560	1,600	222	196	171	145	
1,600	1,640	228	202	177	151	
1,640	1,680	234	208	183	157	
1,680	1,720	240	214	189	163	
1,720	1,760	248	220	195	169	

4. To find the amount that would have been withheld from Luis's check, look at the withholding tables for Single Persons—Monthly Payroll Period. A portion of that table is shown at the left.

On the withholding table, locate Luis's monthly income of $675. It falls on the line for "At least 640, But less than 680." You will use the column for 1 withholding allowance, because on his Form W-4 Luis listed 1 exemption or withholding allowance. Under that column, find the amount withheld. It is $58 per month.

To find the yearly withholding, multiply the monthly amount by 12:

$58 x 12 = $696

The amount withheld from Luis's checks was $696.

5. The amount owed is less than the amount already withheld. The difference is:

$696 – 454 = $242

Luis can expect a refund of $242.

EXERCISE YOUR SKILLS

1. Why is it necessary for people to pay federal income taxes?

2. What is the date by which personal income tax returns must be filed for the previous year?

3. Does the voluntary compliance nature of our income tax system mean that you legally have the right not to pay? If not, what does it mean?

___ Activity 1 ___

Use the Tax Table in the Reference Section of the book to find the taxes owed by each of the following people.

	Filing Status	Taxable Income	Tax Owed
1.	Single	$ 3,500	_____
2.	Married, Filing Jointly	8,870	_____
3.	Married, Filing Separate	47,850	_____
4.	Head of Household	7,280	_____
5.	Single	10,170	_____

	Filing Status	Taxable Income	Tax Owed
6.	Married, Filing Jointly	46,220	_____
7.	Married, Filing Separately	29,470	_____
8.	Head of Household	49,100	_____
9.	Single	4,250	_____
10.	Married, Filing Jointly	16,305	_____
11.	Married, Filing Separately	37,777	_____
12.	Head of Household	15,555	_____
13.	Single	7,180	_____
14.	Married, Filing Jointly	20,900	_____
15.	Married, Filing Separately	29,820	_____
16.	Head of Household	35,500	_____
17.	Single	22,900	_____
18.	Married, Filing Jointly	39,158	_____
19.	Married, Filing Separately	24,630	_____
20.	Head of Household	23,785	_____

_____ **Activity 2** _____

Use the Tax Rate Schedule (X, Y, or Z) in the Reference Section to find the tax owed by each of the following people.

	Filing Status	Taxable Income	Tax Owed
1.	Single	$ 56,280	_____
2.	Married, Filing Jointly	82,400	_____
3.	Married, Filing Separately	59,680	_____
4.	Head of Household	71,700	_____
5.	Single	96,960	_____
6.	Married, Filing Jointly	78,500	_____
7.	Married, Filing Separately	67,333	_____
8.	Head of Household	91,650	_____
9.	Single	66,249	_____
10.	Married, Filing Jointly	60,134	_____
11.	Married, Filing Separately	67,011	_____
12.	Head of Household	93,393	_____
13.	Single	75,313	_____
14.	Married, Filing Jointly	52,808	_____
15.	Married, Filing Separately	43,812	_____
16.	Head of Household	121,750	_____
17.	Single	92,600	_____
18.	Married, Filing Jointly	125,000	_____
19.	Married, Filing Separately	86,234	_____
20.	Head of Household	56,140	_____

_____ **Activity 3** _____

Find the yearly income, the taxable income, the taxes owed, and the amounts to be withheld annually for the people described below. Use a standard deduction of $3,100 for single persons and $5,200 for married couples. The personal exemption is $2,000 for each exemption. Assume the married couples are filing a joint return.

Filing Status	Monthly Income	Yearly Income	No. of Exemptions	Taxable Income	Tax Owed	Annual Amount Withheld	Refund or Money Owed
Single	$ 825	$ 9,900	1	$ 4,800	$ 724	$ 984	$260
Single	1,250	_____	1	_____	_____	_____	_____
Single	462	_____	1	_____	_____	_____	_____
Single	1,555	_____	1	_____	_____	_____	_____
Single	1,298	_____	1	_____	_____	_____	_____
Single	785	_____	1	_____	_____	_____	_____
Single	2,378	_____	0	_____	_____	_____	_____
Single	3,550	_____	0	_____	_____	_____	_____
Single	2,091	_____	0	_____	_____	_____	_____
Single	1,634	_____	0	_____	_____	_____	_____
Married	3,500	42,000	4	28,800	4,324	4,560	236
Married	2,350	_____	3	_____	_____	_____	_____
Married	3,777	_____	5	_____	_____	_____	_____
Married	3,918	_____	4	_____	_____	_____	_____
Married	5,300	_____	2	_____	_____	_____	_____
Married	2,290	_____	3	_____	_____	_____	_____
Married	3,785	_____	4	_____	_____	_____	_____
Married	1,564	_____	5	_____	_____	_____	_____
Married	4,910	_____	6	_____	_____	_____	_____
Married	4,531	_____	2	_____	_____	_____	_____
Married	3,215	_____	3	_____	_____	_____	_____
Head of Household	1,780	21,360	3	_____	_____	_____	_____
Head of Household	2,116	_____	2	_____	_____	_____	_____
Head of Household	1,462	_____	2	_____	_____	_____	_____
Head of Household	3,209	_____	4	_____	_____	_____	_____

FORMS AND MORE FORMS— 1040A AND 1040EZ

Larry learned his lesson about Automatic Teller Machines the hard way. He still remembers the Saturday afternoon when he took so much cash from half a dozen different ATMs around town that he had to rush to the bank on Monday to put some of the money back in. He even had to borrow $100 from his mother to cover some of the checks he had already written on his checking account. Since that weekend he has been working to pay her back; she has hired him to do everything from mowing the lawn to doing the laundry and taking care of his baby cousin.

Larry also has an outside job as a clerk at a sporting goods store. When he received his W-2 form in January, Larry was amazed that his earnings had been so high. Where had all that money gone? He knew he had spent quite a lot on his car; then of course he and Lorrie Anne had gone out most weekends. Larry had bought a few gifts for her, too. But, Larry knew he was supposed to be saving for college.

At least the income taxes on Larry's earnings have been withheld throughout the year. He would certainly be in debt to his mother if he had to borrow $384 to pay the taxes. He could be baby-sitting his cousin until she is 21! As it is, Larry will get a refund. All he has to do now is fill out the proper form. Larry isn't sure whether he should use the 1040EZ or the 1040A form. He wonders if he would still get his refund if he sent in the wrong one.

OBJECTIVE: In this section, we will help Larry to:

● *fill out forms 1040EZ and 1040A*

WHICH FORM IS THE RIGHT ONE?

Larry would like to have his refund as soon as possible; he has not saved very much of the income from his job to use at college next year. Perhaps if he puts his tax refund in a savings account, his mother will think he is at least making an effort to save some! Of course, he could really use a jacket to go with the new skis he just bought.

Larry knows the IRS will not send his refund at all if he does not send in the form. The question is which form? Larry has no idea why they call all the forms 1040; he can choose from the regular, plain 1040, or the 1040A, or the 1040EZ. Larry hopes he can use the 1040EZ; maybe it is E Z to fill out.

1040EZ. As Larry will see when he finally reads the instructions, if he uses the 1040EZ form he must meet all the following requirements:

1. His filing status is single.

2. He does not claim any dependents.

3. He is under 65 and not blind at the end of the year.

4. His taxable income is less than $50,000.

5. His income included only wages, salaries, tips, and taxable scholarships or fellowships.

6. His taxable interest income was $400 or less.

If he does not meet these requirements, he must use 1040 if he has deductions to itemize (See Section 11-3) or 1040A if he has none.

1040A. If Larry chooses the 1040A he can still get the same refund. The 1040A form is longer and more complex because people can use it with more complicated sources of income, tax credits, and so on. It is the form his parents will use. To use it, you must know a little more about exemptions, dependents, and standard deductions.

Exemptions may potentially be claimed for each person filing, his or her spouse, and dependents, depending upon very detailed instructions. You can take an exemption for yourself unless someone (such as your parent) can claim you as a dependent on his or her tax return. On a joint return, you can take an exemption for your spouse if your spouse cannot be claimed as a dependent on another person's return. If you are filing a separate return, you can take an exemption for your spouse only if your spouse is not filing a return, had no income, and cannot be claimed as a dependent on another person's return.

The qualifications for being a dependent are fairly lengthy, too, and if we are uncertain about who can be our dependent, we must read the IRS publications more carefully. However, the basic requirements are that a dependent must:

1. Be a relative

2. Be a citizen or resident of the U.S.

3. Have gross income of less than $2,000

   • unless he or she is under 19 and is your child, or

   • unless he or she is under 24 and qualifies as a student and is your child

4. Have received at least half of his or her support from you

Following are the instructions for finding your **standard deduction**.

The standard deduction is one of the amounts you subtract from your gross income to find your taxable income.

Standard Deduction Chart for Most People	Line 16		

Standard Deduction Chart for Most People

Line 16

DO NOT use this chart if you were 65 or older or blind, OR if someone can claim you as a dependent.

If your filing status is:	enter on Form 1040A, line 16:
Single	$3,100
Married filing a joint return, or Qualifying widow(er) with dependent child	$5,200
Married filing a separate return and spouse does not itemize	$2,600
Head of household	$4,550

Standard Deduction Chart for People Age 65 or Older or Blind

If someone can claim you as a dependent, use the worksheet below, instead.

Enter the number from the box on line 15a of Form 1040A ▶ ☐   **Caution:** *Do not use the number of exemptions from line 6e.*

If your filing status is:	and the number in the box above is:	enter on Form 1040A, line 16:
Single	1	$3,850
	2	$4,600
Married filing a joint return or Qualifying widow(er) with dependent child	1	$5,800
	2	$6,400
	3	$7,000
	4	$7,600
Married filing a separate return	1	$3,200
	2	$3,800
	3	$4,400
	4	$5,000
Head of household	1	$5,300
	2	$6,050

Notice that the instructions for finding your standard deduction are part of the chart itself. The standard deduction is a separate figure from the personal exemptions. There is one standard deduction for every tax return filed. The category head of household is designed for people who are not partners in a married couple but do have dependents. These might be single parents or grown children caring for elderly parents.

Ask Yourself

1. What is the maximum taxable income a person may have and use the 1040EZ form?

2. In order to be claimed as a dependent, a person must meet what basic requirements?

3. What income besides salaries must be reported on tax forms?

SHARPEN YOUR SKILLS

_____ Skill 1 _____

Larry meets the requirements for using form 1040EZ.

Question   How shall he fill it out?

Solution   Larry has completed his form as shown on the following pages. He used the Tax Table and the instructions on the back of the form. He used the checklist in the 1040EZ instruction booklet to verify his work. These are shown after the form.

_____ Skill 2 _____

Larry's parents must complete the more complicated form 1040A.

Question   What steps must they take to complete the form?

Solution   Following Larry's form is the Lenders' 1040A. An explanation of some of the lines begins below. More detailed instructions are available from the IRS.

Step 1   The Lenders have filled in their names and address and social security numbers.

Step 2   Mr. and Mrs. Lender are married filing a joint return.

Step 3   Lines 6a and 6b. The Lenders claim two exemptions, one for each of them.

Line 6c. The Lenders list Larry as their only dependent.

Line 6e is the total of all the numbers in the 4 boxes in 6a, b, and c.

Step 4   Line 7 is the total of Mr. Lender's and Mrs. Lender's income from their salaries. These two amounts were shown on their W-2 forms:

Mr. Lender made $17,600

Mrs. Lender made $31,000

Line 8a is interest income received on a savings account they have at the credit union.

Lines 8b, 9, and 10 are left blank. If the Lenders had received any dividends from stock investments, they would have included these on line 9.

Line 11 is the total of lines 7, 8a, 9, and 10.

Step 5   The Lenders did not have IRA deductions, so lines 12a, 12b, and 12c are blank.

Department of the Treasury - Internal Revenue Service

Form 1040EZ

Income Tax Return for Single Filers With No Dependents (0)

Please print your numbers like this:

9 8 7 6 5 4 3 2 1 0

Name & address	Use the IRS mailing label. If you don't have one, please print.

L
A
B
E
L

H
E
R
E

Larry L. Lender
Print your name above (first, initial, last)

1040 Lesson St.
Present home address (number, street, and apt. no.). (If you have a P.O. box, see back.)

Omaha, INDIANA   45533
City, town, or post office, state, and ZIP code

Your social security number

3 4 5   4 5   6 7 8 9

Instructions are on the back. Also, see the Form 1040A/ 1040EZ booklet, especially the checklist on page 14.

Yes No

Presidential Election Campaign Fund
Do you want $1 to go to this fund?

Note: Checking "Yes" will not change your tax or reduce your refund. ▶

✓ [ ]

	Dollars	Cents

Report your income

Attach Copy B of Form(s) W-2 here.

*Note: You **must** check Yes or No.*

1	Total wages, salaries, and tips. This should be shown in Box 10 of your W-2 form(s). (Attach your W-2 form(s).)	1	5 , 4 6 0 . 0 0
2	Taxable interest income of $400 or less. If the total is more than $400, you cannot use Form 1040EZ.	2	2 0 0 . 0 0
3	Add line 1 and line 2. This is your **adjusted gross income.**	3	5 , 6 6 0 . 0 0
4	Can your parents (or someone else) claim you on their return? ☒ **Yes.** Do worksheet on back; enter amount from line E here. ☐ **No.** Enter 5,100. This is the total of your standard deduction and personal exemption.	4	3 , 1 0 0 . 0 0
5	Subtract line 4 from line 3. If line 4 is larger than line 3, enter 0. This is your **taxable income.**	5	2 , 5 6 0 . 0 0

Figure your tax

| 6 | Enter your Federal income tax withheld from Box 9 of your W-2 form(s). | 6 | 4 7 8 . 0 0 |
| 7 | **Tax.** Use the amount on **line 5** to look up your tax in the tax table on pages 41-46 of the Form 1040A/1040EZ booklet. Use the **single** column in the table. Enter the tax from the table on this line. | 7 | 3 8 4 . 0 0 |

Refund or amount you owe

Attach tax payment here.

| 8 | If line 6 is larger than line 7, subtract line 7 from line 6. This is your **refund.** | 8 | 9 4 . 0 0 |
| 9 | If line 7 is larger than line 6, subtract line 6 from line 7. This is the **amount you owe.** Attach check or money order for the full amount, payable to "Internal Revenue Service." | 9 | , . |

Sign your return

(Keep a copy of this form for your records.)

I have read this return. Under penalties of perjury, I declare that to the best of my knowledge and belief, the return is true, correct, and complete.

Your signature   Date

X *Larry Lender*   4-12—

For IRS Use Only—Please do not write in boxes below.

Form 1040EZ (1989)

Instructions for Form 1040EZ

Use this form if:	• Your filing status is single. • You do not claim any dependents.	• You were under 65 and not blind at the end of 1989. • Your taxable income (line 5) is less than $50,000.

• You had **only** wages, salaries, tips, and taxable scholarships or fellowships, and your taxable interest income was $400 or less. *Caution: If you earned tips (including allocated tips) that are not included in Box 14 of your W-2, you may not be able to use Form 1040EZ. See page 23 in the booklet.*

If you are not sure about your filing status or dependents, see pages 15 through 20 in the booklet.

If you can't use this form, see pages 11 through 13 in the booklet for which form to use.

Completing your return

Please print your numbers inside the boxes. Do not type your numbers. Do not use dollar signs. You may round off cents to whole dollars. To do so, drop amounts under 50 cents and increase amounts that are 50 cents or more. For example, $129.49 becomes $129 and $129.50 becomes $130. If you round off, do so for all amounts. But if you have to add two or more amounts to figure the amount to enter on a line, include cents when adding and round off only the total.

Name & address

Please use the mailing label we sent you. It can help speed your refund. After you complete your return, put the label in the name and address area. Cross out any errors. Print the right information on the label (including apartment number). **If you don't have a label,** print your name, address, and social security number. If your post office does not deliver mail to your home and you have a P.O. box, show your P.O. box number instead of your home address.

Presidential campaign fund

Congress set up this fund to help pay for Presidential election costs. If you want $1 of your tax to go to this fund, check the "Yes" box. If you check "Yes," your tax or refund will not change.

Report your income

Line 1. If you don't get your W-2 by February 15, contact your local IRS office. You must still report your wages, salaries, and tips even if you don't get a W-2 from your employer. Students, if you received a scholarship or fellowship, see page 23 in the booklet.

Line 2. Banks, savings and loans, credit unions, etc., should send you a Form 1099-INT showing the amount of taxable interest paid to you. You must report all your taxable interest even if you don't get a Form 1099-INT. If you had tax-exempt interest, such as on municipal bonds, write "TEI" in the space to the left of line 2. After "TEI," show the amount of your tax-exempt interest. **Do not** add tax-exempt interest in the total on line 2.

Line 4. If you checked "Yes" because someone can claim you as a dependent, fill in this worksheet to figure the amount to enter on line 4.

Standard deduction worksheet for dependents who checked "Yes" on line 4	A. Enter the amount from line 1 on front.	A. _____ 5460
	B. Minimum amount.	B. _____ 500.00
	C. **Compare** the amounts on lines A and B above. Enter the LARGER of the two amounts here.	C. _____ 5460
	D. Maximum amount.	D. _____ 3,100.00
	E. **Compare** the amounts on lines C and D above. Enter the SMALLER of the two amounts here and on line 4 on front.	E. _____ 3100

If you checked "No" because no one can claim you as a dependent, enter 5,100 on line 4. This is the total of your standard deduction (3,100) and personal exemption (2,000).

Figure your tax

Line 6. If you received a Form 1099-INT showing income tax withheld (backup withholding), include the amount in the total on line 6. To the left of line 6, write "Form 1099." If you had two or more employers and had total wages of over $48,000, see page 35 in the booklet.

If you want IRS to figure your tax, skip lines 7 through 9. Then sign and date your return. If you paid too much tax, we will send you a refund. If you didn't pay enough tax, we will send you a bill. We won't charge you interest or a late payment penalty if you pay within 30 days of the notice date or by April 16, 1990, whichever is later. If you want to figure your own tax, complete the rest of your return.

Amount you owe

Line 9. If you owe tax, attach your check or money order for the full amount. Write your social security number, daytime phone number, and "1989 Form 1040EZ" on your payment.

Sign your return

You must sign and date your return. If you pay someone to prepare your return, that person must sign it and show other information. See page 40 in the booklet.

Mailing your return

Mail your return by **April 16, 1990.** Use the envelope that came with your booklet. If you don't have that envelope, see page 49 in the booklet for the address.

Tax Table

For persons with taxable incomes of less than $50,000

2,000					
2,000	2,025	302	302	302	302
2,025	2,050	306	306	306	306
2,050	2,075	309	309	309	309
2,075	2,100	313	313	313	313
2,100	2,125	317	317	317	317
2,125	2,150	321	321	321	321
2,150	2,175	324	324	324	324
2,175	2,200	328	328	328	328
2,200	2,225	332	332	332	332
2,225	2,250	336	336	336	336
2,250	2,275	339	339	339	339
2,275	2,300	343	343	343	343
2,300	2,325	347	347	347	347
2,325	2,350	351	351	351	351
2,350	2,375	354	354	354	354
2,375	2,400	358	358	358	358
2,400	2,425	362	362	362	362
2,425	2,450	366	366	366	366
2,450	2,475	369	369	369	369
2,475	2,500	373	373	373	373
2,500	2,525	377	377	377	377
2,525	2,550	381	381	381	381
2,550	2,575	384	384	384	384
2,575	2,600	388	388	388	388
2,600	2,625	392	392	392	392
2,625	2,650	396	396	396	396
2,650	2,675	399	399	399	399
2,675	2,700	403	403	403	403

Section 2—Checklist for 1040EZ filers

Avoid common mistakes on Form 1040EZ

Most 1040EZ filers can fill out the form using only the instructions on the back of the form. After you have filled in your form, you can use this checklist to make sure you completed it accurately. Errors may delay your refund.

1. Are your name and address correct on the label? If not, did you correct the label?

2. Is your social security number correct?

3. Did you attach your W-2 form(s) to the left margin of your return?

4. Did you add and subtract correctly?

5. If someone (such as your parent) can claim you as a dependent on his or her tax return, did you check the "Yes" box on line 4 and fill out the worksheet on the back of the form?

6. Did you enter an amount on line 4?

7. Did you use the amount from **line 5** of Form 1040EZ to find your tax in the tax table? Also, did you use the column for **single** people in the table?

8. Did you sign and date your return?

9. If you did not receive a preaddressed envelope in this booklet, did you address your envelope to the service center for your area?

Form
1040A

Department of the Treasury—Internal Revenue Service
**U.S. Individual
Income Tax Return** (O)

OMB No. 1545-0085

Step 1

Label

Use IRS label. Otherwise, please print or type.

L A B E L H E R E	Your first name and initial NATHAN S.	Last name LENDER	Your social security no. 432 12 7777
	If a joint return, spouse's first name and initial MAUREEN T.	Last name LENDER	Spouse's social security no. 459 38 4141
	Home address (number and street). (If you have a P.O. box, see page 15 of the instructions.) 1040 LESSON ST.		Apt. no.
	City, town or post office, state and ZIP code. (If you have a foreign address, see page 15.) OMAHA, INDIANA 45533		

For Privacy Act and Paperwork Reduction Act Notice, see page 3.

Presidential Election Campaign Fund

Do you want $1 to go to this fund? . . . . ☑ Yes ☐ No

If joint return, does your spouse want $1 to go to this fund? ☑ Yes ☐ No

Note: *Checking "Yes" will not change your tax or reduce your refund.*

Step 2

Check your filing status

(Check only one.)

1 ☐ Single (See if you can use Form 1040EZ.)

2 ☑ Married filing joint return (even if only one had income)

3 ☐ Married filing separate return. Enter spouse's social security number above and spouse's full name here. _____

4 ☐ Head of household (with qualifying person). (See page 16.) If the qualifying person is your child but not your dependent, enter this child's name here. _____

5 ☐ Qualifying widow(er) with dependent child (year spouse died ▶ 19 ___). (See page 17.)

Step 3

Figure your exemptions

(See page 17 of instructions.)

6a ☑ **Yourself** If someone (such as your parent) can claim you as a dependent on his or her tax return, do not check box 6a. But be sure to check the box on line 15b on page 2.

6b ☑ **Spouse**

No. of boxes checked on 6a and 6b **2**

C Dependents: 1. Name (first, initial, and last name)	2. Check if under age 2	3. If age 2 or older, dependent's social security number	4. Relationship	5. No. of months lived in your home in 1989
LARRY L. LENDER		345 45 6789	SON	12

No. of your children on 6c who:

● lived with you **1**

● didn't live with you due to divorce or separation (see page 20) ___

No. of **other** dependents listed on 6c ___

If more than 7 dependents, see page 20.

Attach Copy B of Form(s) W-2 here.

d If your child didn't live with you but is claimed as your dependent under a pre-1985 agreement, check here . . . . ▶ ☐

e Total number of exemptions claimed.

Add numbers entered on lines above **3**

Step 4

Figure your total income

Attach check or money order here.

7 Wages, salaries, tips, etc. This should be shown in Box 10 of your W-2 form(s). (Attach Form(s) W-2.) **7** | 48600 00

8a **Taxable** interest income (see page 24). (If over $400, also complete and attach Schedule 1, Part II.) **8a** | 300 00

b **Tax-exempt** interest income (see page 24). (DO NOT include on line 8a.) **8b** |

9 Dividends. (If over $400, also complete and attach Schedule 1, Part III.) **9** |

10 Unemployment compensation (insurance) from Form(s) 1099-G. **10** |

11 Add lines 7, 8a, 9, and 10. Enter the total. This is your **total income.** ▶ **11** | 48900 00

Step 5

Figure your adjusted gross income

12a Your IRA deduction from applicable worksheet. Rules for IRAs begin on page 25. **12a** |

b Spouse's IRA deduction from applicable worksheet. Rules for IRAs begin on page 25. **12b** |

c Add lines 12a and 12b. Enter the total. These are your **total adjustments.** **12c** |

13 Subtract line 12c from line 11. Enter the result. This is your **adjusted gross income.** (If this line is less than $19,340 and a child lived with you, see "Earned Income Credit" (line 25b) on page 37 of instructions.) ▶ **13** | 48900 00

Form 1040A

Step 6	**14** Enter the amount from line 13.	14	48 900 00

15a Check if: ☐ **You** were 65 or older ☐ Blind Enter number of boxes checked ▶15a ☐
☐ **Spouse** was 65 or older ☐ Blind

b If someone (such as your parent) can claim you as a dependent, check here . . . . ▶15b ☐

c If you are married filing separately and your spouse files Form 1040 and itemizes deductions, see page 29 and check here . . ▶15c ☐

Figure your standard deduction,

16 Enter your standard deduction. See page 30 for the chart (or worksheet) that applies to you. Be sure to enter your standard deduction here.   16   5200 00

exemption amount, and

17 Subtract line 16 from line 14. Enter the result. (If line 16 is more than line 14, enter -0-.)   17   43700 00

18 Multiply $2,000 by the total number of exemptions claimed on line 6e.   18   6000 00

taxable income

19 Subtract line 18 from line 17. Enter the result. (If line 18 is more than line 17, enter -0-.) This is your **taxable income**.   ▶ 19   37700 00

If You Want IRS To Figure Your Tax, See Page 31 of the Instructions.

Step 7

Figure your tax, credits, supplemental Medicare premium, and payments (including advance EIC payments)

Caution: If you are under age 14 and have more than $1,000 of investment income, check here   ▶ ☐
Also see page 31 to see if you have to use Form 8615 to figure your tax.

20 Find the tax on the amount on line 19. Check if from: ☒ Tax Table (pages 41–46) or ☐ Form 8615   20   6540 00

21 Credit for child and dependent care expenses. Complete and attach Schedule 1, Part I.   21

22 Subtract line 21 from line 20. Enter the result. (If line 21 is more than line 20, enter -0-.)   22

23 Supplemental Medicare premium. See page 35. Complete and attach Schedule 2 (Form 1040A).   23

24 Add lines 22 and 23. Enter the total. This is your **total tax** and any supplemental Medicare premium.   ▶ 24   6540 00

25a Total Federal income tax withheld—from Box 9 of your W-2 form(s). (If any is from Form(s) 1099, check here ▶ ☐ .)   25a   7216 80

b Earned income credit, from the worksheet on page 38 of the instructions. Also see page 37.   25b

26 Add lines 25a and 25b. Enter the total. These are your **total payments**.   ▶ 26   7216 80

Step 8

Figure your refund or amount you owe

27 If line 26 is more than line 24, subtract line 24 from line 26. Enter the result. This is your **refund**.   27   676 80

28 If line 24 is more than line 26, subtract line 26 from line 24. Enter the result. This is the **amount you owe**. Attach check or money order for full amount payable to "Internal Revenue Service." Write your social security number, daytime phone number, and "1989 Form 1040A" on it.   28

Step 9

Sign your return

(Keep a copy of this return for your records.)

Under penalties of perjury, I declare that I have examined this return and accompanying schedules and statements, and to the best of my knowledge and belief, they are true, correct, and complete. Declaration of preparer (other than the taxpayer) is based on all information of which the preparer has any knowledge.

Your signature	Date	Your occupation
X *Nathan Lender*	4-13-	Accountant

Spouse's signature (if joint return, both must sign)	Date	Spouse's occupation
X *Maureen Lender*	4-13-	Systems Analyst

Paid preparer's use only

Preparer's signature	Date	Preparer's social security no.
X		

Firm's name (or yours if self-employed)		Employer identification no.

Address and ZIP code		Check if self-employed ☐

Line 13 is the same as line 11 for the Lenders. If they had made deposits to IRA accounts, lines 12a, 12b, and 12c would have been the place to claim the tax deferral.

Step 6   Line 14 is the same as line 13.

The Lenders are not over 65 or blind so lines 15a, b, and c are left blank.

Line 16 is the standard deduction amount. This is one portion of your income on which you do not have to pay taxes.

Lines 17, 18, and 19: The Lenders followed the instructions printed in the form to arrive at their taxable income.

Step 7   Lines 20 and 24. Following is the portion of the tax table the Lenders used to find their tax.

Lines 21, 22, and 23 are blank. The amount of line 25a is the amount of income tax that was withheld from both their paychecks combined. The amounts were shown on their W-2 forms.

To complete the rest of the form, the Lenders follow the instructions printed on it. In Step 8, they figure their refund or the amount they owe. Both of them must sign the form, then they will mail it, by the deadline, to the IRS.

Tax Table

If 1040A, line 19, OR 1040EZ, line 5 is—		And you are—				If 1040A, line 19, OR 1040EZ, line 5 is—		And you are—			
At least	But less than	Single (and 1040EZ filers)	Married filing jointly *	Married filing separately	Head of a household	At least	But less than	Single (and 1040EZ filers)	Married filing jointly *	Married filing separately	Head of a household
		Your tax is—						Your tax is—			
35,000						**38,000**					
35,000	35,050	7,396	5,784	7,795	6,577	38,000	38,050	8,236	6,624	8,665	7,417
35,050	35,100	7,410	5,798	7,809	6,591	38,050	38,100	8,250	6,638	8,682	7,431
35,100	35,150	7,424	5,812	7,823	6,605	38,100	38,150	8,264	6,652	8,698	7,445
35,150	35,200	7,438	5,826	7,837	6,619	38,150	38,200	8,278	6,666	8,715	7,459
35,200	35,250	7,452	5,840	7,851	6,633	38,200	38,250	8,292	6,680	8,731	7,473
35,250	35,300	7,466	5,854	7,865	6,647	38,250	38,300	8,306	6,694	8,748	7,487
35,300	35,350	7,480	5,868	7,879	6,661	38,300	38,350	8,320	6,708	8,764	7,501
35,350	35,400	7,494	5,882	7,893	6,675	38,350	38,400	8,334	6,722	8,781	7,515
35,400	35,450	7,508	5,896	7,907	6,689	38,400	38,450	8,348	6,736	8,797	7,529
35,450	35,500	7,522	5,910	7,921	6,703	38,450	38,500	8,362	6,750	8,814	7,543
35,500	35,550	7,536	5,924	7,935	6,717	38,500	38,550	8,376	6,764	8,830	7,557
35,550	35,600	7,550	5,938	7,949	6,731	38,550	38,600	8,390	6,778	8,847	7,571
35,600	35,650	7,564	5,952	7,963	6,745	38,600	38,650	8,404	6,792	8,863	7,585
35,650	35,700	7,578	5,966	7,977	6,759	38,650	38,700	8,418	6,806	8,880	7,599
35,700	35,750	7,592	5,980	7,991	6,773	38,700	38,750	8,432	6,820	8,896	7,613
35,750	35,800	7,606	5,994	8,005	6,787	38,750	38,800	8,446	6,834	8,913	7,627
35,800	35,850	7,620	6,008	8,019	6,801	38,800	38,850	8,460	6,848	8,929	7,641
35,850	35,900	7,634	6,022	8,033	6,815	38,850	38,900	8,474	6,862	8,946	7,655
35,900	35,950	7,648	6,036	8,047	6,829	38,900	38,950	8,488	6,876	8,962	7,669
35,950	36,000	7,662	6,050	8,061	6,843	38,950	39,000	8,502	6,890	8,979	7,683

EXERCISE YOUR SKILLS

1. Why do you think the government does not require everyone to file the same income tax form?

2. Why do you think most married people file joint returns?

3. Why do you think people are allowed to subtract standard deductions to find their taxable income?

_____ **Activity 1** _____

Fill out a 1040EZ form for each of the following amounts. For Problems 1–5, make up a name and address; be sure to mark each form with the problem number you are doing. For Problems 6–9, use the given information. All of the people are single. You may choose whether or not to contribute to the election campaign fund; this choice will not affect anything else you fill out. The standard deduction amount for line 4 will be $3,100 unless the adjusted gross income from line 3 is less than that.

	Income	Withholding	Claimed as a Dependent by Someone
1.	$2,400	$ 125	No
2.	4,200	140	Yes
3.	8,500	550	Yes
4.	18,600	2,000	No
5.	2 jobs: 15,400; 2,200	1,600; 0	No

6. Daryl Hawkins
   1234 Sesame Street
   Phoenix, Arizona   85442
   S.S # 551-76-3333
   Wages: $20,650
   Withholding: $2,500
   Interest Income: $50.00
   Daryl will be claimed as a
   dependent on another's return.

7. Yazmin Rogers
   2020 Twentieth Ave.
   Seattle, Washington   98043
   S.S. # 456-78-4321
   Wages: $39,400
   Withholding: $6,200
   Interest Income: $150.00
   Yazmin will not be claimed as a
   dependent elsewhere.

8. Brent Holmes
   1415 16th Ave.
   Dallas, Texas   75277
   S.S. # 432-55-7777
   Wages: $6,200
   Withholding: $638
   Interest Income: $246.80
   Brent will be claimed as a
   dependent elsewhere.

9. Renata Taylor
   2323 Ranger Street
   Cincinnati, Ohio   50303
   S.S. # 543-77-2222
   Wages: $35,170
   Withholding: $11,485
   Interest Income: $310
   Renata will not be claimed
   as a dependent elsewhere.

———— **Activity 2** ————

Fill out a 1040A form for each of the following couples or individuals. Their social security numbers are shown in parentheses.

1. (421-32-4587) (476-58-9023)
Flora and Ernest Jones
10101 Sesame Street
Anaheim, California   98043
Filing a joint return
Wages: Flora $19,400
        Ernest $21,620
Withholding: Flora $2,350
             Ernest $4,195

Dependents:
Bea   (6) (452-79-5644)
Phillip (14) (751-44-9086)
Earl   (17) (555-44-9922)

Interest Income: $200
Dividends: $180

2. (458-29-7011) (492-71-6322)
Emilio and Rosa Ortiz
13422 Euclid Avenue
Des Moines, Iowa 55105
Filing a joint return
Wages: Emilio $48,750
        Rosa $53,790
Withholding: Emilio $12,695
            Rosa $13,476

Dependents:
Rosita (4) (711-42-9086)
Julio   (8) (329-44-7890)
Carlos (12) (666-21-4444)

Interest Income: $280
Dividends: $195

3. (463-44-9292)
Janice Parker
9286 Spring Blvd.
Two Egg, Florida   32304
Filing as head of household
Wages: Janice $38,450
Withholding: Janice $6,750

Dependents:
Dimitri (12) (428-77-4083)
Newton (14) (555-99-6666)
Sophia (16) (444-55-7799)

Interest Income: $40
Dividends: $300

4. (716-432-9026)
John Madison, Jr.
1409 S. Alta Vista
San Remo, Texas 77566
Filing as head of household
Wages: $46,400
Withholding: $8,952

Dependent:
John Madison, Sr.
        (87) (499-602-6710)

Interest Income: $1050
Dividends: $3029

1040, SCHEDULE A, AND HELP!

Evelyn went into business with her friends selling T-shirts and sweatshirts with hand-painted designs. After a few months, they had their production process fairly well settled and began to show a profit. Now it is February and they have been in business since August; Evelyn knows she must file an income tax return for the income she has received from the business.

Evelyn wants her tax return to be completed very carefully. She heard a couple of her classmates talking about Cal's father's problems with stock investments. They were discussing several of his visits to the IRS office; apparently the IRS was re-examining some of his former tax returns. The way Evelyn heard the gossip, he had to pay over $12,000 in back taxes that the IRS said he owed.

Evelyn knew she couldn't begin to scrape together $12,000 to pay the government, especially not at any one time. Her parents assure her that unless her profits are over $60,000 in one year, she will not have to pay that much. They have had years when their tax bill was that high, however, so Evelyn knows that federal income tax is not an insignificant amount to anyone who receives an income.

If Evelyn decides she cannot fill out the proper forms and needs some help, several sources of assistance are available. Evelyn will explore some of these sources.

OBJECTIVES: In this section, we will help Evelyn to:

consider where a taxpayer can go for help in filing a tax return
complete form 1040 and Schedule A

TAX HELP— HELP!

When Evelyn first looked at the array of different tax forms that are available at the local IRS office, she was not even sure which ones to pick up. She finally settled on the 1040 form, a booklet of instructions, and a few other schedules that looked like they might have something to do with business.

Evelyn's parents have been filing the 1040 form every year since they bought their first house. They know that the interest they pay on the mortgage is **deductible,** which means they do not have to pay taxes on it. However, to take advantage of this deduction, they must use the 1040 form.

Evelyn, who cannot tell a deduction from a dependent, looks at the 1040 form and wonders if it is truly written in English. She recognizes the words, but making sense out of what they say appears to be a formidable task. Fortunately for Evelyn, some people make their living interpreting all the rules set up by the IRS.

By the middle of the 1980s, over a third of all taxpayers sought help from the IRS, and millions of others paid from ten dollars to thousands of dollars for tax help from other sources. For Evelyn and millions like her, four major sources of tax help are available: the IRS, mass-market tax preparation services, CPA tax specialists, and tax lawyers. The first three of these are described below.

Internal Revenue Service. The IRS has a toll-free telephone answering service and nearly 1000 tax assistance centers located throughout the United States. Under certain circumstances, the IRS will figure tax on either Form 1040 or Form 1040A for you. Of course, you must provide complete information and appropriate schedules. The IRS has been known to dispense misleading or incorrect advice in its publications, answer questions incorrectly, make mathematical errors, and even give taxpayers the wrong forms. Nevertheless, taxpayers are responsible for any mistakes made by agency employees. Claiming that you were misinformed will not help if a tax audit is made on your return. (A **tax audit** is an examination of your tax return by the IRS.)

Mass-Market Tax Preparation. Some tax preparation services will prepare your 1040A forms for $10 to $25. Since you have to find and provide all the essential records—which is most of the work—this fee hardly represents a bargain. Enormous effort has been made to simplify the forms so you could fill them out yourself and save the money. If you feel that preparation service is necessary, however, you should talk personally with the person who works on the return to find out something about the preparer's background.

Certified Public Accountants. For complicated tax work, a certified public accountant (CPA) who specializes in taxes is the best source of tax help. Beware, however, of accountants who promise spectacular tax savings.

Do-It-Yourself. Being in business for herself with her friends has given Evelyn more confidence, especially since the business has started to grow and make a profit. Evelyn found in the early stages of the business that visits to her local bookstore and library were very beneficial. She did notice in the business section of the bookstore a whole shelf of books offering advice on how to fill out tax returns. Evelyn's parents have read a few of these tax guides, and every year they study the new changes in the tax law.

Ask Yourself

1. What are four major sources of help in filing income taxes?

2. What is a tax audit?

3. What is the best source of tax help for complicated returns?

SHARPEN YOUR SKILLS

___ Skill 1 ___

Mr. and Mrs. Enterprise file the 1040 form each year mainly because of the mortgage interest deduction. Many parts of the 1040 form are similar to those on the 1040A form. Quite a few of the lines on the 1040 do not apply to them.

Questions   **1.** How should the Enterprises complete their 1040 form?

2. How should they use Schedule A to itemize their deductions?

Solutions

1. On the opposite page is the 1040 filled out by Mr. and Mrs. Enterprise. Following is an explanation of some of the lines.

    The 1040 form is divided into sections by heavy lines and titles for each section.

    The sections with names, address, social security numbers, filing status, and exemptions are the same as on the 1040A. The differences in the forms begin to appear in the income section.

Line 7   Wages, salaries (same as on the 1040 form)

Line 8a   Taxable interest (same as on the 1040 form)

Line 9   Divided income (same as on the 1040 form)

Lines 10–22   Places to list various other kinds of income a family might have. Refer to the IRS instruction booklet for the 1040 form for more detail.

Line 23   Total of lines 7–22.

Lines 24–30   Do not apply to Evelyn's parents; they will write 0.00 on line 30.

Lines 31, 32, and 33   Follow instructions printed on the form.

Line 34   One of the major differences in the two forms. If a family finds that the standard deduction is not as much as the itemized deductions they can list on Schedule A, this is the line on which they will enter the total from Schedule A instead of the standard deduction. The standard deduction can be listed here as on the 1040A. Schedule A will be explained later in this section.

Lines 35, 36, and 37   Follow instructions on the form.

Line 38   The tax, found on the portion of the tax table which follows the 1040 tax forms.

Form **1040** Department of the Treasury—Internal Revenue Service
U.S. Individual Income Tax Return 19

For the year Jan.–Dec. 31, 198 , or other tax year beginning , 198 , ending , 19 | OMB No. 1545-0074

Label

Use IRS label.
Otherwise,
please print
or type.

L A B E L H E R E

Your first name and initial   Last name
FREEMONT O. ENTERPRISE

If a joint return, spouse's first name and initial   Last name
ELAINE P. ENTERPRISE

Home address (number and street). (If a P.O. box, see page 7 of Instructions.)   Apt. no.
11300 OAKLAND AVE.

City, town or post office, state and ZIP code. (If a foreign address, see page 7.)
INLAND, INDIANA 12345

Your social security number
526 : 31 : 7055

Spouse's social security number
475 : 42 : 9266

**For Privacy Act and
Paperwork Reduction
Act Notice, see
Instructions.**

**Presidential
Election Campaign**

Do you want $1 to go to this fund?. . . . . ✔ Yes ▢ No
If joint return, does your spouse want $1 to go to this fund? . ✔ Yes ▢ No

Note: *Checking "Yes" will
not change your tax or
reduce your refund.*

Filing Status

Check only
one box.

1 ▢ Single
2 ✔ Married filing joint return (even if only one had income)
3 ▢ Married filing separate return. Enter spouse's social security no. above and full name here.
4 ▢ Head of household (with qualifying person). (See page 7 of Instructions.) If the qualifying person is your child but not your dependent, enter child's name here.
5 ▢ Qualifying widow(er) with dependent child (year spouse died ▶ 19). (See page 7 of Instructions.)

Exemptions

(See
Instructions
on page 8.)

If more than 6
dependents, see
Instructions on
page 8.

6a ▢ **Yourself** If someone (such as your parent) can claim you as a dependent on his or her tax return, do not check box 6a. But be sure to check the box on line 33b on page 2 . .
b ▢ **Spouse** . . . .

c **Dependents:** (1) Name (first, initial, and last name)	(2) Check if under age 2	(3) If age 2 or older, dependent's social security number	(4) Relationship	(5) No. of months lived in your home in 1989
		:		
		:		
		:		
		:		
		:		

d If your child didn't live with you but is claimed as your dependent under a pre-1985 agreement, check here ▶ ▢
e Total number of exemptions claimed . . . .

No. of boxes
checked on 6a
and 6b   **2**

No. of your
children on 6c
who:

● lived with you   **1**

● didn't live with
you due to
divorce or
separation (see
page 9)

No. of other
dependents on 6c

Add numbers
entered on
lines above   ▶ **3**

Income

Please attach
Copy B of your
Forms W-2, W-2G,
and W-2P here.

If you do not have
a W-2, see
page 6 of
Instructions.

Please
attach check
or money
order here.

7 Wages, salaries, tips, etc. *(attach Form(s) W-2)* . . . . | 7 | 47350 00
8a **Taxable** interest income *(also attach Schedule B if over $400)* . . . | 8a | 650 00
  b Tax-exempt interest income (see page 10). DON'T include on line 8a| **8b** | |
9 Dividend income *(also attach Schedule B if over $400)* . . . | 9 |
10 Taxable refunds of state and local income taxes, if any, from worksheet on page 11 of Instructions . . | 10 |
11 Alimony received . . . . | 11 |
12 Business income or (loss) *(attach Schedule C)* . . . . | 12 |
13 Capital gain or (loss) *(attach Schedule D)* . . . . | 13 |
14 Capital gain distributions not reported on line 13 (see page 11) . . | 14 |
15 Other gains or (losses) *(attach Form 4797)* . . . . | 15 |
16a Total IRA distributions . . | 16a | |16b Taxable amount (see page 11) | 16b |
17a Total pensions and annuities | 17a | |17b Taxable amount (see page 12) | 17b |
18 Rents, royalties, partnerships, estates, trusts, etc. *(attach Schedule E)* | 18 |
19 Farm income or (loss) *(attach Schedule F)* . . . . | 19 |
20 Unemployment compensation (insurance) (see page 13) . . . | 20 |
21a Social security benefits . . | 21a | |21b Taxable amount (see page 13) | 21b |
22 Other income (list type and amount—see page 13) . . . . . . | 22 |
23 Add the amounts shown in the far right column for lines 7 through 22. This is your **total income** ▶ | 23 | 48000 00

**Adjustments
to Income**

(See
Instructions
on page 14.)

24 Your IRA deduction, from applicable worksheet on page 14 or 15 | 24 |
25 Spouse's IRA deduction, from applicable worksheet on page 14 or 15 | 25 |
26 Self-employed health insurance deduction, from worksheet on page 15 | 26 |
27 Keogh retirement plan and self-employed SEP deduction | 27 |
28 Penalty on early withdrawal of savings | 28 |
29 Alimony paid. **a** Recipient's last name_____
  and **b** social security number . . : : | 29 |
30 Add lines 24 through 29. These are your **total adjustments** . . . . ▶ | 30 | 0 00

**Adjusted
Gross Income**

31 Subtract line 30 from line 23. This is your **adjusted gross income.** *If this line is less than $19,340 and a child lived with you, see "Earned Income Credit" (line 58) on page 20 of the Instructions. If you want IRS to figure your tax, see page 16 of the Instructions* . . ▶ | 31 | 48000 00

Form 1040   Page **2**

Tax Compu- tation	32	Amount from line 31 (adjusted gross income)	32	*48000*	*00*
	33a	Check if: ☐ **You** were 65 or older ☐ Blind; ☐ **Spouse** was 65 or older ☐ Blind. Add the number of boxes checked and enter the total here . . . . . ▶ 33a			
	b	If someone (such as your parent) can claim you as a dependent, check here . . ▶ 33b ☐			
	c	If you are married filing a separate return and your spouse itemizes deductions, or you are a dual-status alien, see page 16 and check here . . . . . ▶ 33c ☐			
	34	Enter the **larger** of: { ● Your **standard deduction** (from page 17 of the Instructions), **OR** ● Your **itemized deductions** (from Schedule A, line 26). If you itemize, attach Schedule A and check here . . ▶ ☐ }	34	*7590*	*00*
	35	Subtract line 34 from line 32. Enter the result here	35	*40410*	*00*
	36	Multiply $2,000 by the total number of exemptions claimed on line 6e . . .	36	*6000*	*00*
	37	**Taxable income.** Subtract line 36 from line 35. Enter the result (if less than zero, enter zero)	37	*34410*	*00*
		Caution: If under age 14 and you have more than $1,000 of investment income, check here ▶ ☐ and see page 17 to see if you have to use Form 8615 to figure your tax.			
	38	Enter tax. Check if from: **a** ☒ Tax Table, **b** ☐ Tax Rate Schedules, or **c** ☐ Form 8615. (If any is from Form(s) 8814, enter that amount here ▶ **d** ⌐_____.)	38	*5616*	*00*
	39	Additional taxes (see page 18). Check if from: **a** ☐ Form 4970 **b** ☐ Form 4972 . . .	39		
	40	Add lines 38 and 39. Enter the total . . . . ▶	40	*5616*	*00*
Credits (See Instructions on page 18.)	41	Credit for child and dependent care expenses *(attach Form 2441)*	41		
	42	Credit for the elderly or the disabled *(attach Schedule R)* . .	42		
	43	Foreign tax credit *(attach Form 1116)*	43		
	44	General business credit. Check if from: **a** ☐ Form 3800 or **b** ☐ Form (specify) _____	44		
	45	Credit for prior year minimum tax *(attach Form 8801)*	45		
	46	Add lines 41 through 45. Enter the total	46	*000*	*00*
	47	Subtract line 46 from line 40. Enter the result (if less than zero, enter zero) . . . . . . ▶	47	*5616*	*00*
Other Taxes (Including Advance EIC Payments)	48	Self-employment tax *(attach Schedule SE)*	48		
	49	Alternative minimum tax *(attach Form 6251)*	49		
	50	Recapture taxes (see page 18). Check if from: **a** ☐ Form 4255 **b** ☐ Form 8611 . .	50		
	51	Social security tax on tip income not reported to employer *(attach Form 4137)*	51		
	52	Tax on an IRA or a qualified retirement plan *(attach Form 5329)* . . .	52		
	53	Add lines 47 through 52. Enter the total . . . . ▶	53	*5616*	*00*
Medicare Premium	54	Supplemental Medicare premium *(attach Form 8808)*	54		
	55	Add lines 53 and 54. This is your **total tax** and any supplemental Medicare premium . ▶	55	*5616*	*00*
Payments Attach Forms W-2, W-2G, and W-2P to front.	56	Federal income tax withheld (if any is from Form(s) 1099, check ▶ ☐)	56	*7212 00*	
	57	1989 estimated tax payments and amount applied from 1988 return	57		
	58	Earned income credit (see page 20)	58		
	59	Amount paid with Form 4868 (extension request)	59		
	60	Excess social security tax and RRTA tax withheld (see page 20)	60		
	61	Credit for Federal tax on fuels *(attach Form 4136)* . .	61		
	62	Regulated investment company credit *(attach Form 2439)* . .	62		
	63	Add lines 56 through 62. These are your **total payments** . . . . ▶	63	*7212*	*00*
Refund or Amount You Owe	64	If line 63 is larger than line 55, enter amount **OVERPAID** . . . . ▶	64	*1596*	*00*
	65	Amount of line 64 to be **REFUNDED TO YOU** . . . . ▶	65	*1596*	*00*
	66	Amount of line 64 to be **APPLIED TO YOUR 1990 ESTIMATED TAX** ▶ 66			
	67	If line 55 is larger than line 63, enter **AMOUNT YOU OWE.** Attach check or money order for full amount payable to "Internal Revenue Service." Write your social security number, daytime phone number, and "1989 Form 1040" on it	67		
	68	Penalty for underpayment of estimated tax (see page 21) . . 68			

Sign Here

(Keep a copy of this return for your records.)

Under penalties of perjury, I declare that I have examined this return and accompanying schedules and statements, and to the best of my knowledge and belief, they are true, correct, and complete. Declaration of preparer (other than taxpayer) is based on all information of which preparer has any knowledge.

Your signature	Date	Your occupation
Freemont Enterprise	*4/12/–*	*Production Manager*
Spouse's signature (if joint return, BOTH must sign)	Date	Spouse's occupation
Elaine Enterprise	*4/12/–*	*School Teacher*

Paid Preparer's Use Only

Preparer's signature ▶	Date	Check if self-employed ☐	Preparer's social security no.
Firm's name (or yours if self-employed) and address ▶		E.I. No.	
		ZIP code	

Line 39	Will be blank.
Line 40	Follow instructions on the form.
Lines 41–45	Will be blank for the Enterprises.
Line 46	Will show 0.00.
Line 47	Follow instructions on the form.
Lines 48–52	Will be blank.
Line 53	Follow instructions on the form.
Line 54	Blank
Line 55	Follow instructions on the form.
Line 56	Shows combined amount that was withheld from their income for income tax; the amounts were shown on their W-2 forms.
Line 57–62	Blank
Lines 63–67	Follow instructions.

2. Since Mr. and Mrs. Enterprise have paid $4,500 in interest on their home mortgage, and several other expenses that can be listed on Schedule A, they will use Schedule A to find the total of their itemized deductions.

When they finish this form they will enter this total on line 34 on their 1040 form.

On the next page is the Schedule A they completed. Following is an explanation of some of the lines.

The Enterprises have only a few of the simplest deductions, as follows:

Line 1	Medical expenses—$4,250.00
Line 2	Following the instructions—$4,250.00
Line 3	Following the instructions—0.075 x $4,250 = $3,600.00
Line 4	Following the instructions—$650.00
Line 6	Taxes on their home—$1,240
Line 8	Following instructions—$1,240
Line 9a	Interest on their mortgage—$4,500
Line 13	Following instructions—$4,500
Line 14	Contributions to a community charity—$1,200
Line 17	Following instructions—$1,200
Line 26	Totals from lines 4, 8, 13, 17—$7,590
	This amount is entered on their 1040 form
	on line 34.

19__ Tax Table—Continued

If line 37 (taxable income) is—		And you are—			
At least	But less than	Single	Married filing jointly *	Married filing separately	Head of a household
			Your tax is—		
32,000					
32,000	32,050	6,556	4,944	6,955	5,737
32,050	32,100	6,570	4,958	6,969	5,751
32,100	32,150	6,584	4,972	6,983	5,765
32,150	32,200	6,598	4,986	6,997	5,779
32,200	32,250	6,612	5,000	7,011	5,793
32,250	32,300	6,626	5,014	7,025	5,807
32,300	32,350	6,640	5,028	7,039	5,821
32,350	32,400	6,654	5,042	7,053	5,835
32,400	32,450	6,668	5,056	7,067	5,849
32,450	32,500	6,682	5,070	7,081	5,863
32,500	32,550	6,696	5,084	7,095	5,877
32,550	32,600	6,710	5,098	7,109	5,891
32,600	32,650	6,724	5,112	7,123	5,905
32,650	32,700	6,738	5,126	7,137	5,919
32,700	32,750	6,752	5,140	7,151	5,933
32,750	32,800	6,766	5,154	7,165	5,947
32,800	32,850	6,780	5,168	7,179	5,961
32,850	32,900	6,794	5,182	7,193	5,975
32,900	32,950	6,808	5,196	7,207	5,989
32,950	33,000	6,822	5,210	7,221	6,003
33,000					
33,000	33,050	6,836	5,224	7,235	6,017
33,050	33,100	6,850	5,238	7,249	6,031
33,100	33,150	6,864	5,252	7,263	6,045
33,150	33,200	6,878	5,266	7,277	6,059
33,200	33,250	8,892	5,280	7,291	6,073
33,250	33,300	6,906	5,294	7,305	6,087
33,300	33,350	6,920	5,308	7,319	6,101
33,350	33,400	6,934	5,322	7,333	6,115
33,400	33,450	6,948	5,336	7,347	6,129
33,450	33,500	6,962	5,350	7,361	6,143
33,500	33,550	6,976	5,364	7,375	6,157
33,550	33,600	6,990	5,378	7,389	6,171
33,600	33,650	7,004	5,392	7,403	6,185
33,650	33,700	7,018	5,406	7,417	6,199
33,700	33,750	7,032	5,420	7,431	6,213
33,750	33,800	7,046	5,434	7,445	6,227
33,800	33,850	7,060	5,448	7,459	6,241
33,850	33,900	7,074	5,462	7,473	6,255
33,900	33,950	7,088	5,476	7,487	6,269
33,950	34,000	7,102	5,490	7,501	6,283
34,000					
34,000	34,050	7,116	5,504	7,515	6,297
34,050	34,100	7,130	5,518	7,529	6,311
34,100	34,150	7,144	5,532	7,543	6,325
34,150	34,200	7,158	5,546	7,557	6,339
34,200	34,250	7,172	5,560	7,571	6,353
34,250	34,300	7,186	5,574	7,585	6,367
34,300	34,350	7,200	5,588	7,599	6,381
34,350	34,400	7,214	5,602	7,613	6,395
34,400	34,450	7,228	5,616	7,627	6,409
34,450	34,500	7,242	5,630	7,641	6,423
34,500	34,550	7,256	5,644	7,655	6,437
34,550	34,600	7,270	5,658	7,669	6,451
34,600	34,650	7,284	5,672	7,683	6,465
34,650	34,700	7,298	5,686	7,697	6,479
34,700	34,750	7,312	5,700	7,711	6,493
34,750	34,800	7,326	5,714	7,725	6,507
34,800	34,850	7,340	5,728	7,739	6,521
34,850	34,900	7,354	5,742	7,753	6,535
34,900	34,950	7,368	5,756	7,767	6,549
34,950	35,000	7,382	5,770	7,781	6,563

| SCHEDULES A&B
(Form 1040)

Department of the Treasury
Internal Revenue Service (O) | **Schedule A—Itemized Deductions**
(Schedule B is on back)
► Attach to Form 1040. ► See Instructions for Schedules A and B (Form 1040). | OMB No. 1545-0074
19_ _
Attachment
Sequence No. 07 |

Name(s) shown on Form 1040 — Your social security number

Medical and Dental Expenses	1a	Prescription medicines and drugs, insulin, doctors, dentists, nurses, hospitals, medical insurance premiums you paid, etc .	1a	4250 00	
(Do not include expenses reimbursed or paid by others.)	b	Other. (List—include hearing aids, dentures, eyeglasses, transportation and lodging, etc.) ► _____ _____	1b		
(See Instructions on page 23.)	2	Add the amounts on lines 1a and 1b. Enter the total here . . .	2	4250 00	
	3	Multiply the amount on Form 1040, line 32, by 7.5% (.075) . .	3	3600 00	
	4	Subtract line 3 from line 2. If zero or less, enter -0-. **Total** medical and dental . . ►	4		650 00
Taxes You Paid	5	State and local income taxes	5		
	6	Real estate taxes	6	1240 00	
(See Instructions on page 24.)	7	Other taxes. (List—include personal property taxes.) ► _____	7		
	8	Add the amounts on lines 5 through 7. Enter the total here. **Total** taxes . . ►	8		1240 00
Interest You Paid	9a	Deductible home mortgage interest (from Form 1098) that you paid to financial institutions. Report deductible points on line 10.	9a	4500 00	
(See Instructions on page 24.)	b	Other deductible home mortgage interest. (If paid to an individual, show that person's name and address.) ► _____ _____	9b		
	10	Deductible points. (See Instructions for special rules.) . . .	10		
	11	Deductible investment interest. (See page 25.)	11		
	12a	Personal interest you paid. (See page 25.) . 12a			
	b	Multiply the amount on line 12a by 20% (.20). Enter the result	12b		
	13	Add the amounts on lines 9a through 11, and 12b. Enter the total here. **Total** interest ►	13		4500 00
Gifts to Charity	14	Contributions by cash or check. (If you gave $3,000 or more to any one organization, show to whom you gave and how much you gave.) ► _____	14	1200 00	
(See Instructions on page 25.)	15	Other than cash or check. (You must attach Form 8283 if over $500.)	15		
	16	Carryover from prior year	16		
	17	Add the amounts on lines 14 through 16. Enter the total here. **Total** contributions . ►	17		1200 00
Casualty and Theft Losses	18	Casualty or theft loss(es) (attach Form 4684). (See page 26 of the Instructions.) . . . . ►	18		
Moving Expenses	19	Moving expenses (attach Form 3903 or 3903F). (See page 26 of the Instructions.) . . . . ►	19		
Job Expenses and Most Other Miscellaneous Deductions	20	Unreimbursed employee expenses—job travel, union dues, job education, etc. (You MUST attach Form 2106 in some cases. See Instructions.) ► _____	20		
	21	Other expenses (investment, tax preparation, safe deposit box, etc.). List type and amount ► _____ _____	21		
(See page 26 for expenses to deduct here.)	22	Add the amounts on lines 20 and 21. Enter the total.	22		
	23	Multiply the amount on Form 1040, line 32, by 2% (.02). Enter the result here	23		
	24	Subtract line 23 from line 22. Enter the result. If zero or less, enter -0- . . . . . ►	24		
Other Miscellaneous Deductions	25	Other (from list on page 26 of Instructions). List type and amount ► _____ _____ ►	25		
Total Itemized Deductions	26	Add the amounts on lines 4, 8, 13, 17, 18, 19, 24, and 25. Enter the total here. Then enter on Form 1040, line 34, the LARGER of this total or your standard deduction from page 17 of the Instructions . . . . ►	26		7590 00

For Paperwork Reduction Act Notice, see Form 1040 Instructions.   Schedule A (Form 1040) 1989

EXERCISE YOUR SKILLS

1. Why should taxpayers be informed about income tax laws even though they have someone fill out their forms for them?

2. Why should taxpayers with complicated tax work use a certified public accountant who specializes in taxes?

3. When should taxpayers file a Schedule A instead of claiming the standard deduction?

———— Activity 1 ————

Fill out a 1040 form for each of the following married couples filing a joint return. Each couple will include Schedule A with their return to itemize their deductions.

1. (465-88-3333) (543-66-2121)   Dependents:
   Howard and Florence Charisma   Loren   (5)   (355-66-7848)
   4565 Gulfstream   Charlie (17)   (655-22-9878)
   Panama Beach, Florida   32233
   Wages: Howard $37,800
          Florence $21,866   Itemized deductions:
   Withholding: Howard $7,855   Medical bills: $6,500
                 Florence $6,244   Real estate taxes: $1,200
   Interest Income: $250   Home mortgage interest: $6,420
   Dividends: $300   Contributions: $1,300

2. (233-66-5533) (456-56-1232)   Dependents:
   Macon and Milly Logan   Molly   (17)   (531-22-6545)
   12322 Commonwealth   Mark   (17)   (531-44-3333)
   Boston, Massachusetts   21300
   Wages: Macon $53,500
          Milly $51,700   Itemized deductions:
   Witholding: Macon $17,700   Medical bills: $700
                Milly $10,562   Real estate taxes: $2,253
   Interest Income: $875   Home mortgage interest: $7,564
   Dividends: $200   Contributions: $1,600

EXTEND YOUR UNDERSTANDING
PROJECT 11–1:   STATE INCOME TAXES

Assignments

1. Use reference books such as a world almanac to find the methods different states use to determine how much state income tax their residents pay.

2. Evaluate the methods of determining state income taxes to find out in which states people pay the highest taxes.

3. Find out in which states people pay the lowest taxes.

4. Devise a way to report your findings in an interesting way. Show the five highest, the five lowest, the most unusual, and so on. Or make a bar graph comparing the income tax rates in different states.

Extensions

1. Make up some problems based on your findings to calculate the state income taxes for people making the same salaries but living in different states. Have your classmates solve some of the problems.

2. Find which cities have income taxes and what their rate of taxation is.

3. Discuss with your classmates some reasons why some states have higher income taxes than others.

PROJECT 11–2:   THE HISTORY OF INCOME TAXES

Work with a group of classmates to complete this activity. Use reference books such as encyclopedias, history books, and political science books to find out when federal income taxes were first introduced in the United States.

1. What is the name of the law that made federal income taxes legal?

2. Why and how was it passed?

3. When was the Internal Revenue Service established?

4. Who administers the Internal Revenue Service?

5. How are changes in tax laws made?

6. Do income taxes in fact strictly conform to the "earn more, pay more" principle?

1. Organize a debate with your classmates to argue the pros and cons of federal income taxes. Also include how the taxes could be made more equitable.

2. Investigate income tax laws of other countries in the world.

3. Calculate what percent of income the average American pays in taxes—include federal, state, city, county, and social security taxes.

12 OWNING A CAR

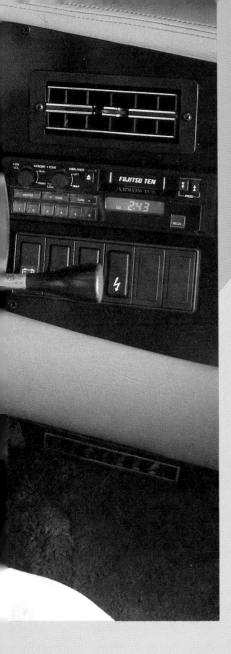

Many young people today have their own cars. Either their parents have bought the cars for them, or they have worked to pay for the cars themselves. In many families the teenager drives the family car. The newly licensed driver may volunteer to do errands, may drive to work or to school, may drive other family members where they need to go, and may even get a chance to go to the beach, or bowling, or to the movies.

In the major metropolitan areas, in which public transportation is accessible and reliable, owning and maintaining an automobile is not essential. In fact, the use of public transportation is usually less expensive under those conditions than the use of private automobiles. The cost to the environment—in air pollution, the depletion of natural resources, and the disposal of metals, tires, batteries, and so on—is lower as well.

We have, however, become a mobile society, very dependent on automobiles. We are accustomed to transporting ourselves rapidly and conveniently over distances that would be impossible to walk and to places that may not be reached by bus or train. In fact, shopping malls, office buildings, and apartments often are designed to be accessible only by automobile.

Drive-in movies have been around for a long time. Many other businesses also offer the convenience of staying in the car. We "drive through" fast food restaurants, banks, cleaners, and car washes. We can make a telephone call or mail a letter from our cars.

After a house, the car is usually the second most expensive item we will purchase. We need to take good care of it. We must pay to insure it, operate it, and maintain it. We must ultimately decide how long to keep repairing it. At some point it will become cost effective to trade in the old one and start over with a new one.

The young people in this chapter explore some of the differences between buying a new car and a used car. They learn what it costs to operate and maintain a car and what protection is provided by the different kinds of insurance. Maria suffers "sticker shock" when she first sees the prices at the new car dealership. She learns, however, that dealers are willing to negotiate on price. They rarely sell their cars for the sticker prices. With separate prices for all of the many options on a car, there is lots of room for negotiation.

After learning that new cars depreciate quickly in value, Alex decides to look for a used van to buy. He considers places to look and learns about the tricks sometimes used to deceive buyers.

Freda looks carefully at the mileage she is getting with her car as she does the driving for the T-shirt business. She also analyzes repairs and maintenance. Finally, Trevor learns about automobile insurance—how much of what kind a driver needs, and how the rates for each driver are determined.

Maria found that saving half of her paycheck every week had its ups and downs. At times she was tempted to give up the idea of having a car of her own. She would like to have some money to spend with her friends from time to time. But she has stuck with her plan.

After saving for six months, however, Maria convinced her father that she could keep up with the payments on the car. What Maria wanted most was a new car, so she and her father visited several new car dealer showrooms. What Maria found there stunned her at first. Each new car had a sheet of paper stuck to the inside of one of the windows. On it was a list of the various features present on that particular car: automatic transmission, power steering, air conditioning, AM/FM stereo with cassette deck, cruise control, power windows, tinted glass—and on and on. Many of the features also had prices listed beside them.

The total price shown at the bottom of each list surprised Maria the most. She could not understand how ordinary people were able to buy new cars at such prices. Her father was not so surprised, however. He explained to Maria after their first dealership that the "sticker price" was not what the dealer actually expected the buyer to pay for the car. Maria became even more confused. If the sticker price is not the real price, how could a buyer know what the real price is?

Maria also wondered if there were other tricks to the car-buying business that she should investigate before shelling out her hard-earned dollars.

OBJECTIVES: In this section, we will help Maria to:

- *find out how to shop for a new car*
- *realize what tricks to watch for*
- *recognize what costs for a new car are reasonable*

SHOP BEFORE GOING TO A CAR DEALER

Maria has never owned a car, but she has seen a lot of them that she would like to own. She knows many factors must be considered, so she has been reading past issues of car reports. She has read automobile and consumer magazines such as *Car and Driver, Auto Mechanics, Motor Trend, Consumer Reports,* and *Changing Times.* She found price information as well as the repair ratings on many cars.

Maria still does not understand why there is such a difference between the **sticker price** and what the dealer actually expects to be paid for the car.

Maria found that she can read a book such as *Edmund's New Car Prices* and calculate exactly what the dealer paid for a specific car. Even the dealer's cost for each option, such as air conditioning and cruise control, was spelled out in detail. On the same list was the manufacturer's suggested retail price, or the amount listed on the sticker in the car window. She found similar information in the *Kelley Blue Book New Car Price Manual*.

Maria also noticed that some cars have a much larger **mark-up**, that is, the price charged above the dealer's cost, than others. Maria noticed certain options were marked-up more than others. She also knows that the purchase price is not everything. She will try to choose a respectable dealer with a good service department—one that is not so far from her home that getting to the dealership for service would be inconvenient.

DEALING WITH DEALERS

Maria has shopped around, and she is prepared to bargain. She knows she must keep her mind open so she can walk away from a car if necessary. She has figured out that if a dealer knows which car she has "fallen in love with," the dealer might also believe that Maria will eventually talk herself into buying it. Maria has learned the three essentials for bargaining:

1. Use competitive market conditions to your advantage.

2. Know the dealer's costs.

3. Be willing to allow the dealer a responsible profit.

She is prepared to go elsewhere or choose a different car if the dealer continues to ask too much.

Maria will remind us again of the essential steps. We have to be well informed about the dealer's cost (and the trade-in price of our used car if we have one), and we must be willing to walk away. One large-volume buyer advises consumers to consider it a good deal to get 8% to 10% off the sticker price on a subcompact, 12% on an intermediate or compact, and 14% on a full-sized model.

Bait and Switch. Maria knows what the dealers probably paid for the three different cars she has decided to choose from. When she saw an advertisement in the newspaper that read "below cost" and "below wholesale," she decided she should visit the dealer in the ad first. But when Maria and her father arrived at the lot they found that the advertised car was not available.

Instead, the salesman was eager to show them another, more expensive car he was sure she would like better. Maria wondered if the salesman thought she had never heard of the bait and switch routine.

Packing. Her father explained to Maria that there are similar reasons why they will borrow their money from the credit union instead of from the auto dealership. He said that sometimes the dealer gets a rebate from the finance company and will try to add special fees, or finance insurance charges to the purchase price. This is a technique known as **packing**. Maria wondered what other tricks she might discover about car buying.

The Balloon Note. Her father was not sure that a **balloon note** is still legal, but Maria wanted to know what that means anyway. With this arrangement, Maria would pay relatively small installments on the loan until the last payment. The last payment, the balloon, is exorbitantly high and usually comes as a surprise.

Bushing. By this time Maria was beginning to realize there was a whole lot more to this car buying business than she had believed. "But wait," her father said. "If we had a car we wanted to trade in when we bought the new one, we would have to be even more aware of what we were doing."

Dealers know they are not the only people offering cars for sale. They want Maria to come back to their lot after having shopped around, or not to look elsewhere at all. They may practice something called **bushing**. If a dealer raises the price after Maria has made a deposit, or offers Maria less for her trade-in than originally promised, the dealer has practiced bushing.

The Highball. If the dealer makes a fantastically attractive-sounding trade-in offer, keeping Maria from comparison shopping, he or she is using the **highball**. However, when it comes time to deliver Maria's new car, the dealer suddenly notices flaws in Maria's old car—which lowers the amount he or she is actually willing to allow Maria on it as a trade-in.

The Lowball. Maria is thoroughly convinced by this time that she must know exactly what real price she is willing to pay for a car. Just when she thought she heard it all, she discovered another dealer with yet another way of figuring the real price. This saleswoman quoted an unrealistically low price for the new car Maria wanted as "insurance" that Maria would return to her dealership after she has made the rounds of other local dealers. Maria did go back only to discover that the quote inevitably expanded to a more realistic level. Maria will begin her search again.

1. How can you recognize what costs for new cars are reasonable?

2. What are three essentials to keep in mind when bargaining with a car dealer?

3. What are three tricks that car dealers use to get sales?

SHARPEN YOUR SKILLS

Maria is comparing the approximate dealer's cost and sticker price on a Starfire car. The dealer's cost is also called the base price. The sticker price corresponds to a suggested list price. Following is a portion of the Starfire Price List she had acquired.

If she chooses these options:	The prices are:	
	Dealer's Cost	Sticker Price
2-door convertible	$31,414	$37,264
Air conditioning	149	180
Carrier, luggage	116	140
Handling package selective ride, electronic	1,407	1,695
Basic equipment group with U1F radio	1,012	1,219

1. What is the difference between the dealer's cost and the sticker price for a Starfire with the features listed above?

2. What is the percent of increase, that is, the dealer's profit?

1. Total the two columns:

   The total sticker price is $40,498.

   The total base price is $34,098.

   Find the difference between them:

   $40,498 – 34,098 = $6400

   The difference between the dealer's cost and the sticker price, the mark-up, is $6400.

2. To find the percent of increase, divide the difference by the dealer price:

   $6400 ÷ $34,098 = 0.188

   The percent of increase is 19%, rounded to the nearest whole percent.

Question   What percent of increase is there for each individual option?

Solution   The difference and percent of increase in the prices for the options are figured in the same way as for the car itself. Following is a summary of the results of Maria's calculations.

Option	Dealer	Sticker	Difference	Percent Increase
2-door convertible	$31,414	$37,264	$5,850	19
Air conditioning	149	180	31	21
Carrier, luggage	116	140	24	21
Handling package selective ride	1,407	1,695	288	20
Basic equipment group with U1F radio	1,012	1,219	207	20

EXERCISE YOUR SKILLS

1. If you were going to buy a car, how would you prepare before you started going to dealerships?

2. What is your best protection against tricks that car dealers use?

3. Why is comparison shopping important to a person who wants to buy a car?

_____ **Activity 1** _____

Following is a portion of the Moonbeam Price List which appears in full in the Reference Section.

MOONBEAM:	Dealer's Cost	Sticker Price
Model A 4-door wagon, 8 cylinder	$12,725	$14,722
Model B 4-door sedan, 6 cylinder	$14,062	$16,295
Model C 4-door sedan, 4 cylinder	$11,053	$12,755
OPTIONS:		
Conventional spare tire	$ 62	$ 73
Air conditioning, manual	695	817
Electronic climate control	850	1000
Anti-lock brake system	838	985
Defroster, rear window	136	160
Radio, AM/FM, cassette player	132	155
Seat, rear facing third (wagons)	132	155
Speed control	178	210
Stripe, paint	52	61

Use the information on the price list to answer the following questions.

1. Find the percent of mark-up for Model A, Model B, and Model C.

2. Find the percent of mark-up for each of the individual options.

3. Find the total dealer cost and the total sticker price for each of the cars and options below.

   a. **Model B**
      Manual air conditioning
      Rear defroster
      AM/FM radio/cassette player
      Speed control

   b. **Model A**
      Electronic climate control
      Rear defroster
      AM/FM radio/cassette player
      Rear facing third seat

   c. **Model C**
      Manual air conditioning
      Rear defroster
      AM/FM radio/cassette player
      Stripe, paint

   d. **Model B**
      Rear defroster
      Anti-lock brake system
      AM/FM radio/cassette player
      Speed control

4. Find the percent of mark-up for each of the total suggested retail prices for each car described in Problem 2.

OWNING A USED CAR: HOW USED IS USED?

When Alex bought his van, he knew he could not afford to buy a new one. If he could have bought a smaller car, he might have been able to get a newer one. But his father, who transports eight 12-year-olds to play basketball every week, hopes to use Alex's van for this purpose.

Alex's father took him to quite a few car lots before he finally made the deal for the van they bought. Alex had seen a number of vans he really liked in the process. At first, Alex did not understand why his father was inspecting some of the vans so closely and insisting on driving several of them out to the freeway and around town.

Alex's father told him about the first used car he ever bought. He knew he had a certain amount of money to spend, so he allowed himself to be talked into buying the second car the salesperson showed him. He and the salesperson drove it around town for a few minutes. The car was only one-and-a-half years old and showed 14,000 miles on the odometer. He did not even notice that the odometer was not hooked up when he tested the car.

Alex's parents really enjoyed the car during the 90-day warranty period; then it started having problems. Among other things, the radiator had to be replaced, as did the alternator, the fuel pump, and the transmission. A mechanic finally told Alex's father that the car was a repainted taxi! He estimated that it had about 90,000 miles on it by then. Alex's parents eventually sold the car, promising themselves to be more careful next time, if they ever decided to buy another used vehicle.

Alex understands now why the van he finally got was thoroughly checked out by their mechanic before they agreed to buy it. Alex was not pleased to learn that some car salespeople are not always honest in their treatment of customers. He wonders what other factors might have an effect on the price of a used car.

OBJECTIVES: In this section, we will help Alex to:

- *examine reasons for choosing a used car*
- *decide where to buy a used car*
- *determine which used car to choose*
- *realize what tricks to watch for*
- *recognize what costs for a used car are reasonable*

WHY CHOOSE USED?

When Alex first knew he would be getting to drive the new van that his family was going to purchase, he looked forward to helping pick it out. What Alex soon realized was that his father intended to buy a van that was new to them, not brand new from the factory. Alex was disappointed, so he decided to do a little research on the subject to find out if he could change his father's mind.

What Alex discovered was very perplexing until he thought about it thoroughly. Alex has looked at the sticker prices on new cars; he also knows dealers do not always expect to sell a car for the sticker price. Alex has also looked at price guides that enumerate the trade-in value of various cars. What really got Alex's attention was the large amount of **depreciation** that the cars experience over the first few years.

The way Alex understands depreciation, it is supposed to be the difference between the actual purchase price of the car or truck and its eventual resale value—divided by the number of years the unit is driven.

Alex found some expert estimates on what he should figure for depreciation each; year the percents shown below are subtracted from the original new car purchase price for each year of the car's life.

Automobile Year	Depreciation Schedule Percent Decrease
1st	30–32%
2nd	24–26
3rd	18–20
4th	7–8
5th	3–5
6th	3–5
7th	3–5
8th	1–2
9th	1–2
10th	1–2

What really puzzled Alex was how heavily the annual depreciation is "front-loaded"—how much greater it is during the early years in contrast to the low rates in the twilight years of the car's life. If depreciation is supposed to have something to do with how long the car lasts, why does it lose so much of its value during the first two years?

Alex knew his parents' other car had been driven over 150,000 miles during a 10-year period before they finally declared it "junk." Alex also knew that during the first three years of its life, that car had had practically no repairs—just the routine replacement of things like tires, fan belts, and spark plugs. The last three years they had the car was when they really had to spend money having it repaired frequently.

Why, then, is a car that is six months to one year old worth 30 to 32% less to a dealer than when it is brand new? The whole scale seemed upside down to Alex. To him, a very "young" car is almost as valuable as a new car since it is less likely to need expensive repairs.

Alex began to see why used-car buyers are in the majority. A smart buyer can take advantage of a new car's rapid depreciation during the first two or three years of the life of the car. Alex understands that the dealer gets a break, too, because although a car that is a year old can be bought from an individual by a dealer for about 30% less than it cost new, the dealer can then sell the car to the next customer and make a profit.

WHERE TO BUY

Alex can see also why there is such a wide variation in the price charged at different places for the same car, and he knows he must be very careful when he chooses both a car and a dealer. His father has pointed out four of the most common places for used car purchases: new car dealers, used car dealers, private sellers, and car rental companies.

New Car Dealers. New car dealers who sell used cars tend to charge more than other sellers. New car dealers are most likely to keep for resale the best used cars traded in for new cars.

Used Car Dealers. Used car dealers may have less extensive service facilities than new car dealers or no facilities at all. There are three types of used car dealers: (1) fly-by-night operators who stay in business until forced to close; (2) small owner-operated lots that obtain top quality trade-ins from the used car managers of new car dealerships; and (3) large, independent dealers who use extensive newspaper and television advertising to get high volume sales. It is helpful to find out how long the dealer has done business in the same location.

Private Sales. Alex tried to find a good used van by checking the classified advertisements in the local newspaper. He followed up on one ad and discovered the ad was placed by a dealer. Alex decided to look elsewhere; he realized that this was a roundabout technique designed to get buyers.

If Alex does decide to buy from a private party, he will check the **title** to the car before giving a deposit or transferring money to the seller. They will want to be sure that the party selling the car actually owns the car and is named in the title.

Car Rental Company Sales. Rental car offices, such as Hertz, Avis, and National, also sell used cars. Most of the cars they sell are nine to twelve months old and have been driven under 25,000 miles.

INSPECTING A USED CAR

Alex already knows from his parents' experience that staring at an engine, kicking the tires, or driving the car around the block, will not tell him what he wants to know about the condition of a used car. Alex knows that the smart used car buyer conducts three types of inspections: on-the-lot, on-the-road, and in-the-garage.

Alex has talked with Maria, too, and knows that some new car dealers practice a few tricks to make sales. Alex will share with Maria, and with us, some of the used car tricks that he will be watching out for.

Doping. We may be told that the used car we want has been completely "reconditioned." The test drive may seem to confirm this claim. But within a few days the car may develop a host of mechanical problems if the dealer has used a variety of methods to temporarily disguise the car's flaws.

The "Almost New" Car. This bargain, late-model, "leftover" car has been used as a demonstrator. It may be last year's model advertised by mail at an unbelievably low price. The catch with a mail-order car is that it may be a repainted taxi or a police car, driven 100,000 miles or more.

Macing. We have sold our own used car to a dealer at a very nice price. The dealer pays us a small amount of cash and the rest of the purchase price in notes or a postdated check. Either the check turns out to be worthless, or when the notes mature, the fly-by-night operator cannot be found and the notes are worthless paper.

Odometer Tampering. The **odometer** on a car is the counter that keeps track of the car's mileage. It is set to 0 when the car is new and is not to be moved artificially. However, an expert can turn an odometer back tens of thousands of miles with no trouble at all.

Alex would remind us that our trusted mechanic will be glad to check the car over before we buy. A good mechanic can examine certain parts and spot most of these gimmicks before we fall for them.

Ask Yourself

1. What is depreciation?

2. Why do new car dealers tend to charge more for their used cars than other sellers?

3. What does "doping" mean in regard to used cars?

SHARPEN YOUR SKILLS

_____ Skill 1 _____

Alex found the Resale Value Table shown on the following page in a reference book at the library.

Alex particularly noticed these details: If he were planning to sell (or trade-in) a Romero 6 Convertible to the dealer, he would get $7300 for it. If he were planning to buy the same car, he would pay $8525 for it.

Resale Value Table for Cosmos Motor Company

Year-Model-Body Type	Original List	Current Whlse	Average Retail
4-YEARS OLD			
ROMERO 4			
Sport Cpe	10414	3600	4500
Z28 Sport Cpe	12963	5925	6850
FLAME 6*			
4 Dr Sdn	11264	3850	4750
FLAME CLASSIC 6*			
2 Dr Sport Cpe	11665	4625	5550
4 Dr Sedan	11829	4750	5675
4 Dr Brougham Sdn	12478	5175	6075
4 Dr Wgn (8 cyl)	12562	5250	6175
* For 8 cylinder models add $400 wholesale and $400 retail.			
CAMEL 4*			
2 Dr Cpe	8258	2950	3850
4 Dr Sdn	8443	3050	3950
4 Dr Wgn	8606	3125	4025
2 Dr CS Htchbk Cpe	8940	3150	4050
4 Dr CS Sedan	8916	3150	4050
4 Dr CS Wgn	9097	3225	4125
2 Dr RS Conv	13996	5500	6425
2 Dr RS Cpe	8988	3250	4150
2 Dr RS Htchbk Cpe	9183	3350	4250
4 Dr RS Sdn	9163	3350	4250
4 Dr RS Wgn	9335	3450	4350
* For 6 cylinder models add $200 wholesale and $200 retail.			
CAMEL 6*			
2 Dr Z24 Sport Cpe	10256	4325	5250
2 Dr Z24 Htchbk Sport Cpe	10451	4425	5350
SPLASH 4*			
2 Dr Cpe	10243	3450	4350
4 Dr Sdn	10444	3550	4450
4 Dr 2 Seat Wgn	10598	3775	4675
4 Dr 3 Seat Wgn	10836	3850	4750
* For 6 cylinder models add $300 wholesale and $300 retail.			
ARROW 4			
CS Htchbk Cpe	7125	1775	2625
CS Htchbk Sdn	7309	1875	2725
CS Diesel Htchbk Cpe	6507	1325	2075
CS Diesel Htchbk Sdn	6712	1425	2175
(Diesel models not available w/air conditioning or automatic transmission)			
HOTSHOT 6			
Htchbk Cpe	27405	14350	16975
Conv	32480	17700	20350
LAMU 5*			
2 Dr Sport Cpe	10344	4350	5275
2 Dr LS Cpe	13640	4450	5375
*For 8 cylinder models add $325 wholesale and $325 retail.			
LAMU 8			
2 Dr SS Sport Cpe	13640	6525	7725
DWARF 4			
4 Dr Htchbk Sdn	9176	3325	4225
5 Dr Htchbk Sdn	9417	3425	4325
RAINBOW 4			
4 Dr Htchbk Sdn	8728	2550	3425
5.0 Liter V8 TPI Eng	745	385	470
5.7 Liter V8 TPI Eng	1045	530	660

Year-Model-Body Type	Original List	Current Whlse	Average Retail
3 YEARS OLD			
ROMERO 6*			
Sport Cpe	11260	4950	5875
Convertible	15659	7300	8525
* For 8 cylinder models add $300 wholesale and $300 retail.			
ROMERO 8*			
Z28 Sport Cpe	14084	7150	8375
Z28 Convertible	18483	10325	12050
FLAME 6*			
4 Dr Sdn	11770	5150	6050
FLAME CLASSIC 6*			
2 Dr Sport Cpe	12167	5950	6875
4 Dr Sedan	12335	6100	7000
FLAME CLASSIC BROUGHAM 6*			
4 Dr Sdn	13324	6550	7750
4 Dr LS Sdn	14580	6925	8150
* For 8 cylinder models add $425 wholesale and $425 retail.			
FLAME 8			
4 Dr Wgn	12770	5725	6625
FLAME CLASSIC 8			
4 Dr Wgn	13361	6650	7875
CAMEL 4*			
2 Dr Cpe	8737	3600	4500
4 Dr Sdn	8961	3700	4600
4 Dr Wgn	9127	3825	4725
2 Dr CS Htchbk Cpe	9368	3850	4750
4 Dr CS Sedan	9343	3850	4750
4 Dr CS Wgn	9530	3975	4875
2 Dr RS Conv	14611	6725	7950
2 Dr RS Cpe	9483	4000	4900
2 Dr RS Htchbk Cpe	9685	4100	5025
4 Dr RS Sdn	9664	4100	5025
4 Dr RS Wgn	9842	4225	5150
* For 6 cylinder models add $200 wholesale and $200 retail.			
4 Dr 2 Seat Wgn	11200	4425	5350
4 Dr 3 Seat Wgn	11447	4525	5450
* For 6-cylinder models add $300 wholesale and $300 retail.			
ARROW 4			
2 Dr CS Htchbk Cpe	6345	2175	3025
4 Dr CS Htchbk Sdn	6845	2275	3125
HOTSHOT 8			
Htchbk Cpe	27999	16350	19000
Conv	33172	19950	22950
LAMU 6*			
2 Dr LS Cpe	12081	5475	6400
* For 8 cylinder models add $350 wholesale and $350 retail.			
LAMU 8			
2 Dr SS Sport Cpe	14238	8100	9325
2 Dr SS Aero Cpe	15613	7550	8775
DWARF 4			
4 Dr Htchbk Sdn	9378	4275	5200
5 Dr Htchbk Sdn	9630	4375	5300
RAINBOW 4			
4 Dr Htchbk Sdn	9200	3325	4225
2 Dr Htchbk Cpe	8903	3225	4125
DASHER 3			
2 Dr Htchbk Cpe	7486	2475	3350
2 Dr ER Htchbk Cpe	7601	2500	3375

Questions

1. How much mark-up is this?

2. What percent profit is the dealer making?

Solutions

1. The mark-up is the difference between $7300 and $8525.

$$\$8525 - 7300 = \$1225$$

The mark-up is $1225.

2. The percent profit is:

$$\$1225 \div \$7300 = 0.1678$$

The percent profit is 17%, rounded to the nearest whole percent.

___ **Skill 2** ___

Alex also noticed two other helpful tables: the Options Valuation Table for the most popular options and the High Mileage Deduction Table. These tables appear in the Reference Section at the back of the book.

First look at the Options Valuation Table. It tells you what value is added or taken away from a trade-in because of its optional features. For instance, if Alex's three-year-old car had no power steering, the dealer would deduct $85 from the wholesale price or $100 from the retail price. If it had power brakes, the dealer would add $40 to the wholesale price or $50 to the retail.

The High Mileage Deduction Table gives additional information about a car's trade-in value. If his car were three years old with 44,000 miles on it, the High Mileage Deduction Table indicates that the dealer would deduct another $200. (The note at the top of the table indicates that lower amount applies to this car.)

Question   If Alex were to trade in a 3-year-old Romero 6 Convertible which has no power steering and 44,000 miles on it, how much would the dealer allow him as a trade-in?

Solution   Subtract the deduction for no power steering:

$$\$7300 - \$85 = \$7215$$

Subtract the deduction for high mileage (the lower amount):

$$\$7215 - 200 = \$7015$$

The dealer would allow Alex $7015 for the trade-in.

___ **Skill 3** ___

Alex would like to know how quickly his car's value depreciated over the first three years. According to the Automobile Depreciation Schedule (which appears in full in the Reference Section), the car depreciated as follows:

1st year—30%   2nd year—24%   3rd year—18%

The original list price of his car was $15,659.

Question   How much is Alex's car worth after three years?

Solution   At the end of the first year, his car's value could be calculated as follows:

$$\$15,659 - (30\% \times 15,659) =$$

$$\$15,659 - 4,697.70 = \$10,961.30$$

At the end of the second year, his car would have been worth:

$$\$10,961.30 - (24\% \times \$10,961.30) =$$

$$\$10,961.30 - 2,630.71 = \$8,330.59$$

At the end of the third year, his car would have been worth:

$$\$8,330.59 - (18\% \times 8,330.59) =$$

$$\$8,330.59 - 1,499.51 = \$6,831.08$$

After 3 years, Alex's car would be worth $6,831.08.

EXERCISE YOUR SKILLS

1. Why do some buyers prefer to buy "young" used cars instead of new ones?

2. From what source do you think a buyer might buy a used car with the best deal?

3. How can a used-car buyer reduce the possibility of getting a "bad deal" on a used car?

_____ Activity 1 _____

Used Car Price Changes

	Original List	Current Wholesale	Average Retail
Car A	$11,260	$4,900	$5,875
Car B	13,324	6,550	7,750
Car C	8,737	3,600	4,500
Car D	9,200	3,325	4,225

Use the information above for the following questions.

1. What is the mark-up between the price the dealer probably paid for each of the used cars above and the price the dealer will try to sell the car for?

2. What percent profit will the dealer receive if each of the cars above are bought and sold for the prices shown?

—————   Activity 2   —————————————————————

Use the information given in Activity 1, and the High Mileage Deduction Table and the Options Valuation Table in the Reference Section of the book to answer the following questions.

1. Car A is three years old. It has been driven 45,000 miles, has no air conditioning, and has power brakes. What is it's trade-in value?

2. Car B is two years old. It has been driven 35,000 miles, has no automatic transmission, and has power brakes and windows. What is the trade-in value of this car?

3. Car C is one year old. It has been driven 10,000 miles, has power brakes, a vinyl top, and power seats. What is the trade-in value of this car?

4. Car D is four years old. It has been driven 60,000 miles, has no automatic transmission, no air conditioning, has power brakes and power windows. What is the trade-in value of this car?

—————   Activity 3   —————————————————————

Original List Price:

Car A – $27,405   **Car B** – $32,480   **Car C** – $40,595

Car D – $12,081   **Car E** – $14,611   **Car F** – $ 9,630

Use the information above and the depreciation rates in Skill 3 of this section to answer the following questions. Use a table like the one shown below to record your answers.

1. How much would each of the cars above depreciate in one year, and how much would each be worth?

2. How much would each of the cars above have depreciated after two years, and how much would each be worth?

3. How much would each of the cars above have depreciated after three years, and how much would each be worth?

	1		2		3	
Car	After 1 Year		After 2 Years		After 3 Years	
	Depreciation	Value	Depreciation	Value	Depreciation	Value
A						
B						
C						
D						
E						
F						

OPERATION AND MAINTENANCE: FEEDING AND FIXING

Freda volunteered to be part of the business being started by her friends Evelyn and Greg. She knows she is a good salesperson; she also knows that neither Evelyn nor Greg has a car. Because she does, Freda can distribute posters and flyers advertising their business. She can also deliver the completed products—painted T-shirts and sweat shirts—to their customers.

Freda does a lot of selling, but her bank account does not show how well she does with it. Freda is not very careful taking care of money and monitoring expenses. Since the business with Evelyn and Greg will include Hari as the money manager, Freda will have to pay more attention to her expenses. Hari will want an accurate record of how much the expenses are when Freda drives. Knowing Hari, he will not be satisfied with a vague estimate.

Freda knows her car will be in need of some repairs, too, as it gets older. She is not sure if these should be included when she calculates the expenses for the business. Freda has also been curious about when a car is no longer worth putting money into for repairs. She wonders if she would save more money eventually if she just bought a new car instead. Freda will investigate the factors that contribute to this import decision.

OBJECTIVES: In this section, we will help Freda to:

- *calculate car mileage per gallon of gasoline*
- *compute operating costs of a car including fuel and repairs*

MILEAGE

Even a poor money manager like Freda knows it does not take a genius with a lot of record keeping skills to figure out what it costs to buy gasoline for her car. She realizes that she should make a note of her odometer reading every time she fills the tank with gas. And she must keep a record of the number of gallons of gas she buys and the cost per gallon.

Freda also knows that driving costs are based to a large degree on driving habits, the type of driving done (such as city or country), the climate, and the size and kind of car. As Alex and Maria noticed when they were shopping for cars, different cars have very different performance records. Even the same car can eventually become less efficient and use more gasoline as its parts become more worn.

Freda's car is not very old, but if she drives a lot of miles this year for the business, it will certainly need some maintenance and, perhaps, some repairs. Freda will keep a record of these expenses as the year progresses. She and her business partners will figure out a way of paying for the business miles.

MAINTENANCE

Since Freda's car has only 12,027 miles on it, expenses for tune-ups, parts, and repairs should be minimal, at least for a while. Even a car under **warranty** requires checkups and service. Freda will keep an accurate record of all maintenance expenses.

Freda does anticipate that sometime during the next 20,000 miles, she will need to buy new tires. If she drives with reasonable care and keeps the wheels properly aligned, she can keep the wear to a minimum. Over- or under-inflation of tires, sharp cornering, rapid acceleration, and quick stops all contribute to tire wear. In addition, high-speed driving generates heat that increases tire wear.

Freda is careful to have the oil changed as frequently as every 3000 miles. This is because she has heard the practice of changing oil often enough will keep her car in good condition. She also checks the water level in the battery and the antifreeze in the radiator. She keeps a spare container of windshield washer fluid in her trunk. Once she ran out of fluid during a drive in messy weather and had trouble seeing through the windshield properly. The experience frightened her and caused her to be especially careful about her supply.

REPAIRS

Freda has been reading several consumer magazines and automobile magazines that give information about caring for a car. She has found some facts she is not too pleased to see, but she will share them with us. Now that her car has passed the 12,000 mile mark, it may need several of the following minor repairs: brake relining, reconditioning of brake drums; replacement or overhauling of the alternator; replacement of hoses, shock absorbers, muffler, batteries, headlights, voltage regulator, and ignition coil. She may also be confronted with problems involving the water and fuel pumps. Freda is certainly hoping her car will not need all of these at once!

If she keeps the car another three years or so and drives it more than 50,000 miles, she knows the car will need some major repairs. These could include work on the transmission, valves, or air conditioning. Freda would like to estimate some of these repair expenses so she will be able to pay for them when the time comes. Perhaps she will take a course in auto mechanics, and learn to do some of the repairs herself.

Ask Yourself

1. What is an odometer reading?

2. How can you keep the wear on your car's tires to a minimum?

3. What are some major car repairs that you can expect as a car gets older?

SHARPEN YOUR SKILLS

_____ Skill 1 _____

Freda has been keeping careful records during the first few weeks she has been driving for the business. Her first set of records looks like this:

Odometer Reading	Gallons of Gas	Cost
11,400		
11,604	12.0	$18.00
11,842	13.6	20.80
12,027	10.3	15.45

Questions

1. How many miles to the gallon is Freda getting?

2. What is her gasoline cost per mile?

Solutions

1. First she must calculate how many miles she has driven. She subtracts the beginning odometer reading from the ending one to find the miles driven:

Ending odometer reading	12,027
Beginning odometer reading	−11,400
Miles driven	627

   Next she must total the gallons of gasoline she has purchased:

	12. gallons
	13.6
	+ 10.3
Total	35.9 gallons

   To find the miles per gallon, she divides the total number of miles she has driven by the number of gallons she has used.

   $$627 \div 35.9 = 17.5$$

   She has gotten 17.5 miles to the gallon.

2. First, she finds the total amount she paid for gas:

$18.00
20.80
+15.45
$54.25

   Then she divides the cost by the number of miles driven:

   $$\$54.25 \div 627 = 8.7$$

   Her cost per mile for gasoline is 8.7 cents.

_____ Skill 2 _____

Freda has been driving for the business for one year. She wants to figure out her costs. She knows her car gets 17.5 miles to the gallon of gasoline. She needs to add up her costs for maintenance and repairs.

Freda has kept the following records:

Miles driven	12,500
Cost per gallon of gas	$1.49

Maintenance:

tune-ups	$ 85.70
oil	3.50
oil change	64.75
filters	35.90
wheel alignment	13.73

Repairs:

brakes	186.75
alternator	125.90
battery	75.00
radiator hose	12.50

Tires (4, new)	$ 485.00

Questions

1.   How much are Freda's total expenses for operating the car for the year?

2.   What is the cost per mile for operating the car?

Solutions

1.   For gasoline, Freda will buy 12,500 ÷ 17.5 gallons at $1.49 per gallon.

12,500 ÷ 17.5= 714.3 gallons, to the nearest tenth

714.3 x $1.49 = $1064.31 for gasoline

The total maintenance expenses are $203.60.

The total repair costs are $403.15.

The cost of the tires is $485.00.

The total for the year is: $1064.31
203.60
403.15
+ 485.00
$2156.06

2. The cost per mile is $2156.06 ÷ 12,500 = 0.1725 or 17.3 cents to the nearest tenth of a cent.

Note: These figures are just for operation of the car. They do not include car payments, depreciation, insurance, taxes, or license fees.

EXERCISE YOUR SKILLS

1. Why should the gas mileage of a car be a factor to consider when buying a car?

2. Why is it important to take care of minor car repairs as soon as they are needed?

3. Why should car owners estimate repair expenses when they prepare their budgets?

———— Activity 1 ————

Use the information in the following table to find the distance traveled, the mileage per gallon, and the cost per mile for the following trips.

	Odometer Readings		Gallons of Gasoline	Cost of Gasoline	Distance	Miles per Gallon	Cost per Mile
	First	Last					
1.	28,431.9	28,848.8	18.4	$25.15	_____	_____	_____
2.	38,715.7	39,326.1	15.7	18.95	_____	_____	_____
3.	11,477.3	11,628.6	9.5	14.00	_____	_____	_____
4.	18,388.4	19,374.2	40.6	63.74	_____	_____	_____
5.	15,428.5	15,639.6	10.9	14.38	_____	_____	_____
6.	8,964.3	9,514.9	23.8	27.40	_____	_____	_____
7.	5,889.9	6,859.2	44.2	52.53	_____	_____	_____
8.	33,886.7	34,939.4	26.8	33.45	_____	_____	_____
9.	8,963.2	9,276.8	12.4	15.75	_____	_____	_____
10.	19,879.4	20,861.3	29.7	31.80	_____	_____	_____

11. Your car's odometer reads 9243. You purchase 10.8 gallons of gas for $17.66. The next week, you purchase 12.4 gallons of gas for $20.70. The third week, you purchase 11.7 gallons of gas for $19.85. At the end of the month, you purchase 10.5 gallons of gas for $17.00; your odometer then reads 9978.

a. How many miles did you drive that month?

    b. How many miles did the car run per gallon?

    c. What was your cost per gallon of gasoline?

_____ Activity 2 _____

Find the total operating expenses and the cost per mile for operating each car listed below with the given expenses. Assume that each car gets 16.5 miles per gallon of gasoline and that gasoline costs $1.56 per gallon.

1. Miles driven   10,400

    Maintenance:

Tune-ups	$ 92.40
Oil changes and filters	$ 57.95
P/S belt	$ 10.09

    Repairs:

Exhaust system	$175.34
Battery	$ 74.95

2. Miles driven   15,328

    Maintenance:

Tune-ups	$ 87.95
Oil changes	$ 60.68
Oil filters	$ 8.35
Rotate tires	$ 22.00

    Repairs:

Alternator	$137.80
Muffler	$ 68.70

3. Miles driven   13,487

    Maintenance:

Tune-ups	$ 84.80
Oil changes	$ 68.30
A/C belt	$ 13.39
Wheel alignment	$ 15.75
Anti-freeze	$ 17.00

    Repairs:

Radiator	$165.25
Brakes	$197.45

4. Miles driven   9,894

    Maintenance:

Tune-ups	$ 92.78
Oil changes	$ 66.50
Grease	$ 8.65
Radiator hose	$ 16.75
Alternator belt	$ 10.95

    Repairs:

F & R shocks	$120.80
Tires	$565.00

5. Miles driven   11,532

    Maintenance:

Tune-ups	$119.50
Oil changes	$ 64.99
Wheel alignment	$ 79.85

    Repairs:

Broken window	$ 89.00
Alternator	$148.00

6. Miles driven   8,394

    Maintenance:

Tune-ups	$ 39.00
Parts	$ 18.00
Oil filters	$ 9.00
Fan belt	$ 8.79

    Repairs:

Brakes	$169.80
Muffler	$ 79.99

INSURANCE: HOW MUCH PROTECTION?

Trevor does not have his own car yet. He knows Alex and Maria have theirs; they have told Trevor how much they enjoy being able to drive to school and do errands with the car. Maria's parents frequently ask her to take her younger brother places he needs to go. Maria usually does not mind that. Trevor has a younger sister, Trácey; she is not such a bad kid either, unless she has four or five of her friends over to visit at once. Then she gets silly and they giggle a lot.

Trevor was once asked to take Tracey and her friends Roy and Leah to a movie. Trevor drove the family car, but after that day he may not be willing 'to do it again.

Trevor knows that driving is a very responsible task, and that the driver must pay attention all the time, not only to what he is doing but also to the other drivers. As he drove to the movie, another car came speeding past Trevor, rapidly changing lanes and weaving back and forth among the other cars. Just as the car passed them, Leah finished telling a funny story and Roy and Tracey squealed with laughter, distracting Trevor for just an instant. When Trevor looked ahead at the traffic again the car that had flashed by had forced another car partially off the road. To avoid this car, a third car was making an emergency stop, causing the driver to lose control of the back end of the car, which finally came to a stop in the middle of Trevor's lane.

Trevor swerved quickly into the left lane, attempting to avoid both cars; he also stepped on the brakes pretty hard. The children in the back seat were wearing their seat belts, but with all the swerving and skidding going on, they were still thrown around a bit. Tracey spilled her cup of juice all over Roy, who squealed even louder. They were acting like riding in a car was some sort of ride at the amusement park!

When Trevor finally got the car stopped, he really lectured them about being so noisy in the car and the hazards of distracting the driver. Even though he did not actually hit anyone, Trevor was pretty shaken up. He knows his parents have insurance on the car for themselves and for Trevor. They have complained about how high the premiums are for young men his age. Trevor's parents have explained to him that if he ever does get his own car, he can plan to pay for the insurance, too.

Trevor is grateful that he did not hit anyone that day; all three cars came pretty close to being in an accident. The driver of the weaving car, who nearly caused an accident, no doubt will have an accident before long if he or she keeps on driving dangerously. What if one of the children had been injured? Tracey may have to find another driver next time. Even with insurance, Trevor is not sure he is ready to take that risk again.

OBJECTIVES: In this section, we will help Trevor to:

- *examine several types of insurance available for car owners*
- *compare rates of auto insurance for different drivers—based on the age, sex, training and marital status of driver, whether the car is owned by the driver and whether it is driven to work*

AUTOMOBILE INSURANCE

Trevor's parents would purchase automobile insurance even if it were not required by law in their state. They know that all states require drivers to prove financial responsibility at the time of an accident. **Financial responsibility laws** require drivers to pay (either through insurance or through personal savings) for damage to other persons or to property of other persons up to the minimum amounts prescribed by law. A driver may be required to put up thousands of dollars as proof of financial responsibility. If a driver fails to do this at the time of an accident, the driver may have his or her driver's license suspended or revoked. To **revoke** a license is to take it away permanently.

Six kinds of automobile insurance are available in most states.

Bodily Injury Liability. Trevor almost hit a car the day he had his sister's friends in the car. Even though he had to swerve, he still might have been considered to have caused the accident. If he had caused an accident and if someone had been injured, **bodily injury liability** coverage would have paid for the personal injuries he caused to someone else. This coverage is protection against claims or lawsuits that are brought against you by pedestrians, riders in your car, and persons in other cars. Bodily injury liability coverage is purchased in amounts ranging from $10,000 to $300,000. The amount purchased is usually expressed as two figures, such as 50/100. The first amount (which stands for $50,000) is the maximum that the insurance company will pay for a claim made by one person. The second amount ($100,000) is the maximum the insurance company will pay for all claims from one accident.

Property Damage Liability. Coverage for **property damage liability** would have paid for the damage done to other peoples' property, such as a car, a light post, a building, or a fence. Property damage insurance is usually sold in amounts ranging from $5000 to $25,000. When property damage liability and bodily injury coverage are purchased together, the policy protection may be expressed in three figures: 100/300/25. In this case, the insurance company will pay bodily injury claims up to $100,000 for one person, or $300,000 for one accident, and $25,000 for property damage.

Medical payments. Coverage for **medical payments** would pay for the medical costs resulting from an auto accident whether Trevor was at fault or not. This coverage applies to Trevor and the members of his family when they are riding in their own car or in the car of another person.

Collision. Coverage for **collision** would have paid for the damage to Trevor's family's car if it hit the other vehicle, or if it is hit while stationary or moving, or if it turns over. If the car is not too valuable, collision insurance may not be worth the cost.

Comprehensive Physical Damage. Coverage for **comprehensive physical damage** pays for damages that result from a fire, falling object, theft, windstorm, flood, earthquake, mischief, flying object, and vandalism. The accident Trevor was almost in had nothing to do with the damages caused by any of these.

Uninsured and Underinsured Motorist Protection. Coverage for **uninsured and underinsured motorist protection** would have paid for Trevor's personal expenses in the accident if it could be shown that the driver of the other car was at fault, and if the other driver had little or no bodily injury liability coverage.

Trevor is glad his parents have the kinds of automobile insurance they think they need, but he is also glad he did not have to test the policies out by filing a claim. He will not volunteer again to drive three little kids anywhere unless he can extract a promise of absolute silence in the car! (He knows his sister will never agree to that!)

THE COST OF INSURANCE

As Trevor keeps hearing from his parents, the cost of insurance is not the same for every driver. Young men are particularly expensive to insure. One way the insurance industry determines premiums is to assign a factor to each classification of the driver.

In the Reference Section you will find a table entitled Driver Rating Factors. It shows separate rating systems for adults and young people.

The **driver rating factor** is based on such characteristics as age, sex, whether the person is married, the kind of driving the person does, and whether the driver has been through a driver training program. The base premium is multiplied by the appropriate factor to find the premium for a specific individual.

Ask Yourself

1. What is bodily injury liability insurance

2. What is property damage liability insurance

3. What does comprehensive physical damage insurance cover

SHARPEN YOUR SKILLS

Trevor is now looking at actual insurance costs. He has found the following list of basic rates.

Car Class Rating	Collision Deductible			Comprehensive Deductible		
	$ 50	**$100**	**$200**	**$ 0**	**$50**	**$100**
1-10	$ 50	$ 43	$ 37	$14	$13	$ 11
11-20	82	75	69	35	31	28
21-30	114	104	94	45	41	37
31-40	128	119	110	67	61	56

AUTOMOBILE INSURANCE
Six-Month Basic Rate Schedule

He noticed that several factors affect the basic rates. One is the **car class rating**. This rating reflects the resale value of the car, a higher rating for a higher value. Another factor is the amount of the deductible. The **deductible** is a means of keeping insurance rates lower, by having the insured pay a part of any claim. The higher the deductible, the more you cover yourself, and the lower your premiums. If you have an accident that costs $500, for instance, and your deductible is $200, the insurance company will only be liable for $300.

_____ Skill 1 _____

Trevor is 17 years old. He has had driver training. He is single. He is not the owner or principal operator of the car he drives. He does errands in the car; he does not use it to drive to work. All these facts are relevant to finding his rating factor on the Driver Rating Factors Table (in the Reference Section of the book).

Question According to the Driver Rating Factors Table, what is Trevor's rating factor?

Solution First, find Part II, Unmarried Youths.

Look in the age column for his age,17. Then under sex find M.

Next, look at the section for "No" under Owner or Usual Driver.

Trevor has had driver's education training and does not drive to work.

The factor for Trevor is 2.45.

Question Will Trevor's premium likely go up or down as he gets older?

Solution Within the section for Trevor's driving classification, the factor goes down with age (from 2.45 at 17 or lower to 2.00 at 21). The cost of insurance will go down as the factor goes down, because the premium is equal to the base premium times the rating factor.

Question   If Trevor were to buy his own car, and nothing else about his classification changed, would his premium go up or down?

Solution   Look at the column for "Owner or Usual Operator." At age 17, with driver training, the factor is 3.60. His premiums would go up sharply.

_____ Skill 2 _____

Trevor is driving a car with a rating of 22. His driver factor rating is 2.45. He plans to buy collision insurance with a deductible of $100 and comprehensive insurance with a $50 deductible.

Question   How much would this insurance coverage cost?

Solution   Use the Six-Month Basic Rate Table in the Reference Section. His car rating is between 21 and 30, so his costs will be on the third line.

Under collision, with a deductible of $100, the base rate is $104.

Under comprehensive, with a deductible of $50, the base rate is $41.

The total base cost of insurance is:

$104 + 41 = $145

Multiply the base rate by the driver rating factor:

$141 x 2.45 = $345.45

His premium for 6 months would be $345.45.

EXERCISE YOUR SKILLS

1. Why do laws require drivers to be financially responsible for damage to other persons or their property?

2. Why is it important for drivers today to have adequate medical payment coverage?

3. What is the advantage of having deductibles in insurance coverage?

_____ Activity 1 _____

Use the Driver Rating Factors Table in the Reference Section of the book to find the driver rating factor for each of the following individuals.

1. A 19-year-old female without driver training who drives to work; not owner or usual driver

2. A 19-year-old unmarried male without driver training who drives to work; not owner or usual driver

3. A 17-year-old female with driver training who drives to work; is the owner

4. A 17-year-old married male with driver training who drives to work; is the owner

5. A 22-year-old female with or without driver training who drives to work; is the owner

6. A 24-year-old unmarried male with or without driver training who does not drive to work; is not the owner or usual driver

7. The usual driver of the car, 33 years of age, drives to work

8. The usual driver of the car, 55 years of age, drives to work

9. The usual driver of the car, 65 years of age who does not drive to work

10. An adult, age 35, who is not the usual driver and does not drive to work

_____ **Activity 2** _____

Use the Six-Month Basic Rate Schedule in the Reference Section to find the 6-month premiums for each of the following situations.

	Driver Rating Factor	Car Class Rating	Collision Deductible	Comprehensive Deductible	Six-Month Premium
1.	2.25	15	$200	$ 0	
2.	1.00	32	$100	$ 50	
3.	2.40	9	$200	$100	
4.	0.80	23	$ 50	$100	
5.	1.10	10	$200	$ 50	
6.	4.05	12	$200	$100	
7.	2.70	27	$100	$100	
8.	1.25	8	$200	$ 50	
9.	2.60	34	$100	$100	
10.	0.75	2	$200	$100	

EXTEND YOUR UNDERSTANDING
PROJECT 12–1: INVESTIGATING PERCENT OF MARK-UP

Assignment

Work with a group of your classmates to complete this activity.

1. Use a reference book which lists the base cost and suggested list (sticker) price such as Edmund's *New Car Prices* or the *Kelley Blue Book New Car Price Manual.*

2. Have each member of the group choose 10 automobiles of various makes and models—try to get a wide range of prices.

3. Have each member of the group choose a list of options for his or her automobiles.

4. Calculate the percent of mark-up for each of the options and for each of the automobiles selected.

5. Turn in a compilation of the percent of mark-ups among various car manufacturers and models of cars.

6. Turn in a list of the percent of mark-ups of various options.

Extensions

1. Share your group's results with the other groups in the class.

2. Try to determine a trend among manufacturers as to which one has the greatest mark-up on sticker prices.

3. Make a graph similar to the one below to summarize your results.

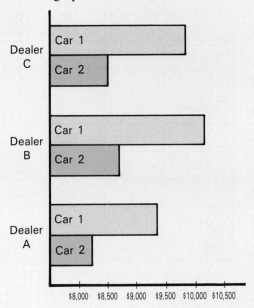

410

PROJECT 12-2: PERCENT OF PROFIT FOR USED CARS

Assignment

Work with a group of classmates to complete this activity.

1. Have each member of the groups select twenty cars advertised in the newspaper or on a used-car lot.

2. Consult a reference book such as Edmund's or the *Blue Book* for used-car prices to use in calculating the trade-in value of the cars you select.

3. Use the prices listed in the newspaper or on the cars in the lot to calculate the percent of profit that the dealer is making on the cars.

4. Turn in a list of the trade-in values and the percent of profit for the cars you researched.

Extensions

1. Share your group's results with the other groups in the class.

2. Compare the mark-up and percent of profit for similar cars from different used-car dealers.

3. Try to determine whether some dealers make higher mark-ups than others.

4. Make a graph similar to the one below to show percent mark-up on 3 cars from each of 3 dealers.

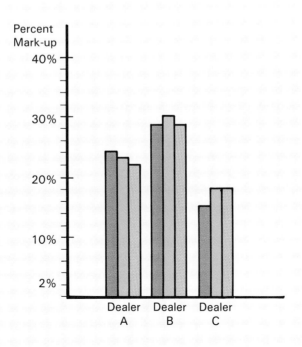

CHAPTER 12 KEY TERMS

CHAPTER 12 REVIEW

1. How do you know what is a reasonable price to pay for a car?

2. If you want to buy a recent model used car, where would you be most likely to find one?

3. If you purchase a new car, what will probably be the most costly factor of operating the car?

4. What are three kinds of protection a driver can get from insurance?

5. Why are there great variations in insurance rates?

6. Find the mark-up and the percent of profit for the dealer in each of the following trade-in deals:

	a.	**b.**
Original list price	$24,875	$15,645
Current wholesale price	11,350	7,185
Average retail price	12,175	7,995

7. Use the information in the Excessive Mileage Deduction Table and the Optional Equipment Table in the Reference Section of the book to find the trade-in value of the following cars.

   a. 1987 Luxury Sedan   Sold at 3-years-old after being driven
   Original List Price   28,078 miles; no automatic transmission;
   $24,875   no air conditioning

b. 1986 Compact
Original List Price
$15,645

Sold at 2-years-old after being driven 23,439 miles; has power brakes and windows

Depreciation Rates:	First Year – 30%
	Second Year – 24%
	Third Year – 18%

8. Use the depreciation rates given above to find the following:

a. The amount of depreciation of a $15,790 car after 2 years and its value at that time.

b. The amount of depreciation of a $38,750 car after 3 years and its value at that time.

Use the information in the following table to find the distance traveled, the mileage per gallon, and the cost per mile for the following periods.

	Odometer Readings		Gallons of Gasoline	Cost of Gasoline
	First	Last		
9.	25,731.5	25,998.8	15.4	$23.15
10.	18,713.2	18,326.1	17.7	28.75
11.	10,475.3	10,627.6	9.6	14.25

Find the total operating expenses and the cost per mile for operating each car listed below with the given expenses. Assume that each car gets 26.4 miles per gallon of gasoline and that gasoline costs $1.47 per gallon.

12. Miles driven 15,400
  Maintenance:
    Tune-ups $ 96.80
    Oil changes and
      filters $ 67.95
    Antifreeze $ 16.89
  Repairs:
    New Radiator $275.38
    Battery $ 64.95

13. Miles driven 25,326
  Maintenance:
    Tune-ups $ 77.95
    Oil changes $ 64.63
    Grease $ 7.35
    Rotate tires $ 25.00
  Repairs:
    Shock absorbers $127.80
    Brakes $168.70

14. Use the Six-Month Basic Rate Schedule in the Reference Section to find the 6-month insurance premium for the following insurance situations.

Driver rating factor	**a.** 0.75	**b.** 4.05
Car class rating	14	32
Collision deductible	$200	$100
Comprehensive deductible	$100	$50

413

1. How can you best make sure you get a fair deal when you purchase a car?

2. Which trade-ins do new car dealers usually keep for resale?

3. How does depreciation affect the cost per mile of operating a car?

4. How can you help the tires on your car to last longer?

5. Why is it wise for drivers to be insured even when it is not required by law?

6. The original list price of a car was $15,475. You were given a trade-in allowance of $7,800 and the dealer then sold the car for $8,900. What was the amount of mark-up? What percent profit did the dealer receive?

7. Use the High Mileage Deduction Table and the Options Valuation Table in the Reference Section of the book to find the trade-in value of a 1988 car, originally priced at $9340, that was traded in after 2 years with 34,000 miles on it. The car has no air conditioning but has power brakes.

8. Use the Automobile Depreciation Schedule in the Reference Section to find how much a $25,865 car would depreciate in 2 years and how much it would then be worth.

9. Find the distance traveled, the mileage per gallon of gas, and the cost per mile for the following period:

   1st odometer reading: 25,431.8

   2nd odometer reading: 25,852.4

   19.2 gallons of gas costing $26.39

10. Use the cost per mile for gas in Problem 9. Then find the total operating expenses and the cost of gas for driving the car 12,500 miles with $150.00 maintenance costs and $340.75 repair costs.

11. Use the Six-Month Basic Rate Schedule in the Reference Section to find the 6-month premium for the following insurance coverage:

    a. Driving rating factor: 1.25   Car class rating: 22
       Collision deductible: $100   Comprehensive deductible: $50

    b. Driving rating factor: 2.60   Car class rating: 9
       Collision deductible: $200   Comprehensive deductible: $100

    c. Driving rating factor: 3.20   Car class rating: 33
       Collision deductible: $50   Comprehensive deductible: $0

1. Your balance from the first of the month through the 15th was $625. Then you made a payment of $125 on the 16th. You make no more charges or payments through the 31st of the month. Find your average daily balance.

2. Your family's take-home pay is $3950 a month, how much can you afford to spend for credit card payments each month?

3. Graph the following changes in stock prices.

   $3\frac{1}{2}$, $5\frac{1}{4}$, $5\frac{3}{8}$, $2\frac{3}{4}$, 7, $6\frac{1}{4}$, $3\frac{5}{8}$, $6\frac{3}{4}$, $4\frac{1}{4}$, $5\frac{1}{2}$

4. Use the Consumer Price Index Chart in the Reference Section to find the expected cost of each of the following items in 1989. The price for each item in 1984 is given.

   a. Man's coat $ 95
   b. Airline ticket $ 189
   c. Compact car $ 7500
   d. House $93,000
   e. Rent $ 535

5. Use the Comparison Table for Term and Whole Life Premiums in the Reference Section to find how much will be paid in premiums in 30 years for a whole life insurance policy of $200,000 purchased at age 35.

6. Use the Tax Table in the Reference Section to find the tax owed by each of the following:

   a. a single person with $35,900 taxable income
   b. a married couple, filing jointly, with $16,950 taxable income

7. Use the Tax Table in the Reference Section to find the tax owed by each of the following:

   a. a single person with $95,950
   b. a married couple, filing jointly, with $103,500 taxable income

8. Fill out a 1040EZ form for the following single person.
   (554-19-6152)   3 exemptions
   Manuel Ramos   Salary: $25,950
   965 Fairlane Avenue   Interest Income: $535
   Columbus, Ohio 49356   Withholding: $2560

9. The original list price of a car was $13,950. You were given a trade-in allowance of $6200 and the dealer then sold the car for $7500. What was the amount of mark-up? What percent profit did the dealer receive?

10. Use the Automobile Depreciation Schedule in the Reference Section to find how much a $21,965 car would depreciate in 3 years and how much it would then be worth.

CHAPTER **13** **TRAVEL PLANS**

The travel and tourism industry knows how much we Americans look forward to getting away from wherever we are and going somewhere else. We probably have as many reasons for wanting to travel as we have travelers. Some of us want to express our pioneering, explorer spirit; others simply wish to be away from a messy house and let someone else do the cleaning for a while. Some of us have so much Puritan work ethic that we cannot have a good time unless we work hard—so we go back-packing and camping in the mountains. When we come home exhausted, we know we have had a wonderful time.

Some trips are easier to look back on rather than living through. Three months afterwards, we will remember how beautiful the beach was and forget how hard it was to find clothes that were comfortable to put over the sunburn. We remember how amazing the science exhibits were and what magnificent works of art we saw at the museums and forget how much our feet hurt from all that walking in the city. We remember how much our four-year-old enjoyed the dolphins at the marine show, and forget that he or she cried all the way home.

The travel and tourism industry is happy to cater to every travel need we can express, and some we can't even anticipate. Even if we wander thousands of miles from home to explore territories completely unknown to us, we can be comforted by the familiarity of many of the same motel chains, gas stations, and fast-food franchises. If we try the local specialty restaurant that is one-of-a-kind, our four-year-old can usually order a kiddie burger and fries.

The smaller cities now have the familiar shopping mall where we can buy what we forgot to bring, rent a video tape, and spend a little time and money at a video game arcade.

So that we do not forget any part of our trip we can buy souvenirs everywhere. The traveler who is really alert can probably buy the same coffee mug, key chain, and sun visor with the local insignia on them everywhere he or she goes. At home, the traveler can then remember the pleasant journey and forget that these vacation trips often cost twice as much as planned.

Perhaps there are ways to anticipate some of these expenses. We already know that our four-year-old will prefer the $25 teddy bear wearing the state insignia T-shirt to the 25-cent picture postcard of the gorgeous scenery. Our teenagers in this chapter will try to help. They will plan a few trips and point out some sources of information that will give us some clues about what to expect the next time we go exploring.

Betty likes to travel. She and her family have taken a vacation trip every other summer for as long as Betty can remember. One of Betty's favorite trips was to the West Coast. She remembers her first encounter, at age four, with the Pacific Ocean. How exciting it was to watch the waves roaring in, gradually subsiding as they washed up on to the beach. She could hardly wait to rush down to run in the surf, splashing as she went. What a shock it was when the water first hit her feet—it was so cold! She quickly changed her mind about wanting to swim. She decided instead to spend her time digging in the sand. She remembers that the surf came up and washed her shovel away; she imagined that it would come ashore somewhere in China.

On that same trip Betty remembers seeing giant sequoia trees that are so old they have little signs on them telling how tall and how old they are. Farther north in California they actually drove their car through one of these huge redwoods. Her father bought Betty a small redwood box and a model truck with tiny redwood logs on the back.

On other trips, Betty remembers seeing the Liberty Bell in Philadelphia, and standing on top of the Empire State Building in New York City. The science museum in Boston was one of her favorites; her little brother, Bruce, who was along on this trip, left his teddy bear on the subway in Boston.

Betty helps her family plan their trips. They usually drive 400 to 500 miles in a day; they stop at the end of two days and stay a couple of nights. On some trips they might travel farther, but they try not to drive more than two days at a time. After that much driving, everybody needs a rest. They usually take a different way home in order to see another area.

Betty isn't sure where they will go this year; she would like to visit New Orleans again—perhaps Florida, or Atlanta, Georgia. They may go west again; Bruce was too young to remember much about the Grand Canyon the last time they went. Of course there is always more than anyone can visit in one trip in Washington, D.C. Bruce was so entranced by the National Air and Space Museum that Betty's parents could hardly get him to leave, even at closing time.

Betty's mother teaches history at the high school and frequently knows interesting stories about the people who have lived in the area they are visiting. Her father makes up riddles and games for them to play as they drive along, partly to keep the kids from pestering each other. Two years ago, Bruce got a hand-held electronic game which can hold his attention for 100 miles at a time. Betty will enjoy traveling even more this year.

OBJECTIVES: In this section, we will help Betty to:

- *consider the factors that affect the choice of a travel plan*
- *use map reading skills to plot a travel route from one point in the U.S. to another*
- *use a map scale and a mileage chart to determine distances traveled*
- *determine the cost of driving specific distances*

WHICH WAY TO GO

Betty's family has discovered several factors that they must consider when they plan a new car trip. Here are some of their suggestions.

What Highways Shall We Use? The type of highway to take is one of the decisions you make when you take a driving trip.

- The driver may prefer to drive as much as possible on interstate highways, which have controlled access and where a fairly constant speed can be maintained. **Interstate highways** are very widespread in our country and they are usually well-marked and well-mapped. The driver can be sure that cars entering or exiting these highways will have special lanes for these actions, and the traffic will move steadily, at least away from major cities. Food, gasoline, lodgings, campgrounds, and rest stops are usually readily available.

- Frequently the driver may prefer not to use interstate highways, but to use **federal and state highways** instead. These highways often offer much more interest and variety than the interstate, because they go through towns not around them. State and federal highways do not have controlled access (entrance and exit lanes) so the driver must look out for other cars crossing or entering the highway with little or no warning. Driving on these highways is not as monotonous as interstate driving.

Betty's family has used both types of highways. Driving on the interstate can be hypnotically boring and frequently the driver has trouble staying awake. Then someone else has to take over the driving. Since the state and federal highways go through small and large towns, driving is usually stop-and-go due to the numerous traffic lights. For a change of pace, Betty's family enjoys visiting some of the smaller towns, seeing local attractions, and buying locally grown fruits and vegetables.

• It is important to keep a fairly new set of maps handy. Betty's family uses a large **road atlas** with all the states in it. When they will be in a large city they often pick up a city map as well, especially if they plan to do anything more than just drive through that city. They belong to an auto club which will map out the entire trip for them if they wish, but they generally prefer making their own plans. Sometimes they change their minds during the trip about their route; they may decide to visit a local attraction that they had not known about.

• They also use a **mileage chart** printed in the road atlas to find the approximate distances they will travel between large cities. To find the distances between smaller towns, they rely on the mileage indicators shown on the road maps themselves. One of the family members is in charge of reading the maps for each portion of the trip, to keep them on course.

Where Are We? Betty and her family want to travel to a place, not just look forward to getting there. They give a lot of thought to these traveling decisions:

• Pace the driving schedule each day so that no one gets too tired of being in the car, including the driver. Betty's family now has three capable drivers, and no one drives more than 1 1/2 to 2 hours at a time. Sometimes Betty drives about an hour before one of her parents takes over.

• Plan to make frequent stops for meals, fuel, short visits, a little exercise. Betty and Bruce can really make everyone uncomfortable if they are cooped up in a car for too many hours at a time with no substantial breaks. The family has found that even an inexpensive visit to a local variety store for an hour can be restful.

• Take along games or activities that you can do in the car. Betty usually takes a book and a few magazines; Bruce prefers a new carton of baseball cards so he can open a package every few hours. Their father brings his favorite snacks. They all enjoy the portable cassette player with headphones. Their mother sometimes tells stories about the history of the places they are traveling through. Together, their parents make up riddles and games for everyone.

Are We There Yet? The family has learned to be flexible in the time schedules on their trips. They realize that many unexpected events can occur to change the timing of their plans. These unexpected events could include:

- Especially heavy traffic during rush hour in larger cities;

- Long stretches of highway construction causing traffic delays;

- A mechanical difficulty with their car. This can cause a serious delay, especially if help is not readily available. They always have their car thoroughly checked by their mechanic before they leave home, but any car can have problems when it is driven at highway speeds for days at a time.

Successful Family Vacations. Betty's family learns something new every time they take a trip. Here are some things they have learned that makes trips more pleasant for everyone:

- Pack the car so that the things you need are easy to get to when you need them.

- Keep a trash bag handy to keep the car from becoming littered with baseball card wrappers, used napkins, empty paper cups, and so on.

- Do not travel more than 8 to 10 hours a day, including stops; after 2 days of driving, stay 2 nights before going on.

- Stop occasionally for some recreation. Betty's family sought out good playgrounds as places to stop a few hours. Before they had children, their parents would stop to play a round of golf on a local course. Now they visit local baseball card shops and sometimes attend major league baseball games if they are in the right city and can get tickets. Betty and Bruce particularly enjoy large motel swimming pools; and the whole family enjoys museums in the big cities.

The best experiences have taught them not to try to do too much in any one day, to give themselves plenty of time to rest and enjoy whatever activities they choose, and to be open to changes in plans if someone is too tired or too hungry to be pleasant company. They all want to look back on their next trip as a time they enjoyed being together.

Ask Yourself

1. What determines which routes you use when you travel by car?

2. Why would people use federal and state highways instead of interstates?

3. What are two unexpected events that can change the timing of travel plans?

SHARPEN YOUR SKILLS

_____ Skill 1 _____

Betty and her family have decided to drive to Georgia to visit cousins. One of Betty's first jobs is to plan their route.

Question   What highways could they use to drive from Indianapolis, Indiana to Milledgeville, Georgia?

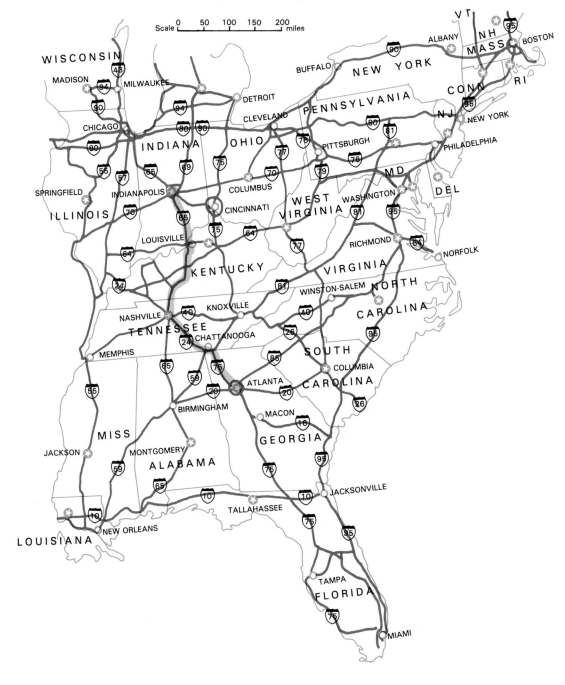

Solution   Betty will use a portion of the U.S. interstate highway map, located on the opposite page, to plan their general route. She will use a portion of the Georgia state map, shown below, to locate their specific destination. Betty has highlighted the highways on the maps she thinks they should take to get to their destination.

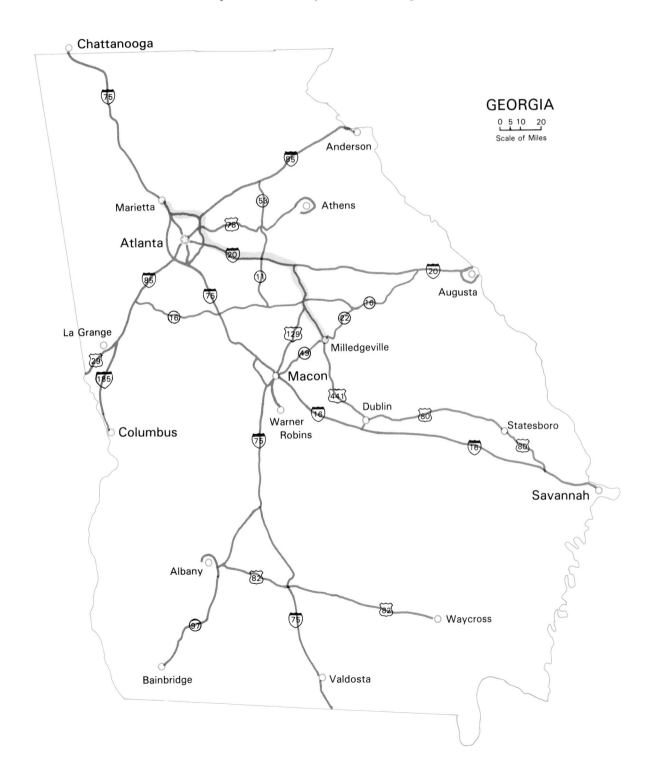

GEORGIA

0 5 10   20
Scale of Miles

United States Mileage Chart

	Atlanta, GA	Boston, MA	Cheyenne, WY	Chicago, IL	Cincinnati, OH	Cleveland, OH	Dallas, TX	Denver, CO	Des Moines, IA	Detroit, MI	Indianapolis, IN	Kansas City, MO	Louisville, KY	Memphis, TN	Milwaukee, WI	Minneapolis, MN	New Orleans, LA	Omaha, NE	Philadelphia PA	Pittsburgh, PA
Albuquerque, NM	1381	2172	517	1281	1372	1560	638	417	977	1525	1266	782	1301	1010	1319	1190	1134	858	1899	1619
Amarillo, TX	1097	1897	511	1043	1096	1285	358	423	742	1269	991	547	1019	726	1084	975	850	643	1624	1344
Atlanta, GA		1037	1442	674	440	672	795	1398	870	699	493	798	382	371	761	1068	479	986	741	687
Austin, TX	919	1911	904	1110	1083	1327	193	906	877	1315	1037	682	982	615	1184	1129	517	837	1615	1367
Birmingham, AL	150	1165	1347	642	465	709	645	1286	787	724	475	697	364	246	728	1006	342	898	869	741
Boston, MA	1037		1907	963	840	628	1748	1949	1280	695	906	1391	941	1296	1050	1368	1507	1412	296	561
Charleston, SC	289	929	1722	877	603	730	1072	1678	1150	842	696	1078	591	660	964	1282	720	1266	633	666
Cheyenne, WY	1442	1907		954	1174	1279	869	100	627	1211	1068	650	1161	1101	987	788	1361	495	1678	1390
Chicago, IL	674	963	954		287	335	917	996	327	266	181	499	292	530	87	405	912	459	738	452
Cleveland, OH	672	628	1279	335	244		1159	1321	652	170	294	779	101	468	374	692	786	693	567	287
Columbus, OH	533	735	1235	308	108	139	1028	1229	618	192	171	656	209	576	395	713	894	750	462	182
Dallas, TX	795	1748	869	917	920	1159		781	684	1143	865	489	819	452	991	936	496	644	1452	1204
Denver, CO	1398	1949	100	996	1164	1321	781		669	1253	1058	600	1120	1040	1029	841	1273	537	1691	1411
Des Moines, IA	870	1280	627	327	571	652	684	669		584	465	195	566	599	361	252	978	132	1051	763
Detroit, MI	699	695	1211	266	259	170	1143	1253	584		278	743	360	713	353	671	1045	716	573	287
Flagstaff, AZ	1704	2495	757	1604	1695	1883	961	657	1300	1848	1589	1105	1624	1333	1642	1481	1457	1171	2222	1942
Harrisburg, PA	700	373	1579	639	468	314	1383	1592	952	474	534	1019	569	931	726	1044	1142	1084	102	189
Indianapolis, IN	493	906	1068	181	106	294	865	1058	465	278		485	111	435	268	586	796	587	633	353
Jackson, MS	391	1406	1257	742	655	899	404	1169	809	914	646	644	554	212	824	1036	178	845	1110	939
Kansas City, MO	798	1391	650	499	591	779	489	600	195	743	485		520	451	537	447	806	201	1118	838
Knoxville, TN	193	911	1372	527	253	485	837	1328	800	512	346	728	241	385	614	932	596	916	615	511
Louisville, KY	382	941	1161	292	101	345	819	1120	566	360	111	520		367	379	697	685	687	668	388
Mackinaw City, MI	935	916	1291	387	495	439	1261	1341	673	284	460	864	562	880	368	508	1247	805	842	556
Miami, FL	655	1504	2097	1329	1095	1264	1300	2037	1525	1352	1148	1448	1037	997	1416	1723	856	1641	1208	1200
Minneapolis, MN	1068	1368	788	405	692	740	936	841	252	671	586	447	697	826	332		1214	357	1143	857
New Orleans, LA	479	1507	1361	912	786	1030	496	1273	978	1045	796	806	685	390	994	1214		1007	1211	1070
Norfolk, VA	540	558	1764	831	604	508	1329	1758	1141	666	700	1162	642	877	918	1236	1019	1273	263	384
Pierre, SD	1361	1726	434	763	1050	1098	943	518	492	1029	944	592	1055	1043	690	394	1394	391	1501	1215
Pittsburgh, PA	687	561	1390	452	287	129	1204	1411	763	287	353	838	388	752	539	857	1070	895	288	
Portland, ME	1139	106	1986	1042	942	707	1850	2028	1359	775	1001	1486	1043	1398	1129	1447	1609	1491	398	663
Portland, OR	2601	3046	1159	2083	2333	2418	2009	1238	1786	2349	2227	1809	2320	2259	2010	1678	2505	1654	2821	2535
San Antonio, TX	983	1988	1027	1187	1160	1404	270	939	954	1392	1114	759	1059	692	1261	1206	550	914	1692	1444
San Francisco, CA	2496	3095	1188	2142	2362	2467	1753	1235	1815	2399	2256	1835	2349	2125	2175	1940	2249	1683	2866	2578
Seattle, WA	2618	2976	1228	2013	2300	2348	2078	1307	1749	2279	2194	1839	2305	2290	1940	1608	2574	1638	2751	2465
Tulsa, OK	772	1537	765	683	736	925	257	681	443	909	631	248	659	401	757	695	647	387	1264	984
Washington, DC	608	429	1611	671	481	346	1319	1616	984	506	558	1043	582	867	758	1075	1078	1116	133	221
Wichita, KS	903	1587	583	696	787	975	365	509	392	940	681	197	710	532	734	644	815	298	1314	1034

_____ Skill 2 _____

Question How far is it from Indianapolis, Indiana to Atlanta, Georgia?

Solution To find out approximately how many miles they will travel on this leg of their trip, Betty will use a mileage chart like the one shown above.

She will find Atlanta on the left-hand side, then look for Indianapolis across the top. She will then find the box in which the row for Atlanta and column for Indianapolis come together. That box contains the number 493. It is approximately 493 miles from Indianapolis to Atlanta.

_____ Skill 3 _____

Betty estimates that the driving distance from Atlanta to Milledgeville is 115 miles. Betty's car gets an average of 17.6 miles to the gallon of gasoline, and one gallon costs $1.39.

Question   How much will Betty's family pay for gasoline to drive 493 miles from Indianapolis to Atlanta plus 115 miles from Atlanta to Milledgeville?

Solution   First, Betty will add 493 to 115 for the total number of miles:

$$493 + 115 = 608 \text{ miles}$$

She will find the number of gallons she needs by dividing the number of miles driven by the number of miles per gallon:

$$608 \div 17.6 = 34.5 \text{ gallons, to the nearest tenth}$$

Finally, she will find the cost of this gasoline by multiplying the number of gallons by the cost of each gallon:

$$34.5 \times \$1.39 = \$47.96$$

The cost of gasoline for Betty's car to drive 608 miles is $47.96.

EXERCISE YOUR SKILLS

1. What are three factors that might affect your travel plans?

2. What is one advantage of traveling by car rather than by air?

3. Why should you use a map to plan your route before you begin a car trip?

_____ Activity 1 _____

Use a copy of a United States interstate map and a copy of a map of Georgia. Highlight the routes from where you live to:

1. Atlanta, Georgia   4. Jesup, Georgia

2. Athens, Georgia   5. Rome, Georgia

3. Waycross, Georgia   6. Valdosta, Georgia

7. Use the mileage chart in the Reference Section of the book or the mileage scale on the maps to find how far it is from your city to each of the cities you located in Georgia (1–6 above).

_____ Activity 2 _____

Use the mileage chart in the Reference Section of the book to find the number of miles between each pair of cities named below.

1. Albuquerque, New Mexico, and Cheyenne, Wyoming

2. Birmingham, Alabama, and Wichita, Kansas

3. Charleston, South Carolina, and Milwaukee, Wisconsin

4. Columbus, Ohio, and Denver, Colorado

5. Dallas, Texas, and Pittsburgh, Pennsylvania

6. Flagstaff, Arizona, and Cleveland, Ohio

7. Harrisburg, Pennsylvania, and Salt Lake City, Utah

8. Kansas City, Missouri, and Boston, Massachusetts

9. Knoxville, Tennessee, and Atlanta, Georgia

10. Mackinaw City, Michigan, and San Francisco, California

11. Minneapolis, Minnesota and Tulsa, Oklahoma

12. Norfolk, Virginia and Cincinnati, Ohio

13. Pierre, South Dakota and Houston, Texas

_____ Activity 3 _____

Find the cost of driving the following distances with the miles-per-gallon and the cost of gasoline shown. Round each number of gallons to the nearest tenth and each cost answer to the nearest penny.

	Miles	Miles per Gallon	Number of Gallons	Cost per Gallon	Total Cost
1.	540	16.2	33.3	$1.29	$42.96
2.	2110	12.6	_____	1.39	_____
3.	750	17.3	_____	1.99	_____
4.	1235	23.4	_____	0.89	_____
5.	840	9.6	_____	1.09	_____
6.	1029	21.3	_____	1.89	_____
7.	926	16.8	_____	1.29	_____
8.	1445	31.2	_____	1.19	_____
9.	693	23.4	_____	1.49	_____
10.	1827	19.3	_____	1.09	_____

What Sylvia enjoys most about traveling is staying in nice motels. She is particularly fond of the ones that have good restaurants nearby so that someone else does all the meal planning, cooking, and cleaning up afterwards. Ever since Sylvia's parents have been divorced, Sylvia and her mother have shared the cooking and cleaning tasks. Sylvia is actually a pretty good cook, but she does enjoy a break from cooking while they travel.

Sylvia and her mother have also done some camping while they travel. Sylvia's uncle owns a van with space for two people to sleep comfortably. They have borrowed it several times for short vacation trips. Sylvia can stay in the van for one night, but by the next night she wants to be back in a motel with maid service. Sylvia and her mother usually wind up combining both types of lodging on their vacations.

Sylvia and her mother know that they must economize if they are to have enough money to do some shopping when they visit a new city. They are also aware of how much it costs to eat out for every meal.

OBJECTIVES: In this section, we will help Sylvia to:

- *calculate the cost of lodging*
- *estimate the cost of food*
- *plan entertainment activities*

MAKING CHOICES ON A BUDGET

Where Shall We Stay? Sylvia and her mother know that lodging can be very expensive, and they have discovered that they can be prepared for the cost if they make **reservations** ahead of time.

When Sylvia and her mother travel, they want to get the most enjoyment they can with their limited time and money. Since they cannot afford to take very many trips, they plan carefully to avoid any expensive surprises. They make a detailed budget before they go, and as they travel, they stick very closely to their plan.

Large motel chains publish directories of their locations throughout the country and will make reservations for customers ahead of time. With advance planning, Sylvia and her mother know before they leave how much they will spend on lodging and where they can stay.

Sometimes they stay at a campground. Sylvia knows these spots can also be reserved, because she has read published campground information that she found in the library and at the bookstore.

Who's Going to Cook? If Sylvia and her mother go camping or stay in a cabin with kitchen facilities, they purchase groceries at local grocery stores and cook some of their meals. They like eating in restaurants the best, and are pretty skilled at predicting how much they will spend to eat in certain places. They have found that many fast-food places are quite inexpensive, although they still cost more than. eating at home. Their food money for the trip is specifically budgeted, so they are careful not to spend too much. Published restaurant guides are found at bookstores and libraries. Sylvia has read several.

What Can We Do Today? Sylvia knows that the cost of entertaining themselves on a trip will vary greatly depending on their choice of activities. If Sylvia were traveling with her father, he might take her to the theater in New York City and not even discuss the cost with her. When Sylvia travels with her mother, she knows ahead of time how much they can spend for activities and shopping. Going to the beach, for instance, is much cheaper than skiing. Visiting a zoo or museum is relatively inexpensive; shopping all afternoon can be very costly. Even public transportation, parking fees, and tolls are figured into their plans. Sylvia's mother enjoys flea markets and resale shops, and they both like going through stores that sell new and used books and sheet music.

A few of their trips have concluded with Sylvia and her mother eating sandwiches on the way home because they had spent all their money, but usually they are pretty faithful about sticking to the plan. They do like peanut butter, but overspending on a shopping trip is not worth sandwiches at the campground for more than one day.

Ask Yourself

1. How can you estimate the cost of lodging when you travel?

2. How can you save money on food costs when you travel?

3. What are two relatively inexpensive ways to entertain yourself in cities that you travel to?

SHARPEN YOUR SKILLS

_____ Skill 1 _____

Sylvia has found the following lodging listings in a travel guide.

LOTUS INN, LOTUS, IOWA

I-123 at 33rd Place, S.W.
Exit 3   666-6666
Location: 3322 South Street,
S.W. 12345. Southwest Lotus.
Downtown 3 1/2 miles. Convention
Center 4 miles. Race Track 1 mile.
Restaurants & shopping nearby.
Airport: 7 miles

1 person, one bed $27.95	2 people, one bed $29.95	
1 person, two beds $39.95	2 people, two beds $35.95	4 people, double room $37.95
1 person, king size $29.95	2 people, king size $35.95	

PLEASURE LODGE MONMOUTH, GEORGIA

Near International Airport
Indoor Pool   HBO
Health Club   Sauna
Location: 1001 Sandwich
Road, Exit Stream Road,
Follow Airport signs.
Downtown 8 miles.
Stadium 6 miles.

Features: Free airport transportation, grand buffet, cable TV.

Rates: Tax 8%. XP $8.
Teens free. RB $8.
        1 person   Standard: $65–83
                   Luxury: $69–90
        2 people   Standard: $73–91
                   Luxury: $77–99
All rooms have two double beds.

WILLOW BRANCH INN OF SILVER GLADE

I-11 to I-12 & downtown area.
Exit 5 & Miller Blvd. Inn located
1 1/2 miles from interstate.
606 Derby Street
Silver Glade, TX 99449

Seasons	RT	1 PRS	2 PRS
1/1–12/31	D	$39–46	$45–52
1/1–12/31	DD	N/A	$48–55
1/1–12/31	K	$43–50	$49–56

3 miles from mountain attractions, 1/2
miles from convention center. 24-hour
full service restaurant. Pets 15 lb and
under. RB $14. Ex Prs $7.

Question How much will it cost Sylvia and her mother to stay at each of these motels if they want a room with two double beds? (Where a range of prices is given, they will choose the lower estimate.)

Solution At the Lotus Inn in Lotus, Iowa, two beds for two people cost $35.95.

The Pleasure Lodge in Monmouth, Georgia, does not charge for teenagers, so there would be no charge for Sylvia; her mother pays for one person, $65. In addition, they will pay 8% tax figured as follows:

0.08 x $65 = $5.20

The total, including tax, is:

$65.00 + 5.20 = $70.20

At the Willow Branch Inn, for two double beds (shown as DD), their rate is $48.

Question How much should Sylvia and her mother plan to spend for food on their 10-day trip?

Solution To answer this question, we will help Sylvia and her mother find an average food cost over a period of four days, based on the information that follows.

Over a four-day period, Sylvia and her mother spend the following amounts for breakfast and lunch:

	Monday	**Tuesday**	**Wednesday**	**Thursday**
Breakfast	$ 7.50	$12.75	$6.28	$11.32
Lunch	12.85	14.50	6.70	9.43

For dinner, they went to the following restaurants and spent the amounts shown:

Monday   **Tower Tops** (dwntwn), 73rd floor of the Stone Plaza (702-9605). A/C. Lunch/dinner daily; brunch Sun. AE, CB, DC, MC, V. Jkt. Specialties; shrimp provencale, peanut soup, meat broiled over a wood fire. *Note:* One of the highest revolving rests. in the world. Creditable cuisine at best, but an exceptional view of the city and its skyscrapers. Resv. necessary. A "must" for tourists. Very good value at lunch. ($25 each)

Tuesday   **Casa Lindo** (vic.), 2001 Brandywine Road. (435-2405). Lunch/dinner daily; closed Thanksgiving, Dec. 25. AE, CB, DC, MC, V. Specialties: chimichangas, chiles rellenos, burritos de sarita, fajitas. *Note:* The best and most authentic Mexican rest. in the city. Agreeable hacienda décor, attentive svce, and a colorful, pleasant atmosphere. Well worth the 30-min. drive from dwntwn. *Mexican.* ($15 each)

Wednesday **Hidden City** (dwntwn), 400 Bay Street (482-1122). A/C. Lunch/dinner daily; closed holidays. AE, CB, DC, MC, V. Specialties: shrimp, moo shoo pork, Mongolian beef, garlic chicken, Peking duck (on order). *Note:* One of the few authentic Chinese rests. in dwntwn. Rather elegant décor and efficient svce. Locally popular. *Chinese.* ($20 each)

Thursday   **The Pennant** (nr. dwntwn), 21 Grant Hill (898-1296). Lunch/dinner daily (until 2 A.M.). No credit cards. Specialties: hamburgers, chili dogs, sandwiches, orange freezes, apple pie. *Note:* By general consensus, the best hamburgers for close to 50 years. An absolute must-see. Right next to the university. An authentic local institution. *American.* ($10 each)

The 11 total breakfast costs were:

$7.50 + 12.75 + 6.28 + 11.32 = $37.85

The average cost for breakfast was:

$37.85 ÷ 4 = $9.46 rounded to the nearest penny

The average cost for lunch was:

($12.85 + 14.50 + 6.70 + 9.43) ÷ 4 = $10.87

The average cost for dinner was:

(50 + 30 + 40 + 20) ÷ 4 = $35.00

Their average for one whole day was:

$ 9.46   for breakfast

10.87   for lunch

35.00   for dinner

$55.33   total

They spent $55.33, on average, for meals each day. For ten days, they multiply this total by 10 to get an estimate of what they should plan for food:

$55.33 x 10 = $553.30

Their total estimated food cost for 10 days is $553.30.

EXERCISE YOUR SKILLS

1. How can you find out which motel chains offer the most inexpensive accommodations?

2. What are some places besides campgrounds that provide kitchen facilities to travelers?

3. What is a good source of places to visit in an unfamiliar city?

___ Activity 1 ___

When Betty and her family reach Milledgeville, they have a choice of two motels in the area where they want to stay. Use the following information to find the cost of staying at each of the motels for six nights. If they stay at the Milledgeville Lodge, Betty and Bruce will each spend $2.00 each evening playing video games. If they stay at the Georgia Inn, each of the family will play a game of miniature golf each evening after dinner and then they will rent a video for later.

1. **Milledgeville Lodge**
   Rates: 2 adults—$46
             Teens—Free
   Tax: 8%
   Free in-room movies
   Game machines

2. **Georgia Inn**
   Rates: 2 adults—$35
             Teens—$10.00
   Tax: 8%
   Video rental: $8.00
   Miniature golf: $2.00/game

_____ **Activity 2** _____

Breakfast

Special, including beverage–$3.75
Juice: orange, grapefruit, tomato–$0.75
Toast or English muffin–$1.25
Cereal: hot or cold–$1.00
Beverages–$0.50

Lunch

Special, including beverage–$4.25
Hamburger and fries–$3.25
Soup and sandwich–$2.75
Salad bar–$2.50; with soup–$3.00
Beverages–$1.00

Dinner

Special; including soup or salad and beverage–$7.95
Steak or chops; including salad bar and beverage–$12.75
Oriental stir fry; including beverage–$9.65
Mexican platter; including beverage–$8.95
Chicken, broiled or fried with salad bar and beverage–$9.
Sandwich special with salad bar–$5.25
Beverages–$1.00
Desserts–$1.00, $1.25, and $1.50

Use the prices above to plan meals for four people for ten days under each of the following conditions:

1. Using the preferences of your own family as to their usual breakfast, lunch, and dinner

2. The cheapest possible cost of three meals each day with a beverage at each meal and dessert with dinner

3. Meals to keep within a budget of $100.00 per day

4. Meals to keep within a budget of $1200.00 for 10 days

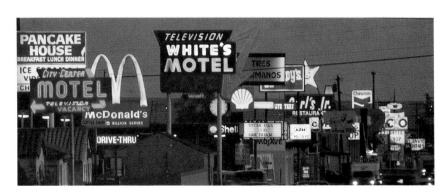

SECTION 13–3
FLYING —THE TIME SAVER

Ramón has made his share of vacation trips by car. Like Sylvia and Betty, he does enjoy seeing new places. He knows that Olivia's mother flew to California last year to be with her sister. He thinks flying must be the best way to travel if you have a long way to go and do not want to spend a lot of time getting there.

Ramón took a flight once; he was quite young. He and his parents flew from Indianapolis to Philadelphia to visit Ramón's grandmother. The flight lasted two hours; Ramón was not as frightened as he thought he would be. He was fascinated how tiny everything on the ground looks from the air—even rivers and mountains and big cities!

This year Ramón's father has a shorter vacation than usual; he is working on a special project at his job and he cannot take extra time off. The whole family would like to make some sort of a trip, though; if Ramón goes away to college next year, this may be their last summer together for a while.

Last winter was especially cold and snowy; another plan that occurs to them is to fly south. Ramón will make out several plans for airline travel to various places and see what his parents like.

OBJECTIVES: In this section, we will help Ramón to:

- *recognize the advantages of flying over other forms of travel*
- *make travel plans based on published airline schedules*
- *estimate the costs of travel plans*

MAKING AIR TRAVEL PLANS

Ramón is learning the major considerations when planning a trip by air.

Why Fly? To Ramón, the obvious advantage to taking a trip by air is that they can go a long distance in a hurry. If their vacation period is to be short anyway, and they want to spend it all in one place, the time saved by flying is a major advantage.

On the other hand, ground transportation to and from the airports at their **departure** and **destination** points can consume time. To get to the airport, Ramón knows that he and his family must either drive themselves and leave their car, take a taxi, or have a friend drive them. When they arrive, they can have someone meet them or pay for their own transportation. Either way,

434

especially if the airports are not convenient, ground transportation will be a factor in their plans.

If they fly, they would not have the lodging expenses of staying overnight while on the road. But, if they were not visiting a family member or other friends with whom they will stay when they reach their vacation spot, they would still have lodging expenses for whatever nights they were away.

Between cities that are connected by Amtrak, Ramón knows that train travel can be an excellent choice. Combining convenience with lower prices for those who travel **coach class**, the train also offers the comparative luxury of sleeping compartments and prepared meals.

Bus service is also a major alternative for those on a budget. Especially when ground transportation to and from airports gets to be significant, a bus can be a logical choice for travel between cities.

When Do You Want to Fly? Ramón knows that several major airlines in the United States fly many times a day to major cities. A lot of smaller cities are connected by the major airlines or by smaller regional airlines. As Ramón started checking on schedules and costs, he was surprised to learn how many different ways there are to get from one place to another by air.

- Some airlines fly exclusively in certain sections of the country; other airlines fly to large cities only. Several different airlines connecting the same cities will have flights at different times of day.

- If you can pay for your ticket weeks or months in advance, you can usually save money. Most often, **advance purchase** offers a savings.

- But many advance airline ticket purchases are **nonrefundable**. If you plan a flight several months ahead of time to save money, you cannot change your travel plans because you will not get your money back. However, to make this option more attractive, some airlines are now offering insurance to cover nonrefundable airline ticket purchases.

- Airlines are in competition with one another. As a way of attracting customers, airlines offer a variety of different nightflight fares, supersaver fares, and company club plans.

Ramón's father reminded him about the weekend he was flying home from a business trip and there was snow and ice in many airports across the country. Flights were cancelled and travelers spent hours trying to rearrange their plans. Ramón's father waited half a day for a later flight, wondering all the time if he might be spending the night in the airport.

Ramón knows that summer travel will not involve much snow and ice, but he understands his father's point: sometimes airline flights are cancelled or delayed, so he must make sure his vacation plans are somewhat flexible. He must also allow for the fact that there are four different time zones across the continental United States. The city to which he is flying could be several hours ahead or behind his own.

Ask Yourself

1. What is the obvious advantage to taking a trip by air?

2. What is one disadvantage to taking a trip by air?

3. Why should you check schedules and costs of several airlines when you are planning a trip?

SHARPEN YOUR SKILLS

_____ Skill 1 _____

WINDWARD AIRLINES SCHEDULE

Leave	Arrive	Stops/Via	Rmks
From Chicago, IL			
To Muscle Shoals, AL		491 mi	
1:00p0	5:10p	ATL	L
4:55p0	9:00p	ATL	D X6
To Myrtle Beach, SC		743 mi	
8:10a0	1:18p	ATL	B
9:54a0	3:15p	ATL	S
Eff. May 15			
1:00p0	6:59p	ATL	L
6:44p0	11:45p	ATL	D X6
To Naples, FL		1136 mi	
8:15a0	1:48p	MCO	B
2:10p0	7:25p	MCO	S
To Nashville, TN		401 mi	
5:30a0	8:45a	CVG	S X67
6:15a0	9:24a	CVG	S X67
7:40a0	10:55a	CVG	X67
9:57a0	12:59p	CVG	X67
11:35aM	2:50p	CVG	X67
3:20pM	6:55p	CVG	X6
3:50p0	6:55p	CVG	
5:35p0	8:43p	CVG	X6
5:40pM	8:43p	CVG	X67
Eff. May 1			
To Nassau, Bah		1301 mi	
8:10a0	1:55p	ATL	
To New Orleans, LA		831 mi	
6:15a0	10:14a	CVG	B/S X67
8:10a0	12:11p	ATL	B
9:25aM	1:35p	CVG	L6
Eff. May 6			
9:57a0	1:35p	CVG	L

Leave	Arrive	Stops/Via	Rmks
10:18a0	2:45p	DFW	X67
11:35a0	3:55p	ATL	L
1:00p0	5:20p	ATL	L
3:14p0	7:20p	ATL	S6
3:20pM	7:45p	CVG	D X6
3:50p0	7:45p	CVG	D
6:44p0	10:35p	ATL	D
8:45p0	12:59a	DFW	S
To New York, NY/			
Newark, NJ		734 mi	
L-LaGuardia; J-Kennedy;			
E-Newark			
7:40aM	12:25pL	CVG	X67
11:35aM	4:40pL	CVG	X67
11:35aM	4:55pE	CVG	X67
3:20pM	7:45pE	CVG	D X6
5:35p0	10:20pL	CVG	
5:40pM	10:20pL	CVG	X67
Eff. May 1			
To Norfolk/Virginia Beach/			
Williamsburg, VA		707 mi	
6:30a0	12:29p	ATL	B X7
9:54a0	3:10p	ATL	S
11:35aM	3:55p	CVG	X67
1:00p0	6:25p	ATL	L
5:35p0	9:40p	CVG	
5:40pM	9:40p	CVG	X67
To Oakland, CA		1843 mi	
Also see San Francisco, San Jose			
8:00a0	12:05p	SLC	B
11:45a0	3:45p	SLC	
3:10p0	7:10p	SLC	D
6:15p0	9:55p	SLC	

Leave	Arrive	Stops/Via	Rmks
To Oklahoma City, OK		695 mi	
8:30a0	12:35p	DFW	B
10:18a0	2:15p	DFW	X67
12:10p0	4:15p	DFW	X7
3:50p0	9:25p	DFW	S
8:45p0	12:35a	DFW	S
To Ontario, CA		1707 mi	
Also see Los Angeles, Burbank,			
Long Beach and Orange County			
8:00a0	11:55a	SLC	B
8:30a0	1:10p	DFW	
11:45a0	3:25p	SLC	
12:10p0	4:20p	DFW	X7
3:50p0	8:10p	DFW	
6:15p0	9:45p		1
To Orange County, CA		1732 mi	
Also see Los Angeles, Burbank,			
Long Beach and Ontario			
6:15a0	12:05p	CVG	X67
8:00a0	12:05p	SLC	B
8:30a0	1:15p	DFW	
9:25aA	3:40p	CVG	6
Eff. May 6			
11:45a0	3:40p	SLC	
3:10p0	7:35p	SLC	S
3:50p0	8:10p	DFW	
To Orlando, FL		995 mi	
5:30a0	10:00a	CVG	B X67
8:15a0	11:42a		B
9:25aM	2:35p	CVG	L6
Eff. May 6			
9:45a0	2:54p	ATL	S
9:57a0	2:35p	CVG	L

As Ramón looked over this list of Windward Airline flights from Chicago to various other cities, he observed that most destinations were reached by way of two flights. The second flight originated at airports with the following labels:

CVG   ATL   DFW   SLC

He consulted the list of airports in the guide and discovered this information:

CVG = Cincinnati, Ohio   DFW = Dallas/Ft. Worth, Texas
ATL = Atlanta, Georgia   SLC = Salt Lake City, Utah

He noticed some other symbols under the Remarks column:

B, L, S, D	Breakfast, Lunch, Snack, Dinner
X6 and X7	The flights travel every day except: 6 (Saturday) and 7 (Sunday)

Ramón knows that the times given are local, and that the city he is traveling to may be in a different time zone from his own. Chicago is in the Central Time Zone. Chicago also has two airports—O'Hare and Midway. The small O or M after the departure time indicates which airport in Chicago these flights leave from.

Questions

1. What would be the quickest flight from Chicago to New Orleans?

2. Which flight takes the longest?

3. Which flight would get him to New Orleans just after noon?

4. Which flights would not get him there until the next day?

5. What time would he arrive if he took the 11:35 P.M. flight?

Solutions   Ramón has found 12 daily flights from Chicago to New Orleans. Five of them go through Atlanta, five through Cincinnati, the other two through Dallas/Ft. Worth. He set up this chart:

	Departure Time	Through Airport	Travel Time
Morning	6:15	CVG	3 hours 59 minutes
	8:10	ATL	4 hours 1 minute
	9:25	CVG	4 hours 10 minutes
	9:57	CVG	3 hours 38 minutes
	10:18	CVG	4 hours 27 minutes
	11:35	DFW	4 hours 20 minutes
Afternoon	1:00	ATL	4 hours 20 minutes
	3:14	ATL	4 hours 6 minutes
	3:20	CVG	4 hours 25 minutes
	3:50	CVG	3 hours 55 minutes
Evening	6:44	ATL	3 hours 51 minutes
	8:45	DFW	4 hours 4 minutes

1. He observed from this list that the fastest trip is the 9:57 A.M. flight through CVG at 3 hours and 38 minutes.

2. The longest flight is the 10:18 A.M. flight through CVG.

3. The 8:10 A.M. flight would get him to New Orleans just after noon.

4. The 8:45 P.M. flight would get him there the next day.

5. He would arrive at 3:55 P.M.

Question   What is the average time it takes to travel from Chicago to New Orleans by air?

Solution   Add the 12 flight times and divide by the number of flights to find the average:

$$44 \text{ hours plus } 316 \text{ minutes} =$$

$$44 \text{ hours} + 5 \text{ hours} + 16 \text{ minutes} =$$

$$49 \text{ hours } 16 \text{ minutes}$$

$$49 \text{ hours} + 16 \text{ minutes} = 49.26 \text{ hours}$$

$$\frac{49.26 \text{ hours}}{12} = 4.11 \text{ hours} = 4 \text{ hours } 7 \text{ minutes}$$

The average length of a flight from Chicago to New Orleans is 4 hours and 7 minutes.

_____ Skill 2 _____

Ramón has found the following list of flights from Chicago to other large cities.

Cities	Days	Number of Stops	60-Day Advance	30-Day Advance	Full Fare
Milwaukee	weekdays, Sat, Sun	NS	$109	$119	$139
Minneapolis	weekdays,	NS	$125	$145	$165
	Sat, Sun	NS	$120	$140	$160
St. Louis	weekdays	1S	$149	$169	$189
	Sat, Sun	1S	$129	$149	$169
	weekdays, Sat, Sun	NS	$169	$189	$209
Louisville	weekdays, Sat, Sun	NS	$114	$142	$192
Columbus	weekdays, Sat, Sun	1S	$119	$119	$119
Detroit	weekdays	NS	$ 69	$ 79	$ 99
	Sat, Sun	NS	$ 69	$ 89	$109
Fargo	weekdays, Sat, Sun	2S	$213	$233	$292
	weekdays	1S	$233	$266	$319

Questions

1. How much could Ramón save over the full fare by making reservations to fly to Milwaukee 60 days in advance?

2. How much would he save by making the reservation 30 days in advance?

3. Does it cost more to fly to St. Louis, with one stop, on weekdays or on weekends?

4. Does a passenger save money by taking a flight that stops in another city on the way to its destination?

5. On which flight would you save the most money reserving 30 days in advance compared with the full fare?

Solutions   Ramón found the following answers by consulting the table.

1. $30

2. $20

3. Weekdays

4. Yes

5. Fargo, all flights

EXERCISE YOUR SKILLS

1. If you want to compare the cost of air travel with car travel, what are some of the costs that must be included in each?

2. Why do you think airlines often charge people less if they pay for a particular flight weeks or months in advance?

3. What is one disadvantage buying an airline ticket months in advance of your flight?

4. How do some airlines provide protection when you buy nonrefundable airline tickets in advance?

_____ Activity 1 _____

Use the Windward Airlines Schedule from the Reference Section of the book to find the following:

1. The shortest flight from Chicago to San Francisco

2. The earliest flight from Chicago to San Diego that goes through Dallas/ Ft. Worth

3. The latest flight from Chicago to Portland, Oregon

4. The shortest flight from Chicago to Ontario, California

5. The longest flight from Chicago to Nashville, Tennessee

6. The average length of the flights from Chicago to Phoenix

7. The average length of the flights from Chicago to Panama City, Florida

8. The average length of the flights from Chicago to Nashville

9. The average length of the flights from Chicago to San Diego

10. The average length of the flights from Chicago to Orlando

_____ **Activity 2** _____

Use the air fare chart in Skill 2 to answer the following questions.

1. What is the least expensive way to get to St. Louis?

2. Will a passenger pay more to fly to Minneapolis on the weekend or a weekday?

3. How much money would you save reserving your weekday flight to Fargo 60 days in advance?

4. How much money would you save reserving your weekday flight to Fargo 30 days in advance?

5. If you found out Wednesday that you needed to be in Milwaukee by Friday, how much would you pay for your flight?

6. If you found out on July 6 that you needed to be in Louisville on November 15, how much would you pay for your ticket?

EXTEND YOUR UNDERSTANDING
PROJECT 13–1: PLAN A CAMPING TRIP

Assignment

Work with a group of classmates to plan a two-week camping trip for a family of four.

1. Decide where you want to go and what sights you want to see along the way.

2. Plan a driving route to include campsites at appropriate places along the way.

3. Estimate the cost of gasoline, lodging, and food for the trip, including the cost of camping at the sites you choose.

4. Find the cost of visiting the sights you want to see.

5. Turn in the costs for the trip, the routes you will travel, and the campsites where you will stop.

Extensions

1. Make a picture collage of the sights you plan to see.

2. Prepare a travel folder describing your camping trip, include illustrations.

PROJECT 13–2: GETTING BARGAIN AIRFARES

Assignment

Work with a group of classmates to find the best bargains for airfares.

1. Each person: choose five cities that you would like to fly to.

2. Get prices from various airlines and travel agents using various flying times.

3. Find the savings on air fares by paying for flights well in advance.

4. Discuss with your group which of the fares were the cheapest.

5. Turn in the cheapest fares to each of the cities, including the airline and the time of day and week.

Extensions

• Prepare tips to travelers regarding the least expensive airlines, best times to travel, and how far in advance to purchase tickets.

CHAPTER 13 KEY TERMS

Section 13–1

federal and state highways
interstate highways
mileage chart
road atlas

Section 13–2

reservations

Section 13–3

advance purchase
coach class
departure
destination
nonrefundable
time zones

CHAPTER 13 REVIEW

1. What are two advantages of using federal and state routes instead of interstates when traveling by car?

2. What are some considerations that would affect your decision about whether to travel on interstates or on federal and state routes?

3. Why should travel plans by car be flexible?

4. Why is it wise to estimate costs of food and lodging before you start out on a car trip?

5. What are two advantages of air travel over car travel?

6. Why is the location of airports in relation to your places of departure and arrival important in planning travel by air?

7. How can you make sure you get the best possible travel arrangements and costs when you travel by air?

Use a United States interstate map to plan the routes you would travel from where you live to the following cities.

8. New Orleans, Louisiana

9. Richmond, Virginia

10. Boston, Massachusetts

11. Little Rock, Arkansas

12. Cincinnati, Ohio

13. Buffalo, New York

Use a mileage chart in a road atlas to find the number of miles between the following pairs of cities:

14. Boston, Massachusetts, and Lexington, Kentucky

15. Austin, Texas, and Detroit, Michigan

16. Cincinnati, Ohio, and Chicago, Illinois

17. Minneapolis, Minnesota, and Spokane, Washington

18. Philadelphia, Pennsylvania, and Omaha, Nebraska

19. Norfolk, Virginia, and Louisville, Kentucky

20. Austin, Texas and Cheyenne, Wyoming

21. Find the cost of driving each of the distances in Problems 14–20 if you get 17.2 miles per gallon and gasoline costs $1.79 per gallon.

22. A family of five want to share a room at the Honolulu Royale. The rates are $86.00 for two people, $10.00 for each extra person, and $4.00 for a rollaway bed; tax is 9.42%. How much will it cost the family to stay at this motel for five nights?

Use the following description to answer Questions 23 and 24.

Atlanta Plaza   Rates: 1 per std. $65–83; 2 per DD $73–91
Tax 8%. XP $8. Teens Free. RB $6

23. What is the least it would cost three adults and one teenager to spend four nights at the Atlanta Plaza? (Assume the third adult and teenager share a double bed.)

24. What is the least it would cost three adults and one teenager to spend three nights at the Atlanta Plaza if each person wanted his or her own bed?

Use the food costs in Activity 2 of Section 2 to find the costs in the following problems.

25. Betty and Bruce go on a 4-day trip. Following are the foods they eat: They each have orange juice, cold cereal, and milk for breakfast each day; Bruce has a hamburger and fries and Betty has soup and a sandwich, both have a beverage for lunch each day; for dinner Bruce chooses the special each day and Betty chooses Oriental stir fry one day, a Mexican platter one day, and broiled or fried chicken for 2 days. Each of them had a dessert costing $1.25 each day for dinner.

What was the daily cost of their food for each of the four days? What was the total cost for four days? What were their average food costs for the four days?

26. If a family of five averaged the same amount as Betty and Bruce did in Problem 25, what would their food costs be for ten days?

Use the Windward Airlines schedule in the Reference Section of the book to find the following:

27. The average length of the flights from Chicago to San Antonio, Texas

28. The average length of the flights from Chicago to Oklahoma City, Oklahoma.

29. The shortest flight from Chicago to Raleigh/Durham, North Carolina

30. The longest flight from Chicago to Roanoke, Virginia

1. What are two advantages of using interstate highways?

2. What are two possible causes of unplanned delays when traveling by car?

3. Why should travelers estimate lodging and food costs before starting on a trip by car?

Plan the routes in Problem 4 and 5 using a United States interstate map.

4. The most direct interstate route between Macon, Georgia, and Tampa, Florida

5. An ocean-view interstate route between the same cities.

6. Use the mileage chart in a road atlas to find the number of miles between Buffalo, New York, and Reno, Nevada.

Find the cost of driving the number of miles indicated in Problems 7–10 with the miles per gallon and the cost of gasoline given. (Round gallons to the nearest tenth and cost to the nearest penny.)

	Miles	Miles per Gallon	Number of Gallons	Cost per Gallon	Total Cost
7.	1768	22.6		$1.57	
8.	976	17.4		.89	
9.	2591	16.8		1.43	
10.	1273	20.3		1.64	

Use the following descriptions to answer Questions 11 and 12.

Humphry Lodge
Rates: 2 per DD – $56
XP – $8.
Tax – 9%

McCarthy Inn
Rates: 2 per DD – $68
Teens Free.
Tax – 8%

11. What is the cost of 3 persons sharing a room at the Humphry Lodge for 6 nights?

12. If 2 adults and 2 teenagers were going to share a room, should they choose the Humphry Lodge or the McCarthy Inn?

Use the Windward Airlines schedule in the Reference Section of the book to find the following information.

13. The average length of flights from Chicago to Myrtle Beach, SC.

14. The shortest flight from Chicago to Richmond/Williamsburg, Virginia.

In this skills preview, you will review skills that you will need to complete the exercises in Chapters 14 and 15. If you do not know how to complete any exercises, be sure to ask for help.

Find the average.

1. 4, 3, 4, 2, 3, 5   **2.** 1½, 2½, 3½, 3, 3

Find each sum.

3. (6 x $936.96) + $93.70 + $18.74   **4.** $742.64 + 3 x $83.55 + 9.29

5. (2 x $928.30) + (2 x $92.30) + 9.29

Find each of the following:

6. 26% of $9600   **7.** 80% of $175,000

8. 28% of $5100   **9.** $825,000 – 20% ($825,000)

Divide.

10. $\dfrac{\$155,500}{3450 \text{ sq. ft.}}$ **11.** $\dfrac{\$121,950}{2880 \text{ sq. ft.}}$

12. $\dfrac{\$2,385,295.20}{\$825,000}$

13. Find what percent $155,500 is of $192,500.

Find each of the following.

14. $\dfrac{\$135,000}{\$180,000}$ x ($1050 – $200)

15. $\dfrac{120,500}{175,000}$ x ($919 – $250)

16. $\dfrac{\$28,950}{52}$ **17.** $\dfrac{\$35,500}{52}$

18. $595 x 52   **19.** $680 x 52   **20.** $921.44 x 52

CHAPTER 14

HOME OWNERSHIP: THE AMERICAN DREAM

The self-contained, single-family home with its nuclear family unit—Mom, Dad, two children, and a dog—is portrayed as every middle-class American's fondest wish. The fact that not every family even wants children, a dog, and a home of its own gets overlooked when the message is broadcast. For those families who do wish to pursue "the American dream," many will find home ownership expensive and laden with responsibilities. Even if they can buy the house, there is always something that needs fixing: the water heater wears out, the toilet does not flush properly, the fan on the furnace burns up, the air conditioner or the roof must be replaced, termites invade.

Because many families still want to own a home no matter what the cost, bankers and lending institutions are still trying to make that possible. At a time when a single-family, three-bedroom home in a moderate neighborhood averages over $100,000 in many cities, most home buyers choose a mortgage as their only means of making the purchase.

Our teenagers in this chapter will examine the process of buying a home and some of the many responsibilities associated with home ownership. Hari will discover why homeowner's insurance is very useful, especially when the temperature falls and the water pipes freeze.

Vernon's family have decided to buy a house when they moved from Chicago to Indiana. They consider the advantages of buying as compared with renting, and they look at the differences between new and older houses. Olivia and her family may move to a larger house; she learns about all the costs associated with buying a house, including the fees and down payment at the time of the purchase and the total financed purchase price through the mortgage.

Rosa and Consuela's parents will be moving to a different house when both sisters are away attending college. Rosa learns about different kinds of mortgages and how a family can determine the size of loan they can afford.

447

CHOOSING A NEW HOUSE

When Vernon's family moved to Indiana from Chicago, where they had lived in a three-bedroom apartment, they decided they would consider buying a house. They knew this was an important and complicated decision. They were making the move because Vernon's mother was transferred to Indiana by the company she works for. Vernon's father is an accountant; he was confident he could find another accounting job in their new city. It seemed unlikely the company would move Vernon's mother again soon, so they thought this would be a good time to buy a house.

Vernon thought this was great news; he had shared a bedroom with his younger brother ever since their sister, P.J., needed a room of her own. Vernon's brother, Kev, never liked sharing the bedroom, either. He always complained about Vernon's choice of music, so Vernon could not play his CD player while Kev was studying. Vernon finally bought a pair of headphones to solve that problem. The neighbors were grateful, too. Vernon had quite a few posters that he liked hanging on the walls, too, but Kev finally insisted that half of the wall space was his, as was half of the closet space.

Vernon and Kev were ecstatic about the idea of having their own rooms in a new house. Vernon also liked the idea that they might have a space for a real recreation room; he could invite friends over—more than one at a time! His mother and father liked the fact that they could decide what kinds of carpets, drapes, and appliances they would have. They also liked being able to control the temperature in the house themselves. In rented apartments, it had always seemed too hot or too cold.

The family knows that buying a house would certainly cost more money than renting an apartment. A lot of responsibility comes with home owner-ship, too. Vernon and Kev would have to help care for the yard. They might all have to help to make repairs and improvements.

To get a whole closet to himself and to have a place where he could close the door and get away from his brother, Vernon was willing to do a lot of painting and lawn mowing. He did more research on the subject and found out all that he could in order to help his parents make the buying decision.

OBJECTIVES: In this section, we will help Vernon to:

- *consider some of the advantages and disadvantages of owning a house*
- *make comparisons among different types of houses available for sale*
- *recognize the relationship between the selling price of a house and its age and amenities*

**CHOOSING
A PLACE
TO LIVE**

Vernon's family were ready to express their feeling of financial independence and family security by buying a house. Like many, they chose to buy a house partly for noneconomic reasons—such as the freedom to have pets, the space to plant a garden, and the ability to make home improvements. Certainly Vernon and Kev were eager to have bedrooms of their own, and the family found this was now possible.

Home ownership usually costs more than renting; but, in the long run, buying a house builds up equity. **Equity** is the difference between what the house (or other property) is worth and what the family still owes on the mortgage. Their monthly payments decrease the debt and increase the amount of equity in the property.When their house is fully paid for, Vernon's family will have 100% equity in the property.

Home ownership has been a particularly good investment in recent years. Because of the increase in property values, many people have been able to experience a large **capital gain**, or increase in the value of their property, when selling their homes. They do not intend to sell this home until Vernon, Kev, and P.J., are through college and perhaps have homes of their own. By then their equity in the house will be substantial.

Advantages of Owning a Home	Disadvantages of Owning a Home
Home ownership often gives a feeling of security and independence.	The money the owner has invested in the home is not readily available for other purchases.
Home ownership usually costs more than renting, but it provides a means of forced savings, that is, setting aside the money invested in the home.	An owner must assume responsibility for financing and maintaining a home; renters leave those responsibilities to the owner.
Home ownership has proven to be a good investment over the years because of a general, widespread increase in property values.	Home ownership makes moving to another community or city more difficult because the old home must be sold.
Interest paid on a mortgage is tax deductible.	Home ownership may require larger monthly payments (including utilities, property tax, and insurance) than does renting.

Vernon's family thought they were ready for home ownership because they could meet these important conditions:

- They could make the monthly payments out of their current income.

- They plan to live in the same place for three years or longer.

- They would get more pleasure and satisfaction from owning than from renting.

- They were prepared to take on the responsibility for the financing, repair, and maintenance of a house.

Usually these responsibilities provide individuals and family members with a sense of pride, enjoyment, and satisfaction. Vernon wasn't sure he would actually enjoy mowing the lawn, but he would have a lot of satisfaction in having his room the way he wanted it!

When they examined the housing market in the new town, Vernon's family realized the next major decision they would make would be whether to buy a new house or an older one.

Buying a New House. A new house often costs more than an older one, but the repairs for a new one are usually less expensive.

If they bought a new house, Vernon's family would also have to consider landscaping or any other general improvements that needed to be made. Items such as furniture, draperies, landscaping, and home modifications can greatly increase the cost of owning a home.

Buying an Older House. If they chose an older house, they could probably buy it at a lower price than a new one. Older homes frequently need repairs, however, such as a new roof, a new furnace, new plumbing, or electrical work. Sometimes a room must be added, or existing rooms must be modified. Many of the improvements or changes Vernon's family made might not appeal to the next owner; therefore such improvements do not always increase the cash value of the home.

Ask Yourself

1. What are some noneconomic reasons people may choose to buy a new home?

2. What is equity?

3. What are some of the advantages of buying a new house as compared with an older one? What are the disadvantages?

SHARPEN YOUR SKILLS

_____ Skill 1 _____

When a house is advertised for sale, one of the figures often listed is the square footage. Following is an example that Vernon found listed in the local paper:

> **30 DAY MOVE-IN $100,050**
> **NEW HOME 2,305 sq. ft., 3**
> **bedrooms, 2 living areas, all**
> **new kitchen. LOADED.**

Question How much does this house cost per square foot?

Solution To find the cost per square foot, divide the full cost by the number of square feet listed:

$$\frac{\$110,050}{2,305} = \$47.744034$$

Round the answer to the nearest penny.

The cost per square foot for the house is $47.74.

_____ Skill 2 _____

The special features of a house are used as selling points. Vernon has found the following features mentioned in house listings he has read:

Usual Rooms

Bedrooms
Bathrooms
Living Room
Kitchen
Dining Room
Garage

Additional Features

WBFP (wood-burning fireplace)
Island Kitchen
Ceiling Fans
Skylights
Sprinklers
Security System
Patio/Deck
Pool
Spa/Jacuzzi
Storage Building

Extra Rooms

Sitting Room
Den/Library/Study/Office
Gameroom/Family Room
Breakfast Area
Formals

Descriptive Phrases

High/Tall ceilings
Split bedrooms
Master bedroom/suite
Large rooms
New carpeting
Hardwood floors
Walk-in closets
Professional landscaping
Multiple living reas
Close to schools /transportation
Well maintained

Question What are the usual rooms, the extra rooms, the additional features, and the descriptive phrases associated with each of the following listings?

a. ENJOY THE GREAT OUTDOORS $45,000

The park is just across the street from this 3-bedroom, $1\frac{1}{2}$ bath house with paneled living room. Covered patio and storage building are bonuses.

b. SWIM AND SUN! $126,500

At your leisure in this charming 4-bedroom, 2.5 bath, traditional, 2-story with trees, bushes & flowers. Enjoy the shimmering private pool & jacuzzi.

c. SEE TO BELIEVE! $235,000

Stunning home priced to sell quickly. Four bedrooms, $3\frac{1}{2}$ baths, lovely formals plus gameroom & party room. 2 fireplaces, spa & decking, sprinklers.

Solution Vernon designed the following table to help him organize the information he was collecting about different houses. He filled it out by reading the ads and transferring the information to the table, as shown.

Usual Rooms	Extra Rooms	Additional Features	Descriptive Phrases
a. 3 bedrooms		covered patio	park across the street
1½ baths		storage building	enjoy great outdoors
paneled living room			
b. 4 bedrooms		pool	traditional
2.5 baths		jacuzzi	2 story
			trees, bushes + flowers
c. 4 bedrooms	game room	2 fireplaces	stunning
3½ baths	party room	spa	priced to sell quickly
		decking	lovely formals
		sprinklers	

After he developed this system, Vernon used it to analyze a number of houses in several price ranges and compare their values. Following is his table.

	Bedrooms	Bathrooms	Den, etc.	Deck, etc.	Extras
Price Range 1 House					
a.	3	1	den	deck, skylights	wooded lot
b.	2	1 1/2	library		near schools
c.	1	1		pool	
d.	2	2			convenient, well kept
e.	2	1 1/2	study	patio	well kept
Price Range 2 House					
a.	5	4	library, den	WBFP pool, spa	large rooms, master bedroom suite
b.	4	3	den	deck, WBFP	tall ceilings, fans, new kitchen
c.	3	2 1/2	study	patio, pool	hardwood floors, walk-in closets
d.	4	3	library den	spa, pool	elegant landscaping, all new kitchen
e.	5	4	study	Security System patio, WBFP pool, sprinklers	exquisite view, wooded lot
Price Range 3 House					
a.	2	2	den	pool	near park
b.	4	2 1/2	study	patio, WBFP	hardwood floors
c.	3	1 1/2	office	deck, spa	large rooms, sunny
d.	3	2	study	patio	walk-in closets, new kitchen
e.	2	1 1/2	library	deck, WBFP	master bdrm suite

Questions

1. **a.** What is the total number of bedrooms in the houses in each price range?

   b. What is the average number of bedrooms in the houses in each price range?

2. **a.** What is the total number of bathrooms in the houses in each price range?

b. What is the average number of bathrooms in each price range?

3. a. How many dens, libraries, and studies are there in each price range?

b. How many decks, patios, pools, and spas are there in each price range?

4. Which of the 3 price ranges is probably the most expensive? The middle? The least expensive?

Solutions

Totals

	Bedrooms	Bathrooms	Dens, etc.	Decks, etc.	Number of Extras
Range 1	10	7	3	3	6
Range 2	21	16.5	7	9	16
Range 3	14	9.5	5	6	9

1. a. The total number of bedrooms in each range is found by adding the column in the table.

b. The average number of bedrooms in each range is found by dividing the total number of bedrooms by the number of houses.

2. a. The total number of bathrooms is found by adding the column.

b. The average number of bathrooms is found by dividing.

3. a. The total number of dens, etc., is found by adding.

b. The total number of decks, etc., is found by adding.

4. Judging by the features and sizes of the houses, Range 2 is probably the most expensive. The least expensive is probably Range 1, and Range 3 is in the middle.

EXERCISE YOUR SKILLS

1. What are some disadvantages of owning a house?

2. In your opinion, do the advantages of owning a house outweigh the disadvantages, or vice versa? Why?

3. Why does owning a house usually cost more than renting an apartment?

_____ Activity 1 _____

List the prices of the following houses in sequence from most expensive to least expensive. Use the features in Skill 2 to compute the cost per square foot. Round your answer to the nearest penny. Use a chart like the following one to record your answers.

Price	Square Feet	Cost per Square Foot
Ex. $835,000	5729	$145.75

a. **$48 PER SQ. FT.**   **$211,000**

5 bedrooms, $3\frac{1}{2}$ baths, library. 4,355 sq. feet. Excellent schools...Sensational!

b. **TERRIFIC VALUE**   **$127,950**

4 bedr., $2\frac{1}{2}$ bath, 2,816 sq. ft. New homes $80,000 to $140,999.

c. **GREAT STYLE & ELEGANCE**   **$190,000**

4 bdrm., library, 3 living, 3 bath, golf course community, approx. 3,600 sq. ft.

d. **3,085 SQ. FT. OF ULTIMATE LUXURY...**

with quiet peaceful setting • lake view on some lots • Hurry, these prices may not last!! • Formals • large rooms • several floor plans to choose from • Great price!!! $110,900.

e. **1.3 ACRES SOUTHLAKE**   **$224,000**

3 fireplaces, Light home! Skylights, planter box at entry! All the amenities • Wooded prop. with creek running through back! Approx. 3,100', 2 story.

f. **$109,950**

Country setting • Over 1/3 acre lot • 3,400 sq. ft. home • 5 huge bedrooms • 4 baths • Custom built home remodeled 8 years ago.

g. **5 BEDROOM/2 STORY**   **$155,900**

Most wanted area! Over 2,850 sq. ft. Lovely 5 bedrooms, 3 full baths, 2 car garage. Beautiful den with wood-burning fireplace, formal living and dining rooms, tile baths, pretty wallpapers. Walk to schools.

h. **COUNTRY ESTATE**   **$375,000**

Ranch features 35 acres with "Country Georgian" 2 story brick home with full basement (4,375 sq. ft. as per bldr.'s plans), 2 barns, 3 ponds, over 10,000 ft. of pipe & cable fence.

i. **GRACIOUS LIVING**   **$239,900**

Perfectly arranged with 3 sep. living areas, incl. huge sunroom overlooking sparkling pool/spa with extensive covered wood deck! Master suite has its own fireplace, opens to sunroom! 3,000 sq. ft. Lots of built-ins!

j. REDUCED $835,000

Estate neighborhood. Custom built home. Appraiser says 5,759 sq. ft. 4 living areas, circular drive, screened-in-outdoor pool plus play yard. Sophisticated luxury. Attic expansion opp. Handsome hardwoods. Country environment in town. Sprinkler & alarm systems.

k. NEW! $595,000

Live in a new home. A home for entertaining. Fenced diving pool & cabana. Large treed yard, 3 car garage, circular drive, outside entrance, patios, paneled library, tile and plank wood floors. Wood shutters, palladium windows. 4,828 sq. ft.

l. CHARM! $79,000

Charming cottage. Hardwood floors. Large backyard w/mature trees. Detached 2 car garage. One year home warranty provided by seller. Bring your decorating expertise. 1,528 sq. ft.

m. LOVERS LANE $99,500

What a doll house! Close-in location. Fashion colors. Decked patio with arboreal off dining room and decked entertainment spa of MBR. Circular drive. 1,314 sq. ft.

n. WELCOME TO TARA! $269,900

Fabulous home with amenities galore! Approx. 4,000 sq. ft. of custom features including all wood spiral staircase–4 HUGE BDRMS, w/WIC-cedar closet–HUGE island kitchen. Sparkling POOL w/waterfall, SPA.

_____ Activity 2 _____

1. Use the list of features in Skill 2 to summarize the following house listings by price range. Use a table like the following to record the information. **NOTE:** 2/2/1 in a listing translates to 2 bedrooms, 2 baths and 1 garage.

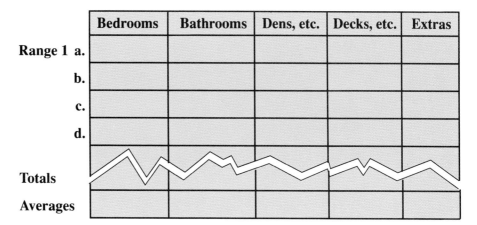

	Bedrooms	Bathrooms	Dens, etc.	Decks, etc.	Extras
Range 1 a.					
b.					
c.					
d.					
Totals					
Averages					

Price Range 1: Under $50,000

a. BIG ROOMY FRAME $38,900

Two bedrooms, 1 bath, office, sitting room. Old knotted pine paneling, fireplace, pool, landscaped. Needs updating/repairs but priced to sell.

b. JUST THE BEGINNING $31,000

A good place to start.home ownership! Well cared for 2/1/1 with large living room. Hardwood floors add charm. Relax on the porch on those casual evenings.

c. EQUITY BUY! $41,000

GREAT for couple just starting out or for the "empty nest." This 2/1/1 is close to shopping, bus line & schools. The brick fireplace makes a cold winter evening look good.

d. JUST STARTING OUT??? $32,000

This home is just for you. It features 3/1.5/den/liv/din/1. Very well kept. Close to schools and public transportation. Large back yard.

e. BUILT IN 1905... $44,444

but updated for today. In-town setting for this two bedroom, one bath home featuring hardwood floors, wood ceilings, lots of shade trees and fenced yard. One car detached garage.

f. RENT RUNNING YOU RAGGED? $45,900

Adorn yourself with home ownership. Try on this affordable 3/2/1. Immaculate condition inside and out. Parklike backyard for the kiddies.

g. FORECLOSURE LIKE NEW! $49,900

Brick 3 bdrm., 2 bath, 2 car garage home. Large den with corner fireplace. Big kitchen dining area. Very open spacious floor plan! Pretty beige carpet! A FAMILY HOME!

h. BOUND TO PLEASE $33,000

Cozy 2/1/1, siding, newish carpet, attic fan, ceiling fans, updated kitchen, brk bar, storage blding, lrg fenced yard, big trees, priced to sell quick.

i. DREAM HOME $35,900

Sparkling 2/1/cp, updated kitchen and bath, central heat and air, din. W/ 2 corner hutches, pretty plush carpet, nice drapes, lots of closets.

j. FOR YOUNG OR OLD $39,900

Attractive 3/1.5, large kitchen & brk., 2 liv. areas, stove, refrigerator to stay, good location near schools, shopping.

Price Range 2: $150,000 to $175,000

a. SPARKLING POOL–BUBBLY SPA $164,900

Beautiful 4 BR, 3 bath. A kitchenette and a full bath are easily accessible to the pool and to the split 4th bedroom. Perfect for an in-law suite or teenager.

b. SWEEPING-VIEW HARMONY $159,000

Stately European-style with hilltop setting. 3 BR/2 BA on large lot...Spa, entertainment area, parquet floors, patio, plus bright skylights and bay windows.

c. THREE CAR GARAGE! $155,000

New custom built home. Four bedrooms with three full baths. Two living areas. Private master suite. Originally priced at $169,900! This is a beautiful buy!

d. SHADED CREEK LOT $154,900

Almost $\frac{3}{4}$ of an acre with huge native trees make for a parklike setting! 4 large bedrooms, $2\frac{1}{2}$ baths. Living room overlooks pool & creek. You'll love it.

e. STAY COOL IN YOUR POOL! $174,900

X-tra large home with 4 bdrms., 3 baths, 3 living areas, dbl. ovens, micro, lots of storage, sprinklers & much more! Walk to school. Call today to see!

f. LOCATION, LOCATION! $159,900

Classic English Tudor located on cul-de-sac street in walking distance to 12 grades of school. 4 bedroom, $2\frac{1}{2}$ bath plus pool/spa. Even has trees.

g. BEST KEPT SECRET $159,900

Owner spared no expense in remodeling this unique custom 4/2/2, 2 living areas, oak hardwood floors, cathedral ceilings, 1/3 acre creek lot with heated pool & spa.

h. EXECUTIVE HOME $159,000

Elegant custom home on beautifully treed lot that backs to Greenbelt. 4 bedrooms with 3 full baths & 2 large living rooms. Incredible kitchen overlooks family room.

i. EVERYTHING UPDATED! $159,900

Circular drive, professional landscaping, sprinkler system and 2 rear yards split by breezeway. 4/3/2 with ceiling fans throughout. Exclusive home and area.

j. EXTREMELY MOTIVATED SELLER $174,900

Superior location, 3 bdrms. & 2-1/2 baths. Romantic master has WBFP + private patio. 2 living areas. Security system, sprinklers & skylights. Plus more.

Price Range 3: $465,000 and up

a. **NATURE'S FINEST $495,000**

3 Acres of beautiful grounds surrounding a magnificent home. Walls of windows front and back to enjoy nature at its finest. 5/4.5/2 living areas/FP/pool/cabana/sauna/tub.

b. **$478,000**

Best buy in the area! This center hall plan has 5 bedrooms, 5-1/2 baths, 2 car garage, sub-zero, security and sprinkler system, hardwoods and MORE!!!

c. **CUSTOM HOME! $469,900**

Exquisite family home custom built w/quaity & tasteful decor! Gorgeous lot w/lush landscaping, Pool, Spa & Hot Tub! Split bedrooms. Ideal teenager's retreat! Wonderful country kitchen! Amenities galore make this SPECIAL! 4/3.5/Frmls/Den/Gameroom/Library!

d. **PRESTIGIOUS $469,000**

Majestic 5 acre estate atop hill. 6/4.5/3. Computer controlled pool/spa. 3 living areas, 3 fireplaces, salon, elegant curved staircase, porte-cochere & circle drive. Luxury abounds.

e. **PERFECT BALANCE OF SIZE... $599,000**

and luxury in generous 5/4.5 on choice golf course lot in Hackberry Creek. 3 living areas offer casual living or gracious entertaining! High ceilings, beautiful views. STYLE!!

f. **FABULOUS! $1,495,000**

This FABULOUS home should be in Architectural Digest! Set on gorgeous lot w/manicured lawn, Pool, Spa & open Cabana! Interior is PERFECTION w/rich appointments & quality! 4/3/Fmrls/Den/2 Sitting Rooms! Lovely view.

g. **ENTERTAINMENT DREAM HOME! $599,000**

Important entry. Gorgeous view of pool. Low maintenance yard. Fabulous home for entertaining! 4/6/3. Wood burning fireplace!

h. **YOU'RE IN LUCK! $639,000**

FABULOUS! French Chateau boasts over 9,000 sq. ft. & set on 10 acres of picturesque grounds! Design excellence—incredible detailing & a wealth of amenities! 5/7.5/Fmls/Den/Garden Room!

i. **GLAMOUR! $679,000**

Stately Traditional on 9/10 Acre w/lovely drive-up! Beautifully remodeled & professionally decorated! Wonderful living areas—Ideal for gracious entertaining & comfortable living! Great Kitchen & Master Suite! 3/4/Fmls/Den/Gameroom/Study!

2. **a.** What is the total number of bedrooms in the houses in each price range?

    b. What is the average number of bedrooms in the houses in each price range?

3. **a.** What is the total number of bathrooms in the houses in each price range?

    b. What is the average number of bathrooms in each price range?

4. **a.** How many houses in each range have a den, library, or study?

    b. How many houses in each range have a deck, patio, pool, or spa?

5. Which item in the additional features list was mentioned most often?

6. How many of the descriptive phrases were mentioned in each price range?

THE COSTS OF BUYING A HOUSE

Olivia's parents are considering buying another house. Since Olivia and Orson have both been attending high school, their parents would allow Olivia to drive herself and her brother to school if they lived a little closer. Olivia's mother has been working for several years and recently received a substantial increase in her salary, so this might be a good time to make that move. They have often talked about wanting more space—especially since Olivia and Orson became teenagers. Olivia and Orson are both pleased about the prospect of having groups of friends over on the weekends.

Olivia has noticed that adults become very secretive when they talk about how much things cost, except of course when they talk about how little things used to cost! Olivia can ask Vernon if he knows about the kinds of costs they would encounter if they decided to buy another home. From what Vernon has already said, Olivia knows that her parents might be in for quite a surprise. If they think the cost of a bicycle has gone up in 35 years, just wait until they see what has happened to the costs of houses!

OBJECTIVES In this section, we will help Olivia to:

- *recognize the major costs to consider when purchasing a house, including the price of the house, the mortgage loan, points, down payment, closing costs, and moving costs;*
- *compute the monthly payments and total costs of paying for a house by using a mortgage plan.*

THE COST OF OWNING YOUR HOME

Since 1980, the prices of houses have consistently outpaced consumer incomes. Since Olivia had studied the effects of inflation and the changes in prices as measured by the Consumer Price Index, she understand why nearly two-thirds of the families buying homes have two incomes. Six out of ten first-time buyers are couples in which both partners hold jobs.

Because of the high cost of new homes, if Olivia's parents were first-time home buyers, they would be facing the following options:

- Buy a condominium as a first home.
- Commute longer distances in order to buy less expensive housing.
- Live in smaller and older homes that may need repairs.
- Borrow money from parents.
- Buy a manufactured home, generally called a mobile home or prefabricated home.
- Accept a more moderate life-style in order to pay for the shelter.

462

How Much to Spend. As Olivia's family considered how much they could afford to spend on another house, their banker suggested this rule of thumb: they should look for housing selling within 2 1/2 times their annual income. Since they are both working, that amounts to quite a lot; and they certainly could not pay that much in cash.

The Mortgage. The family will take a **mortgage**, which is a loan on which both principal (the amount loaned) and interest are paid back over a fixed number of years, usually 15 to 30 years. A mortgage contract is signed between a lender and the borrower for the purpose of buying property. Usually, the amount of the monthly mortgage payment is based upon the amount of the loan, the interest rate, and the length of the loan. The lender may include the cost of taxes and insurance in the mortgage payment. At the end of the 25 or 30 years, the mortgaged home can end up costing two or three times as much as the purchase price of the home. The alternative, however,— saving until they could pay cash for a home—would prevent Olivia's family and most of us from ever being able to buy a home.

Another important factor they have to consider when borrowing for a real estate purchase are the points that the lender may charge. **Points** are a one-time charge; one point means 1% of the value of the mortgage. Points are assessed by a lender when the availability of money is tight, interest rates are high, or other types of loans produce higher interest than home loans.

Down Payment. When they buy the house, they will make a down payment (pay part of the purchase price). Their down payment could range from 0 to 5, 10, 20, 30 percent or more of the purchase price. The higher their original down payment, the lower their monthly mortgage expenses will be. When they sell their other house, they can use the equity they had in it as the down payment on the second one.

Closing Costs. Since they have bought one house, they do know they will also have to have enough cash available for the closing costs that occur at the time the sale is completed. **Closing costs** are the charges and fees associated with the transfer of ownership of a home to a new buyer. These costs are incurred by the buyer for the work involved in preparing and processing all of the documents needed to complete the purchase of the home. A buyer's costs include the following:

- a title search

- mortgage preparation

- an appraisal fee

- recording fees

- a credit report

The seller's costs consist of primarily of paying the realtor's commission and paying for the preparation of the deed, plus any real estate taxes that are due. These costs can run from several hundred to several thousand dollars; the realtor who is handling a sale can estimate the closing costs at the time that final arrangements for the sale are being made.

Moving-in Costs. Olivia's family knows the new expenses have not yet come to an end. When they move into the house, certain other expenses will occur initially that do not occur again until much later, if ever. The cost of curtains, draperies, floor coverings, and landscaping are in this category. Also, they may be required to submit deposits to the utility companies that supply electricity, water, and telephone service.

If they are not moving so far that their utility companies would change, they may already have made those deposits when they bought their first house. If this is the case, they may not be required to make them again. They do know they will want new curtains, bedspreads, draperies, and several new carpets for the new house. They may even want a few new pieces of furniture. They would really like to get a new bedroom suite for Olivia and replace the couch the dog chewed on and damaged the arm. If so, they must plan to have the resources available to meet these moving-in costs.

Ask Yourself

1. What are points?

2. What is the name given to costs incurred by the buyer for work involved in preparing and processing all the documents for a home purchase?

3. What are some of the options first-time buyers have if they find the houses they are looking at are too expensive for them to buy?

SHARPEN YOUR SKILLS

Olivia has noticed that home listings always give the purchase price of the house. But that does not tell her how much her parents would have to pay every month to buy a house. She has found a house listing that appeals to her very much:

GIANT TEEN ROOM ON 3RD FLOOR! Teens can entertain their guests in their own suite. Parents will enjoy the built-in sauna, spa, pool, and large paneled billiard room. A steal at $765,000.

Olivia know that her parents plan to put down 20% on the house they buy. They are hoping for a 30-year mortgage. The prevailing interest rate on a home loan is 11%.

Question   How much would Olivia's family pay every month for the house?

Solution   Olivia discovered that the monthly payment is found in the same way an installment loan monthly payment is found.

First, the down payment is calculated:

$$
\begin{array}{ll}
\$765,000 & \text{purchase price} \\
\underline{\times\ 0.20} & 20\% \\
\$153,000 & \text{down payment}
\end{array}
$$

Next, the down payment is subtracted from the purchase price:

$765,000   purchase price
−153,000   down payment
$612,000   loan amount

Then a table is consulted. The table shows the monthly payments for the interest rate of 11%. A portion of such a table is shown below.

MONTHLY PAYMENT
Necessary to amortize a loan 11%

TERM AMOUNT	29 YEARS	30 YEARS	35 YEARS
$ 25	.24	.24	.24
50	.48	.48	.47
75	.72	.72	.71
100	.96	.96	.94
200	1.92	1.91	1.88
300	2.87	2.86	2.82
400	3.83	3.81	3.75
500	4.79	4.77	4.69
600	5.74	5.72	5.63
700	6.70	6.67	6.56
800	7.66	7.62	7.50
900	8.61	8.58	8.44
1000	9.57	9.53	9.37
2000	19.14	19.05	18.74
3000	28.70	28.57	28.11
4000	38.27	38.10	37.48
5000	47.84	47.62	46.85
6000	57.40	57.14	56.22
7000	66.97	66.67	65.59
8000	76.54	76.19	74.96
9000	86.10	85.71	84.33
10000	95.67	95.24	93.70
15000	143.50	142.85	140.55
20000	191.33	190.47	187.40
25000	239.16	238.09	234.24
30000	286.99	285.70	281.09
35000	334.83	333.32	327.94
36000	344.39	342.84	337.31
37000	353.96	352.36	346.68
38000	363.52	361.89	356.05
39000	373.09	371.41	365.42
40000	382.56	380.93	374.79
51000	487.89	485.69	477.85
52000	497.45	495.21	487.22
53000	507.02	504.74	496.59
54000	516.58	514.26	505.96
55000	526.15	523.78	515.33
56000	535.72	533.31	524.70
57000	545.28	542.83	534.07
58000	554.85	552.35	543.44
59000	564.42	561.88	552.81
60000	573.98	571.40	562.18
65000	621.81	619.02	609.03
70000	669.65	666.63	655.88
75000	717.48	714.25	702.72
80000	765.31	761.86	749.57
100000	956.63	952.33	936.96

The total loan of $612,000 must be broken down into amounts shown on the table:

$612,000 = (6 x $100,000) + $10,000 + $2,000

To find the amount for $100,000, look under the column for 30 years on the line for $100,000. The amount is $952.33. Similarly, the amounts for $10,000 and $2,000 are found. They are $95.24 and $19.05.

The total monthly payment is found by adding up the amounts found:

$5713.98	6 x monthly payment for $100,000
95.24	monthly payment for $10,000
+ 19.05	monthly payment for $2,000
$5828.27	total monthly payment

The total monthly payment for the house is $5828.27. At that amount, Olivia is fairly certain her parents will not share her enthusiasm for the house.

Question   What is the total financed price of the house?

Solution   The total financed cost is found by multiplying the monthly payment by the number of months over the life of the loan and adding the down payment.

First, find the number of months of the loan.

30 years x 12 months = 360 months

Next multiply the monthly payment by the number of months:

$ 5828.27	monthly payment
x 360	number of months
$2,098,177.20	total loan repayment amount

Add the down payment:

$2,098,177.20	total loan repayment amount
+ 153,000.00	down payment
$2,251,177.20	total financed purchase price

The total financed purchase price is $2,251,177.20.

Question   How many times the purchase price is the total financed price?

Solution   Divide the total financed price by the purchase price:

$$\frac{2,251,177.20}{765,000.00} = 2.9427152$$

The buyer would pay 2.94 (to the nearest 0.01) times the purchase price for the house.

EXERCISE YOUR SKILLS

1. What are the major costs to consider when buying a house?

2. How does the amount of the down payment on a house affect the amount that is borrowed in the form of a mortgage?

3. The total financed purchase price for a house is about how many times the purchase price?

_____ **Activity 1** _____

Find the monthly payment, total financed price, and ratio of total financed price (TFP) to purchase price (PP) for the following houses. Use the down payment, interest rate, and time periods given. Refer to the Monthly Payment Tables for 10% and 11% Interest in the Reference Section at the back of the book.

	Price	Percent Down	Down Payment	Loan Amount	Interest Rate	Years	Monthly Payment	Ratio TFP/PP
1.	$289,900	10%		$260,910	10%	25	$2370.83	
2.	35,900	10			11	25		
3.	82,500	10			10	25		
4.	79,900	10			11	30		
5.	112,000	10			10	30		
6.	84,500	10			11	30		
7.	199,000	10			10	25		
8.	85,900	10			11	25		
9.	104,900	20			10	25		
10.	73,950	20			11	30		
11.	77,250	20			10	30		
12.	79,900	20			11	30		
13.	199,000	20			10	25		
14.	253,500	20			11	25		
15.	435,000	20			10	30		
16.	120,000	20			11	30		

SECTION 14-3
SELECTING A MORTGAGE PLAN

Until Vernon and Olivia started discussing the price of buying a home, Rosa had never given it much thought. Her family had bought their house when she was much younger, and she and her sister Consuela have always shared a room. It is a large room, though, for a bedroom, and it has two closets. Rosa and Consuela have been pretty good friends for a couple of years now, so they have been able to accommodate each other's belongings and attitudes about the room fairly well.

Consuela left for college last fall, and Rosa has noticed she has a lot more space and privacy since her sister moved out. Consuela left a lot of her posters and other "kid's stuff" at home when she left. She will probably be coming home in the summer to find a job before she goes back to college, but she is talking about spending next year in France if she can get the right work-study program arranged.

Rosa will be leaving for college next year, and their parents are talking about selling this house and buying one that is more convenient to downtown and their father's job. Though Rosa has not been particularly interested in mortgages, and does not even know there are different kinds, she may see what she can learn from Olivia and Vernon. Rosa's father is a veteran, and the home they live in now was bought with a VA loan. Rosa has never cared about that before, but she will be relying on her parents to help support her when she goes to college. If the family buys a different house, their whole financial plan may undergo some changes that are significant enough to get Rosa's attention.

OBJECTIVES: In this section, we will help Rosa to:

- *learn about several types of mortgages that are available to home-buyers, including the fixed-rate mortgage, the adjustable-rate mortgage, the Federal Housing Administration (FHA) loan, and the Veterans Administration (VA) loan*
- *compute the cost of a home loan for which a family can qualify, based on their monthly and yearly income*

FINANCING THE PURCHASE OF A HOME

When Rosa's family bought their first home, the interest rates and the prices of homes were quite high. As they consider their second home purchase, they will notice that in recent years, interest rates have fluctuated substantially. During the 1980s, interest rates on home loans ranged from as high as 16% to as low as 9%. Consequently, financing for a home purchase has become as important as the purchase price or the construction costs of a home.

Mortgages. Rosa's family expects to consider two types of mortgages: fixed-rate mortgages and adjustable-rate mortgages. **Fixed-rate mortgages (FRMs)** are **amortized** (paid off) on a constant payment basis over a number of years—usually 15, 20, 25, or 30 years. If they select a fixed-rate mortgage, their monthly mortgage payment will remain the same despite rising (or falling) interest rates. Most conventional fixed-rate mortgages are available for loan amounts of up to 80% of the sales price of the home. This would mean the buyer must pay at least 20% as the down payment.

At one time, a fixed-rate mortgage was the only choice available. As interest rates began to rise and fluctuate widely, however, mortgage lenders developed an alternative method of providing mortgages. This alternative is called a variable or adjustable-rate mortgage (**ARM**). An adjustable-rate mortgage is a loan with an interest rate that can be adjusted up or down a number of times during the life of the loan.

In most cases, interest rates for adjustable mortgages are lower than the rates offered on fixed-rate mortgages. Most adjustable mortgages limit rate adjustments using a cap. A **cap** limits the total amount of the increase over the life of the loan.

GOVERNMENT-INSURED REAL ESTATE LOANS

Some fixed-rate mortgages are backed by insurance provided by the federal government. Two of these that Rosa found out about are called FHA loans and VA loans.

Federal Housing Administration Loans. The Federal Housing Administration (FHA) of the Department of Housing and Urban Development provides federal insurance on loans that are obtained through an approved lending institution such as a bank. A buyer who can make only a small down payment can sometimes obtain an FHA loan. With FHA loans, the loan amount ranges between 95 and 100% of the sales price.

Veterans Administration Loans. Rosa's father qualifies for a VA loan because he is a veteran. For persons who served in the armed forces during World War II, the Korean War, the Vietnam War, and during certain Cold War periods, special loan privileges are granted by the Veterans Administration (VA). If Rosa's father, or any other veteran, fails to repay his or her loan, the Veterans Administration has the right to deduct this amount from any pension or other compensation he or she may receive.

In addition to the interest rate, anyone who has a VA loan must also pay a small monthly charge for insurance. A down payment is recommended, but the VA loan law permits the Veterans Administration to guarantee loans up to a specified maximum with no down payment if the lender is willing to make the loan for the full amount of the purchase price. Rosa's father could only qualify for the VA loan if his monthly payments would not exceed a certain amount of his take-home pay. This standard applies to FHA loans as well.

QUALIFYING FOR A MORTGAGE LOAN

Since housing costs have gone up so much since they bought their first house, Rosa's parents will have to find out what size loans they can qualify for now. They know that under current mortgage lending standards, buyers will usually qualify for a mortgage as long as the annual or monthly cost of the house does not exceed 28 percent of the homeowner's gross (total) income.

The bank that will lend them the money for the new house wants to make sure they can afford to make the payments each month. Bankers have found that 28% is a reasonable limit to place upon the size of the mortgage payment. Rosa's parents think that it is reasonable, too; they really do not want to take on a debt larger than that.

Ask Yourself

1. How do fixed-rate and adjustable-rate mortgages differ?

2. What is the main advantage of an adjustable-rate mortgage?

3. Who is eligible for a VA loan?

4. What is the percent of yearly income lending institutions generally agree a family can spend on housing?

_____ **Skill 1** _____

The family's income is $3600 a month. The bank will allow them to borrow enough money to buy a house if the monthly payment is no more than 28% of their monthly income.

Question How much can their monthly mortgage payment be?

Solution 28% = 0.28

0.28 x $3600 = $1008

Their monthly payment can be $1008.

The prevailing interest rate is 10%, and they plan to assume a 30-year mortgage.

Question How much can they borrow?

Solution To find the answer, begin by looking at the Monthly Payment Table for 10% Interest in the Reference Section at the back of the book. A portion of the table is shown below.

The table must be read in reverse—by looking up the monthly payment amount in the correct column and calculating the corresponding total loan amount.

MONTHLY PAYMENT
Necessary to amortize a loan **10%**

TERM AMOUNT	28 YEARS	29 YEARS	30 YEARS
$ 25	.23	.23	.22
50	.45	.45	.44
75	.67	.67	.66
100	.89	.89	.88
200	1.78	1.77	1.76
300	2.67	2.65	2.64
400	3.56	3.53	3.52
500	4.44	4.42	4.39
600	5.33	5.30	5.27

Look at the column for 30-year mortgages. The highest figure on the table is $877.58. Subtract that from the available $1008.

$1008.00   total monthly payment
– 877.58   monthly payment on $100,000
$ 130.42   remainder

Then, locate and subtract the closest amount to the remaining $130.42 without going over. The amount is $87.76. Subtract that amount from the monthly payment. That monthly payment accounts for another $10,000 loan.

$130.42
– 87.76   monthly payment on $10,000
$ 42.66   remainder

Continue using the process until all of the available monthly payment (within $0.22) is accounted for:

$ 42.66 $ 7.55 $ 0.52
– 35.11   ($4,000)   – 7.03   ($800)   – 0.44   ($50)
$ 7.55   remainder $ 0.52   remainder $ 0.08   remainder

Finally, add up the loan amounts accounted for by the monthly payment:

$100,000
10,000
4,000
800
+   50
$114,850

The total loan the family can afford is $114,850.

They intend to put down a 20% down payment.

Question   If the loan is 80% of the purchase price, what price house can they afford?

Solution   You know that $114,850 is 80% of the purchase price. The purchase price is found by dividing the loan amount by 80%.

$$\frac{\$114,850}{0.8} = \$143,562.5$$

The purchase price is $143,562.50.

Question   If the family buys a house at that purchase price with that mortgage, what will be the total financed price of the house over the life of the loan?

Solution   First, find the number of months in the loan.

30 years x 12 months = 360 months

The total price is found by multiplying the monthly payment by the number of months in the loan and then adding the down payment.

$ 1,008.00   monthly payment
x 360   number of months
$362,880.00   total loan repayment amount

The down payment is 20% of the purchase price:

0.20 x $143,562.50 = $28,712.50

The down payment is added to the total loan repayment amount:

$362,880.00   total of monthly payments
+ 28,712.50   down payment
$391,592.50   total loan repayment amount

The result is the total financed price of the house, or $391,592.50.

EXERCISE YOUR SKILLS

1. Why is the interest rate on a mortgage an important factor in a home purchase?

2. In times of inflation, would you rather have an adjustable-rate mortgage or a fixed-rate one?

3. Who provides the insurance for loans made under the FHA and VA programs?

4. Why do lending institutions set a limit on the amount of money a family can borrow?

_____ **Activity 1** _____

Assume the monthly payment is 28% of the monthly income. Find the total cost of the house each family can afford to buy based on the information given. Assume all the mortgages are for 30 years and the interest rate 10%. The first row of figures has been calculated as an example.

Remember the following formula:

Total Cost = Monthly Payment x Months + Down Payment

	Monthly Income	Mortgage Payment	Loan Amount	Percent Down Payment	House Price	Down Payment	Total Cost
	$2500	$700	$79,750	10	$88,611.11	$8861.11	$260,861.11
1.	5900			10			
2.	3500			10			
3.	1200			10			
4.	2650			10			
5.	2899			20			
6.	5245			20			
7.	4350			20			
8.	3495			20			
9.	1600			10			
10.	5777			20			

HOMEOWNER'S INSURANCE

It was three years ago, on a cold New Year's Day, that Hari first realized the importance of home ownership insurance; his family got up to find that all their water pipes had frozen. Since it was their custom to spend the day with Hari's grandparents, who live in a nearby town, they decided to leave early and stop for coffee on the way.

Hari's father does not think too clearly without his morning coffee; he opened the cold water tap in the bathtub to help drain the frozen pipes but forgot to open the drain as well. When Hari opened the front door the following evening when the family arrived home, he could hear the water splashing over the side of the bathtub. The bathroom floor was a small lake; water had run down the hall, soaking the carpets in two bedrooms and slowly seeping into the dining room.

While Hari was eager to help clean up the mess, his mother suggested that they first call the insurance company to find out what they should do. The insurance agent told her to first take photographs of all the areas affected before moving anything and cleaning up. She was also to make a list of all items damaged and any parts of the house needing repair. Hari's mother and the agent then agreed upon a time when an insurance adjuster would come to assist them in filing their claim.

Hari's father pointed out that even though they have a $250 deductible clause in their insurance policy, their settlement from the insurance company would still pay for a new carpet for Hari's room. Hari even got to help pick it out; he chose a color that went well with his computer desk chair, and a type that wouldn't build up static electricity when he walked on it.

OBJECTIVES: In this section, we will help Hari to:

- *understand why homeowner's insurance is important*
- *examine the different categories of coverage in a typical insurance policy*
- *learn about two important factors that affect how much an insurance company pays on claims—deductibles and replacement cost*
- *recognize the value of keeping good records*

THE ROLE OF HOMEOWNER'S INSURANCE

A home is the most important single investment for most families today. But, as Hari discovered, unforeseen events may result in damage to this valuable asset and its contents. Many other incidents can also occur—theft, or accidental injury to someone other than Hari and his family while on their property. The injured person could hold Hari's family liable, and require them to pay medical expenses.

Among potential disasters, homeowner's insurance generally covers the following: fire and lightning, theft, windstorm, hail, explosion, smoke, cave-ins, frozen pipes, falling objects, and water damage. Sometimes insurance for certain coverage costs extra. In areas prone to floods, for instance, it may be difficult or very costly to obtain flood insurance.

Homeowner's insurance protects Hari's family against the financial hardship created by these potentially costly incidents. The requirements for this insurance vary by state. In Hari's case, his family had to prove they had purchased an insurance policy before they were given title to their home. In addition, the financial institution where Hari's parents have their mortgage is required to coordinate payment of the insurance premium by adding an amount for homeowner's insurance to the monthly mortgage payment it collects.

PURCHASING DECISIONS

You may buy insurance from one of three places: from an **independent insurance agent** who sells insurance for many companies; from an agent who sells only one company's insurance; or from the insurance company itself. In general it is very useful to find a local representative who can help file claims, clarify questionable points, and accelerate the payment of claims.

Hari's family made several choices when they purchased their homeowner's insurance policy. Decisions they made on **coverage** (the items and dollar limits for which they are eligible to receive financial compensation) affected their premium (the amount they pay to the insurance company for this coverage). Following are some of the options from which they had to choose when they selected their insurance.

Dwelling (Coverage A). Dwelling coverage includes the dwelling described in the policy, any structures connected to it, outdoor equipment, building equipment used to maintain the property, and permanently attached fixtures. Rented or borrowed property is not included.

Other Structures (Coverage B). Structures that are detached from the dwelling are insured for 10% of the amount of the insurance on the dwelling.

Personal Property (Coverage C). Covers all items owned, regardless of where they are located. If they are not located on the premises, they are covered up to a total of 10% of the coverage. Since many items are excluded, it is important to read this section of any homeowner's policy carefully.

Loss of Use (Coverage D). Had Hari's family not returned when they did, and had the flood damaged their house to the point where they were forced to live somewhere else, their expenses would be covered up to the limit specified in their policy.

Personal Liability (Coverage E). If a visitor had slid and fallen on the flooded bathroom floor, Hari's family would be held liable, or responsible, for any injury that the person suffered as a result. Their insurance company would be required to defend them in court if the injured person decided to bring a lawsuit against them.

Medical Payments to Others (Coverage F). If the injured visitor was admitted to the hospital, Coverage F would help pay for medical expenses, even if Hari's family was not held personally liable.

REIMBURSEMENT FACTORS

The amount Hari's family would receive for any claim would be determined by the original cost of the damaged items, the deductible amount, and the kind of insurance they have.

Deductible. The amount Hari's family pays—in their case, $250—for repairing the eligible damage before the insurance policy begins to reimburse them is the deductible. The deductible applies to each accident or loss. If Hari's father makes the same mistake one week later, they will pay the deductible again. In general, the higher the deductible, the lower the insurance premium.

Replacement Cost. Buildings and other permanent structures (Coverage A and B) automatically have **replacement cost** coverage. If the flooded bathroom floor and part of the walls were completely damaged, the insurance would cover the actual amount it costs to repair or replace these items. Personal property, however, is not automatically covered at replacement cost, but it is covered for the amount that was paid at the time it was purchased. Say the damaged carpeting in Hari's room cost $675 when it was installed four years ago, but will cost $790 to replace today. A standard policy would reimburse $675. Hari's family had decided to pay a higher annual premium for personal property to be covered at replacement cost, so they will receive $790 (after paying the deductible).

RECORD KEEPING

When the insurance adjuster arrived to inspect the damage, Hari quickly learned how important it was to keep detailed information about what they owned. They had kept the receipts that showed where they had purchased the carpeting and exactly what kind it was. This was fortunate, since they had spent a little more to get a better quality of carpeting than most.

Ask Yourself

1. What is the advantage of buying replacement cost insurance?

2. What is included in personal property coverage?

3. Which kinds of coverage protect the family against liability for injury to a non-family member

SHARPEN YOUR SKILLS

_____ Skill 1 _____

Hari's family pays $35.00 in addition to their annual homeowner's insurance premium for replacement cost coverage for their personal property. Their deductible is $150. They filed two insurance claims this year for personal property damage—one for $200 and the other for $800. They calculated that if they had not had the replacement coverage, they would have been reimbursed 10% less for the claims they made.

Question   Was the extra premium they paid for the replacement cost coverage worth it?

Solution

	With Extra Coverage	**Without Extra Coverage**
Claim 1	$200	$180
Less Deductible	– 150	– 150
Reimbursement	$ 50	$ 30
Claim 2	$800	$720
Less Deductible	– 150	– 150
Reimbursement	$650	$570

Total personal property damage claims:

With replacement cost coverage $50 + 650 = $700

Without replacement cost coverage $30 + 570 = $600

Advantage of extra coverage $700 – $600 = 100

Compare the advantage of extra coverage with the $35 cost for the extra coverage.

They paid $35 to receive an extra $100 in reimbursement. The additional coverage was worth it. Their net gain was $65.

_____ Skill 2 _____

Sometimes homeowners underestimate the replacement value of their home. They do this either by mistake or on purpose, thinking this is a good way to pay lower premiums. Hari has found out that if they underestimate by more than 20%, they may be penalized by the insurance company. The amount of the reimbursement with penalty is calculated as follows:

$$\frac{\text{Amt. of insurance carried}}{\text{Amt. of insurance required}} \text{ x (Loss – Deductible)} = \text{Reimbursement}$$

Hari takes note of his family's policy, which can be summarized as follows:

A	Dwelling		$125,000
C	Personal Property		50,000
D	Loss of Use		25,000
E	Personal Liability	Each Occurrence	75,000
F	Medical Payments to Others	Each Person	1,000

Hari knows that the house is now worth $160,000.

Question   Would Hari's family pay a penalty on a claim made today?

Solution   To find out if Hari's house is undervalued by at least 20%, divide the amount for which the house is insured by the amount for which it should be insured (that is, the amount it is worth):

$$\frac{\$125,000}{\$160,000} = 0.78125$$

The house is insured for 0.78 times its worth. Take that amount away from 1.00

$$1.00 - 0.78 = 0.22$$

The house is insured for 22% less than it should be. Therefore a penalty would be deducted from the claim.

Question   If the family had a claim of $950, what would the amount of the reimbursement with penalty be?

Solution   Replace the terms in the formula with the appropriate amounts:

$$\frac{\$135,000}{\$160,000} \text{ x (\$950 – \$150)}$$

$$0.78125 \text{ x } \$800 = \$625$$

The reimbursement with penalty would be $625. The reimbursement without penalty would have been $800 ($950 – 150). That means a penalty of $175 was imposed.

Therefore, it is important to keep your coverage current. When the price of your house appreciates (that is, gains in value over time) you need to increase your insurance.

EXERCISE YOUR SKILLS

1. Why do you think it is more difficult to obtain flood insurance in areas prone to flooding?

2. Why is it important to keep receipts from household appliances and furnishings you buy?

3. Should you clear up the mess from a disaster before or after the insurance adjuster comes to your home? Why?

_____ Activity 1 _____

Li-Ming's family has homeowner's insurance for their house, which is valued at $325,000. They paid $150 this year for replacement cost coverage on their personal property. Their deductible is $250. They filed one insurance claim this year, for $1275. This was for a piece of furniture which they had purchased some years before for $790.

1. a.   What was the amount they recovered?

   b.   What amount would they have recovered if they had not had replacement cost coverage?

   c.   Was the extra premium they paid for the replacement cost coverage worth it?

2. Phillipa's family has the homeowner's insurance described below. Answer questions a, b, and c from Problem 1 for Phillipa's family.

Replacement cost coverage premium	$60
Claim made	$400
Deductible	$150
Original cost of goods	$225

_____ Activity 2 _____

1. Li-Ming's family has been in their house for 10 years. In that time, the value of the house has increased from $249,000 to $325,000. They need to raise the amount that their house is insured for. (Remember that a penalty is charged on any claim if your house is undervalued by more than 20%.)

   a.   Would they pay a penalty if they made a claim today, before they adjusted the amount their house is insured for?

   b.   Using the formula in Skill 2, determine what the reimbursement with penalty would be on a claim for $675.

2. Phillipa's house is valued at $305,000. It is insured for $239,000. Would Phillipa's family pay a penalty on a claim made today? If so, what would the reimbursement with penalty be on a claim for $990?

EXTEND YOUR UNDERSTANDING
PROJECT 14–1   RECYCLING—IS IT WORKING?

Many states have passed laws requiring towns and cities to reduce the amount of waste they put into landfills. One of the methods they use is recycling. Materials such as paper, glass, plastic and metals are sold back to industry. Then the materials are used to make the same product over again (glass bottles become glass bottles) or different products (plastic milk jugs become plastic wood-like park benches and playground equipment).

Assignment

Divide the class in half. One group will investigate recycling in your community. The other will investigate the use of recyclable materials.

Recycling Group—Find the answers to these questions by making telephone calls and visits in your community.

- What kind of recycling program is available? Is there home pickup? A recycling center? A drop-off spot?

- What materials are collected?

- Which are the more valuable materials? How much do they currently sell for? Which are the least valuable? Is your commmunity able to sell them, or must they pay to have them taken away?

- Does the money collected on recyclables help offset the cost of disposing of other garbage?

- What percent of households in your community participate in recycling?

- Has there been a decrease in the last several years in the amount of waste your community buries in a landfill or sends to an incinerator?

Recycled Products Group—Find the answers to the following questions.

- Newspapers. Do the newspapers in your community use any recycled newspaper? If so, what is the percent of recycled paper in their newsprint?

- Printers. Do printers in your community stock recycled paper?

- Where can you buy recycled paper products? Hint: If not in your community, perhaps through the mail.

- Parks. Does your local park system use any recycled plastic benches or playground equipment?

- Restaurants. What kind of containers do restaurants in your area use for food you take out? Are they recyclable?

- Grocery stores. Do stores in your area give you paper or plastic bags? Do they recycle them?

Extensions

- Find out about the methods of solid wast disposal currently in use in your area. Does your city, town, or county have plans to build or expand waste disposal systems? What trends do you see?

- Are there other programs—such as yard waste composting—designed to cut down on trash taken to a landfill?

- Find out how you can safely dispose of hazardous household waste such as oven cleaners, drain cleaners, spot removers, paint, strippers, furniture polish, and batteries. What else is not safe to put in the ordinary trash collection? Are there hazardous household waste collections in your area?

PROJECT 14–2 ASSESSING HOMEOWNER'S INSURANCE

Divide the class into four groups. Give each group the following profiles of three households. Each group is to contact several insurance agents or companies to investigate homeowner's insurance for the households. The aim is to obtain the least expensive coverage for the greatest amount of protection. The groups compete to be the most successful.

Household 1   A townhouse bought for $189,000 two years ago. Household furnishings now ten years old. Some antiques and jewelry.

Household 2   A 5-room student apartment. The roommates have a lot of electronic equipment such as stereos and CD players. The furniture is all secondhand, from resale shops.

Household 3   A 10-room, 3-story house with detached garage and swimming pool. The owner is an amateur photographer who keeps expensive equipment in the home. The house is assessed at $395,000.

The groups should decide what kinds of coverage to ask for, then seek cost quotes from at least three different sources.

CHAPTER 14 KEY TERMS

CHAPTER 14 REVIEW

1. What are the advantages and disadvantages of owning a home?

2. How do fixed rate and adjustable rate mortgages differ?

3. What is the percent of yearly income lending institutions generally agree a family can spend on housing?

4. Complete the following table using the following listings.

   a. GREAT VALUE! $135,450 • 4 bdrm • 3 bath • 3416 sq ft • Excellent schools close by • golf course community

   b. 5 bedroom • $285,900 • Park across the street from this tri-level • 3 1/2 bath • 1 library • game room • walk-in closets • 4344 sq ft

   c. Country Estate • 2986 sq ft of elegance • 4 bdrm • 2 1/2 bath • lake view • quiet • security system • sprinkler system • skylights • pool and spa • Great price!!! $ 175,500

   d. New! Several floor plans to choose from • 3 car garage • circular drive • close to schools and golf course • sprinkler system and alarm system • 3590 sq ft $219,000

House	Price	Square Feet	Cost per sq ft	Bedrooms	Bathrooms	Den, etc.	Extras
a.							
b.							
c.							
d.							

Find the monthly payment, total financed price, and ratio of total financed price (TFP) to purchase price (PP) for the following houses. Use the percent down, interest rate, and time periods given. Refer to the Monthly payment Tables for 10% and 11% Interest in the Reference Section at the back.

	Price	Percent Down	Down Payment	Loan Amount	Interest Rate	Years	Monthly Payment	Ratio TFP/PP
5.	$ 95,500	10%			10%	25		
6.	$115,900	10%			11%	30		
7.	$ 82,600	20%			10%	25		
8.	$105,900	20%			11%	30		
9.	$175,900	10%			10%	30		

Assume the monthly payment is 28% of the monthly income. Find the total cost of the house each family can afford to buy based on the information given. Assume all the mortgages are for 30 years and the interest rate is 10%. Remember: Total Cost = Monthly Payment x Months + Down Payment.

	Monthly Income	Mortgage Payment	Loan Amount	Percent Down Payment	House Price	Down Payment	Total Cost
10.	$2400			10			
11.	$1850			20			
12.	$2690			10			
13.	$3160			20			
14.	$1300			10			

15. Goro Mori's family has homeowner's insurance described below.

Replacement cost coverage premium $125
Claim made $795
Deductible $200
Original cost of goods $465

a. What was the amount they recovered?

b. What amount would they have recovered if they had not had replacement cost coverage?

c. Was the extra premium they paid for the replacement cost coverage worth it?

16. Goro's house is currently worth $210,500. The last time they adjusted the amount, it was $185,000. Would Goro's family pay a penalty on a claim made today? If so, what would the penalty be on a claim for $2695?

1. Find the cost per square foot for each house listed.
   a. 2.5 acres • wooded lot • large rooms • hardwood floors • island kitchen • 4 bdrm • 3 bath • 4395 sq ft • $239,500
   b. $285,900 • Gracious living • den • study • tall ceilings • new kitchen • 5 bdrm • 3½ bath • next to golf course • 4896 sq ft • library • 3 car garage
   c. $139,600 convenient to park and schools • 3 bdrm • 3100 sq ft • storage building • den

Find the monthly payment, total financed price, and ratio of total financed price (TFP) to purchase price (PP) for the following houses. Refer to the amortization tables in the Reference Section for the rates and years given.

	Price	Percent Down	Down Payment	Loan Amount	Interest Rate	Years	Monthly Payment	Ratio TFP/PP
2.	$155,000	10%			10%	25		
3.	$122,500	10%			11%	30		
4.	$103,200	20%			10%	30		

Assume the monthly payment is 28% of the monthly income. Find the total cost of the house each family can afford to buy based on the information given. Assume all the mortgages are for 30 years and the interest rate is 10%. Remember: Total Cost = Monthly Payment x Months + Down Payment.

	Monthly Income	Mortgage Payment	Loan Amount	Percent Down	House Price	Down Payment	Total Cost
5.	$2550			10			
6.	$1600			20			
7.	$2200			10			
8.	$2950			20			

9. Jonathan Johnson's family has homeowner's insurance described below.

   Replacement cost coverage
     premium $95
   Claim made $1350

   Deductible $150
   Original cost of goods $1195

   a. What was the amount they recovered?
   b. What amount would they have recovered if they had not had replacement cost coverage?

1. If you bought 750 shares of stock at a price of 75¾, what would be the total cost of your stock?

2. Use the Future Worth Table for Semiannual Compounding in the Reference Section to find how much would be in the savings account at the end of 30 years if $25,000 was invested at 8½%.

3. Use the Multiples of Salary Chart in the Reference Section to find the amount of life insurance a man at 45 years old who has gross earnings of $50,000 would need in order to provide 75% income replacement.

4. Use the Tax Table in the Reference Section to find the tax owed by each of the following.

   a. a married person, filing separately, with $45,750 taxable income.
   b. a head of a household with $7200 taxable income.

5. Find the distance traveled, the mileage per gallon of gas, and the cost per mile for the following period.

   1st odometer reading: 35,461.9
   2nd odometer reading: 35,953.5
   17.4 gallons of gas costing $24.19

6. Use the information in Problem 5 to find the total operating expenses and the cost per mile of operating a car for 11,750 miles with $250.00 maintenance costs and $274.50 repair costs.

7. Find the monthly payment, total financed price, and ratio of total financed price (TFP) to purchase price (PP) for the following. Refer to the amortization tables in the Reference Section for the interest rates and years given.

	Price	Percent Down	Down Payment	Loan Amount	Interest Rate	Years	Monthly Payment	Ratio TFP/PP
a.	$175.900	10%			10%	30		
b.	$85,600	20%			11%	25		
c.	$153,500	10%			10%	25		

8. Jacob's family has the homeowners insurance described below for their house, which is valued at $225,000.

   Replacement cost coverage   Deductible $100
      premium $115   Original cost of goods $790
   Claim made $960
   a. What was the amount they recovered?
   b. What amount would they have recovered if they had not had replacement cost coverage?

485

Many young people find moving away from their parents and establishing a separate residence an appealing idea. Whether they are going to college, into the work force, or a combination of the two, living on their own can give young people a much desired feeling of independence. With the expression of that independence, however, comes an immediate recognition of the responsibilities involved. If no one in the apartment goes to the grocery store, no food will appear in the refrigerator.

Most young people share an apartment, rented house, or other living quarters with others. Many aspects of sharing living space with another person, which may have been taken for granted in the home in which they grew up—immediately become apparent. Sharing a dormitory room or an apartment with a roommate, a young person learns very quickly whether the living habits in his or her own family differ from those in the roommate's family. Who makes sure that the rent and phone bill get paid? Who buys the groceries? Who prepares the meals? How many dirty dishes can accumulate before being washed? How much noise, quiet, clutter, neatness, dirty laundry, television, extra company, immodesty, late-night snacking, and so on, does each person tolerate? How does each person adjust so that the two—or three, or four—people can live harmoniously?

After renting for a while, many young people hope to be able to purchase a home. When first starting out, they often find that a condominium, townhouse, or mobile home fits their needs and matches their ability to pay.

In this chapter, our teenagers will first look at the factors involved in renting an apartment or house. Then they will study the purchase of smaller-scale housing, for those families and couples who want the advantages of home ownership without paying the price of a full-sized house.

THE HUNT FOR AN APARTMENT

Evelyn and Freda enjoy being in business together. The painted T-shirts and sweatshirts are selling well; however, they have put in a lot of extra hours working on the business. They would like to continue the business over the summer since both are planning to enroll at Community College in the fall. Perhaps they will add beach towels with hand-painted beach scenes to their product list; that way, during the warm season, when sweatshirts do not sell well, they will have a product to market.

Evelyn is planning to study business management at Community College; Freda will pursue advertising and marketing. They have found while working together that they are compatible, sharing the same attitudes about many things. They have even discussed taking an apartment together while they go to college. The drive from home to Community College takes 45 minutes. So, while they could each live at home with their parents another couple of years, that would be inconvenient. And Evelyn is especially ready to be out on her own.

There are several options available to Evelyn and Freda if they do move out. Community College has some very nice dormitories on campus. They are not sure a dormitory is the best choice for them, because they will need space in which to continue their business.

The campus also has a lot of reasonable apartment space around it; most apartments are furnished, several have swimming pools, and shopping areas are conveniently nearby. As summer approaches, Evelyn and Freda will find out what other factors they should discuss before presenting their plans to their parents.

OBJECTIVES: In this section, we will help Evelyn and Freda to:

- *consider the advantages of rental housing*
- *recognize what is involved in sharing living space with a roommate*
- *recognize different types of rental housing*
- *consider the cost of renting as a proportion of monthly income*
- *analyze the amenities, costs, and availability of rental housing*

WHERE DO YOU LOOK?

Apt. for rent. 2 bdrm, carpeted, close to public trans. $800 per month, plus utilities. No pets. Laundry facilities available. References required.

When Evelyn read this ad in the newspaper, she was surprised at the rent—it seemed so high. She had decided what she and Freda needed was a two-bedroom apartment near their classes. It would be nice if the apartment was well kept, sunny, and had room for their business as well. She read on, finding a great variety of bedrooms and features and rents: a very expensive small apartment in an ideal location, an affordable large one that was too far from campus to walk. What would each of these be like? Was there something in between? She would have to look at some of the apartments in the ads to see for herself.

Following are some of the ads she read in one issue of the local paper:

3 br, huge lr & kit, fully crptd. $1\frac{1}{2}$ baths, $975

3 br in vintage 3-flat. 90s kit, 2 frpls, yd, gar, heat incl. $1250

1 br, well maintained bldg. Heat incl. hdwd flrs, nr. trans, shops. $520-655

$\frac{1}{2}$ mo rent free! Extra large bdr, dr. Begin 1 Sept. $495

2 blks to campus. $\frac{1}{2}$ blk to trans. 2 bdr garden, furn, avail now. $750 + utils.

Oct. occup, 3rd floor, 1 br apt. Nr shops & trans, ht/wtr, gar-space incl. No pets. Sec. dep req'd. $600/mo

Charming 2 br, 1 bath, clean, quiet bldg. Great closets. Sep dr, hardwd flrs, remodeled kit. Lndry, no pets. $680

Evelyn noticed the abbreviations that appeared in these ads. Some were familiar—she recognized bdrms as bedrooms and LR & K as living room and kitchen. Some were not so familiar. What was hdwd flrs? Ht/wtr? Fully crptd? Gradually she became accustomed to the lingo—she learned hard-wood floors, hot water, fully carpeted.

She realized that they would have to make the decision based on a number of factors including the rent, the location, the number and size of the rooms, the condition of the apartment, when the apartment would be available, whether it was furnished, and whether they would have to pay for **utilities** (heat, water, electricity) separately.

FACTORS IN THE DECISION TO RENT

Evelyn and Freda will pursue the idea of renting because they see many advantages to it. These advantages of renting include the following:

- knowing exactly how much they must spend each month;

- not being tied down to one location;

- not being responsible for maintenance;

- getting to know the community well before making a commitment to staying there;

- spending less for housing costs than they would as buyers.

Sharing. Evelyn and Freda know that they want to share an apartment. They are already good friends, and they believe this will cut their costs in half. But they are aware that they should discuss the practical arrangements ahead of time. Evelyn's older cousin, Ed, had problems when he and his best friend moved in together. They didn't anticipate the kinds of decisions they would have to make in order to live together amicably. For instance, they had very different opinions about when they could have their friends over. Ed's roommate had so many parties that Ed found it very difficult to get all his studying done. They finally became so angry with each other that they no longer even speak! Evelyn and Freda will discuss some of these problems ahead of time—since they want to remain friends.

The issues they will consider include the following:

Living habits. How will they set hours for listening to music, watching TV, and other activities that might interrupt the other person? How will they divide the responsibility for washing dishes, making beds, cleaning the bathroom, vacuuming, and so on?

Independence vs. companionship. Do they want to spend time together or lead relatively separate lives? Do they want to eat meals together? Do their laundry at the same time?

Sharing expenses. How will they divide the rent, utility bills, food costs, new furniture, household supplies, and the security deposit?

Overnight guests. Who may stay, and how often?

Ending the arrangement. Can either one move out at any time? How would the remaining roommate replace the one who leaves?

HOUSING ALTERNATIVES

Before making their decision to share an apartment, Freda and Evelyn had already considered several other possibilities.

Living with Parents. Many college students do live at home with their parents. It can be a good solution when the college is nearby and the family enjoys being together. For Evelyn and Freda, however, this alternative was not practical. It would have meant a long commute every day; they would have had to own and maintain cars to make the 45-minute drive each way. This would definitely cut into their studying time, the time they still hoped to devote to their business, and their sense of belonging to the college community.

Single Rooms. Another option they have is each renting a single room in a home or hotel; they would want one with kitchen and laundry facilities. Evelyn and Freda think they will need more space than single rooms would provide. However, this can be a good alternative, especially for someone who does not want to invest in furniture and household items or who is not planning to live there for long.

Dormitory. On the campus of Community College is another alternative, dormitories. Dormitories contain sleeping rooms, usually for two people, with separate desk and closet space for each. Some have eating facilities and some do not. Evelyn and Freda have thought about this alternative because it is generally less expensive than private housing. Their reasoning is similar to their thinking about single rooms—they would simply have less space than they would like.

Apartments. Apartments are multiple-unit dwellings which may contain two living units or 200. They can be in high-rise buildings, houses, converted warehouses, or over the coach house of a large, old estate. Most apartments are rented unfurnished, but some are available with furniture. They seldom have any private yard space, but other conveniences such as a parking space and coin-operated washing machines are generally provided.

HOW TO CHOOSE

Freda and Evelyn have decided that what they really want is an apartment. For them, the most important factor in choosing an apartment is location—they want to live near campus. Next, they know they want two bedrooms, a common living room and kitchen, and perhaps a dining room. They really only need one bath. They also need a place to do their laundry and a safe place to keep their bikes.

Other people looking for apartments will have different needs. Elderly people, or others with limited mobility, may prefer the ground floor; commuters may want to be close to train and bus lines. A young couple may want to be near schools and shopping; a single person may choose a large building or one with a common pool or tennis courts so they will be able to meet new people. Apartments are available for people with special needs—a ramp and low counters and extra wide doorways, for instance, for the wheelchair bound. All these choices, and Evelyn and Freda only have two months to find a place to live!

Ask Yourself

1. What are four common types of housing arrangements that college students might choose?

2. What are some economic reasons people might choose to rent a place to live instead of buying one?

3. What are some noneconomic reasons people may choose to rent a place to live instead of buying one?

SHARPEN YOUR SKILLS

_____ **Skill 1** _____

Question Evelyn and Freda have estimated that if they continue their business during the next year, their yearly income will be $18,000. What will their income be per week?

Solution $\dfrac{\$18,000}{52 \text{ weeks}} = \$346.15385$

Weekly income can be calculated from yearly income by dividing the yearly income by 52 weeks.

$$\text{Weekly Income} = \frac{\text{Yearly Income}}{52 \text{ weeks}}$$

Round the answer to the nearest penny.

Their income per week is $346.15

_____ **Skill 2** _____

When selecting a place to live, it is helpful to determine how much money can comfortably be spent on rent. Assume for budgeting purposes that monthly apartment rent must be no more than one week's salary.

Question If a family had an annual income of $67,200, what is the greatest amount of monthly rent they should pay?

Solution First, calculate the family's weekly income:

Weekly income = $67,200/52

Weekly income = $1292.31

Since the rule for determining how much of a family's income should be spent on an apartment states that no more than one week's salary should be spent on each month's rent, the family should spend no more than $1292.31 per month.

EXERCISE YOUR SKILLS

1. What are some of the advantages of sharing an apartment with another person?

2. What are some of the disadvantages of sharing an apartment with another person?

3. If you had a choice, would you prefer to buy a home or rent an equally comfortable apartment? Why?

_____ **Activity 1** _____

Find the weekly income for each of the following positions.

1. SECRETARY/RECEPTIONIST—Attractive suburban offices. Greet clients, visitors, others; order supplies, help with typing, proposals, faxing, etc. $22,000.

2. ENGINEER, CIVIL—Exper. desirable. Exc. benfts. $35,000 to start. Send resume.

3. BANKING OPPORTUNITIES—Our progressive, high performance bank has positions available for responsible applicants with exc. communication and cash handling skills. Exp. pref. but will consider customer oriented trainees. Must be able to work a flexible schedule. $20,000.

4. ACCOUNTING—Jr. Auditor/Accountant. Excellent position avail. for individual w/accounting exp. and college course work. Account reconciliation, preparation of work sheets, determine invoice account distribution. Personal computer exp. desired. $21,500 to start.

5. ADMINISTRATIVE ASSISTANT $18K—Brick Haven Co. needs secretary to work with sales reps not for them. Oppty for growth.

6. SALES—Salaried position as field sales representative. Represent third largest newspaper in the state. Depen. car required. $12/hr. 37.5 hr./week.

─────── **Activity 2** ───

1. The following apartments are available for rent. Laura's annual salary is $35,000. Which of the following apartments rent for an amount within $30 of her weekly salary?

   a. DELUX, 2 BR, util, pool, no pets. $595.

   b. Immac. 2BR, 2ba, 1st flr. Incl. heat & water. $700.

   c. The Oaks/Tiffany Court. Free heat and cook'g gas. Dishwashers, modern appls. Oak kitchen cabinetry. 1 BR apts., lndry. rm. $375.

   d. Jacuzzi, pool, tennis, activities galore. 2 BRs. $775.

   e. Luxury 1 BR. Close to all major freeways, train station, airport. Self cleaning oven, frost free refrig. $525.

   f. Twelve Oaks, furnished apartments. Valet, concierge & maid service available. Immaculately maintained corporate suites. 1 BR. $975.

   g. Bright, 1 BR. Near college and trn. $300.

   h. Northridge—lge, 1BR, new plush crptg, htd, balc. Available immediately. $645.

2. For each apartment in Problem 1, find the annual salary that would be necessary for a renter to earn. Assume that the rent should be equal to one week's pay.

Apartment Rent		Yearly Income	
a.	$595	**a.**	_____
b.	$700	**b.**	_____
c.	$375	**c.**	_____
d.	$775	**d.**	_____
e.	$525	**e.**	_____
f.	$975	**f.**	_____
g.	$300	**g.**	_____
h.	$645	**h.**	_____

WHEN YOU SIGN A LEASE

Ana has begun working as a hostess at the seafood restaurant where Sylvia and her father sometimes eat. The restaurant is located near the mall where Ursula works as a clerk at Joyful Toys. Sometimes the three of them get together after work and do some shopping in the mall or go to the movies.

Ana and Ursula have been thinking of sharing an apartment after high school graduation. Ana will be going on vacation for a while this summer, but the restaurant manager has told her that she can have her job back when she returns. Ursula enjoys her job, and plans to continue working at the toy store after graduation. She may apply for an assistant manager's position in about a year.

Ana and Ursula have been good friends since the 5th grade, when they spent two weeks at girl scout camp together. They discovered that they could prepare a pretty good stew together over an open campfire, and they both like their marshmallows lightly toasted, not burned. Perhaps they would be compatible roommates. Sylvia has promised to show them all the best places to buy towels, dishes, blankets, sheets—and, of course, clothes.

OBJECTIVES: In this section, we will help to:

- *investigate sources of information about rental housing availability*
- *discuss how to choose among rental options*
- *read and comprehend a lease agreement*

HELPERS IN THE SEARCH

Ana does not have to move out of her family's house, but she wants to give it a try. Perhaps if she and Ursula share an apartment for a while, she will discover that being an independent adult carries more responsibility than she is ready for. But she will not know that until she tries. Her parents will support her efforts at independence and help her to cope with the adult decisions she will be making. They have suggested several sources of information useful in a housing search.

Friends. First and easiest is to ask friends if they know of any available places to rent. If they are currently renting, they can also fill you in on the procedures to follow and any problems they have had.

Newspapers. Newspaper classified apartment listings will give Ana and Ursula an idea of the rents being charged for various types and sizes of apartments, in various locations.

Real Estate Agencies. Apartment building owners often list available rental units with a local real estate broker. Avoid people calling themselves **apartment finders**, who pursue your business without your asking. Such services are often operated by people who do not have a real estate broker's license, and they sometimes charge clients for listings that can be obtained from the daily newspaper!

INSPECTING THE APARTMENT

When Ana and Ursula find an apartment they are interested in, they should inspect it carefully and thoroughly. They should look into closets, peer under the sink, tour the basement, flush the toilet, and test the shower. They should ask themselves whether the cabinet space is sufficient and the refrigerator is large enough. Other questions they should ask themselves include: Is the number of electrical outlets sufficient to avoid overloading? Will the size and shape of the rooms fit our needs? Are locks and security systems adequate? Are storage facilities, laundry facilities, and parking areas available?

If they are really interested in an apartment, they should ask other tenants in the building such questions as the following:

- Is routine maintenance adequate and prompt?
- Are complaints responded to quickly, and is the owner accessible?
- Is the building noisy?
- Have rent increases been excessive?
- Does the building have a high turnover of tenants?

Turnover means people moving in and out in rapid succession. In general, it is less desirable to live in a building with a high turnover rate than in one where the population is more stable.

**READING
THE LEASE**

When Ana finds an apartment, she will be sure she understands all of these clauses in the lease, or rental agreement. They include the following:

Term of Lease.   This clause sets the length of time of your lease.

Rent.   You agree to pay this amount on time.

Security Deposit.   The security deposit, usually equal to one month's rent, is collected and held by the landlord in the event you damage the apartment. The security deposit will be required when you move in, in addition to the first month's rent. It will be returned to you when the lease ends and you leave the apartment in the same condition you found it. For this reason, before renting, you should make a written list of damages during your tour of the apartment. This will assist you in settling claims for any damage found in the apartment at the time you leave and ask for your security deposit refund.

Condition of Premises.   You agree that the premises are fine as they are.

Repair.   You agree not to damage the property of the owners.

Use; Sublet Assignment.   You agree that no pets or other persons will live with you.

Right to Relet.   You agree to pay the full term of the lease even if you leave before the time is up. Sometimes it is possible to terminate a lease early, by mutual agreement of the renter and landlord, but you should never count on it.

Holding Over.   You agree to double your rent if you stay beyond the end of the lease.

Access.   You give the owner permission to enter your apartment.

Compliance.   You agree to obey the laws regulating animals, sanitation, and noise.

Default.   You agree that if you fail to pay your rent, the owner has a right to hold your personal property in its place.

Plurals; Successors.   If you have a roommate, both of you share responsibility, equally, for upholding the lease.

Already Ana is realizing that some of these terms of a lease sound quite serious. She will select her apartment carefully, knowing that if she signs a lease for a year, she must be willing to make that year's commitment as an adult.

Ask Yourself

1. What are three sources of information you could consult if you were looking for a new apartment?

2. What types of things should you inspect in any apartment that you are considering renting?

3. What is a lease? Why does a person who is renting an apartment usually have to sign one?

SHARPEN YOUR SKILLS

Skill 1

All apartments have some amenities that make then attractive to a prospective tenant.

Question Does the number of amenities have any relationship to the price of an apartment? Use graph paper (or a computer graphing program) to graph price and number of amenities for the five apartments described below to determine if there is any correlation.

Apartment A has 1 bedroom, cable hookup, extra storage space, a fireplace, a balcony, recreation facilities open to tenants and their guests, a spa and pool, a clubhouse and is close to the bus line. It is also located in a prestigious suburb of a major city. $500/month.

Apartment B has 1 bedroom, cable hookup, a fireplace, a pool, and extra storage space. $250/month.

Apartment C has 1 bedroom, cable hookup and is close to the bus line. $200/month.

Apartment D has 1 bedroom, cable hookup, extra storage, covered parking space, two fireplaces, two balconies, a recreation facility open to tenants and their guests, an exercise facility open 24 hours, a spa, a pool, a club house, and a sauna. It is close to all major bus lines. $600/month.

Apartment E has 1 bedroom, cable hookup, extra storage space, covered parking space, remodeled kitchen, and exercise facility. It is close to major bus line. $350/month.

Solution

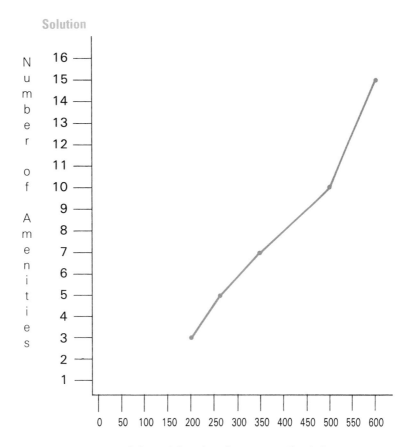

Price of Renting Apartment (in dollars)

Apartment A = 10 amenities and rents for $500
Apartment B = 5 amenities and rents for $250
Apartment C = 3 amenities and rents for $200
Apartment D = 15 amenities and rents for $600
Apartment E = 7 amenities and rents for $350

_____ Skill 2 _____

Larger apartments are usually more expensive than smaller apartments.

Question   From the *Apartment Hunter's Guide* in the Reference Section, locate the Brooktree apartments in the Addison area. Is a 3-bedroom
apartment in this area more or less expensive than an efficiency?

Solution   The 3-bedroom apartment is more expensive since it rents for $414
as opposed to the efficiency which rents for $304.

EXERCISE YOUR SKILLS

1. If you are renting an apartment, why should you take the time to read the lease very carefully before you sign it?

2 Why would it generally be less desirable to live in an apartment building that has a high rate of turnover than in one in which the population is more stable?

3. If you are considering renting an apartment in a certain building, why should you talk to the other tenants of the building before you make your final decision?

4. Why do many landlords require a tenant to pay a security deposit before allowing the tenant to move into an apartment?

5. If you rent an apartment, why should you make a list of everything that is wrong with the apartment before you move in? Why should you ask the landlord (or building manager) to sign that list?

_____ Activity 1 _____

Total the number of amenities for the 20 apartments listed on the *Apartment Hunter's Guide* in the Reference Section. List the rental prices for each 1-bedroom apartment on the *Apartment Hunter's Guide* from lowest to highest. Use graph paper (or a computer graphing program) to graph price versus number of amentities for each apartment to see if there is a correlation between the two.

_____ Activity 2 _____

Use graph paper (or a computer graphing program) to graph price versus number of amentities for each of the three-bedroom apartments listed on the *Apartment Hunter's Guide* in the Reference Section.

CHOOSING A CONDOMINIUM

Yvette and Yvonne have decided they will go to a large university in the Colorado mountains. Yvette wants to study architecture and Yvonne will probably major in art history and secondary education. Since they are twins, they have been close friends for a long time, and have been planning to go to the same college.

The twins are now looking for a place to live in Colorado. Their parents are thinking about trying to buy a townhouse or a condominium, since there does not seem to be much to choose from in the way of apartments in this resort and university town in the mountains. They are thinking that after the young women attend the university, they can sell the condo, or perhaps vacation there themselves in the summer and rent it out to other university students during the school year. It could remain in the family as a vacation or retirement home.

Yvonne likes the condo idea; she would like to learn to ski, too, but she may not be able to talk Yvette into that. Yvette is a serious student and plans to spend a lot of her time in the library.

OBJECTIVE: In this section, we will help Yvette and Yvonne to:

● *Investigate condominiums, townhouses, mobile homes*

MANY CHOICES

The twins' family is attracted to the idea of buying, rather than renting, because of past experience with ownership. The advantages include the following two facts:

- The interest on their mortgage and their property taxes is tax deductible.

- The money they spend builds up equity.

Three types of housing they could buy that might be especially suitable for college-age women are condominiums, townhouses, and mobile homes.

A condominium may be an apartment in a multiple-unit building, or a semi-detached living unit with common areas. **Condominium** means 1) individual ownership of one unit and 2) joint ownership with the other unit

owners of the facilities and common areas (yard, pool, patio, hallways, and so on). All of the unit owners make up the **owners' association**, which is responsible for management of the building, grounds, and common areas. The purchase of a condominium means that the buyer automatically shares in the administration of the building and property. The condominium owner pays a monthly fee to cover the costs of operating and maintaining all of the common areas.

There is no clear-cut distinction between a townhouse and a condominium. **Townhouses** are usually attached houses built side-by-side with no yard between them. Some townhouses are built in a row, others partially above each other. Many are built as fourplexes (four units) and sixplexes (six units).

Some townhouses can be purchased in the conventional manner; the buyer purchases the unit, the land upon which it stands, a lawn out front, and a patio in the rear. Other townhouses can be purchased as condominiums. Under such an arrangement, you own only the interior space, while the grounds belong jointly to you and your neighbors. The condominium townhouse is managed and maintained through a homeowners' association.

A **mobile home** is a portable structure built on a chassis, designed to be used without a permanent foundation. It is usually in a permanent or long-term location. Unlike a recreational vehicle, it is designed as a year-round dwelling. According to the Bureau of the Census, mobile homes have grown in popularity in recent years. In the United States, they now account for more than half of all the new housing sold to people with annual incomes of $18,000 or less.

The mobile home owner must have land on which to park the mobile home or must rent space in a mobile home park and pay a monthly rental fee. Many people choose to rent mobile homes in established mobile home parks. This is especially true in recreational and retirement areas or in other places where temporary housing is in demand. The cost of renting a mobile home is frequently lower than the cost of renting an apartment or house.

Advantages and Disadvantages of Mobile Homes

Advantages	Disadvantages
• The cost is usually much lower than for other forms of housing.	• You can not park mobile homes wherever you please—there are strict zoning regulations governing where you can put them.
• A mobile home can be moved to a new location.	
• The costs to maintain a mobile home are low.	• Living space in a mobile home is limited.
• The small, compact size of a mobile home makes it easier to keep clean and tidy.	• There is usually little yard space around a mobile home.
• Without much yard space, there is little outdoor maintenance needed.	• Because of lightweight construction, mobile homes are not well protected in storms.

Yvonne and Yvette's family have decided to buy a condominium for the twins. The students will not have to take care of maintaining a yard and will have the use of the common facilities. Yvette is looking forward to picking out some appropriate furniture for it; Yvonne is looking forward to the ski season.

Ask Yourself

1. What is a condominium?

2. What advantages could there be to buying a condominium or townhouse rather than buying a single-family home?

3. Why do you think many people who have incomes of less than $18,000 a year choose to buy a mobile home?

SHARPEN YOUR SKILLS

────── Skill 1 ──────

Yvette and Yvonne think they would be happier living in a condo than in an apartment. Their parents are interested in comparing the monthly cost of buying a condo with the rent on an apartment. They have located an apartment that rents for $480 per month, and a condo with a purchase price of $80,000.

Question   How much would Yvette and Yvonne's parents pay every month for the condo assuming a 10% interest rate, a down payment of 20%, and mortgage payments over 30 years?

Solution   Monthly payments on a condo are found in the same way as monthly payments on an installment loan.

First, the down payment is calculated:

$80,000	purchase price
x .20	20%
$16,000	down payment

Then the down payment is subtracted from the purchase price:

$80,000	purchase price
−16,000	down payment
$64,000	loan amount

Then an amortization table is consulted. The table shows the monthly payments for the interest rate of 10%. A portion of such a table is shown on the following page.

10% MONTHLY PAYMENT NECESSARY TO AMORTIZE A LOAN

TERM AMOUNT	24 YEAR	25 YEARS	28 YEARS	29 YEARS	30 YEARS	35 YEARS	40 YEARS
1000	9.18	9.09	8.88	8.83	8.78	8.60	8.50
2000	18.35	18.18	17.76	17.65	17.56	17.20	16.99
3000	27.53	27.27	26.64	26.48	26.33	25.80	25.48
4000	36.70	36.35	35.52	35.30	35.11	34.39	33.97
5000	45.87	45.44	44.40	44.13	43.88	42.99	42.46
6000	55.05	54.53	53.28	52.95	52.66	51.59	50.95
7000	64.22	63.61	62.16	61.78	61.44	60.18	59.45
8000	73.40	72.70	71.04	70.60	70.21	68.78	67.94
9000	82.57	81.79	79.92	79.43	78.99	77.38	76.43
10000	91.74	90.88	88.80	88.25	87.76	85.97	84.92
15000	137.61	136.31	133.20	132.38	131.64	128.96	127.38
20000	183.48	181.75	177.60	176.50	175.52	171.94	169.83
25000	229.35	227.18	222.00	220.62	219.40	214.92	212.29
30000	275.22	272.62	266.39	264.75	263.28	257.91	254.75
35000	321.09	318.05	310.79	308.87	307.16	300.89	297.21
46000	422.00	418.01	408.47	405.94	403.69	395.45	390.61
47000	431.18	427.09	417.35	414.77	412.46	404.05	399.10
48000	440.35	436.18	426.23	423.59	421.24	412.65	407.60
49000	449.53	445.27	435.11	432.42	430.02	421.24	416.09
50000	458.70	454.36	443.99	441.24	438.79	429.84	424.58
51000	467.87	463.44	452.86	450.07	447.57	438.44	433.07
52000	477.05	472.53	461.74	458.89	456.34	447.03	441.56
53000	486.22	481.62	470.62	467.72	465.12	455.63	450.05
54000	495.39	490.70	479.50	476.54	473.89	464.23	458.54
55000	504.57	499.79	488.38	485.37	482.67	472.82	467.04
56000	513.74	508.88	497.26	494.19	491.45	481.42	475.53
57000	522.92	517.96	506.14	503.02	500.22	490.02	484.02
58000	532.09	527.05	515.02	511.84	509.00	498.62	492.51
59000	541.26	536.14	523.90	520.67	517.77	507.21	501.00
60000	550.44	545.23	532.78	529.49	526.55	515.81	509.49

The loan of $64,000 must be broken down into amounts shown on the table:

$64,000 = $60,000 + $4,000

To find the amount for $60,000, look under the column for 30 years on the line for $60,000. The amount is $526.55. The amount for $4,000 is found in the same way. It is $35.11.

The total monthly payment is found by adding up the amounts:

$526.55
+ 35.11
‾‾‾‾‾‾‾
$561.66

The total monthly payment is $561.66.

Question Which alternative would cost more per month? By how much?

Solution The condo would cost $81.66 more per month.

$ 561.66   cost of condo
− 480.00   cost of apartment
‾‾‾‾‾‾‾
$ 81.66

EXERCISE YOUR SKILLS

1. Why is it necessary to have an owner's association for properties that are made up of condominiums or townhouses?

2. Owners' associations for townhouses often have some very strict rules that the individual home owners are obligated to obey. For example, the association may demand that all the townhouses be painted a specific color. Why would associations have such rules?

3. If you had to choose between renting an apartment or buying the same apartment as a condominium, which option do you think you would choose? Why?

_____ **Activity 1** _____

1. Use the amortization table in the Reference Section to help you calculate monthly mortgage payments for each condo and townhouse listed below, assuming a 20% down payment and mortgage payments over 30 years at 10% interest.

a.

GO TO COURT

The tennis courts that is. This 2 story condominium is a 3/2.5/2 with fenced yard, hot tub, atrium, fireplace, separate bedroom suites and offers a pool and lighted bicycle paths and tennis courts.

Purchase Price:	$90,000
Rental Price:	$750/month

b.

DON'T BE A RENT SLAVE!

Rent this beauty for $50/week or purchase it for $44,000. Come see this corporate-owned, 2 bedroom, 1-1/2 bath. Earthtones! Private patio and storage! Fireplace! A real deal at $44,000.

c.

NICE CONDO!

$24,000 purchase price; $230/month to rent. Charming 2 bedroom condo with 1-1/2 baths, washer, dryer, and refrigerator are included. Convenient location.

d.

COZY AND CONVENIENT

$85,000 to buy; $100/week to rent. Condo nestled near creek and greenbelt. Two bedroom, 2.5 bath, two-car garage in excellent condition. See it and fall in love.

e.

STUDIO IN PERRY HEIGHTS

Maximum style & maximum comfort await you in this outstanding condo. Plantation shutters, Mexican tile floors, wet bar, gourmet kitchen, inviting courtyard. Purchase Price, $120,000 or rent for $12,000/year.

f.

LAKEFRONT TOWNHOME

Mellow California-style harmony. 3BR/2.5BA townhome. Security system, Mexican tile floors, upgraded decor, ceramic tile baths, wraparound deck, pecan trees. $140,000 to purchase or rent for $750/month.

2. Compare the monthly rental costs of the above homes with the monthly mortgage payments. Which homes cost more per month to rent than to buy?

	Purchase Price	Monthly Mortgage Price	Rental Price	Monthly Rental Price
a.	$ 90,000	_____	$750/month	_____
b.	$ 44,000	_____	$ 50/week	_____
c.	$ 24,000	_____	$230/month	_____
d.	$ 85,000	_____	$100/week	_____
e.	$120,000	_____	$12,000/year	_____
f.	$140,000	_____	$750/month	_____

EXTEND YOUR UNDERSTANDING
PROJECT 15-1   PRIVATE vs PUBLIC TRANSPORTATION

When the price of gasoline rises, people consider using their private cars less and taking public transportation more often. Where trains or buses are not available, car pooling may be an alternative. In this project you will collect and compare costs for public and private transportation in your community.

Assignment

Answer the following questions for yourself or a member of your family who travels regularly to work or to school.

• Which do you use most regularly—public or private transportation?

• What are your current costs per trip?

• What alternatives are available? List them all. Don't forget to consider walking or biking.

• For each alternative, find out the cost per trip. For a bus or train, this will mean the cost of ticket and possibly a transfer. For car pooling, gas costs divided by the number of passengers. For automobile, use the method described in the Chapter 13. Be sure to include getting to and from the place that a train or bus leaves from.

• Compare the costs of the alternative methods of travel you listed above. Which is the most expensive? Which is the least? What is the difference?

• Which method is the most appealing to you?

• List advantages and disadvantages of public transportation for you personally. To your community.

Extension

• List the environmental costs of the kinds of transportation you studied. How do they compare? How do you compare environmental costs and personal costs? Consider such things as air pollution, cost of rail and road building and maintenance, depletion of natural resources, and the disposal of the vehicles, tires, batteries, and so on.

• Have a class debate. Half the class should prepare evidence and arguments on each side of the proposition: *Resolved that private transportation is superior to public.*

PROJECT 15–2   UTILITIES

Whether you are a renter or homeowner, you often must pay for water, electricity, and heat yourself. Do you know where the natural gas, oil, water, and electricity you use come from? Do you know how they are measured, what they cost, and how their use affects the supply of our natural resources?

Each student should choose one utility to investigate. Collect information through telephone calls, visits, and asking people who pay utility bills.

Assignment

- List some of the ways that a utility is used in your home.

- In your community, how often does the utility send its customers bills?

- How does your utility measure its customers' usage? Does it have a meter in each customer's home?

- In what units is each commodity measured? What is the cost per unit?

- What state or local taxes are added to each bill?

- Collect bills for at least three months and find the average monthly usage.

- Are there regulations in your community limiting the use of any resource—for example, water?

Extensions

- Arrange a visit to a waste water treatment plant. See how the waste water from your community is filtered, cleaned, and discharged. Where is the clean water released? How does this plant deal with sudden heavy flow, such as results from a rainstorm?

- Compare the costs and efficiency of two alternative energy sources—such as natural gas and electricity—when they are used for heat, ovens, and clothes dryers.

- Investigate your community's source of clean drinking water. Does it come from a surface water or ground water source? Is that source vulnerable to any kinds of pollution? Is there a limited supply?

CHAPTER 15 KEY TERMS

utilities

lease
turnover
rent
security deposit

condominium
owner's association
townhouse
mobile home

CHAPTER 15 REVIEW

1. What are the advantages and disadvantages of sharing an apartment with another person?

2. What types of things should you inspect in any apartment that you are considering renting?

3. What are the advantages and disadvantages of owning a condominium?

Find the greatest monthly rent. Rent should not exceed one week's pay.

	Position	Annual Income	Greatest Monthly Rent
4.	A	$73,500	
5.	B	$52,600	
6.	C	$36,500	
7.	D	$27,850	
8.	E	$47,695	
9.	F	$21,500	

For each apartment below, find the annual salary that would be necessary for a renter to earn. Assume that all the rent should be equal to one week's pay.

	Apartment	Apartment Rent	Annual Salary
10.	A	$395	
11.	B	$465	
12.	C	$750	
13.	D	$695	
14.	E	$960	
15.	F	$835	

16. Graph price versus number of amenities for each of the apartments listed below.

Apartment	Number of Amenities	Price
A	5	$425
B	10	$650
C	6	$450
D	8	$595

Use the amortization table in the Reference Section to calculate the monthly mortgage payment for each condo and townhouse listed, assuming a 20% down payment and mortgage payment over 30 years at 10% interest. Compare the monthly rental costs with the monthly mortgage payments.

	Purchase Price	Monthly Mortgage Price	Rental Price	Monthly Rental Price
17.	$95,000		$200/wk	
18.	$65,000		$6000/yr	
19.	$28,500		$250/mo	
20.	$19,400		$225/mo	
21.	$39,000		$95/wk	
22.	$80,000		$190/wk	

Find the weekly income for each of the following positions. What is the greatest amount of monthly rent they should pay?

	Position	Annual Income	Weekly Income	Greatest Monthly Rent
1.	A	$105,000		
2.	B	$ 42,000		
3.	C	$ 32,600		
4.	D	$ 24,800		

For each apartment below, find the annual salary that would be necessary for a renter to earn. Assume that all the rent should be equal to one week's pay.

	Apartment	Apartment Rent	Annual Salary
5.	A	$ 525	
6.	B	$ 295	
7.	C	$ 455	
8.	D	$1025	

9. Graph price versus number of amenities for each of the apartments listed below.

Apartment	Number of Amenities	Price
A	10	$725
B	5	$450
C	12	$960

Use the amortization table in the Reference Section to calculate the monthly mortgage payment for each condo and townhouse listed, assuming a 20% down payment and mortgage payment over 30 years at 10% interest. Compare the monthly rental costs with the monthly mortgage payments.

	Purchase Price	Monthly Mortgage Price	Rental Price	Monthly Rental Price
10.	$ 69,200		$6500/yr	
11.	$ 44,600		$105/mo	
12.	$102,500		$210/wk	

SKILLS PREVIEW

In this skills preview, you will review skills that you will need to complete the exercises in Chapter 16. If you do not know how to complete any exercise, be sure to ask for help.

Find each of the following percents.

1. 28% of $33,500

2. 16% of $45,600

3. 18% of $72,500

4. 17% of $19,450

5. 5% of $28,600

6. 22% of $65,000

7. 25% of $72,400

8. 23.5% of $41,000

9. 19% of $860

10. 12% of $925

11. 7% of $720

12. 9% of $1050

Find each sum.

13. $6.96 + 4.55	**14.** $7.55 +14.95	**15.** $19.43 +12.90
16. $125.92 +693.20	**17.** $192.60 +64.55	**18.** $766.55 +119.95
19. $852.51 321.60 85.20 21.00	**20.** $431.20 55.95 162.01	**21.** $719.95 182.15 75.59 32.86

Divide.

22. $\dfrac{\$2.98}{12}$

23. $\dfrac{\$3.66}{16}$

24. $\dfrac{\$4.51}{18}$

25. $\dfrac{\$0.65}{8}$

26. $\dfrac{\$0.79}{12}$

27. $\dfrac{\$1.23}{14}$

28. $\dfrac{\$14.51}{4}$

29. $\dfrac{\$26.45}{8}$

30. $\dfrac{\$1.79}{18}$

31. $\dfrac{\$32,000}{52}$

32. $\dfrac{\$43,500}{52}$

33. $\dfrac{\$69,500}{52}$

Compare each of the following. Which is larger?

34. $0.00156, $0.00155

35. $0.1155, $0.1096

36. $1.2906, $1.2961

37. $0.00064, $0.00640

38. $0.195550, $0.195545

39. $21.95005, $21.90505

CHAPTER **16** **GAINING CONTROL OVER INCOME AND SPENDING**

514

In this final chapter, several of our teenagers will contribute thoughts about what they have learned in previous chapters. The budgeting process brings together all the pieces of the puzzle, from the wages, salary, interest, and other sources of money coming into the family to the many different directions money must go out again.

Each individual, and every family, will have a unique solution to budgeting problems, but common characteristics can be found. Planning weekly, monthly, and yearly budgets involves more than simply paying the most persistent bill collectors and then trying to figure out how to spend what is left! First, a family must be willing to do some advance planning for expenses they can predict. Then, they can set up some realistic goals and identify steps toward reaching those goals. Finally, they can be reasonably consistent about following their plan, while maintaining enough flexibility to allow for adjustments and changes. Certainly every person who must live with the budgeting decisions and who can understand the budgeting process should have some input into how these decisions are made.

Many families with carefully developed budgets will still find it difficult to stretch the dollars far enough to do everything they want to do. It is important to make long-range plans in which people's desires are included. This makes it easier to stick to the current budget. If family members see that their nonessential needs are included in a plan for the future, and they see the family carrying out the plan, they are likely to be patient and stick to the current limitations. If one family member's wishes are always put aside and never put into the general plan, however, that member will be less likely to cooperate and stay within any kind of budget at all.

Making the plan is easy; carrying it out is the hard part.

Sylvia is well aware of the need for a budget in her family. While they were still married, her mother and father disagreed frequently about how their money should be handled. Since the divorce, she and her mother have had to plan their expenditures very carefully. Last year, Sylvia picked out her dress for the spring dance several months ahead of time and paid for it at the department store on a lay-away plan.

Sylvia wonders exactly how she is going to meet her college expenses. She thinks her father will help, especially since he has been helping her buy the clothes and new set of luggage. Her mother reminded her that one set of luggage and some new clothes are not the same as eight semesters of tuition. Sylvia is hoping she will not have to drop out of college after a year and work to earn the rest of the money before she can continue. Considering her mother's income, however, that is a definite possibility. Sylvia's father has not been very reliable with his child support payments.

Maria thought her father never even made a budget, at least until she started asking about getting a car. When her father suggested that she save half of her paycheck every week, she realized that her father does operate under some kind of plan. Maria and her father have had several discussions about what happened to their friends, Cal and his family, when his father lost so much money with his stock investments. Maria still would like the chance to try investing some of her money in stocks. If she made just a few good choices, the next time she looked at new cars she might not care if the sticker price was the real price—she might just pay it!

As for now, Maria is more aware of how difficult it can be to stick to a financial plan. She is now making car payments every month and buying insurance for her car. How much more complicated it must be for her father, who with her mother, is paying for a house, a car, food, clothing, medical care, insurance, everything the family needs, and who still manages to play golf twice a month and buy season tickets to the symphony orchestra and baseball games.

OBJECTIVES: In this section, we will help Sylvia and Maria to:

- *decide why a family would want to make a budget*
- *approach the decision-making process in terms of*
  —standard of living
  —goals, and
  —alternatives

> *discover the factors that influence standard of living*
>
> *begin planning family budgets by computing income and take-home pay for a variety of family configurations*

LONG- AND SHORT-TERM GOALS

Sylvia wishes she had never heard of budgets. Sometimes she becomes very frustrated because almost everything she does has to fit into some kind of financial plan. There are days she wishes someone would just drop a million dollars in her lap, so she would never have to plan her expenditures again.

Sylvia's mother would like Sylvia to be that lucky, too; but she knows that until that day comes, she and Sylvia must continue to make their financial decisions based on the best information and the most insight and understanding they can gather.

Sylvia wonders why her father never seems to make financial decisions; he just spends money. Her mother reminds her that he may have a plan, but he just does not share it with Sylvia. Sylvia does enjoy being a part of the decision-making process. Simply being told what she can and cannot do is not as comfortable for her.

Sylvia and her mother have worked out several guidelines that they find useful when facing their budget decisions. They include:

- Having a clear idea of what their long-range and short-term goals are
- Recognizing how their standard of living is determined, how it can be raised, and how it affects their goals
- Identifying how their financial goals and planning will change depending on where they are in their life cycle
- Identifying the alternatives they have when they make choices
- Setting up criteria and judging the alternatives

One of Sylvia's long-range goals is going through college and attaining a degree. She isn't quite sure what she will study, but she hopes she can complete a degree without having to drop out in the middle. She would really like to be wealthy, but when she is being realistic, Sylvia realizes her best chance of working at something she would truly enjoy depends upon her getting the best education she can.

Sylvia's mother is helping her see that, to meet her long-range goals, she must be willing to work toward some shorter term goals, such as the creation of their monthly and yearly budget plans. These budgets allow them to save the money Sylvia will need when she does go to college.

Maria understands long- and short-term goals, too. When her father suggested that she could have her car if she knew she could pay for it, Maria learned how much personal satisfaction she could achieve by being able to follow through with her rather ambitious plan.

ELEMENTS THAT DETERMINE THE STANDARD OF LIVING

The phrase standard of living has popped up in the conversations that Sylvia and Maria have had with their parents. They understand that most of us, Maria and Sylvia included, would like to buy more goods and use more services than we do now. We would like our money to go further. We would like to live on a higher economic level than we do at present. Our standard of living is indicated by the quality and quantity of the goods and services we are able to buy. Maria and Sylvia are well aware that the standard of living is higher for some people within a community than for others. They would both like to maintain a high standard of living.

Their standard of living, and ours, depends not only on income and savings, but also on how wisely we spend our money. We have some control over our income. In general, the more skills or training we have or the better we serve in our jobs, the greater our earnings. We also have control over the spending of our income.

Maria and Sylvia realize that raising their standard of living is not an easy task, but it can be approached from two angles: (1) increasing their income; and (2) planning carefully to get the most from the income they receive.

Value of the Dollar. Maria and Sylvia remind us, too, that the amount of money they save or the amount they earn is not so important as what it will buy. Their wages in dollars are indicated by the amount of their paychecks, but their **real wages** are measured by the amount of goods and services the wages will buy. As the years go by, and inflation takes its toll, if the dollar amount of pay stays the same, real wages fall. As Olivia discovered, when she investigated inflation and the Consumer Price Index, today's dollars will not buy what they would ten or even five years ago.

Life Cycle. Maria and Sylvia know that the goals and choices they make now are somewhat determined by the tasks that are appropriate for their age. They will share with us a list of financial tasks that are unique to their place in the life cycle.

Financial Planning Early in The Life Cycle

Age Group	Unique Financial Tasks
13–17	Develop plans for eventual independence
	Evaluate future financial needs and resources
	Explore career options
	Develop an understanding of the financial system
	Develop record-keeping systems
18–24	Establish household
	Train for career
	Attain financial independence
	Purchase risk coverage
	Establish financial identity
	Establish a savings program
	Make a spending plan
	Develop effective financial record-keeping system
	Develop effective financial planning system

Early involvement in family financial affairs is often recommended by financial counselors. Certainly teenagers like Maria and Sylvia should assume some personal and family financial responsibilities.

EXERCISE YOUR SKILLS

___ **Activity 1** ___

Throughout this book, you have been learning a great deal about handling money. In this chapter, you will use what you have learned in the previous chapters to help you put together workable budgets for each of three families.

Choose one family from each of the 3 groups on the following page. You will be developing a budget for each of the families that you choose.

Group 1

The McGrew Family
One adult: Marilyn, who is 43.
One child: JoAnn, who is 17.
Marilyn is a clerk in a local department store. She earns $10 an hour.
JoAnn is still in high school, and she has a driver's license.

The Betts Family
Two adults: Ginni, who is 33, and Jim who is 30.
One child: Eric, who is 10.
Jim is a construction worker and earns $28,000 a year.
Ginni is not currently employed, but she is attending college full time.

Group 2

The Walker Family
Two adults: Hal, who is 40, and Sylvia, who is 38.
Two children: Melanie, who is 16, and Matt, who is 12.
Melanie has a driver's license.
Hal is a Customer Service Representative. He earns $36,000 a year.
Sylvia is not currently employed.

The Scovil Family
Two adults: Bob, who is 30, and May, who is 28.
One child: David, who is 3 years old.
Bob is a truck driver for a local baker. He earns $500 a week.
May is a high-school teacher who makes $29,000 a year.
The family must pay a day-care school for taking care of David during the day.

Group 3

The Isobe Family
Three adults: Rose, who is 43, Umeki, who is 50, and Oki—who is 73 and is Umeki's mother.
Two children: Yuki, who is 18, and Joji, who is 19. Both children are attending a local college and living at home. Both drive.
Rose is a sales representative for a plastics manufacturer. She earns $34,000 a year. Umeki is a laborer for the same company and earns about $31,000 a year. Oki is not employed. The family has two cars.

The Lopez Family
Two adults: Oscar, who is 40, and Miriam, who is 33.
No children
Oscar owns a shoe store and earns $50,000 a year. Miriam earns about $30,000 as a computer programmer. They own two cars.

For most activities in this chapter, you will be creating Family Budget worksheets for each of the families you chose. Your teacher may supply worksheets for you to fill out; otherwise, you will need to create your own worksheets, based on the examples given in each activity.

> **Note:** Remember to save those worksheets after each activity. You will need them for later activities.

Step 1: General Information

The first section of your worksheet for each family should contain the general information about the family. It should look similar to the following:

Family Budget Worksheet   **Student Name** _____

General Information

Family Name _____

Names and ages of adults: _____

_____

_____

Names and ages of children: _____

_____

_____

How many of the children drive? _____

How many of the members are in college? _____

How many of the members of the family are in day care? _____

Does the family have two cars? _____

Step 2: Income and Take-Home Pay

The second section of your Family Budget worksheets should contain a Income and Take-Home Pay chart similar to the one shown on the next page. To complete the chart, do the following:

1. Enter the total number of income tax exemptions for the family. (One exemption for each family member.)

2. Enter the names of each adult wage earner in the family.

3. Enter the amount each person earns, as stated in the textbook.

4. Convert those amounts into monthly incomes. (Assume that 52 weeks or 12 months equal one year and that 40 hours equal one-work week.) Write your answers in the "Monthly Salary" column.

5. Add the monthly incomes of the wage earners together, and write the total in the appropriate place.

6. Using the social security and withholding tables in the Reference Section, find the take-home pay for each wage earner, and then calculate the total take-home pay for the family. Write your answers in the appropriate part of the chart. (If you need help, refer back to Chapter 4.)

INCOME/TAKE-HOME PAY				
Adult's Name	Monthly Salary	Social Security	FICA Withholding	Take-Home Pay
Total Monthly Take-Home Pay –>				

Note: Be sure to save your worksheets. You will need them for later activities.

If Evelyn and Freda do decide to share an apartment near Community College next year, they will certainly plan their finances carefully. They have made quite a lot of money in the business this year, but since they plan to be studying more when they go to college, they will not have time to sell many sweatshirts.

Evelyn thinks her parents will have a specific amount of money they can give her to help pay tuition and expenses. She will have to use the profits from the business to pay for the apartment and living expenses. She and Freda will get together and set up a budget to help them figure out how to pay for everything.

Freda wanted to buy a new bedroom suite to take with her, but when she and Evelyn took a closer look at the money they had, they decided they might be better off renting a furnished apartment. Freda will pick out bedspreads and towels, instead, to give them a sense of setting up housekeeping.

The budget plan for Vernon's parents has undergone some changes as they moved from Chicago. Figuring out ways to pay for housing, food, clothing, and everything else that comes with having three children is more complicated than making the budgeting decisions of Evelyn and Freda. Purchasing the house meant they had to sit down and make a completely new plan. A new category called "home maintenance and repairs" has had to be added.

For Yvette and Yvonne, the housing part of their budget will go toward utility bills and a portion of the mortgage payment on the condominium. Their parents have agreed to help buy the condo if the twins make part of the payment each month. Both young women will work part-time while they are in school, and they have some savings to use as well. The condo is unfurnished, however, so they will be buying some furniture; unless they rent a truck to move them, they may not be able to take their favorite desks from their bedroom at home. Their mother thinks they should buy a small refrigerator to take with them, in which case they will need to rent a truck. Then they could also take a small fold-out couch and the twin beds and assorted other bulky belongings that are hard to get into the car.

For Yvette and Yvonne, moving out and going so far away from home will involve quite a few adjustments and decisions. At least they can both agree on how they want the condo to look inside when they get their things moved in, but one of them will have to learn to cook something more than popcorn unless they plan to have a lot of their meals in the campus cafeteria!

OBJECTIVES: In this section, we will help our teenagers to:

● *consider the factors that determine how we choose a place to live, including life stage, preferences, location, and finances*
● *select the appropriate form of housing for families based on their budget*

HOUSING DECISIONS

Evelyn and Freda, Vernon's family, and Yvette and Yvonne are all faced with the need to provide themselves with shelter. Their situations are quite different, however, and they will make different choices.

Deciding on a place to live can be an exciting, yet sometimes perplexing experience. When choosing a place to live, a person must consider several factors, including stage in life, preferences, the location desired, and the amount of money available to pay for shelter.

Stage in Life. Our stage in life plays a large part in our housing needs. Single persons, the elderly, young married couples, roommates, and older couples without children obviously have housing needs that are different from the needs of families with young children. For Vernon's parents, the need for housing was not the same when their children were small as it is now that the children are older.

Preferences. Different people like different styles in housing. They need space for hobbies, games, and indoor recreation. Some like to entertain friends at home. Our college students may prefer a quiet, peaceful home free from noise and visitors so they can pursue their studies. Vernon's family would like to keep a pet, something they were unable to do in the apartment. Yvette and Yvonne will choose a condo that has access to a swimming pool.

Location. Many experts believe that location should be a top priority when we define our housing needs. We must ask ourselves whether we want to be close to work or school, whether we want to be near friends and family, what kind of community we want to live in, and what kind of social and recreational opportunities we want. Some people want to be close to a place of worship, others close to theaters, a library, or a shopping center. Evelyn, Freda, and the twins want to be close to their college or university. The choice for Vernon's family is more complex. They will also have to consider their transportation needs. For them, the type of transportation available (railroads, buses, taxis, subways, and expressways) is a significant factor in selecting the location of their home.

Price. How much can we afford to pay for housing? Most likely, this factor will determine whether we rent or buy. Costs for housing include not only rent or mortgage payments, but related expenses such as furniture, utilities, property taxes, and insurance.

All of our teenagers and their families will consider carefully what their budgets will allow in the way of cost before they choose their housing. They all know that some of these decisions are very difficult to change if they are not satisfied with their first choice. They will try to weigh the factors carefully and not rush into some choices they might later regret.

EXERCISE YOUR SKILLS

Activity 1

Step 3: Housing

This activity is a continuation of the Family Budget that you started in Section 1 of this chapter. In this activity you will be determining the housing costs for each of the families you chose.

For this section of your worksheet, you will need to create a chart that looks similar to the one shown on the next page. To fill out the chart, follow these steps.

A. Determine the maximum housing payment that each family should be paying by multiplying the family's total take-home pay (from Step 2 of your worksheet) by 28%. Write your answer in the appropriate part of the chart.

B. Using the skills taught in Chapter 14, Section 3, determine the amount of money that the family could borrow towards a house and the maximum price they could pay for a house. Assume they will be paying 11% financing on a 30-year loan and will put 20% down. Write your answer in the appropriate parts of the chart.

C. Find a house that would suit the family and that the family could afford. As a source of house listings, you may either use the housing ads following this chapter or actual ads for housing in your local area. Just be sure to follow the guidelines established in A and B on the preceding page. Write the price of the house you choose in the appropriate column of the chart. Then calculate the down payment and write that amount in the chart.

HOUSING COSTS				
Maximum Housing Payment	Maximum Family Could Borrow	Price of House	Down Payment	Actual Monthly Payments

D. Calculate the monthly payments. Write your answer in the last column of the chart.

Note: Save your worksheets for use with the activities in the next section.

This is Hari's year to learn about money management. When Evelyn and Freda and Greg asked him to keep their accounts for the T-shirt business, he found out quite a lot about fixed and variable expenses. Now his grandmother has retired and he is learning about fixed income with increasing expenses. As a result, Hari's parents are readjusting their budget to be able to help his mother's parents with some of his grandfather's medical bills. Hari has decided that it is easier to be wealthy, especially when you retire, than it is to wonder how you will handle all the expenses adults have to meet.

Trevor got an important lesson about the necessity of keeping up with some fixed expenses—automobile insurance, for one—when he almost had a wreck with his sister and her friends in the car. Trevor thought he wanted to learn to drive when he was old enough, but now he is not too sure! His sister, Tracey, has been pestering him lately to drive her places again. He might be willing, as long as they don't take more than one friend along and Tracey keeps quiet in the car.

Trevor also knows that expensive car insurance is not the only fixed expense in his family's budget, but it is the newest large one. When Trevor started driving, the whole family got together to discuss the impact on the family's budget that additional car insurance would make. Trevor remembers Tracey complaining because her clothing allowance would be cut in half. That was partly why Trevor agreed to drive her on occasion; of course, his clothing allowance was being cut, too.

Daryl knows what his parents' budget looks like—pay off the 23 credit cards every month and then see if anything is left! After Daryl and Sylvia discovered the credit counseling service available through the bank, Daryl's father actually did discuss his situation with someone. He realized that he was in over his head when he began to have trouble making the minimum payments on all his cards every month. He was also having trouble keeping track of his credit purchases. Instead of a convenience, his many credit and charge cards were actually becoming a nuisance. What he has been able to do about the problem is quite encouraging.

Daryl's father has worked out a plan for paying off the VISA and MasterCard accounts over a four year period, and he even has one he can still use as long as he keeps up the payments on the others. He has been allowed to keep the gasoline credit cards and two of the department store charge accounts as long as he pays off the whole balance he owes each month. He has explained to Daryl that his method of budgeting could definitely use some improvement; he hopes Daryl will do better with his own budget plans.

OBJECTIVES: In this section, we will help Hari, Trevor, and Daryl to:

- *enumerate fixed expenses that families must include in their budgets such as utilities, transportation (car payments and insurance), credit payments, other obligations, and other insurance*
- *calculate portions of the budget that will be allocated to cover these fixed expenses*

HOW FIXED IS FIXED?

Hari knows his grandparents' income is a fixed amount, that is, the amount they receive from their retirement plans each month has not gone up. Some retirement plans do include automatic cost-of-living increases under certain conditions to allow retirees to cope with inflationary prices. Hari hopes his grandparents' retirement plans have made some provision for this. He understands now that some expenses in his grandparents' budgets are also fixed, at least until the prices of everything go up again. Hari will list a few that we can all expect to include in a family budget.

Utilities. When Hari encourages his grandfather to tell stories about what life was like when he was a boy, he describes the days before public utilities. He had to draw water up from a well and carry it into their house, they used kerosene lamps for light, huge chunks of ice were delivered by the iceman each day to be put in the icebox for refrigeration, and the nearest telephone was five miles away. Hari is not always sure how much of this actually happened and how much his grandfather makes up. To Hari's grandfather, though, public utilities are not taken for granted.

Hari's parents and grandparents now include payments for electricity, natural gas, water, sewer, and garbage collection as part of their fixed expenses each month. The amounts of these bills may not be exactly the same each month, but there is not so much variation that they cannot consider these amounts as fixed expenses. They also include their telephone and cable television service among the necessary utilities they use each month. Cable television is the newest addition to this list; Hari's grandmother enjoys being able to watch almost all of her favorite baseball teams play on television now that they have started the cable service.

Transportation. Also included on a list of fixed expenses are two types of car expenses: (1) monthly payments for buying a car during the years when the car is still new; (2) automobile insurance, an ever-present need if anyone in the family drives. Trevor's parents know they can choose to pay for this insurance in several ways—twice a year, four times in a year, or twelve times a year. If they pay every month, they must pay a little more in total. They choose to pay twice a year because it saves them money; they set aside an amount each month in anticipation of these semiannual premiums.

Credit Payments. Payments on our credit accounts can be a fixed expense. This expense will not be the same every month for those who use their credit cards for convenience and plan to pay the entire balance when the bill comes. Daryl's father pays the minimum required amount to each of his creditors every month, so this part of his budget is fairly stable.

Other installment loans, such as the home improvement loan that is paying for the new roof on Joan's house, would be included in this part of the budget. So, too, would the tuition loan that Patricia received.

Other Obligations. Hari's parents include as a fixed expense their regular additions to their savings account and contributions to charitable institutions. They also send an amount to his mother's parents each month. Jeff's parents consider their regular contributions to their older son, Jeremy, to help get him through college, as a fixed expense each month; however, Jeremy's "fixed" amount is not so fixed if he needs more money than he has.

Other Insurance. Trevor's father has been careful to buy what he considers adequate life insurance for himself and for Trevor's mother. They do not really notice this as a fixed expense in their budget because the premiums are paid from a payroll deduction; Trevor's father's employer pays part of the cost.

The family's health insurance is paid through the company, too. Health insurance protects a family or an individual against financial loss due to an accident or illness. The most common types of health insurance are hospital, surgical, and general medical. Approximately 84% of all Americans, like Trevor's family, buy health insurance coverage through a **group plan**. Most group plans are provided through an employer, union, or professional association. Some of the ways to provide for health care expense protection are traditional health insurance plans, Health Maintenance Organizations (HMOs), self-insurance, Medicare, and Medicaid.

EXERCISE YOUR SKILLS

_____ Activity 1 _____

In this activity, you will continue to develop the family budgets that you have been working on in Sections 1 and 2. You will need your worksheets.

Step 4:   Transportation

Assume that each of the families you chose owns a car. (Note that some of the families may have two cars.) You will be determining how much each family can afford to spend on car payments, find a car (or two) for each family, and determine what the family's car payments are each month.

A. First, you need to determine how much each family can afford to spend on car payments. To do this, multiply the family's maximum housing payment (see your calculations from Step 3 of your worksheets) by 33%. Write this amount in your worksheet.

B. Next, find each family a car, or two, that will fit within the family budget. Use the classified ads or advertisements for new cars in your local newspaper to help you find at least 3 cars for each family to choose from. These do not necessarily have to be cars they can afford, but they should include a variety of prices.

Cut out the ads and attach them to a piece of paper. Then create a chart like the one shown here and fill in the requested information.

BUYING A CAR		
Type of Car	**Model Year**	**Selling Price**

C. Using the information you acquired in **B** above, and the 11% Amortization Table in the Reference Section, determine what the monthly payments on each of the cars would be. Assume the family would make a 10% down payment. Figure the payments for both a 4-year and a 5-year loan. Write your answers in a chart similar to the one that follows.

COST OF AUTOMOBILE LOANS					
Original Car Price	**10% Down Payment**	**4-year Monthly Payment**	**Total Cost 4-years**	**5-year Monthly Payments**	**Total Cost 5-years**

D. Based on your calculations, choose which car or cars and which payment plan the family can afford. Remember that the total monthly car payments must be equal to or less than the Maximum Monthly Car Payment you calculated in **A**. If all of the cars you chose are too expensive for a

family, you will need to find some less expensive cars and try again. Mark the car or cars you chose on the chart.

E. There are many expenses associated with owning a car. These include the cost of fuel, oil changes, and repairs. To help you calculate these costs, create a chart similar to the one that follows.

OTHER TRANSPORTATION COSTS					
Gasoline Cost per Gallon	Miles Driven per Month	Gasoline Cost per Month	Oil Change Cost per Month	Average Cost of Repairs per Month	Total Costs

To fill in the chart, follow these steps:

1. Find out the price of gasoline in your area. Write your answer in the appropriate column of the chart.

2. Assume that each family drives about 1000 miles a month and that their cars consume about 1 gallon of gas for every 25 miles traveled. Calculate how much the family spends on gasoline each month. Write your answer in the appropriate column of the chart.

3. Find out the typical price of an oil change in your area. Divide the amount by 3, because they may have the oil changed once every 3000 miles. Write the amount in the appropriate column of the chart.

4. Assume that the families in this study spend $25.00 a month on car repairs. Write this amount in the appropriate column of the chart.

5. Calculate the total amount spent in columns 3, 4, and 5 of the chart. Write your answer in the last column of the chart.

> **Note:** Be sure to save your worksheets. You will need them later in this chapter.

_____ Activity 2 _____

Every family has certain types of bills that show up every month. The house and car payments are typical examples. But there are often also water and gas bills, electrical bills, and bills for things the family has put on a charge account.

Step 5: Bills, Bills, Bills

A. The list of bills following this chapter shows you some of the other expenses that each family has. Copy the information for each family into a chart similar to the one shown on the next page.

EXPENSES	
Bill Type	**Minimum Payment**
Water	
Electricity	
Gas	
Department Store	
Charge Card #1	
Charge Card #2	
Education	
Savings	

B. Many families have additional educational expenses, such as tuition for a private school, college tuition, and payments for day-care services. These expenses need to be figured into the family's budget.

Check the first page of your worksheets for each family. Are any of the members of the family in college or in a day-care program? If one or more family members are students in college, find out how much a typical college tuition is for a year in your area. (Your school library should have college catalogs that will supply this information.) If there are children in day-care programs, find out how much a typical full-day program costs in your area.

Convert all such tuitions and fees to their cost per month. Then write the information onto your worksheet.

C. In addition to making payments to other people, many families try to make a payment to themselves every payday. They do this in the form of making deposits to a savings account.

Assume that each family you choose saves 5% of their take-home pay each month. Calculate the amount of money that each family saves each month. Write your answers on your worksheets.

———— **Activity 3** ————

Step 6:   Insurance

Another common expense for many families is insurance. For this activity, assume that all of the families carry medical insurance, life insurance, car insurance, and homeowner's insurance.

A. Use the Annual Group Medical Insurance Premiums table at the end of this chapter to help you create a Medical Insurance Cost chart similar to the one below. This chart shows sample group-insurance premium costs. To complete the chart, follow this procedure.

MEDICAL INSURANCE COSTS		
Number of People in Family	**Annual Premium**	**Monthly Cost**

1. In the first column of the chart, indicate how many people are in the family.

2. In the second column, write the annual premium for the number of people indicated in column 1.

3. Calculate the monthly cost by dividing the annual premium by 12. Write your answer in column 3 of the chart.

B. Using the Annual Life Insurance Premium Rates Table at the end of this chapter, complete the following Life Insurance Cost chart. To complete the chart, follow this procedure.

LIFE INSURANCE COSTS				
Adult's Name	**Cost per $1000**	**Total Amount of Insurance**	**Annual Premium**	**Monthly Cost**
		Total of All Premiums –>		

1. Write the name and age of each adult in the family in column 1.

2. Use the Life Insurance Premium Table to determine how much each $1000 worth of coverage will cost that person.

3. Decide how much insurance each person will need, following the rule that people should generally have life insurance worth 10 times their annual salary. Write that amount in column 3 of the chart.

4. Calculate the annual premium for each person by multiplying the amount in column 2 by the number of thousands of dollars in column 3. Write your answer in column 4.

5. Calculate the monthly cost by dividing the annual premium by 12. Write your answer in column 5.

6. Calculate the total of the monthly costs for each adult. Write that total in the "Total of All Premiums" section of the chart.

C. To complete the Homeowner's Insurance Cost Chart, follow this procedure.

HOMEOWNER'S INSURANCE COSTS		
Total Amount of Insurance Needed	**Annual Premium**	**Monthly Costs**

1. To determine how much insurance is needed, assume that each family needs $50,000 worth of coverage on personal property, $25,000 worth of coverage on loss of use, $75,000 worth of personal liability coverage, and coverage on the house that equals the selling price of the house (from Step 3 of the worksheet). Add those amounts together and write the total in column 1 of the chart.

2. Assume that homeowner's insurance costs approximately $1.00 for each $1000 worth of coverage. To determine the annual premium, divide the total amount of insurance in column 1 by 1000. Write your answer in the Annual Premium column.

3. Finally, calculate the monthly cost of homeowner's insurance by dividing the annual premium by 12. Write your answer in column 3.

D. As you know, determining the cost of car insurance premiums is a complicated task. In real life, before you could compute the cost of insurance premiums, you would not only need to know the age and sex of each driver in the family, you would also need to know their driving record, whether or not they have ever taken a driver's education class, whether they were the primary driver of a car or just an occasional driver, if they drove the car to work or not, the current value of the car, what kind of insurance they wanted on the car, where they lived, and a variety of other facts. To keep this activity simple, we will only use age and sex as determining factors. While this is obviously not totally realistic, it will allow you to see the impact that car insurance can have on a family budget.

Using the 6-Month Car Insurance Premium Table at the end of this chapter complete the chart at the top of the next page. To complete the chart, follow this procedure.

1. Write the name of each driver in the family in column 1.

2. In column 2, tell whether each driver you listed is male or female.

3. In column 3, list each driver's age.

CAR INSURANCE COSTS				
Driver's Name	Male or Female	Driver's Age	6-Month Premium	
	Highest Premium from Above –>			
	Monthly Cost for Car Insurance –>			

4. Next, use the 6-Month Car Insurance Premium Table to find out how much the premium would be for each driver, taking into consideration each driver's age and sex. Write those premiums in column 4.

5. Choose the highest premium from those listed in column 4, and write that premium in the part of the chart labeled "Highest Premium from Above." For the sake of this activity, we will consider this amount to be the cost of 6 months' worth of total car insurance coverage for the family.

6. To find out the family's monthly cost for car insurance, divide the amount in the "Highest Premium" section of the chart by 6. Write your answer in the part of the chart labeled "Monthly Cost for Car Insurance."

Note: Remember to save your worksheets, you will need them for later activities.

SECTION 16-4
VARIABLE EXPENSES

Olivia is pleased that her parents are planning to sell their house and buy another one closer to the school. She will not even mind driving her brother Orson to school if they move: Olivia's talks with Vernon made her more interested in the costs associated with buying a house. When Olivia mentioned these, her mother was willing to discuss the family finances with her. As Olivia read over the list of expenses for things that vary each month, she was surprised that so many items that seemed inexpensive at the time combined to create such a large total. Small things—everyone in the family having a haircut, eating at the cafeteria, going to the movies, or spending the day at a water park—could run into hundreds of dollars over a month's time.

She noticed that groceries take a major portion of the money; this is not surprising as she and Orson have non-stop appetites. Orson has become pretty skilled at preparing his in-between-meals meals, too. His parents have limited the amount of money they let him spend on fast foods—it would cost too much if they did not! Olivia also likes the fact that her parents discuss the budget with her as they work out a way to buy another house.

Jeff's parents will not be selling their house until next year when Jeff goes to college, but their budgets have been revised several times in the last few years. Jeff's older brother, Jeremy, is in college now, so he is part of the reason for the family's fluctuating expenses. One of the reasons Jeremy keeps running out of money is the long distance telephone calls to his girlfriend, Jennifer. His parents are glad that Jeremy has a phone in his room so he can call home frequently, but they are beginning to wonder if they would not save money if they could send Jennifer to college with Jeremy! They can just imagine what the phone bills will look like in another year if Jeremy gets to go to France to study!

OBJECTIVES: In this section, we will help Olivia and Jeff to:

- *enumerate the expenses that vary from month to month in a family budget, including: food, clothing, transportation, education and reading material, personal care, entertainment, and miscellaneous*
- *calculate what a family can determine about the costs of these portions of the budget*

536

**DO WE HAVE
ANYTHING
GOOD TO EAT?**

American eating habits may be changing. At one time, breakfast, lunch, and supper were eaten at the table with all the family members present. This is not as common as it once was. Both of Olivia's parents work all day; Olivia and her brother Orson go to school, then they go to other activities after school and possibly to still other events in the evenings. Their different schedules make it difficult to get together for a family meal. The family members often want to eat different kinds of food. Olivia's father wants to lose weight; Orson wants to gain weight; Olivia is very aware of health and nutrition, and her mother is always experimenting with foods of different countries. One thing that is not changing is that growing teenagers have very substantial appetites.

Olivia was surprised to learn that the family spent more on food last year than on any other single item in their budget. That proportion may change next year if they buy another house. The family must plan their food purchases carefully. They have eaten out quite often, and Olivia's father often brings home food that is already prepared. Orson and Olivia receive a specific amount of money each week for food they buy themselves.

To save on their food costs, Olivia's family try to follow this advice:

- Make a weekly meal plan. Consider good nutrition, personal preferences, preparation time, and cost.

- Watch grocery store ads. Look for those products called **loss leaders** which stores use to attract customers.

- Make a list. Avoid forgetting something you need, and also avoid **impulse buying,** or buying something you do not need.

- Compare prices among brands and stores.

- Buy in quantity.

- Use coupons.

Olivia has been accompanying her parents on grocery shopping trips lately. She has seen at first hand how easy it can be to forget this advice. Her weakness is impulse buying. She would like to try every new product she sees, every item packaged attractively or featured in a display at the end of the aisle. But she sees the wisdom of resisting this impulse.

Another cost-cutting measure Olivia's family takes is to consider the **unit price** of food items they buy. Many foods are available in several size packages—dry cereal, for instance, often comes in boxes of 12, 18, and 24 ounces. The standard unit of that type of food is the ounce (abbreviated oz.). The cost per ounce is the unit price.

Some weights are stated in the metric units. In the metric system, cereal might be labeled in grams. One gram is approximately 0.04 ounces. For a complete list of metric units and their equivalents in the British and American system, see the Measurement Equivalents and Conversion Table in the Reference Section at the back of this book. Some of the most common equivalents are shown on the following page.

Common Conversion Factors

1 centimeter = 0.39 inches
1 meter = 39.4 inches
1 kilometer = 0.62 miles
1 gram = 0.04 ounces
1 kilogram = 2.20 pounds
1 liter = 1.06 quarts

Standard units of heavier products are stated in pounds, or, in the metric system, kilograms. Standard units of liquids are stated in terms of volume. In our system, that means quarts, half-gallons, and gallons. In the metric system, liters.

For paper products, such as tissues, the standard unit is square feet or meters. Some items, such as eggs and vitamins, are sold by count. Eggs are sold by the dozen, vitamins by the 100-count.

Two unit price labels from catsup are shown below.

K
GREAT GROWERS CATSUP
UNIT PRICE   44 OZ BOTTLE
2.25¢   99¢
PER OUNCE

K
LAND OF PLENTY CATSUP
UNIT PRICE   14 OZ BOTTLE
2.38¢   3/$1.00
PER OUNCE

The 44-oz. size of Great Grower's Catsup costs $0.99, or $0.0225 per ounce. The Land of Plenty Catsup, in a 14 oz. bottle costs $0.0238 per ounce. Olivia can easily compare the costs of these two products and conclude that the Great Grower's Catsup is a better buy. This is assuming, of course, that the two products are equivalent. If they are not equivalent, she must take the quality of the product into account as well as the price.

WHAT TO WEAR

Olivia does enjoy shopping for clothes. She knows that the clothes she selects reflect who she is and present a certain image to the world. She looks for clothes that suit her, that make sense for her lifestyle, that are comfortable, and that help her feel confident.

Olivia read an article that said through skillful dressing we can evoke a favorable response from others. The article described research showing that better-dressed people receive better treatment. For Olivia, this might mean making a good impression in a job interview or getting good service in a store. But she realizes that clothes do not have to be trendy or excessively costly to make a good impression. They need to be well chosen and well cared for, that is all.

GETTING AROUND

Most of the time when Jeff does tutoring in algebra for extra money, no one has to take him—he drives himself. Before his brother Jeremy left for college, the family sometimes had to juggle their schedules to get everyone where they needed to go. Now, though, Jeff enjoys the independence of having his own oil company credit card so he can pay for his own gasoline. The first few months he had the card, he was surprised when the bill came. He had not kept track of the number of times he had used the card, and he was not prepared for the large bill he received at the end of the month.

Jeff is learning to pay attention to how much he is spending on transportation; he has also learned to use more public transportation when it is available—public transportation does not get charged on his credit card!

Gasoline and auto maintenance expenses can fluctuate greatly from month to month. When Jeff's family must drive and park in the city, they also include the parking fees and tolls in their budget plan.

WHAT IS LEFT?

Food, clothing, and transportation are large segments in the family budgets. Olivia and Jeff hope there will be money left over for a few other variable expenses in their family budgets, such as sports equipment, books, and movies.

In Olivia's family there is not always a lot left over for these expenses, and certainly every family member will have his or her own views regarding which of these expenses are essential and which are not. What one member considers crucial may be viewed by another member as frivolous. Care must be taken to see that each family member is fairly treated in the budget making process.

Among the optional expenses that add to a family's quality of life are the following:

1. Education and reading material—whatever newspapers, magazines, books, and study materials the family may need. Jeff's mother includes in this category the tuition she paid for a course she is taking in economics.

2. Personal care—visits to the hairdresser or barber; eyeglasses and dental costs that are not covered in the health insurance plan; membership in a health club.

3. Entertainment and miscellaneous—movies, theaters, music, museums, amusement parks, and other optional, but desirable expenses.

SHARPEN YOUR SKILLS

——— Skill 1 ———

Olivia has accompanied her father to the grocery store. He has given her a shopping list, but he did not specify the size of each item to buy. It is up to her to choose.

She comes to a shelf of breakfast cereal and sees three sizes of the Whole Grain Flakes, as follows:

12 oz.	18 oz.	24 oz.
Whole Grain	Whole Grain	Whole Grain
Flakes	Flakes	Flakes
$1.98	$2.69	$3.39

Olivia does not see any unit price labels on the shelf. She has, however, brought her calculator.

Question   Which size package is the best buy?

Solution   Olivia must calculate the cost per standard unit for each of the three sizes. Since the size of the package is stated in ounces on all three packages, she will use the ounce as the standard unit.

She finds the unit price for each size package by dividing its total price by the number of ounces in the package:

$$\frac{\$1.98}{12} \qquad \frac{\$2.69}{18} \qquad \frac{\$3.39}{24}$$

She arrives at the following unit prices:

The 12-ounce package costs $0.165 or $0.17 per ounce.

The 18-ounce package costs $0.149 or $0.15 per ounce.

The 24-ounce package costs $0.141 or $0.14 per ounce.

The best buy, in terms of cost, is the 24-ounce size.

The next time Olivia goes to the grocery store, she finds that the 18-ounce size of Whole Grain Flakes is on sale for $2.29.

Question   Does that make it a better buy than the 24-ounce size?

Solution   The unit price for the sale item is calculated as follows:

$$\frac{\$2.29}{18} = 0.127 = \$0.13$$

The sale makes the 18-ounce size the better buy this week.

Suppose the Whole Grain Flakes company decides to put out a newly packaged version of their cereal. The new package is a box containing 12 separate 1-ounce bags. The cost of the product is $2.98.

Question   How does the unit price of the cereal in the individual bags compare with the unit price of the cereal in the large boxes?

Solution   Calculate the unit price of the new package.

$$\frac{\$2.98}{18} = 0.2483 = \$0.25$$

The cereal in individual bags costs $0.25 an ounce. That is more than any other price per ounce for the cereal.

EXERCISE YOUR SKILLS

_____ Activity 1 _____

Following are the prices and sizes of products you might find in a grocery store. For each one, calculate the unit price and decide which is the best buy in terms of cost. Use a chart like the one below to record your answers.

1. Oil	8 oz $1.10	10 oz $1.29	15 oz $1.89
2. Orange Juice	6 oz $0.79	12 oz $1.29	18 oz $1.79
3. Tuna	6 oz $0.59	13 oz $1.56	16 oz $1.76
4. Raisins	12 oz $1.98	14 1-oz pkgs. $3.04	16 oz $3.50
5. Honey	4 oz $0.80	8 oz $0.96	1 lb $1.33
6. Rice	8 oz $0.78	1 lb $0.59	2 lb $1.05
7. Milk	quart $1.29	1/2 gallon $1.79	1 gallon $2.69
8. Popcorn	1 lb $2.08	32 oz $3.20	45 oz $5.40

	Unit Price			
Product	**Size 1**	**Size 2**	**Size 3**	**Best Buy**

_____ Activity 2 _____

One expense that all families have is the cost of food. Everyone has to eat. In this activity, you will do research to determine how much food could cost each of your families. This activity is a continuation of the Family Budget exercise. You will need your worksheets.

Step 7:   Food, Clothing, and Personal Expenses

A. 1. Create a 3-day meal plan, listing what each family might eat for breakfast, lunch, and dinner each day. Assume that all 3 meals are eaten at home.

   2. List all the groceries needed to feed the number of people in the family for the meals described in your meal plan. Look in fliers and ads from your local grocery stores or visit the stores in person to find the costs for the items.

   3. Add together the cost of the groceries, remembering that this is the cost for 3 days. Then multiply that amount by 10 to find the approximate cost for 30 days, or 1 month.

   4. Keep your meal list, grocery list, and your list of food costs with your worksheets.

Another common expense is clothing. Clothing tends to be expensive, and can take a big bite out of a family's budget. While few people have clothing expenses every month, we can demonstrate the impact of clothing on the budget by choosing 1 outfit of clothing for *one* member of the family.

B. Using department store catalogs or advertising fliers, choose a complete outfit of clothing for one member of the family. The clothing should be appropriate to the person's age and sex. If you do not need to preserve your magazine or flier, cut out pictures of the clothing and attach them to a piece of paper. Keep this information with your worksheets.

Everyone has personal expenses that are not included in any of the categories that have been covered so far. For example, we spend money on haircuts, on newspapers or magazines, on a night out at the movies, renting videos, buying occasional after-school snacks, and so on. If we are not careful, these expenses can quickly add up. For this activity, use your own personal expenses as a model for estimating the personal expenses of members of the families.

C. Keep a daily record of your expenses for 5 days. At the end of that time, total the amount of money you have spent. Then multiply your 5-day total by 6 (to convert the amount to a monthly total). Finally, multiply the monthly total by the number of people in the family to arrive at the personal expenses for each family.

Some families make regular or occasional donations to religious groups or to charities like the American Red Cross or UNESCO.

D. Decide what charitable donations (if any) each of your families make. Choose organizations and causes you would like to support. Choose any amount up to three hundred dollars.

E. For this section of your worksheet, create a chart similar to the one shown here. Copy the food, clothing, personal, and charitable expenses from Exercises A, B, C, and D into the appropriate sections of the chart. Remember to attach the information you have collected to your worksheet.

FOOD, CLOTHING, PERSONAL EXPENSES, CHARITABLE DONATIONS	
	Monthly Cost
Food: Cost for 3 days x 10	
Clothing: Outfit for one person	
Personal: 5-day total x 6	
Charitable Contributions	
To: _____ $ _____ To: _____ $ _____ To: _____ $ _____	
Contributions Total ->	
Total for All Variable Expenses ->	

SECTION 16–5
FITTING IT ALL IN

The budgeting problems our teenagers consider in this chapter do not have simple solutions. In this final section they will begin the difficult task of making the changes in their plans that are necessary when a specific amount of money must meet the needs of a variety of expenses. Some of our young people will find, especially when they leave home and must manage for themselves, "There is always too much month left at the end of my money!"

No matter how well planned the budget is, nor how committed the family is to staying with it, when several people are dependent upon the same income, someone will find some month left at the end of the money. An unexpected expense or added purchase will come along just when the budget is depleted.

Olivia and Maria, Jeff and Hari, Trevor, Daryl, Vernon, Yvette, and Yvonne, have all arrived at an understanding of their family finances. They would perhaps have preferred that their parents just took care of it—as long as they could always buy what they wanted without thinking where the money was coming from. Perhaps some families are operating that way, but most cannot. Parents who are willing to discuss these matters freely and openly with their teenagers, will probably find their teenagers much more willing to be a part of the solution, and less likely to be a part of the problem.

OBJECTIVES: In this section, we will help our teenagers to:

- *look at the reasons a good budget is effective*
- *examine the needs for adjustments within a budget*

BUDGETING PAYS

Some of our teenagers will share with us a few of their thoughts about the benefits of budgeting.

Daryl: Budgets provide an understanding of the individual or family financial condition.

Olivia: Budgets encourage a sensible use of income.

Sylvia: Budgets require examination of goals, values, and priorities.

Maria: Budgets help individuals and families to get maximum value from expenditures.

Freda: Budgets encourage awareness of alternatives.

Trevor: Budgets help individuals or families to live within their current income.

Jeff: Budgets help families or individuals to adjust to irregular or unusual expenditures and to changes in income.

Hari: Budget records are helpful in preparing income tax returns.

**WHEN WHAT
WE HAVE
IS NOT ENOUGH**

Cash shortages can occur in any family because of large, irregular expenses such as insurance, automobile repairs, and clothing. As we saw Trevor's parents doing, you can plan ahead for irregular expenses by setting aside money in a separate **cash-flow savings account.** But there will be times a repair bill or replacement cost will exceed the amount you have set aside. Then you will have to take the money from other parts of the budget.

Adjustment. When adjustments must be made because there still is not enough to go around, every member of the family should participate in the decision making. Young people may have excellent ideas their parents have overlooked. They will most likely be affected by the adjustments that have to be made.

Though every family has its own unique set of budgeting constraints, Maria and Trevor have found a summary of average spending habits for three different income levels prepared by the Bureau of Labor Statistics.

Budget Level			
	Lower	**Intermediate**	**Higher**
Total Budget	$16,809	$25,128	$44,616
Total family consumption	15,736	20,714	30,563
Food	3,309	4,066	5,419
Housing	4,448	5,810	8,516
Clothing	810	1,075	1,851
Transportation	3,377	4,461	6,050
Health care	700	807	1,066
Entertainment	679	916	1,535
Personal care	139	178	272
Other 1,078	1,409	2,612	
Social security and pension	1,195	1,993	3,241
Personal income taxes	1,073	4,414	14,053

Source: Bureau of Labor Statistics, U.S. Department of Labor, Consumer Expenditure Survey, 1984.

**WHO MUST
ADJUST?**

Sylvia is sure that her family is not average in any way. Every time they must make an adjustment in their budget, it means she has to give up something else. The adjustment step in the budget process is supposed to give Sylvia an opportunity to concentrate on ways to get more value out of the money they do have, but she sometimes has doubts.

Sylvia has found the following graph of where the money in family budgets typically goes.

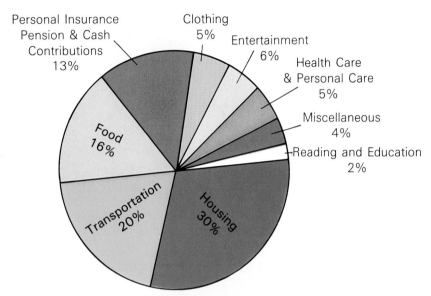

Where the Money Goes: The Distribution of After-Tax Annual Expenditures.
Source: "Consumer Expenditure Survey Results from 1984." *Bureau of Labor Statistics News, USDL 86-258,* 1986.

Sylvia agrees with Jeff when he says that planning a budget is a little like using the space in a closet. We always fill it up no matter how large it is, and there is always something left over that we cannot quite squeeze in. But because the purpose of a budget is to gain control over income and spending, it pays to keep trying.

EXERCISE YOUR SKILLS

_____ Activity 1 _____

Step 8: The Final Monthly Budget

In the activities for Sections 1 through 4, you calculated and estimated income and expenses for three families you chose. Now you will assemble this information into family budgets.

A. Create a budget worksheet like the one on the following page, or create a budget worksheet on a computer, for each of your families. From your worksheets, enter the financial information. Then total the expenses and check that total against the families' actual take-home pay.

B. If any of your families has spent more than its take-home pay, write one or two paragraphs suggesting specific ways that the family could adjust their spending in order to stay within budget.

MONTHLY BUDGET

Income

Salaries and Wages   _____

_____

Total   _____

Expenses

Housing   _____

Food   _____

Clothing   _____

Donations   _____

Savings   _____

Automobile Payments   _____

_____

Other Automobile

Expenses   _____

Utilitities

Water   _____

Gas   _____

Electricity   _____

Credit Payments

Department Store   _____

Charge Cards   _____

Insurance

Life   _____

Homeowner's   _____

Car   _____

Medical   _____

Education   _____

Personal Expenses   _____

Total   _____

EXTEND YOUR UNDERSTANDING
PROJECT 16–1: ELECTRICITY

Electricity is delivered almost invisibly to almost every dwelling in the United States. In some communities, power lines are even buried underground. But the costs of electricity, both direct and indirect, are not inconsequential. First, because our electricity must be made from something else (for instance, water power coal, or nuclear power). Second, because they are among our costs of daily living.

Assignment

1. Make a complete electric appliance inventory of your home, listing all the kitchen appliances, lighting fixtures, radios, televisions, VCRs, hair dryers, computers, and so on. You may be surprised at the length of this list.

2. Ask the person who pays the bills where your household purchases its electricity.

3. How much does the utility company charge its customers per kilowatt hour? Does your utility raise the rates at peak times of the day or year?

4. Find out from the utility how it creates the electricity it sells to you. What are the by-products of generating electricity by this method? What is the effect on our supplies of natural resources?

5. Find out how the electricity reaches your home from the place it is generated.

6. Collect electricity bills for at least three months for your household. Add up the cost and divide by the number of months to find your average monthly cost. Find out whether your usage is higher at certain seasons of the year. How do fluctuations in electricity use affect the household budget?

PROJECT 16–2: COMPARISON SHOPPING FOR GROCERIES

Making the most of your food dollar requires carefully comparing package sizes and prices. You can compare the prices at different stores as well.

Assignment

1. Make a grocery list of 30 items you are going to find prices for at different grocery stores. Include three of each of the following types of food:

   dairy products
   breakfast foods
   canned fruits and vegetables
   fresh fruits and vegetables
   fresh meats
   snack foods
   frozen fruits and vegetables
   frozen dinners or main courses
   fresh bread
   beverages

2. Visit three different grocery stores and record the price of each item on your list. When you visit your first store, be sure to record the brand and size of the items you choose. These must be the same at all three stores. For that reason, do not choose store or generic brands. Record the name and address of each store at the top of your list.

3. On your list, circle the lowest price for each item.

4. Total the cost of the entire list for each store.

5. Answer the following questions:
   Which store had the greatest number of lowest prices?
   Which store had the lowest total cost?
   Which store had the greatest variety of items?
   Which store would you prefer to shop in, and why?

6. Turn in your list of grocery items with prices from three stores, the lowest prices circled and the total costs shown.

Extensions

1. Visit several more stores and include cost comparisons.

2. Make a poster highlighting the values from one store. Show unit prices for the items on sale.

CHAPTER 16 KEY TERMS

CHAPTER 16 REVIEW

Create a monthly Family Budget Worksheet (use the one in the text) for the families considered below. Determine the maximum monthly housing payment if their payments equal 20% of their monthly income. Include monthly automobile, day-care, food, clothing, utilities, and charge card expenses. Subtract total expenses from total income to determine whether the budget balances.

1. The Mendez Family
   Two adults: Vincento, who is 35, and Julin, who is 34.
   Two children: Tom, who is 12, and Maria who is 6.
   Vincento is an engineer and earns $30,000 a year.
   Julin is an elementary school teacher who earns $26,500 a year.
   The family must pay a day-care center for taking care of Maria during the day. This costs them 7% of their monthly income. Their food expenses are 16% of their monthly income. Automobile expenses are 20%, utilities 12%, and clothing 5%. They have no charge card expenses.

2. The Johnson Family
   One adult: Jim, who is 45.
   One child: Jonathan, who is 16.
   Jim is a postal employee and earns $32,500 a year.
   Jonathan is still in high school and has a driver's license.
   The family has two cars. Their total automobile costs are $6,593 per year. Their food costs are 19.5%, and their credit card costs are 10% of their income. They spend approximately $5,500 a year on clothes. The families utilities are 17% of income.

For each item listed below, calculate the unit price and decide which is the best buy in terms of cost.

Item

3.	A	16 oz $1.29	12 oz $1.19	8 oz $0.89
4.	B	14½ oz $1.59	12 oz $1.38	8 oz $0.95
5.	C	6 oz $0.95	10 oz $1.49	12 oz $1.69
6.	D	14½ oz $1.90	6 oz $0.75	16 oz $2.00
7.	E	16 oz $2.15	9 oz $1.15	12 oz $1.75
8.	F	1 quart $1.55	½ gallon $1.89	gallon $2.98
9.	G	32 oz $5.95	18 oz $3.25	1 lb $2.98
10.	H	6 oz $0.95	8 oz $1.29	18 oz $2.50

Using the given budget percentages, determine the weekly, monthly, and yearly budget allotments for the following annual salaries.

	Salary	Budget for wk, mo, yr	Food 16%	Housing 30%	Transportation 20%	Clothing 5%	Pension 13%
11.	$39,000	yr					
		mo					
		wk					
12.	$75,500	yr					
		mo					
		wk					
13.	$45,500	yr					
		mo					
		wk					
14.	$62,400	yr					
		mo					
		wk					
15.	$51,000	yr					
		mo					
		wk					
16.	$42,600	yr					
		mo					
		wk					

1. Create a monthly Family Budget Worksheet for the Gregg family. Determine the maximum monthly housing payment if their housing payment equals 20% of their monthly income. Include monthly automobile, day-care, food, clothing, utilities, and charge card expenses. Subtract total expenses from total income to determine whether the budget balances.

   The Gregg Family
   Two adults: Arnold, who is 42, and Sylvia, who is 43
   Three children: Darrell, who is 17, Ralph, who is 14, and Shari, who is 7
   Arnold is an auto mechanic and earns $29,500 a year.
   Sylvia is a secretary and earns $25,900 a year.
   Darrell is still in high school.
   The family must pay day-care for taking care of Shari during the day. The expenses are 11% of the family's monthly income. Their food expenses are 17% of their income, while credit card costs are 15%. They spend $5,050 a year on utility costs. Their automobile expenses are $4,766 a year, and they spend $500 a month on clothes.

For each item listed below, calculate the unit price and decide which is the best buy in terms of cost.

	Item			
2.	A	16 oz $1.39	14½ oz $1.29	12 oz $1.19
3.	B	32 oz $3.29	16 oz $1.59	12 oz $1.39
4.	C	1 quart $1.65	½ gallon $2.98	gallon $4.20
5.	D	6 oz $0.89	8 oz $0.95	14 oz $1.19

Using the given budget percentages, determine the weekly, monthly, and yearly budget allotments for the following annual salaries.

	Salary	Budget for wk, mo, yr	Food 16%	Housing 30%	Transportation 20%	Clothing 5%	Pension 13%
6.	$36,000	yr					
		mo					
		wk					
7.	$43,500	yr					
		mo					
		wk					

1. Your balance from the first of the month through the 15th was $650. Then you make a payment of $150 on the 16th. You make no more charges or payments through the 31st of the month. Find your average daily balance.

2. Find the whole number of shares that can be bought in the companies listed below if you can spend $90,000 in each company.

   a. Z Mart at $73\frac{5}{8}$ per share
   b. Algin at $33\frac{3}{4}$ per share

3. Use the Tax Rate Schedules X, Y, and Z in the Reference Section of the book to find the tax owed by each of the following.

   a. a married person, filing separately, with $46,945 taxable income
   b. a head of household with $69,450 taxable income

4. Use the Six-Month Basic Rate Schedule in the Reference Section to find the 6-month premium for the following insurance.

   Driving rating factor: 2.25   Collision deductible: $100
   Car class rating: 25   Comprehensive deductible: $50

5. Assume the monthly payment is 28% of the monthly income. Find the total cost of a house based on a monthly income of $3560. Assume a 20% down payment on a 30-year mortgage with 10% interest.

6. Use the amortization table in the Reference Section to calculate the monthly mortgage payment for a condo listed at $79,500, assuming a 20% down payment and a 30-year mortgage at 10% interest. Compare the rental costs ($149/wk) with the monthly mortgage payments.

7. Create a monthly Family Budget Worksheet (use the one in the text) for the Kayoko family. Determine the maximum monthly housing payment if their payments equal 20% of their monthly income. Include monthly automobile, day-care, food, clothing, utilities, and charge card expenses. Subtract total expenses from total income to determine whether the budget balances.

   The Kayoko Family
   Two adults: Saburo, who is 30, and Kato who is 29.
   One child: John, who is 5
   Saburo is a computer programmer and earns $39,500 a year.
   Kato is not employed outside the home. The family has 2 cars which cost them 22% of their monthly income to operate and maintain. They spend $550 a month on food but only 3% of their monthly income on clothes. Their utilities cost them 27% of their monthly income. They have no credit cards.

ASSUMABLE/ $30,000 QUALIFYING LOAN Walk to new elem. school. 3/2/2 with upgraded carpet and vinyl. Window seats in kitchen, new appliances. Great covered patio off kitchen.

ENJOY NOW $72,000 SWIMMING, BOATING... FISHING????Only 2 blocks to lake from this versatile 3/2.5 w/2 large living areas. IMMACULATE condition inside & out. Mstr. w/fg. walk-in closet, top-of-line carpet & appliances. Oversized, fenced yard w/ fruit & pecan trees. Workshop.

SPLISH! SPLASH! $89,900 VACATION AT HOME Spacious 3/2.5, short jog from lake. Large den with fireplace, formal dining & breakfast area in kitchen. All bedrooms up. 32' x 16' gunite diving pool + good-sized yard for entertaining. SUPER BUY!!

BEAUTIFUL FAMILY $34,900 HOME...w/great floor plan. Wonderful location. Walk to school. 3/2/2 with deck and patio. Oak cabinets, window seats, large closets. 2 points paid by seller.

STUNNING HOME... $234,900 In perfect location. Beautiful 3 bdrm, 3 bath home planned for entertaining and comfortable family living. Pool & spa can be viewed from the solarium. Price drastically reduced!!

ATTRACT ATTENTION $299,500 IN...spacious 4/3.5 w/great floor plan. Split bedrooms, raised ceilings, work island in kitchen, fireplace, formal dining, wet bar, wooded lot, lots of extras.

OWNER WANTS $67,900 TO MOVE... to the country. So they are selling this beautiful 3/2/2 with split bedrooms—energy package—corner WBFP—new garage door—new water heater—fresh paint. Be 1st to see.

WELL KEPT!! $50,000 3 bdrms., 1-1/2 baths, 3 car garage with 1 attached garage & 2 detached garages for workshop!

LUXURIOUS MASTER $121,900 SUITE Huge den opens to formal dining! Light & bright! Maintained perfectly throughout! 3-2-2 also has deck & gazebo, sprinkler, rear entry garage & more.

BEAUTIFUL, WELL $103,000 CARED FOR...home in prestigious neighborhood. 3/2/2, extra insulation in well built home. Paneled den w/WBFP. Bring offer!

GORGEOUS $179,900 TRADITIONAL! Professionally decorated and landscaped, 3/2.5/2 living areas,/pool/spa/parquet/French doors/circular drive and 2 WBFP's. Pre-foreclosure/Make offer!

CANYON CREEK $130,000 CHARMER 5 bedrooms, POOL, updated carpet and papers. Near Country Club and Golf Course, 3.5 baths, large lot, gracious home.

2628 REGAL $109,900 Large 4 BR, 3 bath, 2 story home in great location. HAS 3 LIVING AREAS! Close to K-12 grades and shopping centers. STORM WINDOWS AND DOORS!

Bills

The McGrew Family's Bills

Gas $100
Electric $50
Water $10
Charge Card #1 $100
Charge Card #2 $50

The Isobe Family's Bills

Gas $50
Electric $30
Water $20
Charge Card #1 $75
Charge Card #2 $150

The Scovil Family's Bills

Gas $125
Electric $40
Water $15
Charge Card #1 $120
Charge Card #2 $140

The Lopez Family's Bills

Gas $50
Electric $35
Water $10
Charge Card #1 $20
Charge Card #2 $90

The Betts Family's Bills

Gas $50
Electric $25
Water $10
Charge Card #1 $20
Charge Card #2 $0

The Walker Family's Bills

Gas $30
Electric $40
Water $10
Charge Card #1 $90
Charge Card #2 $90

Insurance Tables

ANNUAL GROUP MEDICAL INSURANCE PREMIUMS
One person ....$300.00 annual
Two people ....$500.00 annual
Three people ....$600.00 annual
Four or more people ....$700.00 annual

ANNUAL LIFE INSURANCE PREMIUM RATES PER $1000		
	Cost per $1000	
Age	**Male**	**Female**
20–24	$15.07	$14.03
25–29	$17.08	$15.75
30–34	$19.63	$17.50
35–39	$22.24	$21.00
40–44	$27.19	$26.74
45–49	$32.36	$31.50
50–54	$40.73	$40.02
55–59	$49.34	$48.70
60–64	$62.00	$61.45
65–69	$75.00	$74.50
70–74	$100.25	$100.01
75–79	$125.30	$124.90

6-MONTH CAR INSURANCE PREMIUMS		
Age of Driver	**Male**	**Female**
Under 22	$500	$300
23–28	$300	$250
Over 28	$250	$250

REFERENCE SECTION

USE OF THE GRAPHING CALCULATOR

Many of the activities in the *Mathematics of Money* course lend themselves to the use of the graphing calculator. If you are just getting acquainted with this kind of calculator, the following instructions may be useful to you.

Step One   Use the RANGE key to set the parameters and the scale of a plot.

1. Press the RANGE key. A list of values will appear on the screen. They show the number of units on each axis and an approximate scale factor for each axis.

2. Change these values by using the arrow keys to move from line to line or right to left.

3. Then use the EXE key to lock the new values into the memory of the calculator.

Step Two   Plot two points and graph the line segment between them.

1. Plot a point by using the SHIFT PLOT EXE keys in sequence. Do this twice.

2. Draw a segment to connect the two points by pressing the SHIFT LINE EXE keys in sequence.

Step Three   Graph a line, given the equation of a line.

1. Set the parameters for the graph.

2. Press the GRAPH key. The screen displays y = .

3. Enter the rest of the equation. You may need to use the ALPHA key to enter the variable *x*.

4. Press EXE . The graph will appear.

Sample A   Draw the line determined by the points (2,5) and (-4,3).

1. Press RANGE .
   Set the parameters for the *x*-axis at -5 and 5.
   Set the parameters for the *y*-axis at -6 and 6.
   Set the scale factor for both axes at 1.
   The resulting display will look like this:
   XMIN: -5
   XMAX: 5
   SCL: 1
   YMIN: -6

YMAX: 6
SCL: 1

2. Plot the points. As each point is plotted, a flashing light will appear on the screen at the location of the point.
   Press SHIFT PLOT 2 SHIFT , 5 EXE
   SHIFT PLOT (-) 4 SHIFT , 3 EXE
   Draw the line. Press SHIFT LINE EXE

The following graph will appear.

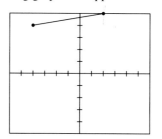

Sample B   Draw the graph of $y = 2x - 1$.

1. Set the parameters for the graph.
   RANGE   XMIN: -2   XMAX: 3
   SCL: 1
          YMIN: -3   YMAX: 4   SCL: 1

2. Press GRAPH .
   $y =$

3. Enter the equation.
   $y = 2x - 1$
   You may need to use the ALPHA key to enter the variable *x*. If you make an error entering the equation, use the arrow keys to correct it.

4. Press the EXE key. The following graph will appear.

Internal Revenue Service Tables:
Federal Income Tax Withholding Table

SINGLE Persons–WEEKLY Payroll Period

(For Wages Paid After December 19_ _)

And the wages are–		And the number of withholding allowances claimed is–										
At least	But less than	0	1	2	3	4	5	6	7	8	9	10
		The amount of income tax to be withheld shall be–										
$0	$25	$0	$0	$0	$0	$0	$0	$0	$0	$0	$0	$0
25	30	1	0	0	0	0	0	0	0	0	0	0
30	35	1	0	0	0	0	0	0	0	0	0	0
35	40	2	0	0	0	0	0	0	0	0	0	0
40	45	3	0	0	0	0	0	0	0	0	0	0
45	50	4	0	0	0	0	0	0	0	0	0	0
50	55	4	0	0	0	0	0	0	0	0	0	0
55	60	5	0	0	0	0	0	0	0	0	0	0
60	65	6	0	0	0	0	0	0	0	0	0	0
65	70	7	1	0	0	0	0	0	0	0	0	0
70	75	7	2	0	0	0	0	0	0	0	0	0
75	80	8	2	0	0	0	0	0	0	0	0	0
80	85	9	3	0	0	0	0	0	0	0	0	0
85	90	10	4	0	0	0	0	0	0	0	0	0
90	95	10	5	0	0	0	0	0	0	0	0	0
95	100	11	5	0	0	0	0	0	0	0	0	0
100	105	12	6	0	0	0	0	0	0	0	0	0
105	110	13	7	1	0	0	0	0	0	0	0	0
110	115	13	8	2	0	0	0	0	0	0	0	0
115	120	14	8	2	0	0	0	0	0	0	0	0
120	125	15	9	3	0	0	0	0	0	0	0	0
125	130	16	10	4	0	0	0	0	0	0	0	0
130	135	16	11	5	0	0	0	0	0	0	0	0
135	140	17	11	5	0	0	0	0	0	0	0	0
140	145	18	12	6	0	0	0	0	0	0	0	0
145	150	19	13	7	1	0	0	0	0	0	0	0
150	155	19	14	8	2	0	0	0	0	0	0	0
155	160	20	14	8	2	0	0	0	0	0	0	0
160	165	21	15	9	3	0	0	0	0	0	0	0
165	170	22	16	10	4	0	0	0	0	0	0	0
170	175	22	17	11	5	0	0	0	0	0	0	0
175	180	23	17	11	5	0	0	0	0	0	0	0
180	185	24	18	12	6	0	0	0	0	0	0	0
185	190	25	19	13	7	1	0	0	0	0	0	0
190	195	25	20	14	8	2	0	0	0	0	0	0
195	200	26	20	14	8	3	0	0	0	0	0	0
200	210	27	21	15	10	4	0	0	0	0	0	0
210	220	29	23	17	11	5	0	0	0	0	0	0
220	230	30	24	18	13	7	1	0	0	0	0	0
230	240	32	26	20	14	8	2	0	0	0	0	0
240	250	33	27	21	16	10	4	0	0	0	0	0
250	260	35	29	23	17	11	5	0	0	0	0	0
260	270	36	30	24	19	13	7	1	0	0	0	0
270	280	38	32	26	20	14	8	2	0	0	0	0
280	290	39	33	27	22	16	10	4	0	0	0	0
290	300	41	35	29	23	17	11	5	0	0	0	0
300	310	42	36	30	25	19	13	7	1	0	0	0
310	320	44	38	32	26	20	14	8	2	0	0	0
320	330	45	39	33	28	22	16	10	4	0	0	0
330	340	47	41	35	29	23	17	11	5	0	0	0
340	350	48	42	36	31	25	19	13	7	1	0	0
350	360	50	44	38	32	26	20	14	8	2	0	0
360	370	51	45	39	34	28	22	16	10	4	0	0
370	380	53	47	41	35	29	23	17	11	5	0	0
380	390	54	48	42	37	31	25	19	13	7	1	0
390	400	56	50	44	38	32	26	20	14	8	3	0
400	410	58	51	45	40	34	28	22	16	10	4	0
410	420	61	53	47	41	35	29	23	17	11	6	0
420	430	64	54	48	43	37	31	25	19	13	7	1
430	440	67	56	50	44	38	32	26	20	14	9	3
440	450	70	58	51	46	40	34	28	22	16	10	4
450	460	72	61	53	47	41	35	29	23	17	12	6
460	470	75	64	54	49	43	37	31	25	19	13	7
470	480	78	67	56	50	44	38	32	26	20	15	9
480	490	81	70	59	52	46	40	34	28	22	16	10
490	500	84	72	61	53	47	41	35	29	23	18	12
500	510	86	75	64	55	49	43	37	31	25	19	13
510	520	89	78	67	56	50	44	38	32	26	21	15
520	530	92	81	70	59	52	46	40	34	28	22	16
530	540	95	84	73	62	53	47	41	35	29	24	18

(Continued on next page)

Internal Revenue Service Tables:
Federal Income Tax Withholding Table

SINGLE Persons–WEEKLY Payroll Period
(For Wages Paid After December 19_ _)

And the wages are–		And the number of withholding allowances claimed is–										
At least	But less than	0	1	2	3	4	5	6	7	8	9	10
		The amount of income tax to be withheld shall be–										
$540	$550	$98	$86	$75	$64	$55	$49	$43	$37	$31	$25	$19
550	560	100	89	78	67	56	50	44	38	32	27	21
560	570	103	92	81	70	59	52	46	40	34	28	22
570	580	106	95	84	73	62	53	47	41	35	30	24
580	590	109	98	87	76	65	55	49	43	37	31	25
590	600	112	100	89	78	67	56	50	44	38	33	27
600	610	114	103	92	81	70	59	52	46	40	34	28
610	620	117	106	95	84	73	62	53	47	41	36	30
620	630	120	109	98	87	76	65	55	49	43	37	31
630	640	123	112	101	90	79	68	56	50	44	39	33
640	650	126	114	103	92	81	70	59	52	46	40	34
650	660	128	117	106	95	84	73	62	53	47	42	36
660	670	131	120	109	98	87	76	65	55	49	43	37
670	680	134	123	112	101	90	79	68	57	50	45	39
680	690	137	126	115	104	93	82	70	59	52	46	40
690	700	140	128	117	106	95	84	73	62	53	48	42
700	710	142	131	120	109	98	87	76	65	55	49	43
710	720	145	134	123	112	101	90	79	68	57	51	45
720	730	148	137	126	115	104	93	82	71	60	52	46
730	740	151	140	129	118	107	96	84	73	62	54	48
740	750	154	142	131	120	109	98	87	76	65	55	49
750	760	156	145	134	123	112	101	90	79	68	57	51
760	770	159	148	137	126	115	104	93	82	71	60	52
770	780	162	151	140	129	118	107	96	85	74	63	54
780	790	165	154	143	132	121	110	98	87	76	65	55
790	800	168	156	145	134	123	112	101	90	79	68	57
800	810	170	159	148	137	126	115	104	93	82	71	60
810	820	173	162	151	140	129	118	107	96	85	74	63
820	830	176	165	154	143	132	121	110	99	88	77	66
830	840	179	168	157	146	135	124	112	101	90	79	68
840	850	182	170	159	148	137	126	115	104	93	82	71
850	860	184	173	162	151	140	129	118	107	96	85	74
860	870	187	176	165	154	143	132	121	110	99	88	77
870	880	190	179	168	157	146	135	124	113	102	91	80
880	890	193	182	171	160	149	138	126	115	104	93	82
890	900	196	184	173	162	151	140	129	118	107	96	85
900	910	198	187	176	165	154	143	132	121	110	99	88
910	920	201	190	179	168	157	146	135	124	113	102	91
920	930	204	193	182	171	160	149	138	127	116	105	94
930	940	207	196	185	174	163	152	140	129	118	107	96
940	950	210	198	187	176	165	154	143	132	121	110	99
950	960	214	201	190	179	168	157	146	135	124	113	102
960	970	217	204	193	182	171	160	149	138	127	116	105
970	980	220	207	196	185	174	163	152	141	130	119	108
980	990	224	211	199	188	177	166	154	143	132	121	110
990	1,000	227	214	201	190	179	168	157	146	135	124	113
1,000	1,010	230	217	204	193	182	171	160	149	138	127	116
1,010	1,020	233	220	207	196	185	174	163	152	141	130	119
1,020	1,030	237	224	211	199	188	177	166	155	144	133	122
1,030	1,040	240	227	214	202	191	180	168	157	146	135	124
1,040	1,050	243	230	217	204	193	182	171	160	149	138	127
1,050	1,060	247	234	221	208	196	185	174	163	152	141	130
1,060	1,070	250	237	224	211	199	188	177	166	155	144	133
1,070	1,080	253	240	227	214	202	191	180	169	158	147	136
1,080	1,090	257	244	231	218	205	194	182	171	160	149	138
1,090	1,100	260	247	234	221	208	196	185	174	163	152	141
1,100	1,110	263	250	237	224	211	199	188	177	166	155	144
1,110	1,120	266	253	240	227	214	202	191	180	169	158	147
1,120	1,130	270	257	244	231	218	205	194	183	172	161	150
1,130	1,140	273	260	247	234	221	208	196	185	174	163	152
1,140	1,150	276	263	250	237	224	211	199	188	177	166	155
1,150	1,160	280	267	254	241	228	215	202	191	180	169	158
1,160	1,170	283	270	257	244	231	218	205	194	183	172	161
1,170	1,180	286	273	260	247	234	221	208	197	186	175	164
1,180	1,190	290	277	264	251	238	225	212	199	188	177	166
1,190	1,200	293	280	267	254	241	228	215	202	191	180	169

$1,200 and over   Use Table 1(a) for a **SINGLE person** on page 22. Also see the instructions on page 20.

SINGLE Persons–MONTHLY Payroll Period

(For Wages Paid After December 19_ _)

And the wages are–		And the number of withholding allowances claimed is–										
At least	But less than	0	1	2	3	4	5	6	7	8	9	10
		The amount of income tax to be withheld shall be–										
$0	$105	$0	$0	$0	$0	$0	$0	$0	$0	$0	$0	$0
105	110	1	0	0	0	0	0	0	0	0	0	0
110	115	2	0	0	0	0	0	0	0	0	0	0
115	120	3	0	0	0	0	0	0	0	0	0	0
120	125	3	0	0	0	0	0	0	0	0	0	0
125	130	4	0	0	0	0	0	0	0	0	0	0
130	135	5	0	0	0	0	0	0	0	0	0	0
135	140	6	0	0	0	0	0	0	0	0	0	0
140	145	6	0	0	0	0	0	0	0	0	0	0
145	150	7	0	0	0	0	0	0	0	0	0	0
150	160	8	0	0	0	0	0	0	0	0	0	0
160	170	10	0	0	0	0	0	0	0	0	0	0
170	180	11	0	0	0	0	0	0	0	0	0	0
180	190	13	0	0	0	0	0	0	0	0	0	0
190	200	14	0	0	0	0	0	0	0	0	0	0
200	210	16	0	0	0	0	0	0	0	0	0	0
210	220	17	0	0	0	0	0	0	0	0	0	0
220	230	19	0	0	0	0	0	0	0	0	0	0
230	240	20	0	0	0	0	0	0	0	0	0	0
240	250	22	0	0	0	0	0	0	0	0	0	0
250	260	23	0	0	0	0	0	0	0	0	0	0
260	270	25	0	0	0	0	0	0	0	0	0	0
270	280	26	1	0	0	0	0	0	0	0	0	0
280	290	28	2	0	0	0	0	0	0	0	0	0
290	300	29	4	0	0	0	0	0	0	0	0	0
300	320	32	6	0	0	0	0	0	0	0	0	0
320	340	35	9	0	0	0	0	0	0	0	0	0
340	360	38	12	0	0	0	0	0	0	0	0	0
360	380	41	15	0	0	0	0	0	0	0	0	0
380	400	44	18	0	0	0	0	0	0	0	0	0
400	420	47	21	0	0	0	0	0	0	0	0	0
420	440	50	24	0	0	0	0	0	0	0	0	0
440	460	53	27	1	0	0	0	0	0	0	0	0
460	480	56	30	4	0	0	0	0	0	0	0	0
480	500	59	33	7	0	0	0	0	0	0	0	0
500	520	62	36	10	0	0	0	0	0	0	0	0
520	540	65	39	13	0	0	0	0	0	0	0	0
540	560	68	42	16	0	0	0	0	0	0	0	0
560	580	71	45	19	0	0	0	0	0	0	0	0
580	600	74	48	22	0	0	0	0	0	0	0	0
600	640	78	52	27	1	0	0	0	0	0	0	0
640	680	84	58	33	7	0	0	0	0	0	0	0
680	720	90	64	39	13	0	0	0	0	0	0	0
720	760	96	70	45	19	0	0	0	0	0	0	0
760	800	102	76	51	25	0	0	0	0	0	0	0
800	840	108	82	57	31	6	0	0	0	0	0	0
840	880	114	88	63	37	12	0	0	0	0	0	0
880	920	120	94	69	43	18	0	0	0	0	0	0
920	960	126	100	75	49	24	0	0	0	0	0	0
960	1,000	132	106	81	55	30	4	0	0	0	0	0
1,000	1,040	138	112	87	61	36	10	0	0	0	0	0
1,040	1,080	144	118	93	67	42	16	0	0	0	0	0
1,080	1,120	150	124	99	73	48	22	0	0	0	0	0
1,120	1,160	156	130	105	79	54	28	2	0	0	0	0
1,160	1,200	162	136	111	85	60	34	8	0	0	0	0
1,200	1,240	168	142	117	91	66	40	14	0	0	0	0
1,240	1,280	174	148	123	97	72	46	20	0	0	0	0
1,280	1,320	180	154	129	103	78	52	26	1	0	0	0
1,320	1,360	186	160	135	109	84	58	32	7	0	0	0
1,360	1,400	192	166	141	115	90	64	38	13	0	0	0
1,400	1,440	198	172	147	121	96	70	44	19	0	0	0
1,440	1,480	204	178	153	127	102	76	50	25	0	0	0
1,480	1,520	210	184	159	133	108	82	56	31	5	0	0
1,520	1,560	216	190	165	139	114	88	62	37	11	0	0
1,560	1,600	222	196	171	145	120	94	68	43	17	0	0
1,600	1,640	228	202	177	151	126	100	74	49	23	0	0
1,640	1,680	234	208	183	157	132	106	80	55	29	3	0
1,680	1,720	240	214	189	163	138	112	86	61	35	9	0
1,720	1,760	248	220	195	169	144	118	92	67	41	15	0

(Continued on next page)

Internal Revenue Service Tables:
Federal Income Tax Withholding Table

SINGLE Persons–MONTHLY Payroll Period
(For Wages Paid After December 19_ _)

And the wages are–		And the number of withholding allowances claimed is–										
At least	But less than	0	1	2	3	4	5	6	7	8	9	10
		The amount of income tax to be withheld shall be–										
$1,760	$1,800	$260	$226	$201	$175	$150	$124	$98	$73	$47	$21	$0
1,800	1,840	271	232	207	181	156	130	104	79	53	27	2
1,840	1,880	282	238	213	187	162	136	110	85	59	33	8
1,880	1,920	293	245	219	193	168	142	116	91	65	39	14
1,920	1,960	304	257	225	199	174	148	122	97	71	45	20
1,960	2,000	316	268	231	205	180	154	128	103	77	51	26
2,000	2,040	327	279	237	211	186	160	134	109	83	57	32
2,040	2,080	338	290	243	217	192	166	140	115	89	63	38
2,080	2,120	349	301	254	223	198	172	146	121	95	69	44
2,120	2,160	360	313	265	229	204	178	152	127	101	75	50
2,160	2,200	372	324	276	235	210	184	158	133	107	81	56
2,200	2,240	383	335	287	241	216	190	164	139	113	87	62
2,240	2,280	394	346	298	251	222	196	170	145	119	93	68
2,280	2,320	405	357	310	262	228	202	176	151	125	99	74
2,320	2,360	416	369	321	273	234	208	182	157	131	105	80
2,360	2,400	428	380	332	284	240	214	188	163	137	111	86
2,400	2,440	439	391	343	295	248	220	194	169	143	117	92
2,440	2,480	450	402	354	307	259	226	200	175	149	123	98
2,480	2,520	461	413	366	318	270	232	206	181	155	129	104
2,520	2,560	472	425	377	329	281	238	212	187	161	135	110
2,560	2,600	484	436	388	340	292	245	218	193	167	141	116
2,600	2,640	495	447	399	351	304	256	224	199	173	147	122
2,640	2,680	506	458	410	363	315	267	230	205	179	153	128
2,680	2,720	517	469	422	374	326	278	236	211	185	159	134
2,720	2,760	528	481	433	385	337	289	242	217	191	165	140
2,760	2,800	540	492	444	396	348	301	253	223	197	171	146
2,800	2,840	551	503	455	407	360	312	264	229	203	177	152
2,840	2,880	562	514	466	419	371	323	275	235	209	183	158
2,880	2,920	573	525	478	430	382	334	286	241	215	189	164
2,920	2,960	584	537	489	441	393	345	297	250	221	195	170
2,960	3,000	596	548	500	452	404	357	309	261	227	201	176
3,000	3,040	607	559	511	463	416	368	320	272	233	207	182
3,040	3,080	618	570	522	475	427	379	331	283	239	213	188
3,080	3,120	629	581	534	486	438	390	342	294	247	219	194
3,120	3,160	640	593	545	497	449	401	353	306	258	225	200
3,160	3,200	652	604	556	508	460	413	365	317	269	231	206
3,200	3,240	663	615	567	519	472	424	376	328	280	237	212
3,240	3,280	674	626	578	531	483	435	387	339	291	244	218
3,280	3,320	685	637	590	542	494	446	398	350	303	255	224
3,320	3,360	696	649	601	553	505	457	409	362	314	266	230
3,360	3,400	708	660	612	564	516	469	421	373	325	277	236
3,400	3,440	719	671	623	575	528	480	432	384	336	288	242
3,440	3,480	730	682	634	587	539	491	443	395	347	300	252
3,480	3,520	741	693	646	598	550	502	454	406	359	311	263
3,520	3,560	752	705	657	609	561	513	465	418	370	322	274
3,560	3,600	764	716	668	620	572	525	477	429	381	333	285
3,600	3,640	775	727	679	631	584	536	488	440	392	344	297
3,640	3,680	786	738	690	643	595	547	499	451	403	356	308
3,680	3,720	797	749	702	654	606	558	510	462	415	367	319
3,720	3,760	808	761	713	665	617	569	521	474	426	378	330
3,760	3,800	820	772	724	676	628	581	533	485	437	389	341
3,800	3,840	831	783	735	687	640	592	544	496	448	400	353
3,840	3,880	842	794	746	699	651	603	555	507	459	412	364
3,880	3,920	853	805	758	710	662	614	566	518	471	423	375
3,920	3,960	864	817	769	721	673	625	577	530	482	434	386
3,960	4,000	876	828	780	732	684	637	589	541	493	445	397
4,000	4,040	887	839	791	743	696	648	600	552	504	456	409
4,040	4,080	900	850	802	755	707	659	611	563	515	468	420
4,080	4,120	913	861	814	766	718	670	622	574	527	479	431
4,120	4,160	926	873	825	777	729	681	633	586	538	490	442
4,160	4,200	940	884	836	788	740	693	645	597	549	501	453
4,200	4,240	953	896	847	799	752	704	656	608	560	512	465
4,240	4,280	966	910	858	811	763	715	667	619	571	524	476
4,280	4,320	979	923	870	822	774	726	678	630	583	535	487
4,320	4,360	992	936	881	833	785	737	689	642	594	546	498

$4,360 and over   Use Table 4(a) for a **SINGLE person** on page 22. Also see the instructions on page 20.

Internal Revenue Service Tables:
Federal Income Tax Withholding Table

MARRIED Persons–MONTHLY Payroll Period
(For Wages Paid After December 19_ _)

And the wages are–		And the number of withholding allowances claimed is–										
At least	But less than	0	1	2	3	4	5	6	7	8	9	10
		The amount of income tax to be withheld shall be–										
$0	$290	$0	$0	$0	$0	$0	$0	$0	$0	$0	$0	$0
290	300	2	0	0	0	0	0	0	0	0	0	0
300	320	4	0	0	0	0	0	0	0	0	0	0
320	340	7	0	0	0	0	0	0	0	0	0	0
340	360	10	0	0	0	0	0	0	0	0	0	0
360	380	13	0	0	0	0	0	0	0	0	0	0
380	400	16	0	0	0	0	0	0	0	0	0	0
400	420	19	0	0	0	0	0	0	0	0	0	0
420	440	22	0	0	0	0	0	0	0	0	0	0
440	460	25	0	0	0	0	0	0	0	0	0	0
460	480	28	2	0	0	0	0	0	0	0	0	0
480	500	31	5	0	0	0	0	0	0	0	0	0
500	520	34	8	0	0	0	0	0	0	0	0	0
520	540	37	11	0	0	0	0	0	0	0	0	0
540	560	40	14	0	0	0	0	0	0	0	0	0
560	580	43	17	0	0	0	0	0	0	0	0	0
580	600	46	20	0	0	0	0	0	0	0	0	0
600	640	51	25	0	0	0	0	0	0	0	0	0
640	680	57	31	5	0	0	0	0	0	0	0	0
680	720	63	37	11	0	0	0	0	0	0	0	0
720	760	69	43	17	0	0	0	0	0	0	0	0
760	800	75	49	23	0	0	0	0	0	0	0	0
800	840	81	55	29	4	0	0	0	0	0	0	0
840	880	87	61	35	10	0	0	0	0	0	0	0
880	920	93	67	41	16	0	0	0	0	0	0	0
920	960	99	73	47	22	0	0	0	0	0	0	0
960	1,000	105	79	53	28	2	0	0	0	0	0	0
1,000	1,040	111	85	59	34	8	0	0	0	0	0	0
1,040	1,080	117	91	65	40	14	0	0	0	0	0	0
1,080	1,120	123	97	71	46	20	0	0	0	0	0	0
1,120	1,160	129	103	77	52	26	0	0	0	0	0	0
1,160	1,200	135	109	83	58	32	6	0	0	0	0	0
1,200	1,240	141	115	89	64	38	12	0	0	0	0	0
1,240	1,280	147	121	95	70	44	18	0	0	0	0	0
1,280	1,320	153	127	101	76	50	24	0	0	0	0	0
1,320	1,360	159	133	107	82	56	30	5	0	0	0	0
1,360	1,400	165	139	113	88	62	36	11	0	0	0	0
1,400	1,440	171	145	119	94	68	42	17	0	0	0	0
1,440	1,480	177	151	125	100	74	48	23	0	0	0	0
1,480	1,520	183	157	131	106	80	54	29	3	0	0	0
1,520	1,560	189	163	137	112	86	60	35	9	0	0	0
1,560	1,600	195	169	143	118	92	66	41	15	0	0	0
1,600	1,640	201	175	149	124	98	72	47	21	0	0	0
1,640	1,680	207	181	155	130	104	78	53	27	2	0	0
1,680	1,720	213	187	161	136	110	84	59	33	8	0	0
1,720	1,760	219	193	167	142	116	90	65	39	14	0	0
1,760	1,800	225	199	173	148	122	96	71	45	20	0	0
1,800	1,840	231	205	179	154	128	102	77	51	26	0	0
1,840	1,880	237	211	185	160	134	108	83	57	32	6	0
1,880	1,920	243	217	191	166	140	114	89	63	38	12	0
1,920	1,960	249	223	197	172	146	120	95	69	44	18	0
1,960	2,000	255	229	203	178	152	126	101	75	50	24	0
2,000	2,040	261	235	209	184	158	132	107	81	56	30	4
2,040	2,080	267	241	215	190	164	138	113	87	62	36	10
2,080	2,120	273	247	221	196	170	144	119	93	68	42	16
2,120	2,160	279	253	227	202	176	150	125	99	74	48	22
2,160	2,200	285	259	233	208	182	156	131	105	80	54	28
2,200	2,240	291	265	239	214	188	162	137	111	86	60	34
2,240	2,280	297	271	245	220	194	168	143	117	92	66	40
2,280	2,320	303	277	251	226	200	174	149	123	98	72	46
2,320	2,360	309	283	257	232	206	180	155	129	104	78	52
2,360	2,400	315	289	263	238	212	186	161	135	110	84	58
2,400	2,440	321	295	269	244	218	192	167	141	116	90	64
2,440	2,480	327	301	275	250	224	198	173	147	122	96	70
2,480	2,520	333	307	281	256	230	204	179	153	128	102	76
2,520	2,560	339	313	287	262	236	210	185	159	134	108	82
2,560	2,600	345	319	293	268	242	216	191	165	140	114	88
2,600	2,640	351	325	299	274	248	222	197	171	146	120	94
2,640	2,680	357	331	305	280	254	228	203	177	152	126	100
2,680	2,720	363	337	311	286	260	234	209	183	158	132	106

(Continued on next page)

MARRIED Persons–MONTHLY Payroll Period

(For Wages Paid After December 19_ _)

And the wages are–		And the number of withholding allowances claimed is–										
At least	But less than	0	1	2	3	4	5	6	7	8	9	10
		The amount of income tax to be withheld shall be–										
$2,720	$2,760	$369	$343	$317	$292	$266	$240	$215	$189	$164	$138	$112
2,760	2,800	375	349	323	298	272	246	221	195	170	144	118
2,800	2,840	381	355	329	304	278	252	227	201	176	150	124
2,840	2,880	387	361	335	310	284	258	233	207	182	156	130
2,880	2,920	393	367	341	316	290	264	239	213	188	162	136
2,920	2,960	399	373	347	322	296	270	245	219	194	168	142
2,960	3,000	405	379	353	328	302	276	251	225	200	174	148
3,000	3,040	415	385	359	334	308	282	257	231	206	180	154
3,040	3,080	426	391	365	340	314	288	263	237	212	186	160
3,080	3,120	437	397	371	346	320	294	269	243	218	192	166
3,120	3,160	448	403	377	352	326	300	275	249	224	198	172
3,160	3,200	460	412	383	358	332	306	281	255	230	204	178
3,200	3,240	471	423	389	364	338	312	287	261	236	210	184
3,240	3,280	482	434	395	370	344	318	293	267	242	216	190
3,280	3,320	493	445	401	376	350	324	299	273	248	222	196
3,320	3,360	504	456	409	382	356	330	305	279	254	228	202
3,360	3,400	516	468	420	388	362	336	311	285	260	234	208
3,400	3,440	527	479	431	394	368	342	317	291	266	240	214
3,440	3,480	538	490	442	400	374	348	323	297	272	246	220
3,480	3,520	549	501	453	406	380	354	329	303	278	252	226
3,520	3,560	560	512	465	417	386	360	335	309	284	258	232
3,560	3,600	572	524	476	428	392	366	341	315	290	264	238
3,600	3,640	583	535	487	439	398	372	347	321	296	270	244
3,640	3,680	594	546	498	450	404	378	353	327	302	276	250
3,680	3,720	605	557	509	462	414	384	359	333	308	282	256
3,720	3,760	616	568	521	473	425	390	365	339	314	288	262
3,760	3,800	628	580	532	484	436	396	371	345	320	294	268
3,800	3,840	639	591	543	495	447	402	377	351	326	300	274
3,840	3,880	650	602	554	506	459	411	383	357	332	306	280
3,880	3,920	661	613	565	518	470	422	389	363	338	312	286
3,920	3,960	672	624	577	529	481	433	395	369	344	318	292
3,960	4,000	684	636	588	540	492	444	401	375	350	324	298
4,000	4,040	695	647	599	551	503	456	408	381	356	330	304
4,040	4,080	706	658	610	562	515	467	419	387	362	336	310
4,080	4,120	717	669	621	574	526	478	430	393	368	342	316
4,120	4,160	728	680	633	585	537	489	441	399	374	348	322
4,160	4,200	740	692	644	596	548	500	453	405	380	354	328
4,200	4,240	751	703	655	607	559	512	464	416	386	360	334
4,240	4,280	762	714	666	618	571	523	475	427	392	366	340
4,280	4,320	773	725	677	630	582	534	486	438	398	372	346
4,320	4,360	784	736	689	641	593	545	497	449	404	378	352
4,360	4,400	796	748	700	652	604	556	509	461	413	384	358
4,400	4,440	807	759	711	663	615	568	520	472	424	390	364
4,440	4,480	818	770	722	674	627	579	531	483	435	396	370
4,480	4,520	829	781	733	686	638	590	542	494	446	402	376
4,520	4,560	840	792	745	697	649	601	553	505	458	410	382
4,560	4,600	852	804	756	708	660	612	565	517	469	421	388
4,600	4,640	863	815	767	719	671	624	576	528	480	432	394
4,640	4,680	874	826	778	730	683	635	587	539	491	443	400
4,680	4,720	885	837	789	742	694	646	598	550	502	455	407
4,720	4,760	896	848	801	753	705	657	609	561	514	466	418
4,760	4,800	908	860	812	764	716	668	621	573	525	477	429
4,800	4,840	919	871	823	775	727	680	632	584	536	488	440
4,840	4,880	930	882	834	786	739	691	643	595	547	499	452
4,880	4,920	941	893	845	798	750	702	654	606	558	511	463
4,920	4,960	952	904	857	809	761	713	665	617	570	522	474
4,960	5,000	964	916	868	820	772	724	677	629	581	533	485
5,000	5,040	975	927	879	831	783	736	688	640	592	544	496
5,040	5,080	986	938	890	842	795	747	699	651	603	555	508
5,080	5,120	997	949	901	854	806	758	710	662	614	567	519
5,120	5,160	1,008	960	913	865	817	769	721	673	626	578	530
5,160	5,200	1,020	972	924	876	828	780	733	685	637	589	541
5,200	5,240	1,031	983	935	887	839	792	744	696	648	600	552
5,240	5,280	1,042	994	946	898	851	803	755	707	659	611	564
5,280	5,320	1,053	1,005	957	910	862	814	766	718	670	623	575

$5,320 and over   Use Table 4(b) for a **MARRIED person** on page 22. Also see the instructions on page 20.

7.65% Social Security Employee Tax Table for 19_ _

Wages at least	But less than	Tax to be withheld	Wages at least	But less than	Tax to be withheld	Wages at least	But less than	Tax to be withheld	Wages at least	But less than	Tax to be withheld
$0.00	$0.07	$0.00	12.75	12.88	.98	25.56	25.69	1.96	38.37	38.50	2.94
.07	.20	.01	12.88	13.01	.99	25.69	25.82	1.97	38.50	38.63	2.95
.20	.33	.02	13.01	13.14	1.00	25.82	25.95	1.98	38.63	38.76	2.96
.33	.46	.03	13.14	13.27	1.01	25.95	26.08	1.99	38.76	38.89	2.97
.46	.59	.04	13.27	13.40	1.02	26.08	26.21	2.00	38.89	39.02	2.98
.59	.72	.05	13.40	13.53	1.03	26.21	26.34	2.01	39.02	39.16	2.99
.72	.85	.06	13.53	13.67	1.04	26.34	26.48	2.02	39.16	39.29	3.00
.85	.99	.07	13.67	13.80	1.05	26.48	26.61	2.03	39.29	39.42	3.01
.99	1.12	.08	13.80	13.93	1.06	26.61	26.74	2.04	39.42	39.55	3.02
1.12	1.25	.09	13.93	14.06	1.07	26.74	26.87	2.05	39.55	39.68	3.03
1.25	1.38	.10	14.06	14.19	1.08	26.87	27.00	2.06	39.68	39.81	3.04
1.38	1.51	.11	14.19	14.32	1.09	27.00	27.13	2.07	39.81	39.94	3.05
1.51	1.64	.12	14.32	14.45	1.10	27.13	27.26	2.08	39.94	40.07	3.06
1.64	1.77	.13	14.45	14.58	1.11	27.26	27.39	2.09	40.07	40.20	3.07
1.77	1.90	.14	14.58	14.71	1.12	27.39	27.52	2.10	40.20	40.33	3.08
1.90	2.03	.15	14.71	14.84	1.13	27.52	27.65	2.11	40.33	40.46	3.09
2.03	2.16	.16	14.84	14.97	1.14	27.65	27.78	2.12	40.46	40.59	3.10
2.16	2.29	.17	14.97	15.10	1.15	27.78	27.91	2.13	40.59	40.72	3.11
2.29	2.42	.18	15.10	15.23	1.16	27.91	28.04	2.14	40.72	40.85	3.12
2.42	2.55	.19	15.23	15.36	1.17	28.04	28.17	2.15	40.85	40.99	3.13
2.55	2.68	.20	15.36	15.50	1.18	28.17	28.31	2.16	40.99	41.12	3.14
2.68	2.82	.21	15.50	15.63	1.19	28.31	28.44	2.17	41.12	41.25	3.15
2.82	2.95	.22	15.63	15.76	1.20	28.44	28.57	2.18	41.25	41.38	3.16
2.95	3.08	.23	15.76	15.89	1.21	28.57	28.70	2.19	41.38	41.51	3.17
3.08	3.21	.24	15.89	16.02	1.22	28.70	28.83	2.20	41.51	41.64	3.18
3.21	3.34	.25	16.02	16.15	1.23	28.83	28.96	2.21	41.64	41.77	3.19
3.34	3.47	.26	16.15	16.28	1.24	28.96	29.09	2.22	41.77	41.90	3.20
3.47	3.60	.27	16.28	16.41	1.25	29.09	29.22	2.23	41.90	42.03	3.21
3.60	3.73	.28	16.41	16.54	1.26	29.22	29.35	2.24	42.03	42.16	3.22
3.73	3.86	.29	16.54	16.67	1.27	29.35	29.48	2.25	42.16	42.29	3.23
3.86	3.99	.30	16.67	16.80	1.28	29.48	29.61	2.26	42.29	42.42	3.24
3.99	4.12	.31	16.80	16.93	1.29	29.61	29.74	2.27	42.42	42.55	3.25
4.12	4.25	.32	16.93	17.06	1.30	29.74	29.87	2.28	42.55	42.68	3.26
4.25	4.38	.33	17.06	17.19	1.31	29.87	30.00	2.29	42.68	42.82	3.27
4.38	4.51	.34	17.19	17.33	1.32	30.00	30.14	2.30	42.82	42.95	3.28
4.51	4.65	.35	17.33	17.46	1.33	30.14	30.27	2.31	42.95	43.08	3.29
4.65	4.78	.36	17.46	17.59	1.34	30.27	30.40	2.32	43.08	43.21	3.30
4.78	4.91	.37	17.59	17.72	1.35	30.40	30.53	2.33	43.21	43.34	3.31
4.91	5.04	.38	17.72	17.85	1.36	30.53	30.66	2.34	43.34	43.47	3.32
5.04	5.17	.39	17.85	17.98	1.37	30.66	30.79	2.35	43.47	43.60	3.33
5.17	5.30	.40	17.98	18.11	1.38	30.79	30.92	2.36	43.60	43.73	3.34
5.30	5.43	.41	18.11	18.24	1.39	30.92	31.05	2.37	43.73	43.86	3.35
5.43	5.56	.42	18.24	18.37	1.40	31.05	31.18	2.38	43.86	43.99	3.36
5.56	5.69	.43	18.37	18.50	1.41	31.18	31.31	2.39	43.99	44.12	3.37
5.69	5.82	.44	18.50	18.63	1.42	31.31	31.44	2.40	44.12	44.25	3.38
5.82	5.95	.45	18.63	18.76	1.43	31.44	31.57	2.41	44.25	44.38	3.39
5.95	6.08	.46	18.76	18.89	1.44	31.57	31.70	2.42	44.38	44.51	3.40
6.08	6.21	.47	18.89	19.02	1.45	31.70	31.84	2.43	44.51	44.65	3.41
6.21	6.34	.48	19.02	19.16	1.46	31.84	31.97	2.44	44.65	44.78	3.42
6.34	6.48	.49	19.16	19.29	1.47	31.97	32.10	2.45	44.78	44.91	3.43
6.48	6.61	.50	19.29	19.42	1.48	32.10	32.23	2.46	44.91	45.04	3.44
6.61	6.74	.51	19.42	19.55	1.49	32.23	32.36	2.47	45.04	45.17	3.45
6.74	6.87	.52	19.55	19.68	1.50	32.36	32.49	2.48	45.17	45.30	3.46
6.87	7.00	.53	19.68	19.81	1.51	32.49	32.62	2.49	45.30	45.43	3.47
7.00	7.13	.54	19.81	19.94	1.52	32.62	32.75	2.50	45.43	45.56	3.48
7.13	7.26	.55	19.94	20.07	1.53	32.75	32.88	2.51	45.56	45.69	3.49
7.26	7.39	.56	20.07	20.20	1.54	32.88	33.01	2.52	45.69	45.82	3.50
7.39	7.52	.57	20.20	20.33	1.55	33.01	33.14	2.53	45.82	45.95	3.51
7.52	7.65	.58	20.33	20.46	1.56	33.14	33.27	2.54	45.95	46.08	3.52
7.65	7.78	.59	20.46	20.59	1.57	33.27	33.40	2.55	46.08	46.21	3.53
7.78	7.91	.60	20.59	20.72	1.58	33.40	33.53	2.56	46.21	46.34	3.54
7.91	8.04	.61	20.72	20.85	1.59	33.53	33.67	2.57	46.34	46.48	3.55
8.04	8.17	.62	20.85	20.99	1.60	33.67	33.80	2.58	46.48	46.61	3.56
8.17	8.31	.63	20.99	21.12	1.61	33.80	33.93	2.59	46.61	46.74	3.57
8.31	8.44	.64	21.12	21.25	1.62	33.93	34.06	2.60	46.74	46.87	3.58
8.44	8.57	.65	21.25	21.38	1.63	34.06	34.19	2.61	46.87	47.00	3.59
8.57	8.70	.66	21.38	21.51	1.64	34.19	34.32	2.62	47.00	47.13	3.60
8.70	8.83	.67	21.51	21.64	1.65	34.32	34.45	2.63	47.13	47.26	3.61
8.83	8.96	.68	21.64	21.77	1.66	34.45	34.58	2.64	47.26	47.39	3.62
8.96	9.09	.69	21.77	21.90	1.67	34.58	34.71	2.65	47.39	47.52	3.63
9.09	9.22	.70	21.90	22.03	1.68	34.71	34.84	2.66	47.52	47.65	3.64
9.22	9.35	.71	22.03	22.16	1.69	34.84	34.97	2.67	47.65	47.78	3.65
9.35	9.48	.72	22.16	22.29	1.70	34.97	35.10	2.68	47.78	47.91	3.66
9.48	9.61	.73	22.29	22.42	1.71	35.10	35.23	2.69	47.91	48.04	3.67
9.61	9.74	.74	22.42	22.55	1.72	35.23	35.36	2.70	48.04	48.17	3.68
9.74	9.87	.75	22.55	22.68	1.73	35.36	35.50	2.71	48.17	48.31	3.69
9.87	10.00	.76	22.68	22.82	1.74	35.50	35.63	2.72	48.31	48.44	3.70
10.00	10.14	.77	22.82	22.95	1.75	35.63	35.76	2.73	48.44	48.57	3.71
10.14	10.27	.78	22.95	23.08	1.76	35.76	35.89	2.74	48.57	48.70	3.72
10.27	10.40	.79	23.08	23.21	1.77	35.89	36.02	2.75	48.70	48.83	3.73
10.40	10.53	.80	23.21	23.34	1.78	36.02	36.15	2.76	48.83	48.96	3.74
10.53	10.66	.81	23.34	23.47	1.79	36.15	36.28	2.77	48.96	49.09	3.75
10.66	10.79	.82	23.47	23.60	1.80	36.28	36.41	2.78	49.09	49.22	3.76
10.79	10.92	.83	23.60	23.73	1.81	36.41	36.54	2.79	49.22	49.35	3.77
10.92	11.05	.84	23.73	23.86	1.82	36.54	36.67	2.80	49.35	49.48	3.78
11.05	11.18	.85	23.86	23.99	1.83	36.67	36.80	2.81	49.48	49.61	3.79
11.18	11.31	.86	23.99	24.12	1.84	36.80	36.93	2.82	49.61	49.74	3.80
11.31	11.44	.87	24.12	24.25	1.85	36.93	37.06	2.83	49.74	49.87	3.81
11.44	11.57	.88	24.25	24.38	1.86	37.06	37.19	2.84	49.87	50.00	3.82
11.57	11.70	.89	24.38	24.51	1.87	37.19	37.33	2.85	50.00	50.14	3.83
11.70	11.84	.90	24.51	24.65	1.88	37.33	37.46	2.86	50.14	50.27	3.84
11.84	11.97	.91	24.65	24.78	1.89	37.46	37.59	2.87	50.27	50.40	3.85
11.97	12.10	.92	24.78	24.91	1.90	37.59	37.72	2.88	50.40	50.53	3.86
12.10	12.23	.93	24.91	25.04	1.91	37.72	37.85	2.89	50.53	50.66	3.87
12.23	12.36	.94	25.04	25.17	1.92	37.85	37.98	2.90	50.66	50.79	3.88
12.36	12.49	.95	25.17	25.30	1.93	37.98	38.11	2.91	50.79	50.92	3.89
12.49	12.62	.96	25.30	25.43	1.94	38.11	38.24	2.92	50.92	51.05	3.90
12.62	12.75	.97	25.43	25.56	1.95	38.24	38.37	2.93	51.05	51.18	3.91

7.65% Social Security Employee Tax Table for 19_ _

Wages at least	But less than	Tax to be withheld	Wages at least	But less than	Tax to be withheld	Wages at least	But less than	Tax to be withheld	Wages at least	But less than	Tax to be withheld
51.18	51.31	3.92	63.86	63.99	4.89	76.54	76.67	5.86	89.22	89.35	6.83
51.31	51.44	3.93	63.99	64.12	4.90	76.67	76.80	5.87	89.35	89.48	6.84
51.44	51.57	3.94	64.12	64.25	4.91	76.80	76.93	5.88	89.48	89.61	6.85
51.57	51.70	3.95	64.25	64.38	4.92	76.93	77.06	5.89	89.61	89.74	6.86
51.70	51.84	3.96	64.38	64.51	4.93	77.06	77.19	5.90	89.74	89.87	6.87
51.84	51.97	3.97	64.51	64.65	4.94	77.19	77.33	5.91	89.87	90.00	6.88
51.97	52.10	3.98	64.65	64.78	4.95	77.33	77.46	5.92	90.00	90.14	6.89
52.10	52.23	3.99	64.78	64.91	4.96	77.46	77.59	5.93	90.14	90.27	6.90
52.23	52.36	4.00	64.91	65.04	4.97	77.59	77.72	5.94	90.27	90.40	6.91
52.36	52.49	4.01	65.04	65.17	4.98	77.72	77.85	5.95	90.40	90.53	6.92
52.49	52.62	4.02	65.17	65.30	4.99	77.85	77.98	5.96	90.53	90.66	6.93
52.62	52.75	4.03	65.30	65.43	5.00	77.98	78.11	5.97	90.66	90.79	6.94
52.75	52.88	4.04	65.43	65.56	5.01	78.11	78.24	5.98	90.79	90.92	6.95
52.88	53.01	4.05	65.56	65.69	5.02	78.24	78.37	5.99	90.92	91.05	6.96
53.01	53.14	4.06	65.69	65.82	5.03	78.37	78.50	6.00	91.05	91.18	6.97
53.14	53.27	4.07	65.82	65.95	5.04	78.50	78.63	6.01	91.18	91.31	6.98
53.27	53.40	4.08	65.95	66.08	5.05	78.63	78.76	6.02	91.31	91.44	6.99
53.40	53.53	4.09	66.08	66.21	5.06	78.76	78.89	6.03	91.44	91.57	7.00
53.53	53.67	4.10	66.21	66.34	5.07	78.89	79.02	6.04	91.57	91.70	7.01
53.67	53.80	4.11	66.34	66.48	5.08	79.02	79.16	6.05	91.70	91.84	7.02
53.80	53.93	4.12	66.48	66.61	5.09	79.16	79.29	6.06	91.84	91.97	7.03
53.93	54.06	4.13	66.61	66.74	5.10	79.29	79.42	6.07	91.97	92.10	7.04
54.06	54.19	4.14	66.74	66.87	5.11	79.42	79.55	6.08	92.10	92.23	7.05
54.19	54.32	4.15	66.87	67.00	5.12	79.55	79.68	6.09	92.23	92.36	7.06
54.32	54.45	4.16	67.00	67.13	5.13	79.68	79.81	6.10	92.36	92.49	7.07
54.45	54.58	4.17	67.13	67.26	5.14	79.81	79.94	6.11	92.49	92.62	7.08
54.58	54.71	4.18	67.26	67.39	5.15	79.94	80.07	6.12	92.62	92.75	7.09
54.71	54.84	4.19	67.39	67.52	5.16	80.07	80.20	6.13	92.75	92.88	7.10
54.84	54.97	4.20	67.52	67.65	5.17	80.20	80.33	6.14	92.88	93.01	7.11
54.97	55.10	4.21	67.65	67.78	5.18	80.33	80.46	6.15	93.01	93.14	7.12
55.10	55.23	4.22	67.78	67.91	5.19	80.46	80.59	6.16	93.14	93.27	7.13
55.23	55.36	4.23	67.91	68.04	5.20	80.59	80.72	6.17	93.27	93.40	7.14
55.36	55.50	4.24	68.04	68.17	5.21	80.72	80.85	6.18	93.40	93.53	7.15
55.50	55.63	4.25	68.17	68.31	5.22	80.85	80.99	6.19	93.53	93.67	7.16
55.63	55.76	4.26	68.31	68.44	5.23	80.99	81.12	6.20	93.67	93.80	7.17
55.76	55.89	4.27	68.44	68.57	5.24	81.12	81.25	6.21	93.80	93.93	7.18
55.89	56.02	4.28	68.57	68.70	5.25	81.25	81.38	6.22	93.93	94.06	7.19
56.02	56.15	4.29	68.70	68.83	5.26	81.38	81.51	6.23	94.06	94.19	7.20
56.15	56.28	4.30	68.83	68.96	5.27	81.51	81.64	6.24	94.19	94.32	7.21
56.28	56.41	4.31	68.96	69.09	5.28	81.64	81.77	6.25	94.32	94.45	7.22
56.41	56.54	4.32	69.09	69.22	5.29	81.77	81.90	6.26	94.45	94.58	7.23
56.54	56.67	4.33	69.22	69.35	5.30	81.90	82.03	6.27	94.58	94.71	7.24
56.67	56.80	4.34	69.35	69.48	5.31	82.03	82.16	6.28	94.71	94.84	7.25
56.80	56.93	4.35	69.48	69.61	5.32	82.16	82.29	6.29	94.84	94.97	7.26
56.93	57.06	4.36	69.61	69.74	5.33	82.29	82.42	6.30	94.97	95.10	7.27
57.06	57.19	4.37	69.74	69.87	5.34	82.42	82.55	6.31	95.10	95.23	7.28
57.19	57.33	4.38	69.87	70.00	5.35	82.55	82.68	6.32	95.23	95.36	7.29
57.33	57.46	4.39	70.00	70.14	5.36	82.68	82.82	6.33	95.36	95.50	7.30
57.46	57.59	4.40	70.14	70.27	5.37	82.82	82.95	6.34	95.50	95.63	7.31
57.59	57.72	4.41	70.27	70.40	5.38	82.95	83.08	6.35	95.63	95.76	7.32
57.72	57.85	4.42	70.40	70.53	5.39	83.08	83.21	6.36	95.76	95.89	7.33
57.85	57.98	4.43	70.53	70.66	5.40	83.21	83.34	6.37	95.89	96.02	7.34
57.98	58.11	4.44	70.66	70.79	5.41	83.34	83.47	6.38	96.02	96.15	7.35
58.11	58.24	4.45	70.79	70.92	5.42	83.47	83.60	6.39	96.15	96.28	7.36
58.24	58.37	4.46	70.92	71.05	5.43	83.60	83.73	6.40	96.28	96.41	7.37
58.37	58.50	4.47	71.05	71.18	5.44	83.73	83.86	6.41	96.41	96.54	7.38
58.50	58.63	4.48	71.18	71.31	5.45	83.86	83.99	6.42	96.54	96.67	7.39
58.63	58.76	4.49	71.31	71.44	5.46	83.99	84.12	6.43	96.67	96.80	7.40
58.76	58.89	4.50	71.44	71.57	5.47	84.12	84.25	6.44	96.80	96.93	7.41
58.89	59.02	4.51	71.57	71.70	5.48	84.25	84.38	6.45	96.93	97.06	7.42
59.02	59.16	4.52	71.70	71.84	5.49	84.38	84.51	6.46	97.06	97.19	7.43
59.16	59.29	4.53	71.84	71.97	5.50	84.51	84.65	6.47	97.19	97.33	7.44
59.29	59.42	4.54	71.97	72.10	5.51	84.65	84.78	6.48	97.33	97.46	7.45
59.42	59.55	4.55	72.10	72.23	5.52	84.78	84.91	6.49	97.46	97.59	7.46
59.55	59.68	4.56	72.23	72.36	5.53	84.91	85.04	6.50	97.59	97.72	7.47
59.68	59.81	4.57	72.36	72.49	5.54	85.04	85.17	6.51	97.72	97.85	7.48
59.81	59.94	4.58	72.49	72.62	5.55	85.17	85.30	6.52	97.85	97.98	7.49
59.94	60.07	4.59	72.62	72.75	5.56	85.30	85.43	6.53	97.98	98.11	7.50
60.07	60.20	4.60	72.75	72.88	5.57	85.43	85.56	6.54	98.11	98.24	7.51
60.20	60.33	4.61	72.88	73.01	5.58	85.56	85.69	6.55	98.24	98.37	7.52
60.33	60.46	4.62	73.01	73.14	5.59	85.69	85.82	6.56	98.37	98.50	7.53
60.46	60.59	4.63	73.14	73.27	5.60	85.82	85.95	6.57	98.50	98.63	7.54
60.59	60.72	4.64	73.27	73.40	5.61	85.95	86.08	6.58	98.63	98.76	7.55
60.72	60.85	4.65	73.40	73.53	5.62	86.08	86.21	6.59	98.76	98.89	7.56
60.85	60.99	4.66	73.53	73.67	5.63	86.21	86.34	6.60	98.89	99.02	7.57
60.99	61.12	4.67	73.67	73.80	5.64	86.34	86.48	6.61	99.02	99.16	7.58
61.12	61.25	4.68	73.80	73.93	5.65	86.48	86.61	6.62	99.16	99.29	7.59
61.25	61.38	4.69	73.93	74.06	5.66	86.61	86.74	6.63	99.29	99.42	7.60
61.38	61.51	4.70	74.06	74.19	5.67	86.74	86.87	6.64	99.42	99.55	7.61
61.51	61.64	4.71	74.19	74.32	5.68	86.87	87.00	6.65	99.55	99.68	7.62
61.64	61.77	4.72	74.32	74.45	5.69	87.00	87.13	6.66	99.68	99.81	7.63
61.77	61.90	4.73	74.45	74.58	5.70	87.13	87.26	6.67	99.81	99.94	7.64
61.90	62.03	4.74	74.58	74.71	5.71	87.26	87.39	6.68	99.94	100.00	7.65
62.03	62.16	4.75	74.71	74.84	5.72	87.39	87.52	6.69			
62.16	62.29	4.76	74.84	74.97	5.73	87.52	87.65	6.70			
62.29	62.42	4.77	74.97	75.10	5.74	87.65	87.78	6.71			
62.42	62.55	4.78	75.10	75.23	5.75	87.78	87.91	6.72			
62.55	62.68	4.79	75.23	75.36	5.76	87.91	88.04	6.73			
62.68	62.82	4.80	75.36	75.50	5.77	88.04	88.17	6.74			
62.82	62.95	4.81	75.50	75.63	5.78	88.17	88.31	6.75			
62.95	63.08	4.82	75.63	75.76	5.79	88.31	88.44	6.76			
63.08	63.21	4.83	75.76	75.89	5.80	88.44	88.57	6.77			
63.21	63.34	4.84	75.89	76.02	5.81	88.57	88.70	6.78			
63.34	63.47	4.85	76.02	76.15	5.82	88.70	88.83	6.79			
63.47	63.60	4.86	76.15	76.28	5.83	88.83	88.96	6.80			
63.60	63.73	4.87	76.28	76.41	5.84	88.96	89.09	6.81			
63.73	63.86	4.88	76.41	76.54	5.85	89.09	89.22	6.82			

Wages	Taxes
100	$7.65
200	15.30
300	22.95
400	30.60
500	38.25
600	45.90
700	53.55
800	61.20
900	68.85
1,000	76.50

19 _ _ Tax Table

Use if your taxable income is less than $50,000. If $50,000 or more, use the Tax Rate Schedules.

Example: Mr. and Mrs. Brown are filing a joint return. Their taxable income on line 37 of Form 1040 is $25,300. First, they find the $25,300–25,350 income line. Next, they find the column for married filing jointly and read down the column. The amount shown where the income line and filing status column meet is $3,799. This is the tax amount they must write on line 38 of their return.

At least	But less than	Single	Married filing jointly *	Married filing separately	Head of a household
			Your tax is—		
25,200	25,250	4,652	3,784	5,051	3,833
25,250	25,300	4,666	3,791	5,065	3,847
25,300	25,350	4,680	(3,799)	5,079	3,861
25,350	25,400	4,694	3,806	5,093	3,875

If line 37 (taxable income) is—		And you are—				If line 37 (taxable income) is—		And you are—				If line 37 (taxable income) is—		And you are—			
At least	But less than	Single	Married filing jointly *	Married filing separately	Head of a household	At least	But less than	Single	Married filing jointly *	Married filing separately	Head of a household	At least	But less than	Single	Married filing jointly *	Married filing separately	Head of a household
			Your tax is—						Your tax is—						Your tax is—		
$0	$5	$0	$0	$0	$0	1,400	1,425	212	212	212	212	2,700	2,725	407	407	407	407
5	15	2	2	2	2	1,425	1,450	216	216	216	216	2,725	2,750	411	411	411	411
15	25	3	3	3	3	1,450	1,475	219	219	219	219	2,750	2,775	414	414	414	414
25	50	6	6	6	6	1,475	1,500	223	223	223	223	2,775	2,800	418	418	418	418
50	75	9	9	9	9	1,500	1,525	227	227	227	227	2,800	2,825	422	422	422	422
75	100	13	13	13	13	1,525	1,550	231	231	231	231	2,825	2,850	426	426	426	426
100	125	17	17	17	17	1,550	1,575	234	234	234	234	2,850	2,875	429	429	429	429
125	150	21	21	21	21	1,575	1,600	238	238	238	238	2,875	2,900	433	433	433	433
150	175	24	24	24	24	1,600	1,625	242	242	242	242	2,900	2,925	437	437	437	437
175	200	28	28	28	28	1,625	1,650	246	246	246	246	2,925	2,950	441	441	441	441
200	225	32	32	32	32	1,650	1,675	249	249	249	249	2,950	2,975	444	444	444	444
225	250	36	36	36	36	1,675	1,700	253	253	253	253	2,975	3,000	448	448	448	448
250	275	39	39	39	39	1,700	1,725	257	257	257	257	**3,000**					
275	300	43	43	43	43	1,725	1,750	261	261	261	261	3,000	3,050	454	454	454	454
300	325	47	47	47	47	1,750	1,775	264	264	264	264	3,050	3,100	461	461	461	461
325	350	51	51	51	51	1,775	1,800	268	268	268	268	3,100	3,150	469	469	469	469
350	375	54	54	54	54	1,800	1,825	272	272	272	272	3,150	3,200	476	476	476	476
375	400	58	58	58	58	1,825	1,850	276	276	276	276	3,200	3,250	484	484	484	484
400	425	62	62	62	62	1,850	1,875	279	279	279	279	3,250	3,300	491	491	491	491
425	450	66	66	66	66	1,875	1,900	283	283	283	283	3,300	3,350	499	499	499	499
450	475	69	69	69	69	1,900	1,925	287	287	287	287	3,350	3,400	506	506	506	506
475	500	73	73	73	73	1,925	1,950	291	291	291	291	3,400	3,450	514	514	514	514
500	525	77	77	77	77	1,950	1,975	294	294	294	294	3,450	3,500	521	521	521	521
525	550	81	81	81	81	1,975	2,000	298	298	298	298	3,500	3,550	529	529	529	529
550	575	84	84	84	84	**2,000**						3,550	3,600	536	536	536	536
575	600	88	88	88	88	2,000	2,025	302	302	302	302	3,600	3,650	544	544	544	544
600	625	92	92	92	92	2,025	2,050	306	306	306	306	3,650	3,700	551	551	551	551
625	650	96	96	96	96	2,050	2,075	309	309	309	309	3,700	3,750	559	559	559	559
650	675	99	99	99	99	2,075	2,100	313	313	313	313	3,750	3,800	566	566	566	566
675	700	103	103	103	103	2,100	2,125	317	317	317	317	3,800	3,850	574	574	574	574
700	725	107	107	107	107	2,125	2,150	321	321	321	321	3,850	3,900	581	581	581	581
725	750	111	111	111	111	2,150	2,175	324	324	324	324	3,900	3,950	589	589	589	589
750	775	114	114	114	114	2,175	2,200	328	328	328	328	3,950	4,000	596	596	596	596
775	800	118	118	118	118	2,200	2,225	332	332	332	332	**4,000**					
800	825	122	122	122	122	2,225	2,250	336	336	336	336	4,000	4,050	604	604	604	604
825	850	126	126	126	126	2,250	2,275	339	339	339	339	4,050	4,100	611	611	611	611
850	875	129	129	129	129	2,275	2,300	343	343	343	343	4,100	4,150	619	619	619	619
875	900	133	133	133	133	2,300	2,325	347	347	347	347	4,150	4,200	626	626	626	626
900	925	137	137	137	137	2,325	2,350	351	351	351	351	4,200	4,250	634	634	634	634
925	950	141	141	141	141	2,350	2,375	354	354	354	354	4,250	4,300	641	641	641	641
950	975	144	144	144	144	2,375	2,400	358	358	358	358	4,300	4,350	649	649	649	649
975	1,000	148	148	148	148	2,400	2,425	362	362	362	362	4,350	4,400	656	656	656	656
1,000						2,425	2,450	366	366	366	366	4,400	4,450	664	664	664	664
1,000	1,025	152	152	152	152	2,450	2,475	369	369	369	369	4,450	4,500	671	671	671	671
1,025	1,050	156	156	156	156	2,475	2,500	373	373	373	373	4,500	4,550	679	679	679	679
1,050	1,075	159	159	159	159	2,500	2,525	377	377	377	377	4,550	4,600	686	686	686	686
1,075	1,100	163	163	163	163	2,525	2,550	381	381	381	381	4,600	4,650	694	694	694	694
1,100	1,125	167	167	167	167	2,550	2,575	384	384	384	384	4,650	4,700	701	701	701	701
1,125	1,150	171	171	171	171	2,575	2,600	388	388	388	388	4,700	4,750	709	709	709	709
1,150	1,175	174	174	174	174	2,600	2,625	392	392	392	392	4,750	4,800	716	716	716	716
1,175	1,200	178	178	178	178	2,625	2,650	396	396	396	396	4,800	4,850	724	724	724	724
1,200	1,225	182	182	182	182	2,650	2,675	399	399	399	399	4,850	4,900	731	731	731	731
1,225	1,250	186	186	186	186	2,675	2,700	403	403	403	403	4,900	4,950	739	739	739	739
1,250	1,275	189	189	189	189							4,950	5,000	746	746	746	746
1,275	1,300	193	193	193	193												
1,300	1,325	197	197	197	197												
1,325	1,350	201	201	201	201												
1,350	1,375	204	204	204	204												
1,375	1,400	208	208	208	208												

* This column must also be used by a qualifying widow(er).

Continued on next page

19. . Tax Table—*Continued*

If line 37 (taxable income) is—		And you are—				If line 37 (taxable income) is—		And you are—				If line 37 (taxable income) is—		And you are—			
At least	But less than	Single	Married filing jointly *	Married filing separately	Head of a household	At least	But less than	Single	Married filing jointly *	Married filing separately	Head of a household	At least	But less than	Single	Married filing jointly *	Married filing separately	Head of a household
		Your tax is—						Your tax is—						Your tax is—			
5,000						**8,000**						**11,000**					
5,000	5,050	754	754	754	754	8,000	8,050	1,204	1,204	1,204	1,204	11,000	11,050	1,654	1,654	1,654	1,654
5,050	5,100	761	761	761	761	8,050	8,100	1,211	1,211	1,211	1,211	11,050	11,100	1,661	1,661	1,661	1,661
5,100	5,150	769	769	769	769	8,100	8,150	1,219	1,219	1,219	1,219	11,100	11,150	1,669	1,669	1,669	1,669
5,150	5,200	776	776	776	776	8,150	8,200	1,226	1,226	1,226	1,226	11,150	11,200	1,676	1,676	1,676	1,676
5,200	5,250	784	784	784	784	8,200	8,250	1,234	1,234	1,234	1,234	11,200	11,250	1,684	1,684	1,684	1,684
5,250	5,300	791	791	791	791	8,250	8,300	1,241	1,241	1,241	1,241	11,250	11,300	1,691	1,691	1,691	1,691
5,300	5,350	799	799	799	799	8,300	8,350	1,249	1,249	1,249	1,249	11,300	11,350	1,699	1,699	1,699	1,699
5,350	5,400	806	806	806	806	8,350	8,400	1,256	1,256	1,256	1,256	11,350	11,400	1,706	1,706	1,706	1,706
5,400	5,450	814	814	814	814	8,400	8,450	1,264	1,264	1,264	1,264	11,400	11,450	1,714	1,714	1,714	1,714
5,450	5,500	821	821	821	821	8,450	8,500	1,271	1,271	1,271	1,271	11,450	11,500	1,721	1,721	1,721	1,721
5,500	5,550	829	829	829	829	8,500	8,550	1,279	1,279	1,279	1,279	11,500	11,550	1,729	1,729	1,729	1,729
5,550	5,600	836	836	836	836	8,550	8,600	1,286	1,286	1,286	1,286	11,550	11,600	1,736	1,736	1,736	1,736
5,600	5,650	844	844	844	844	8,600	8,650	1,294	1,294	1,294	1,294	11,600	11,650	1,744	1,744	1,744	1,744
5,650	5,700	851	851	851	851	8,650	8,700	1,301	1,301	1,301	1,301	11,650	11,700	1,751	1,751	1,751	1,751
5,700	5,750	859	859	859	859	8,700	8,750	1,309	1,309	1,309	1,309	11,700	11,750	1,759	1,759	1,759	1,759
5,750	5,800	866	866	866	866	8,750	8,800	1,316	1,316	1,316	1,316	11,750	11,800	1,766	1,766	1,766	1,766
5,800	5,850	874	874	874	874	8,800	8,850	1,324	1,324	1,324	1,324	11,800	11,850	1,774	1,774	1,774	1,774
5,850	5,900	881	881	881	881	8,850	8,900	1,331	1,331	1,331	1,331	11,850	11,900	1,781	1,781	1,781	1,781
5,900	5,950	889	889	889	889	8,900	8,950	1,339	1,339	1,339	1,339	11,900	11,950	1,789	1,789	1,789	1,789
5,950	6,000	896	896	896	896	8,950	9,000	1,346	1,346	1,346	1,346	11,950	12,000	1,796	1,796	1,796	1,796
6,000						**9,000**						**12,000**					
6,000	6,050	904	904	904	904	9,000	9,050	1,354	1,354	1,354	1,354	12,000	12,050	1,804	1,804	1,804	1,804
6,050	6,100	911	911	911	911	9,050	9,100	1,361	1,361	1,361	1,361	12,050	12,100	1,811	1,811	1,811	1,811
6,100	6,150	919	919	919	919	9,100	9,150	1,369	1,369	1,369	1,369	12,100	12,150	1,819	1,819	1,819	1,819
6,150	6,200	926	926	926	926	9,150	9,200	1,376	1,376	1,376	1,376	12,150	12,200	1,826	1,826	1,826	1,826
6,200	6,250	934	934	934	934	9,200	9,250	1,384	1,384	1,384	1,384	12,200	12,250	1,834	1,834	1,834	1,834
6,250	6,300	941	941	941	941	9,250	9,300	1,391	1,391	1,391	1,391	12,250	12,300	1,841	1,841	1,841	1,841
6,300	6,350	949	949	949	949	9,300	9,350	1,399	1,399	1,399	1,399	12,300	12,350	1,849	1,849	1,849	1,849
6,350	6,400	956	956	956	956	9,350	9,400	1,406	1,406	1,406	1,406	12,350	12,400	1,856	1,856	1,856	1,856
6,400	6,450	964	964	964	964	9,400	9,450	1,414	1,414	1,414	1,414	12,400	12,450	1,864	1,864	1,864	1,864
6,450	6,500	971	971	971	971	9,450	9,500	1,421	1,421	1,421	1,421	12,450	12,500	1,871	1,871	1,871	1,871
6,500	6,550	979	979	979	979	9,500	9,550	1,429	1,429	1,429	1,429	12,500	12,550	1,879	1,879	1,879	1,879
6,550	6,600	986	986	986	986	9,550	9,600	1,436	1,436	1,436	1,436	12,550	12,600	1,886	1,886	1,886	1,886
6,600	6,650	994	994	994	994	9,600	9,650	1,444	1,444	1,444	1,444	12,600	12,650	1,894	1,894	1,894	1,894
6,650	6,700	1,001	1,001	1,001	1,001	9,650	9,700	1,451	1,451	1,451	1,451	12,650	12,700	1,901	1,901	1,901	1,901
6,700	6,750	1,009	1,009	1,009	1,009	9,700	9,750	1,459	1,459	1,459	1,459	12,700	12,750	1,909	1,909	1,909	1,909
6,750	6,800	1,016	1,016	1,016	1,016	9,750	9,800	1,466	1,466	1,466	1,466	12,750	12,800	1,916	1,916	1,916	1,916
6,800	6,850	1,024	1,024	1,024	1,024	9,800	9,850	1,474	1,474	1,474	1,474	12,800	12,850	1,924	1,924	1,924	1,924
6,850	6,900	1,031	1,031	1,031	1,031	9,850	9,900	1,481	1,481	1,481	1,481	12,850	12,900	1,931	1,931	1,931	1,931
6,900	6,950	1,039	1,039	1,039	1,039	9,900	9,950	1,489	1,489	1,489	1,489	12,900	12,950	1,939	1,939	1,939	1,939
6,950	7,000	1,046	1,046	1,046	1,046	9,950	10,000	1,496	1,496	1,496	1,496	12,950	13,000	1,946	1,946	1,946	1,946
7,000						**10,000**						**13,000**					
7,000	7,050	1,054	1,054	1,054	1,054	10,000	10,050	1,504	1,504	1,504	1,504	13,000	13,050	1,954	1,954	1,954	1,954
7,050	7,100	1,061	1,061	1,061	1,061	10,050	10,100	1,511	1,511	1,511	1,511	13,050	13,100	1,961	1,961	1,961	1,961
7,100	7,150	1,069	1,069	1,069	1,069	10,100	10,150	1,519	1,519	1,519	1,519	13,100	13,150	1,969	1,969	1,969	1,969
7,150	7,200	1,076	1,076	1,076	1,076	10,150	10,200	1,526	1,526	1,526	1,526	13,150	13,200	1,976	1,976	1,976	1,976
7,200	7,250	1,084	1,084	1,084	1,084	10,200	10,250	1,534	1,534	1,534	1,534	13,200	13,250	1,984	1,984	1,984	1,984
7,250	7,300	1,091	1,091	1,091	1,091	10,250	10,300	1,541	1,541	1,541	1,541	13,250	13,300	1,991	1,991	1,991	1,991
7,300	7,350	1,099	1,099	1,099	1,099	10,300	10,350	1,549	1,549	1,549	1,549	13,300	13,350	1,999	1,999	1,999	1,999
7,350	7,400	1,106	1,106	1,106	1,106	10,350	10,400	1,556	1,556	1,556	1,556	13,350	13,400	2,006	2,006	2,006	2,006
7,400	7,450	1,114	1,114	1,114	1,114	10,400	10,450	1,564	1,564	1,564	1,564	13,400	13,450	2,014	2,014	2,014	2,014
7,450	7,500	1,121	1,121	1,121	1,121	10,450	10,500	1,571	1,571	1,571	1,571	13,450	13,500	2,021	2,021	2,021	2,021
7,500	7,550	1,129	1,129	1,129	1,129	10,500	10,550	1,579	1,579	1,579	1,579	13,500	13,550	2,029	2,029	2,029	2,029
7,550	7,600	1,136	1,136	1,136	1,136	10,550	10,600	1,586	1,586	1,586	1,586	13,550	13,600	2,036	2,036	2,036	2,036
7,600	7,650	1,144	1,144	1,144	1,144	10,600	10,650	1,594	1,594	1,594	1,594	13,600	13,650	2,044	2,044	2,044	2,044
7,650	7,700	1,151	1,151	1,151	1,151	10,650	10,700	1,601	1,601	1,601	1,601	13,650	13,700	2,051	2,051	2,051	2,051
7,700	7,750	1,159	1,159	1,159	1,159	10,700	10,750	1,609	1,609	1,609	1,609	13,700	13,750	2,059	2,059	2,059	2,059
7,750	7,800	1,166	1,166	1,166	1,166	10,750	10,800	1,616	1,616	1,616	1,616	13,750	13,800	2,066	2,066	2,066	2,066
7,800	7,850	1,174	1,174	1,174	1,174	10,800	10,850	1,624	1,624	1,624	1,624	13,800	13,850	2,074	2,074	2,074	2,074
7,850	7,900	1,181	1,181	1,181	1,181	10,850	10,900	1,631	1,631	1,631	1,631	13,850	13,900	2,081	2,081	2,081	2,081
7,900	7,950	1,189	1,189	1,189	1,189	10,900	10,950	1,639	1,639	1,639	1,639	13,900	13,950	2,089	2,089	2,089	2,089
7,950	8,000	1,196	1,196	1,196	1,196	10,950	11,000	1,646	1,646	1,646	1,646	13,950	14,000	2,096	2,096	2,096	2,096

* This column must also be used by a qualifying widow(er).

Continued on next page

19.. Tax Table—*Continued*

If line 37 (taxable income) is—		And you are—			
At least	But less than	Single	Married filing jointly *	Married filing separately	Head of a household
		Your tax is—			
14,000					
14,000	14,050	2,104	2,104	2,104	2,104
14,050	14,100	2,111	2,111	2,111	2,111
14,100	14,150	2,119	2,119	2,119	2,119
14,150	14,200	2,126	2,126	2,126	2,126
14,200	14,250	2,134	2,134	2,134	2,134
14,250	14,300	2,141	2,141	2,141	2,141
14,300	14,350	2,149	2,149	2,149	2,149
14,350	14,400	2,156	2,156	2,156	2,156
14,400	14,450	2,164	2,164	2,164	2,164
14,450	14,500	2,171	2,171	2,171	2,171
14,500	14,550	2,179	2,179	2,179	2,179
14,550	14,600	2,186	2,186	2,186	2,186
14,600	14,650	2,194	2,194	2,194	2,194
14,650	14,700	2,201	2,201	2,201	2,201
14,700	14,750	2,209	2,209	2,209	2,209
14,750	14,800	2,216	2,216	2,216	2,216
14,800	14,850	2,224	2,224	2,224	2,224
14,850	14,900	2,231	2,231	2,231	2,231
14,900	14,950	2,239	2,239	2,239	2,239
14,950	15,000	2,246	2,246	2,246	2,246
15,000					
15,000	15,050	2,254	2,254	2,254	2,254
15,050	15,100	2,261	2,261	2,261	2,261
15,100	15,150	2,269	2,269	2,269	2,269
15,150	15,200	2,276	2,276	2,276	2,276
15,200	15,250	2,284	2,284	2,284	2,284
15,250	15,300	2,291	2,291	2,291	2,291
15,300	15,350	2,299	2,299	2,299	2,299
15,350	15,400	2,306	2,306	2,306	2,306
15,400	15,450	2,314	2,314	2,314	2,314
15,450	15,500	2,321	2,321	2,321	2,321
15,500	15,550	2,329	2,329	2,335	2,329
15,550	15,600	2,336	2,336	2,349	2,336
15,600	15,650	2,344	2,344	2,363	2,344
15,650	15,700	2,351	2,351	2,377	2,351
15,700	15,750	2,359	2,359	2,391	2,359
15,750	15,800	2,366	2,366	2,405	2,366
15,800	15,850	2,374	2,374	2,419	2,374
15,850	15,900	2,381	2,381	2,433	2,381
15,900	15,950	2,389	2,389	2,447	2,389
15,950	16,000	2,396	2,396	2,461	2,396
16,000					
16,000	16,050	2,404	2,404	2,475	2,404
16,050	16,100	2,411	2,411	2,489	2,411
16,100	16,150	2,419	2,419	2,503	2,419
16,150	16,200	2,426	2,426	2,517	2,426
16,200	16,250	2,434	2,434	2,531	2,434
16,250	16,300	2,441	2,441	2,545	2,441
16,300	16,350	2,449	2,449	2,559	2,449
16,350	16,400	2,456	2,456	2,573	2,456
16,400	16,450	2,464	2,464	2,587	2,464
16,450	16,500	2,471	2,471	2,601	2,471
16,500	16,550	2,479	2,479	2,615	2,479
16,550	16,600	2,486	2,486	2,629	2,486
16,600	16,650	2,494	2,494	2,643	2,494
16,650	16,700	2,501	2,501	2,657	2,501
16,700	16,750	2,509	2,509	2,671	2,509
16,750	16,800	2,516	2,516	2,685	2,516
16,800	16,850	2,524	2,524	2,699	2,524
16,850	16,900	2,531	2,531	2,713	2,531
16,900	16,950	2,539	2,539	2,727	2,539
16,950	17,000	2,546	2,546	2,741	2,546

If line 37 (taxable income) is—		And you are—			
At least	But less than	Single	Married filing jointly *	Married filing separately	Head of a household
		Your tax is—			
17,000					
17,000	17,050	2,554	2,554	2,755	2,554
17,050	17,100	2,561	2,561	2,769	2,561
17,100	17,150	2,569	2,569	2,783	2,569
17,150	17,200	2,576	2,576	2,797	2,576
17,200	17,250	2,584	2,584	2,811	2,584
17,250	17,300	2,591	2,591	2,825	2,591
17,300	17,350	2,599	2,599	2,839	2,599
17,350	17,400	2,606	2,606	2,853	2,606
17,400	17,450	2,614	2,614	2,867	2,614
17,450	17,500	2,621	2,621	2,881	2,621
17,500	17,550	2,629	2,629	2,895	2,629
17,550	17,600	2,636	2,636	2,909	2,636
17,600	17,650	2,644	2,644	2,923	2,644
17,650	17,700	2,651	2,651	2,937	2,651
17,700	17,750	2,659	2,659	2,951	2,659
17,750	17,800	2,666	2,666	2,965	2,666
17,800	17,850	2,674	2,674	2,979	2,674
17,850	17,900	2,681	2,681	2,993	2,681
17,900	17,950	2,689	2,689	3,007	2,689
17,950	18,000	2,696	2,696	3,021	2,696
18,000					
18,000	18,050	2,704	2,704	3,035	2,704
18,050	18,100	2,711	2,711	3,049	2,711
18,100	18,150	2,719	2,719	3,063	2,719
18,150	18,200	2,726	2,726	3,077	2,726
18,200	18,250	2,734	2,734	3,091	2,734
18,250	18,300	2,741	2,741	3,105	2,741
18,300	18,350	2,749	2,749	3,119	2,749
18,350	18,400	2,756	2,756	3,133	2,756
18,400	18,450	2,764	2,764	3,147	2,764
18,450	18,500	2,771	2,771	3,161	2,771
18,500	18,550	2,779	2,779	3,175	2,779
18,550	18,600	2,786	2,786	3,189	2,786
18,600	18,650	2,804	2,794	3,203	2,794
18,650	18,700	2,818	2,801	3,217	2,801
18,700	18,750	2,832	2,809	3,231	2,809
18,750	18,800	2,846	2,816	3,245	2,816
18,800	18,850	2,860	2,824	3,259	2,824
18,850	18,900	2,874	2,831	3,273	2,831
18,900	18,950	2,888	2,839	3,287	2,839
18,950	19,000	2,902	2,846	3,301	2,846
19,000					
19,000	19,050	2,916	2,854	3,315	2,854
19,050	19,100	2,930	2,861	3,329	2,861
19,100	19,150	2,944	2,869	3,343	2,869
19,150	19,200	2,958	2,876	3,357	2,876
19,200	19,250	2,972	2,884	3,371	2,884
19,250	19,300	2,986	2,891	3,385	2,891
19,300	19,350	3,000	2,899	3,399	2,899
19,350	19,400	3,014	2,906	3,413	2,906
19,400	19,450	3,028	2,914	3,427	2,914
19,450	19,500	3,042	2,921	3,441	2,921
19,500	19,550	3,056	2,929	3,455	2,929
19,550	19,600	3,070	2,936	3,469	2,936
19,600	19,650	3,084	2,944	3,483	2,944
19,650	19,700	3,098	2,951	3,497	2,951
19,700	19,750	3,112	2,959	3,511	2,959
19,750	19,800	3,126	2,966	3,525	2,966
19,800	19,850	3,140	2,974	3,539	2,974
19,850	19,900	3,154	2,981	3,553	2,981
19,900	19,950	3,168	2,989	3,567	2,989
19,950	20,000	3,182	2,996	3,581	2,996

If line 37 (taxable income) is—		And you are—			
At least	But less than	Single	Married filing jointly *	Married filing separately	Head of a household
		Your tax is—			
20,000					
20,000	20,050	3,196	3,004	3,595	3,004
20,050	20,100	3,210	3,011	3,609	3,011
20,100	20,150	3,224	3,019	3,623	3,019
20,150	20,200	3,238	3,026	3,637	3,026
20,200	20,250	3,252	3,034	3,651	3,034
20,250	20,300	3,266	3,041	3,665	3,041
20,300	20,350	3,280	3,049	3,679	3,049
20,350	20,400	3,294	3,056	3,693	3,056
20,400	20,450	3,308	3,064	3,707	3,064
20,450	20,500	3,322	3,071	3,721	3,071
20,500	20,550	3,336	3,079	3,735	3,079
20,550	20,600	3,350	3,086	3,749	3,086
20,600	20,650	3,364	3,094	3,763	3,094
20,650	20,700	3,378	3,101	3,777	3,101
20,700	20,750	3,392	3,109	3,791	3,109
20,750	20,800	3,406	3,116	3,805	3,116
20,800	20,850	3,420	3,124	3,819	3,124
20,850	20,900	3,434	3,131	3,833	3,131
20,900	20,950	3,448	3,139	3,847	3,139
20,950	21,000	3,462	3,146	3,861	3,146
21,000					
21,000	21,050	3,476	3,154	3,875	3,154
21,050	21,100	3,490	3,161	3,889	3,161
21,100	21,150	3,504	3,169	3,903	3,169
21,150	21,200	3,518	3,176	3,917	3,176
21,200	21,250	3,532	3,184	3,931	3,184
21,250	21,300	3,546	3,191	3,945	3,191
21,300	21,350	3,560	3,199	3,959	3,199
21,350	21,400	3,574	3,206	3,973	3,206
21,400	21,450	3,588	3,214	3,987	3,214
21,450	21,500	3,602	3,221	4,001	3,221
21,500	21,550	3,616	3,229	4,015	3,229
21,550	21,600	3,630	3,236	4,029	3,236
21,600	21,650	3,644	3,244	4,043	3,244
21,650	21,700	3,658	3,251	4,057	3,251
21,700	21,750	3,672	3,259	4,071	3,259
21,750	21,800	3,686	3,266	4,085	3,266
21,800	21,850	3,700	3,274	4,099	3,274
21,850	21,900	3,714	3,281	4,113	3,281
21,900	21,950	3,728	3,289	4,127	3,289
21,950	22,000	3,742	3,296	4,141	3,296
22,000					
22,000	22,050	3,756	3,304	4,155	3,304
22,050	22,100	3,770	3,311	4,169	3,311
22,100	22,150	3,784	3,319	4,183	3,319
22,150	22,200	3,798	3,326	4,197	3,326
22,200	22,250	3,812	3,334	4,211	3,334
22,250	22,300	3,826	3,341	4,225	3,341
22,300	22,350	3,840	3,349	4,239	3,349
22,350	22,400	3,854	3,356	4,253	3,356
22,400	22,450	3,868	3,364	4,267	3,364
22,450	22,500	3,882	3,371	4,281	3,371
22,500	22,550	3,896	3,379	4,295	3,379
22,550	22,600	3,910	3,386	4,309	3,386
22,600	22,650	3,924	3,394	4,323	3,394
22,650	22,700	3,938	3,401	4,337	3,401
22,700	22,750	3,952	3,409	4,351	3,409
22,750	22,800	3,966	3,416	4,365	3,416
22,800	22,850	3,980	3,424	4,379	3,424
22,850	22,900	3,994	3,431	4,393	3,431
22,900	22,950	4,008	3,439	4,407	3,439
22,950	23,000	4,022	3,446	4,421	3,446

* This column must also be used by a qualifying widow(er).

Continued on next page

19. . Tax Table—*Continued*

23,000 / 24,000 / 25,000

If line 37 (taxable income) is—		And you are—			
At least	But less than	Single	Married filing jointly *	Married filing separately	Head of a household
23,000					
23,000	23,050	4,036	3,454	4,435	3,454
23,050	23,100	4,050	3,461	4,449	3,461
23,100	23,150	4,064	3,469	4,463	3,469
23,150	23,200	4,078	3,476	4,477	3,476
23,200	23,250	4,092	3,484	4,491	3,484
23,250	23,300	4,106	3,491	4,505	3,491
23,300	23,350	4,120	3,499	4,519	3,499
23,350	23,400	4,134	3,506	4,533	3,506
23,400	23,450	4,148	3,514	4,547	3,514
23,450	23,500	4,162	3,521	4,561	3,521
23,500	23,550	4,176	3,529	4,575	3,529
23,550	23,600	4,190	3,536	4,589	3,536
23,600	23,650	4,204	3,544	4,603	3,544
23,650	23,700	4,218	3,551	4,617	3,551
23,700	23,750	4,232	3,559	4,631	3,559
23,750	23,800	4,246	3,566	4,645	3,566
23,800	23,850	4,260	3,574	4,659	3,574
23,850	23,900	4,274	3,581	4,673	3,581
23,900	23,950	4,288	3,589	4,687	3,589
23,950	24,000	4,302	3,596	4,701	3,596
24,000					
24,000	24,050	4,316	3,604	4,715	3,604
24,050	24,100	4,330	3,611	4,729	3,611
24,100	24,150	4,344	3,619	4,743	3,619
24,150	24,200	4,358	3,626	4,757	3,626
24,200	24,250	4,372	3,634	4,771	3,634
24,250	24,300	4,386	3,641	4,785	3,641
24,300	24,350	4,400	3,649	4,799	3,649
24,350	24,400	4,414	3,656	4,813	3,656
24,400	24,450	4,428	3,664	4,827	3,664
24,450	24,500	4,442	3,671	4,841	3,671
24,500	24,550	4,456	3,679	4,855	3,679
24,550	24,600	4,470	3,686	4,869	3,686
24,600	24,650	4,484	3,694	4,883	3,694
24,650	24,700	4,498	3,701	4,897	3,701
24,700	24,750	4,512	3,709	4,911	3,709
24,750	24,800	4,526	3,716	4,925	3,716
24,800	24,850	4,540	3,724	4,939	3,724
24,850	24,900	4,554	3,731	4,953	3,735
24,900	24,950	4,568	3,739	4,967	3,749
24,950	25,000	4,582	3,746	4,981	3,763
25,000					
25,000	25,050	4,596	3,754	4,995	3,777
25,050	25,100	4,610	3,761	5,009	3,791
25,100	25,150	4,624	3,769	5,023	3,805
25,150	25,200	4,638	3,776	5,037	3,819
25,200	25,250	4,652	3,784	5,051	3,833
25,250	25,300	4,666	3,791	5,065	3,847
25,300	25,350	4,680	3,799	5,079	3,861
25,350	25,400	4,694	3,806	5,093	3,875
25,400	25,450	4,708	3,814	5,107	3,889
25,450	25,500	4,722	3,821	5,121	3,903
25,500	25,550	4,736	3,829	5,135	3,917
25,550	25,600	4,750	3,836	5,149	3,931
25,600	25,650	4,764	3,844	5,163	3,945
25,650	25,700	4,778	3,851	5,177	3,959
25,700	25,750	4,792	3,859	5,191	3,973
25,750	25,800	4,806	3,866	5,205	3,987
25,800	25,850	4,820	3,874	5,219	4,001
25,850	25,900	4,834	3,881	5,233	4,015
25,900	25,950	4,848	3,889	5,247	4,029
25,950	26,000	4,862	3,896	5,261	4,043

26,000 / 27,000 / 28,000

If line 37 (taxable income) is—		And you are—			
At least	But less than	Single	Married filing jointly *	Married filing separately	Head of a household
26,000					
26,000	26,050	4,876	3,904	5,275	4,057
26,050	26,100	4,890	3,911	5,289	4,071
26,100	26,150	4,904	3,919	5,303	4,085
26,150	26,200	4,918	3,926	5,317	4,099
26,200	26,250	4,932	3,934	5,331	4,113
26,250	26,300	4,946	3,941	5,345	4,127
26,300	26,350	4,960	3,949	5,359	4,141
26,350	26,400	4,974	3,956	5,373	4,155
26,400	26,450	4,988	3,964	5,387	4,169
26,450	26,500	5,002	3,971	5,401	4,183
26,500	26,550	5,016	3,979	5,415	4,197
26,550	26,600	5,030	3,986	5,429	4,211
26,600	26,650	5,044	3,994	5,443	4,225
26,650	26,700	5,058	4,001	5,457	4,239
26,700	26,750	5,072	4,009	5,471	4,253
26,750	26,800	5,086	4,016	5,485	4,267
26,800	26,850	5,100	4,024	5,499	4,281
26,850	26,900	5,114	4,031	5,513	4,295
26,900	26,950	5,128	4,039	5,527	4,309
26,950	27,000	5,142	4,046	5,541	4,323
27,000					
27,000	27,050	5,156	4,054	5,555	4,337
27,050	27,100	5,170	4,061	5,569	4,351
27,100	27,150	5,184	4,069	5,583	4,365
27,150	27,200	5,198	4,076	5,597	4,379
27,200	27,250	5,212	4,084	5,611	4,393
27,250	27,300	5,226	4,091	5,625	4,407
27,300	27,350	5,240	4,099	5,639	4,421
27,350	27,400	5,254	4,106	5,653	4,435
27,400	27,450	5,268	4,114	5,667	4,449
27,450	27,500	5,282	4,121	5,681	4,463
27,500	27,550	5,296	4,129	5,695	4,477
27,550	27,600	5,310	4,136	5,709	4,491
27,600	27,650	5,324	4,144	5,723	4,505
27,650	27,700	5,338	4,151	5,737	4,519
27,700	27,750	5,352	4,159	5,751	4,533
27,750	27,800	5,366	4,166	5,765	4,547
27,800	27,850	5,380	4,174	5,779	4,561
27,850	27,900	5,394	4,181	5,793	4,575
27,900	27,950	5,408	4,189	5,807	4,589
27,950	28,000	5,422	4,196	5,821	4,603
28,000					
28,000	28,050	5,436	4,204	5,835	4,617
28,050	28,100	5,450	4,211	5,849	4,631
28,100	28,150	5,464	4,219	5,863	4,645
28,150	28,200	5,478	4,226	5,877	4,659
28,200	28,250	5,492	4,234	5,891	4,673
28,250	28,300	5,506	4,241	5,905	4,687
28,300	28,350	5,520	4,249	5,919	4,701
28,350	28,400	5,534	4,256	5,933	4,715
28,400	28,450	5,548	4,264	5,947	4,729
28,450	28,500	5,562	4,271	5,961	4,743
28,500	28,550	5,576	4,279	5,975	4,757
28,550	28,600	5,590	4,286	5,989	4,771
28,600	28,650	5,604	4,294	6,003	4,785
28,650	28,700	5,618	4,301	6,017	4,799
28,700	28,750	5,632	4,309	6,031	4,813
28,750	28,800	5,646	4,316	6,045	4,827
28,800	28,850	5,660	4,324	6,059	4,841
28,850	28,900	5,674	4,331	6,073	4,855
28,900	28,950	5,688	4,339	6,087	4,869
28,950	29,000	5,702	4,346	6,101	4,883

29,000 / 30,000 / 31,000

If line 37 (taxable income) is—		And you are—			
At least	But less than	Single	Married filing jointly *	Married filing separately	Head of a household
29,000					
29,000	29,050	5,716	4,354	6,115	4,897
29,050	29,100	5,730	4,361	6,129	4,911
29,100	29,150	5,744	4,369	6,143	4,925
29,150	29,200	5,758	4,376	6,157	4,939
29,200	29,250	5,772	4,384	6,171	4,953
29,250	29,300	5,786	4,391	6,185	4,967
29,300	29,350	5,800	4,399	6,199	4,981
29,350	29,400	5,814	4,406	6,213	4,995
29,400	29,450	5,828	4,414	6,227	5,009
29,450	29,500	5,842	4,421	6,241	5,023
29,500	29,550	5,856	4,429	6,255	5,037
29,550	29,600	5,870	4,436	6,269	5,051
29,600	29,650	5,884	4,444	6,283	5,065
29,650	29,700	5,898	4,451	6,297	5,079
29,700	29,750	5,912	4,459	6,311	5,093
29,750	29,800	5,926	4,466	6,325	5,107
29,800	29,850	5,940	4,474	6,339	5,121
29,850	29,900	5,954	4,481	6,353	5,135
29,900	29,950	5,968	4,489	6,367	5,149
29,950	30,000	5,982	4,496	6,381	5,163
30,000					
30,000	30,050	5,996	4,504	6,395	5,177
30,050	30,100	6,010	4,511	6,409	5,191
30,100	30,150	6,024	4,519	6,423	5,205
30,150	30,200	6,038	4,526	6,437	5,219
30,200	30,250	6,052	4,534	6,451	5,233
30,250	30,300	6,066	4,541	6,465	5,247
30,300	30,350	6,080	4,549	6,479	5,261
30,350	30,400	6,094	4,556	6,493	5,275
30,400	30,450	6,108	4,564	6,507	5,289
30,450	30,500	6,122	4,571	6,521	5,303
30,500	30,550	6,136	4,579	6,535	5,317
30,550	30,600	6,150	4,586	6,549	5,331
30,600	30,650	6,164	4,594	6,563	5,345
30,650	30,700	6,178	4,601	6,577	5,359
30,700	30,750	6,192	4,609	6,591	5,373
30,750	30,800	6,206	4,616	6,605	5,387
30,800	30,850	6,220	4,624	6,619	5,401
30,850	30,900	6,234	4,631	6,633	5,415
30,900	30,950	6,248	4,639	6,647	5,429
30,950	31,000	6,262	4,650	6,661	5,443
31,000					
31,000	31,050	6,276	4,664	6,675	5,457
31,050	31,100	6,290	4,678	6,689	5,471
31,100	31,150	6,304	4,692	6,703	5,485
31,150	31,200	6,318	4,706	6,717	5,499
31,200	31,250	6,332	4,720	6,731	5,513
31,250	31,300	6,346	4,734	6,745	5,527
31,300	31,350	6,360	4,748	6,759	5,541
31,350	31,400	6,374	4,762	6,773	5,555
31,400	31,450	6,388	4,776	6,787	5,569
31,450	31,500	6,402	4,790	6,801	5,583
31,500	31,550	6,416	4,804	6,815	5,597
31,550	31,600	6,430	4,818	6,829	5,611
31,600	31,650	6,444	4,832	6,843	5,625
31,650	31,700	6,458	4,846	6,857	5,639
31,700	31,750	6,472	4,860	6,871	5,653
31,750	31,800	6,486	4,874	6,885	5,667
31,800	31,850	6,500	4,888	6,899	5,681
31,850	31,900	6,514	4,902	6,913	5,695
31,900	31,950	6,528	4,916	6,927	5,709
31,950	32,000	6,542	4,930	6,941	5,723

* This column must also be used by a qualifying widow(er).

Continued on next page

19..Tax Table—_Continued_

32,000

If line 37 (taxable income) is— At least	But less than	And you are— Single	Married filing jointly *	Married filing separately	Head of a household
32,000	32,050	6,556	4,944	6,955	5,737
32,050	32,100	6,570	4,958	6,969	5,751
32,100	32,150	6,584	4,972	6,983	5,765
32,150	32,200	6,598	4,986	6,997	5,779
32,200	32,250	6,612	5,000	7,011	5,793
32,250	32,300	6,626	5,014	7,025	5,807
32,300	32,350	6,640	5,028	7,039	5,821
32,350	32,400	6,654	5,042	7,053	5,835
32,400	32,450	6,668	5,056	7,067	5,849
32,450	32,500	6,682	5,070	7,081	5,863
32,500	32,550	6,696	5,084	7,095	5,877
32,550	32,600	6,710	5,098	7,109	5,891
32,600	32,650	6,724	5,112	7,123	5,905
32,650	32,700	6,738	5,126	7,137	5,919
32,700	32,750	6,752	5,140	7,151	5,933
32,750	32,800	6,766	5,154	7,165	5,947
32,800	32,850	6,780	5,168	7,179	5,961
32,850	32,900	6,794	5,182	7,193	5,975
32,900	32,950	6,808	5,196	7,207	5,989
32,950	33,000	6,822	5,210	7,221	6,003

33,000

At least	But less than	Single	Married filing jointly *	Married filing separately	Head of a household
33,000	33,050	6,836	5,224	7,235	6,017
33,050	33,100	6,850	5,238	7,249	6,031
33,100	33,150	6,864	5,252	7,263	6,045
33,150	33,200	6,878	5,266	7,277	6,059
33,200	33,250	6,892	5,280	7,291	6,073
33,250	33,300	6,906	5,294	7,305	6,087
33,300	33,350	6,920	5,308	7,319	6,101
33,350	33,400	6,934	5,322	7,333	6,115
33,400	33,450	6,948	5,336	7,347	6,129
33,450	33,500	6,962	5,350	7,361	6,143
33,500	33,550	6,976	5,364	7,375	6,157
33,550	33,600	6,990	5,378	7,389	6,171
33,600	33,650	7,004	5,392	7,403	6,185
33,650	33,700	7,018	5,406	7,417	6,199
33,700	33,750	7,032	5,420	7,431	6,213
33,750	33,800	7,046	5,434	7,445	6,227
33,800	33,850	7,060	5,448	7,459	6,241
33,850	33,900	7,074	5,462	7,473	6,255
33,900	33,950	7,088	5,476	7,487	6,269
33,950	34,000	7,102	5,490	7,501	6,283

34,000

At least	But less than	Single	Married filing jointly *	Married filing separately	Head of a household
34,000	34,050	7,116	5,504	7,515	6,297
34,050	34,100	7,130	5,518	7,529	6,311
34,100	34,150	7,144	5,532	7,543	6,325
34,150	34,200	7,158	5,546	7,557	6,339
34,200	34,250	7,172	5,560	7,571	6,353
34,250	34,300	7,186	5,574	7,585	6,367
34,300	34,350	7,200	5,588	7,599	6,381
34,350	34,400	7,214	5,602	7,613	6,395
34,400	34,450	7,228	5,616	7,627	6,409
34,450	34,500	7,242	5,630	7,641	6,423
34,500	34,550	7,256	5,644	7,655	6,437
34,550	34,600	7,270	5,658	7,669	6,451
34,600	34,650	7,284	5,672	7,683	6,465
34,650	34,700	7,298	5,686	7,697	6,479
34,700	34,750	7,312	5,700	7,711	6,493
34,750	34,800	7,326	5,714	7,725	6,507
34,800	34,850	7,340	5,728	7,739	6,521
34,850	34,900	7,354	5,742	7,753	6,535
34,900	34,950	7,368	5,756	7,767	6,549
34,950	35,000	7,382	5,770	7,781	6,563

35,000

At least	But less than	Single	Married filing jointly *	Married filing separately	Head of a household
35,000	35,050	7,396	5,784	7,795	6,577
35,050	35,100	7,410	5,798	7,809	6,591
35,100	35,150	7,424	5,812	7,823	6,605
35,150	35,200	7,438	5,826	7,837	6,619
35,200	35,250	7,452	5,840	7,851	6,633
35,250	35,300	7,466	5,854	7,865	6,647
35,300	35,350	7,480	5,868	7,879	6,661
35,350	35,400	7,494	5,882	7,893	6,675
35,400	35,450	7,508	5,896	7,907	6,689
35,450	35,500	7,522	5,910	7,921	6,703
35,500	35,550	7,536	5,924	7,935	6,717
35,550	35,600	7,550	5,938	7,949	6,731
35,600	35,650	7,564	5,952	7,963	6,745
35,650	35,700	7,578	5,966	7,977	6,759
35,700	35,750	7,592	5,980	7,991	6,773
35,750	35,800	7,606	5,994	8,005	6,787
35,800	35,850	7,620	6,008	8,019	6,801
35,850	35,900	7,634	6,022	8,033	6,815
35,900	35,950	7,648	6,036	8,047	6,829
35,950	36,000	7,662	6,050	8,061	6,843

36,000

At least	But less than	Single	Married filing jointly *	Married filing separately	Head of a household
36,000	36,050	7,676	6,064	8,075	6,857
36,050	36,100	7,690	6,078	8,089	6,871
36,100	36,150	7,704	6,092	8,103	6,885
36,150	36,200	7,718	6,106	8,117	6,899
36,200	36,250	7,732	6,120	8,131	6,913
36,250	36,300	7,746	6,134	8,145	6,927
36,300	36,350	7,760	6,148	8,159	6,941
36,350	36,400	7,774	6,162	8,173	6,955
36,400	36,450	7,788	6,176	8,187	6,969
36,450	36,500	7,802	6,190	8,201	6,983
36,500	36,550	7,816	6,204	8,215	6,997
36,550	36,600	7,830	6,218	8,229	7,011
36,600	36,650	7,844	6,232	8,243	7,025
36,650	36,700	7,858	6,246	8,257	7,039
36,700	36,750	7,872	6,260	8,271	7,053
36,750	36,800	7,886	6,274	8,285	7,067
36,800	36,850	7,900	6,288	8,299	7,081
36,850	36,900	7,914	6,302	8,313	7,095
36,900	36,950	7,928	6,316	8,327	7,109
36,950	37,000	7,942	6,330	8,341	7,123

37,000

At least	But less than	Single	Married filing jointly *	Married filing separately	Head of a household
37,000	37,050	7,956	6,344	8,355	7,137
37,050	37,100	7,970	6,358	8,369	7,151
37,100	37,150	7,984	6,372	8,383	7,165
37,150	37,200	7,998	6,386	8,397	7,179
37,200	37,250	8,012	6,400	8,411	7,193
37,250	37,300	8,026	6,414	8,425	7,207
37,300	37,350	8,040	6,428	8,439	7,221
37,350	37,400	8,054	6,442	8,453	7,235
37,400	37,450	8,068	6,456	8,467	7,249
37,450	37,500	8,082	6,470	8,484	7,263
37,500	37,550	8,096	6,484	8,500	7,277
37,550	37,600	8,110	6,498	8,517	7,291
37,600	37,650	8,124	6,512	8,533	7,305
37,650	37,700	8,138	6,526	8,550	7,319
37,700	37,750	8,152	6,540	8,566	7,333
37,750	37,800	8,166	6,554	8,583	7,347
37,800	37,850	8,180	6,568	8,599	7,361
37,850	37,900	8,194	6,582	8,616	7,375
37,900	37,950	8,208	6,596	8,632	7,389
37,950	38,000	8,222	6,610	8,649	7,403

38,000

At least	But less than	Single	Married filing jointly *	Married filing separately	Head of a household
38,000	38,050	8,236	6,624	8,665	7,417
38,050	38,100	8,250	6,638	8,682	7,431
38,100	38,150	8,264	6,652	8,698	7,445
38,150	38,200	8,278	6,666	8,715	7,459
38,200	38,250	8,292	6,680	8,731	7,473
38,250	38,300	8,306	6,694	8,748	7,487
38,300	38,350	8,320	6,708	8,764	7,501
38,350	38,400	8,334	6,722	8,781	7,515
38,400	38,450	8,348	6,736	8,797	7,529
38,450	38,500	8,362	6,750	8,814	7,543
38,500	38,550	8,376	6,764	8,830	7,557
38,550	38,600	8,390	6,778	8,847	7,571
38,600	38,650	8,404	6,792	8,863	7,585
38,650	38,700	8,418	6,806	8,880	7,599
38,700	38,750	8,432	6,820	8,896	7,613
38,750	38,800	8,446	6,834	8,913	7,627
38,800	38,850	8,460	6,848	8,929	7,641
38,850	38,900	8,474	6,862	8,946	7,655
38,900	38,950	8,488	6,876	8,962	7,669
38,950	39,000	8,502	6,890	8,979	7,683

39,000

At least	But less than	Single	Married filing jointly *	Married filing separately	Head of a household
39,000	39,050	8,516	6,904	8,995	7,697
39,050	39,100	8,530	6,918	9,012	7,711
39,100	39,150	8,544	6,932	9,028	7,725
39,150	39,200	8,558	6,946	9,045	7,739
39,200	39,250	8,572	6,960	9,061	7,753
39,250	39,300	8,586	6,974	9,078	7,767
39,300	39,350	8,600	6,988	9,094	7,781
39,350	39,400	8,614	7,002	9,111	7,795
39,400	39,450	8,628	7,016	9,127	7,809
39,450	39,500	8,642	7,030	9,144	7,823
39,500	39,550	8,656	7,044	9,160	7,837
39,550	39,600	8,670	7,058	9,177	7,851
39,600	39,650	8,684	7,072	9,193	7,865
39,650	39,700	8,698	7,086	9,210	7,879
39,700	39,750	8,712	7,100	9,226	7,893
39,750	39,800	8,726	7,114	9,243	7,907
39,800	39,850	8,740	7,128	9,259	7,921
39,850	39,900	8,754	7,142	9,276	7,935
39,900	39,950	8,768	7,156	9,292	7,949
39,950	40,000	8,782	7,170	9,309	7,963

40,000

At least	But less than	Single	Married filing jointly *	Married filing separately	Head of a household
40,000	40,050	8,796	7,184	9,325	7,977
40,050	40,100	8,810	7,198	9,342	7,991
40,100	40,150	8,824	7,212	9,358	8,005
40,150	40,200	8,838	7,226	9,375	8,019
40,200	40,250	8,852	7,240	9,391	8,033
40,250	40,300	8,866	7,254	9,408	8,047
40,300	40,350	8,880	7,268	9,424	8,061
40,350	40,400	8,894	7,282	9,441	8,075
40,400	40,450	8,908	7,296	9,457	8,089
40,450	40,500	8,922	7,310	9,474	8,103
40,500	40,550	8,936	7,324	9,490	8,117
40,550	40,600	8,950	7,338	9,507	8,131
40,600	40,650	8,964	7,352	9,523	8,145
40,650	40,700	8,978	7,366	9,540	8,159
40,700	40,750	8,992	7,380	9,556	8,173
40,750	40,800	9,006	7,394	9,573	8,187
40,800	40,850	9,020	7,408	9,589	8,201
40,850	40,900	9,034	7,422	9,606	8,215
40,900	40,950	9,048	7,436	9,622	8,229
40,950	41,000	9,062	7,450	9,639	8,243

* This column must also be used by a qualifying widow(er).

Continued on next page

19_ _ Tax Table—*Continued*

41,000

If line 37 (taxable income) is— At least	But less than	Single	Married filing jointly *	Married filing separately	Head of a household
41,000	41,050	9,076	7,464	9,655	8,257
41,050	41,100	9,090	7,478	9,672	8,271
41,100	41,150	9,104	7,492	9,688	8,285
41,150	41,200	9,118	7,506	9,705	8,299
41,200	41,250	9,132	7,520	9,721	8,313
41,250	41,300	9,146	7,534	9,738	8,327
41,300	41,350	9,160	7,548	9,754	8,341
41,350	41,400	9,174	7,562	9,771	8,355
41,400	41,450	9,188	7,576	9,787	8,369
41,450	41,500	9,202	7,590	9,804	8,383
41,500	41,550	9,216	7,604	9,820	8,397
41,550	41,600	9,230	7,618	9,837	8,411
41,600	41,650	9,244	7,632	9,853	8,425
41,650	41,700	9,258	7,646	9,870	8,439
41,700	41,750	9,272	7,660	9,886	8,453
41,750	41,800	9,286	7,674	9,903	8,467
41,800	41,850	9,300	7,688	9,919	8,481
41,850	41,900	9,314	7,702	9,936	8,495
41,900	41,950	9,328	7,716	9,952	8,509
41,950	42,000	9,342	7,730	9,969	8,523

42,000

At least	But less than	Single	Married filing jointly *	Married filing separately	Head of a household
42,000	42,050	9,356	7,744	9,985	8,537
42,050	42,100	9,370	7,758	10,002	8,551
42,100	42,150	9,384	7,772	10,018	8,565
42,150	42,200	9,398	7,786	10,035	8,579
42,200	42,250	9,412	7,800	10,051	8,593
42,250	42,300	9,426	7,814	10,068	8,607
42,300	42,350	9,440	7,828	10,084	8,621
42,350	42,400	9,454	7,842	10,101	8,635
42,400	42,450	9,468	7,856	10,117	8,649
42,450	42,500	9,482	7,870	10,134	8,663
42,500	42,550	9,496	7,884	10,150	8,677
42,550	42,600	9,510	7,898	10,167	8,691
42,600	42,650	9,524	7,912	10,183	8,705
42,650	42,700	9,538	7,926	10,200	8,719
42,700	42,750	9,552	7,940	10,216	8,733
42,750	42,800	9,566	7,954	10,233	8,747
42,800	42,850	9,580	7,968	10,249	8,761
42,850	42,900	9,594	7,982	10,266	8,775
42,900	42,950	9,608	7,996	10,282	8,789
42,950	43,000	9,622	8,010	10,299	8,803

43,000

At least	But less than	Single	Married filing jointly *	Married filing separately	Head of a household
43,000	43,050	9,636	8,024	10,315	8,817
43,050	43,100	9,650	8,038	10,332	8,831
43,100	43,150	9,664	8,052	10,348	8,845
43,150	43,200	9,678	8,066	10,365	8,859
43,200	43,250	9,692	8,080	10,381	8,873
43,250	43,300	9,706	8,094	10,398	8,887
43,300	43,350	9,720	8,108	10,414	8,901
43,350	43,400	9,734	8,122	10,431	8,915
43,400	43,450	9,748	8,136	10,447	8,929
43,450	43,500	9,762	8,150	10,464	8,943
43,500	43,550	9,776	8,164	10,480	8,957
43,550	43,600	9,790	8,178	10,497	8,971
43,600	43,650	9,804	8,192	10,513	8,985
43,650	43,700	9,818	8,206	10,530	8,999
43,700	43,750	9,832	8,220	10,546	9,013
43,750	43,800	9,846	8,234	10,563	9,027
43,800	43,850	9,860	8,248	10,579	9,041
43,850	43,900	9,874	8,262	10,596	9,055
43,900	43,950	9,888	8,276	10,612	9,069
43,950	44,000	9,902	8,290	10,629	9,083

44,000

At least	But less than	Single	Married filing jointly *	Married filing separately	Head of a household
44,000	44,050	9,916	8,304	10,645	9,097
44,050	44,100	9,930	8,318	10,662	9,111
44,100	44,150	9,944	8,332	10,678	9,125
44,150	44,200	9,958	8,346	10,695	9,139
44,200	44,250	9,972	8,360	10,711	9,153
44,250	44,300	9,986	8,374	10,728	9,167
44,300	44,350	10,000	8,388	10,744	9,181
44,350	44,400	10,014	8,402	10,761	9,195
44,400	44,450	10,028	8,416	10,777	9,209
44,450	44,500	10,042	8,430	10,794	9,223
44,500	44,550	10,056	8,444	10,810	9,237
44,550	44,600	10,070	8,458	10,827	9,251
44,600	44,650	10,084	8,472	10,843	9,265
44,650	44,700	10,098	8,486	10,860	9,279
44,700	44,750	10,112	8,500	10,876	9,293
44,750	44,800	10,126	8,514	10,893	9,307
44,800	44,850	10,140	8,528	10,909	9,321
44,850	44,900	10,154	8,542	10,926	9,335
44,900	44,950	10,169	8,556	10,942	9,349
44,950	45,000	10,185	8,570	10,959	9,363

45,000

At least	But less than	Single	Married filing jointly *	Married filing separately	Head of a household
45,000	45,050	10,202	8,584	10,975	9,377
45,050	45,100	10,218	8,598	10,992	9,391
45,100	45,150	10,235	8,612	11,008	9,405
45,150	45,200	10,251	8,626	11,025	9,419
45,200	45,250	10,268	8,640	11,041	9,433
45,250	45,300	10,284	8,654	11,058	9,447
45,300	45,350	10,301	8,668	11,074	9,461
45,350	45,400	10,317	8,682	11,091	9,475
45,400	45,450	10,334	8,696	11,107	9,489
45,450	45,500	10,350	8,710	11,124	9,503
45,500	45,550	10,367	8,724	11,140	9,517
45,550	45,600	10,383	8,738	11,157	9,531
45,600	45,650	10,400	8,752	11,173	9,545
45,650	45,700	10,416	8,766	11,190	9,559
45,700	45,750	10,433	8,780	11,206	9,573
45,750	45,800	10,449	8,794	11,223	9,587
45,800	45,850	10,466	8,808	11,239	9,601
45,850	45,900	10,482	8,822	11,256	9,615
45,900	45,950	10,499	8,836	11,272	9,629
45,950	46,000	10,515	8,850	11,289	9,643

46,000

At least	But less than	Single	Married filing jointly *	Married filing separately	Head of a household
46,000	46,050	10,532	8,864	11,305	9,657
46,050	46,100	10,548	8,878	11,322	9,671
46,100	46,150	10,565	8,892	11,338	9,685
46,150	46,200	10,581	8,906	11,355	9,699
46,200	46,250	10,598	8,920	11,371	9,713
46,250	46,300	10,614	8,934	11,388	9,727
46,300	46,350	10,631	8,948	11,404	9,741
46,350	46,400	10,647	8,962	11,421	9,755
46,400	46,450	10,664	8,976	11,437	9,769
46,450	46,500	10,680	8,990	11,454	9,783
46,500	46,550	10,697	9,004	11,470	9,797
46,550	46,600	10,713	9,018	11,487	9,811
46,600	46,650	10,730	9,032	11,503	9,825
46,650	46,700	10,746	9,046	11,520	9,839
46,700	46,750	10,763	9,060	11,536	9,853
46,750	46,800	10,779	9,074	11,553	9,867
46,800	46,850	10,796	9,088	11,569	9,881
46,850	46,900	10,812	9,102	11,586	9,895
46,900	46,950	10,829	9,116	11,602	9,909
46,950	47,000	10,845	9,130	11,619	9,923

47,000

At least	But less than	Single	Married filing jointly *	Married filing separately	Head of a household
47,000	47,050	10,862	9,144	11,635	9,937
47,050	47,100	10,878	9,158	11,652	9,951
47,100	47,150	10,895	9,172	11,668	9,965
47,150	47,200	10,911	9,186	11,685	9,979
47,200	47,250	10,928	9,200	11,701	9,993
47,250	47,300	10,944	9,214	11,718	10,007
47,300	47,350	10,961	9,228	11,734	10,021
47,350	47,400	10,977	9,242	11,751	10,035
47,400	47,450	10,994	9,256	11,767	10,049
47,450	47,500	11,010	9,270	11,784	10,063
47,500	47,550	11,027	9,284	11,800	10,077
47,550	47,600	11,043	9,298	11,817	10,091
47,600	47,650	11,060	9,312	11,833	10,105
47,650	47,700	11,076	9,326	11,850	10,119
47,700	47,750	11,093	9,340	11,866	10,133
47,750	47,800	11,109	9,354	11,883	10,147
47,800	47,850	11,126	9,368	11,899	10,161
47,850	47,900	11,142	9,382	11,916	10,175
47,900	47,950	11,159	9,396	11,932	10,189
47,950	48,000	11,175	9,410	11,949	10,203

48,000

At least	But less than	Single	Married filing jointly *	Married filing separately	Head of a household
48,000	48,050	11,192	9,424	11,965	10,217
48,050	48,100	11,208	9,438	11,982	10,231
48,100	48,150	11,225	9,452	11,998	10,245
48,150	48,200	11,241	9,466	12,015	10,259
48,200	48,250	11,258	9,480	12,031	10,273
48,250	48,300	11,274	9,494	12,048	10,287
48,300	48,350	11,291	9,508	12,064	10,301
48,350	48,400	11,307	9,522	12,081	10,315
48,400	48,450	11,324	9,536	12,097	10,329
48,450	48,500	11,340	9,550	12,114	10,343
48,500	48,550	11,357	9,564	12,130	10,357
48,550	48,600	11,373	9,578	12,147	10,371
48,600	48,650	11,390	9,592	12,163	10,385
48,650	48,700	11,406	9,606	12,180	10,399
48,700	48,750	11,423	9,620	12,196	10,413
48,750	48,800	11,439	9,634	12,213	10,427
48,800	48,850	11,456	9,648	12,229	10,441
48,850	48,900	11,472	9,662	12,246	10,455
48,900	48,950	11,489	9,676	12,262	10,469
48,950	49,000	11,505	9,690	12,279	10,483

49,000

At least	But less than	Single	Married filing jointly *	Married filing separately	Head of a household
49,000	49,050	11,522	9,704	12,295	10,497
49,050	49,100	11,538	9,718	12,312	10,511
49,100	49,150	11,555	9,732	12,328	10,525
49,150	49,200	11,571	9,746	12,345	10,539
49,200	49,250	11,588	9,760	12,361	10,553
49,250	49,300	11,604	9,774	12,378	10,567
49,300	49,350	11,621	9,788	12,394	10,581
49,350	49,400	11,637	9,802	12,411	10,595
49,400	49,450	11,654	9,816	12,427	10,609
49,450	49,500	11,670	9,830	12,444	10,623
49,500	49,550	11,687	9,844	12,460	10,637
49,550	49,600	11,703	9,858	12,477	10,651
49,600	49,650	11,720	9,872	12,493	10,665
49,650	49,700	11,736	9,886	12,510	10,679
49,700	49,750	11,753	9,900	12,526	10,693
49,750	49,800	11,769	9,914	12,543	10,707
49,800	49,850	11,786	9,928	12,559	10,721
49,850	49,900	11,802	9,942	12,576	10,735
49,900	49,950	11,819	9,956	12,592	10,749
49,950	50,000	11,835	9,970	12,609	10,763

* This column must also be used by a qualifying widow(er).

50,000 or over—use tax rate schedules

19_ _ Tax Rate Schedules

Caution: *Use ONLY if your taxable income (Form 1040, line 37) is $50,000 or more. If less, use the **Tax Table**.*

Schedule X—Use if your filing status is **Single**

If the amount on Form 1040, line 37, is: Over—	But not over—	Enter on Form 1040, line 38	of the amount over—
$0	$18,550	........15%	$0
18,550	44,900	**$2,782.50 + 28%**	18,550
44,900	93,130	**10,160.50 + 33%**	44,900
93,130	....	Use **Worksheet** below to figure your tax.	

Schedule Z—Use if your filing status is **Head of household**

If the amount on Form 1040, line 37, is: Over—	But not over—	Enter on Form 1040, line 38	of the amount over—
$0	$24,850	........15%	$0
24,850	64,200	**$3,727.50 + 28%**	24,850
64,200	128,810	**14,745.50 + 33%**	64,200
128,810	....	Use **Worksheet** below to figure your tax.	

Schedule Y-1—Use if your filing status is **Married filing jointly or Qualifying widow(er)**

If the amount on Form 1040, line 37, is: Over—	But not over—	Enter on Form 1040, line 38	of the amount over—
$0	$30,950	........15%	$0
30,950	74,850	**$4,642.50 + 28%**	30,950
74,850	155,320	**16,934.50 + 33%**	74,850
155,320	....	Use **Worksheet** below to figure your tax.	

Schedule Y-2—Use if your filing status is **Married filing separately**

If the amount on Form 1040, line 37, is: Over—	But not over—	Enter on Form 1040, line 38	of the amount over—
$0	$15,475	........15%	$0
15,475	37,425	**$2,321.25 + 28%**	15,475
37,425	117,895	**8,467.25 + 33%**	37,425
117,895	....	Use **Worksheet** below to figure your tax.	

Worksheet (Keep for your records)

1. If your filing status is:
   - Single, enter $26,076.40
   - Head of household, enter $36,066.80
   - Married filing jointly or Qualifying widow(er), enter $43,489.60
   - Married filing separately, enter $35,022.35

   1. _____

2. Enter your taxable income from Form 1040, line 37 . . . . 2. _____

3. If your filing status is:
   - Single, enter $93,130
   - Head of household, enter $128,810
   - Married filing jointly or Qualifying widow(er), enter $155,320
   - Married filing separately, enter $117,895

   3. _____

4. Subtract line 3 from line 2. Enter the result. (If the result is zero or less, use the schedule above for your filing status to figure your tax. DO NOT use this worksheet.)   4. _____

5. Multiply the amount on line 4 by 28% (.28). Enter the result . . . . 5. _____

6. Multiply the amount on line 4 by 5% (.05). Enter the result . . . . 6. _____

7. Multiply $560 by the number of exemptions claimed on Form 1040, line 6e. (If married filing separately, see the **Note** below.) Enter the result . . . . 7. _____

8. Compare the amounts on lines 6 and 7. Enter the **smaller** of the two amounts here . . . . 8. _____

9. **Tax.** Add lines 1, 5, and 8. Enter the total here and on Form 1040, line 38 . . . . 9. _____

Note: *If married filing separately and you did **not** claim an exemption for your spouse, multiply $560 by the number of exemptions claimed on Form 1040, line 6e. Add $560 to the result and enter the total on line 7 above.*

Standard Deduction Chart

Standard Deduction Chart for Most People

Standard Deduction Chart for Most People	**Line 16**

DO NOT use this chart if you were 65 or older or blind, OR if someone can claim you as a dependent.

If your filing status is:	enter on Form 1040A, line 16:
Single	$3,100
Married filing a joint return, or Qualifying widow(er) with dependent child	$5,200
Married filing a separate return and spouse does not itemize	$2,600
Head of household	$4,550

Standard Deduction Chart for People Age 65 or Older or Blind

Standard Deduction Chart for People Age 65 or Older or Blind

If someone can claim you as a dependent, use the worksheet below, instead.

Enter the number from the box on line 15a of Form 1040A ▶ ☐ **Caution:** *Do not use the number of exemptions from line 6e.*

If your filing status is:	and the number in the box above is:	enter on Form 1040A, line 16:
Single	1	$3,850
	2	$4,600
Married filing a joint return or Qualifying widow(er) with dependent child	1	$5,800
	2	$6,400
	3	$7,000
	4	$7,600
Married filing a separate return	1	$3,200
	2	$3,800
	3	$4,400
	4	$5,000
Head of household	1	$5,300
	2	$6,050

FUTURE WORTH OF ONE DOLLAR WITH INTEREST
PAYABLE AT <u>BEGINNING</u> OF EACH PERIOD COMPOUNDED <u>MONTHLY</u>

MONTHS	5%	5½%	ANNUAL RATES 6%	7%	7½%	8%
1	1.0041667	1.0045833	1.0050000	1.0058333	1.0062500	1.006667
2	1.0083507	1.0091877	1.0100250	1.0117007	1.0125391	1.013378
3	1.0125522	1.0138131	1.0150751	1.0176023	1.0188674	1.020134
4	1.0167711	1.0184598	1.0201505	1.0235383	1.0252354	1.026935
5	1.0210077	1.0231277	1.0252513	1.0295089	1.0316431	1.033781
6	1.0252619	1.0278170	1.0303775	1.0355144	1.0380908	1.040673
7	1.0295338	1.0325279	1.0355294	1.0415549	1.0445789	1.047610
8	1.0338235	1.0372603	1.0407070	1.0476306	1.0511075	1.054595
9	1.0381311	1.0420144	1.0459106	1.0537418	1.0576770	1.061625
10	1.0424567	1.0467903	1.0511401	1.0598886	1.0642874	1.068703
11	1.0468002	1.0515881	1.0563958	1.0660713	1.0709392	1.078827
12	1.0511619	1.0564079	1.0616778	1.0722901	1.0776326	1.083000
13	1.0555417	1.0612497	1.0669862	1.0785451	1.0843678	1.090220
14	1.0599398	1.0661138	1.0723211	1.0848366	1.0911451	1.097488
15	1.0643562	1.0710011	1.0776827	1.0911648	1.0979648	1.104804
16	1.0687911	1.0759089	1.0830712	1.0975300	1.1048270	1.112169
17	1.0732444	1.0808401	1.0884865	1.1039322	1.1117322	1.119583
18	1.0777162	1.0857940	1.0939289	1.1103718	1.1186805	1.127047
19	1.0822067	1.0907706	1.0993986	1.1168490	1.1256723	1.134561
20	1.0867159	1.0957699	1.1048956	1.1233639	1.1327077	1.142125
21	1.0912439	1.1007922	1.1104201	1.1299169	1.1397872	1.149739
22	1.0957907	1.1058375	1.1159722	1.1365081	1.1469108	1.157404
23	1.1003565	1.1109059	1.1215520	1.1431377	1.1540790	1.165120
24	1.1049413	1.1159976	1.1271598	1.1498060	1.1612920	1.172888
YEARS						
3	1.1614722	1.1789486	1.1966805	1.2329256	1.2514461	1.270237
4	1.2208954	1.2454506	1.2704892	1.3220539	1.3485992	1.375666
5	1.2833587	1.3157038	1.3488502	1.4176253	1.4532944	1.489846
6	1.3490177	1.3899198	1.4320443	1.5201055	1.5661174	1.613502
7	1.4180361	1.4683222	1.5203696	1.6299941	1.6876992	1.747422
8	1.4905855	1.5511471	1.6141427	1.7478265	1.8187197	1.892457
9	1.5668466	1.6386440	1.7136995	1.8741770	1.9599116	2.049530
10	1.6470095	1.7310764	1.8193967	2.0096614	2.1120646	2.219640
11	1.7312736	1.8287227	1.9316131	2.1549400	2.2760297	2.403869
12	1.8198489	1.9318771	2.0507508	2.3107207	2.4527238	2.603389
13	1.9129558	2.0408501	2.1772366	2.4777629	2.6431351	2.819469
14	2.0108262	2.1559701	2.3115238	2.6568806	2.8483286	3.053484
15	2.1137039	2.2775838	2.4540936	2.8489467	3.0694517	3.306921
16	2.2218450	2.4060574	2.6054567	3.0548973	3.3077412	3.581394
17	2.3355188	2.5417779	2.7661556	3.2757361	3.5645298	3.878648
18	2.4550084	2.6851542	2.9367660	3.5125393	3.8412535	4.200574
19	2.5806113	2.8366180	3.1178993	3.7664611	4.1394600	4.549220
20	2.7126403	2.9966256	3.3102045	4.0387388	4.4608170	4.926803
21	2.8514241	3.1656588	3.5143706	4.3306996	4.8071219	5.335725
22	2.9973084	3.3442268	3.7311293	4.6437662	5.1803112	5.778588
23	3.1506564	3.5328675	3.9612572	4.9794645	5.5824722	6.258207
24	3.3118499	3.7321490	4.2055789	5.3394304	6.0158541	6.777636
25	3.4812905	3.9426716	4.4649698	5.7254182	6.4828804	7.340176
26	3.6593999	4.1650692	4.7403594	6.1393092	6.9861633	7.949407
27	3.8466217	4.4000119	5.0327344	6.5831203	7.5285173	8.609204
28	4.0434222	4.6482071	5.3431424	7.0590146	8.1129757	9.323763
29	4.2502913	4.9104025	5.6726958	7.5693113	8.7428071	10.097631
30	4.4677443	5.1873878	6.0225752	8.1164975	9.4215339	10.935730
31	4.6963226	5.4799973	6.3940345	8.7032397	10.1529521	11.843390
32	4.9365954	5.7891122	6.7884045	9.3323976	10.9411521	12.826385
33	5.1891610	6.1156636	7.2070985	10.0070374	11.7905422	13.890969
34	5.4546483	6.4606351	7.6516165	10.7304470	12.7058726	15.043913
35	5.7337184	6.8250658	8.1235515	11.5061518	13.6922625	16.292550
36	6.0270664	7.2100530	8.6245944	12.3379325	14.7552285	17.644824
37	6.3354225	7.6167568	9.1565405	13.2298426	15.9007152	19.109335
38	6.6595547	8.0464017	9.7212959	14.1862290	17.1351290	20.695401
39	7.0002702	8.5002820	10.3208841	15.2117527	18.4653736	22.413109
40	7.3584173	8.9797648	10.9574537	16.3114115	19.8988886	24.273386

FUTURE WORTH OF ONE DOLLAR PER PERIOD WITH INTEREST PAYABLE AT <u>END</u> OF EACH PERIOD COMPOUNDED <u>MONTHLY</u>

ANNUAL RATES

MONTHS	7%	7½%	8%	8½%	MONTHS
1	1.0000 000 000	1.0000 000 000	1.0000 000 000	1.0000 000 000	1
2	2.0058 333 333	2.0062 500 000	2.0066 666 667	2.0070 833 333	2
3	3.0175 340 278	3.0187 890 625	3.0200 444 444	3.0213 001 736	3
4	4.0351 363 096	4.0376 564 941	4.0401 780 741	4.0427 010 498	4
5	5.0586 746 047	5.0628 918 472	5.0671 125 946	5.0713 368 489	5
6	6.0881 835 399	6.0945 349 213	6.1008 933 452	6.1072 588 183	6
7	7.1236 979 439	7.1326 257 645	7.1415 659 675	7.1505 185 683	7
8	8.1652 528 486	8.1772 046 756	8.1891 764 073	8.2011 680 748	8
9	9.2128 834 902	9.2283 122 048	9.2437 709 167	9.2592 596 820	9
10	10.2666 253 106	10.2859 891 561	10.3053 960 561	10.3248 461 047	10
11	11.3265 139 582	11.3502 765 883	11.3740 986 965	11.3979 804 313	11

YEARS	7%	7½%	8%	8½%	MONTHS
1	12.3925 852 896	12.4212 158 170	12.4499 260 211	12.4787 161 260	12
2	25.6810 315 719	25.8067 228 988	25.9331 897 618	26.0604 372 748	24
3	39.9301 007 103	40.2313 816 823	40.5355 577 431	40.8426 590 595	36
4	55.2092 362 089	55.7758 642 148	56.3499 150 651	56.9314 948 188	48
5	71.5929 016 481	72.5271 053 242	73.4768 562 452	74.4424 373 457	60
6	89.1609 435 866	90.5787 888 150	92.0253 250 965	93.5011 879 456	72
7	107.9989 806 974	110.0318 714 089	112.1133 077 144	114.2445 587 761	84
8	128.1988 210 340	130.9951 473 604	133.8685 829 824	136.8214 549 457	96
9	149.8589 094 619	153.5858 569 044	157.4295 353 681	161.3939 434 199	108
10	173.0848 074 335	177.9303 419 404	182.9460 351 817	188.1384 164 104	120
11	197.9897 074 475	204.1647 526 176	210.5803 918 953	217.2468 575 961	132
12	224.6949 846 973	232.4358 087 750	240.5083 865 871	248.9282 202 674	144
13	253.3307 885 987	262.9016 204 944	272.9203 900 780	283.4099 272 851	156
14	284.0366 770 795	295.7325 723 538	308.0225 738 733	320.9395 036 228	168
15	316.9622 967 213	331.1122 763 290	346.0382 216 115	361.7863 532 108	180
16	352.2681 120 693	369.2385 986 705	387.2091 493 629	406.2436 928 367	192
17	390.1261 876 635	410.3247 665 002	431.7972 438 125	454.6306 569 857	204
18	430.7210 266 035	454.6005 603 156	480.0861 281 110	507.2945 887 293	216
19	474.2504 697 328	502.3135 990 713	532.3829 659 904	564.6135 331 075	228
20	520.9266 598 255	553.7307 250 249	589.0204 156 215	626.9989 509 042	240
21	570.9770 754 741	609.1394 960 920	650.3587 456 387	694.8986 722 943	252
22	624.6456 397 168	668.8497 940 564	716.7881 267 958	768.8001 115 680	264
23	682.1939 088 081	733.1955 576 303	788.7311 138 265	849.2337 660 059	276
24	743.9023 469 251	802.5366 500 558	866.6453 332 989	936.7770 240 238	288
25	810.0716 930 231	877.2608 716 938	951.0263 945 609	1032.0583 099 227	300
26	881.0244 265 007	957.7861 288 550	1042.4110 422 915	1135.7615 949 968	312
27	957.1063 388 184	1044.5627 710 033	1141.3805 707 135	1248.6313 073 827	324
28	1038.6882 187 293	1138.0761 094 015	1248.5645 211 836	1371.4776 758 941	336
29	1126.1676 593 353	1238.8491 312 872	1364.6446 866 803	1505.1825 462 040	348
30	1219.9709 957 759	1347.4454 247 566	1490.3594 486 634	1650.7057 111 227	360
31	1320.5553 829 925	1464.4723 307 141	1626.5084 738 895	1809.0918 004 170	372
32	1428.4110 236 938	1590.5843 395 171	1773.9578 010 617	1981.4777 796 249	384
33	1544.0635 573 822	1726.4867 513 105	1933.6453 496 682	2169.1011 116 981	396
34	1668.0766 220 821	1872.9396 205 222	2106.5868 860 525	2373.3086 400 598	408
35	1801.0546 012 565	2030.7620 065 807	2293.8824 846 631	2595.5662 568 435	420
36	1943.6455 692 975	2200.8365 546 266	2496.7235 255 857	2837.4694 257 163	432
37	2096.5444 499 475	2384.1144 318 366	2716.4002 728 651	3100.7546 348 240	444
38	2260.4964 030 425	2581.6206 469 672	2954.3100 818 258	3387.3118 620 729	456
39	2436.3004 560 833	2794.4597 828 686	3211.9662 875 950	3699.1981 422 284	468
40	2624.8133 983 333	3023.8221 740 283	3491.0078 313 688	4038.6523 332 224	480
41	2826.9539 564 210	3270.9905 636 936	3793.2096 856 547	4408.1111 876 673	492
42	3043.7072 717 972	3537.3472 778 037	4120.4941 448 027	4810.2268 449 467	504
43	3276.1297 018 678	3824.3819 558 528	4474.9430 526 457	5247.8858 694 467	516
44	3525.3539 682 009	4133.6998 819 208	4858.8110 450 281	5724.2299 715 942	528
45	3792.5946 768 987	4467.0309 624 621	5274.5398 914 574	6242.6785 604 472	540
46	4079.1542 380 362	4826.2394 010 654	5724.7740 271 061	6806.9532 897 277	552
47	4386.4292 130 186	5213.3341 242 884	6212.3773 739 614	7421.1047 735 016	564
48	4715.9171 207 875	5630.4800 168 787	6740.4515 581 235	8089.5416 632 816	576
49	5069.2237 360 502	6080.0100 292 129	7312.3556 391 288	8817.0622 952 813	588
50	5448.0709 150 972	6564.4382 246 684	7931.7274 767 987	9608.8891 349 990	600

FUTURE WORTH OF ONE DOLLAR WITH INTEREST
PAYABLE AT <u>BEGINNING</u> OF EACH PERIOD COMPOUNDED <u>QUARTERLY</u>

QUARTERS	ANNUAL RATES					
	5%	5½%	6%	6½%	7%	7½%
1	1.0125000	1.0137500	1.0150000	1.0162500	1.0175000	1.0187500
2	1.0251563	1.0276891	1.0302250	1.0327641	1.0353062	1.0378516
3	1.0379707	1.0418198	1.0456784	1.0495465	1.0534241	1.0573113
4	1.0509453	1.0561448	1.0613636	1.0666016	1.0718590	1.0771359
5	1.0640822	1.0706668	1.0772840	1.0839339	1.0906166	1.0973322
6	1.0773832	1.0853885	1.0934433	1.1015478	1.1097024	1.1179071
7	1.0908505	1.1003126	1.1098449	1.1194480	1.1291221	1.1388679
8	1.1044861	1.1154419	1.1264926	1.1376390	1.1488818	1.1602217
9	1.1182922	1.1307792	1.1433900	1.1561256	1.1689872	1.1819758
10	1.1322708	1.1463274	1.1605408	1.1749127	1.1894445	1.2041379
11	1.1464242	1.1620894	1.1779489	1.1940050	1.2102598	1.2267155
12	1.1607545	1.1780681	1.1956182	1.2134076	1.2314393	1.2497164
13	1.1752639	1.1942666	1.2135524	1.2331255	1.2529895	1.2731486
14	1.1899547	1.2106877	1.2317557	1.2531637	1.2749168	1.2970201
15	1.2048292	1.2273347	1.2502321	1.2735277	1.2972279	1.3213392
16	1.2198895	1.2442105	1.2689855	1.2942225	1.3199294	1.3461143
17	1.2351382	1.2613184	1.2880203	1.3152536	1.3430281	1.3713540
18	1.2505774	1.2786616	1.3073406	1.3366265	1.3665311	1.3970669
19	1.2662096	1.2962432	1.3269507	1.3583466	1.3904454	1.4232619
20	1.2820372	1.3140665	1.3468550	1.3804198	1.4147782	1.4499480
21	1.2980627	1.3321349	1.3670578	1.4028516	1.4395368	1.4771346
22	1.3142885	1.3504518	1.3875637	1.4256479	1.4647287	1.5048308
23	1.3307171	1.3690205	1.4083772	1.4488147	1.4903615	1.5330464
24	1.3473511	1.3878445	1.4295028	1.4723580	1.5164428	1.5617910
YEARS						
7	1.4159923	1.4657648	1.5172222	1.5704194	1.6254129	1.6822611
8	1.4881305	1.5480599	1.6103243	1.6750118	1.7422135	1.8120238
9	1.5639438	1.6349754	1.7091395	1.7865703	1.8674073	1.9517958
10	1.6436195	1.7267708	1.8140184	1.9055588	2.0015973	2.1023493
11	1.7273542	1.8237200	1.9253330	2.0324720	2.1454302	2.2645158
12	1.8153549	1.9261124	2.0434783	2.1678379	2.2995987	2.4391912
13	1.9078387	2.0342536	2.1688734	2.3122194	2.4648457	2.6273403
14	2.0050342	2.1484664	2.3019631	2.4662170	2.6419671	2.8300025
15	2.1071813	2.2690916	2.4432198	2.6304710	2.8318163	3.0482972
16	2.2145324	2.3964893	2.5931444	2.8056646	3.0353079	3.2834302
17	2.3273525	2.5310398	2.7522690	2.9925264	3.2534221	3.5367005
18	2.4459203	2.6731445	2.9211580	3.1918334	3.4872099	3.8095069
19	2.5705285	2.8232277	3.1004106	3.4044147	3.7377974	4.1033565
20	2.7014849	2.9817373	3.2906628	3.6311542	4.0063919	4.4198725
21	2.8391130	3.1491464	3.4925895	3.8729949	4.2942874	4.7608032
22	2.9837526	3.3259546	3.7069072	4.1309426	4.6028707	5.1280318
23	3.1357608	3.5126897	3.9343762	4.4060700	4.9336285	5.5235870
24	3.2955132	3.7099090	4.1758035	4.6995213	5.2881543	5.9496537
25	3.4634043	3.9182011	4.4320456	5.0125170	5.6681559	6.4085854
26	3.6398486	4.1381878	4.7040117	5.3463587	6.0754641	6.9029172
27	3.8252819	4.3705255	4.9926666	5.7024348	6.5120411	7.4353797
28	4.0201622	4.6159078	5.2990343	6.0822261	6.9799901	8.0089141
29	4.2249707	4.8750671	5.6242019	6.4873122	7.4815654	8.6266886
30	4.4402132	5.1487768	5.9693229	6.9193776	8.0191834	9.2921157
31	4.6664214	5.4378539	6.3356217	7.3802193	8.5954342	10.0088711
32	4.9041538	5.7431612	6.7243980	7.8717538	9.2130938	10.7809141
33	5.1539976	6.0656099	7.1370309	8.3960252	9.8751378	11.6125092
34	5.4165607	6.4061624	7.5749845	8.9552140	10.5847556	12.5082501
35	5.6925187	6.7658351	8.0398124	9.5516457	11.3453659	13.4730848
36	5.9825260	7.1457017	8.5331638	10.1878007	12.1606329	14.5123429
37	6.2873078	7.5468957	9.0567891	10.8663246	13.0344842	15.6317650
38	6.6076168	7.9706147	9.6125458	11.5900393	13.9711296	16.8375348
39	6.9442440	8.4181234	10.2024057	12.3619545	14.9750814	18.1363126
40	7.2980209	8.8907573	10.8284616	13.1852806	16.0511763	19.5352728

FUTURE WORTH OF ONE DOLLAR WITH INTEREST
PAYABLE AT <u>BEGINNING</u> OF EACH PERIOD COMPOUNDED <u>QUARTERLY</u>

QUARTERS	8%	8½%	ANNUAL RATES 9%	9½%	10%	10½%
1	1.0200000	1.0212500	1.0225000	1.0237500	1.0250000	1.0262500
2	1.0404000	1.0429516	1.0455062	1.0480641	1.0506250	1.0531891
3	1.0612080	1.0651143	1.0690301	1.0729251	1.0768906	1.0808353
4	1.0824322	1.0877480	1.0930833	1.0984383	1.1038129	1.1092072
5	1.1040808	1.1108626	1.1176777	1.1245262	1.1314082	1.1383239
6	1.1261624	1.1344684	1.1428254	1.1512337	1.1596934	1.1682049
7	1.1486857	1.1585759	1.1685390	1.1785755	1.1886858	1.1988703
8	1.1716594	1.1831956	1.1948311	1.2065667	1.2184029	1.2303406
9	1.1950926	1.2083385	1.2217148	1.2352226	1.2488630	1.2626371
10	1.2189944	1.2340157	1.2492034	1.2645591	1.2800845	1.2957813
11	1.2433743	1.2602386	1.2773105	1.2945924	1.3120867	1.3297955
12	1.2682418	1.2870186	1.3060500	1.3253390	1.3448888	1.3647027
13	1.2936066	1.3143678	1.3354361	1.3568158	1.3785110	1.4005261
14	1.3194788	1.3422981	1.3654834	1.3890402	1.4129738	1.4372899
15	1.3458683	1.3708219	1.3962068	1.4220299	1.4482982	1.4750188
16	1.3727857	1.3999519	1.4276215	1.4558031	1.4845056	1.5137380
17	1.4002414	1.4297009	1.4597429	1.4903784	1.5216183	1.5534737
18	1.4282462	1.4600820	1.4925872	1.5257749	1.5596587	1.5942523
19	1.4568112	1.4911088	1.5261704	1.5620121	1.5986502	1.6361015
20	1.4859474	1.5227948	1.5605092	1.5991098	1.6386164	1.6790491
21	1.5156663	1.5551542	1.5956207	1.6370887	1.6795819	1.7231242
22	1.5459797	1.5882012	1.6315221	1.6759696	1.7215714	1.7683562
23	1.5768993	1.6219505	1.6682314	1.7157738	1.7646107	1.8147755
24	1.6084372	1.6564170	1.7057666	1.7565235	1.8087259	1.8624134
YEARS						
7	1.7410242	1.8017642	1.8645450	1.9294326	1.9964950	2.0658023
8	1.8845406	1.9598653	2.0381030	2.1193626	2.2037569	2.2914028
9	2.0398873	2.1318395	2.2278164	2.3279890	2.4325353	2.5416405
10	2.2080397	2.3189041	2.4351890	2.5571523	2.6850638	2.8192060
11	2.3900531	2.5223832	2.6618644	2.8088739	2.9638081	3.1270836
12	2.5870704	2.7437172	2.9096396	3.0853747	3.2714896	3.4685836
13	2.8003282	2.9844727	3.1804785	3.3890936	3.6111123	3.8473779
14	3.0311653	3.2463541	3.4765280	3.7227102	3.9859924	4.2675393
15	3.2810308	3.5312151	3.8001348	4.0891674	4.3997897	4.7335853
16	3.5514932	3.8410720	4.1538639	4.4916980	4.8565446	5.2505269
17	3.8442505	4.1781183	4.5405194	4.9338530	5.3607166	5.8239223
18	4.1611404	4.5447396	4.9631660	5.4195330	5.9172281	6.4599365
19	4.5041522	4.9435313	5.4251540	5.9530225	6.5315126	7.1654081
20	4.8754392	5.3773161	5.9301453	6.5390278	7.2095678	7.9479223
21	5.2773321	5.8491648	6.4821429	7.1827184	7.9580139	8.8158926
22	5.7123540	6.3624168	7.0855223	7.8897728	8.7841583	9.7786516
23	6.1832357	6.9207060	7.7450862	8.6664285	9.6960672	10.8465507
24	6.6929332	7.5279838	8.4660027	9.5195368	10.7026439	12.0310722
25	7.2446461	8.1885490	9.2540463	10.4566236	11.8137164	13.3449519
26	7.8418379	8.9070775	10.1154436	11.4859557	13.0401324	14.8023167
27	8.4882576	9.6886554	11.0570227	12.6166134	14.3938662	16.4188363
28	9.1879630	10.5388152	12.0862471	13.8585711	15.8881351	18.2118915
29	9.9453466	11.4635747	13.2112751	15.2227860	17.5375285	20.2007612
30	10.7651630	12.4694801	14.4410244	16.7212897	19.3581498	22.4068298
31	11.6525587	13.5636515	15.7852429	18.3673047	21.3677753	24.8538170
32	12.6131043	14.7538343	17.2545857	20.1753506	23.5860258	27.5680328
33	13.6528297	16.0484532	18.8606998	22.1613774	26.0345594	30.5786605
34	14.7782619	17.4566722	20.6163163	24.3429052	28.7372822	33.9180704
35	15.9964660	18.9884596	22.5353514	26.7391789	31.7205826	37.6221680
36	17.3150892	20.6546583	24.6330167	29.3713377	35.0135879	41.7307796
37	18.7424094	22.4670624	26.9259397	32.2626016	38.6484497	46.2880813
38	20.2873867	24.4385014	29.4322955	35.4384766	42.6606570	51.3430731
39	21.9597198	26.5829300	32.1719513	38.9269793	47.0893831	56.9501064
40	23.7699070	28.9155280	35.1666232	42.7588841	51.9778681	63.1694681

FUTURE WORTH OF ONE DOLLAR WITH INTEREST
PAYABLE AT BEGINNING OF EACH PERIOD COMPOUNDED QUARTERLY

QUARTERS	ANNUAL RATES					
	11%	11½%	12%	12½%	13%	13½%
1	1.0275000	1.0287500	1.0300000	1.0312500	1.0325000	1.0337500
2	1.0557562	1.0583266	1.0609000	1.0634766	1.0660563	1.0686391
3	1.0847895	1.0887535	1.0927270	1.0967102	1.1007031	1.1047056
4	1.1146213	1.1200551	1.1255088	1.1309824	1.1364759	1.1419894
5	1.1452733	1.1522567	1.1592741	1.1663256	1.1734114	1.1805316
6	1.1767684	1.1853841	1.1940523	1.2027733	1.2115473	1.2203745
7	1.2091295	1.2194639	1.2298739	1.2403599	1.2509226	1.2615622
8	1.2423806	1.2545235	1.2667701	1.2791212	1.2915775	1.3041399
9	1.2765460	1.2905910	1.3047732	1.3190937	1.3335538	1.3481546
10	1.3116510	1.3276955	1.3439164	1.3603154	1.3768943	1.3936548
11	1.3477214	1.3658667	1.3842339	1.4028253	1.4216434	1.4406907
12	1.3847838	1.4051354	1.4257609	1.4466635	1.4678468	1.4893140
13	1.4228653	1.4455331	1.4685337	1.4918718	1.5155518	1.5395783
14	1.4619941	1.4870921	1.5125897	1.5384928	1.5648072	1.5915391
15	1.5021990	1.5298460	1.5579674	1.5865707	1.6156635	1.6452536
16	1.5435094	1.5738291	1.6047064	1.6361510	1.6681725	1.7007809
17	1.5859559	1.6190767	1.6528476	1.6872807	1.7223881	1.7581822
18	1.6295697	1.6656251	1.7024331	1.7400083	1.7783658	1.8175209
19	1.6743829	1.7135119	1.7535061	1.7943835	1.8361626	1.8788622
20	1.7204284	1.7627753	1.8061112	1.8504580	1.8958379	1.9422738
21	1.7677402	1.8134551	1.8602946	1.9082848	1.9574527	2.0078255
22	1.8163531	1.8655920	1.9161034	1.9679187	2.0210699	2.0755896
23	1.8663028	1.9192277	1.9735865	2.0294162	2.0867546	2.1456408
24	1.9176261	1.9744055	2.0327941	2.0928354	2.1545742	2.2180562
YEARS						
7	2.1374268	2.2114430	2.2879277	2.3669600	2.4486217	2.5329967
8	2.3824214	2.4769380	2.5750828	2.6769901	2.7827996	2.8926555
9	2.6554975	2.7743071	2.8982783	3.0276287	3.1625847	3.3033821
10	2.9598740	3.1073769	3.2620378	3.4241948	3.5942014	3.7724275
11	3.2991385	3.4804334	3.6714523	3.8727040	4.0847234	4.3080724
12	3.6772899	3.8982772	4.1322519	4.3799601	4.6421898	4.9197732
13	4.0987855	4.3662853	4.6508859	4.9536578	5.2757370	5.6183291
14	4.5685934	4.8904801	5.2346130	5.6024998	5.9957481	6.4160725
15	5.0922514	5.4776073	5.8916031	6.3363286	6.8140234	7.3270871
16	5.6759316	6.1352221	6.6310512	7.1662762	7.7439736	8.3674561
17	6.3265141	6.8717868	7.4633065	8.1049322	8.8008395	9.5555466
18	7.0516671	7.6967800	8.4000173	9.1665357	10.0019423	10.9123334
19	7.8599380	8.6208178	9.4542934	10.3671905	11.3669666	12.4617695
20	8.7608540	9.6557910	10.6408906	11.7251100	12.9182839	14.2312093
21	9.7650341	10.8150181	11.9764161	13.2608930	14.6813187	16.2518908
22	10.8843147	12.1134163	13.4795618	14.9978366	16.6849653	18.5594878
23	12.1318885	13.5676939	15.1713656	16.9622892	18.9620615	21.1947391
24	13.5224608	15.1965649	17.0755056	19.1840505	21.5499264	24.2041684
25	15.0724223	17.0209902	19.2186320	21.6968235	24.4909726	27.6409049
26	16.8000424	19.0644471	21.6307396	24.5387255	27.8334008	31.5656216
27	18.7256844	21.3532315	24.3455880	27.7528666	31.6319901	36.0476067
28	20.8720459	23.9167961	27.4011738	31.3880037	35.9489953	41.1659865
29	23.2644261	26.7881297	30.8402625	35.4992797	40.8551678	47.0111221
30	25.9310239	30.0041817	34.7109871	40.1490605	46.4309147	53.6862052
31	28.9032705	33.6063371	39.0675218	45.4078807	52.7676169	61.3090798
32	32.2161998	37.6409497	43.9708400	51.3555139	59.9691264	70.0143220
33	35.9088612	42.1599382	49.4895678	58.0821823	68.1534685	79.9556168
34	40.0247801	47.2214543	55.7009446	65.6899259	77.4547764	91.3084705
35	44.6124708	52.8906313	62.6919038	74.2941500	88.0254889	104.2733097
36	49.7260084	59.2404220	70.5602901	84.0253760	100.0388492	119.0790192
37	55.4256661	66.3525376	79.4162281	95.0312213	113.6917440	135.9869831
38	61.7786258	74.3184990	89.3836644	107.4786386	129.2079303	155.2956995
39	68.8597696	83.2408147	100.6021018	121.5564486	146.8417025	177.3460498
40	76.7525632	93.2343002	113.2285518	137.4782038	166.8820602	202.5273171

FUTURE WORTH OF ONE DOLLAR WITH INTEREST
PAYABLE AT <u>BEGINNING</u> OF EACH PERIOD COMPOUNDED <u>SEMIANNUALLY</u>

SEMIANNUAL PERIODS		ANNUAL RATES			
	5%	5½%	6%	6½%	7%	7½%
1	1.0250000	1.0275000	1.0300000	1.0325000	1.0350000	1.0375000
2	1.0506250	1.0557562	1.0609000	1.0660563	1.0712250	1.0764063
3	1.0768906	1.0847895	1.0927270	1.1007031	1.1087179	1.1167715
4	1.1038129	1.1146213	1.1255088	1.1364759	1.1475230	1.1586504
5	1.1314082	1.1452733	1.1592741	1.1734114	1.1876863	1.2020998
6	1.1596934	1.1767684	1.1940523	1.2115473	1.2292553	1.2471785
7	1.1886858	1.2091295	1.2298739	1.2509226	1.2722793	1.2939477
8	1.2184029	1.2423806	1.2667701	1.2915775	1.3168090	1.3424708
9	1.2488630	1.2765460	1.3047732	1.3336538	1.3628974	1.3928134
10	1.2800845	1.3116510	1.3439164	1.3768943	1.4105988	1.4450439
11	1.3120867	1.3477214	1.3842339	1.4216434	1.4599697	1.4992331
12	1.3448888	1.3847838	1.4257609	1.4678468	1.5110687	1.5554543
13	1.3785110	1.4228653	1.4685337	1.5155518	1.5639561	1.6137839
14	1.4129738	1.4619941	1.5125897	1.5648072	1.6186945	1.6743008
15	1.4482982	1.5021990	1.5579674	1.6156635	1.6753488	1.7370870
16	1.4845056	1.5435094	1.6047064	1.6681725	1.7339860	1.8022278
17	1.5216183	1.5859559	1.6528476	1.7223881	1.7946756	1.8698113
18	1.5596587	1.6295697	1.7024331	1.7783658	1.8574892	1.9399293
19	1.5986502	1.6743829	1.7535061	1.8361626	1.9225013	2.0126766
20	1.6386164	1.7204284	1.8061112	1.8958379	1.9897889	2.0881520
21	1.6795819	1.7677402	1.8602946	1.9574527	2.0594315	2.1664577
22	1.7215714	1.8163531	1.9161034	2.0210699	2.1315116	2.2476999
23	1.7646107	1.8663028	1.9735865	2.0867546	2.2061145	2.3319886
24	1.8087259	1.9176261	2.0327941	2.1545742	2.2833285	2.4194382
YEARS						
13	1.9002927	2.0245457	2.1565913	2.2968973	2.4459586	2.6042984
14	1.9964950	2.1374268	2.2879277	2.4486217	2.6201720	2.8032830
15	2.0975676	2.2566017	2.4272625	2.6103684	2.8067937	3.0174714
16	2.2037569	2.3824214	2.5750828	2.7827996	3.0067076	3.2480251
17	2.3153221	2.5152563	2.7319053	2.9666209	3.2208603	3.4961945
18	2.4325353	2.6554975	2.8982783	3.1625847	3.4502661	3.7633256
19	2.5556824	2.8035581	3.0747835	3.3714932	3.6960113	4.0508672
20	2.6850638	2.9598740	3.2620378	3.5942014	3.9592597	4.3603788
21	2.8209952	3.1249055	3.4606959	3.8316209	4.2412580	4.6935389
22	2.9638081	3.2991385	3.6714523	4.0847234	4.5433416	5.0521547
23	3.1138509	3.4830861	3.8950437	4.3545449	4.8669411	5.4381709
24	3.2714896	3.6772899	4.1322519	4.6421898	5.2135890	5.8536811
25	3.4371087	3.8823218	4.3839060	4.9488355	5.5849269	6.3009389
26	3.6111123	4.0987855	4.6508859	5.2757370	5.9827133	6.7823700
27	3.7939249	4.3273184	4.9341248	5.6242324	6.4088320	7.3005855
28	3.9859924	4.5685934	5.2346130	5.9957481	6.8653011	7.8583958
29	4.1877832	4.8233211	5.5534010	6.3918047	7.3542822	8.4588264
30	4.3997897	5.0922514	5.8916031	6.8140234	7.8780909	9.1051336
31	4.6225291	5.3761762	6.2504017	7.2641322	8.4392079	9.8008227
32	4.8565446	5.6759316	6.6310512	7.7439736	9.0402905	10.5496668
33	5.1024072	5.9924003	7.0348822	8.2555114	9.6841852	11.3557273
34	5.3607166	6.3265141	7.4633065	8.8008395	10.3739413	12.2233759
35	5.6321029	6.6792568	7.9178219	9.3821900	11.1128253	13.1573182
36	5.9172281	7.0516671	8.4000173	10.0019423	11.9043362	14.1626195
37	6.2167877	7.4448416	8.9115783	10.6626331	12.7522226	15.2447322
38	6.5315126	7.8599380	9.4542934	11.3669666	13.6604996	16.4095250
39	6.8621704	8.2981787	10.0300599	12.1178258	14.6334687	17.6633152
40	7.2095678	8.7608540	10.6408906	12.9182839	15.6757375	19.0129029

FUTURE WORTH OF ONE DOLLAR WITH INTEREST
PAYABLE AT <u>BEGINNING</u> OF EACH PERIOD COMPOUNDED <u>SEMIANNUALLY</u>

SEMIANNUAL PERIODS		ANNUAL RATES			
8%	8½%	9%	9½%	10%	10½%
1 1.0400000	1.0425000	1.0450000	1.0475000	1.0500000	1.0525000
2 1.0816000	1.0868063	1.0920250	1.0972562	1.1025000	1.1077562
3 1.1248640	1.1329955	1.1411661	1.1493759	1.1576250	1.1659135
4 1.1698586	1.1811478	1.1925186	1.2039713	1.2155062	1.2271239
5 1.2166529	1.2313466	1.2461819	1.2611599	1.2762816	1.2915479
6 1.2653190	1.2836788	1.3022601	1.3210650	1.3400956	1.3593542
7 1.3159318	1.3382352	1.3608618	1.3838156	1.4071004	1.4307203
8 1.3685691	1.3951102	1.4221006	1.4495468	1.4774554	1.5058331
9 1.4233118	1.4544024	1.4860951	1.5184003	1.5513282	1.5848893
10 1.4802443	1.5162145	1.5529694	1.5905243	1.6288946	1.6680960
11 1.5394541	1.5806536	1.6228530	1.6660742	1.7103394	1.7556711
12 1.6010322	1.6478314	1.6958814	1.7452128	1.7958563	1.8478438
13 1.6650735	1.7178642	1.7721961	1.8281104	1.8856491	1.9448556
14 1.7316764	1.7908734	1.8519449	1.9149456	1.9799316	2.0469605
15 1.8009435	1.8669855	1.9352824	2.0059055	2.0789282	2.1544259
16 1.8729812	1.9463324	2.0223702	2.1011860	2.1828746	2.2675333
17 1.9479005	2.0290516	2.1133768	2.2009924	2.2920183	2.3865788
18 2.0258165	2.1152862	2.2084788	2.3055395	2.4066192	2.5118742
19 2.1068492	2.2051859	2.3078603	2.4150526	2.5269502	2.6437476
20 2.1911231	2.2989063	2.4117140	2.5297676	2.6532977	2.7825443
21 2.2787681	2.3966098	2.5202412	2.6499316	2.7859626	2.9286279
22 2.3699188	2.4984657	2.6336520	2.7758034	2.9252607	3.0823809
23 2.4647155	2.6046505	2.7521663	2.9076540	3.0715238	3.2442059
24 2.5633042	2.7153482	2.8760138	3.0457676	3.2250999	3.4145267

YEARS

	8%	8½%	9%	9½%	10%	10½%
13	2.7724698	2.9510574	3.1406790	3.3419875	3.5556727	3.7824633
14	2.9987033	3.2072276	3.4297000	3.6670167	3.9201291	4.1900473
15	3.2433975	3.4856350	3.7453181	4.0236570	4.3219424	4.6415511
16	3.5080587	3.7882099	4.0899810	4.4149828	4.7649415	5.1417072
17	3.7943163	4.1170502	4.4663615	4.8443674	5.2533480	5.6957583
18	4.1039326	4.4744359	4.8773785	5.3155124	5.7918161	6.3095119
19	4.4388135	4.8628449	5.3262192	5.8324792	6.3854773	6.9894012
20	4.8010206	5.2849702	5.8163645	6.3997243	7.0399887	7.7425529
21	5.1927839	5.7437387	6.3516155	7.0221375	7.7615876	8.5768613
22	5.6165151	6.2423311	6.9361229	7.7050843	8.5571503	9.5010718
23	6.0748227	6.7842045	7.5744196	8.4544519	9.4342582	10.5248716
24	6.5705282	7.3731158	8.2714556	9.2767001	10.4012696	11.6589923
25	7.1066833	8.0131483	9.0326363	10.1789172	11.4673998	12.9153216
26	7.6865887	8.7087397	9.8638646	11.1688805	12.6428083	14.3070282
27	8.3138143	9.4647127	10.7715868	12.2551240	13.9386961	15.8487000
28	8.9922216	10.2863089	11.7628420	13.4470114	15.3674125	17.5564964
29	9.7259869	11.1792249	12.8453176	14.7548173	16.9425722	19.4483186
30	10.5196274	12.1496514	14.0274079	16.1898155	18.6791859	21.5439965
31	11.3780290	13.2043171	15.3182801	17.7643762	20.5938024	23.8654968
32	12.3064762	14.3505344	16.7279449	19.4920728	22.7046672	26.4371532
33	13.3106846	15.5962504	18.2673340	21.3877987	25.0318956	29.2859217
34	14.3968365	16.9501025	19.9483854	23.4678958	27.5976649	32.4416628
35	15.5716184	18.4214773	21.7841356	25.7502954	30.4264255	35.9374548
36	16.8422624	20.0205767	23.7888207	28.2546725	33.5451342	39.8099401
37	18.2165910	21.7584878	25.9779869	31.0026160	36.9835104	44.0997100
38	19.7030648	23.6472606	28.3686111	34.0178142	40.7743202	48.8517294
39	21.3108349	25.6999906	30.9792326	37.3262592	44.9536880	54.1158085
40	23.0497991	27.9309104	33.8300964	40.9564712	49.5614411	59.9471251

581

**FUTURE WORTH OF ONE DOLLAR WITH INTEREST
PAYABLE AT <u>BEGINNING</u> OF EACH PERIOD COMPOUNDED <u>SEMIANNUALLY</u>**

SEMIANNUAL PERIODS		ANNUAL RATES			
	11%	**11½%**	**12%**	**12½%**	**13%**	**13½%**
1	1.0550000	1.0575000	1.0600000	1.0625000	1.0650000	1.0675000
2	1.1130250	1.1183063	1.1236000	1.1289063	1.1342250	1.1395563
3	1.1742414	1.1826089	1.1910160	1.1994629	1.2079496	1.2164763
4	1.2388247	1.2506089	1.2624770	1.2744293	1.2864664	1.2985884
5	1.3069600	1.3225189	1.3382256	1.3540812	1.3700867	1.3862432
6	1.3788428	1.3985637	1.4185191	1.4387112	1.4591423	1.4798146
7	1.4546792	1.4789811	1.5036303	1.5286307	1.5539865	1.5797021
8	1.5346865	1.5640225	1.5938481	1.6241701	1.6549957	1.6863320
9	1.6190943	1.6539538	1.6894790	1.7256807	1.7625704	1.8001594
10	1.7081445	1.7490562	1.7908477	1.8335358	1.8771375	1.9216701
11	1.8020924	1.8496269	1.8982986	1.9481318	1.9991514	2.0513829
12	1.9012075	1.9559805	2.0121965	2.0698900	2.1290962	2.1898512
13	2.0057739	2.0684493	2.1329283	2.1992581	2.2674875	2.3376661
14	2.1160915	2.1873852	2.2609040	2.3367117	2.4148742	2.4954586
15	2.2324765	2.3131598	2.3965582	2.4827562	2.5718410	2.6639021
16	2.3552627	2.4461665	2.5403517	2.6379285	2.7390107	2.8437155
17	2.4848021	2.5868211	2.6927728	2.8027990	2.9170464	3.0356663
18	2.6214663	2.7355633	2.8543392	2.9779740	3.1066544	3.2405737
19	2.7656469	2.8928582	3.0255995	3.1640270	3.3085869	3.4593125
20	2.9177575	3.0591975	3.2071355	3.3618534	3.5236451	3.6928160
21	3.0782342	3.2351014	3.3995636	3.5719693	3.7526820	3.9420811
22	3.2475370	3.4211197	3.6035374	3.7952173	3.9966063	4.2081716
23	3.4261516	3.6178341	3.8197497	4.0324184	4.2563857	4.4922232
24	3.6145899	3.8258596	4.0489346	4.2844446	4.5330508	4.7954483
YEARS						
13	4.0231289	4.2784827	4.5493830	4.8367363	5.1414996	5.4646830
14	4.4778431	4.7846539	5.1116867	5.4602218	5.8316173	6.2273137
15	4.9839513	5.3507084	5.7434912	6.1640785	6.6143662	7.0963742
16	5.5472624	5.9837306	6.4533867	6.9586668	7.5021795	8.0867176
17	6.1742417	6.6916433	7.2510253	7.8556824	8.5091595	9.2152696
18	6.8720854	7.4833066	8.1472520	8.8683290	9.6513014	10.5013181
19	7.6488028	8.3686285	9.1542523	10.0115120	10.9467474	11.9668426
20	8.5133088	9.3586896	10.2857179	11.3020584	12.4160745	13.6368903
21	9.4755255	10.4658810	11.5570327	12.7589644	14.0826221	15.5400036
22	10.5464968	11.7040602	12.9854819	14.4036747	15.9728621	17.7087082
23	11.7385146	13.0887236	14.5904875	16.2603984	18.1168195	20.1800691
24	13.0652602	14.6372015	16.3938717	18.3564653	20.5485496	22.9963239
25	14.5419612	16.3688739	18.4201543	20.7227285	23.3066787	26.2056047
26	16.1855664	18.3054140	20.6968853	23.3940177	26.4350176	29.8627606
27	18.0149400	20.4710588	23.2550204	26.4096528	29.9832579	34.0302954
28	20.0510786	22.8929130	26.1293409	29.8140221	34.0077607	38.7794359
29	22.3173518	25.6012877	29.3589274	33.6572358	38.5724523	44.1913485
30	24.8397704	28.6300801	32.9876909	37.9958639	43.7498397	50.3585274
31	27.6472855	32.0171975	37.0649694	42.8937682	49.6221620	57.3863746
32	30.7721199	35.8050321	41.6461997	48.4230430	56.2826967	65.3950019
33	34.2501388	40.0409911	46.7936699	54.6650759	63.8372416	74.5212831
34	38.1212607	44.7780906	52.5773675	61.7117459	72.4057954	84.9211939
35	42.4299162	50.0756186	59.0759302	69.6667756	82.1244633	96.7724773
36	47.2255575	55.9998773	66.3777151	78.6472584	93.1476194	110.2776813
37	52.5632262	62.6250128	74.5820007	88.7853816	105.6503586	125.6676210
38	58.5041848	70.0339432	83.8003360	100.2303722	119.8312779	143.2053229
39	65.1166203	78.3193964	94.1580576	113.1506936	135.9156312	163.1905208
40	72.4764263	87.5850705	105.7959935	127.7365252	154.1589068	185.9647779

FUTURE WORTH OF ONE DOLLAR PER PERIOD WITH INTEREST
PAYABLE AT <u>END</u> OF EACH PERIOD COMPOUNDED <u>SEMIANNUALLY</u>

ANNUAL RATES

HALF YEARS	7%	7¹/₂%	8%	8¹/₂%	HALF YEARS
1	1.0000 000 000	1.0000 000 000	1.0000 000 000	1.0000 000 000	1
YEARS					
1	2.0350 000 000	2.0375 000 000	2.0400 000 000	2.0425 000 000	2
2	4.2149 428 750	4.2306 777 344	4.2464 640 000	4.2623 017 656	4
3	6.5501 521 813	6.5914 279 550	6.6329 754 624	6.6747 961 983	6
4	9.0516 867 704	9.1325 542 472	9.2142 262 601	9.2967 102 258	8
5	11.7313 931 606	11.8678 384 702	12.0061 071 230	12.1462 227 778	10
6	14.6019 616 385	14.8121 155 033	15.0258 054 642	15.2430 908 288	12
7	17.6769 863 562	17.9813 537 034	18.2919 111 901	18.6087 863 820	14
8	20.9710 297 094	21.3927 415 098	21.8245 311 432	22.2666 453 449	16
9	24.4996 913 004	25.0647 806 658	25.6454 128 845	26.2420 293 274	18
10	28.2796 818 133	29.0173 865 636	29.7780 785 758	30.5625 014 857	20
11	32.3289 021 505	33.2719 962 557	34.2479 697 876	35.2580 176 303	22
12	36.6665 282 061	37.8516 847 196	39.0826 041 223	40.3611 339 232	24
13	41.3131 016 776	42.7812 900 052	44.3117 446 187	45.9072 326 048	26
14	46.2906 273 446	48.0875 479 447	49.9675 829 796	51.9347 673 151	28
15	51.6226 772 772	53.7992 371 548	56.0849 377 507	58.4855 297 104	30
16	57.3345 024 663	59.9473 351 187	62.7014 686 711	65.6049 392 238	32
17	63.4531 524 044	66.5651 861 926	69.8579 085 147	73.3423 579 793	34
18	70.0076 031 845	73.6886 824 501	77.5983 138 495	81.7514 330 416	36
19	77.0288 947 213	81.3564 583 436	85.9703 362 596	90.8904 683 761	38
20	84.5502 777 478	89.6101 002 389	95.0255 156 984	100.8228 290 966	40
21	92.6073 712 804	98.4943 719 603	104.8195 977 794	111.6173 808 049	42
22	101.2383 312 998	108.0574 575 679	115.4128 769 582	123.3489 670 674	44
23	110.4840 314 467	118.3512 226 852	126.8705 677 180	136.0989 283 398	46
24	120.3882 565 864	129.4314 957 935	139.2632 060 438	149.9556 659 380	48
25	130.9979 101 618	141.3583 710 189	152.6670 836 570	165.0152 549 644	50
26	142.3632 363 131	154.1965 340 546	167.1647 176 834	181.3821 104 406	52
27	154.5380 578 195	168.0156 129 847	182.8453 586 463	199.1697 112 651	54
28	167.5800 309 877	182.8905 559 143	199.8055 399 119	218.5013 870 136	56
29	181.5509 186 948	198.9020 374 521	218.1496 719 687	239.5111 730 400	58
30	196.5168 828 788	216.1368 962 512	237.9906 852 013	262.3447 398 047	60
31	212.5487 978 619	234.6886 059 804	259.4507 251 137	287.1604 028 744	62
32	229.7225 859 896	254.6577 822 811	282.6619 042 830	314.1302 205 964	64
33	248.1195 771 767	276.1527 284 585	307.7671 156 725	343.4411 870 581	66
34	267.8268 940 611	299.2900 228 673	334.9209 123 114	375.2965 286 021	68
35	288.9378 645 906	324.1951 511 770	364.2904 587 560	409.9171 128 881	70
36	311.5524 639 960	351.0031 869 466	396.0565 601 905	447.5429 802 687	72
37	335.7777 882 442	379.8595 241 992	430.4147 755 021	488.4350 080 997	74
38	361.7285 612 119	410.9206 659 701	467.5766 211 830	532.8767 195 215	76
39	389.5276 779 842	444.3550 731 044	507.7708 734 716	581.1762 492 555	78
40	419.3067 868 486	480.3440 779 088	551.2449 767 468	633.6684 800 424	80
41	451.2069 127 419	519.0828 676 115	598.2665 668 494	690.7173 645 381	82
42	485.3791 251 019	560.7815 429 649	649.1251 187 043	752.7184 487 635	84
43	521.9852 532 873	605.6662 577 321	704.1337 283 906	820.1016 146 065	86
44	561.1986 529 527	653.9804 452 369	763.6310 406 272	893.3340 603 895	88
45	603.2050 270 092	705.9861 386 308	827.9833 335 424	972.9235 401 691	90
46	648.2033 050 580	761.9653 920 356	897.5867 735 595	1059.4218 842 279	92
47	696.4065 854 607	822.2218 102 708	972.8698 542 819	1153.4288 251 657	94
48	748.0431 445 102	887.0821 954 618	1054.2960 343 913	1255.5961 561 203	96
49	803.3575 174 779	956.8983 194 588	1142.3665 907 976	1366.6322 499 475	98
50	862.6116 566 603	1032.0488 316 799	1237.6237 046 067	1487.3069 706 945	100
51	926.0861 719 059	1112.9413 127 255	1340.6537 989 026	1618.4570 114 193	102
52	994.0816 594 999	1200.0144 849 009	1452.0911 488 931	1760.9916 953 668	104
53	1066.9201 256 978	1293.7405 916 379	1572.6217 866 428	1915.8992 807 228	106
54	1144.9465 116 506	1394.6279 587 177	1702.9877 244 328	2084.2538 126 600	108
55	1228.5303 269 429	1503.2237 511 885	1843.9915 227 465	2267.2225 701 852	110
56	1318.0673 994 794	1620.1169 409 277	1996.5012 310 027	2466.0741 594 184	112
57	1413.9817 500 074	1745.9415 009 455	2161.4557 314 525	2682.1873 094 194	114
58	1516.7276 001 516	1881.3798 437 521	2339.8705 191 390	2917.0604 315 477	116
59	1626.7915 234 724	2027.1665 224 387	2532.8439 535 007	3172.3220 086 337	118
60	1744.6947 497 318	2184.0922 145 438	2741.5640 201 064	3449.7418 859 957	120

**FUTURE WORTH OF ONE DOLLAR WITH INTEREST
PAYABLE AT <u>BEGINNING</u> OF EACH PERIOD COMPOUNDED <u>ANNUALLY</u>**

YEARS	5%	5½%	ANNUAL RATES 6%	6½%	7%	7½%
1	1.0500000	1.0550000	1.0600000	1.0650000	1.0700000	1.0750000
2	1.1025000	1.1130250	1.1236000	1.1342250	1.1449000	1.1556250
3	1.1576250	1.1742414	1.1910160	1.2079496	1.2250430	1.2422969
4	1.2155062	1.2388247	1.2624770	1.2864664	1.3107960	1.3354691
5	1.2762816	1.3069600	1.3382256	1.3700867	1.4025517	1.4356293
6	1.3400956	1.3788428	1.4185191	1.4591423	1.5007304	1.5433015
7	1.4071004	1.4546792	1.5036303	1.5539865	1.6057815	1.6590491
8	1.4774554	1.5346865	1.5938481	1.6549957	1.7181862	1.7834778
9	1.5513282	1.6190943	1.6894790	1.7625704	1.8384592	1.9172387
10	1.6288946	1.7081445	1.7908477	1.8771375	1.9671514	2.0610316
11	1.7103394	1.8020924	1.8982986	1.9991514	2.1048520	2.2156089
12	1.7958563	1.9012075	2.0121965	2.1290962	2.2521916	2.3817796
13	1.8856491	2.0057739	2.1329283	2.2674875	2.4098450	2.5604131
14	1.9799316	2.1160915	2.2609040	2.4148742	2.5785342	2.7524440
15	2.0789282	2.2324765	2.3965582	2.5718410	2.7590315	2.9588774
16	2.1828746	2.3552627	2.5403517	2.7390107	2.9521637	3.1807932
17	2.2920183	2.4848021	2.6927728	2.9170464	3.1588152	3.4193526
18	2.4066192	2.6214663	2.8543392	3.1066544	3.3799323	3.6758041
19	2.5269502	2.7656469	3.0255995	3.3085869	3.6165275	3.9514894
20	2.6532977	2.9177575	3.2071355	3.5236451	3.8696845	4.2478511
21	2.7859626	3.0782342	3.3995636	3.7526820	4.1405624	4.5664399
22	2.9252607	3.2475370	3.6035374	3.9966063	4.4304017	4.9089229
23	3.0715238	3.4261516	3.8197497	4.2563857	4.7405299	5.2770921
24	3.2250999	3.6145899	4.0489346	4.5330508	5.0723670	5.6728741
25	3.3863549	3.8133923	4.2918707	4.8276901	5.4274326	6.0983396
26	3.5556727	4.0231289	4.5493830	5.1414996	5.8073529	6.5557151
27	3.7334563	4.2444010	4.8223459	5.4756970	6.2138676	7.0473937
28	3.9201291	4.4778431	5.1116867	5.8316173	6.6488384	7.5759482
29	4.1161356	4.7241244	5.4183879	6.2106725	7.1142570	8.1441444
30	4.3219424	4.9839513	5.7434912	6.6143662	7.6122550	8.7549552
31	4.5380395	5.2580686	6.0881006	7.0443000	8.1451129	9.4115768
32	4.7649415	5.5472624	6.4533867	7.5021795	8.7152708	10.1174451
33	5.0031885	5.8523618	6.8405899	7.9898211	9.3253398	10.8762535
34	5.2533480	6.1742417	7.2510253	8.5091595	9.9781135	11.6919725
35	5.5160154	6.5138250	7.6860868	9.0622549	10.6765815	12.5688704
36	5.7918161	6.8720854	8.1472520	9.6513014	11.4239422	13.5115357
37	6.0814069	7.2500501	8.6360871	10.2786360	12.2236181	14.5249009
38	6.3854773	7.6488028	9.1542523	10.9467474	13.0792714	15.6142684
39	6.7047512	8.0694870	9.7035075	11.6582859	13.9948204	16.7853386
40	7.0399887	8.5133088	10.2857179	12.4160745	14.9744578	18.0442390

FUTURE WORTH OF ONE DOLLAR WITH INTEREST
PAYABLE AT <u>BEGINNING</u> OF EACH PERIOD COMPOUNDED <u>ANNUALLY</u>

YEARS	8%	8½%	9%	9½%	10%	10½%
			ANNUAL RATES			
1	1.0800000	1.0850000	1.0900000	1.0950000	1.1000000	1.1050000
2	1.1664000	1.1772250	1.1881000	1.1990250	1.2100000	1.2210250
3	1.2597120	1.2772891	1.2950290	1.3129324	1.3310000	1.3492326
4	1.3604890	1.3858587	1.4115816	1.4376610	1.4641000	1.4909021
5	1.4693281	1.5036567	1.5386240	1.5742387	1.6105100	1.6474468
6	1.5868743	1.6314675	1.6771001	1.7237914	1.7715610	1.8204287
7	1.7138243	1.7701422	1.8280391	1.8875516	1.9487171	2.0115737
8	1.8509302	1.9206043	1.9925626	2.0668690	2.1435888	2.2227889
9	1.9990046	2.0838557	2.1718933	2.2632216	2.3579477	2.4561818
10	2.1589250	2.2609834	2.3673637	2.4782276	2.5937425	2.7140808
11	2.3316390	2.4531670	2.5804264	2.7136592	2.8531167	2.9990593
12	2.5181701	2.6616862	2.8126648	2.9714569	3.1384284	3.3139606
13	2.7196237	2.8879296	3.0658046	3.2537453	3.4522712	3.6619264
14	2.9371936	3.1334036	3.3417270	3.5628511	3.7974983	4.0464287
15	3.1721691	3.3997429	3.6424825	3.9013219	4.1772482	4.4713037
16	3.4259426	3.6887210	3.9703059	4.2719475	4.5949730	4.9407906
17	3.7000181	4.0022623	4.3276334	4.6777825	5.0544703	5.4595736
18	3.9960195	4.3424546	4.7171204	5.1221719	5.5599173	6.0328288
19	4.3157011	4.7115632	5.1416613	5.6087782	6.1159090	6.6662759
20	4.6609571	5.1120461	5.6044108	6.1416121	6.7274999	7.3662348
21	5.0338337	5.5465700	6.1088077	6.7250653	7.4002499	8.1396895
22	5.4365404	6.0180285	6.6586004	7.3639465	8.1402749	8.9943569
23	5.8714636	6.5295609	7.2578745	8.0635214	8.9543024	9.9387644
24	6.3411807	7.0845736	7.9110832	8.8295559	9.8497327	10.9823346
25	6.8484752	7.6867624	8.6230807	9.6683637	10.8347059	12.1354798
26	7.3963532	8.3401372	9.3991579	10.5868583	11.9181765	13.4097051
27	7.9880615	9.0490488	10.2450821	11.5926098	13.1099942	14.8177242
28	8.6271064	9.8182180	11.1671395	12.6939077	14.4209936	16.3735852
29	9.3172749	10.6527665	12.1721821	13.8998290	15.8630930	18.0928117
30	10.0626569	11.5582516	13.2676785	15.2203127	17.4494023	19.9925569
31	10.8676694	12.5407030	14.4617695	16.6662424	19.1943425	22.0917754
32	11.7370830	13.6066628	15.7633288	18.2495354	21.1137767	24.4114118
33	12.6760496	14.7632291	17.1820284	19.9832413	23.2251544	26.9746100
34	13.6901336	16.0181036	18.7284109	21.8816492	25.5476699	29.8069441
35	14.7853443	17.3796424	20.4139679	23.9604059	28.1024368	32.9366732
36	15.9681718	18.8569120	22.2512250	26.2366445	30.9126805	36.3950239
37	17.2456256	20.4597495	24.2538353	28.7291257	34.0039486	40.2165014
38	18.6252756	22.1988282	26.4366805	31.4583926	37.4043434	44.4392340
39	20.1152977	24.0857286	28.8159817	34.4469399	41.1447778	49.1053536
40	21.7245215	26.1330156	31.4094201	37.7193992	45.2592556	54.2614157

FUTURE WORTH OF ONE DOLLAR WITH INTEREST
PAYABLE AT <u>BEGINNING</u> OF EACH PERIOD COMPOUNDED <u>ANNUALLY</u>

YEARS			ANNUAL RATES			
	11%	11½%	12%	12½%	13%	13½%
1	1.1100000	1.1150000	1.1200000	1.1250000	1.1300000	1.1350000
2	1.2321000	1.2432250	1.2544000	1.2656250	1.2769000	1.2882250
3	1.3676310	1.3861959	1.4049280	1.4238281	1.4428970	1.4621354
4	1.5180704	1.5456084	1.5735194	1.6018066	1.6304736	1.6595237
5	1.6850582	1.7233534	1.7623417	1.8020325	1.8424352	1.8835593
6	1.8704146	1.9215390	1.9738227	2.0272865	2.0819518	2.1378399
7	2.0761602	2.1425160	2.2106814	2.2806973	2.3526055	2.4264482
8	2.3045378	2.3889053	2.4759632	2.5657845	2.6584442	2.7540187
9	2.5580369	2.6636294	2.7730788	2.8865076	3.0040419	3.1258113
10	2.8394210	2.9699468	3.1058482	3.2473210	3.3945674	3.5477958
11	3.1517573	3.3114907	3.4785500	3.6532362	3.8358612	4.0267482
12	3.4984506	3.6923121	3.8959760	4.1098907	4.3345231	4.5703592
13	3.8832802	4.1169280	4.3634931	4.6236270	4.8980111	5.1873577
14	4.3104410	4.5903748	4.8871123	5.2015804	5.5347525	5.8876510
15	4.7845895	5.1182679	5.4735658	5.8517779	6.2542704	6.6824839
16	5.3108943	5.7068687	6.1303937	6.5832502	7.0673255	7.5846193
17	5.8950927	6.3631586	6.8660409	7.4061564	7.9860778	8.6085429
18	6.5435529	7.0949218	7.6899658	8.3319260	9.0242680	9.7706961
19	7.2633437	7.9108378	8.6127617	9.3734167	10.1974228	11.0897401
20	8.0623115	8.8205842	9.6462931	10.5450938	11.5230878	12.5868550
21	8.9491658	9.8349513	10.8038483	11.8632306	13.0210892	14.2860805
22	9.9335740	10.9659707	12.1003101	13.3461344	14.7138308	16.2147013
23	11.0262672	12.2270574	13.5523473	15.0144012	16.6266288	18.4036860
24	12.2391566	13.6331690	15.1786289	16.8912013	18.7880905	20.8881836
25	13.5854638	15.2009834	17.0000644	19.0026015	21.2305423	23.7080884
26	15.0798648	16.9490965	19.0400721	21.3779267	23.9905128	26.9086804
27	16.7386500	18.8982426	21.3248808	24.0501675	27.1092794	30.5413522
28	18.5799014	21.0715405	23.8838665	27.0564385	30.6334858	34.6644347
29	20.6236906	23.4947676	26.7499305	30.4384933	34.6158389	39.3441334
30	22.8922966	26.1966659	29.9599221	34.2433050	39.1158980	44.6555915
31	25.4104492	29.2092825	33.5551128	38.5237181	44.2009647	50.6840963
32	28.2055986	32.5683500	37.5817263	43.3391828	49.9470901	57.5264493
33	31.3082145	36.3137102	42.0915335	48.7565807	56.4402118	65.2925200
34	34.7521180	40.4897869	47.1425175	54.8511533	63.7774394	74.1070101
35	38.5748510	45.1461124	52.7996196	61.7075474	72.0685065	84.1114565
36	42.8180846	50.3379153	59.1355739	69.4209909	81.4374123	95.4665031
37	47.5280740	56.1267756	66.2318428	78.0986147	92.0242759	108.3544811
38	52.7561621	62.5813548	74.1796639	87.8609415	103.9874318	122.9823360
39	58.5593399	69.7782106	83.0812236	98.8435592	117.5057979	139.5849514
40	65.0008673	77.8027048	93.0509704	111.1990041	132.7815516	158.4289198

586

**FUTURE WORTH OF ONE DOLLAR PER PERIOD WITH INTEREST
PAYABLE AT <u>END</u> OF EACH PERIOD COMPOUNDED <u>ANNUALLY</u>**

ANNUAL RATES

YEARS

	7%	7¹/₂%	8%	8¹/₂%
1	1.0000000	1.0000000	1.0000000	1.0000000
2	2.0700000	2.0750000	2.0800000	2.0850000
3	3.2149000	3.2306250	3.2464000	3.2622250
4	4.4399430	4.4729219	4.5061120	4.5395141
5	5.7507390	5.8083910	5.8666010	5.9253728
6	7.1532907	7.2440203	7.3359290	7.4290295
7	8.6540211	8.7873219	8.9228034	9.0604970
8	10.2598026	10.4463710	10.6366276	10.8306393
9	11.9779887	12.2298488	12.4875578	12.7512436
10	13.8164480	14.1470875	14.4865625	14.8350993
11	15.7835993	16.2081191	16.6454875	17.0960828
12	17.8884513	18.4237280	18.9771265	19.5492498
13	20.1406429	20.8055076	21.4952966	22.2109360
14	22.5504879	23.3659207	24.2149203	25.0988656
15	25.1290220	26.1183647	27.1521139	28.2322692
16	27.8880536	29.0772421	30.3242830	31.6320120
17	30.8402173	32.2580352	33.7502257	35.3207331
18	33.9990325	35.6773879	37.4502437	39.3229954
19	37.3789648	39.3531919	41.4462632	43.6654500
20	40.9954923	43.3046813	45.7619643	48.3770132
21	44.8651768	47.5525324	50.4229214	53.4890594
22	49.0057392	52.1189724	55.4567552	59.0356294
23	53.4361409	57.0278953	60.8932956	65.0536579
24	58.1766708	62.3049874	66.7647592	71.5832188
25	63.2490377	67.9778615	73.1059400	78.6677924
26	68.6764704	74.0762011	79.9544151	86.3545548
27	74.4838233	80.6319162	87.3507684	94.6946919
28	80.6976909	87.6793099	95.3388298	103.7437407
29	87.3465293	95.2552582	103.9659362	113.5619587
30	94.4607863	103.3994025	113.2832111	124.2147252
31	102.0730414	112.1543577	123.3458680	135.7729768
32	110.2181543	121.5659345	134.2135374	148.3136799
33	118.9334251	131.6833796	145.9506204	161.9203427
34	128.2587648	142.5596331	158.6266701	176.6835718
35	138.2368784	154.2516056	172.3168037	192.7016754
36	148.9134598	166.8204760	187.1021480	210.0813178
37	160.3374020	180.3320117	203.0703198	228.9382298
38	172.5610202	194.8569126	220.3159454	249.3979793
39	185.6402916	210.4711810	238.9412210	271.5968076
40	199.6351120	227.2565196	259.0565187	295.6825362

ORGANIZATION OF THE FEDERAL RESERVE SYSTEM

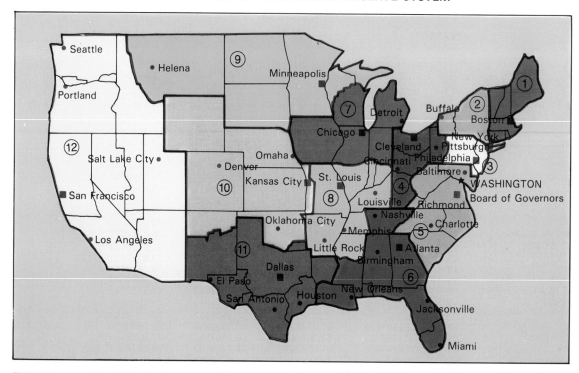

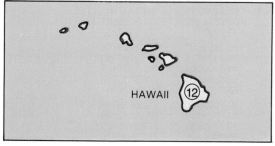

LEGEND

— **BOUNDARIES OF FEDERAL RESERVE DISTRICTS**

★ **BOARD OF GOVERNORS OF THE FEDERAL RESERVE SYSTEM**

• **CITY WHERE A BRANCH OF FEDERAL RESERVE BANK IS LOCATED**

BOUNDARIES OF FEDERAL RESERVE BRANCH TERRITORIES

■ **CITY WHERE FEDERAL RESERVE BANK IS LOCATED**

③ **FEDERAL RESERVE DISTRICT NUMBER. THIS NUMBER APPEARS ON THE CURRENCY ISSUED BY THE FEDERAL RESERVE BANK IN THE DISTRICT.**

Source: Board of Governors of the Federal Reserve System, *Federal Reserve Bulletin* 73, no. 2 (February 1987): A86.

Hypothetical Credit-Scoring Table

Fill out your credit profile by answering the nine questions below in Table 1. Circle the one response that applies to you, and then find your total score by adding up the points you got for each response. The points are found in the lower right-hand corner of each box. (For example: if you are 25 years old, you get 12 points.) Once you've totaled your score, look at Table 2 to find out how good a credit "bet" you may be.

1.

1. age?	under 25 **12**	25–29 **5**	30–34 **0**	35–39 **1**	40–44 **18**	45–49 **22**	50 or over **31**	
2. time at address?	less than 1 yr. **9**	1–2 yrs. **0**	2–3 yrs. **5**	3–5 yrs. **0**	5–9 yrs. **5**	10 yrs. or more **21**		
3. age of auto?	none **0**	0–1 yrs. **12**	2 yrs. **16**	3–4 yrs. **13**	5–7 yrs. **3**	8 yrs. or more **0**		
4. monthly auto payment?	none **18**	less than $125 **6**	$126-$150 **1**	$151-$199 **4**	$200 or more **0**			
5. housing cost?	less than $274 **0**	$275-$399 **10**	$400 or more **12**	owns clear **12**	lives with relatives **24**			
6. checking and savings accounts	both **15**	checking only **2**	savings only **2**	neither **0**				
7. finance company reference	yes **0**	no **15**						
8. major credit cards?	none **0**	1 **5**	2 or more **15**					
9. ratio of debt to income?	no debts **41**	1%–5% **16**	6%–15% **20**	16% or over **0**				

2.

A lender using this scoring table selects a cutoff point from a table like this, which gauges how likely applicants are to repay loans.

Total Score	Probability of Repayment
90	89 in 100
95	91 in 100
100	92 in 100
105	93 in 100
110	94 in 100
115	95 in 100
120	95.5 in 100
125	96 in 100
130	96.25 in 100

Source: Federal Reserve Board. Developed by Fair, Isaac, and Co., Inc. Modified to update.

ANNUAL PERCENTAGE RATES

APR	10.00%	10.25%	10.50%	10.75%	11.00%	11.25%	11.50%	11.75%	12.00%	12.25%	12.50%
TERM	FINANCE CHARGE PER $100 OF AMOUNT FINANCED										
6	2.94	3.01	3.08	3.16	3.23	3.31	3.38	3.45	3.53	3.60	3.68
12	5.50	5.64	5.78	5.92	6.06	6.20	6.34	6.48	6.62	6.76	6.90
18	8.10	8.31	8.52	8.73	8.93	9.14	9.35	9.56	9.77	9.98	10.19
24	10.75	11.02	11.30	11.58	11.86	12.14	12.42	12.70	12.98	13.26	13.54
30	13.43	13.78	14.13	14.48	14.83	15.19	15.54	15.89	16.24	16.60	16.95
36	16.16	16.58	17.01	17.43	17.86	18.29	18.71	19.14	19.57	20.00	20.43

APR	12.75%	13.00%	13.25%	13.50%	13.75%	14.00%	14.25%	14.50%	14.75%	15.00%	15.25%
6	3.75	3.83	3.90	3.97	4.05	4.12	4.20	4.27	4.35	4.42	4.49
12	7.04	7.18	7.32	7.46	7.60	7.74	7.89	8.03	8.17	8.31	8.45
18	10.40	10.61	10.82	11.03	11.24	11.45	11.66	11.87	12.08	12.29	12.50
24	13.82	14.10	14.38	14.66	14.95	15.23	15.51	15.80	16.08	16.37	16.65
30	17.31	17.66	18.02	18.38	18.74	19.10	19.45	19.81	20.17	20.54	20.90
36	20.86	21.30	21.73	22.17	22.60	23.04	23.48	23.92	24.35	24.80	25.24

APR	15.50%	15.75%	16.00%	16.25%	16.50%	16.75%	17.00%	17.25%	17.50%	17.75%	18.00%
6	4.57	4.64	4.72	4.79	4.87	4.94	5.02	5.09	5.17	5.24	5.32
12	8.59	8.74	8.88	9.02	9.16	9.30	9.45	9.59	9.73	9.87	10.02
18	12.72	12.93	13.14	13.35	13.57	13.78	13.99	14.21	14.42	14.64	14.85
24	16.94	17.22	17.51	17.80	18.09	18.37	18.66	18.95	19.24	19.53	19.82
30	21.26	21.62	21.99	22.35	22.72	23.08	23.45	23.81	24.18	24.55	24.92
36	25.68	26.12	26.57	27.01	27.46	27.90	28.35	28.80	29.25	29.70	30.15

APR	18.25%	18.50%	18.75%	19.00%	19.25%	19.50%	19.75%	20.00%	20.25%	20.50%	20.75%
6	5.39	5.46	5.54	5.61	5.69	5.76	5.84	5.91	5.99	6.06	6.14
12	10.16	10.30	10.44	10.59	10.73	10.87	11.02	11.16	11.31	11.45	11.59
18	15.06	15.28	15.49	15.71	15.93	16.14	16.36	16.57	16.79	17.01	17.22
24	20.11	20.40	20.69	20.98	21.27	21.56	21.86	22.15	22.44	22.74	23.03
30	25.29	25.66	26.03	26.40	26.77	27.14	27.52	27.89	28.26	28.64	29.01
36	30.60	31.05	31.51	31.96	32.42	32.87	33.33	33.79	34.25	34.71	35.17

APR	21.00%	21.25%	21.50%	21.75%	22.00%	22.25%	22.50%	22.75%	23.00%	23.25%	23.50%
6	6.21	6.29	6.36	6.44	6.51	6.59	6.66	6.74	6.81	6.89	6.96
12	11.74	11.88	12.02	12.17	12.31	12.46	12.60	12.75	12.89	13.04	13.18
18	17.44	17.66	17.88	18.09	18.31	18.53	18.75	18.97	19.19	19.41	19.62
24	23.33	23.62	23.92	24.21	24.51	24.80	25.10	25.40	25.70	25.99	26.29
30	29.39	29.77	30.14	30.52	30.90	31.28	31.66	32.04	32.42	32.80	33.18
36	35.63	36.09	36.56	37.02	37.49	37.95	38.42	38.89	39.36	39.82	40.29

APR	23.75%	24.00%	24.25%	24.50%	24.75%	25.00%	25.25%	25.50%	25.75%	26.00%	26.25%
6	7.04	7.12	7.19	7.27	7.34	7.42	7.49	7.57	7.64	7.72	7.79
12	13.33	13.47	13.62	13.76	13.91	14.05	14.20	14.34	14.49	14.64	14.78
18	19.84	20.06	20.28	20.50	20.72	20.95	21.17	21.39	21.61	21.83	22.05
24	26.59	26.89	27.19	27.49	27.79	28.09	28.39	28.69	29.00	29.30	29.60
30	33.57	33.95	34.33	34.72	35.10	35.49	35.88	36.26	36.65	37.04	37.43
36	40.77	41.24	41.71	42.19	42.66	43.14	43.61	44.09	44.57	45.05	45.53

5% MONTHLY PAYMENT NECESSARY TO AMORTIZE A LOAN

TERM AMOUNT	1 YEAR	2 YEARS	3 YEARS	4 YEARS	5 YEARS	6 YEARS	7 YEARS
25	2.14	1.10	.75	.58	.47	.40	.36
50	4.28	2.19	1.50	1.15	.95	.81	.71
75	6.42	3.29	2.25	1.73	1.42	1.21	1.07
100	8.56	4.39	3.00	2.31	1.89	1.61	1.42
200	17.12	8.77	5.99	4.61	3.77	3.22	2.83
300	25.68	13.16	8.99	6.91	5.66	4.83	4.24
400	34.24	17.54	11.98	9.21	7.54	6.44	5.65
500	42.80	21.93	14.98	11.51	9.43	8.05	7.06
600	51.36	26.31	17.97	13.81	11.31	9.65	8.47
700	59.91	30.70	20.97	16.11	13.20	11.26	9.88
800	68.47	35.08	23.96	18.41	15.08	12.87	11.29
900	77.03	39.47	26.96	20.71	16.97	14.48	12.70
1000	85.59	43.85	29.95	23.01	18.85	16.09	14.11
2000	171.17	87.70	59.90	46.02	37.70	32.17	28.22
3000	256.76	131.55	89.85	69.02	56.55	48.25	42.33
4000	342.34	175.40	119.80	92.03	75.40	64.33	56.44
5000	427.92	219.25	149.74	115.04	94.24	80.41	70.55
6000	513.51	263.10	179.69	138.04	113.09	96.49	84.66
7000	599.09	306.94	209.64	161.05	131.94	112.57	98.77
8000	684.68	350.79	239.59	184.05	150.79	128.65	112.88
9000	770.26	394.64	269.54	207.06	169.63	144.74	126.99
10000	855.84	438.49	299.48	230.07	188.48	160.82	141.10
15000	1283.76	657.73	449.22	345.10	282.72	241.22	211.65
20000	1711.68	876.97	598.96	460.13	376.96	321.63	282.20
25000	2139.60	1096.22	748.70	575.16	471.20	402.03	352.75
30000	2567.52	1315.46	898.44	690.19	565.44	482.44	423.30
35000	2995.44	1534.70	1048.18	805.22	659.68	562.85	493.85
36000	3851.28	1578.55	1078.13	828.23	678.53	578.94	507.96
37000	3856.87	1622.40	1108.08	851.24	697.38	595.03	522.07
38000	3942.46	1666.25	1138.03	874.25	716.23	611.12	536.18
39000	4028.05	1710.10	1167.98	897.26	735.08	627.21	550.29
40000	3423.36	1753.94	1197.92	920.25	753.91	643.25	564.40
41000	4199.22	1797.80	1227.88	943.28	772.78	659.38	578.51
42000	4284.81	1841.65	1257.83	966.29	791.63	675.47	592.62
43000	4370.40	1885.50	1287.78	989.30	810.48	691.56	606.73
44000	4375.99	1929.35	1317.73	1012.31	829.33	707.65	620.84
45000	3851.28	1973.18	1347.66	1035.28	848.15	723.66	634.95
46000	4547.16	2017.05	1377.63	1058.33	867.03	739.82	649.06
47000	4552.75	2060.90	1407.58	1081.34	885.88	755.82	663.17
48000	4638.34	2104.75	1437.53	1104.35	904.73	771.91	677.28
49000	4723.93	2148.60	1467.48	1127.36	923.58	788.00	691.39
50000	4279.20	2192.43	1497.40	1150.31	942.39	804.06	705.50
51000	4895.10	2236.30	1527.38	1173.38	961.28	820.17	719.61
52000	4900.69	2280.15	1557.33	1196.39	980.13	836.26	733.72
53000	4986.28	2324.00	1587.28	1219.40	998.63	852.35	747.83
54000	5071.87	2367.85	1617.23	1242.41	1017.48	868.44	761.94
55000	5077.46	2411.35	1647.18	1265.42	1036.33	884.53	776.05
56000	5163.05	2455.20	1677.13	1288.43	1055.18	900.62	790.16
57000	5248.64	2499.05	1707.08	1311.44	1074.03	916.71	804.27
58000	5334.23	2542.90	1737.03	1334.45	1092.88	932.80	818.38
59000	5419.82	2586.75	1766.98	1357.46	1111.38	948.89	832.49
60000	5505.41	2630.60	1796.93	1380.47	1129.88	964.98	846.60
65000	5933.33	2849.85	1946.67	1495.51	1224.12	1045.39	917.15
70000	6361.25	3069.10	2096.41	1610.55	1318.36	1125.80	987.70
75000	6789.17	3288.35	2246.15	1725.59	1412.60	1206.21	1058.25
80000	7217.07	3507.60	2395.89	1840.63	1506.84	1286.62	1128.80
100000	8928.77	4384.57	2994.85	2300.76	1883.80	1608.25	1411.00

591

$8^3/_4\%$ **MONTHLY PAYMENT**
NECESSARY TO AMORTIZE A LOAN

TERM AMOUNT	1 YEAR	2 YEARS	3 YEARS	4 YEARS	5 YEARS	6 YEARS	7 YEARS
$ 25	2.18	1.14	.79	.62	.52	.45	.40
50	4.37	2.28	1.59	1.24	1.03	.89	.80
75	6.55	3.42	2.38	1.86	1.55	1.34	1.20
100	8.73	4.56	3.17	2.48	2.06	1.79	1.60
200	17.47	9.11	6.34	4.95	4.13	3.58	3.19
300	26.20	13.67	9.51	7.43	6.19	5.37	4.79
400	34.93	18.23	12.68	9.91	8.25	7.16	6.39
500	43.67	22.79	15.84	12.38	10.32	8.95	7.98
600	52.40	27.37	19.02	14.86	12.38	10.74	9.58
700	61.13	31.90	22.19	17.34	14.44	12.53	11.18
800	69.86	36.46	25.36	19.82	16.50	14.32	12.78
900	78.59	41.02	28.53	22.30	18.56	16.11	14.38
1000	87.34	45.57	31.68	24.77	20.64	17.90	15.96
2000	174.67	91.14	63.37	49.53	41.27	35.80	31.92
3000	262.01	136.71	95.05	74.30	61.91	53.70	47.88
4000	349.35	182.28	126.73	99.07	82.55	71.60	63.84
5000	436.68	227.85	158.42	123.83	103.19	89.51	79.81
6000	524.01	273.42	190.10	148.60	123.82	107.41	95.77
7000	611.35	318.99	221.78	173.37	144.46	125.31	111.74
8000	698.68	364.56	253.47	198.13	165.10	143.21	127.70
9000	786.02	410.13	285.15	222.90	185.74	161.12	143.66
10000	873.36	455.70	316.84	247.67	206.37	179.02	159.62
15000	1310.03	683.55	475.25	371.50	309.56	268.53	239.44
20000	1746.71	911.40	633.67	495.33	412.74	358.03	319.25
25000	2183.39	1139.25	792.09	619.16	515.93	447.54	399.06
30000	2620.07	1367.10	950.51	743.00	619.12	537.05	478.87
35000	3056.75	1594.95	1108.92	866.83	722.30	626.56	558.69
36000	3144.08	1640.52	1140.61	891.59	742.94	644.46	574.65
37000	3231.42	1686.09	1172.29	916.36	763.58	662.36	590.61
38000	3318.75	1731.66	1203.97	941.13	784.21	680.26	606.57
39000	3406.09	1777.23	1235.66	965.89	804.85	698.17	622.54
40000	3493.42	1822.80	1267.34	990.66	825.49	716.07	638.50
41000	3580.76	1868.38	1299.02	1015.43	846.13	733.97	654.46
42000	3668.09	1913.95	1330.71	1040.19	866.76	751.87	670.42
43000	3755.43	1959.52	1362.39	1064.96	887.40	769.77	686.39
44000	3842.77	2005.09	1394.07	1089.73	908.04	787.68	702.35
45000	3930.10	2050.66	1425.76	1114.49	928.68	805.58	718.31
46000	4017.44	2096.23	1457.44	1139.26	949.31	823.48	734.27
47000	4104.77	2141.80	1489.12	1164.03	969.95	841.38	750.24
48000	4192.11	2187.37	1520.81	1188.79	990.59	859.28	766.20
49000	4279.44	2232.94	1552.49	1213.56	1011.22	877.18	782.16
50000	4366.78	2278.51	1584.18	1238.33	1031.86	895.09	798.12
51000	4454.11	2324.08	1615.86	1263.09	1052.50	912.99	814.09
52000	4541.45	2369.65	1647.54	1287.86	1073.14	930.89	830.05
53000	4628.79	2415.22	1679.23	1312.62	1093.77	948.79	846.01
54000	4716.12	2460.79	1710.91	1337.39	1114.41	966.69	861.97
55000	4803.46	2506.36	1742.59	1362.16	1135.05	984.59	877.94
56000	4890.79	2551.93	1774.28	1386.92	1155.69	1002.50	893.90
57000	4978.13	2597.50	1805.96	1411.69	1176.32	1020.40	909.86
58000	5065.46	2643.07	1837.64	1436.46	1196.96	1038.30	925.82
59000	5152.80	2688.64	1869.33	1461.22	1217.60	1056.20	941.79
60000	5240.14	2734.21	1901.01	1485.99	1238.23	1074.10	957.75
65000	5676.81	2962.06	2059.43	1609.82	1341.42	1163.61	1037.56
70000	6113.49	3189.91	2217.85	1733.66	1444.61	1253.12	1117.37
75000	6550.17	3417.76	2376.26	1857.49	1547.79	1342.63	1197.19
80000	6986.85	3645.61	2534.68	1981.32	1650.98	1432.14	1277.00
100000	8733.56	4557.01	3168.35	2476.65	2063.72	1790.17	1596.25

10% MONTHLY PAYMENT NECESSARY TO AMORTIZE A LOAN

TERM AMOUNT	1 YEAR	2 YEARS	3 YEARS	4 YEARS	5 YEARS	6 YEARS	7 YEARS
$ 25	2.20	1.16	.81	.64	.54	.47	.42
50	4.40	2.31	1.62	1.27	1.07	.93	.84
75	6.60	3.47	2.43	1.91	1.61	1.40	1.26
100	8.80	4.62	3.23	2.54	2.13	1.86	1.67
200	17.59	9.23	6.46	5.08	4.25	3.71	3.33
300	26.38	13.85	9.69	7.61	6.38	5.56	4.99
400	35.17	18.46	12.91	10.15	8.50	7.42	6.65
500	43.96	23.08	16.14	12.69	10.63	9.27	8.31
600	52.75	27.69	19.37	15.22	12.75	11.12	9.97
700	61.55	32.31	22.59	17.76	14.88	12.97	11.63
800	70.34	36.92	25.82	20.30	17.00	14.83	13.29
900	79.13	41.54	29.05	22.83	19.13	16.68	14.95
1000	87.92	46.15	32.27	25.37	21.25	18.53	16.61
2000	175.84	92.29	64.54	50.73	42.50	37.06	33.21
3000	263.75	138.44	96.81	76.09	63.75	55.58	49.81
4000	351.67	184.58	129.07	101.46	84.99	74.11	66.41
5000	439.58	230.73	161.34	126.82	106.24	92.63	83.01
6000	527.50	276.87	193.61	152.18	127.49	111.16	99.61
7000	615.42	323.02	225.88	177.54	148.73	129.69	116.21
8000	703.33	369.16	258.14	202.91	169.98	148.21	132.81
9000	791.25	415.31	290.41	228.27	191.23	166.74	149.42
10000	879.16	461.45	322.68	253.63	212.48	185.26	166.02
15000	1318.74	692.18	484.01	380.44	318.71	277.89	249.02
20000	1758.32	922.90	645.35	507.26	424.95	370.52	332.03
25000	2197.90	1153.63	806.68	634.07	531.18	463.15	415.03
30000	2637.48	1384.35	968.02	760.88	637.42	555.78	498.04
35000	3077.06	1615.08	1129.36	887.70	743.65	648.41	581.05
36000	3164.98	1661.22	1161.62	913.06	764.90	666.94	597.65
37000	3252.89	1707.37	1193.89	938.42	786.15	685.46	614.25
38000	3340.81	1753.51	1226.16	963.78	807.39	703.99	630.85
39000	3428.72	1799.66	1258.43	989.15	828.64	722.51	647.45
40000	3516.64	1845.80	1290.69	1014.51	849.89	741.04	664.05
41000	3604.56	1891.95	1322.96	1039.87	871.13	759.56	680.65
42000	3692.47	1938.09	1355.23	1065.23	892.38	778.09	697.25
43000	3780.39	1984.24	1387.49	1090.60	913.63	796.62	713.86
44000	3868.30	2030.38	1419.76	1115.96	934.87	815.14	730.46
45000	3956.22	2076.53	1452.03	1141.32	956.12	833.67	747.06
46000	4044.14	2122.67	1484.30	1166.68	977.37	852.19	763.66
47000	4132.05	2168.82	1516.56	1192.05	998.62	870.72	780.26
48000	4219.97	2214.96	1548.83	1217.41	1019.86	889.25	796.86
49000	4307.88	2261.11	1581.10	1242.77	1041.11	907.77	813.46
50000	4395.80	2307.25	1613.36	1268.13	1062.36	926.30	830.06
51000	4483.72	2353.40	1645.63	1293.50	1083.61	944.83	846.67
52000	4571.64	2399.55	1677.90	1318.87	1104.86	963.36	863.28
53000	4659.56	2445.70	1710.17	1344.24	1126.11	981.89	879.89
54000	4747.48	2491.85	1742.44	1369.61	1147.36	1000.42	896.56
55000	4835.38	2537.98	1774.70	1394.95	1168.59	1018.93	913.07
56000	4923.32	2584.14	1806.98	1420.34	1189.86	1037.48	929.71
57000	5011.24	2630.29	1839.25	1445.71	1211.11	1056.01	946.32
58000	5098.44	2676.44	1871.52	1471.08	1232.36	1074.54	962.93
59000	5186.36	2722.59	1903.79	1496.45	1253.61	1093.07	979.54
60000	5274.96	2768.70	1936.04	1521.76	1274.83	1111.56	996.08
65000	5714.54	2999.43	2097.37	1648.57	1381.06	1204.18	1079.08
70000	6154.12	3230.15	2258.71	1775.39	1487.30	1296.81	1162.09
75000	6593.70	3460.87	2420.04	1902.20	1593.53	1389.44	1245.09
80000	7033.28	3691.60	2581.38	2029.01	1699.77	1482.07	1328.10
100000	8791.60	4614.50	3226.73	2536.27	2124.72	1852.59	1660.13

10% MONTHLY PAYMENT NECESSARY TO AMORTIZE A LOAN

TERM AMOUNT	24 YEAR	25 YEARS	28 YEARS	29 YEARS	30 YEARS	35 YEARS	40 YEARS
$ 25	.23	.23	.23	.23	.22	.22	.22
50	.46	.46	.45	.45	.44	.43	.43
75	.69	.69	.67	.67	.66	.65	.64
100	.92	.91	.89	.89	.88	.86	.85
200	1.84	1.82	1.78	1.77	1.76	1.72	1.70
300	2.76	2.73	2.67	2.65	2.64	2.58	2.55
400	3.67	3.64	3.56	3.53	3.52	3.44	3.40
500	4.59	4.55	4.44	4.42	4.39	4.30	4.25
600	5.51	5.46	5.33	5.30	5.27	5.16	5.10
700	6.43	6.37	6.22	6.18	6.15	6.02	5.95
800	7.34	7.27	7.11	7.06	7.03	6.88	6.80
900	8.26	8.18	8.00	7.95	7.90	7.74	7.65
1000	9.18	9.09	8.88	8.83	8.78	8.60	8.50
2000	18.35	18.18	17.76	17.65	17.56	17.20	16.99
3000	27.53	27.27	26.64	26.48	26.33	25.80	25.48
4000	36.70	36.35	35.52	35.30	35.11	34.39	33.97
5000	45.87	45.44	44.40	44.13	43.88	42.99	42.46
6000	55.05	54.53	53.28	52.95	52.66	51.59	50.95
7000	64.22	63.61	62.16	61.78	61.44	60.18	59.45
8000	73.40	72.70	71.04	70.60	70.21	68.78	67.94
9000	82.57	81.79	79.92	79.43	78.99	77.38	76.43
10000	91.74	90.88	88.80	88.25	87.76	85.97	84.92
15000	137.61	136.31	133.20	132.38	131.64	128.96	127.38
20000	183.48	181.75	177.60	176.50	175.52	171.94	169.83
25000	229.35	227.18	222.00	220.62	219.40	214.92	212.29
30000	275.22	272.62	266.39	264.75	263.28	257.91	254.75
35000	321.09	318.05	310.79	308.87	307.16	300.89	297.21
36000	330.26	327.14	319.67	317.70	315.93	309.49	305.70
37000	339.44	336.22	328.55	326.52	324.71	318.08	314.19
38000	348.61	345.31	337.43	335.35	333.48	326.68	322.68
39000	357.79	354.40	346.31	344.17	342.26	335.28	331.17
40000	366.96	363.49	355.19	353.00	351.03	343.87	339.68
41000	376.13	372.57	364.07	361.82	359.81	352.47	348.15
42000	385.31	381.66	372.95	370.65	368.59	361.07	356.65
43000	394.48	390.75	381.83	379.47	377.36	369.66	365.14
44000	403.66	399.83	390.71	388.29	386.14	378.26	373.63
45000	412.83	408.92	399.59	397.12	394.91	386.86	382.12
46000	422.00	418.01	408.47	405.94	403.69	395.45	390.61
47000	431.18	427.09	417.35	414.77	412.46	404.05	399.10
48000	440.35	436.18	426.23	423.59	421.24	412.65	407.60
49000	449.53	445.27	435.11	432.42	430.02	421.24	416.09
50000	458.70	454.36	443.99	441.24	438.79	429.84	424.58
51000	467.87	463.44	452.86	450.07	447.57	438.44	433.07
52000	477.05	472.53	461.74	458.89	456.34	447.03	441.56
53000	486.22	481.62	470.62	467.72	465.12	455.63	450.05
54000	495.39	490.70	479.50	476.54	473.89	464.23	458.54
55000	504.57	499.79	488.38	485.37	482.67	472.82	467.04
56000	513.74	508.88	497.26	494.19	491.45	481.42	475.53
57000	522.92	517.96	506.14	503.02	500.22	490.02	484.02
58000	532.09	527.05	515.02	511.84	509.00	498.62	492.51
59000	541.26	536.14	523.90	520.67	517.77	507.21	501.00
60000	550.44	545.23	532.78	529.49	526.55	515.81	509.49
65000	596.31	590.66	577.18	573.62	570.43	558.79	551.95
70000	642.18	636.10	621.58	617.74	614.31	601.78	594.41
75000	688.05	681.53	665.98	661.86	658.18	644.76	636.86
80000	733.92	726.97	710.37	705.99	702.06	687.74	679.32
100000	917.39	908.71	887.97	882.48	877.58	859.68	849.15

594

11% MONTHLY PAYMENT NECESSARY TO AMORTIZE A LOAN

TERM AMOUNT	24 YEARS	25 YEARS	28 YEARS	29 YEARS	30 YEARS	35 YEARS	40 YEARS
$ 25	.25	.25	.25	.24	.24	.24	.24
50	.50	.50	.49	.48	.48	.47	.47
75	.75	.74	.73	.72	.72	.71	.70
100	.99	.99	.97	.96	.96	.94	.93
200	1.98	1.97	1.93	1.92	1.91	1.88	1.86
300	2.97	2.95	2.89	2.87	2.86	2.82	2.79
400	3.96	3.93	3.85	3.83	3.81	3.75	3.72
500	4.95	4.91	4.81	4.79	4.77	4.69	4.65
600	5.93	5.89	5.77	5.74	5.72	5.63	5.57
700	6.92	6.87	6.74	6.70	6.67	6.56	6.50
800	7.91	7.85	7.70	7.66	7.62	7.50	7.43
900	8.90	8.83	8.66	8.61	8.58	8.44	8.36
1000	9.89	9.81	9.62	9.57	9.53	9.37	9.29
2000	19.77	19.61	19.23	19.14	19.05	18.74	18.57
3000	29.65	29.41	28.85	28.70	28.57	28.11	27.85
4000	39.53	39.21	38.46	38.27	38.10	37.48	37.14
5000	49.41	49.01	48.08	47.84	47.62	46.85	46.42
6000	59.29	58.81	57.69	57.40	57.14	56.22	55.70
7000	69.17	68.61	67.31	68.97	66.67	65.59	64.99
8000	79.05	78.41	76.92	76.54	76.19	74.96	74.27
9000	88.93	88.22	86.54	86.10	85.71	84.33	83.55
10000	98.81	98.02	96.15	95.67	95.24	93.70	92.83
15000	148.21	147.02	144.23	143.50	142.85	140.55	139.25
20000	197.61	196.03	192.30	191.33	190.47	187.40	185.66
25000	247.01	245.03	240.37	239.16	238.09	234.24	232.08
30000	296.41	294.04	288.45	286.99	285.70	281.09	278.49
35000	345.81	343.04	336.52	334.83	333.32	327.94	324.91
36000	355.69	352.85	346.14	344.39	342.84	337.31	334.19
37000	365.57	362.65	355.75	353.96	352.36	346.68	343.47
38000	375.46	372.45	365.37	363.52	361.89	356.05	352.76
39000	385.34	382.25	374.98	373.09	371.41	365.42	362.04
40000	395.22	392.05	384.60	382.66	380.93	374.79	371.32
41000	405.10	401.85	394.21	392.22	390.46	384.16	380.61
42000	414.98	411.65	403.83	401.79	399.98	393.53	389.89
43000	424.86	421.45	413.44	411.36	409.50	402.90	399.17
44000	434.74	431.25	423.06	420.92	419.03	412.27	408.45
45000	444.62	441.06	432.67	430.49	428.55	421.64	417.74
46000	454.50	450.86	442.29	440.05	438.07	431.01	427.02
47000	464.38	460.66	451.90	449.62	447.60	440.38	436.30
48000	474.26	470.46	461.52	459.19	457.12	449.74	445.59
49000	484.14	480.26	471.13	468.75	466.64	459.11	454.87
50000	494.02	490.06	480.74	478.32	476.17	468.48	464.15
51000	503.90	499.86	490.36	487.89	485.69	477.85	473.44
52000	513.78	509.66	499.97	497.45	495.21	487.22	482.72
53000	523.66	519.46	509.59	507.02	504.74	496.59	492.00
54000	533.54	529.27	519.20	516.58	514.26	505.96	501.28
55000	543.42	539.07	528.82	526.15	523.78	515.33	510.57
56000	553.30	548.87	538.43	535.72	533.31	524.70	519.85
57000	563.18	558.67	548.05	545.28	542.83	534.07	529.13
58000	573.06	568.47	557.66	554.85	552.35	543.44	538.42
59000	582.94	578.27	567.28	564.42	561.88	552.81	547.70
60000	592.82	588.07	576.89	573.98	571.40	562.18	556.98
65000	642.22	637.08	624.97	621.81	619.02	609.03	603.40
70000	691.62	686.08	673.04	669.65	666.63	655.88	649.81
75000	741.02	735.09	721.11	717.48	714.25	702.72	696.23
80000	790.43	784.10	769.19	765.31	761.86	749.57	742.64
100000	988.03	980.12	961.48	956.63	952.33	936.96	928.30

595

12¹/₂%   MONTHLY PAYMENT NECESSARY TO AMORTIZE A LOAN

TERM AMOUNT	1 YEAR	2 YEARS	3 YEARS	4 YEARS	5 YEARS	6 YEARS	7 YEARS
$ 25	2.23	1.19	.84	.67	.57	.50	.45
50	4.46	2.37	1.68	1.33	1.13	1.00	.90
75	6.69	3.55	2.51	2.00	1.69	1.49	1.35
100	8.91	4.74	3.35	2.66	2.25	1.99	1.80
200	17.82	9.47	6.70	5.32	4.50	3.97	3.59
300	26.73	14.20	10.04	7.98	6.75	5.95	5.38
400	35.64	18.93	13.39	10.64	9.00	7.93	7.17
500	44.55	23.66	16.73	13.29	11.25	9.91	8.97
600	53.45	28.39	20.08	15.95	13.50	11.89	10.76
700	62.36	33.12	23.42	18.61	15.75	13.87	12.55
800	71.27	37.85	26.77	21.27	18.00	15.85	14.34
900	80.18	42.58	30.11	23.93	20.25	17.84	16.13
1000	89.09	47.31	33.46	26.58	22.50	19.82	17.93
2000	178.17	94.62	66.91	53.16	45.00	39.63	35.85
3000	267.25	141.93	100.37	79.74	67.50	59.44	53.77
4000	356.34	189.23	133.82	106.32	90.00	79.25	71.69
5000	445.42	236.54	167.27	132.90	112.49	99.06	89.61
6000	534.50	283.85	200.73	159.48	134.99	118.87	107.53
7000	623.59	331.16	234.18	186.06	157.49	138.68	125.45
8000	712.67	378.46	287.63	212.64	179.99	158.49	143.37
9000	801.75	425.77	301.09	239.22	202.49	178.31	161.30
10000	890.83	473.08	334.54	265.80	224.98	198.12	179.22
15000	1336.25	709.61	501.81	398.70	337.47	297.17	268.82
20000	1781.66	946.15	669.08	531.60	449.96	396.23	358.43
25000	2227.08	1182.69	836.35	664.50	562.45	495.28	448.04
30000	2672.49	1419.22	1003.61	797.40	674.94	594.34	537.64
35000	3117.91	1655.76	1170.88	930.30	787.43	693.40	627.25
36000	3206.99	1703.07	1204.34	956.88	809.93	713.21	645.17
37000	3296.07	1750.38	1237.79	983.46	832.43	733.02	663.09
38000	3385.15	1797.68	1271.24	1010.04	854.93	752.83	681.01
39000	3474.24	1844.99	1304.70	1036.62	877.42	772.64	698.93
40000	3563.32	1892.30	1338.15	1063.20	899.92	792.45	716.85
41000	3652.40	1939.60	1371.60	1089.78	922.42	812.26	734.78
42000	3741.49	1986.91	1405.06	1116.36	944.92	832.07	752.70
43000	3830.57	2034.22	1438.51	1142.94	967.42	851.89	770.62
44000	3919.65	2081.53	1471.96	1169.52	989.91	871.70	788.54
45000	4008.73	2128.83	1505.42	1196.10	1012.41	891.51	806.46
46000	4097.82	2176.14	1538.87	1222.68	1034.91	911.32	824.38
47000	4186.90	2223.45	1572.33	1249.26	1057.41	931.13	842.30
48000	4275.98	2270.76	1605.78	1275.84	1079.91	950.94	860.22
49000	4366.07	2318.06	1639.23	1302.42	1102.40	970.75	878.15
50000	4454.15	2365.37	1672.69	1329.00	1124.90	990.58	896.07
51000	4543.23	2412.68	1706.14	1355.58	1147.40	1010.38	913.99
52000	4632.31	2459.99	1739.59	1382.16	1169.90	1030.19	931.91
53000	4721.40	2507.29	1773.05	1408.74	1192.40	1050.00	949.83
54000	4810.48	2554.60	1806.50	1435.32	1214.89	1069.81	967.75
55000	4899.56	2601.91	1839.95	1461.90	1237.39	1089.62	985.67
56000	4988.65	2649.21	1873.41	1488.48	1259.89	1109.43	1003.59
57000	5077.73	2696.52	1906.86	1515.06	1282.39	1129.24	1021.52
58000	5166.81	2743.83	1940.32	1541.64	1304.89	1149.05	1039.44
59000	5255.89	2791.14	1973.77	1568.22	1327.38	1168.86	1057.36
60000	5344.98	2838.44	2007.22	1594.80	1349.88	1188.68	1075.28
65000	5790.39	3074.98	2174.49	1727.70	1462.37	1287.73	1164.89
70000	6235.81	3311.52	2341.76	1860.60	1574.86	1386.79	1254.49
75000	6681.22	3548.05	2509.03	1993.50	1687.35	1485.84	1344.10
80000	7126.63	3784.59	2676.30	2126.40	1799.84	1684.90	1433.70
100000	8908.29	4730.74	3345.37	2658.00	2249.80	1981.12	1792.13

13% MONTHLY PAYMENT NECESSARY TO AMORTIZE A LOAN

TERM AMOUNT	1 YEAR	2 YEARS	3 YEARS	4 YEARS	5 YEARS	6 YEARS	7 YEARS
$ 25	2.23	1.18	.84	.67	.57	.50	.46
50	4.47	2.38	1.69	1.34	1.14	1.00	.91
75	6.70	3.56	2.53	2.01	1.71	1.50	1.37
100	8.93	4.75	3.37	2.68	2.28	2.01	1.82
200	17.86	9.51	6.74	5.37	4.55	4.01	3.64
300	26.79	14.26	10.11	8.05	6.83	6.02	5.46
400	35.09	19.01	13.48	10.73	9.11	8.03	7.28
500	44.66	23.77	16.85	13.41	11.38	10.04	9.10
600	52.95	28.52	20.22	16.10	13.66	12.04	10.92
700	61.88	33.27	23.59	18.78	15.94	14.05	12.12
800	70.81	38.02	26.96	21.46	18.22	16.06	13.94
900	79.74	42.77	30.33	24.14	20.50	18.07	15.76
1000	89.32	47.54	33.69	26.83	22.75	20.07	18.19
2000	178.63	95.08	67.39	53.65	45.51	40.15	36.38
3000	267.95	142.62	101.08	79.95	68.26	60.22	54.57
4000	357.27	190.16	134.77	106.78	91.01	80.29	72.76
5000	446.59	237.71	168.47	134.14	113.77	100.37	90.96
6000	535.90	285.25	202.16	160.96	136.52	120.44	109.15
7000	625.22	332.79	235.86	187.79	159.27	140.52	127.34
8000	714.54	380.33	269.55	214.62	182.02	160.59	145.54
9000	803.86	427.88	303.25	241.45	204.78	180.67	163.73
10000	893.17	475.42	336.94	268.27	227.53	200.74	181.92
15000	1339.76	713.13	505.41	402.41	341.30	301.11	272.88
20000	1786.35	950.84	673.88	536.55	455.06	401.48	363.84
25000	2232.93	1188.55	842.35	670.69	568.83	501.85	454.80
30000	2679.52	1426.25	1010.82	804.82	682.59	602.22	545.76
35000	3126.10	1663.96	1179.29	938.96	796.36	702.59	636.72
36000	3215.42	1711.51	1212.98	965.79	819.11	722.67	654.91
37000	3304.74	1759.05	1246.68	992.62	841.86	742.74	673.10
38000	3394.06	1806.59	1280.37	1019.44	864.62	762.82	691.29
39000	3483.37	1854.13	1314.06	1046.27	887.37	782.89	709.49
40000	3572.69	1901.67	1347.76	1073.10	910.12	802.96	727.68
41000	3662.01	1949.21	1381.45	1099.93	932.88	823.04	745.87
42000	3751.33	1996.76	1415.15	1126.75	955.63	843.11	764.06
43000	3840.64	2044.30	1448.84	1153.58	978.38	863.19	782.25
44000	3929.96	2091.84	1482.53	1180.41	1001.14	883.26	800.45
45000	4019.28	2139.38	1516.23	1207.24	1023.89	903.33	818.64
46000	4108.59	2186.92	1549.92	1234.06	1046.64	923.41	836.83
47000	4197.91	2234.47	1583.62	1260.89	1069.39	943.48	855.02
48000	4287.23	2282.01	1617.31	1287.72	1092.15	963.56	873.21
49000	4376.55	2329.55	1651.00	1314.55	1114.90	983.63	891.41
50000	4465.86	2377.09	1684.70	1341.37	1137.65	1003.71	909.60
51000	4555.18	2424.63	1718.39	1368.20	1160.41	1023.78	927.79
52000	4644.50	2472.17	1752.09	1395.03	1183.16	1043.85	945.98
53000	4733.82	2519.72	1785.78	1421.86	1205.91	1063.93	964.17
54000	4823.13	2567.26	1819.47	1448.68	1228.67	1084.00	982.37
55000	4912.45	2614.80	1853.17	1475.51	1251.42	1104.08	1000.56
56000	5001.77	2662.34	1886.86	1502.34	1274.17	1124.15	1018.75
57000	5091.08	2709.88	1920.56	1529.17	1296.93	1144.22	1036.94
58000	5180.40	2757.43	1954.25	1555.99	1319.68	1164.30	1055.13
59000	5269.72	2804.97	1987.94	1582.82	1342.43	1184.37	1073.33
60000	5359.04	2852.51	2021.64	1609.65	1365.18	1204.45	1091.52
65000	5805.62	3090.22	2190.11	1743.79	1478.95	1304.82	1182.48
70000	6252.21	3327.93	2358.58	1877.92	1592.72	1405.19	1273.44
75000	6698.80	3565.64	2527.05	2012.06	1706.48	1505.56	1364.40
80000	7145.38	3803.35	2695.52	2146.20	1820.25	1605.93	1455.36
100000	8931.73	4754.18	3369.40	2682.75	2275.31	2007.41	1819.20

597

MONTHLY MORTGAGE PAYMENT COMPARISONS

30-YEAR MORTGAGE LOAN AMOUNTS

RATES	54000	56000	58000	60000	62000	64000	66000	68000	70000
9.50	454.06	470.88	487.69	504.51	521.33	538.15	554.96	571.78	588.60
9.75	463.94	481.13	498.31	515.49	532.68	549.86	567.04	584.23	601.41
10.00	473.89	491.44	508.99	526.54	544.09	561.65	579.20	596.75	614.30
10.25	483.89	501.82	519.74	537.66	555.58	573.50	591.43	609.35	627.27
10.50	493.96	512.25	530.55	548.84	567.14	585.43	603.73	622.02	640.32
10.75	504.08	522.75	541.42	560.09	578.76	597.43	616.10	634.77	653.44
11.00	514.25	533.30	552.35	571.39	590.44	609.49	628.53	647.58	666.63
11.25	524.48	543.91	563.33	582.76	602.18	621.61	641.03	660.46	679.88
11.50	534.76	554.56	574.37	594.17	613.98	633.79	653.59	673.40	693.20
11.75	545.08	565.27	585.46	605.65	625.83	646.02	666.21	686.40	706.59
12.00	555.45	576.02	596.60	617.17	637.74	658.31	678.88	699.46	720.03
12.25	565.86	586.82	607.78	628.74	649.70	670.65	691.61	712.57	733.53
12.50	576.32	597.66	619.01	640.35	661.70	683.05	704.39	725.74	747.08
12.75	586.81	608.55	630.28	652.02	673.75	695.48	717.22	738.95	760.69
13.00	597.35	619.47	641.60	663.72	685.84	707.97	730.09	752.22	774.34

20-YEAR MORTGAGE LOAN AMOUNTS

RATES	54000	56000	58000	60000	62000	64000	66000	68000	70000
9.50	503.35	521.99	540.64	559.28	577.92	596.56	615.21	633.85	652.49
9.75	512.20	531.17	550.14	569.11	588.08	607.05	626.02	644.99	663.96
10.00	521.11	540.41	559.71	579.01	598.31	617.61	636.92	656.22	675.52
10.25	530.09	549.72	569.35	588.99	608.62	628.25	647.88	667.52	687.15
10.50	539.13	559.09	579.06	599.03	619.00	638.96	658.93	678.90	698.87
10.75	548.22	568.53	588.83	609.14	629.44	649.75	670.05	690.36	710.66
11.00	557.38	578.02	598.67	619.31	639.96	660.60	681.24	701.89	722.53
11.25	566.60	587.58	608.57	629.55	650.54	671.52	692.51	713.49	734.48
11.50	575.87	597.20	618.53	639.86	661.19	682.52	703.84	725.17	746.50
11.75	585.20	606.88	628.55	650.23	671.90	693.57	715.25	736.92	758.60
12.00	594.59	616.61	638.63	660.65	682.67	704.70	726.72	748.74	770.76
12.25	604.02	626.40	648.77	671.14	693.51	715.88	738.25	760.62	783.00
12.50	613.52	636.24	658.96	681.69	704.41	727.13	749.85	772.58	795.30
12.75	623.06	646.13	669.21	692.29	715.36	738.44	761.52	784.59	807.67
13.00	632.65	656.08	679.51	702.95	726.38	749.81	773.24	796.67	820.10

15-YEAR MORTGAGE LOAN AMOUNTS

RATES	54000	56000	58000	60000	62000	64000	66000	68000	70000
9.50	563.88	584.76	605.65	626.53	647.42	668.30	689.19	710.07	730.96
9.75	572.06	593.24	614.43	635.62	656.81	677.99	699.18	720.37	741.56
10.00	580.29	601.78	623.27	644.76	666.26	687.75	709.24	730.73	752.22
10.25	588.57	610.37	632.17	653.97	675.77	697.57	719.37	741.17	762.96
10.50	596.92	619.02	641.13	663.24	685.35	707.46	729.56	751.67	773.78
10.75	605.31	627.73	650.15	672.57	694.99	717.41	739.83	762.25	784.66
11.00	613.76	636.49	659.23	681.96	704.69	727.42	750.15	772.88	795.62
11.25	622.27	645.31	668.36	691.41	714.45	737.50	760.55	783.60	806.64
11.50	630.82	654.19	677.55	700.91	724.28	747.64	771.01	794.37	817.73
11.75	639.43	663.12	686.80	710.48	734.16	757.85	781.53	805.21	828.89
12.00	648.09	672.09	696.10	720.10	744.10	768.11	792.11	816.11	840.12
12.25	656.80	681.15	705.45	729.78	754.11	778.43	802.76	827.08	851.41
12.50	665.56	690.21	714.86	739.51	764.16	788.82	813.47	838.12	862.77
12.75	674.37	699.35	724.33	749.30	774.28	799.26	824.23	849.21	874.19
13.00	683.23	708.53	733.84	759.14	784.45	809.75	835.06	860.36	885.67

30-YEAR MORTGAGE LOAN AMOUNTS

RATES	134000	136000	138000	140000	142000	144000	146000	148000	150000
9.50	1126.74	1143.56	1160.38	1177.19	1194.01	1210.83	1227.65	1244.46	1261.28
9.75	1151.27	1168.45	1185.63	1202.82	1220.00	1237.18	1254.37	1271.55	1288.73
10.00	1175.95	1193.50	1211.05	1228.60	1246.15	1263.70	1281.26	1298.81	1316.36
10.25	1200.78	1218.70	1236.62	1254.54	1272.46	1290.39	1308.31	1326.23	1344.15
10.50	1225.75	1244.05	1262.34	1280.64	1298.93	1317.23	1335.52	1353.82	1372.11
10.75	1250.87	1269.53	1288.20	1306.87	1325.54	1344.21	1362.88	1381.55	1400.22
11.00	1276.11	1295.16	1314.21	1333.25	1352.30	1371.34	1390.39	1409.44	1428.48
11.25	1301.49	1320.92	1340.34	1359.77	1379.19	1398.62	1418.04	1437.47	1456.89
11.50	1326.99	1346.80	1366.60	1386.41	1406.21	1426.02	1445.83	1465.63	1485.44
11.75	1352.61	1372.80	1392.99	1413.18	1433.36	1453.55	1473.74	1493.93	1514.12
12.00	1378.34	1398.91	1419.49	1440.06	1460.63	1481.20	1501.77	1522.35	1542.92
12.25	1404.18	1425.14	1446.10	1467.05	1488.01	1508.97	1529.93	1550.89	1571.84
12.50	1430.13	1451.47	1472.82	1494.16	1515.51	1536.85	1558.20	1579.54	1600.89
12.75	1456.17	1477.90	1499.64	1521.37	1543.10	1564.84	1586.57	1608.31	1630.04
13.00	1482.31	1504.43	1526.55	1548.68	1570.80	1592.93	1615.05	1637.17	1659.30

MONTHLY MORTGAGE PAYMENT COMPARISONS

30-YEAR MORTGAGE LOAN AMOUNTS

RATES	110000	112000	114000	116000	118000	120000	122000	124000	126000
9.00	885.08	901.18	917.27	933.36	949.45	965.55	981.64	997.73	1013.82
9.25	904.94	921.40	937.85	954.30	970.76	987.21	1003.67	1020.12	1036.57
9.50	924.94	941.76	958.57	975.39	992.21	1009.02	1025.84	1042.66	1059.48
9.75	945.07	962.25	979.44	996.62	1013.80	1030.99	1048.17	1065.35	1082.54
10.00	965.33	982.88	1000.43	1017.98	1035.54	1053.09	1070.64	1088.19	1105.74
10.25	985.71	1003.63	1021.55	1039.48	1057.40	1075.32	1093.24	1111.17	1129.09
10.50	1006.21	1024.51	1042.80	1061.10	1079.39	1097.69	1115.98	1134.28	1152.57
10.75	1026.83	1045.50	1064.17	1082.84	1101.51	1120.18	1138.85	1157.52	1176.19
11.00	1047.56	1066.60	1085.65	1104.69	1123.74	1142.79	1161.83	1180.88	1199.93
11.25	1068.39	1087.81	1107.24	1126.66	1146.09	1165.51	1184.94	1204.36	1223.79
11.50	1089.32	1109.13	1128.93	1148.74	1168.54	1188.35	1208.16	1227.96	1247.77
11.75	1110.35	1130.54	1150.73	1170.92	1191.10	1211.29	1231.48	1251.67	1271.86
12.00	1131.47	1152.05	1172.62	1193.19	1213.76	1234.34	1254.91	1275.48	1296.05
12.25	1152.69	1173.64	1194.60	1215.56	1236.52	1257.48	1278.43	1299.39	1320.35
12.50	1173.98	1195.33	1216.67	1238.02	1259.36	1280.71	1302.05	1323.40	1344.75

20-YEAR MORTGAGE LOAN AMOUNTS

RATES	110000	112000	114000	116000	118000	120000	122000	124000	126000
9.00	989.70	1007.69	1025.68	1043.68	1061.67	1079.67	1097.66	1115.66	1133.65
9.25	1007.46	1025.77	1044.09	1062.41	1080.73	1099.04	1117.36	1135.68	1153.99
9.50	1025.34	1043.98	1062.63	1081.27	1099.91	1118.56	1137.20	1155.84	1174.48
9.75	1043.37	1062.34	1081.31	1100.28	1119.25	1138.22	1157.19	1176.16	1195.13
10.00	1061.53	1080.83	1100.13	1119.43	1138.73	1158.03	1177.33	1196.63	1215.93
10.25	1079.81	1099.44	1119.07	1138.71	1158.34	1177.97	1197.60	1217.24	1236.87
10.50	1098.22	1118.19	1138.15	1158.12	1178.09	1198.06	1218.03	1237.99	1257.96
10.75	1116.75	1137.06	1157.36	1177.67	1197.97	1218.28	1238.58	1258.88	1279.19
11.00	1135.41	1156.05	1176.69	1197.34	1217.98	1238.62	1259.27	1279.91	1300.56
11.25	1154.18	1175.17	1196.15	1217.14	1238.12	1259.11	1280.09	1301.08	1322.06
11.50	1173.07	1194.40	1215.73	1237.06	1258.39	1279.72	1301.04	1322.37	1343.70
11.75	1192.08	1213.75	1235.43	1257.10	1278.78	1300.45	1322.13	1343.80	1365.47
12.00	1211.19	1233.22	1255.24	1277.26	1299.28	1321.30	1343.33	1365.35	1387.37
12.25	1230.42	1252.79	1275.16	1297.53	1319.91	1342.28	1364.65	1387.02	1409.39
12.50	1249.76	1272.48	1295.20	1317.92	1340.65	1363.37	1386.09	1408.82	1431.54

15-YEAR MORTGAGE LOAN AMOUNTS

RATES	110000	112000	114000	116000	118000	120000	122000	124000	126000
9.00	1115.69	1135.97	1156.26	1176.54	1196.83	1217.11	1237.40	1257.68	1277.97
9.25	1132.12	1152.70	1173.28	1193.87	1214.45	1235.03	1255.62	1276.20	1296.79
9.50	1148.64	1169.53	1190.41	1211.30	1232.18	1253.07	1273.95	1294.84	1315.72
9.75	1165.30	1186.49	1207.68	1228.86	1250.05	1271.24	1292.43	1313.61	1334.80
10.00	1182.07	1203.56	1225.05	1246.54	1268.04	1289.53	1311.02	1332.51	1354.00
10.25	1198.94	1220.74	1242.54	1264.34	1286.14	1307.94	1329.74	1351.54	1373.34
10.50	1215.94	1238.05	1260.16	1282.27	1304.37	1326.48	1348.59	1370.70	1392.81
10.75	1233.04	1255.46	1277.88	1300.30	1322.72	1345.14	1367.56	1389.98	1412.40
11.00	1250.25	1272.99	1295.72	1318.45	1341.18	1363.91	1386.65	1409.38	1432.11
11.25	1267.58	1290.63	1313.67	1336.72	1359.77	1382.82	1405.86	1428.91	1451.96
11.50	1285.01	1308.37	1331.74	1355.10	1378.46	1401.83	1425.19	1448.56	1471.92
11.75	1302.55	1326.23	1349.91	1373.60	1397.28	1420.96	1444.65	1468.33	1492.01
12.00	1320.19	1344.19	1368.19	1392.20	1416.20	1440.20	1464.21	1488.21	1512.21
12.25	1337.93	1362.25	1386.58	1410.91	1435.23	1459.56	1483.88	1508.21	1532.54
12.50	1355.78	1380.43	1405.08	1429.73	1454.38	1479.03	1503.68	1528.33	1552.98

MONTHLY EDUCATIONAL LOAN PAYMENT COMPARISONS

5-YEAR LOAN AMOUNTS

RATES	2000	4000	6000	8000	10000	12000	14000	16000	18000
5.00	37.74	75.48	113.23	150.97	188.71	226.45	264.19	301.93	339.68
5.25	37.97	75.94	113.92	151.89	189.86	227.83	265.81	303.78	341.75
5.50	38.20	76.40	114.61	152.81	191.01	229.21	267.42	305.62	343.82
5.75	38.43	76.87	115.30	153.74	192.17	230.61	269.04	307.47	345.91
6.00	38.67	77.33	116.00	154.66	193.33	231.99	270.66	309.32	347.99
6.25	38.90	77.80	116.69	155.59	194.49	233.39	272.29	311.19	350.08
6.50	39.13	78.27	117.40	156.53	195.66	234.80	273.93	313.06	352.19
6.75	39.37	78.73	118.10	157.47	196.83	236.20	275.57	314.94	354.30
7.00	39.60	79.20	118.81	158.41	198.01	237.61	277.22	316.82	356.42
7.25	39.84	79.68	119.52	159.36	199.19	239.03	278.87	318.71	358.55
7.50	40.08	80.15	120.23	160.30	200.38	240.45	280.53	320.61	360.68
7.75	40.31	80.63	120.94	161.26	201.57	241.89	282.20	322.51	362.83
8.00	40.55	81.11	121.66	162.21	202.76	243.32	283.87	324.42	364.98
8.25	40.79	81.58	122.38	163.17	203.96	244.75	285.55	326.34	367.13
8.50	41.03	82.07	123.10	164.13	205.17	246.20	287.23	328.27	369.30

5-YEAR LOAN AMOUNTS

RATES	20000	22000	24000	26000	28000	30000	32000	34000	36000
5.00	377.42	415.16	452.90	490.64	528.39	566.13	603.87	641.61	679.35
5.25	379.72	417.70	455.67	493.64	531.61	569.59	607.56	645.53	683.50
5.50	382.02	420.23	458.43	496.63	534.83	573.03	611.24	649.44	687.64
5.75	384.34	422.78	461.21	499.64	538.08	576.51	614.95	653.38	691.82
6.00	386.66	425.32	463.99	502.65	541.32	579.98	618.65	657.31	695.98
6.25	388.98	427.88	466.78	505.68	544.57	583.47	622.37	661.27	700.17
6.50	391.33	430.46	469.59	508.72	547.86	586.99	626.12	665.25	704.39
6.75	393.67	433.04	472.40	511.77	551.14	590.50	629.87	669.24	708.61
7.00	396.02	435.63	475.23	514.83	554.43	594.03	633.64	673.24	712.84
7.25	398.39	438.23	478.07	517.91	557.74	597.58	637.42	677.26	717.10
7.50	400.76	440.83	480.91	520.98	561.06	601.14	641.21	681.29	721.36
7.75	403.14	443.46	483.77	524.08	564.40	604.71	645.03	685.34	725.66
8.00	405.53	446.08	486.63	527.19	567.74	608.29	648.84	689.40	729.95
8.25	407.92	448.72	489.51	530.30	571.09	611.89	652.68	693.47	734.26
8.50	410.33	451.37	492.40	533.43	574.47	615.50	656.53	697.57	738.60

10-YEAR LOAN AMOUNTS

RATES	2000	4000	6000	8000	10000	12000	14000	16000	18000
5.00	21.21	42.43	63.64	84.85	106.06	127.28	148.49	169.70	190.92
5.25	21.46	42.92	64.38	85.83	107.29	128.75	150.21	171.67	193.13
5.50	21.71	43.41	65.12	86.82	108.53	130.23	151.94	173.64	195.35
5.75	21.95	43.91	65.86	87.82	109.77	131.72	153.68	175.63	197.59
6.00	22.20	44.41	66.61	88.82	111.02	133.22	155.43	177.63	199.84
6.25	22.46	44.91	67.37	89.82	112.28	134.73	157.19	179.65	202.10
6.50	22.71	45.42	68.13	90.84	113.55	136.26	158.97	181.68	204.39
6.75	22.96	45.93	68.89	91.86	114.82	137.79	160.75	183.72	206.68
7.00	23.22	46.44	69.66	92.89	116.11	139.33	162.55	185.77	208.99
7.25	23.48	46.96	70.44	93.92	117.40	140.88	164.36	187.84	211.32
7.50	23.74	47.48	71.22	94.96	118.70	142.44	166.18	189.92	213.66
7.75	24.00	48.00	72.01	96.01	120.01	144.01	168.02	192.02	216.02
8.00	24.27	48.53	72.80	97.06	121.33	145.59	169.86	194.12	218.39
8.25	24.53	49.06	73.59	98.12	122.65	147.18	171.71	196.24	220.77
8.50	24.80	49.59	74.39	99.19	123.99	148.78	173.58	198.38	223.18

10-YEAR LOAN AMOUNTS

RATES	20000	22000	24000	26000	28000	30000	32000	34000	36000
5.00	212.13	233.34	254.55	275.77	296.98	318.19	339.40	360.62	381.83
5.25	214.59	236.04	257.50	278.96	300.42	321.88	343.34	364.80	386.25
5.50	217.05	238.76	260.46	282.17	303.87	325.58	347.28	368.99	390.69
5.75	219.54	241.50	263.45	285.40	307.36	329.31	351.27	373.22	395.17
6.00	222.04	244.24	266.45	288.65	310.86	333.06	355.27	377.47	399.67
6.25	224.56	247.01	269.47	291.93	314.38	336.84	359.29	381.75	404.20
6.50	227.10	249.81	272.52	295.23	317.94	340.65	363.36	386.07	408.78
6.75	229.65	252.61	275.58	298.54	321.51	344.47	367.44	390.40	413.37
7.00	232.22	255.44	278.66	301.88	325.10	348.32	371.55	394.77	417.99
7.25	234.80	258.28	281.76	305.24	328.72	352.20	375.68	399.17	422.65
7.50	237.40	261.14	284.88	308.62	332.36	356.10	379.84	403.58	427.32
7.75	240.02	264.02	288.03	312.03	336.03	360.03	384.04	408.04	432.04
8.00	242.66	266.92	291.19	315.45	339.72	363.98	388.25	412.51	436.78
8.25	245.30	269.84	294.37	318.90	343.43	367.96	392.49	417.02	441.55
8.50	247.97	272.77	297.57	322.36	347.16	371.96	396.76	421.55	446.35

MONTHLY EDUCATIONAL LOAN PAYMENT COMPARISONS

15-YEAR LOAN AMOUNTS

RATES	2000	4000	6000	8000	10000	12000	14000	16000	18000
5.00	15.82	31.63	47.45	63.26	79.08	94.89	110.71	126.53	142.34
5.25	16.08	32.16	48.23	64.31	80.39	96.47	112.54	128.62	144.70
5.50	16.34	32.68	49.03	65.37	81.71	98.05	114.39	130.73	147.08
5.75	16.61	33.22	49.83	66.43	83.04	99.65	116.26	132.87	149.48
6.00	16.88	33.75	50.63	67.51	84.39	101.26	118.14	135.02	151.89
6.25	17.15	34.30	51.45	68.59	85.74	102.89	120.04	137.19	154.34
6.50	17.42	34.84	52.27	69.69	87.11	104.53	121.96	139.38	156.80
6.75	17.70	35.40	53.09	70.79	88.49	106.19	123.89	141.59	159.28
7.00	17.98	35.95	53.93	71.91	89.88	107.86	125.84	143.81	161.79
7.25	18.26	36.51	54.77	73.03	91.29	109.54	127.80	146.06	164.32
7.50	18.54	37.08	55.62	74.16	92.70	111.24	129.78	148.32	166.86
7.75	18.83	37.65	56.48	75.30	94.13	112.95	131.78	150.60	169.43
8.00	19.11	38.23	57.34	76.45	95.57	114.68	133.79	152.90	172.02
8.25	19.40	38.81	58.21	77.61	97.01	116.42	135.82	155.22	174.63
8.50	19.69	39.39	59.08	78.78	98.47	118.17	137.86	157.56	177.25

15-YEAR LOAN AMOUNTS

RATES	20000	22000	24000	26000	28000	30000	32000	34000	36000
5.00	158.16	173.97	189.79	205.60	221.42	237.23	253.05	268.87	284.68
5.25	160.78	176.85	192.93	209.01	225.09	241.17	257.24	273.32	289.40
5.50	163.42	179.76	196.10	212.44	228.78	245.13	261.47	277.81	294.15
5.75	166.08	182.69	199.30	215.91	232.52	249.13	265.73	282.34	298.95
6.00	168.77	185.65	202.53	219.40	236.28	253.16	270.03	286.91	303.79
6.25	171.48	188.63	205.78	222.93	240.08	257.23	274.37	291.52	308.67
6.50	174.22	191.64	209.07	226.49	243.91	261.33	278.76	296.18	313.60
6.75	176.98	194.68	212.38	230.08	247.77	265.47	283.17	300.87	318.57
7.00	179.77	197.74	215.72	233.69	251.67	269.65	287.62	305.60	323.58
7.25	182.57	200.83	219.09	237.35	255.60	273.86	292.12	310.37	328.63
7.50	185.40	203.94	222.48	241.02	259.56	278.10	296.64	315.18	333.72
7.75	188.26	207.08	225.91	244.73	263.56	282.38	301.21	320.04	338.86
8.00	191.13	210.24	229.36	248.47	267.58	286.70	305.81	324.92	344.03
8.25	194.03	213.43	232.83	252.24	271.64	291.04	310.44	329.85	349.25
8.50	196.95	216.64	236.34	256.03	275.73	295.42	315.12	334.81	354.51

Stock Closing Prices

	HMNP Company	**EVS Company**
June 3	7⅜	12½
June 4	7¼	12⅞
June 5	6¾	12⅝
June 6	7	12¼
June 7	7⅝	12⅛
June 10	7¾	11½
June 11	7½	11⅝
June 12	7¼	11⅝
June 13	7¼	12
June 14	6⅞	12⅛
June 17	6¾	12⅛
June 18	6¾	12½
June 19	7	12⅜
June 20	7⅛	12½
June 21	7	12⅛
June 24	7¼	12
June 25	7⅜	11¾
June 26	7¾	12
June 27	7⅜	12⅛
June 28	7⅜	12⅛

CONSUMER PRICE INDEX FOR ALL URBAN CONSUMERS 1984 = 100		
Group	**March 1989**	**March 1988**
All items	122.3	116.5
Food	123.5	115.9
Apparel and upkeep	119.3	114.3
Men's and boys' apparel	115.9	111.6
Women's and girls' apparel	119.4	115.3
Footwear	114.1	107.3
		(continued)

602

CONSUMER PRICE INDEX FOR ALL URBAN CONSUMERS
1984 = 100   (continued)

Group	March 1989	March 1988
Housing, total	121.5	117.0
Rent	138.6	132.9
Gas and electricity	104.8	101.7
Fuel oil, coal, bottled gas	81.5	80.5
House operation	110.5	108.3
House furnishings	105.1	104.7
Transportation	111.9	106.5
Medical care	146.1	136.3
Personal care	123.6	118.1
Entertainment	124.7	119.0
Personal and educational expenses	154.6	145.0

Source: The 1990 Information Please Almanac

Percentage of Advertising Expenditures by Medium, 1984

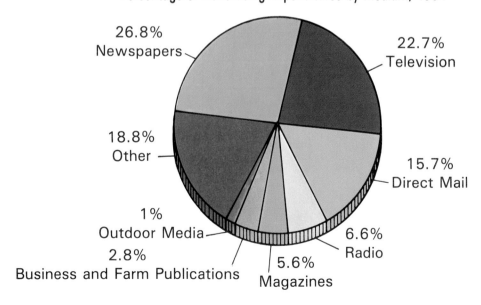

26.8% Newspapers
22.7% Television
18.8% Other
15.7% Direct Mail
1% Outdoor Media
2.8% Business and Farm Publications
5.6% Magazines
6.6% Radio

Multiples-of-Salary Chart for Net Income Replacement

Present Gross Earnings	Present Age							
	25 Years		35 Years		45 Years		55 Years	
	75%	60%	75%	60%	75%	60%	75%	60%
$ 7,500	4.0	3.0	5.5	4.0	7.5	5.5	6.5	4.5
9,000	4.0	3.0	5.5	4.0	7.5	5.5	6.5	4.5
15,000	4.5	3.0	6.5	4.5	8.0	6.0	7.0	5.5
23,500	6.5	4.5	8.0	5.5	8.5	6.5	7.5	5.5
30,000	7.5	5.0	8.0	6.0	8.5	6.5	7.0	5.5
40,000	7.5	5.0	8.0	6.0	8.0	6.0	7.0	5.5
65,000	7.5	5.5	7.5	6.0	7.5	6.0	6.5	5.0

Comparison Table for Term and Whole Life Premiums
Policy face value is $100,000.

Age	5-Year Renewable Term	Whole Life	First Year Difference
20	$205	$ 775	$ 570
25	207	918	711
30	218	1,112	894
35	254	1,374	1,120
40	363	1,729	1,366
45	562	2,127	1,565
50	878	2,689	1,811

Accumulated Cash Value of $100,000 Whole Life Policy						
Age at Issue	After Paying Premiums for:					At Age 65
	5 years	10 years	15 years	17 years	20 years	
25	$2212	$7105	$12840	$16139	$19438	$57716
30	3011	8898	15667	19432	23197	55890
35	3999	11027	18837	23088	27339	53533
40	5151	13369	22203	27031	31759	50453
45	6367	15921	26016	31211	36407	46426
50	7737	18715	29992	35586	41181	41181
55	9210	21707	34080	39915	45751	34080
60	10842	24827	37980	43954	49928	24827

The cash value is the amount of money you will receive if you decide to cancel your policy. Most policies have no cash value for the first three years. The cash value increases as the policy increases in age. Also, the amount depends on the type and face value of the policy as well as the age of the insured when the policy was issued.

AUTOMOBILE INSURANCE Six-Month Basic Rate Schedule						
Car Class Rating	Collision Deductible			Comprehensive Deductible		
	$ 50	$100	$200	$ 0	$50	$100
1-10	$ 50	$ 43	$ 37	$14	$13	$ 11
11-20	82	75	69	35	31	28
21-30	114	104	94	45	41	37
31-40	128	119	110	67	61	56

STARFIRE PRICE LIST

Starfire (8 Cylinder)
2 Dr Hatchback Coupe 26958   31979
2 Dr Convertible Coupe 31414   37264
Destination Charge: All models 525   525

Mfgs. Code	Description	Base Cost	Sgstd. List

STANDARD EQUIPMENT:

5.7 liter TPI V8 engine, 4 speed automatic overdrive transmission, driver's side supplemental inflatable restraint system, engine oil cooler, driver's side illuminated visor vanity mirror, power operated retractable halogen headlamps, halogen fog lamps, dual electrically adjusted and heated mirrors, one-piece removable fiberglass roof panel (Coupe), full-folding roof (Convertible), anti-theft system, intermittent wiper system, electronic speed control with resume speed, air conditioning, heated rear window (Coupe), leather wrapped steering wheel, radio (AM/FM stereo with seek and scan, cassette, 4 speakers, automatic power antenna), power door locks, power windows, cloth bucket seats with lateral support and back angle adjustment plus wool-pad comfort liner, outside engine air induction, radial tires, 17″ x 9½″ cast aluminum wheels, power 4-wheel disc brakes, anti-lock braking system, power rack and pinion steering, heavy duty gas charged shock absorbers, underhood lamps, accoustical insulation package, uniframe design body structure with corrosion-resistant coating.

ACCESSORIES

Description	Base Cost	Sgstd. List
Coupe Base Equipment Group—included w/model	NC	NC
- with UU8 radio add	683	823
- with U1F radio add	1012	1219
Coupe Preferred Equipment Group 1—includes: electronic air conditioning; electronically tuned music system—includes AM/FM stereo radio with seek and scan, stereo cassette tape and digital clock, special tone and balance control and four speakers); power seat—six-way driver's side only	1057	1273
- with U1F radio add	329	396
Convertible Base Equipment Group—included with model	NC	NC
- with UU8 radio add	683	823
- with U1F radio add	1012	1219
Convertible Preferred Equipment Group 1—includes: electronic air conditioning; electronically tuned music system - includes AM/FM stereo radio with seek and scan, stereo cassette tape and digital clock, special tone and balance control and four speakers), power seat—six-way driver's side only	1057	1273
- with U1F radio add	329	396
Interior Trim		
cloth bucket seats	NC	NC
leather bucket seats	353	425
leather adjustable sport bucket seat	872	1050
Engine—5.7 liter V8	NC	NC
Air Conditioning, Electronic Control	149	180
Axle, Performance Ratio	18	22
Carrier, Luggage—black	116	140
Cooler, Engine Oil—included with performance handling package	91	110
California Emission Requirements—includes all testing necessary for registration in the State of California	83	100
Standard Emission Equipment	NC	NC
Handling Package		
performance: includes KC4 engine oil cooler and heavy duty brakes	382	460
selective ride, electronic	1407	1695
Heater, Engine Block	17	20
Low Tire Pressure Warning Indicator	270	325
Radio Equipment—for specific radio pricing, please refer to radio information included with each preferred equipment group		
electronically tuned music system; (includes AM/FM stereo radio with seek and scan, stereo cassette tape and digital clock, special tone and balance control and four speakers)		
electronically tuned music system; (includes AM/FM stereo radio with seek and scan, stereo cassette tape, compact disc player, and digital clock, special tone and balance control and four speakers.		
Roof Panels—removable		
blue tint (transparent)	510	615
bronze tint (transparent)	510	615

MOONBEAM PRICE LIST

Mfgs. Code	Description	Base Cost	Sgstd. List
P57	4 Dr GL Wagon	12725	14722
P54	4 Dr SHO Sedan	18599	21633
P53	4 Dr LX Sedan	13964	16180
P58	4 Dr LX Wagon	15316	17771
MOONBEAM (4 Cylinder) (New York State)			
P50	4 Dr L Sedan	11053	12755
P52	4 Dr GL Sedan	11455	13228
MOONBEAM (6 Cylinder) (New York State)			
P55	4 Dr L Wagon	12440	14387
P57	4 Dr GL Wagon	12823	14837
P54	4 Dr SHO Sedan	18697	21748
P53	4 Dr LX Sedan	14062	16295
P58	4 Dr LX Wagon	15414	17886
Destination Charge: All Models		470	470
Tires			
all models except SHO, have four tires as standard equipment:			
spare tire, conventional		62	73
Air Conditioning, Electronic Climate Control		**850**	**1000**
Air Conditioning, Manual		695	817
Anti-Lock Braking System		838	985
Autolamp System		62	73
Battery, Heavy-Duty		23	27
Cargo Area Cover		56	66
Cornering Lamps		58	68
Defroster, Rear Window		136	160
Engine Block Immersion Heater		17	20
Floor Mats, Front and Rear		36	43
Decklid and Fuel Door, Remote—Sedans		78	91
- Wagons (fuel door only)		35	41
Fuel Tank, Extended Range		39	46
Illuminated Entry System		69	82
Instrument Cluster, Diagnostic		85	100
Instrument Cluster, Electronic		203	239
Keyless Entry System		186	218
Light Group		50	59
Load Floor Extension—"picnic table"		77	90
Locks, Power Door		192	226
Mirrors, Dual Illuminated Visor		85	100
Moldings, Rocker Panel		47	55
Moonroof, Power		659	766
Paint, Clearcoat		160	188
Parking Brake Release, Automatic		10	12
Radio Systems			
audio digital disc		418	491
audio system, high level		285	335
radio, electronic AM/FM stereo search with cassette player		132	155
sound system premium		143	168
radio antenna, power		69	82
Audio System		447	526
Seat, Rear Facing Third		132	155
Seat, 6-Way Power Driver's		247	290
Seats, 6-Way Power Dual Control		247	290
Speed Control		178	210
Steering Wheel, Leather Wrapped		54	63
Stripe, Paint		52	61
Suspension, Heavy-Duty (Load Carrying)		22	26
Speed Sensitive Steering Variable Power Assist		88	104

607

Resale Value Table for Cosmos Motor Company

Year-Model-Body Type	Original List	Current Whlse	Average Retail
4-YEARS OLD			
ROMERO 4			
Sport Cpe	10414	3600	4500
Z28 Sport Cpe	12963	5925	6850
FLAME 6*			
4 Dr Sdn	11264	3850	4750
FLAME CLASSIC 6*			
2 Dr Sport Cpe	11665	4625	5550
4 Dr Sedan	11829	4750	5675
4 Dr Brougham Sdn	12478	5175	6075
4 Dr Wgn (8 cyl)	12562	5250	6175
* For 8 cylinder models add $400 wholesale and $400 retail.			
CAMEL 4*			
2 Dr Cpe	8258	2950	3850
4 Dr Sdn	8443	3050	3950
4 Dr Wgn	8606	3125	4025
2 Dr CS Htchbk Cpe	8940	3150	4050
4 Dr CS Sedan	8916	3150	4050
4 Dr CS Wgn	9097	3225	4125
2 Dr RS Conv	13996	5500	6425
2 Dr RS Cpe	8988	3250	4150
2 Dr RS Htchbk Cpe	9183	3350	4250
4 Dr RS Sdn	9163	3350	4250
4 Dr RS Wgn	9335	3450	4350
* For 6 cylinder models add $200 wholesale and $200 retail.			
CAMEL 6*			
2 Dr Z24 Sport Cpe	10256	4325	5250
2 Dr Z24 Htchbk Sport Cpe	10451	4425	5350
SPLASH 4*			
2 Dr Cpe	10243	3450	4350
4 Dr Sdn	10444	3550	4450
4 Dr 2 Seat Wgn	10598	3775	4675
4 Dr 3 Seat Wgn	10836	3850	4750
* For 6 cylinder models add $300 wholesale and $300 retail.			
ARROW 4			
CS Htchbk Cpe	7125	1775	2625
CS Htchbk Sdn	7309	1875	2725
CS Diesel Htchbk Cpe	6507	1325	2075
CS Diesel Htchbk Sdn	6712	1425	2175
(Diesel models not available w/air conditioning or automatic transmission)			
HOTSHOT 6			
Htchbk Cpe	27405	14350	16975
Conv	32480	17700	20350
LAMU 5*			
2 Dr Sport Cpe	10344	4350	5275
2 Dr LS Cpe	13640	4450	5375
*For 8 cylinder models add $325 wholesale and $325 retail.			
LAMU 8			
2 Dr SS Sport Cpe	13640	6525	7725
DWARF 4			
4 Dr Htchbk Sdn	9176	3325	4225
5 Dr Htchbk Sdn	9417	3425	4325
RAINBOW 4			
4 Dr Htchbk Sdn	8728	2550	3425
5.0 Liter V8 TPI Eng	745	385	470
5.7 Liter V8 TPI Eng	1045	530	660
3 YEARS OLD			
ROMERO 6*			
Sport Cpe	11260	4950	5875
Convertible	15659	7300	8525
* For 8 cylinder models add $300 wholesale and $300 retail.			
ROMERO 8*			
Z28 Sport Cpe	14084	7150	8375
Z28 Convertible	18483	10325	12050
FLAME 6*			
4 Dr Sdn	11770	5150	6050
FLAME CLASSIC 6*			
2 Dr Sport Cpe	12167	5950	6875
4 Dr Sedan	12335	6100	7000
FLAME CLASSIC BROUGHAM 6*			
4 Dr Sdn	13324	6550	7750
4 Dr LS Sdn	14580	6925	8150
* For 8 cylinder models add $425 wholesale and $425 retail.			
FLAME 8			
4 Dr Wgn	12770	5725	6625
FLAME CLASSIC 8			
4 Dr Wgn	13361	6650	7875
CAMEL 4*			
2 Dr Cpe	8737	3600	4500
4 Dr Sdn	8961	3700	4600
4 Dr Wgn	9127	3825	4725
2 Dr CS Htchbk Cpe	9368	3850	4750
4 Dr CS Sedan	9343	3850	4750
4 Dr CS Wgn	9530	3975	4875
2 Dr RS Conv	14611	6725	7950
2 Dr RS Cpe	9483	4000	4900
2 Dr RS Htchbk Cpe	9685	4100	5025
4 Dr RS Sdn	9664	4100	5025
4 Dr RS Wgn	9842	4225	5150
* For 6 cylinder models add $200 wholesale and $200 retail.			
4 Dr 2 Seat Wgn	11200	4425	5350
4 Dr 3 Seat Wgn	11447	4525	5450
* For 6-cylinder models add $300 wholesale and $300 retail.			
ARROW 4			
2 Dr CS Htchbk Cpe	6345	2175	3025
4 Dr CS Htchbk Sdn	6845	2275	3125
HOTSHOT 8			
Htchbk Cpe	27999	16350	19000
Conv	33172	19950	22950
LAMU 6*			
2 Dr LS Cpe	12081	5475	6400
* For 8 cylinder models add $350 wholesale and $350 retail.			
LAMU 8			
2 Dr SS Sport Cpe	14238	8100	9325
2 Dr SS Aero Cpe	15613	7550	8775
DWARF 4			
4 Dr Htchbk Sdn	9378	4275	5200
5 Dr Htchbk Sdn	9630	4375	5300
RAINBOW 4			
4 Dr Htchbk Sdn	9200	3325	4225
2 Dr Htchbk Cpe	8903	3225	4125
DASHER 3			
2 Dr Htchbk Cpe	7486	2475	3350
2 Dr ER Htchbk Cpe	7601	2500	3375

608

Automobile Depreciation Schedule

Year	Percent Decrease
1st	30–32%
2nd	24–26
3rd	18–20
4th	7–8
5th	3–5
6th	3–5
7th	3–5
8th	1–2
9th	1–2
10th	1–2

Options Valuation Table

Deduct from resale value if car does not have:

Years Old		Radio	Auto Trans	Power Steering	Air Conditioning
1	Whsle	$ 50	$145	$125	$400
	Retail	60	175	150	500
2	Whsle	40	130	105	325
	Retail	50	155	125	400
3	Whsle	35	105	85	285
	Retail	45	130	100	350
4	Whsle	30	90	85	225
	Retail	35	110	100	275
5	Whsle	25	75	85	185
	Retail	30	90	100	225
6	Whsle	15	55	85	170
	Retail	20	65	100	200
7	Whsle	10	35	85	170
	Retail	15	45	100	200

Add to resale value if car has:

Years Old		Radio	Auto Trans	Power Steering	Air Conditioning
1	Whsle	$ 60	$115	$140	$ 85
	Retail	75	140	170	100
2	Whsle	40	100	85	60
	Retail	50	120	100	75
3	Whsle	40	85	60	60
	Retail	50	100	75	75
4	Whsle	40	60	40	40
	Retail	50	75	50	50
5	Whsle	40	60	40	40
	Retail	50	75	50	50
6	Whsle	40	40	20	20
	Retail	50	50	25	25
7	Whsle	40	40	20	20
	Retail	50	50	25	25

High Mileage Deduction Table

Note: Deduct the lower amount for sub-compacts, compacts, and intermediate cars. Deduct the higher amount for standard and luxury cars.

Years Old	15000 or less	15000-20000	20000-25000	25000-30000	30000-35000	35000-40000	40000-45000
	Dollars						
1		150/200	205/300	305/400	405/500	505/600	765/700
2					200/250	255/325	330/425
3							200/250
4							
5							
6							
7							

Years Old	45000-50000	50000-55000	55000-60000	60000-65000	65000-70000	Usual Mileage for Years
	Dollars					
1						10000-15000
2	430/525	530/625	630/725	730/825	830/925	15000- 30000
3	255/325	330/425	430/525	525/575	580/675	30000- 40000
4	110/150	155/250	255/325	330/400	405/525	40000- 50000
5		100/150	155/250	255/325	330/425	45000-50000
6			75/100	105/150	155/250	50000-55000
7				75/100	105/125	55000-60000

DRIVER RATING FACTORS (Part I)
Category: Married Youths

Age	Sex	Owner or Usual Driver	Driver Training	Drive to Work	Rating Factor
16-17	F	Yes	Yes	Yes	2.40
				No	2.25
			No	Yes	2.60
				No	2.45
		No	Yes	Yes	1.90
				No	1.75
			No	Yes	2.05
				No	1.90
	M	Yes	Yes	Yes	2.45
				No	2.30
			No	Yes	2.70
				No	2.55
		No	Yes	Yes	2.45
				No	2.30
			No	Yes	2.70
				No	2.55
18-21	F	Yes	Yes	Yes	1.95
				No	1.80
			No	Yes	2.10
				No	1.95
		No	Yes	Yes	1.55
				No	1.40
			No	Yes	1.65
				No	1.50
	M	Yes	Yes	Yes	2.00
				No	1.85
			No	Yes	2.15
				No	2.00
		No	Yes	Yes	2.00
				No	1.85
			No	Yes	2.15
				No	2.00

DRIVER RATING FACTORS (Part II)
Category: Unmarried Youths

Age	Sex	Owner or Usual Driver	Driver Training	Drive to Work	Rating Factor
16-17	F	Yes	Yes	Yes	2.40
				No	2.25
			No	Yes	2.60
				No	2.45
		No	Yes	Yes	1.90
				No	1.75
			No	Yes	2.05
				No	1.90
	M	Yes	Yes	Yes	3.75
				No	3.60
			No	Yes	4.20
				No	4.05
		No	Yes	Yes	2.60
				No	2.45
			No	Yes	2.85
				No	2.70
18-21	F	Yes	Yes	Yes	1.95
				No	1.80
			No	Yes	2.10
				No	1.95
		No	Yes	Yes	1.55
				No	1.40
			No	Yes	1.65
				No	1.50
	M	Yes	Yes	Yes	3.00
				No	2.85
			No	Yes	3.35
				No	3.20
		No	Yes	Yes	2.15
				No	2.00
			No	Yes	2.30
				No	2.15

DRIVER RATING FACTORS (Part III)
Category: All Adults

Age	Sex	Owner or Usual Driver	Drive to Work	Rating Factor
21-24	F	Yes	Yes	1.50
			No	1.35
		No	Yes	1.40
			No	1.25
	M	Yes	Yes	2.25
			No	2.10
		No	Yes	1.55
			No	1.40
25-29	Both	Yes	Yes	1.65
			No	1.50
30-49	Both	Yes	Yes	1.25
			No	1.00
50-64	Both	Yes	Yes	1.15
			No	0.90
65 +	Both	Yes	Yes	1.05
			No	0.80

Interstate Highway Map (Eastern U. S.)

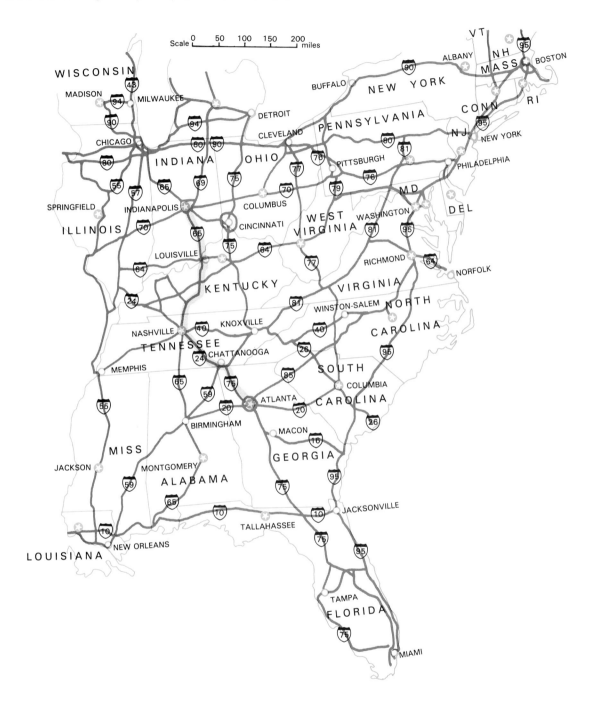

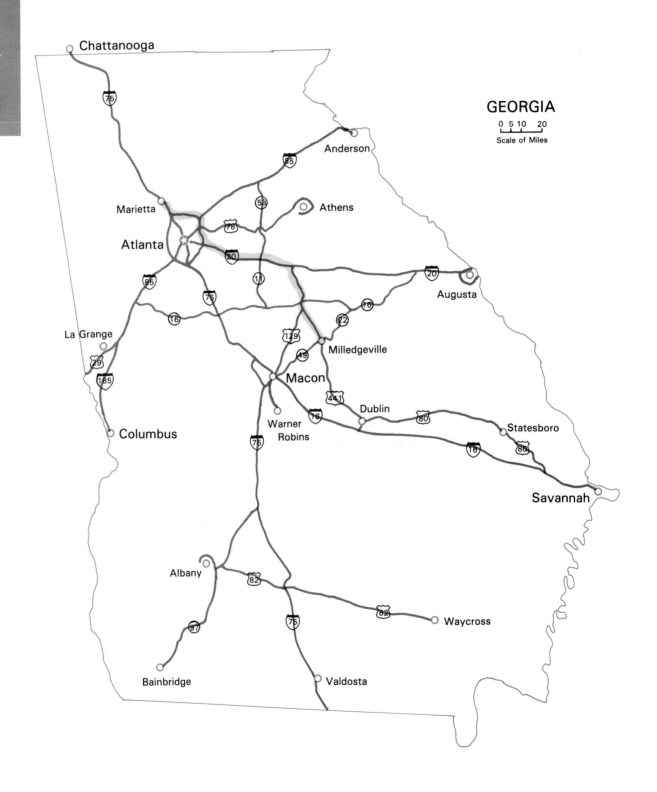

GEORGIA

0 5 10   20
Scale of Miles

Chattanooga

Anderson

Athens

Marietta

Atlanta

Augusta

La Grange

Milledgeville

Macon

Columbus

Warner
Robins

Dublin

Statesboro

Savannah

Albany

Waycross

Bainbridge

Valdosta

United States Mileage Chart

	Atlanta, GA	Boston, MA	Cheyenne, WY	Chicago, IL	Cincinnati, OH	Cleveland, OH	Dallas, TX	Denver, CO	Des Moines, IA	Detroit, MI	Indianapolis, IN	Kansas City, MO	Louisville, KY	Memphis, TN	Milwaukee, WI	Minneapolis, MN	New Orleans, LA	Omaha, NE	Philadelphia, PA	Pittsburgh, PA	Portland, OR	St. Louis, MO	Salt Lake City, UT	San Francisco, CA	Seattle, WA	Toledo, Ohio	Tulsa, OK	Washington, DC	Wichita, KS
Albuquerque, NM	1381	2172	517	1281	1372	1560	638	417	977	1525	1266	782	1301	1190	1319	1134	1190	858	1899	1619	1371	1038	604	1115	1440	1469	645	1824	593
Amarillo, TX	1097	1897	511	1043	1096	1285	358	423	742	1269	991	547	1019	726	1084	975	850	643	1624	1344	1655	761	888	1399	1724	1210	361	1549	350
Atlanta, GA		1037	1442	674	440	672	795	1398	870	699	493	798	382	371	761	1068	479	986	741	687	2601	541	1878	2496	2618	640	772	608	903
Austin, TX	919	1911	994	1110	1083	1327	193	906	877	1315	1037	682	982	1184	1129	615	517	837	1615	1748	2069	823	1302	1781	2138	1256	450	1482	548
Birmingham, AL	150	1165	1347	642	465	709	645	906	787	724	465	697	364	246	728	1006	342	898	869	741	2505	465	1781	2343	2366	665	647	736	778
Boston, MA	1037		1907	963	840	628	1748	1949	1280	695	906	1391	941	1296	1050	1368	1507	1412	296	561	3046	1141	2343	3095	2976	739	1537	429	1587
Charleston, SC	289	929	1722	963	603	730	1072	1678	1150	842	696	1211	591	660	964	1282	783	1266	633	666	2881	821	2158	2785	2890	783	1061	500	1192
Cheyenne, WY	1442	1907		954	877	1174	869	100	627	1211	1068	650	1101	987	292	436	1361	495	1678	1390	1159	901	436	1188	1228	1176	765	1611	583
Chicago, IL	674	963	954		287	335	917	996	327	266	181	499	292	530	87	405	912	459	738	452	2083	289	1390	2142	2013	232	683	671	696
Cleveland, OH	672	628	1174	335	244		1279	996	652	170	294	266	375	779	335	738	1321	693	567	133	2333	340	1610	2467	2348	111	925	346	975
Columbus, OH	533	735	1279	287	108	139	1028	917	618	192	171	656	294	656	209	576	894	750	462	133	2391	406	1671	2423	2321	133	802	387	852
Dallas, TX	795	1748	287	917	920	1159		781	684	1143	865	489	819	452	991	936	496	644	1452	1691	2009	630	1242	1753	2078	1084	257	1319	365
Denver, CO	1398	1949	100	1321	1164	627	781		669	1253	1120	600	1040	841	566	841	1273	537	1691	1051	1238	857	504	1235	1307	1218	681	1616	509
Des Moines, IA	870	1280	627	652	571	259	684	652		595	278	278	1058	465	195	252	978	132	1051	842	1786	333	1063	1749	1815	549	443	775	392
Detroit, MI	699	695	1211	266	259	170	1143	899	404		278	743	358	743	360	671	1045	716	573	278	2349	513	1647	2279	2399	59	909	506	940
Flagstaff, AZ	1704	2495	757	1604	1695	1883	961	657	1300	1848	1589	1105	1624	1481	1642	1457	1457	1171	2222	1942	1241	1361	511	792	1347	1792	968	2147	916
Harrisburg, PA	700	373	1579	639	468	314	1383	1592	952	373	474	534	569	726	931	1044	1142	1084	102	189	2722	769	2015	2767	2652	415	1165	107	1215
Indianapolis, IN	493	906	1257	181	106	294	465	268	278	278		485	111	435	268	586	796	587	633	353	2227	235	1504	2256	2194	219	631	558	681
Jackson, MS	391	1406	1257	742	655	899	404	1169	809	914	809	646	554	212	824	1036	178	845	1110	939	2401	495	1646	2470	2157	855	527	977	708
Kansas City, MO	798	1391	650	499	591	779	489	600	195	743	485		520	451	212	447	806	201	1809	838	2505	257	1086	1835	1839	687	248	1043	197
Knoxville, TN	193	911	1372	527	253	485	837	1328	800	512	346	666	385	537	614	932	596	916	615	511	2531	471	1808	2540	2540	453	786	482	871
Louisville, KY	382	941	1161	292	101	345	819	1120	566	360	111	700		385	379	697	685	687	668	388	2320	263	1597	2349	2305	301	659	607	710
Mackinaw City, MI	935	916	1291	387	495	439	1261	1341	673	284	460	864	562	880	368	508	1247	805	842	556	2128	651	1691	2058	2443	328	1047	760	1061
Miami, FL	655	1504	2097	1329	1095	1261	1300	2037	1525	1148	1352	1001	775	1037	1416	1723	856	1208	1208	1200	3256	1196	2532	3273	3053	1293	1398	1075	1529
Minneapolis, MN	1068	1368	788	405	692	740	936	1238	252	252	252	671	759	697	332		1214	357	1641	856	1678	552	1186	1940	1737	636	172	636	172
New Orleans, LA	479	1507	1361	912	786	1030	270	1273	978	1141	978	666	806	390	685	994		1143	1211	1070	2505	673	1738	2574	2249	986	637	1078	816
Norfolk, VA	540	558	1764	831	604	508	1329	1758	1141	743	877	700	806	877	642	994	1162	1211	263	384	2914	905	2200	2952	2952	607	1278	188	1352
Pierre, SD	1361	1726	434	763	1050	1098	943	518	492	1758	492	944	592	918	394	690	1394	1273	263	501	1353	824	823	1575	1283	995	760	1434	578
Pittsburgh, PA	687	561	1390	452	287	129	1204	1411	763	566	492	287	353	838	388	752	1055	391	1501	288	2535	539	1826	2578	2349	228	964	221	1034
Portland, ME	1139	106	1291	1042	942	707	1850	2028	1359	673	763	775	659	1486	1043	857	1394	895	288	895	3125	636	2422	3174	3174	328	1632	221	1682
Portland, OR	2601	3046	2083	1850	2009	2418	1264	707	1786	2037	1525	775	775	1486	997	1416	1609	1208	2821	2535		1236	767	636	172	2315	1293	3055	1682
San Antonio, TX	983	1988	1027	1187	1160	1404	270	939	954	1392	1114	759	692	1206	1261	1261	550	856	1692	1654	2086	900	1319	1737	2155	1333	527	1559	625
San Francisco, CA	2496	3095	1188	2142	2362	2467	1753	939	1815	2362	1815	1835	1835	1940	2125	1261	1940	2249	2866	1683	636	2089	752		808	2364	1760	2799	1695
Seattle, WA	2618	2976	1228	2013	2300	2348	2078	2078	1749	1307	1749	1839	1839	2305	2290	2290	1608	2574	2751	1638	172	2081	836	808		2245	1982	2684	1808
Tulsa, OK	772	1537	765	683	736	925	257	925	443	681	443	248	659	248	659	401	757	647	2505	387	1913	396	1172	1913	1913	850		1189	182
Washington, DC	608	429	1611	671	481	346	1319	1616	984	506	984	1043	582	1043	582	867	1075	1078	133	221	2754	793	2047	2799	2684	447	1189		1239
Wichita, KS	903	1587	583	696	787	975	365	509	392	940	392	197	710	197	710	532	734	815	298	1314	1739	447	1003	1695	1808	884	182	1239	

Time Zone World Map

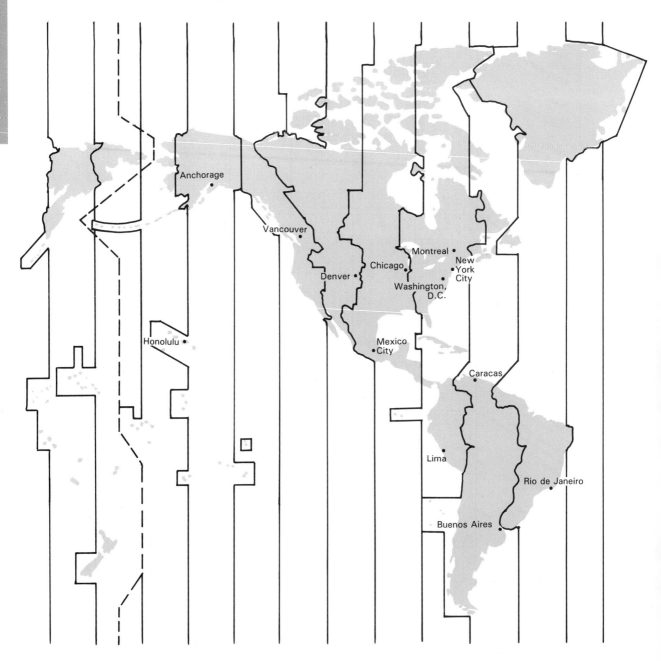

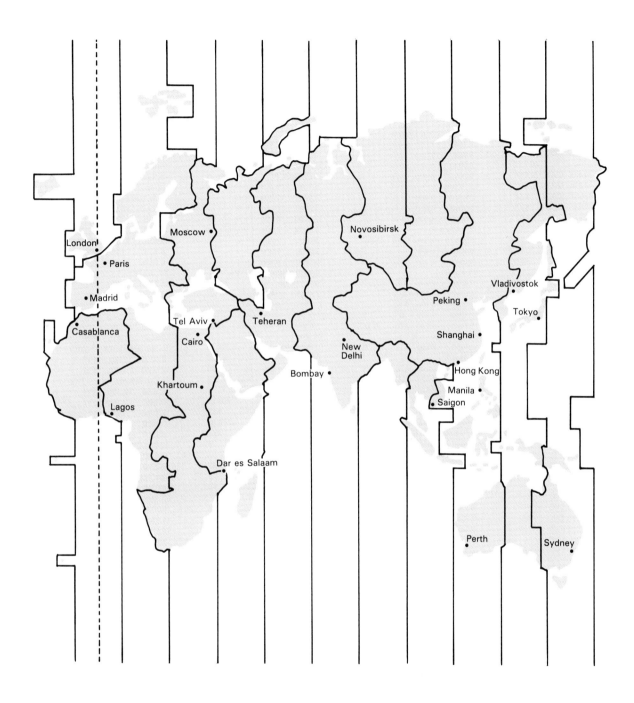

WINDWARD AIRLINES SCHEDULE

Leave	Arrive	Stops/Via	Rmks
From Chicago, IL			
To Muscle Shoals, AL		491 mi	
1:00p0	5:10p	ATL	L
4:55p0	9:00p	ATL	D X6
To Myrtle Beach, SC		743 mi	
8:10a0	1:18p	ATL	B
9:54a0	3:15p	ATL	S
Eff. May 15			
1:00p0	6:59p	ATL	L
6:44p0	11:45p	ATL	D X6
To Naples, FL		1136 mi	
8:15a0	1:48p	MCO	B
2:10p0	7:25p	MCO	S
To Nashville, TN		401 mi	
5:30a0	8:45a	CVG	S X67
6:15a0	9:24a	CVG	S X67
7:40aM	10:55a	CVG	X67
9:57a0	12:59p	CVG	X67
11:35aM	2:50p	CVG	X67
3:20pM	6:55p	CVG	X6
3:50p0	6:55p	CVG	
5:35p0	8:43p	CVG	X6
5:40pM	8:43p	CVG	X67
Eff. May 1			
To Nassau, Bah		1301 mi	
8:10a0	1:55p	ATL	
To New Orleans, LA		831 mi	
6:15a0	10:14a	CVG	B/S X67
8:10a0	12:11p	ATL	B
9:25aM	1:35p	CVG	L6
Eff. May 6			
9:57a0	1:35p	CVG	L
10:18a0	2:45p	DFW	X67
11:35a0	3:55p	ATL	L
1:00p0	5:20p	ATL	L
3:14p0	7:20p	ATL	S6
3:20pM	7:45p	CVG	D X6
3:50p0	7:45p	CVG	D
6:44p0	10:35p	ATL	D
8:45p0	12:59a	DFW	S
To New York, NY/			
Newark, NJ		734 mi	
L-LaGuardia; J-Kennedy;			
E-Newark			
7:40aM	12:25pL	CVG	X67
11:35aM	4:40pL	CVG	X67
11:35aM	4:55pE	CVG	X67
3:20pM	7:45pE	CVG	D X6
5:35p0	10:20pL	CVG	
5:40pM	10:20pL	CVG	X67
Eff. May 1			
To Norfolk/Virginia Beach/			
Williamsburg, VA		707 mi	
6:30a0	12:29p	ATL	B X7
9:54a0	3:10p	ATL	S
11:35aM	3:55p	CVG	X67
1:00p0	6:25p	ATL	L
5:35p0	9:40p	CVG	
5:40pM	9:40p	CVG	X67
To Oakland, CA		1843 mi	
Also see San Francisco, San Jose			
8:00a0	12:05p	SLC	B
11:45a0	3:45p	SLC	
3:10p0	7:10p	SLC	D
6:15p0	9:55p	SLC	
To Oklahoma City, OK		695 mi	
8:30a0	12:35p	DFW	B
10:18a0	2:15p	DFW	X67
12:10p0	4:15p	DFW	X7
3:50p0	9:25p	DFW	S
8:45p0	12:35a	DFW	S
To Ontario, CA		1707 mi	
Also see Los Angeles, Burbank,			
Long Beach and Orange County			
8:00a0	11:55a	SLC	B
8:30a0	1:10p	DFW	
11:45a0	3:25p	SLC	
12:10p0	4:20p	DFW	X7
3:50p0	8:10p	DFW	
6:15p0	9:45p	1	
To Orange County, CA		1732 mi	
Also see Los Angeles, Burbank,			
Long Beach and Ontario			
6:15a0	12:05p	CVG	X67
8:00a0	12:05p	SLC	B
8:30a0	1:15p	DFW	
9:25aM	3:40p	CVG	6
Eff. May 6			
11:45a0	3:40p	SLC	
3:10p0	7:35p	SLC	S
3:50p0	8:10p	DFW	
To Orlando, FL		995 mi	
5:30a0	10:00a	CVG	B X67
8:15a0	11:42a		B
9:25aM	2:35p	CVG	L6
Eff. May 6			
9:45a0	2:54p	ATL	S
9:57a0	2:35p	CVG	L
11:35a0	5:00p	ATL	L
2:10p0	5:37p	0	S
3:14p0	8:29p	ATL	S X6
Disc. Apr. 30			
3:14p0	8:29p	ATL	S
Eff. May 1			
3:14p0	8:29p	ATL	S6
3:20pM	8:52p	CVG	DX6
3:50p0	8:52p	CVG	D
4:55p0	9:44p	ATL	D
6:44p0	11:35p	ATL	D
7:59p0	12:55a	ATL	S
To Palm Springs, CA		1658 mi	
8:00a0	11:45a	SLC	B
Disc. Apr. 30			
11:45a0	3:45p	SLC	
3:10p0	8:25p	SLC	S
6:15p0	10:25p	SLC	X5
To Panama City, FL		812 mi	
6:30a0	10:15a	ATL	B X7
8:10a0	12:05p	ATL	B
9:54a0	1:35p	ATL	S
11:35a0	3:29p	ATL	L
1:00p0	5:07p	ATL	L
3:14p0	6:59p	ATL	S X6
Disc. Apr. 30			
3:14p0	6:59p	ATL	S
Eff. May 1			
3:14p0	6:59p	ATL	S6
4:55p0	8:45p	ATL	D
6:44p0	10:30p	ATL	D X6
To Paris, Fra		4154 mi	
Orly Airport			
11:35aM	7:25a	CVG	X67
Eff. May 8; aircraft change enroute			
11:35aM	7:25a	CVG	X67
Disc. May 5; aircraft change enroute			
1:00p0	7:25a	ATL	
To Pasco/Richland/			
Kennewick, WA		1579 mi	
8:00a0	11:40a	SLC	B
3:10p0	7:33p	SLC	S
6:15p0	9:40p	SLC	
To Pensacola, FL		787 mi	
8:10a0	11:53a	ATL	B
11:35a0	3:12p	ATL	L
3:14p0	6:50p	ATL	S X6
Disc. Apr. 30			
3:14p0	6:50p	ATL	S
Eff. May 1			
3:14p0	6:50p	ATL	S6
6:44p0	10:20p	ATL	D
To Philadelphia, PA		669 mi	
6:15a0	11:50a	CVG	B/SX67
11:35aM	4:23p	CVG	X67
5:35p0	10:05p	CVG	
5:40pM	10:05p	CVG	X67
Eff. May 1			
To Phoenix, AZ		1445 mi	
6:15a0	9:50a	CVG	X67
8:00a0	11:30a	SLC	B
8:30a0	12:15p	DFW	
12:10p0	3:35p	DFW	X7
3:20pM	7:39p	CVG	X6
3:50p0	7:22p	DFW	
3:50p0	7:39p	CVG	
6:15p0	9:45p	SLC	
6:44p0	10:40p	DFW	
To Pittsburgh, PA		403 mi	
7:40aM	11:45a	CVG	X67
11:35aM	3:50p	CVG	X67
5:35p0	9:40p	CVG	
5:40pM	9:40p	CVG	X67
Eff. May 1			
To Pocatello, ID		1268 mi	
8:00a0	12:55p	SLC	B X67
11:45a0	4:59p	SLC	X6
3:10p0	6:45p	SLC	S
6:15p0	10:25p	SLC	
To Portland, ME		894 mi	
11:35aM	6:30p	CVG	X67
To Portland, OR		1749 mi	
6:15a0	11:00a	CVG	X67
8:00a0	12:00n	SLC	B
11:45a0	3:35p	SLC	
12:10p0	6:19p	DFW	X7
3:10p0	7:05p	SLC	D
3:20pM	10:20p	CVG	X6
6:15p0	10:20p	SLC	
To Raleigh/Durham, NC		636 mi	
5:30a0	9:20a	CVG	B/SX67
6:15a0	12:43p	CVG	B/SX67
6:30a0	11:30a	ATL	B X7
7:40aM	12:43p	CVG	X67
9:54a0	2:55p	ATL	S
1:00p0	5:57p	ATL	L
3:20pM	7:50p	CVG	S X6
3:50p0	7:50p	CVG	S
4:55p0	9:50p	ATL	D
To Reno, NV/Tahoe		1680mi	
8:00a0	11:30a	SLC	B
11:45a0	4:27p	SLC	
3:10p0	6:20p	1	S
6:15p0	9:21p	SLC	
To Richmond/			
Williamsburg, VA		632 mi	
6:15a0	11:35a	CVG	B/SX67
6:30a0	11:25a	ATL	B X7
7:40aM	11:35a	CVG	X67
9:54a0	3:05p	ATL	S
11:35aM	3:55p	CVG	X67
1:00p0	6:40p	ATL	L
5:35p0	9:50p	CVG	
5:40pM	9:50p	CVG	X67
Eff. May 1			
To Roanoke, VA		520 mi	
5:30a0	9:50a	CVG	S X67
6:15a0	11:45a	CVG	S X67
7:40aM	11:45a	CVG	X67
11:35aM	3:50p	CVG	X367
11:35aM	4:25p	CVG	3
5:35p0	9:55p	CVG	X6
5:40pM	9:55p	CVG	X67
Eff. May 1			
To Rock Springs, WY		1099 mi	
11:45a0	4:30p	SLC	
To Sacramento, CA		1790 mi	
8:00a0	11:50a	SLC	B
11:45a0	3:40p	SLC	
3:10p0	6:40p	SLC	S
6:15p0	9:50p	SLC	
To St. George, UT		1414 mi	
6:15p0	10:37p	SLC	X67
To Salt Lake City, UT		1257mi	
7:40aM	1:55p	CVG	X67
8:00a0	10:09a	0	B
8:30a0	1:36p	DFW	
9:25aM	2:14p	CVG	
Eff. May 6			
11:35aM	5:28p	CVG	S X67
11:45a0	1:57p	0	
3:10p0	5:21p	0	S
3:20pM	8:34p	CVG	X6
6:15p0	8:25p	0	
6:44p0	11:41p	DFW	
To San Angelo, TX		1011 mi	
8:30a0	12:58p	DFW	B
12:10p0	4:30p	DFW	X7
To San Antonio, TX		1040 mi	
8:30a0	12:38p	DFW	B
10:18a0	2:25p	DFW	X67
12:10p0	4:05p	DFW	X7
3:50p0	7:50p	DFW	S
8:45p0	12:40a	DFW	S
To San Diego, CA		1729 mi	
6:15a0	10:20a	CVG	X67
8:00a0	11:50a	SLC	B
Disc. Apr. 30			
8:00a0	11:50a	SLC	B
Eff. May 1			
8:30a0	12:55p	DFW	
11:45a0	3:30p	SLC	
12:10p0	5:25p	DFW	W X7
3:20pM	9:11p	CVG	X6
3:50p0	7:40p	DFW	
6:15p0	10:00p	SLC	
6:44p0	11:05p	DFW	
To San Francisco, CA		1854 mi	
Also see Oakland and San Jose			
6:15a0	11:15a	CVG	X67
8:00a0	12:00n	SLC	B
8:30a0	1:20p	DFW	
11:45a0	3:45p	SLC	C
12:10p0	4:45p	DFW	X7
3:10p0	7:10p	SLC	D
3:20pM	8:35p	CVG	X6
3:50p0	8:35p	CVG	
3:50p0	8:50p	DFW	
6:15p0	10:00p	SLC	
6:44p0	11:45p	DFW	
To San Jose, CA		1837 mi	
Also see San Francisco and			
Oakland			
7:40aM	3:45p	CVG	X67
8:00a0	12:10p	SLC	B

Measurement Equivalents and Conversion Table

American and British System

Length
1 inch
12 inches = 1 foot
36 inches = 3 feet = 1 yard

Volume or Capacity
1 pint   = 1/2 quart = 1/8 gallon
2 pints = 1 quart   = 1/4 gallon
4 pints = 2 quarts = 1/2 gallon
8 pints = 4 quarts = 1 gallon

Dry Measure
1 pint
2 pints = 1 quart
16 pints = 8 quarts = 1 peck
64 pints = 32 quarts = 4 pecks = 1 bushel

Weight
1 ounce (oz)
16 ounces = 1 pound (lb)
2000 pounds = 1 ton

Metric System

Length
1 meter (m) = 100 cm = 1000 m
1 millimeter (mm)   = 0.001   m
1 centimeter (cm)   = 0.01   m
1 decimeter (dm)   = 0.1   m
1 decameter (dkm)   = 10   m
1 hecktometer (hm) = 100   m
1 kilometer (km)   = 1000   m

Volume or Capacity
1 liter (l) = 100 cl = 1000 ml
1 milliliter (ml)   = 0.001   l
1 centiliter (cl)   = 0.01   l
1 decukuter (dl)   = 0.1   l
1 decacliter (dkl) = 10   l
1 hectoliter (hl)   = 100   l
1 kiloliter (kl)   = 1000   l

Weight
1 gram (g) = 100 cg = 1000 mg
1 milligram (mg)   = 0.001   g
1 centigram (cg)   = 0.01   g
1 decigram (dg)   = 0.1   g
1 decagram (dkg)   = 10   g
1 hectogram (hg)   = 100   g
1 kilogram (kg)   = 1000   g

Conversion Factors
Metric System   British & American System

Meters	Yards	Inches
1	1.093	39.37
0.914	1	36

Centimeters	Inches	Feet
1	0.394	0.0328
2.54	1	0.0833
30.48	12	1

Kilometers	Miles
1	0.621
1.609	1

Grams	Ounces	Pounds
1	0.035	0.0022
28.36	1	0.0625
453.59	16	1
1000	35.274	2.205

Kilograms	Ounces	Pounds
1	35.274	2.205
0.028	1	0.0625
0.454	16	1

Liters	Pints	Quarts	Gallons
1	2.113	1.057	0.264
0.473	1	0.5	0.125
0.946	2	1	0.25
3.785	8	4	1

Common Conversion Factors
1 centimeter = 0.39 inches
1 meter = 39.4 inches
1 kilometer = 0.62 miles
1 gram = 0.04 ounces
1 kilogram = 2.20 pounds
1 liter = 1.06 quarts

Chapter 3

SECTION 3-1

Activity 1

1. 4 weeks $240
2. 8 weeks $480
3. 12 weeks $720
4. 26 weeks $1560
5. 52 weeks $3120

Activity 3

1. Total amount needed: $139.99

Amount per Week	Number of Weeks Needed	Total Amount Saved
$15	10	$150
20	7	$140
25	6	$150
50	3	$150

2. Total amount needed: $199.99

Amount per Week	Number of Weeks Needed	Total Amount Saved
$15	14	$210
20	10	$200
25	8	$200
50	4	$200

3. Total amount needed: $149.99

Amount per Week	Number of Weeks Needed	Total Amount Saved
$15	10	$150
20	8	$160
25	6	$150
50	3	$150

4. Total amount needed: $179.99

Amount per Week	Number of Weeks Needed	Total Amount Saved
$15	12	$180
20	9	$180
25	8	$200
50	4	$200

5. Total amount needed: $369.99

Amount per Week	Number of Weeks Needed	Total Amount Saved
$15	25	$375
20	19	$380
25	15	$375
50	8	$400

SECTION 3-2

Activity 1

	Principal	Interest Rate	Compounded	Interest Earned	New Balance
1.	$1000	6%	annually	1st per: $60	$1060.00
				2nd per: $63.60	$1123.60
2.	$1000	6%	semi-annually	1st per: $30	$1030.00
				2nd per: $30.90	$1060.90
				3rd per: $31.82	$1092.72
				4th per: $32.78	$1125.50
3.	$1000	6%	quarterly	1st per: $15	$1015.00
				2nd per: $15.22	$1030.22
				3rd per: $15.45	$1045.67
				4th per: $15.68	$1061.35
				5th per: $15.92	$1077.27
				6th per: $16.15	$1093.42
				7th per: $16.40	$1109.82
				8th per: $16.64	$1126.46
4.	$5000	8%	annually	1st per: $400	$5400.00
				2nd per: $432	$5832.00
5.	$5000	8%	semi-annually	1st per: $200	$5200.00
				2nd per: $208	$5408.00
				3rd per: $216.32	$5624.32
				4th per: $224.97	$5849.29
6.	$5000	8%	quarterly	1st per: $100	$5100.00
				2nd per: $102	$5202.00
				3rd per: $104.04	$5306.04
				4th per: $106.12	$5412.16
				5th per: $108.24	$5520.40
				6th per: $110.40	$5630.80
				7th per: $112.61	$5743.41
				8th per: $114.86	$5858.27

Activity 2

1. Using Compound Interest Table

	Principal	Interest Rate	Compounded	New Balance
a.	$1000	6%	annually	1st yr: $1060.00
				2nd yr: $1123.60
b.	$1000	6%	semi-annually	1st yr: $1060.90
				2nd yr: $1125.51
c.	$1000	6%	quarterly	1st yr: $1061.35
				2nd yr: $1126.46

2. Using Formula $A = P\left(1 + \dfrac{i}{n}\right)^{nt}$

	Principal	Interest Rate	Compounded	New Balance
a.	$1000	6%	annually	2nd yr: $1123.60
b.	$1000	6%	semiannually	2nd yr: $1125.50
c.	$1000	6%	quarterly	2nd yr: $1126.30
d.	$5000	8%	annually	2nd yr: $5832.00
e.	$5000	8%	semiannually	2nd yr: $5849.29
f.	$5000	8%	quarterly	2nd yr: $5859.30
g.	$10,000	12%	annually	2nd yr: $12,544.00
h.	$10,000	12%	semiannually	2nd yr: $12,624.77
i.	$10,000	12%	quarterly	2nd yr: $12,667.70

Activity 3

Three Years' Interest

Principal $3000	Annually	Semiannually	Quarterly	Monthly
Total in Account	$3779.14	$3795.96	$3804.73	$3810.71
Interest Only	$ 779.14	$ 795.96	$ 804.73	$ 810.71

SECTION 3-3

Activity 1

1.

Level	Begin With		Reserve		Loans
1	500	=	100	+	400
2	400	=	80	+	320
3	320	=	64	+	256
4	256	=	51.20	+	204.80
5	204.80	=	40.96	+	163.84
6	163.84	=	32.77	+	131.07
7	131.07	=	26.21	+	104.86
8	104.86	=	20.97	+	83.89
9	83.89	=	16.78	+	67.11
10	67.11	=	13.42	+	53.69

Total extra money created $1785.26.

2.

Level	Begin With		Reserve		Loans
1	2500	=	500	+	2000
2	2000	=	400	+	1600
3	1600	=	320	+	1280
4	1280	=	256	+	1024
5	1024	=	204.80	+	819.20
6	819.20	=	163.84	+	655.36
7	655.36	=	131.07	+	524.29
8	524.29	=	104.86	+	419.43
9	419.43	=	83.89	+	335.55
10	355.55	=	67.11	+	268.44

Total extra money created $8926.27.

3.

Level	Begin With		Reserve		Loans
1	12500	=	2500	+	10000
2	10000	=	2000	+	8000
3	8000	=	1600	+	6400
4	6400	=	1280	+	5120
5	5120	=	1024	+	4096
6	4096	=	819.20	+	3276.80
7	3276.80	=	655.36	+	2621.44
8	2621.44	=	524.29	+	2097.15
9	2097.15	=	419.43	+	1677.72
10	1677.72	=	335.54	+	1342.18

Total extra money created $44,631.29.

CHAPTER REVIEW

1. 180.00
2. 540.00
3. 1170.00
4. 2340.00

	Number of Weeks	Total Amount Saved
5.	11	$165
6.	7	175
7.	4	200

	Total Amount Saved	Interest Earned	Total in Account
8.	$1300	$ 78.00	$1378.00
9.	1690	101.40	1791.40
10.	3536	212.16	3748.16
11.	5720	343.20	6063.20

	Years	Total Value
12.	1	$6420
	2	6869.40
	3	7350.25
	4	7864.77
	5	8415.31
13.	1	$6427.35
	2	6885.13
	3	7375.53
	4	7900.85
	5	8463.59
14.	1	$6431.15
	2	6893.29
	3	7388.63
	4	7919.57
	5	8488.66
15.	1	$6433.74
	2	6898.83
	3	7397.55
	4	7866.32
	5	8505.75

16.

Level	Begin With		Reserve		Loans
1	2000	=	400	+	1600
2	1600	=	320	+	1280
3	1280	=	256	+	1024
4	1024	=	204.80	+	819.20
5	819.20	=	163.84	+	655.36
6	655.36	=	131.07	+	524.29

Total extra money = $5902.85

SKILLS PREVIEW

1. $50.00
2. $573.42
3. $944.00
4. $24.00
5. $3.33
6. 61
7. $16
8. C
9. $200.00
10. 30%
11. $44.40
12. 500
13. $34.57
14. 4%
15. $25.00

Chapter 4

SECTION 4-1

Activity 1

Payroll registers for earnings and deductions should look like those in Sharpen Your Skills. They should include the following information.

PAYROLL REGISTER for WEEK 1
EARNINGS

Employee	Number of Exemptions	Marital Status	Hourly Rate	Hours Worked	Gross Earnings
Catlyn	0	S	$3.75	16	$ 60.00
Sara	1	S	4.50	20	90.00
Joleen	0	S	8.00	26	208.00
Hernando	1	S	6.25	14	87.50
				Total Payroll	$445.50

Activity 2

DEDUCTIONS for WEEK 1

Employee	Gross Earnings	Federal Income Tax	FICA (Social Security)	Total Deductions	Take-Home Pay
Catlyn	$ 60.00	$ 6.00	$ 4.59	$10.59	49.41
Sara	90.00	5.00	6.89	11.89	78.11
Joleen	208.00	27.00	15.91	42.91	165.09
Hernando	87.50	4.00	6.69	10.69	76.81
Totals	$445.50	$42.00	$34.08		$369.42

Activity 3

MONTHLY PAYROLL SUMMARY
Employee: Catlyn

Week	Gross Earnings	Federal Income Tax	FICA (Social Security)	Take-Home Pay
1	$ 60.00	$ 6.00	$ 4.59	$ 49.41
2	52.50	4.00	4.02	44.48
3	78.75	8.00	6.02	64.73
4	120.00	15.00	9.18	95.82
Totals	$311.25	$33.00	$23.81	$254.44

SECTION 4-2

Activity 1

1. $443.00	8. 390.00
2. 502.50	9. 512.50
3. 334.50	10. 434.00
4. 452.50	11. 441.50
5. 299.50	12. 501.50
6. 460.00	13. 411.25
7. 387.50	14. 544.50

SECTION 4-3

Activity 1

1. a. Loss	$ 43.00	6. a. Loss	121.25
b. Profit	53.00	b. Profit	40.00
c. Profit	149.00	c. Profit	201.25
2. a. Loss	2.50	7. a. Profit	12.50
b. Profit	267.50	b. Profit	137.50
c. Profit	537.50	c. Profit	262.50
3. a. Loss	34.50	8. a. Loss	102.50
b. Profit	113.50	b. Loss	15.00
c. Profit	261.50	c. Profit	72.50
4. a. Loss	52.50	9. a. Loss	205.00
b. Profit	27.50	b. Loss	137.80
c. Profit	107.50	c. Loss	70.00
5. a. Loss	36.00	10. a. Loss	83.25
b. Profit	200.50	b. Profit	66.00
c. Profit	437.00	c. Profit	215.25

11. a. Loss	141.50	13. a. Profit	88.75
b. Loss	83.50	b. Profit	385.00
c. Loss	25.50	c. Profit	681.25
12. a. Loss	75.25	14. a. Loss	134.50
b. Loss	1.50	b. Loss	44.50
c. Profit	87.25	c. Profit	45.50

SECTION 4-4

Activity 1

	Fixed Costs	Variable Costs	Number Produced	Total Costs	Average Sale	Total Sales
1. Bumper stickers	$235.00	$1.04	200	$443.00	$ 2.00	$ 443.00
			300	547.00		547.00
			400	651.00		651.00
2. Towels	$272.50	$2.30	100	$502.50	$ 5.00	$ 500.00
			200	732.50		1000.00
			300	962.50		1500.00
3. Stationary	$182.50	$1.52	100	$334.50	$ 3.00	$ 300.00
			200	486.50		600.00
			300	638.50		900.00
4. Pennants	$212.50	$1.20	200	$452.50	$ 2.00	$ 400.00
			300	572.50		600.00
			400	692.50		800.00
5. Cards	$272.50	$1.34	25	$306.10	$10.00	$ 250.00
			50	339.70		500.00
			75	373.30		750.00
6. Mugs	$282.50	$3.55	25	$371.25	$10.00	$ 250.00
			50	460.00		500.00
			75	548.75		750.00
7. Tennis Balls	$112.50	$2.75	100	$387.50	$ 4.00	$ 400.00
			200	662.50		800.00
			300	937.50		1200.00
8. Book Bags	$190.00	$4.00	25	$290.00	$ 7.50	$ 187.50
			50	390.00		375.00
			75	490.00		562.50
9. Lunch Boxes	$272.50	$4.80	25	$392.50	$ 8.00	$ 200.00
			50	512.50		400.00
			75	632.50		600.00
10. Racket Covers	$232.50	$4.03	25	$333.25	$10.00	$ 250.00
			50	434.00		500.00
			75	534.75		750.00
11. Book Marks	$257.50	$0.92	200	$441.50	$ 1.50	$ 300.00
			300	533.50		450.00
			400	625.50		600.00
12. Cookies	$356.50	$1.45	75	$465.25	$ 5.00	$ 375.00
			100	501.50		500.00
			125	537.75		625.00
13. Blankets	$207.50	$8.15	25	$411.25	$20.00	$ 500.00
			50	615.00		1000.00
			75	818.75		1500.00
14. Organizers	$224.50	$6.40	25	$384.50	$10.00	$ 250.00
			50	544.50		500.00
			75	704.50		750.00

Activity 2

1.

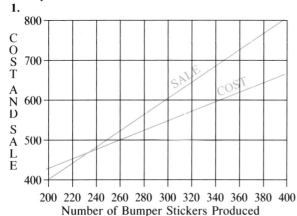

Number of Bumper Stickers Produced

Activity 3

1. 245	**8.** 54
2. 101	**9.** 85
3. 123	**10.** 39
4. 266	**11.** 444
5. 31	**12.** 100
6. 44	**13.** 18
7. 90	**14.** 62

CHAPTER REVIEW

1. $145.10
2. 195.00
3. 930.70
4. 325.60

	Federal Income Tax With-holding	FICA Social Security	Take-Home Pay
5.	$ 10.00	$ 9.74	$107.56
6.	20.00	14.92	160.08
7.	196.00	71.20	663.50
8.	39.00	24.91	261.69

9. $162.90
10. 208.30
11. 253.70

12. Loss $ 22.90
13. Profit   71.70
14. Profit   166.30

	Fixed Costs	Variable Costs (per unit)	Number Produced	Total Costs	Average Sale (per unit)	Total Sales	Profit (Loss)
15.	117.50	2.27	20	162.90	7.00	140	(22.90)
16.	117.50	2.27	40	208.30	7.00	280	71.70
17.	117.50	2.27	60	253.70	7.00	420	166.30

18. Graph as appropriate.
19. Graph as appropriate.
20. 25

21. Answers will vary. Before starting a business, you should know if a market for your product or service exists, what the potential costs of going into business will be, who your competitors are, and what differentiates your product or service from the others.
22. Businesses must make a profit in order to stay in business. You should know how much profit or loss a business makes in order to determine if changes need to be made.
23. If a company does not make enough money to break even, it may decide to make changes on the product or service, to discontinue certain products, or to increase or change its advertising efforts.
24. Oscar should consider how much profit the company is making.

CUMULATIVE REVIEW

1. $192.88
2. $132.00
3. $4600
4. $73.81
5. $16,275 + 3,580.50 = $19,855.50
6. $1.49
7. Answers will vary.
8. Balance Forward $ 982.61
     Check, Date, To: − 243.50
                  For: 739.11
9. 7 weeks
10. $500 × .0425 = 21.25
     500 + 21.25 = 521.25
     521.25 × .0425 = 22.15
     521.25 + 22.15 = 543.40
     Simple interest = $43.40
11. $A = \$1,000(1 + .08)^{2 \times 6}$
     $A = 1,000(1.08)^{12}$
     $A = 1,000(2.5181696)$
     $A = \$2518.17$
12. 510
13. $10 less
14.

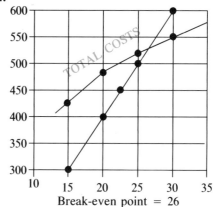

Break-even point = 26

Chapter 5

SECTION 5-1

Activity 1

	Yrs.	Monthly Payments	Total Payments	Amount of Interest	Percent of Interest
a.	3	217.46	7828.56	1328.56	20%
	4	172.77	8292.96	1792.96	28%
	5	146.24	8774.40	2274.40	35%
b.	3	317.82	11441.52	1941.52	20%
	4	252.51	12120.48	2620.48	28%
	5	213.74	12824.40	3324.40	35%
c.	3	200.73	7226.28	1226.28	20%
	4	159.48	7655.04	1655.04	28%
	5	134.99	8099.40	2099.40	35%
d.	3	401.45	14452.20	2452.20	20%
	4	318.96	15310.08	3310.08	28%
	5	269.98	16198.80	4198.80	35%
e.	3	585.45	21076.20	3576.20	20%
	4	465.15	22327.20	4827.20	28%
	5	393.72	23623.20	6123.20	35%
f.	3	313.56	11288.16	2513.16	29%
	4	309.66	14863.68	3213.68	28%
	5	262.11	15726.60	4076.60	35%
g.	3	293.56	10568.16	1793.16	20%
	4	233.25	11196.00	2421.00	28%
	5	197.43	11845.80	3070.80	35%
h.	3	184.84	6654.24	1129.24	20%
	4	146.86	7049.28	1524.28	28%
	5	124.31	7458.60	1933.60	35%

SECTION 5-2

Activity 1

	Yrs.	Interest	Percent	Total Payments
a.	3	1328.56	20	$ 7828.56
	4	1792.96	28	8292.96
	5	2274.40	35	8774.40
b.	3	1941.52	20	11,441.52
	4	2620.48	28	12,120.48
	5	3324.40	35	12,824.40
c.	3	1226.28	20	7226.28
	4	1655.04	28	7655.04
	5	2099.40	35	8099.40
d.	3	2452.20	20	14,452.20
	4	3310.08	28	15,310.08
	5	4198.80	35	16,198.80
e.	3	3576.20	20	21,076.20
	4	4827.20	28	22,327.20
	5	6123.20	35	23,623.20
f.	3	2381.36	20	14,031.36
	4	3213.68	28	14,863.68
	5	4076.60	35	15,726.60
g.	3	1793.16	20	10,568.16
	4	2421.00	28	11,196.00
	5	3070.80	35	11,845.80
h.	3	1129.24	20	6654.24
	4	1524.28	28	7049.28
	5	1933.60	35	7458.63

SECTION 5-3

Activity 1

	3 Yrs	5 Yrs	Savings
a.	$ 7828.56	$ 8774.40	$ 945.84
b.	11,441.52	12,824.40	1382.88
c.	7226.28	8099.40	873.12
d.	14,452.20	16,198.80	1746.60
e.	21,076.20	23,623.20	2547.00
f.	14,031.36	15,726.60	1695.24

CHAPTER REVIEW

	Monthly Payment	Total Payments
1.	205.73	7406.28
2.	275.20	13,209.60
3.	167.86	10,071.60
4.	81.84	2921.04
5.	83.73	4019.04
6.	101.25	6075.00

	Amount of Interest	Percent
7.	1280	20
8.	3052	28
9.	2791.25	35
10.	714	28
11.	890.40	28
12.	1631	35

	Down	Loan	Monthly Payment	Total Payments	Total Cost
13.	299.50	2695.50	60.19	3611.40	3910.90
14.	599.25	3395.75	85.61	4109.28	4708.53
15.	2090	8360	269.45	9700.20	11790.20
16.	1045	9405	211.49	12689.40	13734.40
17.	1799.25	10195.75	270.46	12982.08	14781.33
18.	2373	9492	305.75	11007.00	13380.00

SKILLS PREVIEW

1. $2.31		14. $320.00	
2. $450.27		15. $106,666.67	
3. $583.24		16. $50.00	
4. 0.18		17. $520.00	
5. 0.015		18. $67.50	
6. 2.35		19. $93.69	
7. $13,991.67		20. $855.24	
8. $250.41		21. $55.24	
9. $957.38		22. 50	
10. $22,500		23. 20	
11. $181.34		24. 70	
12. $25.13		25. 110	
13. $14.27			

Chapter 6

SECTION 6-1

Activity 1

1.

	Balance	Interest	Amount Owed	Payment
a.	$2000.00	$30.00	$2030.00	$203
b.	1827.00	27.41	1854.41	185
c.	1669.41	25.04	1694.45	169
d.	1525.45	22.88	1548.33	155
e.	1393.33	20.90	1414.23	141
f.	1273.23	19.10	1292.33	129
g.	1163.33	17.45	1180.78	118
h.	1062.78	15.94	1078.72	108
i.	970.72	14.56	985.28	99
j.	886.28	13.29	899.57	90
k.	809.57	12.14	821.71	82
l.	739.71	11.10	750.81	75
		Total Interest = $229.81		

2.

	Balance	Interest	Amount Owed	Payment
a.	$4690.00	$70.35	$4760.35	$476
b.	4284.35	64.27	4348.62	435
c.	3913.62	58.70	3972.32	397
d.	3575.32	53.63	3628.95	363
e.	3265.95	48.99	3314.94	331
f.	2983.94	44.76	3028.70	303
g.	2725.70	40.89	2766.59	277
h.	2489.59	37.34	2526.93	253
i.	2273.93	34.11	2308.04	231
j.	2077.04	31.16	2108.20	211
k.	1897.20	28.46	1925.66	193
l.	1732.66	25.99	1758.65	176
	Total	$538.65		

3.

	Balance	Interest	Amount Owed	Payment
a.	$1358.00	$20.37	$1378.37	$138
b.	1240.37	18.61	1258.98	126
c.	1132.98	16.99	1149.97	115
d.	1034.97	15.52	1050.49	105
e.	945.49	14.18	959.67	96
f.	863.67	12.96	876.63	88
g.	788.63	11.83	800.46	80
h.	720.46	10.81	731.27	73
i.	658.27	9.87	668.14	67
j.	601.14	9.02	610.16	61
k.	549.16	8.24	557.40	56
l.	501.40	7.52	508.92	51
	Total	$155.92		

SECTION 6-2

Activity 1

1.

	Balance	Interest	Amount Owed	Payment
a.	$2000.00	$30.00	$2030.00	$102
b.	1928.00	28.92	1956.92	98
c.	1858.92	27.88	1886.80	94
d.	1792.80	26.89	1819.69	91
e.	1728.69	25.93	1754.62	88
f.	1666.62	25.00	1691.62	85
g.	1606.62	24.10	1630.72	82
h.	1548.72	23.23	1571.95	79
i.	1492.95	22.39	1515.34	76
j.	1439.34	21.59	1460.93	73
k.	1387.93	20.82	1408.75	70
l.	1338.75	20.08	1358.83	68
	Total	$296.83		

2.

	Balance	Interest	Amount Owed	Payment
a.	$4690.00	$70.35	$4760.35	$238
b.	4522.35	67.84	4590.19	230
c.	4360.19	65.40	4425.59	221
d.	4204.59	63.07	4267.66	213
e.	4054.66	60.82	4115.48	206
f.	3909.48	58.64	3968.12	198
g.	3770.12	56.55	3826.67	191
h.	3635.67	54.54	3690.21	185
i.	3505.21	52.58	3557.79	178
j.	3379.79	50.70	3430.49	172
k.	3258.49	48.88	3307.37	165
l.	3142.37	47.14	3189.51	159
	Total	$696.51		

3.

	Balance	Interest	Amount Owed	Payment
a.	$1358.00	20.37	1378.37	69
b.	1309.37	19.64	1329.01	66
c.	1263.01	18.95	1281.96	64
d.	1217.96	18.27	1236.23	62
e.	1174.23	17.61	1191.84	60
f.	1131.84	16.98	1148.82	57
g.	1091.82	16.38	1108.20	55
h.	1053.20	15.80	1069.00	53
i.	1016.00	15.24	1031.24	52
j.	979.24	14.69	993.93	50
k.	943.93	14.16	958.09	48
l.	910.09	13.65	923.74	46
	Total	$201.74		

For $2000: $296.83 − 229.81 = $67.02 more interest paid.
For $4690: $696.51 − 538.65 = $157.86 more interest paid.
For $1358: $201.74 − 155.92 = $45.82 more interest paid.

4.

	Balance	Interest	Amount Owed	Payment
a.	$2500.00	$43.75	$2543.75	$254
b.	2289.75	40.07	2329.82	233
c.	2096.82	36.69	2133.51	213
d.	1920.51	33.61	1954.12	195
e.	1759.12	30.78	1789.90	179
f.	1610.90	28.19	1639.09	164
g.	1475.09	25.81	1500.90	150
h.	1350.90	23.64	1374.54	137
i.	1237.54	21.66	1259.20	126
j.	1133.20	19.83	1153.03	115
k.	1038.03	18.17	1056.20	106
l.	950.20	16.63	966.83	97
	Total	$338.83		

5.

Balance	Interest	Amount Owed	Payment
2500.00	29.25	2529.25	253
2276.25	26.63	2302.88	230
2072.88	24.25	2097.13	210
1887.13	22.08	1909.21	191
1718.21	20.10	1738.31	174
1564.31	18.30	1582.61	158
1424.61	16.67	1441.28	144
1297.28	15.18	1312.46	131
1181.46	13.82	1195.28	120
1075.28	12.58	1087.86	109
978.86	11.45	990.31	99
891.31	10.43	901.74	90
	220.74		

$118.09 more interest was paid at 21% per year.

Activity 2

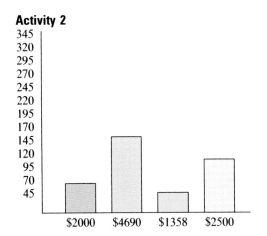

SECTION 6-3

Activity 1

1.

Number of Days	Sum of Balances
7	$13,639.50
1	1,850.50
23	42,561.50

Average Daily Balance = $1872.63
Finance Charge = $28.09
New Balance = $1878.59

2.

Number of Days	Sum of Balances
10	$18,785.90
1	1,785.59
17	30,355.03

Average Daily Balance = $1818.80
Finance Charge = $27.28
New Balance = $1812.87

3.

Number of Days	Sum of Balances
15	$27,193.05
1	1,724.87
15	25,873.08

Average Daily Balance = $1767.45
Finance Charge = $26.51
New Balance = $1751.38

4.

Number of Days	Sum of Balances
12	$21,016.56
1	1,668.38
17	28,362.49

Average Daily Balance = $1701.58
Finance Charge = $25.52
New Balance = $1693.90

5.

Number of Days	Sum of Balances
20	$33,878.07
1	1,614.90
10	16,149.00

Average Daily Balance = $1665.87
Finance Charge = $24.99
New Balance = $1639.89

6.

Number of Days	Sum of Balances
13	$21,318.57
1	1,564.89
16	25,038.24

Average Daily Balance = $1597.39
Finance Charge = $23.96
New Balance = $1588.85

7.

Number of Days	Sum of Balances
18	$28,599.30
1	1,517.85
12	18,214.20

Average Daily Balance = $1559.08
Finance Charge = $23.39
New Balance = $1541.24

8.

Number of Days	Sum of Balances
9	$13,871.13
1	1,473.24
21	30,938.04

Average Daily Balance = $1597.39
Finance Charge = $22.39
New Balance = $1495.63

9.

Number of Days	Sum of Balances
13	$19,443.19
1	1,431.63
16	22,905.60

Average Daily Balance = $1459.35
Finance Charge = $21.89
New Balance = $1453.49

10.

Number of Days	Sum of Balances
21	$30,523.92
1	1,392.52
9	12,532.41

Average Daily Balance = $1433.83
Finance Charge = $21.51
New Balance = $1414.00

CHAPTER REVIEW

1.

	Balance	Interest	Amount Owed	Payment
a.	$1200.00	$18.00	$1218.00	$122
b.	1096.00	16.44	1112.44	111
c.	1001.44	15.02	1016.46	102
d.	914.46	13.72	928.18	93
e.	835.18	12.53	847.71	85
f.	762.71	11.44	774.15	77
Total		$87.15		

2.

	Balance	Interest	Amount Owed	Payment
a.	$1200.00	$21.00	$1221.00	$61
b.	1160.00	20.30	1180.30	59
c.	1121.30	19.62	1140.92	57
d.	1083.92	18.97	1102.89	55
e.	1047.89	18.34	1066.23	53
f.	1013.23	17.73	1030.96	52
Total		$115.96		

3.

Number of Days	Sum of Balances
16	$20,012.00
1	1,125.75
13	14,634.75

Average Daily Balance = $1192.42.

4.

Number of Days	Sum of Balances
18	$177,688.80
1	9,378.60
12	112,543.20

Average Daily Balance = $9664.86
Finance Charge = $144.97
New Balance = $9523.57

CUMMULATIVE REVIEW

1. $355.25
2. $11,600
3. $67,500
4. 85 cents
5. First name, middle initial, and full last name.
6. One hundred ten dollars & 23/100
7. $64.65
8. $608.00
9. $152.00
10. $3996.00
11. $596.00
12. $1800.00
13. 20%
14.

540.00	8.10	548.10	55
493.10	7.40	500.50	50
450.50	6.76	457.26	46

15.

15	450 =	6750.00
1	350 =	350.00
15	350 =	5250.00

Avg. Daily Bal. = $398.39

Chapter 7

SECTION 7-1

Activity 1
1. **Family A** $630 − 151 = $479; dishwasher
   Family B $454 − 238 = $216; car stereo
   Family C $299 − 235 = $64; 9″ candlesticks or silver-plated tray
   Family D $856 − 222 = $634; 26″ stereo TV
   Family E $438 − 199 = $239; removable car stereo
   Family F $328 − 179 = $149; reverse cassette car stereo
   Family G $600 − 159 = $441; dishwasher
2. **Family A** CD Changer with remote, $199.99 car stereo
   Family B $139.99 car stereo, 9″ candlesticks or silver-plated tray
   Family C 4½″ candlesticks or 8″ bowl, set of napkin rings
   Family D dishwasher, $199.99 removable car stereo
   Family E $199.99 removable car stereo, set of napkin rings
   Family F 9″ candlesticks, silverplated tray
   Family G dishwasher, 4½″ candlesticks or 8″ bowl
3. none
4. It will take 8 months to pay for the items, which cost $1,709.97 altogether.

SECTION 7-2

Activity 1
Credit Score: **1.** 95 **2.** 119 **3.** 66 **4.** 146 **5.** 41
              6. 154 **7.** 79 **8.** 96

SECTION 7-3

Activity 1
1. Car Price $10,100

	Plan A	Plan B
Rebate	$900	none
Loan Amount	$9,200	$10,100.00
Rate/Time	13%/48 months	5%/48 months
Monthly Payment	$246.82	$232.38
Total Financed Price	$11,847.36	$11,154.24

2. Car Price $12,000

	Plan A	Plan B	Plan C
Rebate	$1,500	$800	none
Loan Amount	$10,500.00	$11,200.00	$12,000
Rate/Time	13%/48 mo	8¾% 48 mo	5%/48 mo
Monthly Payment	$281.68	$277.39	$276.09
Total Financed Price	$13,520.64	$13,314.72	$13,252.32

3. Car Price $9,400

	Plan A	Plan B	Plan C
Rebate	$1,500	$1,200	none
Loan Amount	$7,900	$8,200	$9,400
Rate/Time	13%/48 mo	8¾%/48 mo	5%/48 mo
Monthly Payment	$211.93	$203.08	$216.27
Total Financed Price	$10,172.64	$9,747.84	$10,380.96

4. Car Price $6,500

	Plan A	Plan B	Plan C
Rebate	$1,500	$1,000	none
Loan Amount	$5,000	$5,500	$6,500
Rate/Time	13%/48 mo	8¾%/48 mo	5%/48 mo
Monthly Payment	$134.14	$136.21	$149.55
Total Financed Price	$6,438.72	$6,538.08	$7,178.40

SECTION 7-4

Activity 1

1.

Purchase	Balance	Interest	Amount Owed	Payment
$ 0.00	$554.75	$8.32	$563.07	$56
76.35	583.42	8.75	592.17	59
0.00	533.17	8.00	541.17	54
0.00	487.17	7.31	494.48	49
75.99	521.47	7.82	529.29	53
22.80	499.09	7.49	506.59	51
0.00	455.59	6.83	462.42	46
97.88	514.30	7.71	522.01	52
75.00	545.01	8.18	553.19	55
31.00	529.19	7.94	537.13	54
66.00	549.13	8.24	557.37	56
67.00	568.37	8.53	576.90	58
	Total Interest	$87.12		

Owes more than at beginning

2.

Purchase	Balance	Interest	Amount Owed	Payment
$ 0.00	$875.66	$13.13	$888.79	$89
0.00	799.79	12.00	811.79	81
0.00	730.79	10.96	741.75	74
0.00	667.75	10.02	677.77	68
0.00	609.77	9.15	618.92	62
158.00	714.92	10.72	725.64	73
0.00	652.64	9.79	662.43	66
85.00	681.43	10.22	691.65	69
92.00	714.65	10.72	725.37	73
0.00	652.37	9.79	662.16	66
0.00	596.16	8.94	605.10	61
123.00	667.10	10.01	677.11	68
	Total Interest	$125.45		

Owes less than at beginning

3.

Purchase	Balance	Interest	Amount Owed	Payment
$ 0.00	$1450.63	$21.76	$1472.39	$147
0.00	1325.39	19.88	1,345.27	135
0.00	1210.27	18.15	1228.42	123
234.00	1339.42	20.09	1359.51	136
0.00	1223.51	18.35	1241.86	124
0.00	1117.86	16.77	1134.63	113
0.00	1021.63	15.32	1036.95	104
0.00	932.95	13.99	946.94	95
0.00	851.94	12.78	864.72	86
314.00	1092.72	16.39	1109.11	111
45.00	1043.11	15.65	1058.76	106
68.00	1020.76	15.31	1036.07	104
	Total Interest	$204.44		

Owes less than at beginning

SECTION 7-5

Activity 1

1. Family A spends 15% on credit payments. They are not spending too much.
2. Family B spends 11% on credit payments. They are not spending too much.
3. Family C spends 11% on credit payments. They are not spending too much.
4. Family D spends 18% on credit payments. They are not spending too much, but are getting close.

CHAPTER REVIEW

1. Family A—135, Family B—94
2. Accept any reasonable answer. Possible answer: So people will have enough money to pay for food, household expenses, and medical expenses.
3. Accept any reasonable answer. Possible answer: Because they will have established credit when they are ready to furnish an apartment or buy a home.
4. Accept any reasonable answer. Possible answer: Because the person who cosigns is responsible for the debt if the friend does not make the payments.
5. Answers may vary, but students will probably say it is good because people who need credit, such as widows, the elderly, and others, may not be discriminated against if they are able to make payments. Accept any reasonable answers.
6. Up to $700

13. 33¾
14. 104⅝
15. 415⅛
16. 5066¼
17. $828
18. $1,212
19. $347
20. $1,246
21.

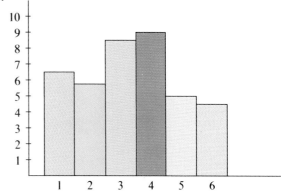

22. $321.72
23. $662.07
24. $320.25

7.

	Plan A	Plan B	Plan C
Rebate	$1,200	$750	none
Loan Amount	11,300	11,750	$12,500
Time of Loan	48 mo.	48 mo.	36 mo.
Monthly Payment	276.02	283.21	370.58
Total Financed Price	13,248.96	13,594.08	13,340.88
Total Interest	1,948.96	1,844.08	840.88
Dealer's Profit	3,148.96	2,594.08	840.88

8.

	Purchase	Balance	Interest	Amount Owed	Payment
a.	$ 0	$500.00	$7.50	$507.50	$51
b.	125	581.50	8.72	590.22	59
c.	0	531.22	7.97	539.19	54
d.	0	485.19	7.28	492.47	49
e.	0	443.47	6.65	450.12	45
f.	0	405.12	6.08	411.20	41
	Total Interest	$44.20			

9. 18% of their income is spent on credit bills. 13% of their income is spent on installment payments. No, because it does not exceed 20% of their income.

SKILLS PREVIEW

1. $21.5 million
2. $49.3 million
3. $16.6 million
4. $377,000 or $400,000 rounded
5. 20.6%
6. 31.3%
7. 50.6%
8. 5.3%
9. $250 less
10. $6,349 less
11. $403,123 more
12. $375.14 more

Chapter 8

SECTION 8-1

Activity 1
1. a. $18.20 billion
   b. $15.41 billion
   c. $10.66 billion
   d. $4.48 billion
   e. $3.80 billion
   f. $1.90 billion
   g. $679,000,000
2. a. $23.53 billion
   b. $19.93 billion
   c. $13.78 billion
   d. $5.79 billion
   e. $4.92 billion
   f. $2.46 billion
   g. $878,000,000
3. a. $28.22 billion
   b. $23.90 billion
   c. $16.53 billion
   d. $6.95 billion
   e. $5.90 billion
   f. $2.95 billion
   g. $1.05 billion

Activity 2
1. 55%
2. 55%
3. 55%
4. 55%
5. 55%
6. 55%
7. 55%

SECTION 8-2

Activity 1
1. Bigger Than Life; Save Money
2. Save Money
3. Save Money; Act Now
4. Bigger Than Life
5. Save Money
6. Save Money
7. Save Money; Healthy or Nutritious; Scientific or Statistical
8. Save Money; Act Now
9. Bigger Than Life; Young and Beautiful
10. Remember Me
11. Bigger Than Life; Healthy or Nutritious
12. Bigger Than Life; Young and Beautiful
13. Scientifc or Statistical
14. Save Money
15. Save Money; Scientific or Statistical
16. Save Money
17. Save Money; Act Now; Young and Beautiful
18. Bigger Than Life; Scientific or Statistical; Act Now; Young and Beautiful; Join the Crowd; Healthy or Nutritious
19. Healthy or Nutritious
20. Act Now; Join the Crowd; Healthy or Nutritious

SECTION 8-3

Activity 1
1. Weasel Claim
2. Unique Claim
3. Ours is Better Than Theirs
4. Unfinished Claim
5. Unfinished Claim
6. Ours is Better Than Theirs; Unique Claim
7. Weasel Claim
8. Ours is Better Than Theirs
9. Ours is Better Than Theirs; Weasel Claim
10. Unique Claim
11. Unfinished Claim
12. Ours is Better Than Theirs
13. Unique Claim
14. Weasel Claim; Ours is Better Than Theirs
15. Unique Claim

SECTION 8-4

Activity 1

1. Monday   106,000
   Tuesday   104,000
   Wednesday   67,000
   Thursday   66,000
   Friday   82,000
   Saturday   51,000
   Sunday   86,000
2. $154.22
3. $93.83
4. $3.18
5. Answers will vary.

Activity 2

1. Program Y
2. Program Y
3. Program X
4. Yes
5. Program X because more women of child-bearing age watch the show.
6. Program X
7. Program Y

CHAPTER REVIEW

1. Answers will vary.
2. Answers will vary.
3. Answers will vary. Products would include those that would make people more popular, richer, more successful, and more accepted by their colleagues.
4. Answers will vary. Scientific or statistical messages could be targeted to people with average income and intelligence who might believe the impact of numbers of scientific appeals. Healthy or nutritious messages affect older people or those who are concerned with their health, watch their diets, and engage in sports or health-related activities.
5. Answers will vary.
6. Answers will vary, although they should reflect the fact that each network has program demographics, and you would want to choose the demographics that most closely match your target audience's. You also want to buy cost-effective advertising spots.
7. a. $17.8 billion
   b. $20.9 billion
   c. 2%
8. Program A
9. Program B
10. 8.8%
11. 20%
12. 300,000
13. 74,000
14. Program A
15. Program B
16. Program A

CUMULATIVE REVIEW

1. $131.38
2. $10,100
3. $1.74
4. $1177.50
5. $16.50
6. $21,540 $8,040

7.

Balance	Interest	New Balance
$825	12.38	837.38
735.38	11.30	764.68
833.68	12.51	846.18
761.18	11.42	772.60
695.60	10.43	706.03
635.03	9.53	644.56

Payment	Additional
84	
76	145
85	
77	
71	
64	

$67.57 is the total interest that will be paid over the 6 months.

8. **Plan A**
   Total financed price = $13,260
   Total interest = $3,260
   Dealer's profit = $3760
   Plan B
   Total financed price = $14,040
   Total interest = $3,540
   Dealer's profit = $3,540
9. a. $19 billion
   b. 3.42%

Chapter 9

SECTION 9-1

Activity 1

	Number of Shares	Total Cost
1.	7692	$49,998.00
2.	2010	$49,998.75
3.	5479	$49,995.88
4.	4651	$49,998.25
5.	5633	$49,992.88
6.	4705	$49,990.63
7.	5555	$49,995.00
8.	15384	$49,998.00
9.	10256	$49,998.00
10.	932	$49,978.50
11.	8000	$50,000.00
12.	1294	$49,980.75
13.	2721	$49,998.38
14.	1058	$49,990.50
15.	5063	$49,997.13

Activity 2
1. NOLT
2. LUKO
3. ⅜
4. MIMT
5. Down ⅛
6. MIMT
7. $64.00
8. 16½
9. NAJ

SECTION 9-2

Activity 1

	Total Cost of Shares
1.	$6337.50
2.	$14,231.25
3.	$208; $187.50
4.	$1462.50
5.	$22,500.00
6.	$665.00
7.	$14,535
8.	$36,312.50
9.	$73,000
10.	$49,275
11.	$68.437.50
12.	$83,947.50
13.	$77,152.50
14.	$34,590.38
15.	$34,500

Activity 2

	First Total	Second Total	Difference (Profit or Loss)
1.	$12,813.75	$13,272.75	$459 pr
2.	$2203.75	$2687.50	$483.75 pr
3.	$17,000	$16,350	$650 loss
4.	$120,000	$138,000	$18,000 pr
5.	$4406.25	$3956.25	$50.00 loss
6.	$3061.25	$3487.50	$426.25 pr
7.	$52,875	$56,700	$3825 pr
8.	$3609.38	$3478.75	$130.63 loss
9.	$9223.75	$7065	$2158.75 loss
10.	$4004.00	$4207	$203 pr
11.	$6016.75	$7117.38	$1100.63 pr
12.	$60,480	$62,370	$1890 pr
13.	$2819.63	$2678	$141.63 loss
14.	$109,500	$113,437.50	$3937.50 pr
15.	$37,300	$34,900	$2400 loss
16.	$5871.25	$5005	$866.25 loss
17.	$20,250	$22,406.25	$2156.25 pr
18.	$48,500	$52,750	$44,250 pr
19.	$26,355	$25,620	$4735 loss
20.	$13,333.75	$11,082.50	$1251.25 loss

Activity 3

1.	+2%	11.	+18%
2.	+22%	12.	+3%
3.	−4%	13.	−5%
4.	+15%	14.	+4%
5.	−1%	15.	−6%
6.	+14%	16.	−15%
7.	+7%	17.	+11%
8.	−4%	18.	+9%
9.	−23%	19.	−3%
10.	+5%	20.	−10%

SECTION 9-3

Activity 1

Graph 1

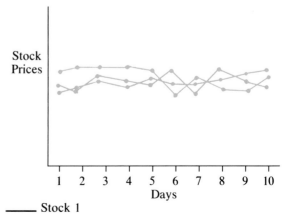

Days

_____ Stock 1
_____ Stock 2
_____ Stock 3

Graph 2

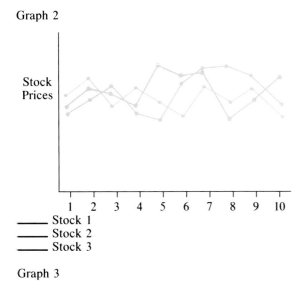

Stock Prices

_____ Stock 1
_____ Stock 2
_____ Stock 3

Graph 3

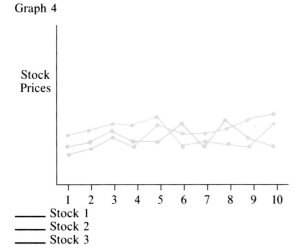

Stock Prices

_____ Stock 1   _____ Stock 2   _____ Stock 3

Graph 4

Stock Prices

_____ Stock 1
_____ Stock 2
_____ Stock 3

Graph 5

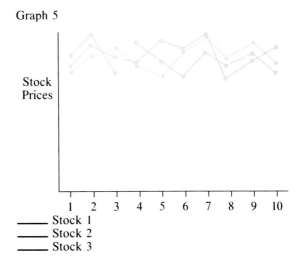

Stock Prices

_____ Stock 1
_____ Stock 2
_____ Stock 3

Activity 2

	Week 1	Week 2	Week 3
AP & P	350	625	325
Zoca Z1	200	600	305
Graft	160	460	220
Gepsi	300	460	300
Cara Lou	500	950	700
Zola	1000	1050	570
Elmand	30,000	32,000	22,000
Disnel	450	464	366
ADT	50	300	200
Parity	196	308	188

	Week 4	Week 5	Week 6
AP & P	575	1275	1185
Zoca Z1	105	225	530
Graft	470	670	825
Gepsi	150	800	675
Cara Lou	820	200	280
Zola	270	120	290
Elmand	22,180	7680	5680
Disnel	246	196	31
ADT	400	520	710
Parity	138	538	908

SECTION 9-4

Activity 1

1.	**1989 Price**	2.	**1984 Price**
a.	$11,801.95	a.	$192.80
b.	.37	b.	14.79
c.	26.84	c.	78.22
d.	50,76	d.	80,658.44
e.	111.25	e.	339.37
f.	78,975	f.	404.38
g.	464.31	g.	30.80
h.	112.76	h.	18.59
i.	80.28	i.	33.68
j.	418.73	j.	1196.64

CHAPTER REVIEW

1. By selling them for more money than you paid for them
2. When you buy a bond you give money to the government or school district to use for a period of time, paying you interest, and then repaying you in full.
3. A mutual fund allows a small investor to participate in the stock or bond market without having to investigate individual stocks.
4. Answers will differ, but may include: The stability of the company and its prospects for the future.
5. Stocks and bonds are traded through brokers; for each sale there must be a person or institution willing to buy.
6. The SEC protects investors by requiring security firms to make accurate and complete information available to the buyer and acting against fraud and misrepresentation.
7. People try to predict the future of the stock market so as to buy stocks at their lowest prices and sell them at their peak.

	Total Value of Purchase	**Total Value of Sale**	**Profit**
8.	$158,125	$171,250	$13,125
9.	46,250	50,625	4375
10.	60,937.50	67,187.50	6250
11.	122,812.50	132,500	9687.50
12.	117,500	126,250	8750
13.	42,187.50	53,437.50	11,250
14.	108,750	112,500	3750

	Total Value	**Balance**
15.	$47,437.50	$247,437.50
16.	24,312.50	271,750
17.	11,593.75	283,343.75
18.	37,500	245,843.75
19.	28,875	216,968.75
20.	3537.50	220,506.25
21.	35,787.50	184,718.75
22.	37,625	222,343.75
23.	24,743.75	197,600
24.	163,500	34,100
25.	16,000	50,100

	Number of Whole Shares	**Total Value**
26.	1090	$79,978.75
27.	1237	79,941.13
28.	939	79,932.38
29.	1292	79,942.50
30.	3764	79,985
31.	2519	79,978.25
32.	1993	79,969.13
33.	26,666	79,998
34.	2831	79,975.75
35.	2077	79,964.50

36–37. Different graphs possible. A line graph would probably be the most useful for these situations.

SKILLS PREVIEW

1. $254
2. $1003
3. $878
4. $88,800
5. $69,050
6. $99.880
7. $11,896.10
8. $12,851.20
9. $12,552.76
10. $8961
11. $8730
12. $9258
13. $32,800
14. $51,400
15. $152,750
16. $255,000
17. $487,500
18. $2748
19. $459
20. $8067
21. $634,352.84
22. $209,639.20
23. $380,102.06
24. $534,334.79
25. $18,660
26. $29,400
27. $266.25
28. $334.13
29. $6633

Chapter 10

SECTION 10-1

Activity 1
$357,500
390,000
280,000
200,000
240,000
195,000
176,250
105,750
97,500
90,000

SECTION 10-2

Activity 1
1. **a.** $207
   b. $918
   c. $508
   d. $2748
   e. $1686
   f. $6381
   g. $109
   h. $556
   i. $544.50
   j. $2593.50
   k. $2195
   l. $6722.50

2. **a.** and **b.** $711 Term
   c. and **d.** $2240 Term
   e. and **f.** $4695 Term
   g. and **h.** $447 Term
   i. and **j.** $2049 Term
   k. and **l.** $4527.50 Term

SECTION 10-3

Activity 1
1. $91,523.92 (20 years)
2. $146,211.88 (25 years)
3. $226,566.42 (30 years)
   30 vs 20 years = +$135,042.50
   30 vs 25 years = +$80,354.54

Activity 3
1. $1112 ÷ 2 = $556
2. $352,319.67
3. Policy cash value = $ 57,716.00
   Interest investment = <u>352,319.67</u>
   Interest + $294,603.67

CHAPTER REVIEW

1. To replace income lost due to a death.
2. A person must decide whether they want pure protection–term insurance or protection plus savings–cash-value insurance.
3. Policy builds up cash value much like a savings account.
4. Social security payments will not match the lifestyle you were use to prior to retiring.
5. $240,000
6. $255,000
7. $459

8. $843
9. $726
10. $3435
11. $226,566.42
12. $292,423.76
13. 30 years = $226,566.42
    20 years = <u> 91,523.92</u>
             $135,042.50
14. $2061 × 30 = $61,830
15. $256,006.54
16. Cash value of insurance policy = $ 80,299.50
    Annual Compounding Interest = <u>$256,006.54</u>
             + $175,707.04
17. $2061 ÷ 12 = $171.75
18. $255,969.23
19. Cash value of insurance policy = $ 80,299.50
    Monthly Compounding Interest = <u> 255,969.23</u>
             + $175,669.73
20. $256,006.54 − $255,969.23 = +$37.31 Problem 15

CUMULATIVE REVIEW

1. $92.38
2. $1380
3.

Balance	Interest	Amount Owed	Payment
$690.00	$10.35	$700.35	$70.04
630.31	9.45	639.76	63.98
575.75	8.64	584.39	58.44

4. $860
5.

Purchases	Balance	Interest	Amount Owed	Payment
	$720.00	$10.80	$730.80	$73.08
125.00	782.72	11.74	794.46	79.45
	715.01	10.73	725.74	72.57
	653.17	9.80	662.97	66.30
	596.67	8.95	605.62	60.56
	545.06	8.18	553.24	55.32

6.

	Plan A	Plan B
Total Financed Price	14,188.80	14,644.80
Total Interest	2788.80	1744.80
Dealer's Profit	4288.80	1744.80

7. **a.** $87,375
   b. $10,875
   c. 12% gain
8.

	Total Value	Balance
		$150,000
Von Comp	$66,750	216,750
Abon	21,250	238,000
Etra	59,625	178,375
XXMC	44,212.50	222,587.50
Imoco	29,025	193,562.50
Zelta	33,000	226,562.50
Diti Corp	10,000	236,562.50

9. **a.** 1796
   b. 2790
   c. 2303
   d. 4240
10. $320,000
11. $2748

Chapter 11

SECTION 11-1

Activity 1
1. $529
2. $1331
3. $11,916
4. $1091
5. $1526
6. $8920
7. $6241
8. $10,525
9. $641
10. $2449
11. $8583
12. $2336
13. $1076
14. $3139
15. $6339
16. $6717
17. $4008
18. $6946
19. $4883
20. $3566

Activity 2
1. $13,915.90
2. $19,426
3. $15,811.40
4. $17,220.50
5. $27,340.30
6. $18,139
7. $18,336.89
8. $23,804
9. $17,205.67
10. $12,814.02
11. $18,230.63
12. $24,379.19
13. $20,196.79
14. $10,762.74
15. $10,574.96
16. $33,737
17. $25,901.50
18. $33,484
19. $24,574.22
20. $12,488.70

Activity 3

Yearly Income	Taxable Income	Tax Owed	Annual Amount Withheld	Refund or Money Owe
$15,000	$ 9,900	$ 1,489	$ 1,776	$ 287
5,544	444	66	360	294
18,660	13,560	2,036	2,280	244
15,576	10,476	1,571	1,848	277
9,420	4,320	649	912	263
28,536	25,436	4,708	5,136	428
42,600	39,500	8,656	9,024	368
25,092	21,992	3,742	4,188	446
19,608	16,508	2,479	2,736	257
28,200	17,000	2,554	2,784	230
45,324	30,124	4,519	4,752	233
47,016	33,816	5,448	5,640	192
63,600	54,400	11,208	11,484	276
27,480	16,280	2,441	2,712	271
45,420	32,220	5,000	5,232	232
18,768	3,568	536	792	256
58,920	41,720	7,660	7,848	388
54,372	47,272	9,214	8,940	274
38,580	29,480	4,421	4,368	53
21,360	12,260	1,841	2,100	259
25,392	18,292	2,741	3,048	307
17,544	10,444	1,564	1,836	272
38,508	27,408	4,449	5,664	1,215

CHAPTER REVIEW

1. Filing status—category which helps you determine the amount of tax you owe, based on the fact of whether you are single, married and filing jointly or head of a household.
2. Because most of us would not be willing to do without the many services our government provides.
3. As the number of dependents increase, your taxes decrease for your income bracket.
   1. $5,002
   2. $529
   3. $1,264
   4. $7,529
   5. $152
   6. $4,466
   7. $33,588.50
   8. $11,161.50
   9. $32,263
   10. $11,161.50

SKILLS PREVIEW

1. $3,350; 13% increase
2. $1,651; 9% decrease
3. $4,240; 26% decrease
4. $4,275; $18, 525
5. $6,957; $30, 147
6. $2,595; $11,245
7. $8,525
8. 21.7
9. 19.5
10. .08
11. 1,064
12. 369
13. $58.75
14. 77
15. $9.22
16. 6.78 hours
17. 9:36
18. .40 hours or $\frac{2}{5}$ hour

Chapter 12

SECTION 12-1

Activity 1
1. Model A $1997
   Model B $2233
   Model C $1702
2. $11
   $22
   $150
   $147
   $24
   $23
   $23
   $32
   $9

3.

	Dealer Cost	Sticker Price
a.	$15,203	$17,637
b.	$13,975	$16,192
c.	$12,068	$13,948
d.	$15,346	$17,805

4. a. 16%
   b. 15.9%
   c. 15.6%
   d. 16%

SECTION 12-2

Activity 1
1. a. $975
   b. $1200
   c. $900
   d. $900
2. a. 20%
   b. 18%
   c. 25%
   d. 27%

Activity 2
1. a. $4400
   b. $6305
   c. $3885
   d. $2780

Activity 3

Car	AFTER 1 YEAR Deprec./Value	AFTER 2 YEARS Deprec./Value	AFTER 3 YEARS Deprec./Value
A	$822.15/$26,582.85	$6379.88/$20,202.97	$3636.53/$16,566.44
B	$9744/$22,736	$5456.64/$17,279.36	$3110.28/$14,169.08
C	$12,178.50/$28,416.50	$6819.96/$21,596.54	$3887.38/$17,709.16
D	$3624.30/$8456.70	$2029.61/$6427.09	$1156.88/$5270.21
E	$4383.30/$10,227.70	$2454.65/$7773.05	$1399.15/$6373.90
F	$2889/$6741	$1617.84/$5123.16	$922.17/$4200.99

SECTION 12-3

Activity 1

	Distance	Miles/gallon	Cost/mile
1.	416.90	22.7	$.06
2.	610.40	38.9	$.03
3.	151.30	15.9	$.09
4.	985.80	24	$.065
5.	211.10	19.4	$.07
6.	550.60	23.1	$.05
7.	969.30	21.9	$.05
8.	1052.70	39.3	$.03
9.	313.60	25.3	$.05
10.	981.90	33.1	$.03

11. a) 735
    b) 16.2 miles per gallon
    c) $1.66

Activity 2

	Operating expense	Cost per mile
1.	$1394	$.13
2.	$1834.67	$.12
3.	$1837.07	$.14
4.	$1816.86	$.09
5.	$1591.64	$.14
6.	$1118.19	$.13

SECTION 12-4

Activity 1
1. 1.65
2. 2.30
3. 2.40
4. 2.45
5. 1.50
6. 1.40
7. 1.25
8. 1.15
9. .80
10. 1.00

Activity 2
1. $234
2. $180
3. $115.20
4. $120.80
5. $55
6. $392.85
7. $380.70
8. $62.50
9. $455
10. $36

CHAPTER REVIEW

1. By consulting books such as Edmund's *New Car Prices* or the *Kelley Blue Book New Car Price Manual* so the buyer will know exactly what the dealer paid for a specific car.
2. Possible answer is car rental companies
3. Gasoline
4. **a.** Coverage for property damage liability
   b. Coverage for medical payments
   c. Coverage for collision
5. Because the rates are affected by the car class rating which reflects the resale value of the car, by the amount of the deductible and by the driver rating factor.

6.

	Mark up	Percent of profit
a.	$825	7.3%
b.	$810	11.3%

7. **a.** $10,461.47
   b. $8463.14
8. **a.** Depreciation amount = $7389.72; Value = $8400.28
   b. Depreciation amount = $21,845; Value = $16,905

	Distance traveled	Mileage/gal	Cost/mile
9.	267.30	17.4	8.7¢
10.	387.10	21.9	7.4¢
11.	152.30	15.9	9.4¢

	Operating expenses	Cost/mile
12.	$1379.47	9¢
13.	$1881.63	7.4¢

14. **a.** $72.75 **b.** $729

CUMULATIVE REVIEW

1. $560.48
2. Less than $790 dollars a month
3. Different graphs possible. A line graph would probably be the most useful for this situation.
4. **a.** $110.10
   b. $211.49
   c. $24.70
   d. $112,995
   e. $741.51
5. $82,440
6. **a.** $7648
   b. $2546
7. **a.** $27,007
   b. $26,389
8. (See Form 1040EZ)
9. 1300, 21%
10. $9582.01

Chapter 13

SECTION 13-1

Activity 1

1-6. Answers will vary. Students should turn in map of Georgia highlighting the routes from their city to the six cities listed.

7. Answers will vary. Students to give the miles from their city to the six cities in Activity 1.

Activity 2

1. 517
2. 778
3. 964
4. 1229
5. 1204
6. 1883
7. 2015
8. 1319
9. 193
10. 2443
11. 695
12. 604
13. 1186

Activity 3

2. 167.5; $232.83
3. 43.4; $86.37
4. 52.8; $46.99
5. 87.5; $95.38
6. 48.3; $91.29
7. 55.1; $71.08
8. 46.3; $55.10
9. 29.6; $44.10
10. 94.7; $103.22

SECTION 13-2

Activity 1

1. $322.08
2. $387.60

SECTION 13-3

Activity 1

1. 6:15 P—3hrs, 45 min
2. 8:30 A
3. 6:15 P
4. 6:15 P
5. 3:20 P
6. 3 hrs, 47 min
7. 3 hrs, 55 min
8. 3 hrs, 12 min
9. 4 hrs, 13 min
10. 4 hrs, 63 min

CHAPTER REVIEW

1. Possible answer: More things of interest and variety; driving not as monotonous as interstates.
2. Possible answer: Whether you need to get where you are going quickly or have time to drive more slowly.
3. Possible unexpected delays: rush hour heavy traffic; long stretches of highway construction; mechanical difficulty with the car.
4. Food and lodging costs can vary widely. Therefore, it is important to estimate costs before the trip to ensure you will have sufficient funds to cover them.
5. Possible answers: Speed, no lodging expenses of staying overnight while on the road.
6. Ground transportation to and from the airport can consume time. Taxis fees increase with distance.
7. Contact various airlines since each offer a variety of different night flight fares, supersaver fares, and company club plans. Most often, advance purchase offers a savings.

8–13. Answers will vary
14. 896 miles
15. 1315 miles
16. 287 miles
17. 1330 miles
18. 1183 miles
19. 642 miles
20. 944 miles
21. (14) $93.25
    (15) $136.85
    (16) $29.87
    (17) $138.41
    (18) $123.11
    (19) $66.81
    (20) $103.45
22. $656.52
23. $85.32
24. $99.36
25. Cost per day = $28.65, $29.35, $28.70, $28.70
    Total cost = $115.40
    Average = $28.85
26. $721.25
27. 4 hours, 1 minute
28. 4 hours, 20 minutes
29. 5:30 A.M.
30. 7:40 A.M.

SKILLS PREVIEW

1. 3.5
2. 2.7
3. 5734.2
4. 1002.58
5. 2050.49
6. $660,000
7. $140,000
8. $1428
9. $2496
10. $45.07 per square foot
11. $42.34 per square foot
12. 2.89
13. 81%
14. 637.50
15. 460.65
16. 556.73
17. $682.70
18. $30,940
19. $35,360
20. $47,914.88

Chapter 14

SECTION 14-1

Activity 1

	Price	Square Feet	Cost per Square Foot
j.	$835,000	5759	$144.99
k.	595,000	4828	123.24
h.	375,000	4375	85.71
n.	269,900	4000	67.48
i.	239,900	3000	79.97
e.	224,000	3100	72.26
a.	211,000	4355	48.45
c.	190,000	3600	52.78
g.	155,900	2850	54.70
b.	127,950	2816	45.44
m.	99,500	1314	75.72
l.	79,000	1528	51.70

SECTION 14-2

Activity 1

	Price	Percent Down	Down Payment	Loan Amount	Interest Rate	Years	Monthly Payment	Ratio TFP/PP
1.	$289,900	10%	$28,990	$260,910	10%	25	$2370.83	2.73
2.	35,900	10	3590	32,310	11	25	316.60	2.94
3.	82,500	10	8250	74,250	10	25	674.73	2.73
4.	79,900	10	7990	71,910	11	30	684.74	3.43
5.	112,000	10	11,200	100,800	10	30	884.61	3.16
6.	84,500	10	8450	76,050	11	30	724.26	3.43
7.	199,000	10	19,900	179,100	10	25	1627.50	2.73
8.	85,900	10	8590	77,310	11	25	757.65	2.94
9.	104,900	20	20,980	83,920	10	25	762.42	2.73
10.	73,950	20	14,790	59,160	11	30	563.32	3.43

Activity 1

	Monthly Income	Mortgage Payment	Loan Amount	Percent Down Payment	House Price	Down Payment	Total Cost
	$2500	$ 700.00	$ 79,750	10	$ 88,611.11	$ 8861.11	$260,861.11
1.	5900	1652.00	188,225	10	209,138.88	20,913.89	615,633.89
2.	3500	980.00	111,650	10	124,055.55	12,405.56	365,205.56
3.	1200	336.00	38,275	10	42,527.78	4252.78	125,212.78
4.	2650	742.00	84,550	10	93,944.44	9394.44	276,514.44
5.	2899	811.72	92,475	20	115,593.75	21,118.75	313,337.95

SECTION 14-4

Activity 1

1. a. Claim 1 $1,275
    Less Deductible   − 250
            $1,025

The Li-Ming family would have recovered $1,025.

b. Claim 2 $1,275.00
    Less Replacement   − 127.50
            1,147.50
    Less Deductible   − 250.00
            $ 897.50

They would have recovered $897.50.

c. Claim 1 $1,025.00
    Claim 2   − 897.50
            127.50
    Less Replacement Cost   − 150.00
            $ 22.50

Yes. Their net gain was $22.50.

2. a. $250
b. $210
c. No. Net loss $20.00

CHAPTER REVIEW

1. Accept all reasonable answers. See Section 14-1 for full discussion.
2. A fixed-rate mortgage is amortized on a constant payment basis over a number of years. An adjustable-rate mortgage, the interest rate, and therefore the payments, can be adjusted up or down a number of times during the life of the loan.
3. 28%
4.

House	Price	Square Feet	Cost per sq ft	Bedrooms	Bathrooms	Den, etc.	Extras
a.	$135,450	3416	$39.65	4	3		Schools close by Golf course area
b.	285,900	4344	65.81	5	3.5	Library Game room	Park across street Tri-level Walk-in closets
c.	175,500	2986	58.77	4	2.5		Country estate Lake view, quiet
d.	219,900	3590	61.25	–	–		New, several flr plans, circ drive, close to sch & golf

	Price	Percent Down	Down Payment	Loan Amount	Interest Rate	Years	Monthly Payment	Ratio TFP/PP
5.	$ 95,500	10%	$ 9550	$ 85,950	10%	25	$ 781.05	2.73
6.	$115,900	10%	11,590	104,310	11%	30	993.03	3.43
7.	$ 82,600	20%	16,520	66,080	10%	25	600.44	2.73
8.	$105,900	20%	21,180	84,720	11%	30	806.63	3.43
9.	$175,900	10%	17,590	158,310	10%	30	1389.22	3.16

	Monthly Income	Mortgage Payment	Loan Amount	Percent Down Payment	House Price	Down Payment	Total Cost
10.	$2400	672.00	76,550	10	85,055.56	8505.56	250,425.56
11.	$1850	518.00	59,025	20	73,781.25	14,756.25	201,236.25
12.	$2690	753.20	85,825	10	95,361.11	9,536.11	280,688.11
13.	$3160	884.80	100,800	20	126,000.00	25,200.00	343,728.00
14.	$1300	364.00	41,475	10	46,033.33	4608.33	135,648.33

15. a. $595.00
  b. $265
  c. Yes
16. Yes. 12%

CUMULATIVE REVIEW

1. $56,812.50
2. $303,741.27
3. 400,000
4. a. $11,223
  b. $1084
5. Distance = 491.6
  MPG = 28.3
  Cost per mile = $0.05
6. $1112/$0.09 per mile
7.

	Price	Percent Down	Down Payment	Loan Amount	Interest Rate	Years	Monthly Payment	Ratio TRP/PP
a.	$175,900	10%	17,590	158,310	10%	30	1389.22	3.16
b.	$ 85,600	20%	17,120	68,480	11%	25	671.16	2.94
c.	$153,500	10%	15,350	138,150	10%	25	1255.39	2.73

8. a. $860
  b. $764

Chapter 15

SECTION 15-1

Activity 1
1. $423.08
2. $673.08
3. $384.62
4. $413.46
5. $346.15
6. $450.00

SECTION 15-2

Activity 1
Draw graph—price vs number of amenities for 1-bedroom apartments from lowest to highest as listed in the Apartment Hunter's Guide in the Reference Section.

Activity 2
Draw graph—price vs number of amenities for 3-bdrm apts listed in Apartment Hunter's Guide in the Reference Section.

SECTION 15-3

Activity 1
1. a. $631.89
   b. $308.92
   c. $168.51
   d. $596.76
   e. $842.48
   f. $982.92
2. a, c, and e.

CHAPTER REVIEW

1. Advantages include sharing expenses with another person and ready companionship. Disadvantages include combining different living habits and the need to find a new roommate if the old one moves out.
2. You should look in the closets and under the sinks. Test showers and toilets. Decide if electrical outlets are sufficient to avoid overloading and if the locks and security systems are adequate. Decide if the space is sufficient for your needs.
3. Advantages include joint ownership and joint responsibility for the yard, pool, patio, and hallways, as well as lower monthly payments. The disadvantages are that you have to pay for inside repairs, there are usually no private yards, residents share common walls.
4. $1413.46
5. $1011.54
6. $701.92
7. $535.58
8. $917.21
9. $413.46
10. $20,540
11. $24,180
12. $39,000
13. $36,140

14. $49,420
15. $43,420

16.

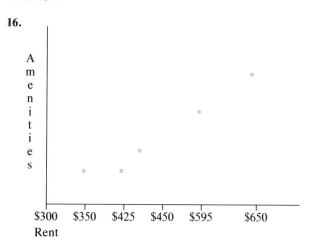

Amenities vs Rent

	Purchase Price	Monthly Mortgage Price	Rental Price	Monthly Rental Price
17.	$95,000	$666.96	$200/wk	$866.67
18.	$65,000	$456.34	$6000/yr	$115.38
19.	$28,500	$200.11	$250/mo	$250.00
20.	$19,400	$136.03	$225/mo	$225.00
21.	$39,000	$273.82	$95/wk	$411.67
22.	$80,000	$561.66	$190/wk	$823.33

SKILLS PREVIEW

1. $9380
2. $7296
3. $13,050
4. $3306.50
5. $1430
6. $14,300
7. $18,100
8. $9635
9. $163.40
10. $111
11. $50.40
12. $94.50
13. $11.51
14. $22.50
15. $32.33
16. $819.12
17. $257.15
18. $886.50
19. $1280.31
20. $649.16
21. $1010.55
22. $.25
23. $.23
24. $.25
25. $.08
26. $.07
27. $.09
28. $3.63
29. $3.31
30. $.10
31. $615.38
32. $836.54
33. $1336.54
34. $0.00156
35. $0.1155
36. $1.2961
37. $0.00640
38. $0.195550
39. $21.95005

Chapter 16

SECTION 16-4

Activity 1

Product	Unit Price Size 1	Size 2	Size 3	Best Buy
Oil	$0.137	$0.129	$0.126	15 oz
Orange Juice	$0.1316	$0.1075	$0.0994	18 oz
Tuna	$0.983	$0.12	$0.11	16 oz
Raisins	$0.165	$0.217	$0.218	12 oz
Honey	$0.20	$0.12	$0.083	1 lb
Rice	$0.0975	$0.0368	$0.0328	2 lbs
Milk	$0.0403	$0.0279	$0.0210	1 gal
Popcorn	$0.13	$0.10	$0.12	32 oz

CHAPTER REVIEW

Monthly Budget

1. *Income* $4616.67
   Expenses
   Housing $ 941.67
   Food   753.33
   Automobile   941.67
   Utilities   565.00
   Day-care   329.58
   Clothing   235.42
       Total Expenses   3766.67

The family is within their budget since $4708.33 (Income) − $3766.67 (Expenses) = $941.66

2. *Income* $2708.33
   Expenses
   Housing $ 541.67
   Food   528.12
   Automobile   549.42
   Utilities   460.42
   Clothes   458.33
   Credit cards   270.83
       Total Expenses   2808.79

The family is over budget since $2708.33 (Income) − $2808.79 (Expenses) = $-100.46

3. .08/oz.; .10/oz.; .11/oz. The 16 oz. size is the best buy.
4. .11/oz.; .12/oz.; .12/oz. The 14½ oz. size is the best buy.
5. .16/oz.; .15/oz.; .14/oz. The 12 oz. size is the best buy.
6. .13/oz.; .13/oz.; .13/oz. They are all the same price—13¢ per oz.
7. .13/oz.; .13/oz.; .15/oz. The 16 oz. & 9 oz. are both the better buys.
8. $1.565/qt.; $.95/qt.; $.75/qt. The gallon is the best buy.
9. .19/oz.; .18/oz.; .19/oz. The 18 oz. size is the best buy.
10. .16/oz.; .16/oz.; .14/oz. The 18 oz. size is the best buy.

	Salary	Budget for wk, mo, yr	Food 16%	Housing 30%	Transportation 20%	Clothing 5%	Pension 13%
11.	$39,000	yr	$ 6240	$ 11,700	$ 7800	$ 1950	$ 5070
		mo	520	975	650	162.50	422.50
		wk	120	225	150	37.50	97.50
12.	$75,500	yr	$12,080	$ 22,650	$ 15,100	$ 3775	$ 9815
		mo	1006.67	1887.50	1258.33	314.58	817.92
		wk	232.31	435.58	290.38	72.60	188.75
13.	$45,500	yr	$ 7280	$ 13,650	$ 9100	$ 2275	$ 5915
		mo	606.67	1137.50	758.33	189.58	492.92
		wk	140	262.50	175 ·	43.75	113.75
14.	$62,400	yr	$ 9984	$ 18,720	$ 12,480	$ 3120	$ 8112
		mo	832	1560	1040	260	676
		wk	192	360	240	60	156
15.	$51,000	yr	$ 8160	$ 15,300	$ 10,200	$ 2550	$ 6630
		mo	680	1275	850	212.50	552.50
		wk	156.92	294.23	196.15	49.04	127.50
16.	$42,600	yr	$ 6816	$ 12,780	$ 8520	$ 2130	$ 5538
		mo	568	1065	710	177.50	461.50
		wk	131.08	245.77	163.85	40.96	106.50

CUMULATIVE REVIEW

1. $572.58
2. a. 1222
   b. 2666
3. a. $11,608.85
   b. $16,478
4. $326.25
5. $142,000
6. $558.15
7.   **Monthly Budget**
   Income $3291.66
   Expenses
   Housing $ 658.33
   Automobile   724.17
   Food   550.00
   Clothes   98.75
   Utilities   888.75
      Total Expenses $ 2920
   The family is not over budget since $3291.66
   (Income) − $2920 (Expenses) = $371.66

GLOSSARY

add-on costs Expenses that add to the price of a product as it goes through processing, marketing, and distribution. Examples include labor, packaging, advertising, energy, and transportation.

adjustable-rate mortgage (ARM) Loan with an interest rate that can be adjusted up or down during the life of the loan

advance purchase Paying ahead of time; if you pay for an airline ticket ahead of time you may get a lower price.

advertising Communicating with people, in a variety of media, with the aim of promoting and presenting information about goods and services

all-purpose bank cards Credit cards widely accepted by businesses who do not have their own charge account systems; examples include MasterCard and VISA.

amortized Paid off; a mortgage is usually amortized over a period of from 15 to 30 years.

annual percentage rate (APR) The percent cost of credit on a yearly basis

annuity Investment plan that provides income upon retirement; tax-deferred annuities put off taxes on the income until the owner is in a lower tax bracket

automated tellers Automated teller machines (ATMs) perform banking services quickly and automatically at convenient locations and during nonbanking hours.

average-balance account Checking account in which a fee is charged if the average balance for the month falls below the minimum

average daily balance The average of daily balances over the month, found by figuring the unpaid balance for each day of the billing cycle, adding these balances together, and dividing the total by the number of days

bait and switch Unethical sales practice in which one product is used to draw customers to the store and another, more expensive, product is then urged on them

balloon note A form of loan in which the initial payments are low and there is a large payment at the end

bear market When prices on the stock exchange are going down

beneficiary The person designated to receive the death benefit in a life insurance policy

blank endorsement Your signature on the back of a check with no additional message

bodily injury liability Insurance that covers injuries to others in an automobile accident caused by the insured person

bond A security; a bond amounts to a loan to a government or corporation for which the holder receives interest on the money over the life of the bond, and the full amount at the maturity date.

brand Product or service which has an identifying name and characteristics to make it stand out in the marketplace

broker Salesperson who specializes in buying and selling stocks and bonds

bull market When prices on the stock exchange are going up

bushing Shady practice of car dealers in which the dealer offers less for a trade-in or charges more for a car than originally promised

business-to-business advertising Advertising not aimed at the consumer but at another business; examples include the business of advertising, the promotion of office equipment and computers.

canceled checks Checks drawn on an account that have cleared through the bank and been returned to the account holder for record keeping

cap A limit to the total amount of increase allowable in an adjustable-rate mortgage

capital gain Increase in the market value of a security or other asset; increase in the value of property during the time that it is owned

car class rating Rating applied to a car which reflects

657

its resale value

cash discount A lower price given to a customer who pays cash instead of using credit

cash-flow savings account Account used to hold money which will be needed at times of heavy demand on the budget

cash-value insurance Insurance plus savings plan; one of two main types of life insurance; *compare* term insurance.

collision Insurance that pays for damage to the insured person's car in an accident

commercial banks Banks offering a wide variety of services in addition to savings accounts: checking accounts, credit cards, loans, financial counseling, safe-deposit boxes, traveler's checks, money order and transfers, and trust and investment services.

commission Money paid a salesperson for each item sold; a percentage of the cost of the item. Also, broker's fee for buying and selling securities.

common stock Stock which entitles the owner to receive dividends and vote for the company board of directors

comparison shopping Gathering price and product information from a number of sources or stores before making a decision to buy

competition The striving of one company or product against another for the consumers' dollars; the competition, rival companies that sell competing products.

compounded quarterly Interest applied to a savings account every three months, or four times a year

certificate of deposit (CD) Special form of savings in which a fixed amount of money must be deposited for a specified amount of time. The longer the time, the higher the interest rate; penalties are imposed for early withdrawal.

charge account A charge account customer at a store or business has the right to make purchases there for later billing.

charge card A card that allows you to make purchases for later billing

check register A record of checks written, fees charged, and deposits made in a checking account

checks Forms filled out and signed by the owner of a

checking account authorizing the bank to pay the amount shown to the person designated

closing costs Charges and fees associated with the transfer of ownership of a home to a new buyer

coach class The economical fare on an airplane or train; *compare* first class.

collateral Something of value offered as assurance that a loan will be repaid; also security.

collection agency A firm that is hired by creditors to collect outstanding debts or repossess items not paid for

compound interest Interest paid on a savings account more than one time a year; interest earned in the first part of the year earns interest itself in the next part. Interest is commonly compounded semiannually or quarterly.

comprehensive physical damage Insurance that pays for damage to a car that results from fire, falling object, theft, windstorm, flood, earthquake, mischief, flying objects, and vandalism

condominium Living space in which individual units are privately owned and common spaces are jointly owned

Consumer Price Index (CPI) An economic tool for comparing prices from one era to another

consumers Purchasers of goods and users of services; all the members of a society who need to buy things. *Contrast* producers.

corporate bond Bond issued by a private company to raise money for plant expansion or other operations

corporation A business made up of a number of owners who have shares of stock in the company

cosign Parents or others can cosign a loan with a young borrower; this makes the parents or other cosigner responsible for repaying the loan if the borrower does not.

cost-per-check accounts Checking accounts that charge a small fee for every check which clears during the month, often in addition to requiring a minimum balance

coverage The items and dollar amounts for which an insurance company will compensate a policy holder; homeowner's insurance coverage may include dwelling, personal property, loss of use, personal liability, and medical payments.

credit A form of debt that occurs when cash, goods, or services are provided in exchange for a promise to pay at a future date

credit card A small plastic card that identifies the holder and gives the holder privileges of making purchases on credit; the holder is not required to pay the total outstanding bill every month, but to pay a minimum required amount.

credit limit The maximum value of purchases a credit card holder can charge on an account; once the balance is partly paid back the holder can again make purchases up to the limit

credit rating An indication of a person's ability to secure goods, services, and money in return for the promise to pay

credit risk A customer who is unlikely to be able to pay for purchases made on credit is referred to as a poor credit risk.

credit unions Not-for-profit savings and lending financial institutions in which all members belong to the same social or professional organization

creditor Business, bank, or individual who extends credit

decreasing term Kind of term life insurance in which the death benefits decrease over time and the premium is lower than for renewable term insurance

deductible Any amount which you may deduct from your gross income to find the amount on which you owe taxes; interest paid on a mortgage, charitable contributions, and medical expenses are deductible.

deductible The portion of a loss that the insured person pays; the insurance company pays the costs above the deductible

deferred payment price The amount including interest you pay for an item you buy on installment

deflation A general decrease in prices

demand deposits Checks

demographics Characteristics used to sort the general population into identifiable groups that can be used as target groups for advertising; sex, age, income, family configuration, education, employment.

departure Leave; the point of departure is the city you are leaving when you begin a trip.

dependents People supported by another; a tax payer's dependents include children and a husband or wife supported by the person

depreciation The difference between the original purchase price of a car or other asset, and its eventual resale price

destination The place to which you are traveling when making a trip

direct mail Marketing technique in which a customer learns about a product through the mail, but is not given a coupon or order form to use to make a purchase. *Compare* direct response.

direct response Marketing technique in which a customer receives a coupon or order form, orders products from a catalog, and has them delivered directly to his or her home.

disability insurance Benefits paid through social security to those who can no longer work because of injury or illness

discretionary income Income remaining after you pay for basic needs such as food, clothing, and shelter

diversify Acquire a balanced variety of securities rather than owning too much of any one; diversification cuts down the risk of investment.

dividend The part of the profits of a corporation that each stockholder receives

down payment The amount of a purchase you make in cash before taking out a loan for the remainder

drawer The person who writes and signs a check

driver rating factor The multiple applied to a base premium to determine the insurance costs for an individual; in general, the factor for a young person is higher than for an older person, so the younger person pays higher premiums.

easy money policy An easy money policy results when the reserve requirement is lowered and money is thus freed up.

efficient Working well; a business is efficient when it is producing a product with a minimum of energy, expense, and waste.

endorsement Signature and directions to the bank on the back of a check

endowment policy Type of cash-value life insurance which builds up value quickly through high premiums

entrepreneurship Putting together the ingredients of a business, including making plans, hiring workers, obtaining raw materials, and obtaining equipment

Equal Credit Opportunity Act Law that prohibits discrimination in granting credit on the basis of sex, marital status, race, color, religion, age, or national origin

equity The difference between what a home is worth and what the buyer still owes on it in the form of a mortgage

excess reserves Money remaining from a deposit after the required reserves have been subtracted; money available for investment or loans by a bank.

face value The amount of the death benefit in a life insurance policy

Fair Credit Billing Act Law that allows people to preserve their good credit rating while settling a dispute with a store or credit card company

Fair Credit Reporting Act Law giving people the right to examine their own credit files and have incorrect information removed

Fair Debt Collection Practices Act Law which prohibits violence, the threat of violence, harassment, public embarrassment and other methods in the collection of debts

federal and state highways Highways that pass through towns, offering more interest and variety to the driver than interstates which go around them; they do not have controlled access.

Federal Reserve note Currency issued by the Federal Reserve; our paper money.

finance charge A charge levied on the unpaid balance in a single-purpose or all-purpose credit account

finance charges The amount over the loan amount that you pay to a lending institution for a loan; also called interest.

financial responsibility laws Laws requiring drivers

to pay, either with insurance or with personal funds, for damage to other people or others' property

first class The expensive fare on an airplane; service, meals, and seating are superior to those in coach class.

fixed costs A company's costs that remain constant over a period of time; may include labor, transportation, advertising, energy, and so on.

fixed-rate mortgage (ARM) A mortgage paid off in equal monthly payments on a regular schedule over the years of the loan; *compare* adjustable-rate mortgage.

form W-4 Filled out at the beginning of employment, the form provides the IRS with information used to determine how much of the worker's wages to withhold for income tax

fringe benefits Benefits given to workers in addition to wages or salary; paid vacations, life and health insurance, free uniforms, retirement plans, and stock options are examples.

full endorsement Your signature on the back of a check made out to you and directions to the bank to transfer the check to someone else

garnishment To hold a part of a debtor's earnings for the payment of a debt; a legal method of debt collection.

graduated commission Commission plan in which a salesperson receives a higher rate of commission for sales above a certain amount

gross pay Total pay, before deductions have been made

group life insurance Insurance purchased through the place of employment covering all employees as a group

group plan Means of buying health insurance through an employer or other organization

health insurance Hospital and medical insurance; for senior citizens, Medicare

highball Shady car dealer practice in which a fantastic trade-in offer is withdrawn after the deal is made

homeowner's insurance Insurance covering a dwelling and personal property against damage or loss from fire and lightning, theft, windstorm, hair, explosion, and so on. Mortgage lenders typically require the homeowner to take out this insurance.

hourly rate Amount of money paid for each hour of work

impulse buying Making consumer decisions on the spur of the moment. Sellers encourage it; consumers on a budget avoid it.

incentive Motivation; profit is one incentive to businesses to do well.

income The money a person receives from work or investments

income security A guarantee that a source of income will continue

income tax Tax on an individual's earnings from wages, salary, tips, interest, rents, dividends, and capital gains. In the U.S., the largest revenue producing tax for the federal government. The U.S. income tax is based on ability to pay, voluntary compliance, and paying-as-you-earn through withholding.

independent insurance agent One who sells insurance from a number of different insurance companies

inflation A general increase in prices

insider trading Illegal trading activity; trading stocks on the basis of information that should only have been known within the companies themselves

installment loan Borrowed money paid back in installments, often monthly; a common way to buy expensive items.

insured The person who is insured, the holder of a life insurance policy

interest 1. The amount over the loan amount that you pay to a lending institution for a loan; also called finance charges. **2.** Money paid to you by a financial institution for the privilege of using your money to make investments and loans to others.

interstate highways Major, controlled access highways linking cities in the U.S.

investing Putting money into a device such as a security in the expectation of realizing a gain

joint return Married couples have a choice of filing their income tax returns jointly (together) or separately.

labor Work; the use of the efforts and skills of workers in manufacturing a product or extending a service

late payment penalties Possible extra charge imposed if payment on a credit account is late

lease Rental agreement between renter and landlord

legal tender Money that by law must be accepted for paying debts and taxes

life insurance A contract to pay a specified amount of money to a designated person upon the death of the insured

limited payment insurance Cash-value life insurance which accumulates value more quickly than ordinary life because higher premium payments are made over a shorter period of time

liquidation bankruptcy Outright bankruptcy, an extreme measure in which a debtor who cannot pay must sell most assets and then is left free of debt; the person cannot reapply for credit for seven years.

liquidity The ease and speed with which you can withdraw money from deposit

loan sharks Illegal money lenders who charge extremely high interest for short-term cash loans and may use violence to collect the debt

loss leader Product sold for less than it cost in order to bring customers into a store

low balance account Checking account in which a fee is charged if the balance falls below the minimum any time during the month

lowball Shady car dealer practice in which an unrealistically low price is mentioned for a car but is later raised

management Leadership in a company; those people who make decisions affecting labor, production, advertising, distribution, and so on.

market basket List of goods and services which are tracked in the CPI

market rate The interest rate currently charged by lending institutions such as banks and credit unions

mark-up Profit; the difference between the price at which a retailer bought an item and the price at which the retailer sells it.

medical payments Insurance coverage for medical costs resulting from an automobile accident

mileage chart Chart showing distances between cities or towns

minimum balance accounts Checking accounts that require you to keep a minimum amount—often $300—on deposit at all times

mobile home A portable living space designed to be used without a permanent foundation, intended as a year-round dwelling

money supply How much money (in the form of coins, currency, and demand deposits) is in circulation in the economy; regulated by the Federal Reserve System.

mortgage Loan for the purpose of buying property; usually paid in monthly payments, of principal and interest, over a period of from 15 to 30 years.

multiplier effect In the multiplier effect, money is loaned or invested over and over again, by different institutions, each institution keeping the required proportion in reserve but passing on the larger portion for additional investment or loan making.

multi-purpose credit cards Credit cards often used for travel and entertainment for which an annual fee is charged and for which the total balance must be paid each month; examples include American Express, Diners Club, and Carte Blanche.

municipal bond Issued by states, cities, counties, school districts or other governmental bodies to raise money for schools, hospitals, streets, and so on

mutual fund A means of pooling funds with many other investors to acquire a wide variety of stocks, bonds, and other kinds of investments

nonprice competition Competing for consumers' dollars by product differentiation, advertising, customer service, product design, or product improvement

nonrefundable A purchase, such as an airline ticket, is nonrefundable when you cannot return it for money

NOW account Negotiable Order of Withdrawal account; checking account in which the balance earns interest but which may also charge a service or per-check fee.

odd lot A stock trade of fewer than 100 shares

odometer The counter on the dashboard of a car that shows the number of miles the car has been driven

ordinary life Cash-value life insurance which combines a savings feature with protection; also called whole life or straight life.

outstanding checks All checks on an account that have been written but have not yet cleared through the bank

overtime hours Hours worked in addition to regular hours; pay for overtime is usually higher than for regular hours.

owner's association The group of owners of individual units in a condominium; responsible for maintenance of building, grounds, and common areas.

packing Car dealer's attempt to add special fees or finance insurance charges to the purchase price of a car

pawnbroker A person who will make a cash loan for about 40 percent of the value of an item left with the lender

payee The person to whom a check is written

payroll deduction Money deducted directly from a salary by an employer for U.S. Savings Bonds, annuities, donations to community charities, and so on

points One-time charge by the lending institution at the time of buying a home with a mortgage; each point is equal to 1% of the value of the mortgage.

preferred stock Stock which entitles the owner to receive dividends ahead of common stock owners, but which does not usually entitle the owner to vote for the board of directors

prepayment penalty Charge that may be imposed when a person pays back the full amount of the loan ahead of the payment schedule

price competition Competing for consumers' dollars by lowering the price of a product

producers Those who manufacture goods. *Contrast* consumers.

profit The amount of money a business makes above the cost of the products or services it produces

profit The amount of money a business makes above the cost of the products or services it produces

property damage liability Insurance that pays for damage done to other people's property

push money Money paid to a salesperson by a manufacturer to sell its goods ahead of others

---

rating point Measure by which television programs are compared and upon which advertising rates are based; stands for the percent of the television audience that had their television tuned to a particular channel.

real wages The value of wages in terms of the goods and services it will buy. In times of inflation, even when the dollar amount of wages goes up, the real wage may fall.

reconciliation The process of finding the correct balance in a checking account by comparing the bank statement with the check register

regular hours The hours an employee is required to work each week

regular savings accounts The most flexible and liquid kind of deposit, used for money you may need in an emergency

renewable-convertible term Term life insurance in which a specified death benefit will be paid at any time during the term at which the holder dies

rent Money paid to landlord, usually by the month, for the use of an apartment or house

rent-to-own plan A purchase plan in which you pay in monthly installments to rent an item; later you can choose to buy the item, applying the payments already made to the purchase price.

replacement cost Insurance coverage which compensates owners for lost or damaged items of personal property at the amount it would cost to replace them; standard coverage reimburses at the amount originally paid.

repossess For the store to take back an item purchased on credit but not fully paid for

required reserve Percentage of deposits a bank must hold in reserve to repay depositors. This money is not free for the bank to use for loans or investments.

reservation A hotel's or restaurant's agreement to hold a room or a table for the person making the reservation; sometimes a deposit, or part of the price in advance, is required to hold the reservation.

restrictive endorsement Your signature on the back of a check and the words "for deposit only"; it protects the check against being cashed by someone else.

retirement insurance Monthly social security payments made to a retired worker or the worker's surviving spouse

revoke To take away permanently; a driver's license can be revoked for a very serious infraction

road atlas Book of maps showing highways and local roads, land forms, cities, towns, and distances; useful in planning and taking road trips.

round lot A stock trade of 100 shares

---

salary Weekly, monthly, or yearly rate of pay

savings banks Similar to commercial banks in offering services, but specializing in making real estate loans

securities Investments

security Something of value offered as assurance that a loan will be repaid; also collateral.

security deposit Money, often equal to one month's rent, given to the landlord when a lease is signed; the deposit is refunded when the renter leaves the property in good condition.

self-employment income Income earned by people working for themselves—as physicians, farmers, writers, consultants, and so on

simple interest Interest paid one time a year at the end of the year on the total balance in a savings account

single-purpose credit cards Credit cards issued by companies and businesses for use in purchasing their products and services; examples include oil companies and department stores.

Social Security System Compulsory federal insurance program which provides a level of income security for workers who have retired, surviving dependents of workers, and others

speculating Investing in which more money is risked in less secure investments

standard deduction One of the amounts you are permitted to deduct from your income to determine your taxable income; alternatively you may choose to itemize deductions for such things as charitable contributions, medical expenses, and interest paid on a mortgage loan.

standard of living The quality of goods and services a family can afford, determined by their income

standard unit The amount used to calculate and compare unit prices. May be weight (pounds, ounces), volume (pint, quart, gallon), square feet, or number (100-count).

statement Record of the month's activity in a checking account sent to the account holder every month

sticker price The price shown in a car window in a show room; usually higher than the dealer actually expects to receive

survivor's insurance Money for living expenses paid to survivors of workers who would have been eligible for social security

take-home pay Amount of money a worker receives after deductions have been made for social security, income tax, and other purposes

target market The portion of the general population to which advertisers pitch their promotion for a given product

tax audit An examination of your tax return by the IRS

taxable income Your gross income minus personal exemptions (for self and dependents) and standard deduction or itemized deductions; the amount you use to look up your taxes on the tax table.

tax liability The amount of income tax you owe

technology The development of new machines or labor-saving methods; may improve manufacturing but also may enable work to be done by fewer workers, thus reducing employment.

term insurance Kind of life insurance which pays death benefits but does not include savings; one of two major kinds; *compare* whole life.

thrift institutions Savings and loan associations; lend money for the purchase and construction of homes.

tight money policy A tight money policy results when the reserve requirement is higher so that less money is available for investments and loans.

timely medium Advertising medium, like radio and unlike monthly magazines, in which information about products, prices, and sales can be communicated to consumers quickly

title Document stating the ownership of a car

total financed price The total dollar amount you actually pay for a credit loan; includes the original loan plus interest payments.

townhouse Living space attached to others in row or other configuration; attached house.

transfer payments The federal government transfers money—by means of taxation and spending—from those who owe it to those who are in need. Social security, disability payments, and disaster relief are examples.

Truth in Lending Act Law that requires creditors to tell customers the exact cost of buying on credit

turnover Rate at which people move out and new people move into apartments or other rental units

unfinished claim Advertising claim technique in which a product is said to be superior but does not say to what; examples include, "fresher, more natural, less work," and so on.

uninsured and underinsured motorist protection Insurance that pays for damage to your car if you are in an accident caused by a driver who had little or no bodily injury insurance

unit price The cost per standard unit of a product; the cost used to compare different size packages of the product.

U.S. Securities and Exchange Commission (SEC) Federal agency whose purpose is to correct unsound stock selling practices

utilities Suppliers of heat, water, electricity, and natural gas to households; households pay periodic bills for service.

variable costs A company's costs that vary depending upon the quantity of items they produce; may include materials, packaging, and so on.

wage Hourly or daily rate of pay

wage earner plan A plan under Chapter XIII of the Federal Bankruptcy Act in which people can restructure their debt without declaring bankruptcy

warranty The guarantee to keep a car in good repair; the period during which the guarantee is in force.

weasel words Advertising technique in which a quality is implied which could not be stated directly; for example, "this product has the look and feel of the finest porcelain."

INDEX

PHOTO ACKNOWLEDGMENTS

All photographs Image Bank Chicago unless indicated by (*).

Cover photograph © Comstock, Inc.

CHAPTER 1   p. 2: Don Klumpp; **p. 4:** Colin Molyneux(1983); **p. 5:** David J. Maenza; **p. 6:** Garry Gay; **p. 7:** Alvis Upitis; **p. 9:** Michael Melford; **p. 11:** Sobel/Klonsky; **p. 12:** Gianalberto Cigolini; **p. 15:** Bill Varie; **p. 16:** ITTC Productions; **p. 20:** Al Satterwhite; **p. 21:** Mel DiGiacomo; **p. 28:** J. Carmichael, Jr.; **p. 30:** Luis Castaneda; **p. 32:** Alvis Upitis; **p. 34:** Robert J. Herko.

CHAPTER 2   p. 38: Janeart Ltd. (1986); **p. 40:** Jeffrey M. Spielman, Stockphotos, Inc.*; **p. 41:** Janeart Ltd.; **p. 42:** Mary Lyons Photography; **p. 44:** Murray Alcosser; **p. 46:** Jay Freis; **p. 53:** Photogenie(1989); **p. 54:** Sobel/Klonsky(1988); **p. 55:** Alvis Upitis; **p. 56:** Alvis Upitis; **p. 57:** Alfred Gescheidt; **p. 65:** Alvis Upitis; **p. 66:** David W. Hamilton; **p. 66:** Ted Kawalerski; **p. 66:** Weinberg-Clark; **p. 70:** David W. Hamilton.

CHAPTER 3   p. 72: Michael Melford; **p. 74:** Gary Gladstone; **p. 75:** Bill Varie(1987); **p. 78:** Tim Bieber; **p. 79:** Antonio Rosario; **p. 81:** Ira Block; **p. 82:** Luis Castaneda(1988); **p. 83:** Benn Mitchell; **p. 92:** Alvis Upitis; **p. 93:** Murray Alcosser; **p. 95:** Stephen Marks, Stockphotos, Inc.*; **p. 100:** Louis H. Jawitz; **p. 102:** C.L. Chryslin.

CHAPTER 4   p. 106: Mel DiGiacomo; **p. 108:** Antonio Rosario; **p. 110:** Janeart Ltd.; **p. 115:** Kaz Mori; **p. 116:** Jake Rajs; **p. 118:** Don Klumpp; **p. 121:** G.V. Faint; **p. 122:** Ellen Schuster; **p. 123:** Michael Melford (1989); **p. 124:** Charles C. Place; **p. 125:** Gary Gladstone; **p. 129:** Antonio Rosario; **p. 130:** Jay Freis; **p. 135:** Michael Melford(1988).

CHAPTER 5   p. 140: Jeff Spielman, Stockphotos, Inc.*; **p. 142:** Patti McConville; **p. 144:** Antonio Luiz Hamdan; **p. 148:** Gary Bistram;

p. 149: Steve Niedorf; **p. 151:** Steve Dunwell; **p. 153:** Maria Taglienti; **p. 154:** Janeart Ltd.; **p. 155:** Steve Proehl; **p. 157:** Murray Alcosser; **p. 158:** Steve Niedorf; **p. 159:** Obremski; **p. 161:** Michael Salas (1988); **p. 162:** Michael Quackenbush; **p. 163:** Jay Freis; **p. 163:** Jean Pierre Pieuchot; **p. 166:** Murray Alcosser.

CHAPTER 6   p. 168: Stephen Marks, Stockphotos, Inc.*; **p. 170:** P.+G. Bowater; **p. 177:** Obremski; **p. 179:** Benn Mitchell; **p. 180:** Walter Bibikow; **p. 180:** Jay Freis; **p. 183:** Steve Krongard(1985); **p. 187:** W. Von dem Bussche; **p. 189:** Bill Varie; **p. 190:** Marc Romanelli.

CHAPTER 7   p. 200: Alvis Upitis (1988); **p. 202:** Gary Gladstone; **p. 203:** Robert Kristofik; **p. 206:** C.L. Chryslin; **p. 207:** Bill Varie(1989); **p. 208:** Janeart Ltd.; **p. 209:** Marc Romanelli; **p. 210:** Murray Alcosser; **p. 213:** Luis Castaneda; **p. 215:** Grafton Marshall Smith; **p. 216:** Richard Pan, Stockphotos, Inc.*; **p. 217:** A.T. Willett; **p. 219:** Kay Chernush; **p. 222:** Jay Freis; **p. 223:** Elyse Lewin; **p. 225:** Gill C. Kenny; **p. 228:** Obremski; **p. 231:** DC Productions.

CHAPTER 8   p. 242: John William Banagan; **p. 244:** Kevin Forest; **p. 245:** N. Felberg; **p. 250:** Ulf E. Wallin(1988); **p. 251:** Michael Salas; **p. 252:** Gerald Brimacombe; **p. 258:** John Ramey; **p. 259:** Ted Kawalerski(1984); **p. 261:** Gerhard Gscheidle(1987); **p. 266:** Michel Tcherevkoff; **p. 269:** Butch Martin; **p. 274:** David W. Hamilton; **p. 275:** Mel DiGiacomo.

CHAPTER 9   p. 280: G.V. Faint; **p. 282:** Nick Pauloff; **p. 284:** Michael Quackenbush; **p. 289:** Benn Mitchell; **p. 291:** David W. Hamilton; **p. 294:** Michael Salas; **p. 295:** Butch Martin; **p. 305:** Garry Gay; **p. 307:** Steve Dunwell; **p. 311:** Robert Kristofik.

CHAPTER 10   p. 319: Kuhn, Inc.; **p. 321, 322:** Stephen Marks, Stockphotos, Inc.*; **p. 325:** Michael Melford; **p. 325:** Sobel/Klonsky; **p. 326:** Elyse Lewin; **p. 331:** GaryBistram;

p. 333: Walter Bibikow (1984); **p. 336:** Frank Wing.

CHAPTER 11   p. 345: William Rivelli; **p. 347:** Mel DiGiacomo; **p. 357:** Michael Salas; **p. 369:** Jay Freis; **p. 376:** Elyse Lewin; **p. 376:** Al Satterwhite; **p. 377:** Michael Melford.

CHAPTER 12   p. 382: Frank Bates(1988); **p. 384:** Pamela Zilly; **p. 386:** Michael Salas(1988); **p. 389:** Alvis Upitis; **p. 390:** Janeart Ltd. (1985); **p. 398:** Joe Azzara(1982); **p. 404:** David W. Hamilton.

CHAPTER 13   p. 416: Kathleen O'Donell, Stockpotos, Inc.*; **p. 418:** John Kelly; **p. 419:** Hans Wendler; **p. 421:** SUMO; **p. 427:** Nancy Brown; **p. 428:** Charles C. Place; **p. 433:** Guido Alberto Rossi; **p. 434:** Giparo; **p. 440:** Michael Melford(1987); **p. 445:** Steve Satushek.

CHAPTER 14   p. 446: Charles C. Place; **p. 448:** Don A. Sparks; **p. 450:** Walter Bibikow; **p. 452:** Roger Miller (1981); **p. 461:** Nancy Brown; **p. 462:** Ira Block(1989); **p. 465:** Patti McConville; **p. 467:** Antonio Rosario; **p. 468:** David W. Hamilton; **p. 469:** Ted Kawalerski; **p. 472:** Jeff Smith; **p. 474:** Michael Salas(1988).

CHAPTER 15   p. 486: Kay Chernush; **p. 488:** Robert Kristofik; **p. 490:** Kay Chernush; **p. 491:** Benn Mitchell; **p. 495:** Charles Mahaux; **p. 496:** A.T. Willett; **p. 500:** Schmid/Langsfeld; **p. 501:** Magnus Rietz; **p. 502:** Al Hamdan; **p. 512:** Michael Salas(1989).

CHAPTER 16   p. 514: Tim Bieber; **p. 516:** Elyse Lewin; **p. 518:** Obremski; **p. 522:** Regine Mahaux; **p.523:** Murray Alcosser; **p. 525:** Geo Sipp; **p. 526:** Michael Salas; **p. 527:** Jay Brousseau; **p. 531:** Swedowsky; **p. 535:** Gerald Brimacombe; **p. 536:** DW Productions; **p. 538:** Gregg Mancuso, Stockphotos, Inc.*; **p. 540:** Whitney Lane; **p. 541:** Michael Melford; **p. 544:** Margaret W. Cusack; **p. 545:** Alfred Gescheidt; **p. 546:** Luis Castaneda; **p. 549:** Roger Miller.